NUGGETS
of truth

A BIBLE STUDENT'S DEVOTIONAL
and
A BIBLE TEACHER'S
RESOURCE HANDBOOK

DR. JOHN MANNION

DAN,
From one life-long
Bible student/teacher to another,
I hope this Resource is a blessing
to you.   Bless you in the name of Jehova-Rophe,
John
Jeff Mannion
(January 17)

AMBASSADOR INTERNATIONAL
GREENVILLE, SOUTH CAROLINA & BELFAST, NORTHERN IRELAND
www.ambassador-international.com

Nuggets of Truth

ISBN: 978-1-62020-932-5
eISBN: 978-1-62020-948-6

Unless otherwise marked, Scripture quotations taken from the New American Standard Bible (NASB) Copyright © 1960, 1962, 1963, 1968, 1971, 1972, 1973, 1975, 1977, 1995 by The Lockman Foundation.

Scripture marked NIV taken from The Holy Bible, New International Version, NIV Copyright 1984 by Biblica, Inc. Used by permission. All rights reserved worldwide.

Scripture marked KJV taken from the King James Version. Public Domain.

Scripture marked TLB taken from The Living Bible copyright © 1971 by Tyndale House Foundation. Used by permission of Tyndale House Publishers Inc., Carol Stream, Illinois 60188. All rights reserved.

Scripture marked NKJV taken from the New King James Version®. Copyright © 1982 by Thomas Nelson. Used by permission. All rights reserved.

Cover Design and Interior Typesetting by Hannah Nichols
eBook edition by Anna Riebe Raats

AMBASSADOR INTERNATIONAL
Emerald House
411 University Ridge, Suite B14
Greenville, SC 29601, USA
www.ambassador-international.com

AMBASSADOR BOOKS
The Mount
2 Woodstock Link
Belfast, BT6 8DD, Northern Ireland, UK
www.ambassadormedia.co.uk

The colophon is a trademark of Ambassador, a Christian publishing company.

To the all merciful, gracious, patient, and faithful love of my life . . . His name is Jesus!

"May he kiss me with the kisses of his mouth!

For your love is better than wine.

"Your oils have a pleasing fragrance,

Your name is like purified oil;

Therefore the maidens love you.

"Draw me after you and let us run together!

The king has brought me into his chambers."

"We will rejoice in you and be glad;

We will extol your love more than wine.

Rightly do they love you."

Song of Solomon 1:2-4

And to the loves of my life that the love of my life so graciously gave me: Audrey, Katie, John, Heidi, Luke, Abby, and Carlie.

"I want those already wise to become the wiser and become leaders by exploring the depths of meaning in these nuggets of truth" (Proverbs 1:5-6, TLB).

Contents

INTRODUCTION

INSPIRATIONAL WRITING MEETS BIBLE COMMENTARY, *Nuggets of Truth* stands as a different kind of devotional. It is, perhaps, more in keeping with Oswald Chamber's *My Utmost for His Highest* in that it is meant to teach more than it is meant to simply inspire. Not that each *Nugget* does not inspire. On the contrary, it stands as a very inspirational book even as the Scriptures themselves never fail to inspire. The content of each individual devotional is full of Scripture. Each one is designed to provide the reader with a short Bible study. Hence, the reader is more of a student than simply a reader. The considerable content of each day's study digs deep enough with a pointed focus that the student effectively goes through a mini Bible college program once having gone through the entire year.

Each excerpt should be read and studied. The reader/student should have both the devotional and the Bible open at the same time. Many of the Scriptures are included word for word within the context of the study. These Scriptures can still be looked up to take in a little bit more of the passage's context. Some Scriptures are simply referenced. Here it is, perhaps, more important and helpful to look up the passages in one's Bible. At the end of each devotional there is some space provided for the student to take notes. As students are studying the Scriptures, they will find it useful to take some notes and document some thoughts and insights.

The subtitle of *Nuggets of Truth, A Bible Student's Devotional and A Bible Teacher's Resource Handbook,* reveals the two-fold purpose and use of this book. It is meant to be a devotional for Bible students ***and*** for Bible teachers. In keeping with this second purpose, the devotional is exhaustively indexed. The indexes include a more general category/topical index (organized according to the major doctrinal studies of systematic theology including theology proper, Christology, pneumatology, eschatology, soteriology, anthropology, ecclesiology, and practical theology), as well as a much more detailed Scripture index and word/subject index. The idea with these indexes is the devotional can be used by Bible teachers/preachers as a resource for their teaching/preaching ministries. Lessons/messages can be developed as teachers/preachers find, via the indexes, pertinent material to use in building their lessons/messages.

And so it is hoped that *Nuggets of Truth* will be a blessing for Bible students and Bible teachers. It is for those who want to study the Scriptures daily and grow in wisdom. It is for those who want to teach the Scriptures and grow in leadership. May Proverbs 1:5-6 become the voice of *Nuggets of Truth* . . .

"I want those already wise to become the wiser and become leaders by exploring the depths of meaning in these nuggets of truth" (The Living Bible).

January

I WANT TO KNOW WHAT PLEASES HIM . . .

"And without faith it is impossible to please Him, for he who comes to God must believe that He is and that He is a rewarder of those who seek Him."

Hebrews 11:6

Ever since man fell away from God in the garden due to sin, God has been asking man, **"Where are you?"** God's desire was to **walk** with man "in the cool of the day" but "the man and his wife hid themselves from the **presence** of the Lord" (Genesis 3:8-9). Walk. Presence. Where are you? God wants to be with you!

What is it that pleases God? It is the **walking** with Him that pleases Him: " . . . so that you will walk in a manner worthy of the Lord, to please Him in all respects" (Colossians 1:10); " . . . brethren, we request and exhort you in the Lord Jesus, that as you received from us instruction as to how you ought to walk and please God (just as you actually do walk), that you excel still more" (1 Thessalonians 4:1). What pleases God? God's pleasure is found in the **walking**!

Soon after the Fall, and its disruption of this **walking** with God and being in God's **presence**, the Scripture again references one who **walked** with God. It was Enoch . . . "and he was not, for God took him" (Genesis 5:24). A little girl heard about the story of Enoch in Sunday school and explained it to her mother: "You know, Mom, Enoch made God so happy that God took him home with Him. He used to go for walks with God. One day they walked so far God said to Enoch, 'You're a long ways from home. You had better come in and stay with Me!'"

Do you want to know what pleases God? The Scripture is clear. It is impossible to please Him without faith because by faith we come to God and that is what pleases Him; He is pleased when we "seek Him." Sometimes, life seems so complicated . . . so difficult to know what really matters. If God is God, then what matters is what pleases Him. That is the bottom line and sometimes it is the bottom line that makes sense of everything in an otherwise senseless fallen world.

That must have been the longing of those in John 6:28 who asked Jesus "What shall we do, that we may work the works of God?" Give us the bottom line! What pleases God? Jesus replied, "This is the work of God that you believe in Him whom He has sent." There it is again—that "come to God" and "seek Him" thing that is the action of faith/believe—that **walking, presence, "Where are you?"** thing that goes back to the garden.

Sometimes I find myself asking that John 6:28 question in search of a sense of purpose and meaning. I find encouragement in its simplification of things; I find encouragement and motivation in answering the question of purpose in my life from the perspective of God's desires and I begin to turn my face toward Him and see Him smile. Life makes sense again. This is the very essence of repentance. It is turning away from not walking with God (which is to be in the flesh) as "those who are in the flesh cannot please God" (Romans 8:8), and it is turning to walking with God as "he who comes to God" pleases Him (Hebrews 11:6). Repentance = turning away from not pleasing God and turning toward pleasing Him.

Hence, the reason why prayer is important (and the motivation behind engaging in it) is because **it pleases God**! God wants to walk with you in the garden. He wants you to be in His presence. Do you want to know what pleases Him? What pleases Him is *what matters*. He is pleased when you seek Him. *Prayer matters!* It matters so much that "He is a rewarder of those who seek Him" (Hebrews 11:6).

———

JANUARY 2

NO FEAR, GOD IS STILL ON THE THRONE . . .

"Are not five sparrows sold for two cents? Yet not one of them is forgotten before God. Indeed, the very hairs of your head are all numbered. Do not fear; you are of more value than many sparrows."

Luke 12:6-7

The greatness of God is, perhaps, seen in no more grand light than through the lens of the attribute of His sovereignty. God's sovereignty can be defined as His unchallengeable power for good. It is described by His "three C" actions; He **C**reates, He **C**auses, and He **C**ontrols. Nothing exists apart from Him. Nothing is set into motion that did not begin with His action. And nothing is outside of His control.

The extent of the sovereignty of God is complete and thorough. Even each hair of your head is numbered and known (the average human head has 100,000 strands of hair). God is fully aware of each strand. The picture of God's sovereignty in Luke 12:6-7 goes beyond His omniscience, however. It is not simply that He knows how many hairs you have but that He is intimately in control of those hairs. God is still on the throne (in control) even if you are going bald! Perhaps, this is more poignantly pictured when the passage proclaims, in its build-up of its lesser-to-greater argument (sparrows are of less importance than people), "not one of them is forgotten before God." To not be forgotten by God is to be within His control. All is within this wondrous sphere . . . the sale of sparrows and the number of hairs on our heads!

Man is completely dependent on the sovereignty of God. John the Baptist proclaimed, "A man can receive nothing, unless it has been given him from heaven" (John 3:27). Ultimately, success in ministry depends on God since a man cannot receive (which is his responsibility) if it is not first given to him (God's responsibility). To boast, then, is to not understand God's sovereignty. At the same time, to fear evil is to not understand God's sovereignty. Satan must ask permission from God regarding what he can do to God's people (Luke 22:31-32). Finally, to live behind a mask is to not understand God's sovereignty. It is impossible to hide from God not simply because of His omnipresence but because of the fullness of His sovereignty.

The Pharisaical masks that we all sometimes try to wear are foolishness before God. He cannot be fooled. He knows your heart (see Luke 16:15).

In any case, God is never flustered, no matter the situation. When you are going through those "flustery" times of life, when things just don't seem to make sense, remember, God is not shaken. He is not running up and down the hall screaming "Oh Myself . . . what am I going to do?" He still knows where you are and what you are going through. He still loves you, and He is **still on the throne**!

———————

JANUARY 3

JESUS, THE GREAT ILLUMINATOR . . . AND ILLUMINATION!

"He who has My commandments and keeps them is the one who loves Me;
and he who loves Me will be loved by My Father,
and I will love him and will disclose Myself to him."

John 14:21

Jesus is the great illuminator *and* illumination. This makes sense because He is the Word of God (Revelation 19:13). It is God's revealed Word that gives us understanding of truth (revelation or illumination). On the Road to Emmaus it was Jesus Who "opened their minds to understand the Scriptures" (Luke 24:45). It is Jesus, the Son of God, Who reveals the Father: "All things have been handed over to Me by My Father, and no one knows who the Son is except the Father, and who the Father is except the Son, and anyone to whom the Son wills to reveal Him" (Luke 10:22). This makes sense because "He is the image of the invisible God" in whom "it was the Father's good pleasure for all the fullness to dwell" (Colossians 1:14, 19), and He "is the radiance of His glory and the exact representation of His nature" (Hebrews 1:3). Jesus is "the way, and the truth, and the life" and He says, "no one comes to the Father but through Me" (John 14:6). Jesus is the revealer. He is the revelation of God!

But how do we receive revelation? In John 14:21, the receiving of revelation ("and will disclose Myself to him") is clearly connected to obedience ("He who has My commandments and keeps them"). It is also connected to love (" . . . is the one who loves Me; and he who loves Me will be loved by My Father, and I will love him"). Herein, we have a clue as to how to answer our question. How do we receive revelation? It all begins with God's revelation of love to us in Christ. Paul understands this as the starting point and so his prayer for the Ephesians is that they would know that love:

> For this reason I bow my knees before the Father, from whom every family in heaven and on earth derives its name, that He would grant you, according to the riches of His glory, to be strengthened with power through His Spirit in the inner man, so that Christ may dwell in your hearts through faith; *and* that you, being rooted and grounded in love, may be able to comprehend with all the saints what is the breadth and length and height and depth, and to know the love of Christ which surpasses knowledge, that you may be filled up to all the fullness of God (Ephesians 3:14-19).

When we know His love for us then we love God; "we love, because He first loved us" (1 John 4:19). When we love God, then we obey Him; Jesus said, "If you love Me, you will keep My commandments" (John 14:15). When we obey God, then God reveals Himself to us (John 14:21; John 7:17; Mark 3:33-35). This process (God reveals His love to us in Christ → we love God → we obey God → God reveals Himself to us) continues and results in more and more knowledge of God/truth; revelation or illumination. Thus, the process starts with Jesus (He is the great illuminator) and ends with Jesus (He is the illumination itself). He is "the Alpha and the Omega, the beginning and the end" (Revelation 21:6). Jesus is both illuminator and illumination; He says "I" (illuminator) "will disclose Myself" (illumination). He is "all in all" (Ephesians 1:23) in whom is "the summing up of all things" (Ephesians 1:10). It is all about Jesus!

JANUARY 4

THE COMMANDMENT OF FELLOWSHIP . . .

"Behold, how good and how pleasant it is for brothers to dwell together in unity! It is like the
precious oil upon the head, coming down upon the beard, even Aaron's beard, coming down

upon the edge of his robes. It is like the dew of Hermon coming down upon the mountains of Zion; for there the Lord commanded the blessing—life forever."

Psalm 133:1-3

Why would Christians choose to not take advantage of the blessing and joy of fellowship? Perhaps the real question is, "Is it even possible for a Christian to negate the blessing and joy of fellowship? Is fellowship and its ensuing blessing simply an optional aspect of the Christian life?" The biblical answer to this question is, "No!" Fellowship and its blessing is not an option, it is a **commandment**. And so, when the Psalmist proclaims, "Behold, how good and how pleasant it is for brothers to dwell together in unity!," he then concludes "for there the Lord **commanded** the blessing" (Psalm 133).

Some Christians think the type of fellowship seen in the New Testament church is a "radical" aspect of Christianity. However, the New Testament passages do not read like that. The accounts of this "radical" form of Christianity are presented in a "matter of fact" way. The New Testament practice of fellowship was "normative," not "radical"! For example, Acts 2:44—"And all those who had believed were together, and had all things in common"—is presented very naturally. We do not get the idea there was a forced fellowship. It was the fellowship that comes from the understanding we have been born into the same family. A brother does not say to his sister, "Let's try to organize a family. We can get a mother, father, and a little brother and form our own family." No, the family is not humanly pieced together, but is divinely appointed. A father asked his daughter, "Are you glad that Billy is your brother?" The daughter replied, "Well, I really did not have a choice!"

Our minds must be renewed with respect to our spiritual families. Fellowship is not an option in the church. It is a requirement. It is required in order to obey God. It is required in order to grow in your relationship with God. The sharing that we see in the fellowship of the New Testament church is not "radical." Compared to worldly fellowship, it is radical. However, relative to the Bible it is normative. The members of the church must renew their minds to understand and accept the implications of the requirements of living in a family. Families spend time together and share things. The members of a family share their lives with each other.

Are fellowship and its ensuing blessing simply an optional aspect of the Christian life? No! Fellowship and its blessing is not an option, it is a *commandment*. Yes, "the Lord *commanded* the blessing" (Psalm 133:3). So, **fellowship**!

———————

GOD CHOOSES ONE BUT NOT THE OTHER. IS THAT FAIR?

"For many are called, but few are *chosen."*

Matthew 22:14

God chooses one (Jacob), but not the other (Esau) . . . Is that fair (Malachi 1:2-3)? It may be helpful here to read Romans 9:6-33: "So then He has mercy on whom He desires, and He hardens whom He desires. You will say to me then, 'Why does He still find fault? For who resists His will?' On the contrary, who are you, O man, who answers back to God?" (Romans 9:18-20). Here we see that first, and foremost, God is sovereign. This should be the end of the discussion ("who are you, O man, who answers back to God?"). God, as the Creator, has authority to choose as He wishes. Nevertheless, God does give us more of an explanation: "But it is not as though the word of God has failed. For they are not all Israel who are descended from Israel" (Romans 9:6). The justice of God is different than the justice of man. Man defines justice and fairness in terms of everything being the same. God defines justice and fairness in terms of how people respond to what they are given. For example, in the parable of the talents the owner judges each slave "according to his own ability" (Matthew 25:15). God's justice or fairness is based on whether or not He has kept His promises. Man's understanding of justice focuses on his own evaluation of the contents of God's promises. God's understanding of justice focuses on His faithfulness to His promises. The contents of those promises are unaffected by man's evaluation because God is sovereign (Romans 9:19-21).

It should also be understood that God's choosing is not an exclusive act, but rather, it is designed to be an inclusive act; God's chosen ones are blessed **so that** they can be a blessing to others (Genesis 12:2-3). It should also be understood that "election" is not reserved for a certain people group: "For they are not all Israel who are descended from Israel" (Romans 9:6). So, just because you are born into a Christian family, does not mean you are automatically a Christian. You still must respond to God's offer (promise) yourself; you have to make your own decision to trust in Christ and not yourself for salvation. But you may say, "It is still not fair that some are born into Christian families while others are born into Muslim families!" It is fair because regardless of your birth situation God responds to you as you respond to what He has given you (Mark 4:9, 24, 25), and God has given everyone some degree of revelation of Himself.

"What shall we say then? There is no injustice with God, is there? May it never be!" (Romans 9:14). The invitation is there ("For many are called"), but few accept it ("but few are chosen"); many reject God's provision (Matthew 22:14). Just as with the Edomites, God's sovereign control overwhelms man's proud self-reliance—"Though Edom says, 'We have been beaten down, but we will return and build up the ruins'; thus says the Lord of hosts, 'They may build, but I will tear down'" (Malachi 1:4)—so, too, does the king reject those who reject him:

> And he sent out his slaves to call those who had been invited to the wedding feast, and they were unwilling to come. Again he sent out other slaves saying . . . 'come to the wedding feast.' But they paid no attention and went their way . . . Then he said to his slaves, 'The wedding is ready, but those who were invited were not worthy . . . ' But when the king came in to look over the dinner guests, he saw a man there who was not dressed in wedding clothes, and he said to him, 'Friend, how did you come in here without wedding clothes?' And the man was speechless. Then the king said to the servants, 'Bind him hand and foot, and throw him into the outer darkness; in that place there will be weeping and gnashing of teeth.' For many are called, but few *are* chosen (Matthew 22:3-5, 8, 11-14).

Worthiness is based on how you respond to God. The proper response is to trust in and rely on His **provision**. It is to say, "I cannot **provide** for myself. I need God's **provision**. I need His 'wedding clothes' that He has **provided** for me, for without them I cannot get into the wedding feast" (Matthew 22:11-12). By faith we must accept and wear His wedding clothes that He has provided for us. This is what it means to be chosen (Matthew 22:14). You are called. Are you chosen? Are you wearing His wedding clothes or your own? At the end of the day (literally), you better be sure to have on the right "clothes" (Revelation 16:15).

JANUARY 6

WHEN THE CHOSEN BECOME FROZEN . . .

"The oracle of the word of the Lord to Israel through Malachi. 'I have loved you,' says the Lord. But you say, 'How have You loved us?' . . . 'You also say,' 'My, how tiresome it is!' 'And you disdainfully sniff at it,' says the Lord of hosts . . . "

Malachi 1:1-2, 13

The book of Malachi presents the love that God has for His chosen people even though they refuse to acknowledge it or respond to it. Why do the chosen become frozen? Difficult times for the people of Israel led them to turn from God. Their main problems were disappointment and impatience. Expectation and reality were two different things. After the exile to Babylon had ended, the people of Israel began to look with hope at the predictions made by earlier prophets. It had been prophesied that there would be a fruitfulness for the land (Ezekiel 34:26-30), a fruitfulness for the people (Isaiah 54:1-3), and a fruitfulness for the nation (Jeremiah 23:5-6). However, reality was not consistent with these expectations. Instead there was drought (Malachi 3:10), Persian rule (Malachi 1:8), and a low population in Israel.

The book of Malachi was written around 460 B.C. The exile of the Jews to Babylon that began in 586 had ended about seventy-five years earlier. The temple was already rebuilt. The sacrificial system was functioning. The knowledge of the Law (as communicated by Ezra) was evident. Yet, it was a waiting period for God's chosen people as opposed to a period of great change, and God's chosen people were proving themselves to not be very good at waiting as they showed no honor or respect for God, but instead despised His name (Malachi 1:6). And so, God sends His "messenger" (the name Malachi means "My messenger") with an "oracle of the word of the Lord" (Malachi 1:1). The Hebrew word for "oracle" often signifies an ominous occasion. It could be translated as "burden." The word is used twenty-seven times in the Old Testament, and in 25 occurrences it is found in the context of a coming judgment.

This "burden" is addressed to Israel (Malachi 1:1), God's chosen people; the Jewish people in general as there is no longer any distinction between "Israel" (the ten northern tribes) and "Judah" (the two southern tribes). When the 10 tribes went into their own exile earlier in Assyria, they never really came out as an identifiable people—hence, the "ten lost tribes of Israel"—since they intermarried with their captors which would later result in the people known as the Samaritans. Whereas, when Judah and Benjamin went into exile in Babylon, they obeyed God's command and did not intermarry, thus, retaining their identification as Jews.

The impatience of Israel—God's chosen people—had turned them into God's frozen people. They were so cold toward God that their very offerings were useless: "Oh that there were one among you who would shut the gates, that you might not *uselessly* kindle fire on My altar!" (Malachi 1:10). How did they become "frozen"? Disappointment and impatience . . . impatience with a lack of desired results: "You have wearied the Lord with your words. Yet you say, 'How have we wearied Him?' In that you say, 'Everyone who does evil is good in the sight of the Lord, and He delights in them,' or, 'Where is the God of justice?'" (Malachi 2:17). God's people must be careful. They must not evaluate and question God simply on the grounds of their own perception and understanding of the timing of desired results (Malachi 1:2: "'I have loved you,' says the Lord. But you say, 'How have You loved us?'"), nor should they question God's integrity by challenging the value of worshiping Him (Malachi 1:13: "You also say, 'My, how tiresome it is!' And you disdainfully sniff at it, says the Lord of hosts . . . "). If you have a problem in this area of your life of faith and are a bit frozen, then thaw yourself out by renewing your trust in the sovereignty of God!

———————

THE EMPOWERING WORK OF THE HOLY SPIRIT . . .

" . . . but you will receive power when the Holy Spirit has come upon you;
and you shall be My witnesses both in Jerusalem, and in all Judea and Samaria,
and even to the remotest part of the earth."

Acts 1:8

After initially being understood as the second volume of the writings of Luke (it was originally attached to Luke's Gospel) what came to be called "The Acts of the Apostles" began to be recognized in the second century A.D. as a separate book. This, of course, is consistent with the way the author, Luke, understood it: "The first account I composed, Theophilus, about all that Jesus began to do and teach" (Acts 1:1). And so, in the Gospel of Luke we see the ministry of Jesus on earth, and in Luke's second volume, the book of Acts, we see the ministry of Jesus on earth as it is done through His people by the power of the Holy Spirit.

The book of Acts mainly refers to the ministries of two of the apostles (Peter, chapters 1-12 and Paul, chapters 13-28). "The Acts of Peter and Paul" may have been a more suitable title. Even more suitable may have been the title "The Acts of the Holy Spirit." His presence and actions in extending the influence and growth of the church is the focus of the book; thus, perhaps, a fuller title may be "The continuation and extension of the ministry of Jesus through the church by the power of the Holy Spirit." In any case, the three key themes in Acts are the power of the Holy Spirit, the spread of the gospel, and the growth of the church.

The purpose of the sending of the Holy Spirit is for believers to receive empowering: " . . . but you will receive power when the Holy Spirit has come upon you; and you shall be My witnesses both in Jerusalem, and in all Judea and Samaria, and even to the remotest part of the earth" (Acts 1:8). Jesus clearly explained that the Holy Spirit was sent in order that believers might have "power" (the Greek term is *"dunamis"* from which we get the English word "dynamite"). He also made a clear connection between the **power** of the Holy Spirit and the **witness** of the church (also consider Luke 24:47-49). We might say that the **power** of the Spirit is directly connected to the **mission** of the church. The word "witness" is the translation of the Greek word *"martus."* From *"martus"* we get the English word "martyr." The foundational idea of "martus" or "witness" is to be willing "to die for what has been seen and testified to." Thus, we see a biblical connection that is the foundation of the sending and receiving of the Holy Spirit. Throughout the Bible we see that power and death are, related. Power is perfected in weakness (2 Corinthians 12:9). Life is connected with death (Matthew 16:24-25; John 12:24-25). Moreover, power is connected with suffering (2 Timothy 1:8).

And so, we see that the Spirit is sent to give us power. This power enables us to die to ourselves so that we can witness for Christ (this death may be spiritual and/or physical). To witness was originally understood as a proclamation of the resurrection of Jesus Christ; the idea of a witness was often directly connected with what someone had seen and heard (Acts 22:15) regarding the resurrection. It follows, then, that the common greeting between believers in the early church was "He is alive" and its response "He is alive indeed!" No chest bumping, no secret handshakes . . . just "**He is alive**!" And so, the ultimate act of power becomes the ultimate greeting which is certainly nothing less than a definitive expression of praise and worship. **He is alive! He is alive indeed!**

JANUARY 8

BROKEN TO BE MADE WHOLE . . .

"The sacrifices of God are a broken spirit; A broken and a contrite heart, O God, You will not despise."

Psalm 51:17

Someone might say confidently, "I may bend but I will not break." However, it is brokenness that God "will not despise" (Psalm 51:7). It is coming to the end of yourself that brings you to the beginning of God, for to come to God you must recognize and confess your need. You must be broken to be made whole. Oppositely, sin is very closely linked with a lack of recognition of your need; it is associated with a lack of brokenness (John 9:41). It is true that our greatest need is to see that we are in need of God.

The process of coming to Jesus is the process of being "broken." Jesus will "break" us again and again as He transforms us into His own image (Matthew 21:44; Romans 12:1-2; Romans 8:28-29). We must avoid allowing the opposite of brokenness—self-righteousness—to become a stumbling block on the way to Jesus. Self-righteousness (the lack of brokenness) denies the need for God's help. Peter fell over this stumbling block (Mark 14:29). We must accept the fact that we need God and His provision for salvation. Those who cannot see that they have need will "have no part" with Jesus (John 13:8).

Being justified and forgiven (made whole) is associated with humility and brokenness before God. It is associated with trusting only in God and refusing to trust in yourself. Someone might proudly declare, "I may bend but I will not break" while another person might humbly cry, "I am broken. Help!" In any case, as the Pharisee and the tax collector found out, you must be broken to be made whole . . .

> Two men went up into the temple to pray, one a Pharisee and the other a tax collector. The Pharisee stood and was praying this to himself: 'God, I thank You that I am not like other people: swindlers, unjust, adulterers, or even like this tax collector. I fast twice a week; I pay tithes of all that I get.' But the tax collector, standing some distance away, was even unwilling to lift up his eyes to heaven, but was beating his breast, saying, 'God, be merciful to me, the sinner!' I tell you, this man went to his house justified rather than the other; for everyone who exalts himself will be humbled, but he who humbles himself will be exalted (Luke 18:10-14).

To exalt yourself is to trust in yourself. To humble yourself is to trust in God. You cannot have God's rule (His kingdom) without your poverty (Matthew 5:3). You cannot see God's ability without seeing your inability (John 15:5). You cannot experience God's power without first experiencing your own weakness (2 Corinthians 12:9). You cannot see unless you are first blind (John 9:39-41). You cannot get help from a physician unless you are first sick (Matthew 9:12). God does not want your sacrifices (Psalm 51:16). He wants your broken and contrite heart (Psalm 51:17). So, go before God in all your brokenness and watch as He puts you back together!

JANUARY 9

THE SUPREMACY OF LOVE . . .

"'Teacher, which is the great commandment in the Law?' And He said to him, 'YOU SHALL LOVE THE LORD YOUR GOD WITH ALL YOUR HEART, AND WITH ALL YOUR SOUL, AND WITH ALL YOUR MIND. This is the great and foremost commandment. The second is like it, YOU SHALL LOVE YOUR NEIGHBOR AS YOURSELF. On these two commandments depend the whole Law and the Prophets.'"

Matthew 22:36-40

The whole of the Old Testament is boiled down to two commandments. Both commandments have one thing in common; that is, love. The supremacy of love is seen in the fact that it is the central idea within the summing up of God's commandments; our love for God and our love for others.

Your love for God will depend on your perception of how much you have been forgiven; your perception of the degree to which you **need** forgiveness. In a parable about a moneylender and two debtors—one of which is forgiven little and, thus, loves little and one of which is forgiven much and, thus, loves much—Jesus describes the connection between love and forgiveness when He says, " . . . he who is forgiven little, loves little" (Luke 7:40-47). Perhaps, this is why in comparison to our love for Jesus we should "hate" those whom we, otherwise, would be understood to love (Luke 14:26). Forgiveness is found in Jesus alone. The degree to which we need Jesus for forgiveness (not anyone else) is so absolute that our love for Him supersedes our love for anyone else.

Yet, the supremacy of love is also established by the commandment to love others. This is not in spite of our love for Jesus, but an expression of that love. Jesus challenged Peter (John 21:15) to express his love for Him via his willingness to give of himself on behalf of those who are followers of Jesus. Our love for Jesus can be measured by our love for others (John 15:12-14). Disciples of Jesus are known by their love for one another (John 13:35).

What are the results of love? Evidence of your love for God is your **obedience** to Him. Obedience is a result of love. **Revelation** is a result of obedience, and therefore, also a result of love (John 14:15, 21). Those who love their God, obey and know their God (Exodus 5:2). **Service** is also a result of love. The service of the foot washing is preceded by the declaration of Jesus' love for His disciples (John 13:1). Finally, it should be noted that **giving** is the action of love: "For God so loved the world that He gave . . . " (John 3:16). Perhaps in its most clear application, true love results in giving. To love is to give of oneself for the good of the other, and in so doing, reigns supreme in its reflection of God. And so, one who is loved and who then loves is one who is an obedient servant who knows his God and gives of himself for the sake of others in reflecting that very God whom He knows. The supremacy of love is found in the cross (John 3:16) and then found in those who take up their cross daily (Luke 9:23).

JANUARY 10

THERE IS A CURE FOR HYPOCRISY . . .

"But let your statement be, 'Yes, yes' or 'No, no'; anything beyond these is of evil."

Matthew 5:37

Pointing to God or reality (as opposed to superficiality; see 1 Samuel 16:7) exposes hypocrisy. God is the God of reality (the "I AM"), not superficiality. Thus, the fullness (or reality) of the law is not found in its sacrificial aspect, but in its compassion (Matthew 12:7). Compassion reflects the heart of the law. Compassion points to reality. Alternatively, sacrifice can often be very superficial. The Law and the Prophets are based on reality, not hypocrisy/superficiality. The reality is to treat others as you would have others treat you. Anything else is superficial (Matthew 7:12). The superficial must be distinguished from the profound. For example, defiling yourself is the result of what is said, thought, and done (reality/profound). It is not the result of what is eaten (superficiality/external); rather, it has to do with what comes out of the heart (Matthew 15:11).

When it came to hypocrisy, Jesus was very direct and did not hesitate to confront it and expose it (Luke 16:15). Jesus did not allow hypocrites to be in control of the conversation or situation. Rather, He used superior wisdom to remain in control and to expose their hypocrisy (Luke 20:1-8). How is hypocrisy exposed? In general, when you speak forth truth (reality) you will often expose hypocrisy (including the exposing of your own hypocrisy which is why confession or "self-truth-speak" is so important in the Christian walk). This speaking forth of truth (Luke 11:45) will insult and irritate the hypocrites (or the hypocrite in you). Nevertheless, speak forth truth/confession and let truth do the judging/convicting (John 3:18). Sometimes, hypocrisy may fool others now, but its folly will ultimately be exposed (Luke 12:2). In the end everything will be revealed for what it really is (reality always wins the day). Thus, the "final justice" of God brings comfort to the righteous who sometimes feel like Habakkuk felt (see Habakkuk 1:1-4, 12-14).

True religion includes the contents of the heart (reality/profound) along with appropriate outward forms of expression that can contain those contents. Religiosity or hypocrisy is satisfied with the form only. Thus, a cure for hypocrisy is to evaluate your outward forms, not necessarily throw them out. Do your forms include real heartfelt contents, or are they just a show? Make sure you fill them with real contents. When all is "said" and done, integrity is the greatest cure for hypocrisy (Matthew 5:37). Practice and treasure integrity and you will avoid hypocrisy. Hypocrisy begins when you allow your "yes" to be something less than "yes" or your "no" to be something more than "no." Let truth be the medicine you take to cure hypocrisy. Speak truth and the truth will set you free from hypocrisy (John 8:32).

————————

JANUARY 11

FATHER TO THE SON: "GREAT JOB . . . HAVE A SEAT!"

"So then, when the Lord Jesus had spoken to them, He was received up into heaven and sat down at the right hand of God."

Mark 16:19

When you finally finish a big job, it is "oh so nice" to just sit down and enjoy the satisfaction of your accomplishment. So, it is with Jesus! He "sat down at the right hand of God" in a dramatic indication and visible demonstration of the completion of His work of redemption. This aspect of the gospel story—Christ in heaven seated at the right hand of God the Father—is called the session (1 Peter 3:22; Ephesians 1:20; Acts 7:56; Revelation 5:6-10). He is "seated"—He is enthroned, marking His victory and authority as in Revelation 3:21—"at the right hand of God." He is God and He is with God as in John 1:1. He and the Father are distinct yet One, a singular plurality, a unity in diversity, different yet not divided as in Revelation 22:3 where there is God and the Lamb yet only one throne on which they sit.

In the session there is honor and glory (Hebrews 2:9), joy (Psalm 16:11; Hebrews 12:2), and authority (Ephesians 1:20-23; 1 Corinthians 15:23-25; 1 Peter 3:22). Most significantly for us, the session is associated with the pouring out of the Holy Spirit on the church: "Therefore having been exalted to the right hand of God, and having received from the Father the promise of the Holy Spirit, He has poured forth this which you both see and hear" (Acts 2:33).

Jesus came to earth from heaven (incarnation), returned to heaven from earth (ascension), is seated at the right hand of the Father (session), and "This Jesus, who has been taken up from you into heaven, will come in just the same way as you have watched Him go into heaven" (Acts 1:11). He is coming back, and when He returns, He will come as Judge (Psalm 110). Be sure you are ready!

THE LORD *says to my Lord:*

"Sit at My right hand

Until I make Your enemies a footstool for Your feet."

THE LORD *will stretch forth Your strong scepter from Zion,* saying,

"Rule in the midst of Your enemies."

Your people will volunteer freely in the day of Your power;

In holy array, from the womb of the dawn,

Your youth are to You as the dew.

THE LORD *has sworn and will not change His mind,*

"You are a priest forever

According to the order of Melchizedek."

The Lord is at Your right hand;

He will shatter kings in the day of His wrath.

He will judge among the nations,

He will fill them with corpses,

He will shatter the chief men over a broad country.

He will drink from the brook by the wayside;

Therefore He will lift up His head (Psalm 110).

———————

JANUARY 12

A DISCIPLE OF JESUS IS MARKED BY LOVE . . .

"A new commandment I give to you, that you love one another,
even as I have loved you, that you also love one another.
By this all men will know that you are My disciples,
if you have love for one another."

John 13:34-35

A disciple of Jesus is marked by love. A follower of Jesus is a follower of love. The disciple's love for Jesus is such that it would almost seem that he hates everything/anything else; the disciple prefers Jesus above all else: "If anyone comes to Me, and does not hate his own father and mother and wife and children and brothers and sisters, yes, and even his own life, he cannot be My disciple" (Luke 14:26). It is not to say that a disciple should actually hate his wife, his child, or even his own sense of success and self-fulfillment. It is to say, however, that disciples of Jesus are to give such a degree of preference to Jesus that other people or other things seem to never even be candidates for that top spot. Real Christianity is a complete commitment to Christ. Christ is placed first in all aspects of your life. You must unconditionally surrender to Jesus. You are willing to give your whole life to Him. For the disciple, nothing can ever take Jesus' "top-spot" place because He always comes before all things: "But seek ***first*** His kingdom and His righteousness, and all these things will be added to you" (Matthew 6:33). One thing that is "added to you" is the ability to love others. It is a mark of disciples that they love one another: "A new commandment I give to you, that you love one another, even as I have loved you, that you also love one another. By this all men will know that you are My disciples, if you have love for one another" (John 13:34-35). Thus, love for one another becomes a way to put Jesus first, and in so doing, even becomes a way to make Him known to other people ("By this all men will know that you are My disciples").

Disciples also love the Word of God. They hold onto the teachings of Christ: "Jesus was saying to those Jews who had believed Him, 'If you continue in My word, then you are truly disciples of Mine; and you will know the truth, and the truth will make you free'" (John 8:31-32). Consistency in the Word of God yields a consistency in one's walk with Jesus; you are not "wishy-washy." And so, Jesus says to them, "No one, after putting his hand to the plow and looking back, is fit for the kingdom of God" (Luke 9:62).

A disciple chooses to deny himself, live the life of the cross, and follow Christ (Matthew. 16:24). A disciple denies himself by laying down his rights for the sake of Christ and others. In so doing, he follows (he is a disciple) Christ who amazingly did not claim His rights as God but laid them down (Philippians 2:7 says: He "emptied Himself" or "laid aside His privileges"). The disciple lives the life of the cross—which may include shame, persecution, and abuse—living a life set against the ways of the world. He will not simply do this on a few sacred holidays but will do it every day: "And He was saying to them all, 'If anyone wishes to come after Me, he must deny himself, and take up his cross daily and follow Me'" (Luke 9:23). The disciple (follower) must walk and live like Christ walked and lived. In so doing, he will bear fruit as Christ bore fruit and glorify God by showing himself to be Jesus' disciple: "My Father is glorified by this, that you bear much fruit, and so prove to be My disciples" (John 15:8). There is much fruit to be harvested but the primary/first fruit is love (Galatians 5:22-23; 1 Corinthians 13:13). A disciple will be willing to abandon everything to follow Christ. Jesus says, "So then, none of you can be My disciple who does not give up all his own possessions" (Luke 14:33). In summary, a disciple works hard, consumes very little, and gives and loves very much (Matthew 6:19-21).

JANUARY 13

SPIRITUAL LAWS . . . THE UNSEEN BUT REAL ORDER!

"God is not mocked; for whatever a man sows, this he will also reap."

Galatians 6:7

There are spiritual principles. For example, violence cannot find its justification by claiming that it is being done in the name/reputation of Jesus (Luke 9:54-56). This is the spiritual principle that still rebukes the Crusades which occurred hundreds of years ago. It is a principle that leads to some difficult discussions about the idea of "just war" and any sort of violent civil disobedience. Those who go to war and take up the sword may also die in that war by the sword (Matthew 26:52). This principle can be said to be consistent with the law of sowing and reaping.

There are spiritual laws, albeit unseen, that establish the real order of the universe, for example, the law of sowing and reaping. Spiritual laws keep things real. Another way to say this is: "God is not mocked." It is a clear spiritual law that you will reap exactly what you sow. In Matthew 5:4, we see that "blessed are those who mourn, for they shall be comforted." For those who mourn over their sin (are uncomfortable with it), there is comfort (forgiveness). For those who do not mourn over their sin (are comfortable with it), there is no comfort (forgiveness). If you sow your own comfort, you do not reap the comfort of God. Jesus once said it this way: "For judgment I came into this world, so that those who do not see may see, and that those who see may become blind . . . If you were blind, you would have no sin; but since you say, 'We see,' your sin remains" (John 9:39, 41).

Another way to say that you will reap what you sow is "You will produce what you are" or "A good tree cannot produce bad fruit, nor can a bad tree produce good fruit" (Matthew 7:18). To some extent we will even determine how we will be judged by others due to the law of reaping and sowing: "Do not judge so that you will not be judged. For in the way you judge, you will be judged; and by your standard of measure, it will be measured to you" (Matthew 7:1-3).

The Bible tells us to do unto others as we would want them to do unto us (Luke 6:31). You are to sow what you would want to reap. It is in this context that we also read about the law of sowing and reaping with respect to mercy and judgment and giving and receiving (Luke 6:37-39). Do you want to reap mercy? Then sow it! Do you want to reap "getting"? Then give! The spiritual law of sowing and reaping, although unseen, is real.

JANUARY 14

GOD MADE YOU TO FELLOWSHIP . . .

"Then God said, 'Let Us make man in Our image, according to Our likeness . . .
God created man in His own image, in the image of God He created him;
male and female He created them.'"

Genesis 1:26-27

In the New Testament, the Bible refers to believers as saints. Of the sixty-two times this reference is used, sixty-one times the word *saint* is in the plural form. The Bible assumes the fellowship of believers even as it assumes that the people of God are a group, not an individual. It assumes that the church is a community in fellowship, not an individual alone. It is the "people of God" not the "person of God"! Fellowship is assumed in the Word of God because it is inherent in God's plan.

First, fellowship is inherent in who we are in creation. We are made in the image of an "Us." "Then God said, 'Let **Us** make man in **Our** image, according to **Our** likeness'" (Genesis 1:26) which is a reference to the Trinity. The essence of the Trinity is relationship. The Trinity is the manifestation of the perfect community (fellowship). To be created in the image of an "Us" is to be created in the image of a perfect fellowship. And so, mankind is then created as a fellowship—"And God created man in His own image, in the image of God He created him; male and female He created them" (Genesis 1:27)—or as a plurality; that is, male and female. The man, alone, was incomplete. Thus, God created the most basic community or fellowship—"For this cause a man shall leave his father and his mother, and shall cleave to his wife; and they shall become one flesh"—when He instituted marriage. A sense of fellowship is inherent to who we are in creation. We are inherently social beings.

Second, fellowship is inherent in who we are in the Fall. Man is by nature a social being. However, in the Fall, man's nature was distorted. He became alienated from God, himself, and others. Nonetheless, fellowship is inherent to who we are in the Fall inasmuch as the Fall points to all that we have in common. We are all sinners (Romans 3:23). There is only one, all-encompassing, solution (John 14:6). Thus, we have a common problem and a common solution. This is the basis for fellowship in the church that is made up of those who are part of the Fall of man—"Since there is one bread, we who are many are one body; for we all partake of the one bread" (1 Corinthians 10:17)—and so we are described as "one body." Some of the strongest communities or "fellowships" of people have formed around a common problem and a common solution. Soviets and Americans came together in World War II because they had a common problem (Hitler) and a common solution (victory in war). How much truer should this dynamic of bringing people together be in the church? We have a common problem, and a common solution of eternal significance, not simply temporal importance.

Third, fellowship is inherent in who we are in Christ. The initial purpose that Jesus had for His followers was to have fellowship with them. Fellowship ("that they might be with Him") precedes evangelism and ministry (Mark 3:14). Jesus develops a community (the twelve), provides an example of how it should operate (serving each other), and then encourages the community (fellowship) to continue (John 13:15)—"A new commandment I give to you, that you love one another, even as I have loved you, that you also love one another. By this all men will know that you are My disciples, if you have love for one another" (John 13:34-35). God made you to fellowship, so, **fellowship**!

JANUARY 15

THE KINGDOM OF GOD IS ALREADY AND NOT YET

"'YOU HAVE PUT ALL THINGS IN SUBJECTION UNDER HIS FEET.'
For in subjecting all things to him,
He left nothing that is not subject to him.

But now we do not yet see all
things subjected to him."

Hebrews 2:8-9

What is the kingdom of God? The Greek term *basileia*, translated "kingdom," is most directly translated as "reign" or "rule." The kingdom of God is the rule of God. God's rule, ultimately, is exhaustive as "the Lord has established His throne in the heavens, and His sovereignty rules over all" (Psalm 103:19). His kingdom, presently, is marked by His authority or rule in the hearts of those who yield themselves to Him; thus, the "kingdom of heaven is at hand" or "in your midst" (Matthew 4:17). The kingdom of God is already **and** not yet; "he left nothing that is not subject to him" **and** "now we do not yet see all things subjected to him" (Hebrews 2:8-9).

The two Ages overlap. The powers of the "Age to Come" have penetrated this Age, even while we still live in this present evil Age. We are transformed and no longer conform to the powers of this Age. The kingdom of God is a present reality (Mark 1:15; Matthew 12:28; Luke 17:20; Romans 12:1-2). At the same time, the kingdom of God will not come in its fullness until the Second Coming of Christ and the resurrection of the dead. This will lead to the "Age to Come" when all evil is destroyed. The kingdom of God is a future reality (Luke 22:18; Mark 9:1; John 18:36).

Eternal life belongs to the kingdom of God, the "Age to Come," but it has also entered this present evil age. Man may experience this life by being born again. Eternal life is to know God through personal relationship and actual experience in this lifetime (John 17:3; John 3:3; Romans 14:17). The righteousness of the kingdom of God is imparted to us as we allow God to reign in our heart. No one can attain the standard required by the righteousness of the kingdom of God. We must receive it like a child through God's unmerited grace (Ephesians 2:8-9; Mark 10:15; Luke 22:29). The kingdom of God makes one fundamental demand; the demand for a decision to allow God to rule your life. This requires repentance, which is to turn around, to reverse your course of life, and to embrace the direction of the kingdom of God (Mark 1:15; Luke 9:23; Matthew 6:33; Matthew 19:16).

And so, the kingdom of God is already *and* not yet. For those who live in the kingdom of God now, the obvious question, then, is: "What can I do to move the kingdom of God from the "already" to the "not yet"?" The answer to this question is quite clear in the Scripture: "this gospel of the kingdom shall be preached in the whole world for a witness to all the nations, and then the end shall come" (Matthew 24:14). What can you do? Preach the gospel . . . be a witness. Then the end shall come. The kingdom of God "not yet" will become the kingdom of God "already." Maranatha . . . Come, Lord Jesus! (Revelation 22:20).

TWO KINGDOMS AS DIFFERENT AS NIGHT AND DAY

"Any kingdom divided against itself is laid waste; and a house divided against itself falls. If Satan also is divided against himself, how will his kingdom stand?"

Luke 11:17-18

The kingdom of God "is not of this world" (John 18:36). This world has its own god (2 Corinthians 4:4) who heads up a counterfeit kingdom (Luke 11:17-18). Satan's kingdom is very different than the kingdom of God . . . they're as different as night and day!

The kingdom of God is associated with light (Isaiah 58:8; Revelation 21:23; 1 Timothy 6:16) while the kingdom of Satan is associated with darkness (Ephesians 6:12; 1 John 2:9; Revelation 16:10; Colossians 1:13). The kingdom of God is marked by love (Matthew 22:37) and redemption (Matthew 8:11) while the kingdom of Satan is marked by separation from God (Matthew 13:19; 1 John 3:8). The kingdom of God is centered in truth (John 14:6) while the kingdom of Satan is centered in lies (2 Thessalonians 2:9; John 8:44). The kingdom of God includes the power of God (Luke 21:27) and the kingdom of Satan is defeated by that power (Matthew 16:18; 1 John 3:8). Ultimately, the kingdom of God will remain forever (2 Peter 1:11) while the kingdom of Satan is only temporary (Revelation 20:10).

The extreme distinctions between the two kingdoms can be seen clearly in their character. The kingdom of God is marked by unity, harmony, and peace (John 10:16; Luke 2:14) while the kingdom of Satan is marked by confusion (1 Corinthians 14:33; Isaiah 41:29). The kingdom of God is linked to sacrifice (Romans 12:1) and humility (1 Peter 5:5) while the kingdom of Satan is linked to pride (Proverbs 16:18; James 4:6). The kingdom of God is associated with justice and righteousness (Psalm 11:7; Isaiah 54:14; Romans 10:4) while the kingdom of Satan is associated with wickedness (1 John 3:12; 3 John 11). Perhaps most significantly as to the character of the two kingdoms, the kingdom of God is marked by mercy (2 Corinthians 1:3) but the kingdom of Satan is marked by death (Romans 6:23).

And so, the kingdom of God is linked to victory over sin and death (1 John. 5:12) by faith (Ephesians 2:8-9) while the kingdom of Satan is linked to the destruction that comes from sin (Romans 5:12) by deception (2 Thessalonians 2:3). The kingdom of God is marked by the incorruptible (1 Corinthians 15:50) but the kingdom of Satan is marked by the corruptible (Romans 8:19-21). Ultimately, the kingdom of God is associated with free will/freedom (Joshua 24:15; John 8:36), joy (Psalm 126:5), and victory (Romans 8:37) while the kingdom of Satan is associated with slavery (2 Peter 2:19), punishment (Matthew 18:8), and defeat (Genesis 3:15; 1 John 3:8).

The two kingdoms are very different. One is real and associated with Him who is real; the "I Am Who I Am" (Exodus 3:14). The other is a counterfeit and associated with him who is a counterfeiter; the deceiver (Revelation 12:9) and disguiser (2 Corinthians 11:14). Satan's kingdom of darkness is the opposite of God's kingdom of light. These two opposites in no way attract!

JANUARY 17

SIN SICKENS, JESUS HEALS, AND THE SOVEREIGN GOD IS GLORIFIED

". . . and the power of the Lord was present *for Him to perform healing."*

Luke 5:17

Where does sickness come from? Certainly, it is a result of the Fall of man in the garden; that is, a result of sin. Jesus links sickness with sin when he instructs the man who was healed at the pool in Bethesda saying, "Behold, you have become well; do not sin anymore, so that nothing worse happens to you" (John 5:14). Sickness and death (sickness' ultimate manifestation) are the wages of sin (Romans 6:23) and all have sinned (Romans 3:23) since all have the nature of sin in them (Psalm 51:5; Ephesians 2:3). Sickness, then, comes from the corruption of the Fall whether that corruption be directly or indirectly associated with the victim; thus, "As He passed by, He saw a man blind from birth. And His disciples asked Him, 'Rabbi, who sinned, this man or his parents, that he would be born blind?' Jesus answered, 'It was neither that this man sinned, nor his parents; but it was so that the works of God might be displayed in him'" (John 9:1-3). Sickness may not be a direct result of your own sin but it is a result of sin; a result of the corruption of the Fall. Regardless, like all other dynamics of evil (corruption), it is subject to the sovereignty of God and, thus, used by Him for His purposes and glory.

What is the purpose of healing? Just as death can be used to glorify God through the manifestation of His power in salvation, so too, sickness can be used to glorify God through the manifestation of His power in healing. And so with regard to sickness, Jesus would say things like: "This sickness is not to end in death, but for the glory of God, so that the Son of God may be glorified by it" (John 11:4). Jesus healed as a way to demonstrate His authority to forgive sins (Matthew 9:6). Healing can even be used as a sign of the gospel's authenticity as it is ministered through its adherents: "And He said to them, 'Go into all the world and preach the gospel to all creation . . . these signs will accompany those who have believed: in My name . . . they will lay hands on the sick, and they will recover'" (Mark 16:15-18).

What is the cause of healing? Just as salvation is a result of God's love (John 3:16), so, too, healing is the result of God's compassion. "When He went ashore, He saw a large crowd, and felt compassion for them and healed their sick" (Matthew 14:14).

Compassion is often linked with healing (Luke 7:13; Mark 1:41; John 11:35; Matthew 20:34). So too, faith is often linked with healing: "But Jesus turning and seeing her said, 'Daughter, take courage; your faith has made you well'" (Matthew 9:22). Even these "causes" of healing, however, are not a recipe for it. Ultimately, God is sovereign over healing. The power of the Lord must be present to perform healing (Luke 5:17). The implication is that sometimes the power of the Lord is not present. He is a sovereign God. Most importantly then, healing is the result of the presence of the power of the Lord to heal.

JANUARY 18

THE GOD OF MERCY AND GRACE . . . HOPE FOR ALL!

"A BATTERED REED HE WILL NOT BREAK OFF, AND A SMOLDERING WICK HE WILL NOT PUT OUT, UNTIL HE LEADS JUSTICE TO VICTORY. AND IN HIS NAME THE GENTILES WILL HOPE."

Matthew 12:20-21

Variety, it is said, is the spice of life. Hope, then, is its caffeine. It is hope that spurs life on while the absence of it yields a sense of sickness . . . lifelessness . . . depression (Proverbs 13:12). Perhaps nothing is more depressing than when you fall. You fall and seemingly cannot get up. Your legs are broken, and the mountain is steep. It is hopeless. What caffeine will spur you on? Is there hope? God is a God of mercy and grace . . . a strong cup of coffee! It is His mercy and grace that spurs you on . . . that gives you hope.

God's mercy is great. He does not need much of a response from you to be able to bless you. Even as with Sodom in Genesis 18:22-32—hope in the midst of seemingly certain destruction that could be avoided if there were fifty responses or forty-five or forty or thirty or twenty or even just ten—the existence of even a smoldering wick is enough. He will not put it out (Matthew 12:20). His great mercy allows Him to respond to any amount of response to Him. Of course, this must be respected as even the mercy and patience of God has a limit (Luke 13:6-8). Nevertheless, it is in this mercy that even a battered reed will not be broken off and may find hope . . . caffeine for the weary.

This hope is for all since all need hope. God's mercy and grace is available for all people "and in His name the gentiles will hope" (Matthew 12:21). God's spontaneous expressions of favor to the undeserving (His grace) is, in that sense, common. Perhaps, the most common thing about mankind is sin (Romans 3:23) and its most grand depression that comes from the grandest Fall. You fall and seemingly cannot get up. Yet, God is kind to ungrateful and evil men (Luke 6:35). God has grace upon all (Romans 2:4) and so all have hope:

From one man he made every nation of men, that they should inhabit the whole earth; and he determined the times set for them and the exact places where they should live. God did this so that men would seek him and perhaps reach out for him and find him, though he is not far from each one of us. For in him we live and move and have our being (Acts 17:26-28).

So, no matter where you are today in your journey through the caverns and dark holes of the grand Fall, you have hope. Why? Because God's grace and mercy puts you in a place where even if you are badly battered and almost broken or even if you are barely smoldering and almost out, God is not far off and can be moved by even the weakest of reeds and the slightest of flames. So, do not give up. Just reach out!

―――――――――

JANUARY 19

THE UNIVERSALITY OF THE FIRST AND LAST ADAM

"For if by the transgression of the one, death reigned through the one, much more those who receive the abundance of grace and of the gift of righteousness will reign in life through the One, Jesus Christ. So then as through one transgression there resulted condemnation to all men, even so through one act of righteousness there resulted justification of life to all men. For as through the one man's disobedience the many were made sinners, even so through the obedience of the One the many will be made righteous."

Romans 5:17-19

The Hebrew term *Adam* is properly translated as "Man" or "mankind." The first man, Adam, was a real historical person who universally represents mankind/humanity. Thus, the Adamic covenant is a covenant made with mankind. When it was broken, it was broken by mankind. When we understand that God made a covenant with man and man broke the covenant, then we understand the need for the universal atonement. Jesus, as the "last Adam" (1 Corinthians 15:45), died for **all** men. He died for Jew and gentile (notice that Paul does not call Jesus the "last Moses"). Jesus died for all men because all men are guilty of breaking the covenant. He died for all men because "All have sinned and fallen short of the glory of God" (Romans 3:23).

Just as Luke was careful to trace the genealogy of Jesus all the way back to Adam (Luke 3:38), Paul was also careful to recognize Adam and the universality of his sin as it relates to the plan of redemption. And so, Paul points out the need for the gentiles to be redeemed (Ephesians 2:11-12). He was also careful to point out the need for the Jews to also be redeemed (Ephesians 2:1-3). A "common need" requires a "common solution." The first Adam fostered a universal need and the last Adam fostered a universal solution. The universal Fall of man demands universal redemption/atonement. And so, "then as through one transgression there resulted condemnation to all men, even so through one act of righteousness there resulted justification of life to all men" (Romans 5:18).

To the Jew, when Adam sinned, all sinned in Adam; after Adam sinned all of mankind would have a sin nature (this is often referred to as the doctrine of original sin). As the Psalmist says, we are born in sin (Psalm 51:5) and as Paul says, we have a sin nature (Ephesians 2:3). "The wicked are estranged from the womb" (Psalm 58:3), "the intent of man's heart is evil from his youth" (Genesis 8:21), and "Therefore, just as through one man sin entered into the world, and death through sin, and so death spread to all men, because all sinned" (Romans 5:12).

The universality of the first and last Adam is a theological reality. Universal salvation (salvation for Jew and Gentile) is a theological necessity because universal sin and death are theological realities. We all have the same problem (Romans 3:9), thus, we all have the same solution (John 3:16). How much more, then, should we (those who recognize the problem and receive the solution) be unified with each other "since there is one bread, we who are many are one body; for we all partake of the one bread . . ." (1 Corinthians 10:17).

JANUARY 20

CHRISTIAN FELLOWSHIP . . . MORE THAN AN ICE CREAM SOCIAL!

" . . . my companion and my familiar friend; We who had sweet fellowship together . . ."

Psalm 55:13-14

Although it is true that fellowship is described at one point in the Bible as being "sweet"— " . . . my companion and my familiar friend. We who had sweet fellowship together" (Psalm 55:13-14)—it must be said that Christian fellowship is more than an ice cream social! It consists of more than simply hanging out together and taking part in the church program (no matter how much you may enjoy Cookies and Cream or Vanilla Fudge Ripple).

Christian fellowship is based on relationship. The word relationship is an intimate word. Especially among Christians, its meaning and manifestation should not simply rest on the superficial. Christian fellowship should be personal, intimate, and authentic. We must get beyond superficial and casual concerns. We must become familiar with each other's lives in a more profound way. How else could we have compassion for (to suffer with) our brother (Mark 8:2)? Our fellowship with God is intimate. We speak to God from the depths of our souls. Our fellowship with each other must be intimate also (1 John 1:3).

One of the fastest ways to destroy intimate fellowship is to base our relationships on accomplishing tasks. We cannot have intimate, real relationships when the primary reason for meeting together is to accomplish a task or to organize a project. The main reason to come together must be to commune with God and each other. We must come together as brothers and sisters who desire the good of each other through seeking the good of the Father. When the main reason to come together is simply to accomplish a task, we invert the order of the gospel. Faith before works is changed and becomes works before faith. Jesus required a deep relationship with His disciples. He did not promote casual acquaintances or "working relationships."

The tragedy of Western Christianity is that the focus that Christ had on filling up the community with loving hearts has been replaced by a focus on filling up the community numerically. In some of our gatherings we would never notice if twenty-five percent of the people who were at the previous gathering were not there as long as the twenty-five percent who were not there were replaced by other people. When we look at the members of the community as simply representing a filled place in the community, then we necessarily forfeit true community and fellowship. The result is a focus on filled chairs instead of on filled lives. This does not happen in a community that understands what real, intimate, and personal relationships require. The members must interact with each other and share their lives. It is not enough to meet together and share a building.

How can we promote and experience authentic relationships in our fellowship? We must realize that the Christian community is "a called out" people who are members of a covenant community. The covenant is with their Father and with each other. We must make this covenant something specific, concrete, and defined. In order to do this, we must make a covenant with a small group of believers. A small group is necessary for fellowship to become actual, real, personal, and intimate. To think that we can have that kind of fellowship with 500 people is to make fellowship an unrealistic theory, instead of a reality.

Yes, "we who had sweet fellowship together" (Psalm 55:14) must not simply be "we who ate ice cream together." Nothing wrong with ice cream, but Christian fellowship is more than an ice cream social!

JANUARY 21

A WISE MAN SAID: THE PROOF IS IN THE PUDDING!

"... Yet wisdom is vindicated by her deeds."

Matthew 11:19

Wisdom is vindicated (declared or proven) by her deeds. It is that which we do that proves that the wisdom of God is in us. Wisdom can be defined as practical knowledge or the proper application of knowledge. It is much more action oriented than thought oriented (although the popular understanding of wisdom is the opposite). Wisdom comes to light by its fruits or results. Wisdom is said, in Luke 7:35, to be vindicated by "all her children." If you think you are wise, then, you have to ask yourself "What is my so-called wisdom birthing?" If the kids running around the room are fools, then it is probably not wisdom! What do children look like who are birthed from wisdom? They look like those who are willing to do God's will (John 7:17).

True wisdom is effectual. It has results. It is so practical that it will "set you free." Wisdom (the application of truth) results in sanctification (the opposite of being enslaved to sin):

> So Jesus was saying to those Jews who had believed Him, 'If you continue in My word, then you are truly disciples of Mine; and you will know the truth, and the truth will make you free.' They answered Him, 'We are Abraham's descendants and have never yet been enslaved to anyone; how is it that You say, "You will become free?"' Jesus answered them, 'Truly, truly, I say to you, everyone who commits sin is the slave of sin' (John 8:31-34).

Wisdom is practical. It is powerful. It can win battles ... battles of the wits! Jesus instructed His followers, that when they would be brought before officials for His name's sake, to not take time to defend themselves, but rather, to decide ahead of time to use the opportunity to testify about Jesus, and then He would give them the wisdom to overwhelm their opponents (Luke 21:10-15).

This "battle of the wits" type of wisdom is often seen in Jesus' interactions with the hypocritical Pharisees. Jesus does not allow hypocrisy to be in control of a situation; rather, He uses superior wisdom to remain in control and to expose hypocrisy:

> On one of the days while He was teaching the people in the temple and preaching the gospel, the chief priests and the scribes with the elders confronted Him, and they spoke, saying to Him, 'Tell us by what authority You are doing these things, or who is the one

who gave You this authority?' Jesus answered and said to them, 'I will also ask you a question, and you tell Me: "Was the baptism of John from heaven or from men?"' They reasoned among themselves, saying, 'If we say, "From heaven," He will say, "Why did you not believe him?" But if we say, "From men," all the people will stone us to death, for they are convinced that John was a prophet.' So they answered that they did not know where it came from. And Jesus said to them, 'Nor will I tell you by what authority I do these things' (Luke 20:1-8).

JANUARY 22

FEW ARE CHOSEN . . . BUT WHOSE CHOICE IS IT?

"For many are called, but few are chosen."

Matthew 22:14

The conclusion to the parable of the wedding feast is that "many are called, but few are chosen" (Matthew 22:14). In the parable (Matthew 22:1-14), those who are chosen are those have been invited (called) *and* who come to the feast wearing the wedding clothes provided by the host. You cannot enter the wedding feast wearing your own clothes; you cannot enter (be chosen) by your own provision. It is one thing to be invited (called). It is another thing to respond to that call consistent with its provision (chosen). In order to be chosen **you have to wear the clothes provided for you!** And so, whose choice is it? It is God's choice that we choose! In a very real sense, everyone is invited (called), but only a few come to the feast in the proper attire (chosen).

God desires all to be saved (1 Timothy 2:4) and does not want anyone to perish (2 Peter 3:9). God is sovereign, yet man has a free will. God chooses (John 15:16) yet does "not send the Son into the world to judge the world" (John 3:17). How do these components of salvation live together? How can many be called yet few be chosen? God is sovereign *and* man has a free will. They paradoxically live together; neither negates the other. This "living together" is, perhaps, best exemplified in John 1:12-13 where we see a picture of the dynamics of salvation in which "as many as received Him, to them He gave the right to become children of God (man's free will/choice) who were born not of blood, nor of the will of the flesh, nor of the will of man, but of God" (God's sovereignty/choice). So then whose choice is it? It is God's choice that we choose. God's choice becomes our choice; herein, is the seeming contradiction (paradox) as it "lives together." We choose God's choice which only God can make available and to which God must draw us (John 6:44, 65). At the same time, it should be stated that the unwillingness of people can hinder the realization of what God intends, even when God desires to draw them to Himself (Matthew 23:37; John 6:70).

How, then, are we saved? We are born of God. Our free will is not a will that creates since we are not creators (and our free will must be consistent with who we are). We are creations (receivers), and thus, our free will is a will that receives or rejects that which is already created and offered (which can only come from the Creator and Offerer, the Sovereign God). It has been said, "The free will of man is so powerfully influenced by God's sovereignty as to allow man to freely accept or reject, and yet conclude what God has concluded beforehand." We should remember that it is man's free will that rejects God, and that God, in that sense, does not disqualify anyone. Man disqualifies himself. We might say that God's drawing influence is available to everyone (many are called), but God does not draw some (few are chosen) because of their own actions. Man puts himself outside of the influence of God. His own actions result in the hardness of his heart (consider John 3:18; Mark 4:11-12; 6:52; Ephesians 4:17-19).

The foundational way in which man places himself outside of the influence of God (or, as in the parable of the wedding feast, outside of the wedding feast) is to not see/confess his need for God. Jesus comes for the sick not for the healthy (Matthew 9:12) and "If you were blind you would have no sin; but since you say, 'We see,' your sin remains" (John 9:41). In other words, since you say you are without need, then the thing you need is not applied to you. In the parable of the wedding feast those who are chosen are those who confess their need for God, as it were, by wearing the wedding clothes provided by the host. You cannot enter the wedding feast wearing your own clothes; you cannot enter by your own provision. You can only enter by accepting the provision of the host. It is a foundational theological truth: **you have to wear the clothes provided for you!** In this sense God says, "You did not choose me, but I chose you" (John 15:16). Whose choice is it? It is God's choice (provision) that we choose (accept that provision)! God's choice becomes our choice, and in so doing God's sovereignty and man's free will "live together."

———————

JANUARY 23

DOES GOD STILL SPEAK TODAY? . . . DOES HE SPEAK TO YOU?

"And after the earthquake a fire, but *the Lord* was *not in the fire;*
and after the fire a sound of a gentle blowing."

1 Kings 19:12

Does God still speak today? Does God still guide His people? Does God still communicate with them (perhaps with a gentle blowing or a still small voice)? Is He still around/involved in an interactive way with His people to apply His Word to their lives? Or is He gone? Has he left the applied scene of day to day life? Is He, as Nietzsche implied, interpersonally dead (by *dead* Nietzsche meant "not relevant/pertinent") or as Thomas Jefferson surmised, not involved (the mantra of deists)? Does the "closing of the Canon" necessitate the "closing of God's mouth"? If so, does the understanding of one's relationship with God verge on an incipient deism with respect to God's communicative involvement with His people?

To some degree, these questions are answered as we understand the idea of what might be called subordinate revelation (sometimes called illumination). Subordinate revelation is additional revelation only in the sense that it can further explain and clarify the revelation that already exists. This revelation is always subordinate and secondary to the special revelation of the Scriptures. Subordinate revelation must be consistent with special revelation. It must answer to it. Subordinate revelation consists of things like guidance through circumstances, understanding in Bible study (illumination of the Word as it is applied to you/your life), guidance through gifts of the Spirit like prophecy and word of wisdom, and communication in prayer that is sometimes described as God's communication with us via a "gentle blowing" (1 Kings 19:12) or "a still small voice" (1 Kings 19:12, KJV). Prayer seen as only one-way communication is, to some degree, incipient deism with respect to God's communicative involvement with His people.

A balanced understanding of subordinate revelation is important. Subordinate revelation is not additional revelation in the sense of new revelation. God's truth has been fully declared in His Word. It is not new truth. It is a deeper appreciation, understanding, and application of what has already been revealed. At the same time, we must accept the existence and the importance of subordinate revelation. A desired balanced approach must seek to avoid extremes. We must not fall into the extreme that uses subordinate revelation to gain new knowledge that is not consistent with or goes beyond the Scriptures. There is a sufficiency about Scripture; what we need to know can be found in God's Word. At the same time, we must not fall into the extreme that understands the closing of the Canon (final organization of the Bible) as signifying the closing of God's mouth. This extreme says that God no longer communicates with His people or reveals Himself. However, the sufficiency of Scripture does not cause God to stop revealing Himself, or His ways, or His direction through a variety of means (the content of which is consistent with Scripture).

God is not dead. His revelation of Himself is not static. Truth is not static in its application. "The word of God is living and active" (Hebrews 4:12). God still speaks to His people because God is alive and His relationship with His people is interactive. So, whether we are more comfortable theologically with saying, "God illuminated me" or "God spoke to me," Nietzsche and Jefferson were wrong. God is not dead on a practical, relational, or communicative level. He is alive!

JANUARY 24

SOCIAL CONCERNS FOUND IN GOD'S COVENANT . . .

"You shall not pervert the justice due to your needy brother in his dispute. Keep far from a false charge . . . You shall not take a bribe, for a bribe blinds the clear-sighted and subverts the cause of the just. You shall not oppress a stranger . . . "

Exodus 23:6-9

God is a just God. So, it only stands to reason that His covenant with His people would be full of social concerns. God is a social activist! For example, He is concerned about the rights of individuals. Each person has the right to be secure and protected: "If a man is caught kidnapping any of his countrymen of the sons of Israel, and he deals with him violently or sells him, then that thief shall die" (Deuteronomy 24:7). Again, God exhibits His justice, this time in that individuals shall enjoy protection against false accusation: "You shall not bear a false report; do not join your hand with a wicked man to be a malicious witness . . . to pervert justice" (Exodus 23:1-3). More specifically, the God of justice insists that women not be treated unfairly: "It shall be, if you are not pleased with her, then you shall let her go wherever she wishes; but you shall certainly not sell her for money, you shall not mistreat her, because you have humbled her" (Exodus 21:14).

The God of justice insists on equal rights. This is seen in His instructions for the Sabbath: " . . . but the seventh day is a Sabbath of the Lord your God; in it you shall not do any work, you or your son or your daughter, your male or your female servant or your cattle or your sojourner who stays with you" (Exodus 20:10). In addition, God insists on a fair trial: "You shall do no injustice in judgment; you shall not be partial to the poor nor defer to the great, but you are to judge your neighbor fairly" (Leviticus 19:15). God also speaks of rights regarding inheritance: "Then the Lord spoke to Moses, saying, 'Among these the land shall be divided for an inheritance according to the number of names. To the larger group you shall increase their inheritance, and to the smaller group you shall diminish their inheritance; each shall be given their inheritance according to those who were numbered of them'" (Numbers 26:52-54). Another issue of justice is the security of property: "You shall not see your countryman's ox or his sheep straying away, and pay no attention to them; you shall certainly bring them back to your countryman" (Deuteronomy 22:1). Similarly, God proposes that there be job security: "You shall not oppress a hired servant who is poor and needy, whether he is one of your countrymen or one of your aliens who is in your land in your towns. You shall give him his wages on his day before the sun sets, for he is poor and sets his heart on it . . ." (Deuteronomy 24:14-15).

Very much on God's heart is justice for the poor. He repeatedly promotes sharing with those in need: "You shall sow your land for six years and gather in its yield, but on the seventh year you shall let it rest and lie fallow, so that the needy of your people may eat" (Exodus 23:10-11). Those in need were not to be exploited: "You shall not wrong a stranger or oppress him . . . If you lend money to My people, to the poor among you, you are not to act as a creditor to him; you shall not charge him interest" (Exodus 22:21, 25). Finally, God even looks out for the "rights" of animals; animals should be cared for and respected: "You shall not see your countryman's donkey or his ox fallen down on the way, and pay no attention to them; you shall certainly help him to raise them up" (Deuteronomy 22:4). And so, God is a God of social concerns because "the Lord is a God of justice" (Isaiah 30:18).

––––––––––

JANUARY 25

ISAIAH POINTS TO JESUS . . .

"Behold, a virgin will be with child and bear a son, and she will call His name Immanuel."

Isaiah 7:14

The New Testament is the continuation and fulfillment of the Old Testament. And so, we see Jesus in the Exodus and in the Tabernacle. Jesus is found throughout the Old Testament. Jesus says, "that all things which are written about Me in the Law of Moses and the Prophets and the Psalms must be fulfilled" (Luke 24:44), and "You search the Scriptures . . . it is these that bear witness of me" (John 5:39), and "For if you believed in Moses, you would also believe me; for he wrote of me"

(John 5:46). The book of Isaiah quite often points to Christ. Isaiah references the history of Christ, the mission of Christ, and the titles of Christ.

With regard to the history of Christ, Isaiah points to His birth: "Therefore the Lord Himself will give you a sign: Behold, a virgin will be with child and bear a son, and she will call His name Immanuel" (Isaiah 7:14; Matthew 1:23). Here, we not only see a picture of Jesus' birth, but we also see a declaration of the incarnation and divinity of Jesus ("Immanuel" means "God is with us"). Isaiah also points to the lineage of Jesus and His anointing: "Then a shoot will spring from the stem of Jesse, and a branch from his roots will bear fruit. The Spirit of the Lord will rest on Him (Isaiah 11:1-2; Revelation 5:5; Matthew 3:16).

With regard to the mission of Christ, Isaiah points to Him as Illuminator: "The people who walk in darkness will see a great light; those who live in a dark land, the light will shine on them" (Isaiah 9:2; Luke 1:79). Isaiah also refers to Christ as Judge: "And He will delight in the fear of the Lord, and He will not judge by what His eyes see, nor make a decision by what His ears hear; but with righteousness He will judge" (Isaiah 11:3-4; John 2:25). In addition, Isaiah points to Christ as Reprover: "But with righteousness He will judge the poor, and decide with fairness for the afflicted of the earth; and He will strike the earth with the rod of His mouth, and with the breath of His lips He will slay the wicked" (Isaiah 11:4; Revelation 19:15). Christ is also seen as Law Giver: "He will not be disheartened or crushed until He has established justice in the earth; and the coastlands will wait expectantly for His law" (Isaiah 42:4; Matthew 12:18). He is seen as Liberator (Isaiah 42:7; Matthew 20:34), Burden bearer (Isaiah 53:4; John 19:7), Suffering Savior (Isaiah 53:5; 1 Corinthians 15:3), Sin Bearer (Isaiah 53:6; Hebrews 9:28), and Intercessor (Isaiah 53:12; Mark 15:28).

With regard to the titles of Christ, Isaiah refers to Him, perhaps most profoundly, as Immanuel (Isaiah 7:14; Matthew 1:23). Then he identifies Him as Mighty God, Everlasting Father, and Prince of Peace (Isaiah 9:6; Matthew 1:23). Christ is also referred to as Righteous King (Isaiah 32:1; Matthew 21:5), Divine Servant (Isaiah 42:1; Mark 1:11), Arm of the Lord (Isaiah 53:1; John 12:38), Anointed Preacher (Isaiah 61:1; Mark 1:38), and Mighty Savior (Isaiah 63:1; Matthew 18:11). And so, Isaiah, who is a writer of the Word of God, makes references throughout his book to Jesus, the Word of God (John 1:1). Jesus is all these functions and titles. He is Immanuel . . . He is the Suffering Savior . . . He is Mighty God! He is all these things and so much more. He is the Alpha and Omega (Revelation 22:13), and eventually we will see "the summing up of all things in Christ": "He made known to us the mystery of His will . . . which He purposed in Him with a view to an administration suitable to the fullness of the times, the summing up of all things in Christ, things in the heavens and things on the earth" (Ephesians 1:9-10). Glory be to Christ!

GOD THE SOVEREIGN SAVIOR . . .

" . . . who were born not of blood, nor of the will of the flesh nor of the will of man, but of God."

John 1:13

God is sovereign over salvation. This is not to say that man plays no part (John 1:12). Directly before the Scripture establishes that someone can become a child of God only by the will of God (and not by the will of man), we see that salvation is for "as many as received Him" (signifying human action/decision). Man is involved. God is sovereign. Man must decide. God must source that decision. The fact that God is the sovereign savior and not just the savior is good news. The more I come to know my fallen self (and my equally as fallen free will), the more I erupt with the same question asked long ago . . . "Then who can be saved?" Salvation is impossible if we only depend on man and his free will. It is only possible through God, and thus finds its source in God (Mark 10:26-27).

God is the source of all good things . . . "And God saw all that He had made, and behold, it was very good" (Genesis 1:31; James 1:17). He is the source of salvation. It is God who draws the person to Himself. The person does not come in his own ability; he is not born of the will of man, but of God (John 6:44). In John 6:41-66, Jesus seemed to be making His point about the need for God to draw a man to Himself in the context of responding to those who were "grumbling." They were grumbling because they could not accept the words of Jesus. The implication seems to be that Jesus was explaining why some could not accept His words. They could not accept His words because they were not being drawn by the Father. This points to the sovereignty of God over salvation and is, of course, a very controversial and difficult part of theology for finite man to understand. "As a result of this many of His disciples withdrew, and were not walking with Him anymore" (John 6:66). The ultimate application of having to count on God and not being able to count on yourself is seen in "God the sovereign savior." Is this not the ultimate "stumbling block"? God had to do it all and I could not do anything (John 15:5).

It has been said, "The free will of man is so powerfully influenced by God's sovereignty as to allow man to freely accept or reject, and yet conclude what God has concluded beforehand." The lesson from John 6 is that the free will of man first needs God's sovereign influence to draw him. We do not grumble because God does not draw us; rather, we grumble because rebellion parades in our hearts. Man's free will is free. In its freedom it chooses to reject God. It rejects God's drawing influence. Then, without God's drawing influence, man cannot come to God. In a certain sense, then (in the same sense that man does not create evil since evil is not created but, rather, is a distortion of that which is created), man becomes the source (or perhaps better stated, the corruption) of God not being the source (Ephesians 4:17-19). Then who can be saved? Jesus answers as He references the sovereign savior: "With men it is impossible, but not with God; for all things are possible with God" (Mark 10:27).

JANUARY 27

IT IS THE PEOPLE OF GOD, NOT THE PERSON OF GOD!

"...but now you are THE PEOPLE OF GOD..."

1 Peter 2:10

During World War II, Adolph Hitler's scientists conducted experiments to find the most effective type of punishment or torture for eliciting information from prisoners. They found solitary confinement was the most effective form of torture. After a few weeks of solitary confinement, most would cooperate with the enemy. Fellowship with other people is a fundamental human need. The word *fellowship* is an Old English word (derived from the Greek term *koinonia*) which means "sharing" or "togetherness." It is a basic part of human life. We must have social interaction. It could be said it is a life or death situation. Studies have shown newborn babies are more adversely affected by a lack of human contact than by a lack of food. A newborn baby will live longer without food than it will without human contact and affection. And so, solitary confinement (a lack of human sharing and togetherness) resulted in weakness. The prisoner fell to the temptation and abandoned his own value of loyalty.

In the same way, Christians who lack spiritual fellowship with other Christians will be weakened. They will inevitably abandon their values and fall to the temptations of the enemy. The Christian's need for spiritual fellowship with others is more than a need. It is a basic part of the Christian life. Without it Christianity cannot exist because without it Christianity cannot be practiced in its fullness. Spiritual lives die when there is no spiritual fellowship with others. No Christian can stand alone. God has formed the **people** of God—"but now you are the people of God" (1 Peter 2:10)—not simply the **person** of God. His goal is to have a **family**—"Brethren, sons of Abraham's family, and those among you who fear God, to us the word of this salvation is sent out" (Acts 13:26)—not simply an **individual**.

The necessity of fellowship in the church does not automatically mean that there is fellowship in the church or that it is easy to practice that fellowship. From the beginnings of the church we can see that life in the family of God is not always practiced the way it should be practiced. It is difficult to live in such a large family and always get along with each member. There is a certain sting of reality in the following poem: *To dwell above with saints we love, O, that will sure be glory. But to dwell below with saints we know, well, that's another story.* This is not just a church phenomenon; it is a human phenomenon. It is hard to live with and share life with others. Many people might say, "I love people, I just don't like my neighbors!"

Having admitted the difficulty of engaging in fellowship while at the same time recognizing the critical need for it, we might add that its actuality in the church is a powerful witness in a fallen world (John 13:35). Lucian (120-200 A.D.) was a very famous Greek writer in the days of the early church. He was not a Christian, but when he observed the strong fellowship between Christians, he wrote the following words: "It is incredible to see the fervor with which the people of that religion help each other in their wants. They spare nothing. Their first legislator has put it into their heads that they are brethren." Lucian was skeptical, but he could not ignore the fact that these Christians were sincere in their fellowship. The sincere fellowship between Christians was a great testimony of the early church. We need to ask ourselves today: "Is the fellowship in our churches providing a positive testimony to unbelievers?"

———————

JANUARY 28

WHAT IS WISDOM? . . .

"THE PROVERBS of Solomon . . . : To know wisdom and instruction, TO DISCERN the sayings of understanding, TO RECEIVE instruction in wise behavior, RIGHTEOUSNESS, justice and equity; TO GIVE prudence to the naive, TO THE youth knowledge and discretion, A WISE man will hear and increase in learning, AND A man of understanding will acquire wise counsel, TO UNDERSTAND a proverb and a figure, THE WORDS of the wise and their riddles.

Proverbs 1:1-6

The Hebrew word for wisdom is *"hokmah."* It can refer to a practical skill: "I have filled him with the Spirit of God in wisdom, in understanding, in knowledge, and in all kinds of craftsmanship, to make artistic designs for work in gold, in silver, and in bronze, and in the cutting of stones for settings, and in the carving of wood, that he may work in all kinds of craftsmanship" (Exodus 31:3-5). It can also be associated with ability in military and secular activities: " . . . by the power of my hand and by my wisdom I did this, for I have understanding; and I removed the boundaries of the peoples and plundered their treasures, and like a mighty man I brought down their inhabitants" (Isaiah 10:13).

In the book of Proverbs, wisdom refers to "skill in living." It is sometimes associated with discretion and good judgment in governing: "A wise king winnows the wicked, and drives the threshing wheel over them" (Proverbs 20:26). It also may refer to practical moral intelligence that works within the laws of God's universe to avoid problems: "The mouth of the righteous man utters wisdom, and his tongue speaks what is just. The law of his God is in his heart; his feet do not slip" (Psalm 37:30-31).

In a very specific definition of wisdom as spoken by God to man, we see that "the fear of the Lord" is wisdom: "And to man He said, 'Behold, the fear of the Lord, that is wisdom'" (Job 28:28). The word "fear" does not refer to being scared. It does include regarding God as holy: "It is the Lord of hosts whom you should regard as holy. And He shall be your fear" (Isaiah 8:13). To fear the Lord is to be in awe of Him, to praise Him, and to glorify Him: "You who fear the Lord, praise Him; all you descendants of Jacob, glorify Him, and stand in awe of Him, all you descendants of Israel" (Psalm 22:23). It is to acknowledge the greatness of God: "The Almighty— we cannot find Him; He is exalted in power and He will not do violence to justice and abundant righteousness. Therefore men fear Him" (Job 37:23).

A person who fears God will obey Him: "The fear of the Lord is the beginning of wisdom; a good understanding have all those who do His commandments" (Psalm 111:10). God-fearers are God-servers: "Now, therefore, fear the Lord and serve Him in sincerity and truth; and put away the gods which your fathers served beyond the River and in Egypt, and serve the Lord" (Joshua 24:14). God-fearers will turn from evil: "Do not be wise in your own eyes; fear the Lord and turn away from evil" (Proverbs 3:7). In addition, those who fear the Lord will seek Him and have a relationship with Him: "The secret of the Lord is for those who fear Him, and He will make them know His covenant" (Psalm 25:14). Wisdom is gained by someone who is teachable and able to be corrected: "The fear of the Lord is the beginning of knowledge; fools despise wisdom and instruction" (Proverbs 1:7). Finally, wisdom is acquired against the backdrop of humility: "The fear of the Lord is the instruction for wisdom, and before honor comes humility" (Proverbs 15:33).

So, humble yourself before God and make it your prayer . . . "God, build in me Your wisdom!"

JANUARY 29

WHAT KEEPS YOU FROM FELLOWSHIP?

"Let us hold fast the confession of our hope . . . consider how to stimulate one another to love
and good deeds, not forsaking our own assembling together, as is the habit of some,
but encouraging one another . . . "

Hebrews 10:23-25

The Bible seems to anticipate our tendency toward "forsaking our own assembling together, as is the habit of some" (Hebrews 10:25), and so, encourages us not to do so. Why are we inclined to sleep in and not go to church on Sunday morning? Why do we tend to skip our small group meeting on Friday night? Why do we forsake assembling together with other Christians? What hindrances to fellowship exist that we should be aware of to avoid them and not forsake "our own assembling together"?

Two general hindrances to fellowship are individualism and institutionalism. The result of our culture's emphasis on individualism can be a denial of the existence of fellowship. Individualism can hinder our ability to "regard one another as more important than himself" (Philippians 2:3), to "bear one another's burdens" (Galatians 6:2), to "be subject to one another" (Ephesians 5:21), and to "be devoted to one another in brotherly love" giving "preference to one another in honor" (Romans 12:10). All these attitudes and actions assume the existence of fellowship, while the championing of individualism tends to deny it by excusing oneself from it. Similarly, the result of our culture's insistence on institutionalism can be a denial of the existence of authentic fellowship. Institutionalism can hinder us from engaging in genuine fellowship as it tends to "manufacture" it or regulate it, turning fellowship into a formula or recipe. In either case—individualism's "being your own person" or institutionalism's "putting form before function/substance"—the result is often the same; that is, the forsaking of fellowship.

In addition to general hindrances to fellowship that exist in our culture, there are specific fears that spring forth from our cultural emphases that tend to steer us away from fellowship/community. One of those fears is the fear of dependency. Western culture puts such a high value on independence that being dependent on others is thought of as a weakness. However, true biblical fellowship accepts and desires the mutual dependency of its members. The foot's recognition of its dependency on the hand is only natural when it is time to take off its shoe. The eye does not question its dependence on the mouth when it sees something good to eat. The recognition and acceptance of unity in diversity (mutual dependence) within the body of Christ is essential for true fellowship (1 Corinthians 12:14-27).

Another fear that hinders our fellowship is the fear of commitment. Fellowship without a clear declaration of commitment is like a marriage without wedding vows. Neither will make it through the storms that will, inevitably, arrive. It will be easy to forsake it. A marriage is built on covenant and commitment. A husband and a wife do not need to decide in each situation (each storm) whether or not they will help each other or be there for each other. They have *already* made that decision in their covenant with one another ("in good times and in bad . . . in sickness and in health"). As members of the body of Christ, we must realize that, by definition, we are *already* committed to each other. We cannot create this commitment. It *already* exists. We must actively accept it. We do not strive to be committed. We surrender to be committed. Some Christians might say, "I do not want to commit myself to this church or to that small group," but the reality is that if they are Christians, then they *already* are committed to other Christians. They must choose to accept or reject that commitment.

So, throw off the claws of individualism, institutionalism, fear of dependency, and the fear of commitment—enter into fellowship—and "Let us hold fast the confession of our hope . . . consider how to stimulate one another to love and good deeds, not forsaking our own assembling together, as is the habit of some, but encouraging one another . . ." (Hebrews 10:23-25). What keeps you from fellowship?

———————

JANUARY 30

WHAT A REVELATION! . . .

" . . . according to the revelation of the mystery which has been kept secret for long ages past . . . "

Romans 16:25

Revelation and mystery, by definition, live together. Something needs to be revealed because it is not seen or known (it is a mystery). Something that is a mystery needs to be demystified (revealed). Revelation assumes mystery. Here, one might think of the eventual outworking (the wedding day) of an arranged marriage. An incredible moment of revelation would be realized by the husband-to-be as the mystery of the arranged marriage comes to light when the veil is finally removed from the bride and the man views his wife-to-be for the first time. The removing of the veil ("re" "vela") assumed the existence of an unknown arrangement . . . a mystery (at least to the husband-to-be). The mystery needed to be demystified by the removing of the veil. In some cultures, this is called the wedding ceremony. This gives a whole new twist to the "anticipation of the wedding day!"

The gospel is full of mystery. Salvation itself (the new birth) is described in terms of mystery (John 3:8). It is comparable to the mystery of the blowing of the wind ("you do not know where it comes from and where it is going"). The gospel is described as "the revelation of the mystery":

> Now to Him who is able to establish you according to my gospel and the preaching of Jesus Christ, according to the revelation of the mystery which has been kept secret for long ages past, but now is manifested, and by the Scriptures of the prophets, according to the commandment of the eternal God, has been made known to all the nations, *leading* to obedience of faith; to the only wise God, through Jesus Christ, be the glory forever. Amen (Romans 16:25-27).

The gospel is full of revelation. To know the mysteries of the kingdom of God is granted to some, but not to others (Matthew 13:11). Revelation is controlled by God (Luke 9:45). Those who are granted to know the mysteries are those who are His *followers* as opposed to those who are *outside* (Mark 4:10-12); those who follow Him and are in relationship with Him receive revelation. It is the personal relationship that we have with Jesus that leads to receiving revelation. Jesus calls us by name and transforms our hearts through His relationship with us. The result is revelation (John 20:16). Ultimately, to be in relationship with Jesus is to follow Him (to obey Him) and so revelation assumes obedience (John 7:17; Mark 3:33-35). And so, at the most significant "ceremony" of revelation (the revealing of who will go where . . . heaven or hell) Jesus says:

> Not everyone who says to Me, 'Lord, Lord,' *will enter* the kingdom of heaven, but he who does the will of My Father who is in heaven will enter. Many will say to Me on that day, 'Lord, Lord, did we not prophesy in Your name, and in Your name cast out demons, and in Your name perform many miracles?' And then I will declare to them, 'I never knew you; DEPART FROM ME, YOU WHO PRACTICE LAWLESSNESS' (Matthew 7:21-23).

This gives a whole new twist to the "anticipation of the wedding day"! ("The wedding supper of the Lamb" in Revelation 19:9).

JANUARY 31

CONTEXTS OF PRAYER . . .

"And He came to the disciples and found them sleeping, and said to Peter, 'So, you men could not keep watch with Me for one hour? Keep watching and praying . . ."

Matthew 26:40-41

Think about your daily schedule. Consider some of the things that you do for an hour or more each day. What about prayer? Jesus challenges us, "could you not keep watch with Me for one hour

. . . keep watching and praying" (Matthew 26:40-41). The average American watches more than four hours of television every day. Yet, to pray for one hour . . . that may be difficult! Jesus' challenge continues to ring in our ears, "Can you give Me one hour of your time?" To be able to answer this challenge, it may be helpful to understand that there are different types of prayer (petition, intercession, praise, and confession). Praying in a variety of ways can help us to be able to spend more time in prayer. There are also different contexts in which to pray (private prayer, praying with someone else, praying in small groups, and congregational prayer). Praying in a variety of contexts can also help us to be able to spend more time in prayer.

There is, of course, private prayer. All other contexts of praying begin here. It is the foundational context of prayer in which "when you pray, go into your inner room, and when you have shut your door, pray to your Father" (Matthew 6:6). It is important to have an "inner room." The results of the prayers of individuals are great (James 5:16).

There is also the context of two believers praying in agreement (Matthew 18:19). In this context, the focus is on harmony. To pray in agreement is to be in unity. Perhaps, the most natural example of this is the husband and wife praying together.

There is also the context of praying in small groups. Jesus says, "where two or three have gathered together in My name, there I am in their midst" (Matthew 18:20). The Wesleyan revivals of eighteenth-century England were, to a large degree, a result of the prayers of people praying in small groups.

Of course, another context for prayer is congregational praying. You could say that the first church meeting was a prayer meeting: "These all with one mind were continually devoting themselves to prayer, along with the women, and Mary the mother of Jesus, and with His brothers" (Acts 1:14). Congregational prayer is powerful (Acts 12:5-12).

Jesus' challenge continues to ring in our ears, "Can you give Me one hour of your time?" To be able to answer this challenge, it may be helpful to understand that there are different contexts in which to pray. Perhaps, you may pray privately in your "inner room" for some time each day, pray with another person and/or in a small group for some time each day, and pray with your congregation from time to time. As we participate in prayer in multiple contexts on a daily basis, we may find that "giving Jesus one hour of our time" is more possible.

NOTES

February

PRACTICAL LOVE . . .

"But now faith, hope, love, abide these three; but the greatest of these is love."

1 Corinthians 13:13

Hope is very important. "Hope deferred makes the heart sick . . ." (Proverbs 13:12). Certainly, faith is critical in the plan of God. The Scripture even asserts that "you have been saved through faith . . ." (Ephesians 2:8). Yet, as vital as hope and faith are, love stands out and runs ahead of them as "the greatest of these" (1 Corinthians 13:13). Since "God is love" (1 John 4:16), "we also ought to love one another" (1 John 4:11). We are commanded to love as it becomes our badge of authenticity: "A new commandment I give to you, that you love one another, even as I have loved you, that you also love one another. By this all men will know that you are My disciples . . ." (John 13:34-35).

As we study "the love chapter" (1 Corinthians 13) we see a portrait of the nature of love. Most obvious in that portrait is that love is manifested by selflessness; love blooms in being other-oriented. Love is maximized in sacrifice on behalf of others: "Greater love has no one than this, that one lay down his life for his friends" (John 15:13). The selflessness of love is not simply philosophical or political or a social awareness issue that fills one's good works closet. Love is, instead, that which is full of practical, selfless, other orientated actions that meet the practical needs of others. Of course, there is no greater example of this "practical, selfless, other oriented action" called love than the mind boggling fact that God sacrificed His "privileges" as God (Philippians 2:6-7) to lower Himself to our level and likeness (incarnation) in order to stand in our deserved wretched place to provide blood-bought forgiveness for our salvation (propitiation): "By this the love of God was manifested in us, that God has sent His only begotten Son into the world so that we might live through Him. In this is love, not that we loved God, but that He loved us and sent His Son to be the propitiation for our sins" (1 John 4:9-10).

Two of these practical actions that reflect love are the act of giving and the use of our time. Love meets the material needs of others. The Scripture challenges us that "whoever has the world's goods, and sees his brother in need and closes his heart against him, how does the love of God abide in him? Little children, let us not love with word or with tongue, but in deed and truth" (1 John 3:17-18). Ultimately, of course, our giving is to God (Proverbs 3:9-10) and so we are called to give joyfully (2 Corinthians 9:6-8). It is a blessing to give (Luke 6:38). It is even "more blessed to give than to receive" (Acts 20:35) as "The generous man will be prosperous, and he who waters will himself be watered" (Proverbs 11:25). So, be one who loves. Be a giver!

It might be said that who you love is who you spend your time with (Galatians 5:13). The Scripture reminds us that life is short (James 4:14) which yields a sense of the urgency of time (Romans 13:11). And so, we are not to waste time (Proverbs 31:27), rather we are to redeem the time or make the most of our time: "Therefore be careful how you walk . . . making the most of your time" (Ephesians 5:15). Two ways in which we can do this is, first, by planning our time in asking God to "teach us to number our days" (Psalm 90:12), and second, in setting priorities (Ecclesiastes 3:1). In any case, we know that time is precious, and it is most appropriately used in loving God and others. Do not allow yourself to come to the end of your life and regret the way in which you used your time that was not devoted to loving others. It is a haunting picture of the celebrity David Cassidy as he lay dying in his hospital bed surrounded by family members as he uttered his last words, "so much wasted time." His daughter expressed her reaction to the sorrowful moment by stating, "My father's last words were 'so much wasted time.' This will be a daily reminder for me to share my gratitude with those I love as to never waste another minute."

FEBRUARY 2

IF ALL ELSE FAILS IN THE PROCESS OF DISCIPLINE . . .

" . . . and do not associate with him . . . Yet do not regard him as an enemy,
but admonish him as a brother."

2 Thessalonians 3:14-15

Perhaps, surprising to many is that the idea of excommunication is biblical. It is the final step in the biblical process of church discipline. There seems to be two levels of excommunication. The first level is described with phrases like, "Do not associate with him" (2 Thessalonians 3:14; 1 Corinthians 5:9). Both the Thessalonian and the Corinthian passages use the same Greek word ("*sunanamignomi*") which is a term not found in any other place in the New Testament. This word is used to tell others not to have fellowship with the person who has reached this level of church discipline. Obviously, this level of excommunication is very serious. It is exhaustive. It includes "not even to eat with such a one" (1 Corinthians 5:11; 2 Thessalonians 3:10-12). Of course, much fellowship is done in the context of eating together (consider Acts 2:46). If the one being disciplined could not eat with the others, then the lack of association would be complete. Nevertheless, the discipline is not done with a spirit of hatred, but it is done as to a brother: "And yet do not regard him as an enemy, but admonish him as a brother" (2 Thessalonians 3:15).

Perhaps it appears as though there is a contradiction here. To not associate with someone does not seem to be consistent with brotherhood. However, there is no contradiction. The tension that exists between the two concepts is necessary and understandable even as there is tension between the fact that God is both fully holy and at the same time fully love. To "not associate" with the offender and at the same time to do it as to a "brother" is the same tension between hating the sin while still loving the sinner. It is the tension between "the method of discipline" and the "motive of discipline." Within this tension we can have balance, just as within the character of God there is balance. He is one hundred percent holy. He is one hundred percent love. These two attributes do not work against each other. They work together. The same is true in church discipline. It can be direct and firm. Yet it is done in love.

The second level of excommunication is clearly more extreme: "to deliver such a one to Satan for the destruction of his flesh" (1 Corinthians 5:5; 1 Timothy 1:20). This level of excommunication is somewhat more difficult to understand. To understand it, we need to consider the sovereignty of God. God can even use Satan to accomplish His own purposes. Satan can be used as the vehicle of discipline. God can use what is negative to manifest what is positive (see Psalm 76:10 and Romans 8:28). This type of principle is similar to the principle found in 2 Corinthians 12:7: " . . . there was given me a thorn in the flesh, a messenger of Satan to torment me—to keep me from exalting myself!" A negative messenger of Satan was used as a positive thing in the life of Paul. Even if Satan is the agent of discipline, the purposes of God are still positive. The hope of excommunication is that it will result in repentance. It is so "that his spirit may be saved in the day of the Lord Jesus" (1 Corinthians 5:5). After all, to deliver someone to Satan is not an extra step of church discipline. It is a consequence of excommunication. To be excommunicated is like marching alone during a war. A soldier who gets separated from his army is very vulnerable to the attacks of the enemy. It is the same for a Christian who is excommunicated. He does not have the protection of the army of God.

Herein, we see the importance of the ideas of communion and community within the church body. To a certain degree, we truly are dependent on each other. There is protection within the community of the people of God. And so, the discipline occurs when that protection is taken away. This is called excommunication. We might consider the parable of the prodigal son to understand this principle (Luke 15:11-32). Many times people will not repent until they realize what they have lost. This is true of the prodigal son.

FEBRUARY 3

THE NEED TO BE IN NEED AND THE POWER OF WEAKNESS/SUFFERING

"Let us therefore draw near with confidence to the throne of grace, that we may receive mercy and may find grace to help in time of need."

Hebrews 4:16

We need help because we are weak. There is power in that weakness. The power lies in the tendency for the weakness to point to our need, and thus, prompt us to scream for help. Of course, to be helped requires the need to be helped; thus, the need to be in need. Jesus can "sympathize with our weaknesses" and it is for that reason that we should "draw near with confidence to the throne of grace, that we may receive mercy and may find grace to help in time of need" (Hebrews 4:15-16). It is those who need help who God helps; "it is not those who are healthy who need a physician, but those who are sick" (Matthew 9:12) and it is those who do not see who may, in turn, see (John 9:39). In God's economy, there is a need to be in need . . . a need to express that need. "The sacrifices of God are a broken spirit; A broken and a contrite heart, O God, You will not despise" (Psalm 51:17). The need to be in need lies in the fact that "the Lord hears the needy" (Psalm 69:33). God notices and responds to need: "And the sons of Israel sighed because of the bondage, and they cried out; and their cry for help because of their bondage rose up to God. So God heard their groaning . . . God saw the sons of Israel, and God took notice of them" (Exodus 2:23-25).

To be helped requires the need to be helped . . . and the need to be helped is necessarily linked to suffering: "Help! Heeeeelp!" It sounds like someone is suffering. To a certain degree, to be needy is to be in pain. And so, the needy are often associated with those who suffer. Jesus, in his humanity and fight against temptation/sin, expresses great need—help!—and that expression of need is linked to suffering: "In the days of his flesh, Jesus offered up prayers and supplications, with loud cries and tears, to him who was able to save him from death, and he was heard because of his reverence. Although he was a son, he learned obedience through what he suffered" (Hebrews 5:7-8). Suffering is then linked to helping: "For since He Himself was tempted in that which He has suffered, He is able to come to the aid of those who are tempted" (Hebrews 2:18); we are able to "draw near with confidence to the throne of grace, that we may receive mercy and may find grace to help in time of need" (Hebrews 4:16). The "receiving help—suffering" connection is a spiritual one: "for if you are living according to the flesh, you must die; but if by the Spirit you are putting to death the deeds of the body, you will live . . . if we suffer with Him so that we may also be glorified with Him" (Romans 8:13-14, 17). Peter encourages us, "Therefore, since Christ has suffered in the flesh, arm yourselves also with the same purpose, because he who has suffered in the flesh has ceased from sin" (1 Peter 4:1-2), and Paul proclaims, "that I may know Him and the power of His resurrection and the fellowship of His sufferings, being conformed to His death" (Philippians 3:10-11).

The necessary connection between need, help/power, and suffering is most emphatically and concisely seen in the life of Paul: "And He has said to me, 'My grace is sufficient for you, for power is perfected in weakness.' Most gladly, therefore, I will rather boast about my weaknesses, so that the power of Christ may dwell in me. Therefore I am well content with weaknesses, with insults, with distresses, with persecutions, with difficulties, for Christ's sake; for when I am weak, then I am strong" (2 Corinthians 12:9-10). Herein, we see "the need to be in need and the power of weakness/suffering."

FEBRUARY 4

TO UNDERSTAND SIN IS TO UNDERSTAND TEMPTATION

"And He, when He comes, will convict the world concerning sin and righteousness and judgment; concerning sin, because they do not believe in Me . . . "

John 16:8-9

What is the underlying issue of sin? Sin is most fundamentally related to not believing in Jesus (John 16:9). Jesus means "God saves." Thus, to not believe in Jesus is to not believe/trust in the fact that God must save you and that you cannot save yourself; that you need God. The underlying issue of sin is to not trust in God and to not see your need for Him. Sin is very closely linked with a lack of recognition of your need . . . a lack of recognition of your "blindness" . . . a lack of brokenness and humility (John 9:41). Who will convince/convict me of that need? The Holy Spirit (John 16:8). That is why blasphemy against the Holy Spirit is considered an "unforgivable sin" (Mark 3:28). It is not that God will not forgive you; rather, it is that the rejecting of the Holy Spirit is the rejecting of the conviction that will lead you to that forgiveness. To be forgiven of sin (not confessing your need for God) requires that you are first convinced/convicted of that need. That is what the Holy Spirit does (He "convicts the world concerning sin, because they do not believe" in Jesus). He convinces you to "trust in the Lord with all your heart" and to "not lean on your own understanding" (Proverbs 3:5) as opposed to sinning (the pride of trusting/relying not on God but trusting/relying on yourself).

To understand this underlying issue of sin—to trust/rely on yourself rather than to trust/rely on God—is to understand the underlying issue of temptation. Temptation is that which tries to push or lure you into the place of self-trust/self-reliance. In Matthew 4:1-10 we see the ways in which temptation attacked Jesus. In each case, it tried to lure Jesus into a place of self-reliance. Jesus, however, "led by the Spirit" (verse 1), did not fall into its trap. Jesus relied, instead, on the Word of God (verses 4, 7, 10) and defeated the devil and his temptations . . . He did not sin (Hebrews 4:15). Each time He did this, He seemed to gain more strength and ability to do it again (we might refer to this as the "momentum of obedience/trust"). Notice the progression from "It is written . . ." (verse 4) to "On the other hand, it is written . . ." (verse 7) to "Begone, Satan! For it is written . . ." (verse 10). Jesus gained a sort of momentum with each victory as He became increasingly more aggressive and on the offensive in the fight. This was the power of the Holy Spirit! This was the power of reliance on God!

And so, we must understand that with respect to temptation and sin, the spirit is willing, but the flesh is weak. In order to protect ourselves against the flesh and avoid falling into temptation, it is necessary to keep watching and praying (Matthew 26:41; Mark 14:38). We should pray that we will not enter into temptation (Luke 22:40; Matthew 6:13); we should pray that we will not enter into the place of self-trust/self-reliance. Prayer, by its very nature, is the greatest expression of this; when we pray, we are saying we do not rely on ourselves but, rather, we rely on God.

And so, after the command to "trust in the Lord with all your heart" and to "not lean on your own understanding" we are told to "in all your ways acknowledge Him" (Proverbs 3:5-6a); herein, lies the victory: "And He will make your paths straight" (Proverbs 3:6b). To understand sin is to understand temptation. More importantly, to understand sin is to understand and have victory over temptation. To God be the glory (Philippians 1:9-11)!

FEBRUARY 5

FEAR FLIES AWAY IN THE FACE OF THE SOVEREIGN GOD

" . . . do not worry . . . And which of you by worrying can add a single hour to his life's span? . . . But seek for His kingdom . . . "

Luke 12:22, 25, 31

What are you doing? What do you mean, "What am I doing? I am worrying about stuff so I can get something done about it! Leave me alone to my worrying . . . I have a lot to accomplish."

Someone with even a speck of pragmatic inclination looks at this discussion and laughs. The problem with worrying is that it just does not work. The absurdity of worrying is that worrying cannot even accomplish the most miniscule of advancements. We worry about things that we cannot control. Instead of worrying, we should realize that God is sovereign . . . that God is in control. This will free us to do what we can control (what we are responsible for); to seek the kingdom of God.

In an argument that is built by moving from the lesser to the greater, Jesus assures you (the greater) that God is sovereign over your death as he claims that God is sovereign over the death of a sparrow (the lesser). Just as the sparrow will not "fall to the ground apart from your Father," so, too, your life will not end outside of the control of God. Certainly, you should not fear death due to your hope for eternal life in Christ, but also because of your understanding of the sovereignty of God. Perhaps nothing more than death makes us feel a sense of a lack of control. Worry is a by-product of a feeling of a lack of control. Herein, however, is where the absurdity begins. Death is not an out of control issue. God is in total control with respect to your death. When you realize that God is sovereign over your death you will no longer fear or worry about death since the very fuel that feeds that worry no longer is pumped into your gas tank (Matthew 10:29-31).

Our response to the sovereignty of God includes a lack of the fear of men (Luke 12:4-7). After all, why fear someone who does not control your ultimate outcome? When the Bible uses such a phrase as "His hour had not yet come" it is referencing this whole issue of God's control of things behind the scenes played out in this life (John 7:30; 8:20). Although the actors on the stage may seem ominous and intimidating, you should not find yourself memorizing lines while full of fear and worry since you know who is editing the final cut.

Moreover, when we know the sovereign Writer/Producer/Director of the film we are not simply passive players on the stage of life; rather, we become proactive and bold actors. This is why after using the "sparrow argument" to explain God's sovereign control in our lives, Jesus calls us to a logical response of boldness and says, "everyone who confesses Me before men, the Son of Man shall confess him also before the angels of God" (Luke 12:7-9). Fear flies away in the face of the sovereign God. Fear is bondage but the lack of fear is freedom . . . freedom to be bold for God . . . freedom to "seek for His kingdom."

———————

ANOINTING OF THE SPIRIT IS GOD ACTING WITH PURPOSE

"THE SPIRIT of the Lord GOD is upon me, Because the LORD has anointed me To bring good news to the afflicted; He has sent me to bind up the brokenhearted, To proclaim liberty to captives And freedom to prisoners . . . that He may be glorified."

Isaiah 61:1, 3

Throughout the Old Testament, the coming Messiah is depicted as Him whom the Spirit will come upon to anoint/empower for service so that God may be glorified: "The Spirit of the Lord is upon me, because the Lord has anointed me . . . that He may be glorified" (Isaiah 61:1, 3). The anointing of the Spirit is effectual because it is purposeful. God is a God of mission. He is a strategic manager of His resources. He acts with purpose. He does not empower and enable someone by His Spirit simply to display that power; rather, He empowers so that His purposes might be accomplished. His anointing yields results because His anointing is given in order to yield results; thus, "so shall My word be that goes forth from My mouth; it shall not return to Me void, but it shall accomplish what I please, and it shall prosper in the thing for which I sent it" (Isaiah 55:11). And so, in Isaiah 61:1, the coming Messiah is depicted as Him who would complete His mission—"to bring good news to the afflicted . . . to bind up the brokenhearted, to proclaim liberty to captives and freedom to prisoners"—by the anointing of the Spirit.

The quantity and the quality of the Spirit that would be upon the coming One goes beyond that of any other person before Him. It includes the anointing of judges, prophets, priests, and kings. The anointing is complete because the ministry would be complete. Moreover, the results of the ministry would be complete (John 17:4; 19:30). The anointing of the Spirit is wide-ranging because its associated purpose is far-reaching . . . a thorough anointing is the result of a comprehensive purpose: "I have put My Spirit upon Him; He will bring forth justice to the nations . . . a bruised reed He will not break . . . He will not be disheartened or crushed until He has established justice in the earth" (Isaiah 42:1-4). The effect of the anointing is consistent with the purposes of that anointing. The results are that justice, humility, tenderness, steadfastness, and patience would be identified with His ministry.

You are anointed by God with His Spirit consistent with God's purposes; that is to say, God's anointing is effectual in your life. Thus, you grow into your anointing. Even Jesus, the Messiah, grew into His anointing: "And Jesus kept increasing in wisdom and stature, and in favor with God and men" (Luke 2:52). His anointing would include a physical component ("increasing in **stature**"), an intellectual component ("increasing in **wisdom**"), a social component ("increasing in **favor with men**"), and a spiritual component ("increasing in **favor with God**"). This thorough anointing was provided purposely and, thus, was manifested definitively: "The Spirit of the Lord will rest on Him, the spirit of **wisdom and understanding**, the spirit of **counsel** and **strength**, the spirit of **knowledge and the fear of the Lord**" (Isaiah 11:1).

Prophesied long ago were the physical component ("**strength**"), the intellectual component ("**wisdom and understanding**"), the social component ("**counsel**"), and the spiritual component ("**knowledge and the fear of the Lord**"). This model of anointing can translate into a prayer that parents pray over their children: "God, increase my child physically, intellectually, socially, and spiritually." Of course, the motivation behind the prayer must be consistent with the principle associated with God's anointing; that He anoints/empowers so that His purposes might be accomplished. Ultimately, the purpose of "the Spirit of the Lord God is upon me" is "that He may be glorified" (Isaiah 61:1, 3). So, the more exact parental prayer is: "God, increase my child physically, intellectually, socially, and spiritually for Your glory . . . so that this child will be used for Your glory!"

FEBRUARY 7

YOU DON'T HAVE TO FIGURE IT OUT IN THE END . . .

"For just as the lightning comes from the east and flashes even to the west, so will the coming of the Son of Man be."

Matthew 24:27

When will the end come? How will I know if Jesus has returned? What if I miss Him because I don't recognize Him or because I am deceived into thinking an imposter is Jesus? Don't worry! According to Jesus as seen in Matthew 24:23-26, you don't have to figure it out in the end:

> Then if anyone says to you, 'Behold, here is the Christ,' or 'There *He is*,' do not believe *him*. For false Christs and false prophets will arise and will show great signs and wonders, so as to mislead, if possible, even the elect. Behold, I have told you in advance. So if they say to you, 'Behold, He is in the wilderness,' do not go out, *or*, 'Behold, He is in the inner rooms,' do not believe *them*.

Perhaps the most practical biblical point of eschatological teaching for the Christian is that there will be no need to "figure it out" in the end. There is no decision that needs to be/is able to be made "in a moment, in the twinkling of an eye" (1 Corinthians 15:52) or "as the lightning comes from the east and flashes even to the west" (Matthew 24:27). "So will the coming of the Son of Man be."

So what will be happening in the end times? (Mark 13:6-13). False christs will appear and will try to lead people (even Christians) away from Jesus by performing great signs and wonders (Mark 13:20). Many will appear and say that they are Jesus. Do not follow them (Luke 21:8). Christians will be hated by many and killed by family members because of their testimony for Christ (Luke 21:12-17). There will be wars, earthquakes, plagues, famines, terrors, and miracles from heaven (Luke 21:7, 10, 11). Ultimately, Jerusalem will be surrounded by armies and it will be destroyed (Luke 21:20-24).

The return of Christ is inextricably linked to the end times and His return seems to occur after the great tribulation:

> But in those days, after that tribulation, THE SUN WILL BE DARKENED AND THE MOON WILL NOT GIVE ITS LIGHT, AND THE STARS WILL BE FALLING from heaven, and the powers that are in the heavens will be shaken. Then they will see THE SON OF MAN COMING IN CLOUDS with great power and glory. And then He will send forth the angels, and will gather together His elect from the four winds, from the farthest end of the earth to the farthest end of heaven (Mark 13:24-27).

It is after the tribulation that Jesus returns "in clouds" and gathers (raptures) the elect (the church) as is consistent with the picture of the rapture in 1 Thessalonians 4:16-17:

> For the Lord Himself will descend from heaven with a shout, with the voice of *the* archangel and with the trumpet of God, and the dead in Christ will rise first. Then we who are alive and remain will be caught up together with them in the clouds to meet the Lord in the air, and so we shall always be with the Lord.

When Jesus returns, it is the end (there is only one second coming/no third coming; there is only one return of Christ/not two returns of Christ). Tribulation on earth does not then continue in the absence of Christians. God shortens the days of the great tribulation for the sake of the elect, thus, showing that Christians are on the earth during it (Mark 13:20). Furthermore, the Scripture reveals that when the abomination of desolation positions himself in the temple it will be time for believers to flee (Matthew 24:15). This seems to be associated with the great tribulation (note the words, "tribulation like never before and never again"). Again, we see that the elect (Christians) are still in the picture during the great tribulation. Christians can be comforted with regard to the end times even though tribulation is a big part of the picture. The bottom line is that, for Christians, there will be no need to "figure it out" in the end. Jesus will return and He, along with those who are His, will be victorious (Malachi 4:1-3; Revelation 17:14). This will be the end as Jesus returns and raptures His people in order that they might meet Him in the air so as to return to the earth with Him (Matthew 25:1-13; Acts 28:14-16) and gain the final victory. "Therefore comfort one another with these words" (1 Thessalonians 4:18).

FEBRUARY 8

THERE IS A WAR AND SO THERE ARE WEAPONS . . .

"From the days of John the Baptist until now the kingdom of heaven suffers violence, and violent men take it by force."

Matthew 11:12

The war is real. It (casting out demons, for example) is depicted as part of the Christian life (Mark 16:17). The war is real because there are real enemies. Perhaps our most consistent enemy is our own flesh. And so, the kingdom of God advances forcefully because it has a strong opponent (especially the fallen nature of man/the flesh), and forceful men must take it by force because they have that opponent (Matthew 11:12; 1 Corinthians 9:27). The spirit is willing, but the flesh is weak, and so, we need weapons. In order to protect ourselves against the flesh and avoid falling into temptation, it is necessary to keep watching and praying (Mark 14:38). That becomes our greatest weapon (Matthew 26:41).

There is also an enemy named Satan. The war against Satan includes a "deliverance ministry" (Mark 9:25). In order to overpower the enemy and take away his armor, he must be bound (Mark 3:27). And so, it might be said that there are four steps in the deliverance ministry: attack the enemy; overpower the enemy; take away the armor of the enemy; distribute the plunder (Luke 11:22). More specifically, two things are needed to cast out an evil spirit: authority and power (Luke 4:36). This authority and power is most definitively found in the Word of God; Jesus uses the Word of God to fight the devil and his temptations (Luke 4:4, 8, 12).

Perhaps, a subtler weapon for the Christian in the war against Satan is the awareness of the weapons that Satan tends to use in the war. It is important to understand that the nature of the devil is to lie and that he uses lies as potentially effective weapons (John 8:44). He may even send spies who pretend to be righteous in order to win your confidence and trap you (Luke 20:20). In the war, it is helpful to know deception is one of the most often used weapons of the enemy. Of course, one of Satan's greatest weapons against us is to encourage us to focus on worldly interests. This can cause us to deny suffering and hardship, which can lead us away from Christ (Matthew

16:23). In the war, it is helpful to know the offer of a comfortable life has been one of Satan's most used weapons.

He will try to tempt us with the comforts and success of the world in order to keep us from the way of God, which is the way of the cross (Mark 8:31-33). The key is to be aware of his weapons so as "not to be caught unawares" (Jude 1:4). In this way, we use the weapons of our enemy against him!

FEBRUARY 9

ATTITUDES ON THE ROAD TO KNOWING GOD . . .

"The fear of the LORD *is the beginning of knowledge . . . "*

Proverbs 1:7

Attitudes impact actions. The attitude of humility leads us to seek God as we look to Him instead of ourselves. Similarly, a variety of other attitudes are necessary to have on the road to knowing God. The fear of God (not being "afraid of God" but having respect for or being in awe of God) moves us down the road to knowing God. There is, in Scripture a strong connection between the knowledge of God and the fear of God (Isaiah 11:2, Psalm 25:12). "The fear of the Lord is the beginning of knowledge" (Proverbs 1:7).

Since "the fear of the Lord is to hate evil" (Proverbs 8:13), the person who desires to know God must avoid sin. How do we avoid sin? One way to do it is to have **the attitude of a sufferer**. Even Jesus "in the days of His flesh" avoided sin via an attitude of a sufferer as "He offered up both prayers and supplications with loud crying and tears to the One able to save Him form death . . . although He was a Son, He learned obedience from the things which He suffered" (Hebrews 5:7-8). Therefore, we are directed to adopt the attitude of a sufferer "since Christ has suffered in the flesh, arm yourselves also with the same purpose, because he who has suffered in the flesh has ceased from sin" (1 Peter 4:1). Paul understood this connection between suffering and knowing God, and desired to have this very same attitude (Philippians 3:10). He wanted to have the light (knowledge) that comes from suffering (James 1:2-4; Romans 5:3-5).

As much as we might adopt the attitude of a sufferer and in so doing avoid sin, we still sin (1 John 1:8). Thus, on the road to knowing God, we must include **an attitude of repentance**. Without an attitude of repentance our relationship with God, to some degree, will be disrupted after every sin. We will not move ahead on the road to knowing God. To repent is to turn; it is to turn away from the wall that stands between us and God. To know God is to turn to Him (Hosea 6:1-3). Repentance and knowing God are inextricably linked.

Finally, we might consider the most important attitude that we can have if we want to know God. We could call it **the eternal attitude** (2 Corinthians 4:18). Setting our minds on eternal things brings us closer to the Eternal One. Thus, Paul instructs us to "set your mind on the things above, not on the things that are on earth" (Colossians 3:2). It is an awesome thing to realize how close we actually are to God by having an eternal attitude. We can live with Christ in heaven now (Colossians 3:1; 1 Corinthians 15:48; Ephesians 1:3; Ephesians 2:6; John 14:3). According to the Scripture we have been raised up with Christ and we sit with Him in the heavenly places. This should be no surprise, since we know that eternal life (heaven) is to know (sit with) God (John 17:3). We cannot get closer to God than the immediate closeness of sitting with Him. This is as close as we can get. It happens through engaging in an eternal attitude and "living life backwards"—a perspective that considers all things against the larger backdrop of eternity instead of the limited and incomplete backdrop of this life.

On the level of **Awareness,** we know that **Christ lives**. On the level of **Attributes,** we know that **Christ lives in us**. On the level of **Actions,** we know that **Christ works through us**. On the level of **Attitudes,** we know that **we live with Christ**. We have reached the climax of knowing God. Incredibly, we leave the worldly realm and live with Christ "in the heavenly places." We live the eternal life by knowing God. Growing in relationship with God is an inexpressible joy. Certainly, it is the cry of every Christian's heart. **My God, I want to know you more. I need to know you more. I have to know you more.**

FEBRUARY 10

THE NEED FOR SMALL GROUPS . . .

"Day by day . . . breaking bread from house to house, they were taking their meals together with gladness and sincerity of heart, praising God and having favor with all the people. And the Lord was adding to their number day by day those who were being saved."

Acts 2:46-47

Church history has always born out the need for and use of small groups. In the New Testament church, community was practiced in small groups as "day by day . . . breaking bread from house to house, they were taking their meals together with gladness and sincerity of heart" (Acts 2:46). The result was that there was a great revival as they were "having favor with all the people. And the Lord was adding to their number day by day those who were being saved" (Acts 2:47). From the beginning of the organizing of the church, fellowship in small groups has proven to be of great value. The dynamics of small groups are uniquely able to meet critical social and ministerial needs. Are you in a small group?

Small groups meet the need for intimate interpersonal relationships. As human beings, we have a need to have intimate relationships. The world often offers "shallow" relationships to try to fill this need. The Christian small group can replace the emptiness of these shallow relationships with the fullness of real, intimate relationships. Relationships that grow in small group settings tend to foster a commitment to care, love, and serve one another.

Small groups meet the need for individual expression. All people need to feel like they are a part of something. They need to be participators. This is especially true in the church. Each member of the body of Christ must participate (1 Corinthians 12:20-22). However, often times in the larger group, many Christians cannot find their place in the body. In a small group, individual ministries and gifts can be discovered, used and developed. The small group can be a "practice field" and a "proving ground" for the operation of the gifts of the Spirit. The small group gives each Christian the opportunity to find his place in the body. It can promote and multiply ministry.

Small groups meet the need for effective outreach. In the New Testament church, the body of believers ("the sheep") not the shepherds (pastors), gave birth to "the lambs." The small group provides a natural training ground for new ministries to be developed. The focus should be on training and motivating for evangelism. The small group can also provide for a place to invite those who are interested but are not yet believers. Interested unbelievers will often respond to an invitation to come to someone's house before they will respond to an invitation to come to a wider church meeting.

Small groups meet the need for training future leadership. Leadership must be formed from within the church. The small group can provide a place where potential leaders can be trained and given the opportunity to lead. Small groups can be multiplied as leaders are multiplied. This is a very effective strategy for church growth.

Small groups meet the need for improved oversight. It is impossible for one pastor to effectively shepherd 350 people. The pastor must work with a team of leaders. He must delegate responsibility and authority to others. These other leaders can effectively shepherd ten to fifteen people in a small group. For church growth (both in numbers and in quality) to occur there must be a continuous multiplication of leaders. The sheep and the shepherds must be divided into small groups. If this does not happen then there will be limited growth. The sheep will not be cared for and the shepherd will "burn out," or become frustrated and ineffective from overwork.

FEBRUARY 11

MARRIAGE, DIVORCE, AND REMARRIAGE . . .

"And He answered and said, 'Have you not read that He who created them *from the beginning MADE THEM MALE AND FEMALE,' and said, 'FOR THIS REASON A MAN SHALL LEAVE HIS FATHER AND MOTHER AND BE JOINED TO HIS WIFE, AND THE TWO SHALL BECOME ONE FLESH? So they are no longer two, but one flesh. What therefore God has joined together, let no man separate.'"*

Matthew 19:4-6

Marriage is not for everyone. It seems that angels do not marry and that there is no marriage in heaven (Matthew 22:30). Even here on earth, singleness (Matthew 19:12), it seems, is a God-sourced option (the ability to remain single is a God-given gift and should not be forced on someone who does not have that gift!). Marriage, nevertheless, seems to be the norm for most people. What is marriage? Marriage is immediately—at the very creation of Man it is set as a foundation of human society—instituted by God (Genesis 2:24) and is represented by a man leaving his father and mother and cleaving to his wife. The result is that God joins them together and the man and woman become one (Matthew 19:4-6). What is divorce? Divorce is to separate and destroy what God has done; "what God has joined together" (Matthew 19:6). How did divorce begin (certainly it was not God's desire according to Malachi 2:16, God hates it!)? In the Scripture, we can find instructions that were given to men by God but were not consistent with His desire and original intentions (note God's instructions given regarding the people's desire for a king in 1 Samuel 8:4-9). Some things, like divorce, were allowed or permitted because of the sin of man (Matthew 19:8). Divorce is not natural. It is not God's idea! It exists only because of man's sin. It is rebellious in the sense that it goes against God's plan (Mark 10:5-8).

So, what about remarriage (with respect to divorce)? Divorce and remarriage seems to equal adultery unless biblically justified (here one might consider in addition to the unfaithfulness of a spouse, the abandonment of a spouse, as well as remarriage after the death of a spouse). According to Matthew 19:9, we could refer to the following equation as a principle:

$$D - BJ + R = A$$

Divorce – Biblical Justification + Remarriage = Adultery

The remarriage of a divorced person constitutes adultery if their divorce was not rooted in biblical justification. Likewise, remarriage to a divorced person (whose divorce was not biblically justified) also, seemingly, constitutes adultery (Luke 16:18). In a certain sense, divorce is not even recognized by God. If you divorce and remarry, without biblical justification, then you commit adultery. The implication, it seems, is that in God's eyes you are still married (Mark 10:11-12).

Most significantly, it is to be understood how important the institution of marriage is to God (Hebrews 13:4). Its importance, most fundamentally, is rooted in the fact that marriage was instituted by God Himself. It is a "God thing" and God things must not be treated lightly, responded to flippantly, redefined, or in any way undervalued. The treating or perceiving of marriage in these unnatural ways by a society is done at its own peril for once the foundations of a building begin to erode, the entire building is in danger of falling.

FEBRUARY 12

DOES GOD REALLY LOVE SOME AND HATE OTHERS?

"'Was not Esau Jacob's brother?' declares the Lord. 'Yet I have loved Jacob;
but I have hated Esau, and I have made his mountains a desolation and
appointed his inheritance for the jackals of the wilderness.'"

Malachi 1:2-3

The fact that God "hated Esau" is not the result of God's random rejection of a certain people. God did not reject Esau (Edom). Edom rejected God through rejecting God's chosen people, Israel. The focus here is on God's sovereignty. He is sovereign to establish His own system of blessing people. He sovereignly chose Israel as His conduit of blessing by blessing those who bless her and cursing those who do not (Genesis 12:3). He sovereignly uses (appoints) others to carry out His justice against those who do not want to follow His system (the reference to "jackals of the wilderness" probably refers to the fierce Nabatean Arabs that roamed that part of the world at that time). Is this "system" of God's a just system? God's justice is not determined by whether we like or agree with His system. It is determined by the availability of that system to everyone and by Him holding to the promises that hold that system together (Romans 9:4, 6, 8). And so, yes, God is just!

Does God really hate people ("I have hated Esau")? Just as "loved" should be understood as "chosen," "hated" should be understood as "not chosen" (which does not necessarily mean rejected or excluded). Jacob "hated" Leah (Genesis 29:31). The implication is not that he had an emotional hatred for her (the word "more" in verse 30 implies that he actually loved Leah). The idea is that he chose Rachel and did not choose Leah (see also Deuteronomy 21:15-17). The word "hated" in Luke 14:26 is interpreted by Matthew 10:37 in much the same way as in the previous two examples. The understanding is not that we have an emotional hatred for our parents, children, etc. (Again note how the word "more" in Matthew 10:37 implies that we love our parents, children, etc.). The idea is that Christians choose Jesus and do not choose others. Again, this does not mean that we reject or exclude others. It means that others are included in our lives through choosing Jesus. Practically, we might say that husbands are actually able to be better husbands because they have chosen Jesus and not their wives (put Jesus first; as in Matthew 6:33). A husband can only truly love his wife when He makes the commitment to allow Jesus to have first place in his life. A husband who "hates" (does not choose) his wife can more truly love his wife. Leah could only be loved by Jacob correctly in that he chose Rachel. We might say that he had to be a "one-woman man" in order to correctly love either one of them (Matthew 6:24: "you cannot serve two masters"/"you cannot serve God and wealth"). Jacob had to choose one in order to love both. He would love Leah (ideally, in a different way that would be consistent with a monogamous lifestyle) because of his love for Rachel.

This idea of a monogamous relationship is consistent with what God calls us to as Christians (see the book of Hosea). He calls us to a complete commitment to Him, the only God. Those who make that decision can be better family members and better citizens, not because family and country are a priority—or are high on some sort of pecking order—but because their complete commitment to God allows them to be and equips them to be better family members and citizens. And so, in Matthew 6:33 the Greek term for "first" implies "only" ("Seek only the kingdom of God and everything else will be added to you"). Now we can better understand what it means that God "hated" Esau. Israel, the missionary nation (Genesis 12:1-3), was chosen so that God could love the world (John 3:16). God chooses Israel in order to choose others. He loves us in order that we would love others (1 John 4:19) so that others could be loved by Him.

FEBRUARY 13

RELIGIOSITY: THE CONTRADICTION OF A WHITEWASHED TOMB

"So you, too, outwardly appear righteous to men,
but inwardly you are full of hypocrisy and lawlessness."

Matthew 23:28

What is "religiosity?" It is an outward form without contents. It is a "mold" without the filling. It is a mold that is inconsistent with its filling . . . a whitewashed tomb. In terms of religious practices, it is dead ritual (Matthew 23:25-28). It is dead because the more superficial/surface/ external actions or appearances are championed at the expense of the more **profound**/weighty/ internal contents or realities: "Woe to you, scribes and Pharisees, hypocrites! For you tithe mint and dill and cummin, and have neglected the **weightier** provisions of the law: justice and mercy and faithfulness; but these are the things you should have done without neglecting the others" (Matthew 23:23). It is not so much because there is anything inherently wrong with outward forms (tithing, for example); rather, it is that those forms need to be filled with real and appropriate contents (compassion and justice, for example). True religion includes both the contents of the heart along with their outward forms (. . . "but these are the things you should have done without neglecting the others"). So, be sure not to be "blind guides, who strain out a gnat and swallow a camel!" (Matthew 23:24). You can change the outward appearance and still be polluted inside, but if you clean up the pollution inside then it will also change the outward appearance (Matthew 23:25-26).

Religiosity is satisfaction with form only. Religiosity insists on the "form" at the expense of the contents; it holds on to it no matter what and, thus, it often takes the shape of "traditionalism" (Luke 5:36-39). Sometimes this results in irrelevant churches; churches that are unable to walk in the new move of the Spirit. It is "form" without function . . . externalism. When this externalism begins to be paraded about—"practicing your righteousness before men" as in Matthew 6:1 or "when you are praying" using "meaningless repetition" as in Matthew 6:8—then it becomes hypocrisy (the essence of "religiosity"). Hypocrisy is often associated with the process of judging others. To a large degree, judging others is an expression of hypocrisy or religiosity. It is the approving of your own externalism at the expense of another (Matthew 7:3-5).

Hypocrisy is a leaven. A very real danger of religiosity is that it tends to expand or spread (Luke 12:1). Jesus warns us to beware of empty religious teaching (Matthew 16:11). Hypocritical leaders do not enter the kingdom of God. They also hinder others from entering the kingdom of God (Matthew 23:13; Luke 11:52). Ultimately, the result of hypocrisy is futility. Hypocritical worship is good for nothing. Without obedience (contents), the form of worship is futile (Matthew 15:8-9). Jesus' actions, attitudes, and words towards hypocrites indicate that they will be judged with a greater degree of judgment. Thus, the eventual result of hypocrisy is judgment (Mark 12:40). And so, we should avoid hypocrisy/religiosity like the plague. Stay out of whitewashed tombs! They may look nice, but they stink to high heaven.

———————

SPIRITUAL LAWS ... THE LAW OF THE FRUIT!

"For there is no good tree which produces bad fruit, nor, on the other hand,
a bad tree which produces good fruit."

Luke 6:43-44

There are spiritual laws, albeit unseen, that establish the real order of the universe. Light exposes darkness (John 3:20). Darkness does not want to be revealed so it avoids the light. It is a spiritual law that light and darkness oppose each other.

Another example of a spiritual law is the negative impact that sin has on our lives. When we sin we separate ourselves from God (Romans 6:23). This spiritual law is so real that it even resulted in God being, paradoxically, separated from Himself (Matthew 27:46; 2 Corinthians 5:21). These spiritual laws involve the very foundations of our lives. A lack of obedience to the Word of God weakens the foundation and can produce weak Christians (Matthew 7:26-27). This is a spiritual law. Obedience leads to God. Sin leads to other things, particularly death (James 1:15).

A general category of spiritual laws might be classified as the laws of consistency. It is in this category that we find the law of the fruit. A tree will always bear its kind of fruit. So, too, good men will do good things and wicked men will do bad things. More specifically, the words that we speak reveal what is in our hearts (character, will, emotions). There is a consistent correlation between what we speak and who we are (Luke 6:45).

Spiritual laws, although unseen, are by no means impractical. Another spiritual law of consistency can be applied to the very practical field of leadership/management. The **more** authority you are given, the **more** responsibility you will have. The **more** opportunities that you have, the **more** that is expected of you (Luke 12:48). Good leaders/managers are aware of this unseen law and seek to manage people accordingly since workers who are given much authority and little responsibility become bored/unproductive and workers who are given much responsibility and little authority become frustrated/overwhelmed—unseen but very real!

And so, in our lives there exist a variety of ways, within a variety of contexts, in which the "law of the fruit" applies: "For there is no good tree which produces bad fruit, nor, on the other hand, a bad tree which produces good fruit" (Luke 6:43-44). There are always consequences to our actions. We do not live in a sort of "behavior vacuum" since "he who sows sparingly will also reap sparingly, and he who sows bountifully will also reap bountifully" (2 Corinthians 9:6). And so, please ...

Do not be deceived, God is not mocked; for whatever a man sows, this he will also reap. For the one who sows to his own flesh will from the flesh reap corruption, but the one who sows to the Spirit will from the Spirit reap eternal life. Let us not lose heart in doing good, for in due time we will reap if we do not grow weary. So then, while we have opportunity, let us do good to all people, and especially to those who are of the household of the faith (Galatians 6:7-10).

FEBRUARY 15

THE RESURRECTION HAS MANY CONVINCING PROOFS!

"To these He also presented Himself alive after His suffering,
by many convincing proofs, appearing to them over a period *of forty days*
and speaking of the things concerning the kingdom of God."

Acts 1:3

The resurrection of Jesus Christ is not questioned in the Scripture (1 Corinthians 15:20). Jesus is said to have "presented Himself alive . . . by many convincing proofs" (Acts 1:3; John 20:20). There is the empty tomb (John 20:1-9), the testimony of the angels (Matthew 28:5-7), the testimony (through their actions) of His enemies (Matthew 28:11-15), the establishment of Sunday as the Lord's day (John 20:1, 19; 1 Corinthians 16:2), and the testimony and preaching of the apostles and many others (Matthew 28:1-20; Mark 16:1-14; Luke 24:1-53; John 20:1-31; Acts 2:22-32; 4:33). There are "many convincing proofs" (Acts 1:3) for the resurrection of Jesus . . . many points that can be made to build the argument.

How can you explain the quality of the testimonies? They all had the same testimony. If it was a conspiracy it would be impossible for hundreds of people to have the same story, detail by detail. Moreover, there was a rational tone to their explanations. Furthermore, there is no historical record of refutation of the testimonies even though Paul seems to invite people to investigate, and potentially, refute them (1 Corinthians 15:6) when he reports that Jesus appeared to more than 500 "most of whom remain until now" (as if to say, "Go ask them . . . see if they come forth and say it did not happen . . . see if you think they are deluded or are lying . . . ").

How can you explain the great change in the disciples? Immediately after the crucifixion of Christ, they were afraid (John 20:19), they were doubting (John 20:25; Luke 24:21; Mark 16:11-14), and they were hiding (Matthew 27:55-56; John 20:19). They were discouraged (Luke 24:21)! Suddenly, they became bold (Acts 4:31). They were convinced (John 20:8, 28-29). They were out on the streets evangelizing (Mark 16:20). They were encouraged (Luke 24:52-53)! What changed? What happened? The resurrection happened! They were discouraged because Jesus was dead. They were encouraged because Jesus was alive!

How can you explain that the disciples were willing to die for the testimony of the resurrection? Only a real experience could produce that type of courage. There are evidences . . . there are proofs. Ultimately, however, we come back to the bottom-line question in the "resurrection trial": Is Jesus *alive* in your life? What is really on trial? Relationship with God! Is Christianity a creed or a relationship? Do you know about God or do you know God? Is Jesus dead or alive in your life? And so the closing argument in the trial ends with this statement: "If you confess with your mouth Jesus as Lord, and believe in your heart that God raised Him from the dead, you shall be saved" (Romans 10:9).

FEBRUARY 16

DO YOU KNOW YOUR GRANDFATHER
. . . OF THEOLOGY?

"For Your salvation I wait, O Lord."

Genesis 49:18

Soteriology (the theology of salvation) is often referred to as the "grandfather" of theology since it is so fundamental to the message of Scripture and serves as its main theme. There exists a variety of theological concepts that can be used to describe Christian soteriology. According to the Christian religion, what is the nature of the problem and what is the essence of the solution to that problem; that is, what is its soteriology? In order to understand Christian soteriology, it may be helpful to consider seven of its components.

First, redemption is the plan or strategy of salvation. It is to buy back that which was lost. The problem, is that we are lost, and the solution to that problem is to find us by buying us back. And so, we look to " . . . our great God and Savior, Christ Jesus, who gave Himself for us, that He might redeem us from every lawless deed and purify for Himself a people for His own possession . . . " (Titus 2:13-14).

Second, regeneration is the reality and energy of salvation. It is to bring back to life, to give new life, or to give birth again. The problem is that we are dead in our sin, and the solution to that problem is to bring us back to life. And so, " . . . unless one is born again he cannot see the kingdom of God" (John 3:3).

Third, reconciliation is the relational aspect of salvation. It is to make peace between enemies. The problem is that we are estranged from God, and the solution to the problem is to make us to be friends again. And so, " . . . we shall be saved from the wrath of God . . . For if while we were enemies, we were reconciled to God through the death of His Son, much more, having been reconciled, we shall be saved by His life" (Romans 5:9-10).

Fourth, atonement is the work or cost of salvation. It is the reconciliation of the guilty by divine sacrifice. The problem is that God's wrath must be satisfied (sin must be paid for), and the solution to the problem is that God paid the price Himself. And so, " . . . you were not redeemed with perishable things . . . but with precious blood, as of a lamb unblemished and spotless, the blood of Christ" (1 Peter 1:18-19).

Fifth, justification is the legal result of salvation. It is, in a sense, to enter a "court of law" and account the guilty "just" before God. It is to make it "just as if I'd" (justified) never sinned. The problem is that we are guilty of sin, and the solution to the problem is to assign Christ's righteousness (lack of sin) to our account. And so, " . . . having been justified by His blood, we shall be saved from the wrath of God through Him" (Romans 1:9).

Sixth, righteousness is the position of salvation. It is the position of right standing before God. The problem is that in our sin we are out of favor with God, and the solution to the problem is that Christ's blood ushers us into the presence of God. And so, "not having a righteousness of my own derived from the Law, but that which is through faith in Christ, the righteousness which comes from God on the basis of faith, that I may know Him . . . " (Philippians 3:9-10).

Seventh, sanctification is the process of salvation. It is the process of increasingly purifying and setting apart the one who has been saved. The problem is that we are separated from God by our sin, and the solution to the problem is to separate us from our sin by God. And so, "examine everything carefully; hold fast to that which is good; abstain from every form of evil . . . may the God of peace Himself sanctify you entirely; and may your spirit and soul and body be preserved complete, without blame . . . " (1 Thessalonians 5:21-23).

And so, we can more fully understand the "grandfather" of theology as we understand its components. These seven theological concepts describe Christian soteriology. What is the nature of the problem and what is the essence of the solution to that problem? It is the story of two Adams. The first Adam is the problem, and the second Adam is the solution. Herein, is the doctrine of salvation! "For Your salvation I wait, O Lord" (Genesis 49:18).

FEBRUARY 17

THE SUPREMACY OF THE HOLY SPIRIT . . .

" . . . but whoever blasphemes against the Holy Spirit never has forgiveness,
but is guilty of an eternal sin."

Mark 3:29

Who is the Holy Spirit? Most significantly, the Holy Spirit is God. In Acts 5:3-4 the Scripture presents the Holy Spirit and God as interchangeable: "But Peter said, 'Ananias, why has Satan filled your heart to lie to the Holy Spirit and to keep back some of the price of the land? While it remained unsold, did it not remain your own? And after it was sold, was it not under your control? Why is it that you have conceived this deed in your heart? You have not lied to men but to God.'" To lie to the Holy Spirit is to lie to God because the Holy Spirit is God.

His supremacy is established in His divinity. As part of the Trinity, the Holy Spirit is both equal to the Father and the Son, yet distinct from them. The three divine Persons of the Trinity are different, yet One. Thus, the Holy Spirit is both supreme as the one and only God, and supreme as God distinct from the Father and the Son.

And so blasphemy against the Son can be forgiven but blasphemy against the Holy Spirit cannot be forgiven (Luke 12:10). Why? Are they not both equally God? Yes, but they are distinct in their divine roles. It is the Holy Spirit who "will convict the world concerning sin" (John 16:8). That is his distinct divine role. To reject Him is to reject the source of conviction and conviction is what leads one to forgiveness. Blasphemy (rejection) of the One who convicts is unforgivable in the same sense that shutting off the source of forgiveness makes forgiveness impossible. As long as the source of the river is dammed up, no water will flow!

And so, the Son says it is to our advantage that He "go away" (John 16:7) because then He will send the Holy Spirit. It is God sending God. How is that an advantage? It is an advantage because of the nature of the divine role of the Holy Spirit; that He convicts the world of sin (John 16:8). Jesus—"who, although He existed in the form of God, did not regard equality with God a thing to be grasped, but emptied Himself, taking the form of a bond-servant, and being made in the likeness of men . . . " (Philippians 2:6-7)—did not stop being God in the incarnation but He did lay aside ("emptied Himself") His divine privileges; the expressing of all His abilities (for example, His omnipresence). Thus, it would be advantageous to the work of the Trinity that the space and time bound Jesus would go, and the space and time boundless Holy Spirit would come. So, God the Father sends God the Son (John 3:16) and God the Son sends God the Holy Spirit. The supremacy of the Holy Spirit (just like the supremacy of God the Father and God the Son) is rooted in His divinity . . . as the one and only God, and as God distinct from the other members of the Trinity.

———————

FEBRUARY 18

THE WISE MAN IS A MAN OF ACTION . . .

"Therefore everyone who hears these words of Mine and acts on them, may be compared to a wise man who built his house on the rock."

Matthew 7:24

Where does wisdom come from? Who or what is the source of it? Wisdom is associated with *both* hearing and doing; it is connected to God and His words (hearing) as source *and* man and his actions (doing) as response.

First and foremost, it should be understood that Jesus is the source of wisdom. It is He who opens our minds to understanding the Scriptures (Luke 24:45).

Jesus, the Word of God, is the source of wisdom. At the same time, man is involved (action). It is not enough to hear the Word; it must be acted upon. Obedience to the Word of God results in knowing truth/having wisdom. Jesus explains, "If you hold to my teaching, you are really my disciples. Then you will know the truth, and the truth will set you free" (John 8:31-32). Obeying the Word results in knowing truth and knowing truth and having wisdom result in freedom from sin. It begins with obedience.

Obedience and relationship with Jesus (knowing Him) are often linked together. When people asked Jesus what they should do to do the works of God, Jesus answered by saying that relationship with Him/belief in Him is the "work of God" (John 6:28). And so we see in Mark 4:11 that those who are granted to know the mysteries are those who are "about" Jesus (following Him/in relationship with Him); those who follow Him and are in relationship with Him receive revelation/gain wisdom. Knowledge and wisdom are available through spending time with Jesus. Furthermore, in Matthew 13:12 we see that those who have ears to hear will increase in their understanding. Those who do not have ears to hear (they are described in verses 14-15 as those who are dull-hearted due to, perhaps, the hardening effects of sin) will decrease in their understanding. It should be noted that this reference to having ears to hear is placed in the context of being in relationship with Jesus.

And so the wise man must act. "Everyone who hears these words of Mine and acts on them, may be compared to a wise man" (Matthew 7:24). The actions of the wise man are the actions of following Jesus; the actions of relationship with Him and obedience to Him. Are you wise?

———————

FEBRUARY 19

EXAMINE YOURSELF! DON'T "EAT" IN AN "UNWORTHY MANNER"

"Therefore whoever eats the bread or drinks the cup of the Lord in an unworthy manner, shall be guilty of the body and the blood of the Lord. But let a man examine himself, and in so doing he is to eat of the bread and drink of the cup. For he who eats and drinks, eats and drinks judgment to himself if he does not judge the body rightly."

1 Corinthians 11:27-29

For the church, the Lord's Supper is a celebration and remembrance of all that Christ has done for it. A holy ritual, it stands as a profound activity for those who profess Christ as their God. It is a sacred event that is not to be engaged in flippantly. One should "examine himself" (1 Corinthians 11:28) so as to participate in the Lord's Supper in a worthy manner. Paul warns the Corinthian believers to not eat the Lord's Supper "in an unworthy manner," but instead to, "judge the body rightly" (1 Corinthians 11:27, 29). What does it mean to eat "in an unworthy manner" and to "judge the body rightly?" Let's examine ourselves!

What is an "unworthy manner?" The word "unworthy" is the translation of the Greek word *anaxios* (*an* and *axios*). *Axios* means to "bring up the other end of the scale" or to "bring into equality." Equality is the central idea. *An* means "not." Thus, the term *anaxios* or "unworthy" means "unbalanced" or "not equal." To take the Lord's Supper in an "unworthy manner" is to take it in an attitude or manner of inequality. It describes those who were taking the Lord's Supper with an attitude or action of prejudice or discrimination. The cross of Christ—that which the Lord's Supper celebrates—engenders unity, equality, and the destruction of discrimination (Ephesians 3:11-16). Engaging in it in any other way risks contradicting it. The spirit of His death was one of sacrifice, love, and self-denial. Some of the Corinthian Christians were celebrating the Lord's Supper in a way that was completely contradictory to that spirit. Instead of sacrifice, they were filling themselves while others went hungry (1 Corinthians 11:21). Instead of love, they were showing apathy toward their brothers (1 Corinthians 11:22). Instead of self-denial, they were denying others (1 Corinthians 11:33). To take the Lord's Supper with these attitudes and actions was to sin against the body and blood of Christ. It was to despise the work of the cross and to undervalue one's own redemption.

Taking the Lord's Supper in a selfish and prejudicial way would be like having a remembrance supper "in honor" of Dr. Martin Luther King—who gave his life for the cause of equal rights for

African-Americans—and making all the African-Americans sit in the back. The supper **for** Martin Luther King would be **against** him. It would be to "come together not for the better but for the worse" (1 Corinthians 11:17). It would be an insult and sin against his shed blood (1 Corinthians 11:27). The supper would be **unworthy** of Dr. King and would be a mockery of him! So too, when Christians take the Lord's Supper in an unworthy manner, it is a mockery of the work of Christ on the cross and a devaluing of the salvation it provides.

What is "not judging the body rightly?" (1 Corinthians 11:29). The general context of 1 Corinthians 11 revolves around a variety of instructions for the church; that is the body of Christ. The immediate context of 1 Corinthians 11:29 relates to the actions of different members of the church or the "body." To not judge the "body" rightly is to pre-judge (prejudice) the members of the church incorrectly. It is to act in discrimination against another equal member of the "body" through one's actions or attitudes. The result is judgment (1 Corinthians 11:29-30).

Disunity, selfishness, and inequality are not consistent with the celebration of the cross (the Lord's Supper) that brought unity, selflessness, and equality. Be careful! What Supper are you eating? Examine yourself. Eat in a worthy manner that judges the body rightly. Make sure your fellowship with others is couched in a spirit of unity, an attitude of selflessness, and a proclamation of equality. Examine yourself!

———————

FEBRUARY 20

THE FEMALE INFERIORITY COMPLEX IS ABSURD . . .

"However, in the Lord, neither is woman independent of man, nor is man independent of woman. For as the woman originates from the man, so also the man has his birth *through the woman; and all things originate from God."*

1 Corinthians 11:11-12

To say that women are inferior to men is an absurd statement just as to say that men are superior to women is an absurd statement. Women are not inferior to men—they are equal to them—and, thus, any kind of female inferiority complex is absurd! Women are equal to men in the context of creation. God formed the man. God also formed the woman. God was directly and equally involved in both creations. It is not that the woman was made *by* the man—the man was sleeping during her creation—but that the woman was made *from* the man. Thus, there is an order of creation, and therefore, an order within the marriage relationship (there are different marriage roles). The man and the woman are different—they are not the same—but that does not mean they are unequal. The woman was made by God (thus, inferior to Him, but not inferior to the man who did not make her). And so, the difference between men and women is based on the divine order of creation, while the equality of men and women is based on the fact that both have the same Creator. The absurdity that the woman is inferior to the man comes from the misunderstanding concerning who made the woman.

Women are equal to men in the continuation of the human race: "However, in the Lord, neither is woman independent of man, nor is man independent of woman. For as the woman originates from the man, so also the man has his birth through the woman; and all things originate from God" (1 Corinthians 11:11-12). If one person relies on a second person for existence, then the second person cannot be considered inferior. They are equally and mutually dependent. This is true with both men and women. They rely on each other to continue their kind. Two women cannot continue the human race. Two men cannot continue the human race. It takes a man and a woman. God naturally fit things together in this way. They rely on each other for their own existence, and therefore are equal to each other.

The doctrinal error of the "inferiority of women" is based on bad logic. The old Hebrew rabbis said women were inferior because Eve was formed from Adam. This type of logic would mean men are inferior to dirt because Adam was formed from dirt! The old Hebrew rabbis also said women were inferior to men because Eve was formed after Adam. Is man, then, inferior to the animals that were formed before him? The fact that woman was made from man establishes her equality with him. She is, as Adam proclaimed, bone of his bones and flesh of his flesh (Genesis 2:23). They are part of each other and therefore equal in their nature or identity. That, of course, does not mean they are the same. Their equality does not negate their difference. The woman was formed from man and after man. There is a divine order of things. Thus, there is a divine order within the foundational relationship between the man and the woman. This is the basis for "marriage roles." Husbands and wives are equal, yet different. There is equality without sameness. And so, Jesus rebuked the double standards of the Pharisees that were formed by their discrimination and prejudice against women (Matthew 5:28). However, Jesus never became an advocate of the "sameness" agenda of the modern women's liberation movement. He understood men and women are different. Jesus addresses women as equal to men, but not the same. As obvious as this should be, it is not seen by a futile, sinful world (Romans 1:18-32).

The Scripture repeatedly declares the equality of men and women (Genesis 1:27; Genesis 5:1-2; Galatians 3:28; Ephesians 5:28; 1 Peter 3:7). Women are not inferior to men—they are equal to them—and, thus, any kind of female inferiority complex is absurd!

———————

HOW SHALL WE THEN . . . STUDY THE BIBLE?

"Be diligent to present yourself approved to God as a workman who does not need to be ashamed, handling accurately the word of truth."

2 Timothy 2:15

God calls His people to study His Word in a certain way: "Be diligent to present yourself approved to God as a workman who does not need to be ashamed, handling accurately the word of truth" (2 Timothy 2:15). What are we to do? We are to study ("be diligent . . . as a workman"). What are we to study? We are to study the Bible ("the word of truth"). How are we to study? We are to study with an inductive approach that respects the Scripture ("who does not need to be ashamed") and insists on the Scripture saying what the Scripture says ("handling accurately"). How shall we then . . . ? **Inductive Bible Study**!

What is the Bible? The Bible is the inspired Word of God (2 Timothy 3:16). Its author is the Holy Spirit. The instrument used by the author is man (2 Peter 1:21). The Bible did not come down from heaven via a celestial typewriter with angel wings pumping out hundreds of pages of text. It came from heaven (source) via human writers (method). Therefore, the Bible is **God's word in human language**. It is God's word. It is, therefore, without error (Psalm 19:7). It can be trusted (Psalm 119:89; Matthew 24:35). It is not just a book. It is alive. It has power (Hebrews 4:12). Yes, it is in human language. Because the Bible was written in human language, it must be studied grammatically, historically, culturally, and contextually. The Bible was written by men. We must consider the human form of communication (grammatical). We must consider the human events (historical). We must consider the human habits or customs (cultural). Finally, we must consider the human flow of thought (contextual). As Dr. Charles Holman writes:

> Just as it is wrong to deny the humanity of Jesus Christ, so it is erroneous to deny the humanity of the Bible. We are **not** saying that the Bible is a fallible book and teaches error, but nevertheless we must reckon with God's message coming to us through the ordinary processes of human thought in given times and cultures, if we are to handle the Word of God correctly.[1]

We must **study** the **Bible**. It is not enough to casually read the Bible. It must be studied diligently in order to be handled accurately (2 Timothy 2:15). It must be studied prayerfully (Psalm 119:12-18). It must be studied persistently (1 Peter 2:2-3). It cannot simply be studied with the mind. It must be studied with the spirit for it is "spiritually appraised" (1 Corinthians 2:14-15). The teacher of the Bible is the Holy Spirit (John 16:13-15).

We must **study** the **Bible** in an **inductive** way. Inductive Bible study seeks to discover what the Bible says. It does not try to tell the Bible what to say (deductive Bible study). Inductive Bible study begins with the particulars of Scripture and follows them to *their* conclusions. Deductive Bible study begins with *its* conclusions and then tries to use (abuse) the Bible to prove its point. Inductive Bible study tries to be neutral in its approach. It has no "predefined doctrines" that it wants to protect. It has one desire:

Let the Bible say what the Bible says! This desire results in the Bible being read as if it has never been read before. This perspective helps the Bible student to study in an inductive mode. Study the Bible as if it were a love letter from a boyfriend or girlfriend. This perspective helps the Bible student study more inductively as it tends to push the student to observe details, ask questions, and search for answers in the text. Get in the habit of studying the Bible with a hyper-awareness and focus on "connector words" so as to see the pieces of the text and how those pieces are pieced together. All of these perspectives and focuses make it more likely that you will study inductively, allowing the Bible to say what it says, and thus, "handling accurately the word of truth" (2 Timothy 2:15). How shall we then . . . ? **Inductive Bible study**!

FEBRUARY 22

THE FAITH TO RELEASE . . .

"I thank my God in all my remembrance of you, always offering prayer
with joy in my every prayer for you all, in view of your participation
in the gospel from the first day until now. For I am *confident of this very thing,*
that He who began a good work in you will perfect it
until the day of Christ Jesus."

Philippians 1:3-6

Paul founded the church at Philippi with Lydia and the Philippian jailer being his first converts there (Acts 16:12-40). In his letter to them, Paul tells the Philippians that he prays for them with thanks and joy (Philippians 1:3-4). Why is Paul so thankful and joyful? It is "in view of" two things: their "participation in the gospel" and his faith in God with respect to the ultimate success of the Philippians (Philippians 1:5-6). Paul is not a leader who wants to do everything while others do nothing. He joyfully thanks God for *their* involvement in the ministry. Their involvement is Paul's goal. Furthermore, Paul is not a leader who needs to control everything in order to have a sense that all will be completed. Through faith in God to complete ("perfect") that which He has started, Paul has thanks and joy instead of doubt and fear. How is Paul able to have this "faith to release"? Paul says that it is only right for him to feel this way about them because of his care and concern for them and his love for them (Philippians 1:7-8).

To relinquish a ministry and trust in God for its completion does not mean to forget that ministry. It is not like the relinquishing of a girlfriend because you have found another girl and really do not want to be bothered by the original girlfriend anyway. It is more like releasing children. Every parent must do this at some time. It is painful. The result is a deep longing for the child–even as Paul says, "I long for you all with the affection of Christ Jesus" ("affection" in verse 8 means "the bowels of" and is the strongest Greek term available to convey the most profound sense of compassion; it should be noted that it is not the "bowels of Paul" but it is the "bowels of Christ" as it is understood that Paul lived so close to Christ that he felt His compassion for others which meant that he could have this degree of compassion for the Philippians only because Christ lived in Him)—nevertheless, the releasing of the child is done for the child's own good.

To relinquish a ministry and trust in God for its completion does not mean to abandon that ministry. Faith in God does not mean that we are inactive. On the contrary, it points to and leads to our action. Paul's faith in what God will do (and is doing) in the Philippians is based on what God is doing (and will do) in him. Paul's proof (and therefore his faith) that God is working in and caring for the Philippians is the care and compassion of Jesus for the Philippians that God is working in him; the "bowels of Christ" that Paul is experiencing and feeling in himself. Paul is part of the process of the perfecting of the ministry that he is releasing. He is active in his faith because his faith is based on the fact that Jesus lives in him. Thus, his faith is not separate from his works since Paul is the vessel through which the works of Christ (or the "affections/bowels of Christ") are manifested.

Do you participate with other Christians or do you participate alone? Moreover, do you *encourage* and *allow* others to participate? Do you have a sincere desire to see others grow, succeed, and be fruitful in their own ministries? Or do you secretly rejoice when another fails or when his or her ministry is diminished? Are you able to relinquish ministry? Are you able to delegate authority to others and trust God for its completion? Or do you lack faith because your focus is on your own ability and not on the ability of God? Do you try to hold on to everything in order to have a sense of (self) control (the opposite of faith)? Or do you have **the faith to release**?!

———————

FEBRUARY 23

WHERE'S JESUS? . . . HE IS IN HEAVEN!

"And after He had said these things, He was lifted up while they were looking on, and a cloud received Him out of their sight. And as they were gazing intently into the sky while He was going . . . Jesus, who has been taken up from you into heaven . . . "

Acts 1:9-11

Where is Jesus? He is in heaven (Acts 1:11). Forty days after the resurrection (Acts 1:3) came the ascension (Luke 9:51) which is described as Jesus being "taken up from us" (Acts 1:22), "lifted up . . . taken up from you into heaven" (Acts 1:11), and "ascended on high" (Ephesians 4:8-9). Jesus references the ascension saying, "I ascend to My Father" (John 20:17) and "behold the Son of Man ascending where He was before" (John 6:62). Where is Jesus? He is in heaven for "He parted from them and was carried up into heaven" (Luke 24:50) just as it had been prophesied (Psalm 68:18; Ephesians 4:8-10; Psalm 24).

What is the purpose of the ascension? Jesus ascended so that the Holy Spirit would come (John 16:7). He ascended to receive glory and honor (Hebrews 2:9), to rule on the throne of David (Acts 2:29-36), and to sit next to the Father (Ephesians 1:20; Hebrews 1:3). Jesus ascended to be able to intercede for believers (Romans 8:34; Hebrews 7:25), to prepare a place for His people (John 14:2), and to minister as a Priest (Hebrews 4:14-16; 8:1-2). Furthermore, Jesus ascended to rule in victory (1 Corinthians 15:24-28), to show the greatness of His victory (Ephesians 4:8), to show the greatness of His exaltation (Acts 5:31; Philippians 2:9), to give gifts to men (Ephesians 4:8), to raise up believers with Him (Colossians 3:1-3; Ephesians 2:6), and to point to His return (Acts 1:11).

Jesus is the great "I Am." He is the "Alpha and Omega." He is eternal. Jesus has been. He is now. He always will be. So, from where He was, He came. From where He came, He went back. From where He went back, He will return. Jesus came to earth from heaven (incarnation). He returned to heaven from earth (ascension). He will come back to earth from heaven (return of Christ).

And so, the angels declared, "This Jesus, who has been taken up from you into heaven, will come in just the same way as you have watched Him go into heaven" (Acts 1:11). He is coming back . . . "Amen. Come, Lord Jesus" (Revelation 22:20). Maranatha!

———————

FILLED WITH THE HOLY SPIRIT!
HOW DID THEY KNOW?

"WHEN THE DAY of Pentecost had come . . . suddenly there came from heaven
a noise like a violent rushing wind, and it filled the whole house . . .
And they were all filled with the Holy Spirit and began to speak with other tongues,
as the Spirit was giving them utterance."

Acts 2:1-2, 4

One of the more debated topics in the church today (one that has even formed denominations) has to do with what is called the "baptism of the Holy Spirit" or "the filling with the Holy Spirit" or "the gift of the Holy Spirit." More specifically, the debate revolves around the question: Is there an initial evidence that provides proof that this "filling" has occurred in an individual? So, let's take a look at it.

There are seven different accounts in the book of Acts in which we may find people being "filled with" the Holy Spirit. What exactly happened when the Holy Spirit came in the book of Acts? Let's consider the various accounts in order to answer this question. As we will see, there are many things that happened (evidences) when the Holy Spirit "fell" on people. Biblically, it is difficult to say that any one specific thing is the conclusive sign or proof of the "filling" of the Spirit. On the day of Pentecost "evidences" include speaking "with other tongues" (Acts 2:4), preaching (Acts 2:14-36; 3:11-26), things that were *both* "seen and heard" (Acts 2:33), souls being saved (Acts 2:41, 47), the spiritual disciplines of prayer, fellowship (sharing), study, and breaking bread (worship) were practiced (Acts 2:42), signs and wonders (Acts 2:43), sharing (Acts 2:44-46), praise (Acts 2:47), and healing (Acts 3:1-10). So, in this account alone there are nine different "evidences" that can be found.

After the "second shaking" (Acts 4:31), evidences include boldness (Acts 4:31), sharing (Acts 4:32-35), witness or preaching (Acts 4:33), a word of knowledge (Acts 5:3), signs and wonders (Acts 5:12), unity (Acts 5:12), souls being saved (Acts 5:14), and the manifestation of healing and deliverance (Acts 5:16). Next, in the Samarian account, there were things that were "seen" by Simon (Acts 8:18), and the laying on of hands. In Paul's conversion we see healing (Acts 9:18), preaching and proclaiming (Acts 9:20), a word of wisdom (Acts 9:22), and boldness (Acts 9:27-28). In the Cornelius account, evidences include, once again, tongues (Acts 10:46), as well as praise and exaltation of God (Acts 10:46). In addition, in another "continual" filling (Acts 13:52), evidences include preaching (Acts 14:1, 7), the use of spiritual gifts (Acts 14:1, 6), boldness (Acts 14:3), signs and wonders (Acts 14:3), and healing (14:10). Finally, in the Ephesian account (Acts 19), we find tongues (19:6), prophecy (19:6), and the laying on of hands.

To summarize the so called "evidences" of the "baptism of the Holy Spirit," let's add up how many times each evidence occurs in the seven accounts in the book of Acts. Healing and preaching occur four times. Tongues, signs and wonders, boldness, and spiritual gifts occur three times. Sharing, praise, souls being saved, and that which is "seen and heard" occur twice each. Finally, we find prophecy and spiritual disciplines one time each.

The laying on of hands is not one of the evidences of the coming of the Spirit (as are the rest) but is included to show that sometimes it was used as a method to bestow the gift of the Holy Spirit and sometimes it was not. When all is said and done, the "totals" show that there are various significant effects, results, signs, proofs, or "evidences" of the filling of the Holy Spirit. None of the effects appear in all the accounts and no single "evidence" stands out above the rest.

FEBRUARY 25

BE CAREFUL NOT TO TRIP OVER THE CROSS . . .

"Peter said to Him, 'Never shall You wash my feet!' Jesus answered him, 'If I do not wash you, you have no part with Me.'"

John 13:8

I sat high on a hill looking down on an outdoor stage on which actors, in the *Passion Play*, were portraying the crucifixion of Jesus Christ. Jesus took the cross on his back and began to climb the hill depicting his trek up Calvary. As the actor passed by me (I was seated directly on an "aisle") I found myself having to look away. I could not stand to watch. It did not seem right. This perfect Jesus—God Himself who did not deserve this humiliation and agony—did not resonate with my assessment of what should be happening. He should not have to do this.

The **scandal**—the Greek term "e**skandal**on" in 1 Corinthians 1:23 is translated "stumbling block"—of the cross ran up my flesh like a feeling of nausea. My near regurgitation was nothing less than the tendency of the flesh to stumble over the cross . . . to trip over the very thing that would save me because it is revolting to my flesh to think that I should not save myself but, instead, God would have to save me . . . that I could do nothing, and He had to do it all. The issue of the "stumbling block of the cross" (Galatians 5:11) makes it so the danger is to trip over it.

Peter certainly struggled with this. In the Garden of Gethsemane where the civil and religious posse came to arrest Jesus, Peter tripped as he tried to fight his way through that nauseous feeling.

Jesus responded, "Put the sword into the sheath; the cup which the Father has given Me, shall I not drink it?" (John 18:10-11). Some hours earlier in the upper room, Peter was tripping over the cross as Jesus depicted it in the washing of the disciples' feet. Peter expressed his nausea saying, "Lord, do you wash my feet . . . Never shall you wash my feet!" Jesus responded to his tendency to regurgitate (trip over the cross) by saying, "If I do not wash you, you have no part with Me" (John 13:6-8). The cross is a stumbling block because it is difficult for us to accept the fact that God Himself must save us . . . that we could not save ourselves. That fact crawls up our flesh and, if we are not careful, causes us to trip.

There is only one way to follow Jesus. You must accept Him; you have to accept the cross (Luke 14:27). You must accept your need for Him and not trust in yourself (Proverbs 3:5-6; John 15:5). This is divisive (Luke 12:51-53). It divides people from each other, and it divides within individuals (Hebrews 4:12). Ultimately, it will divide the sheep from the goats in the final Judgment (Matthew 25:32). The cross is the kindling wood of the fire of judgment (Luke 12:49-50; John 3:17-20). It is a stumbling block. Don't trip over it!

———————

FEBRUARY 26

THE HOLY CLUB . . .
A DIFFERENT KIND OF CLUB!

" . . . discipline yourself for the purpose of godliness . . . "

1 Timothy 4:7

John Wesley, the founder of the Methodist movement, led a life of discipline with respect to knowing God. Before the Methodist Revivals began in England, Wesley had formed a group called the Holy Club. This "Club" was organized based on a desire to lead a disciplined life in seeking God. The following schedule shows a typical day in the life of a member of the Holy Club: wake up at 5:00 a.m., sing psalms, and read Scriptures until 8:00 a.m.; pray from 8:00 a.m. until 9:00 a.m.; five nights each week meet together for fellowship and mutual encouragement in reading religious books; each night, from 6:00 to 7:00 p.m., pray for the petitions of the poor and plan for ministry for the next day.

Discipline is a method, not a goal. The Holy Club members were disciplined, but that was not the goal. They did not do what they did simply for the sake of discipline; rather, they did what they did in order to know God more fully (the motivation/goal is the love of God and the desire to know Him, and discipline is simply a method toward that end). When discipline is the goal, then it quickly turns into mere ritual. Perhaps it could be said that religiosity is the practice of spiritual disciplines as a motive/goal while knowing God is merely a method toward that goal; whereas, Christianity is the practice of spiritual disciplines as a method toward the goal/motive of knowing God.

The reality of a disciplined life of seeking God will lead to a disciplined life of serving and loving others. This is consistent with the progression of the two greatest commandments: "The foremost is . . . 'you shall love the Lord your God with all your heart, and with all your soul, and with all your mind, and with all your strength.'" The second is this, 'You shall love your neighbor as yourself'" (Mark 12:29-31). This is consistent with what happened in the Holy Club. They soon began a disciplined schedule of visiting and ministering to those in hospitals and prisons and praying for the poor.

We can join all kinds of "clubs." Some like to join the "gossip club." They are very disciplined in gabbing about others and speculating on things they have no business talking about! But there are other ways to use your time and so Paul exhorts Timothy, "But have nothing to do with worldly fables fit only for old women. On the other hand, discipline yourself for the purpose of godliness; for . . . godliness is profitable for all things, since it holds promise for the present life and also for the life to come" (1 Timothy 4:7-8). The "Holy Club" is a different kind of Club!

———————

FEBRUARY 27

GOOD TEAMMATES AVOID GRUMBLING AND DISPUTING . . .

"Do all things without grumbling or disputing; so that you will prove yourselves to be blameless and innocent, children of God above reproach in the midst of a crooked and perverse generation, among whom you appear as lights in the world . . . "

Philippians 2:14-15

Have you ever been part of a team? Maybe you were on a soccer team in high school. Maybe you are part of a team in a business that is trying to solve a problem or develop a new product. No matter what kind of team you are on, you will find that the quickest way to destroy the "team" is to grumble and dispute. Complainers and murmurers, as well as those who are inclined to be contentious and argumentative, serve as a cancer in the body of a team. Relative to the idea and spirit of "teamwork," there is nothing more opposite, and therefore damaging, than complaining and disputing.

If you are on the "children of God team" then you are advised to be especially careful about and to avoid like the plague—lest it become a plague that would eat away at the health of the team—the tendency toward grumbling and disputing. Paul admonishes the Philippians, "Do all things without grumbling or disputing; that you may prove yourselves to be blameless and innocent, children of God above reproach in the midst of a crooked and perverse generation, among whom you appear as lights in the world" (Philippians 2:14-15). Why is this so important? It is "that you may prove yourselves to be blameless and innocent . . . above reproach . . . as lights in the world" and "so that in the day of Christ I may have cause to glory because I did not run in vain nor toil in vain" (Philippians 2:16).

Teammates have a responsibility to their identity and to their heritage. In each aspect of responsibility, the bottom-line motivation to avoid grumbling and disputing is to honor and advance the effectiveness of the team. Teams that are torn apart within—not holding to a responsibility to their identity—are ineffective and disabled with respect to achieving their goals. A soccer team that is full of grumblers and disputers will not be able to play together on the field. Their grumbling and disputing with each other will result in no goals. They will lose! The "children of God team" that is full of grumblers and disputers will not be able to exhibit their "innocence" to a warped world around them, and their light—that would otherwise transform that warped world around them—will turn dark. They will not keep their testimony pure, and thus, will be ineffective. They will score no goals. They will lose! Teams that are torn apart within—not holding to a responsibility to their heritage—are ineffective and disabled with respect to achieving their goals. When the final whistle is blown (in "the day of Christ") the work done to form and shape the team will be in vain as the team's effectiveness will not be realized.

Avoiding the "team cancers" of grumbling and disputing requires an attitude that sees the team as larger than self. Paul had already trained the team to "have this attitude in yourselves which was also in Christ Jesus, who . . . emptied Himself . . . humbled Himself" (Philippians 2:5-8). He trained the team to "do nothing from selfishness or empty conceit, but with humility of mind let each of you regard one another as more important than himself" (Philippians 2:3). The team is bigger than the individual member. Without this understanding, things like grumbling and disputing can overtake a team and cause it to disqualify itself.

Herein lies the challenge in being on the "children of God team." Do you seek to protect the team's unity? Do you avoid complaints and disputes for the sake of the gospel witness? In your life, is the importance of the gospel witness greater than the importance of winning your arguments or expressing your dissatisfactions? Are you a responsible teammate, disciplining yourself to retain a responsibility to your identity and heritage? Do you avoid grumbling and disputing like the plague? Good teammates avoid grumbling and disputing! They avoid the disease. They stay healthy!

FEBRUARY 28

I DESIRE COMPASSION AND NOT SACRIFICE . . .

"But when the Pharisees saw this, they said to Him, 'Look, Your disciples do what is not lawful to do on a Sabbath.' But He said to them, . . . 'But if you had known what this means, 'I DESIRE COMPASSION, AND NOT A SACRIFICE,' you would not have condemned the innocent."

Matthew 12:2-3, 7

In the Old Testament, God commands His people to offer sacrifices. In response to the Pharisees, however, Jesus seems to discard "a sacrifice." Is Jesus contradicting the commands of God and the law? Not at all! Jesus says, "Do not think that I came to abolish the Law or the Prophets; I did not come to abolish but to fulfill" (Matthew 5:17). Jesus is going deeper. He is getting at the heart of the law. The fullness of the law is not found in its sacrificial aspect but in its compassion. The heart of the law is found in attitudes (like compassion) not simply in actions (like sacrifices). This is not to discard sacrifice at all; rather, it is to make it real. Action is not to be done away with but action without attitude is empty and fake (like the lives of the Pharisees). And so, Jesus would later say, "Woe to you, scribes and Pharisees, hypocrites! For you tithe mint and dill and cummin, and have neglected the weightier provisions of the law: justice and mercy and faithfulness; but these are the things you should have done without neglecting the others" (Matthew 23:23-24). It is not that the actions (tithing mint and dill and cumin) should be discarded, but that the attitudes (justice and mercy and faithfulness) must establish the actions. The heart of the law is more profound than mere actions because the heart of the law must come from the heart.

Attitudes lead to actions and are, thus, more vital. Compassion—from the Greek terms "con" and "pati" meaning "to suffer with"—leads to sacrifice; however, sacrifice without compassion is dead and empty. Sacrifice, in this sense, is subordinate (superficial/surface) while compassion is central (profound/heart). Compassion is more associated with humility while sacrifice is more associated with ability. Perhaps, here we find the core of the matter. The heart of the law comes down to how you view yourself and others. Do you view man as unable or able? Jesus responds to the Pharisaical mindset (the mindset that trusts in human ability) when He says, "It is not those who are healthy who need a physician, but those who are sick; I did not come to call the righteous, but sinners" (Mark 2:17) and "But go and learn what this means: 'I DESIRE COMPASSION, AND NOT

SACRIFICE,' for I did not come to call the righteous, but sinners" (Matthew 9:13). The proper response to God is to show compassion to others. Compassion is the response of someone who views himself and others as being sick (sinners/unable). Sacrifice alone is often the response of someone who views himself and others as being healthy (righteous/able).

The law—at least the heart of it that is found in attitudes like compassion—is very practical for it does not simply "go through the motions." Often in the Scripture we see that the very outworking and action of repentance itself is directly associated with compassion (consider Luke 3:10-11). Compassion is even often associated with something as practical as healing (consider Matthew 14:14, Luke 7:13, Mark 1:41, John 11:35, Matthew 20:34). The heart of the law is practical and powerful because it is real. The mere appearance of the law is impotent because it is fake/empty. Herein, lies the difference between ordinary religion and a living faith. Is your faith alive?

NOTES

March

THE LIFE PRODUCING SOUND SYSTEM . . . GOD SPEAKS!

"Moses said, 'THE LORD GOD WILL RAISE UP FOR YOU A PROPHET LIKE ME
FROM YOUR BRETHREN; TO HIM YOU SHALL GIVE HEED
to everything He says to you.'"

Acts 3:22

Revelation is life. God is a revealer of Himself. He **speaks**. He speaks life. He has always spoken. From the initial, "Then God **said** . . ." (Genesis 1:3) to the culminating "He who testifies to these things **says** . . ." (Revelation 22:20), God's revelation of Himself is, ultimately, verbal. This is the idea of the Hebrew word *naviim* or "prophecy" (to speak forth God's words). And so, special revelation was expressed through the Old Testament prophets. The prophet held a unique position. The Scripture reports "Surely the Lord God does nothing unless He reveals His secret counsel to His servants the prophets" (Amos 3:7). The prophet was important. The prophet was used to put the events of history in divine perspective (for example, the Exodus). Historical events were interpreted by the prophets as special revelations of God's purposes. The prophet declared God's special revelation in many ways and in many different forms (poetry, law, history, parables, proverbs). The importance of prophecy, however, is not in its form but in its message. The purpose of the prophet was to prepare for the greater revelation of Jesus Christ (John 5:39; Luke 24:27).

The climax of special revelation—of God's speaking—comes through Jesus Christ. Jesus, the Prophet whom "the Lord God shall raise up" (Acts 3:22) is referenced in Hebrews 1:1-2: "God, after He spoke long ago to the fathers in the prophets in many portions and in many ways, in these last days has spoken to us in His Son, whom He appointed heir of all things, through whom also He made the world." The revelation through Jesus was greater (clearer/fuller) than the revelation through the Old Testament prophets. It was more direct in that a prophet would say, "thus says the Lord," but Jesus says, "I say to you" (Matthew 12:22-28; John 7:46). It was with personal and final authority. A prophet was told something, but Jesus speaks what He was "taught" (John 8:28) and what He had "seen" (John 8:38). It was full. A prophet would say that he knew the way, but Jesus says that He is the way (John 14:6).

Special revelation was revealed through the New Testament apostles. Since the gospel includes the birth, death, resurrection, ascension, and second coming of Jesus, the apostles were needed to make known the meaning of the latter events. The apostles were also used to explain such things as the outpouring of the Holy Spirit, the formation of the church, and the inclusion of the gentiles (Ephesians 3:4-6). As the Old Testament prophets pointed to Jesus, so too, the New Testament apostles point to Him. In each case, the same thing is true. God reveals Himself through His speakers . . . through His speech . . . through, you might say, His incredible life producing "sound system." Revelation is life and God, as revealer of Himself, produces life as He speaks; He has always spoken . . . He has always produced life!

MARCH 2

WHAT SUPPER ARE YOU EATING, THE LORD'S OR . . . ?

"Therefore when you meet together, it is not to eat the Lord's Supper,
for in your eating each one takes his own supper first;
and one is hungry and another is drunk."

1 Corinthians 11:20-21

In the New Testament church, the Lord's Supper was often served in the context of the "agape love feast" (a communal fellowship meal as seen in Jude 12). However, in Corinth the atmosphere of fellowship and love was replaced by division and selfishness. Oxymoronically, instead of exhibiting the unity of the "household of God," the Lord's Supper exposed the divisive social status distinctions of various members of the family. Factions in the Corinthian church were obvious "for, in the first place, when you come together as a church, I hear that divisions exist among you . . . for there must also be factions among you, in order that those who are approved may have become evident among you" (1 Corinthians 11:18-19). In their "tribal" distinctions/divisions, they were taking the Lord's Supper together, yet they were actually dividing the Lord as "each one of you is saying, 'I am of Paul,' and 'I of Apollos,' and 'I of Cephas,' . . . has Christ been divided?" (1 Corinthians 1:12-13). This contradiction actually restricted their growth as believers as seen in Paul's rebuke, "I gave you milk to drink, not solid food; for you were not yet able to receive it . . . for you are still fleshly. For since there is jealousy and strife among you, are you not fleshly . . . " (1 Corinthians 3:2-3).

This "jealousy and strife" manifesting itself in "factions" and "divisions" was probably rooted in ethnic rifts (the Corinthian church consisted of both Jews and Gentiles) and, perhaps to an even greater degree, rooted in economic distinctions. Some of the Corinthian believers were slaves or ex-slaves (1 Corinthians 7:20-24) and not many were of noble birth (1 Corinthians 1:26). Many were probably very poor. At the same time, some of the Corinthian believers were very wealthy. Gaius had the economic means to host the whole church and Erastus was the city treasurer (Romans 16:23). Crispus was the leader of the synagogue (Acts 18:8). In the midst of social differences, Paul focused on the Lord's Supper as a way to teach about the need for unity in the church. And so, Paul rebukes the Corinthians in reference to the taking of the Lord's Supper, saying "therefore when you meet together, it is not to eat the **Lord's** Supper, for in your eating each one takes his own supper first; and one is hungry and another is drunk" (1 Corinthians 11:20-21).

In the social clubs of that time, there were organized feasts where the members of the club came together to eat. Food was allotted to each member according to social status. At the feast, certain members ate more food and better food than other members. The same thing, apparently, was happening at the Corinthian love feasts where the Lord's Supper was served. The wealthier Christians were eating and drinking until they were full, while the poorer Christians had nothing. The Lord's Supper became a manifestation of inequality instead of a celebration of unity. Therefore, when they met together it was not to eat the **Lord's** Supper. Their form of the Lord's Supper negated the real Lord's Supper. It was a contradiction: "coming together as a church" versus "divisions" (1 Corinthians 11:18); "hungry" versus "drunk" (1 Corinthians 11:21); "Lord's Supper" versus "own supper" (1 Corinthians 1:20-21); "come together for the better" versus "come together for the worse" (1 Corinthians 1:17).

Disunity, selfishness, and inequality are not consistent with the celebration of the cross (the Lord's Supper) that brought unity, selflessness, and equality. Be careful! What Supper are you eating, the Lord's *or . . . ?*

MARCH 3

ORDER IN THE MARRIAGE!

"For it was Adam who was first created and then Eve."

1 Timothy 2:13

There is a divine order within the marriage relationship in which the wife is subject to the husband and the husband is the head of the wife (Ephesians 5:22-23). There is order in the marriage because there is a divinely ordained authority structure that is rooted in creation. And so, different roles or functions for men and women are justified by Paul when he explains, "for it was Adam who was first created and then Eve" (1 Timothy 2:13). There is an authority structure that results in different roles. This is the biblical basis for the existence of marriage roles.

Marriage roles are the result of divine choices and organization at creation. The woman is made from the man (Genesis 2:22), made for the man (Genesis 2:18), given to the man (Genesis 2:22-24), and named by the man (Genesis 2:23). None of these dynamics make one superior or inferior to the other, but they do reflect an order of things. And so, the husband and the wife are equal, but not the same. The differences, reflected in divine choices and organization at creation, yield marriage roles.

Marriage roles, then, do not come into existence because of the Fall of man. Marriage roles are inherent to creation. Thus, the redeeming of the marriage relationship does not negate the different functions or roles of husband and wife. Instead, it makes the functions healthy again, after they have been distorted by a fallen society. When the functions and roles are healthy, then the marriage is healthy. Without a proper understanding and practice of these functions or roles, the family will be thrown into chaos. It will lack order and unity. There must be order in a family! Someone must lead. This responsibility of leadership is clearly given to the husband. His taking initiative/authority must be practiced (headship) and accepted (submission).

Certainly, there is a need for order in all types of fellowships. Consider the local church. There is a certain hierarchy of function within a local church. A church member needs to submit to a pastor (1 Corinthians 16:16; 1 Thessalonians 5:12-13). At the same time a pastor or leader must selflessly serve and be devoted to the members of the church (1 Corinthians 16:15). Similarly, there is a certain hierarchy of function within a family—interestingly, the same Greek word (*upotaso*) that is used in 1 Corinthians 16:16 to describe the submission of a church member to a church leader is also used in Ephesians 5:21-22 to describe the submission of a wife to a husband—in which a wife needs to submit to a husband (Ephesians 5:22) and a husband needs to selflessly serve, love, and be devoted to his wife (Ephesians 5:25-29).

Each member of either type of fellowship must respect these relational positions in order for the fellowship to exist and function correctly. They must also respect the equality of their members. The church leader and the church member are different in their structural and functional roles in the church. However, they are equal in their identity because their identity is in Christ. The husband and the wife are different in their structural and functional roles in the family. However, they are equal in their identity because their identity is in Christ. Husbands and wives must understand their equality. They must also understand that they are different, and both must submit to Christ in serving Him within their divinely ordained functional roles. There is order in the marriage!

———————

MARCH 4

DO YOU SEE YOUR INITIATIVES AS "OF," "IN," AND "FROM" JESUS?

"Paul and Timothy, bond-servants of Christ Jesus,
To all the saints in Christ Jesus who are in Philippi . . .
Grace to you and peace from God our Father
and the Lord Jesus Christ."

Philippians 1:1-2

How do you introduce a letter? Maybe it is something like, "To Whom It May Concern . . . I am an alarmed customer who would like to offer a suggestion . . ." Or maybe it is less formal and something like, "Hey Dave . . . your old friend Bob here to just say hello and see if we could get together some time to catch up with each other . . ." Many of the New Testament "books" are actually letters, and those letters include conventional introductions consistent with the way a letter would be written in that respective culture. Paul wrote many letters to various churches that then became Scripture. He wrote to the Philippians and traditionally began the letter in the conventional way of his culture. He identified the sender, the recipient, and the basic contents that served as a general greeting and introduction: "Paul and Timothy, bond-servants of Christ Jesus, to all the saints in Christ Jesus who are in Philippi . . . grace to you and peace from God our Father and the Lord Jesus Christ" (Philippians 1:1-2). The most profound observation one can make about this greeting is that "Jesus" is repeated three times (in two short verses) and stands as the obvious focus from the get-go. It is Jesus who is the focus of the letter as He is, in a very real sense, both the sender and the recipient, as well as the very contents themselves! The letter is sent via those "of Christ Jesus" (sender) to those "in Christ Jesus" (recipient) with its contents being "from . . . Jesus" (Philippians 1:1-2). It is "of," "in," and "from" Jesus. Jesus is "the Alpha and the Omega, the beginning and the end" (Revelation 21:6). He is "Him who fills all in all" (Ephesians 1:23)!

Paul identifies himself as a bond-servant of Christ Jesus. The literal translation is "slave" of Christ Jesus. He does not identify himself as "Paul, the founder of your church" or as "Paul, the great and famous apostle." No. Paul only sees himself as the "sender" of the letter inasmuch as he is a "bond-servant *of* Christ Jesus." Paul lived his life as a slave of Christ because he considered himself a slave. How would you identify yourself? Do you see yourself as a slave of Jesus? Or are you more like an employee? Or are you more like the boss? Or are you merely a temporary, volunteer worker? Remember, a slave does not expect anything in return for his efforts nor earn anything for his labors. His Master controls his life. Does this conflict with your description of yourself? Are you a slave?

Jesus is the Alpha and the Omega. In terms of an introduction to a letter, He is the sender and the recipient. He is the beginning and the end. And so Paul is "confident of this very thing, that He who began a good work in you will perfect it until the day of Christ Jesus" (Philippians 1:6). Jesus is also the in-between or the contents and process. And so Paul tells the Philippians to "work out your salvation with fear and trembling for it is God who is at work in you, both to will and to work for His good pleasure" (Philippians 2:12-13). He is "all in all" (Ephesians 1:23). Do you see it that way? Do you see your initiatives as "of," "in," and "from" Jesus? In the introduction of the "letter regarding your life" do you see Him as the beginning, the end, and everything in-between? Do you see Jesus as your *all in all*? Perhaps, a more concise way to say this is simply, "Is He your Lord?" (Romans 10:9).

MARCH 5

WERE ADAM AND EVE REAL PEOPLE? . . .

"They heard the sound of the L*ORD* *God walking in the garden in the cool of the day, and the man and his wife hid themselves from the presence of the* L*ORD* *God among the trees of the garden. Then the* L*ORD* *God called to the man, and said to him, 'Where are you?" He said, 'I heard the sound of You in the garden, and I was afraid because I was naked; so I hid myself.' And He said, 'Who told you that you were naked? Have you eaten from the tree of which I commanded you not to eat?' The man said, 'The woman whom You gave to be with me, she gave me from the tree, and I ate.'"*

Genesis 3:8-12

Were Adam and Eve real people or are they just part of an allegory used as an extended parable to explain the origin of mankind? Does the historicity of Adam even matter? Does it really matter whether Adam and Eve were real historical people or not?

The theological implications of denying a historical Adam are problematic. If the first Adam was not real, then why would we need a second Adam/"last Adam"? (1 Corinthians 15:45). The awkward results of following this type of thinking are obvious. The historicity of Jesus starts to be questioned as His deity and working of miracles are rejected (it is not surprising that the deistic view that the Adam-Eve story is but a myth resulted in Thomas Jefferson's "Jeffersonian Bible" that was a severely edited New Testament that totally eliminated any references to the miracles or deity of Jesus Christ).

Moreover, with respect to the historicity of Adam, those who propose the "teaching model" (allegorical myth) viewpoint do not see a separation between sin and creation. Sin and creation are viewed as existing right next to each other. Thus, sin is seen as an inherent part of man and creation. It belongs to man in a natural, original sense. If this is true, then Jesus cannot represent original man. Furthermore, it weakens humanity's sense of guilt over sin (after all it is only his original nature). The lack of guilt results in a lack of a need for repentance, which results in a lack of confession, which results in a lack of forgiveness of sins. All of this, again, results in the lack of a need for a historical Jesus and the redemption that He provides.

When we start to play with Scripture and reject its inerrancy as we explain away its truths by saying they are just stories made up by man to explain observed realities, we launch theological avalanches that end in the burial of the entire message of Scripture. The rejection of the historicity of Adam results in just that; the burial of the gospel message itself. Man is a sinner who needs to be saved from his sin. That is fundamental. It begins with the fundamental events found in Genesis 1-3 in which actual real people named Adam and Eve really sinned against their Creator. If those fundamental events were mere "cartoons" then maybe, we don't have anything else to talk about!

––––––––––

MARCH 6

GOOD HABITS . . .

"And He came out and proceeded as was His custom to the Mount of Olives;
and the disciples also followed Him."

Luke 22:39

You can have bad habits and you can have good habits. Jesus had certain customs (Luke 22:39), habits, or disciplines. His habit of prayer was a good habit (Mark 1:35; Matthew 14:23; Mark 6:46; Luke 6:12; 9:28). Jesus Himself is our example to strive for a disciplined prayer life. We pray in the name (John 14:13) of the One who, then, shows us how to pray. We should be consistent in praying (habitual). The Scripture indicates that asking, seeking, and knocking should be continual. The context of Luke 11:8-10 includes the idea of persistent prayer. Our prayers should not be overly repetitive (Matthew 6:7-8), but they should be persistent. Keep knocking until God answers the door! Jesus is our example. By His example, Jesus teaches us to pray according to God's will (Luke 22:42). Jesus' ultimate prayer is that God's will be done. This is a very important example to follow. Our prayers must include the attitude that is able to sincerely say to God: "Not My will but Your will be done" (Mark 14:36, 39).

How can we be "successful" in prayer? First, we must understand that we must pray. Getting an answer ("success") is not possible until we ask. Success in prayer depends, to a large degree, on how much we pray (Matthew 7:7). We must also understand that we are praying to a Father who wants the best for us; He wants our "success" (Luke 11:11-13). And so, success in prayer depends, to a large degree, on the strength of your relationship with God (John 15:7). Faith is the ingredient that makes prayer work (Matthew 21:21-22). Furthermore, fear of God and obedience to Him lead to success in prayer (John 9:31). Finally, there is a relationship between successful prayer and Christian fellowship and unity (Matthew 18:19).

You can have bad habits and you can have good habits. The habit of prayer is a good habit. Do you have that habit?

MARCH 7

GOD AS A "SEEMING CONTRADICTION" . . .

"IN THE beginning was the Word, and the Word was with God, and the Word was God."

John 1:1

Part of the wonder of God is, to some degree, His paradoxical nature. He stands before us as a "seeming contradiction." He is three, yet one; what we call the Trinity. Someone that **is** God (the Word) is also said to be **with** God (John 1:1). Here we see the paradox of the Trinity, and at the same time, a description of it. To say that God is with Himself is a paradox. It is also a definition or picture of what the Trinity looks like. As is consistent with the nature of "paradox," the Trinitarian nature of God is not something we can fully comprehend; it is only something we can describe. In John 1:1, 14, 18 we see that the Word **is** God and we beheld Him (God), yet no man has seen God, yet God has explained God. To say that God explained Himself by being seen, yet without ever being seen is certainly a paradox. It is also a good description of the Trinity. The Son gives life to whom **He** wishes, yet He can only do what He sees the Father doing (John 5:19-21). Again, we see the paradox of the Trinity and at the same time a description or picture of it. The will of the Father and the Son are exact, yet distinct, yet not separated. That is a paradox. That is the nature of God; the Trinity.

Jesus came to earth as God in the flesh, yet He remained under the authority (the commandment) of the Father (John 14:31). This points to the essence of the Trinity; that is, perfect relationship. Our union with Jesus should reflect that perfect relationship. Moreover, the example of the Trinity provides us with motivation in our relationships with others. When we understand

(Genesis 1:26-27) that man (a "them") was made in the image of God (an "Us"), it is not surprising that the Scripture makes a connection between God as a singular plurality (paradox) and the equal but not the same dynamic between husband and wife in the marriage relationship (Genesis 2:24). Similarly, that paradox of the marriage relationship is then connected to the relationships we have in the body of Christ (Ephesians 5:28-32).

Our model for our most foundational relationships (family and church), in many ways, stems from the relationships found within the Trinity (John 17:10-11). A healthy marriage is a unity within diversity; that is, a "singular plurality." A husband and wife understand and apply the dynamic of equality without confusing it with sameness. They are equal in their identity (Galatians 3:28) yet distinct in their roles (Ephesians 5:22-23). Similarly, a healthy church (Romans 12:4-5) is made up of those individual members who do not have the same function (distinct in their roles), yet who are one body (equal in their identity). Although, we may not be able to fully comprehend God as a seeming contradiction, we can apply the description of the paradoxical Trinity to our own relationships and reap the divine fruit of love.

MARCH 8

FELLOWSHIP IS TO SHARE . . . WHAT DO WE SHARE?

" . . . what we have seen and heard we proclaim to you also,
that you too may have fellowship with us; and indeed our
fellowship is with the Father, and with His Son Jesus Christ."

1 John 1:3

The Greek term *koinonia* is the biblical term from which we get our idea of church fellowship. The fundamental meaning of the term *koinonia* revolves around the idea of sharing. Christians are called to this *koinonia*, this fellowship, this sharing. What is it that we share?

First, there is that which we share in. We understand that it is our fellowship with God that is the basis for our fellowship with each other; "what we have seen and heard we proclaim to you also, that you also may have fellowship with us; and indeed our fellowship is with the Father, and with His Son Jesus Christ" (1 John 1:3). Even as we necessarily share much with our natural siblings simply because we have common parents, so too we share much with our spiritual brothers and sisters since we share in a common Father. Our fellowship with other believers is based on a common belief in the divinity of Jesus Christ. We share in a "common salvation" (Jude 3) and "a common faith" (Titus 1:4). Christians are called to fellowship with each other, first of all, because of what we share in.

Second, there is that which we "share out." Christians have in common with each other what they are called to give to others. We are all called to give of our spiritual wealth. In evangelism, we give out a shared gospel (Luke 5:10) and are all called to do so (Matthew 28:19). We are all called to give of our material wealth. We have a common responsibility to share our material possessions with those in need (Hebrews 13:16). Christians are called to fellowship with each other, second of all, because of what we "share out."

Third, there is that which we "share with." Christians share with each other reciprocal responsibilities (Philippians 4:15) and relationships (Romans 15:27). Within the Christian community, there exists a give and take relationship—"For I long to see you in order that I may impart some spiritual gift to you, that you may be established; that I may be encouraged with you while among you, each of us by the other's faith, both yours and mine" (Romans 1:11-12)—as Christians are called to share with each other. To a large degree, the practice of community in the church is based on a series of New Testament commandments that require us to do certain things "one to another" ("serve one another," "encourage one another," and "confess sins to one another"). We are to give and to receive. Christians are called to fellowship with each other, third of all, because of what we "share with."

You might be like the person who recites the poem, *To dwell above with saints we love, O, that will sure be glory. But to dwell below with saints we know, well, that's another story.* It is not necessarily the easiest thing to share life with others (to be in fellowship). Nevertheless, Christians must remain in fellowship (Hebrews 10:25) and are persuaded to do so since we share in, share out, and share with. In a very real sense, then, we share (fellowship) simply because . . . we share!

––––––––––

MARCH 9

YES, CHRISTIANS ARE NARROW MINDED . . .

*"For the gate is small, and the way is narrow that leads to life,
and there are few who find it."*

Matthew 7:14

You are *soooo* narrow minded! Meaning it as a rebuke, our humanistic/pluralistic culture accuses Christians of being narrow minded (intolerant of other beliefs). To the degree that being "intolerant" means that you adhere to the "onlyness" of Jesus (John 14:6; Acts 4:12), being accused of intolerance is actually a complement. You are *soooo* narrow minded! Thank you very much! The way (Jesus is the Way) is narrow (Matthew 7:14) and to pretend that it is not for the sake of political correctness helps no one as few are those who find it.

The way to heaven is narrow (Matthew 7:13). The world hates this assertion. It prefers many ways to heaven because it wants to define the way itself. However, there is only one Definer who has defined the one and only way: "And there is salvation in on one else; for there is no other name under heaven that has been given among men, by which we must be saved" (Acts 4:12); "I am the way . . . no one comes to the Father, but through Me" (John 14:6). That is so "pig-headed . . . " so bigoted . . . so prejudiced . . . so insular . . . so intolerant . . . so narrow-minded. Yes, it is! The truth is that way.

The entrance to salvation is a narrow door. Many will try to enter but will not be able to because the door is so narrow (Luke 13:24). However, it is impossible to get to God without going through that narrow door (John 10:9). It is the only entrance (John 14:6). Herein, lies a mystery. To some "has been given the mystery of the kingdom of God" (Mark 4:11) because the truth is sown on "good soil" (Mark 4:20); repentant soil that is able to hear, accept, and obey the implications of the mystery of the kingdom of God. The mystery of the kingdom of God is that there is **only one way** to salvation for all people, Christ Jesus (Ephesians 3:4-6). The world hates this . . . man's sinful flesh hates this. It prefers many ways; "The gate is wide and the way is broad that leads to destruction" (Matthew 7:13). The idea of only one way is repulsive because it necessarily negates the many other ways, and man, at his very core, wants his own way. This, however, is what needs to be rejected; our insistence on our own way. That is hard. We must deny self (Luke 9:23) . . . we must deny our own way. We must reject the "way to destruction" and choose the "way to life." So be narrow minded . . . and live!

MARCH 10

JOIN JESUS IN HIS PURPOSE AND SPREAD THE NEWS . . .

"But He said to them, 'I must preach the kingdom of God to the other cities also, for I was sent for this purpose."

Luke 4:43

Jesus self-proclaimed purpose was to engage in evangelism . . . the preaching of the *good news* and the kingdom of God (Luke 4:43). Evangelists preach because that same purpose is in those who no longer live but, instead, have Christ living in them (Galatians 2:20). The evangelist is the representative of Jesus (Luke 10:16). The responsibility (position) of the evangelist is not to "produce the crop" (save people/change their hearts); rather, it is a position that involves preaching ("casts seed") and inviting ("puts in the sickle"). The growth or outcome is the responsibility of God (Mark 4:26-29). And so, you do not have to be a great preacher to be effective in evangelism. Results depend more on the condition of the soil than on the preacher, and it is God who prepares and is sovereign over the condition of the soil. The key is the sovereign God, not the preacher (Mark 4:30-32; 1 Corinthians 3:7).

The realization that God is sovereign can actually result in motivation to evangelize (Luke 12:7-9). Moreover, the motivation to evangelize is part of a Christian's new nature since his new nature is that of Christ whose purpose it is to evangelize (Luke 4:43). A Christian is naturally ("new naturally") motivated to evangelize. We are designed to evangelize as a lamp is designed to give light. A light that does not give light has lost its purpose. A Christian who does not evangelize has lost his purpose. And so, Christians evangelize others (Matthew 5:14-16). We are motivated to evangelize because we want to bear fruit (Luke 8:16). Evangelism is the result of knowing God (John 17:21). It is the result of following Jesus (Matthew 4:19; Mark 1:17). It is the result of being called and instructed by Him (Matthew 10:5).

The necessity of evangelism cannot be overstated. The gospel must be preached to all nations before Jesus will return (Matthew 24:14). Evangelism is necessary because there are many people who are ripe to be picked for the kingdom of God (Matthew 9:37; Luke 10:2). And so, Jesus breathes upon the new church in a context of evangelistic commission; the church of the Lord Jesus Christ is an apostolic church; it is a "sent-one" into the world (John 20:21-22).

The spreading of the good news is the greatest commission. Jesus has all authority in heaven and on earth and so those who would spread the news have authority to go to spread it to everyone, everywhere (Matthew 28:18). Furthermore, "the spreaders" are assured of His constant presence (Matthew 28:20). So, join Jesus in His self-proclaimed purpose and spread the news!

———————

MARCH 11

TO DEEM SOMEONE AGAIN IS TO REDEEM . . .

"For the Son of Man has come to save that which was lost."

Matthew 18:11

Perhaps Hollywood is at its best when it sets itself in the timeless themes . . . themes like redemption. Set in France after the Revolution, *Les Misérables* is a powerful story of redemption. Jean Valjean, a seemingly heartless thief, is certainly deemed a bad man who could never change into a good man. Then, in a powerful scene that includes the dynamics that fuel redemption, the bishop who references the silver that Valjean stole from him and that he allowed him to keep—and thus, the character who represents the forgiving redeemer in the movie—says to Valjean, "Don't ever forget, you've promised to become a new man. Jean Valjean, my brother, you no longer belong to evil. With this silver I've bought your soul. I've ransomed you from fear and hatred. And now I give you back to God." As we see in the film, Valjean does go on to become a new man. He was deemed to be a bad man but then deemed again as a good man . . . He was **redeemed**.

In Matthew 18:11, we see that Jesus came in order to **save** the **lost**. To "save the lost" is a good definition of the essence of redemption. Consistent with the lamb of sacrifice in the Old Testament that took away the sins of Israel, Jesus is the "lamb of God who takes away the sin of the world" (John 1:29). God's redemption is thorough. God has provided a way for all people to be deemed differently than they were originally deemed . . . to be deemed again; to be **redeemed**. There is, however, a price. To "save that which was lost" requires loss!

The bishop in *Les Misérables* suffered loss . . . the loss of his silver. The lamb suffers loss . . . the loss of its life. The lamb (of God) suffers the greatest loss imaginable (to win the greatest gain imaginable). He (God) suffers the loss of separation from Himself. On the cross, Jesus cries out, "my god, my god, why have you forsaken me?" (Mark 15:34). To save the lost He had to suffer loss. He had to become sin in order to take away sin (2 Corinthians 5:21). He had to accept the wages of death/separation (Romans 6:23) in order to offer the pension of life/unification. There is, in a sense then, a great irony in redemption. In order for me to be deemed good (from bad), God Himself had to be deemed bad (from good); He had to bear my sin. He had to become my sin. He had to forsake Himself in order for me to be endorsed . . . in order for me to be deemed again (redeemed). Today, through Christ's death on the cross, you can be deemed again!

———————

ALL THAT IS IN THE WORLD
. . . YOU ARE NOT ALONE!

"For all that is in the world, the lust of the flesh and the lust of the eyes and the boastful pride of life, is not from the Father, but is from the world."

1 John 2:16

When it comes to temptation, there is nothing new under the sun. According to 1 John 2:16, temptations ("all that is in the world") can be put into three general categories: 1) the lust of the flesh; 2) the lust of the eyes; 3) the boastful pride of life. Man encountered these three temptations in the Garden of Eden: "When the woman saw that the tree was good for food, and that it was a delight to the eyes, and that the tree was desirable to make one wise, she took from its fruit and ate; and she gave also to her husband with her, and he ate" (Genesis 3:6). This action was "not from the Father." Thus, it was sin, that which goes against the Definer . . . that which "is from the world"; "all that is in the world" is as old as the Fall of Man in the Garden of Eden: 1) lust of the flesh equals "the tree was good for food"; 2) lust of the eyes equals "it was a delight to the eyes"; 3) boastful pride of life equals "the tree was desirable to make one wise" (1 John 2:16; Genesis 3:6). All that is in the world now is all that was in the world then. You are not alone!

You are not alone in your battle against the world . . . against temptation. Jesus can relate to you. He understands your weaknesses in a way that is as mysterious as the incarnation itself. Every temptation that you experience He has also encountered. Incredibly, the Scripture tells us that "we do not have a high priest who cannot sympathize with our weaknesses, but One who has been tempted in all things as we are, yet without sin" (Hebrews 4:15). Jesus came into the world and fully experienced "all that is in the world." He encountered all that is in the world in the temptations in the wilderness (Luke 4:1-13): 1) lust of the flesh equals "tell this stone to become bread" (verse 3); 2) lust of the eyes equals "showed him all the kingdoms of the world" (verse 5); 3) boastful pride of life equals "throw yourself down from here" (to show how special you are . . . verse 9).

And so, Jesus, the second Adam, in order to redeem man, had to experience the same temptations as the first Adam. He experienced all that is in the world. He experienced what you experience. He can relate to you. He understands. He sympathizes with your "weaknesses" as He "has been tempted in all things as we are." There is, of course, one very important difference. Where you fail, He is victorious; "tempted in all things as we are, yet without sin" (Hebrews 4:15). Until Jesus overcame the final temptations of His life (consider the very real battle in Luke 22:44), His sinlessness was only the relative sinlessness that Adam had before the Fall. The good news is, and forever will be, that Jesus Christ was victorious over these temptations . . . over "all that is in the world." This, then, becomes your hope since "greater is He who is in you than he who is in the world" (1 John 4:4). You are not alone in your battle against "all that is in the world" . . . against temptation. Jesus can relate to you. And so, "Let us therefore draw near with confidence to the throne of grace, that we may receive mercy and may find grace to help in time of need" (Hebrews 4:16).

_____

MARCH 13

QUALITIES OF A LEADER WHO IS EITHER BORN OR MADE

" . . . appoint elders in every city . . . if any man is . . .
holding fast the faithful word . . . so that he will
be able both to exhort in sound doctrine
and to refute those who contradict."

Titus 1:5-6, 9

One of the classic questions of philosophers is, "Are leaders born or made?" Of course, the answer is—at least to some degree—**both**! Leaders are born in the sense that leadership is a calling from God. Leadership is a gift (Romans 12:8; 1 Thessalonians 5:12; 1 Timothy 3:4-12; 1 Timothy 5:17). Not all people are called or gifted to be leaders. Leaders are born. At the same time, leaders are made at least in the sense that leadership is an ability that needs to be developed (Proverbs 1:5). If this is true—that leaders are made—then what are the particular qualities that leaders need to develop?

First, leaders need to develop courage. In Paul's list to Titus in which he provides requirements for leaders in the church, he includes: " . . . holding fast the faithful word which is in accordance with the teaching, so that he will be able both to exhort in sound doctrine and to refute those who contradict" (Titus 1:9). Certainly, in the context of the persecution against the first century church, "refuting those who contradict" would take considerable courage.

Another important quality is practical intelligence. This is especially true in the areas of good judgment and discretion (Galatians 6:1). We might include common sense, poise, and wisdom (bring your problems to a few trusted and respected Christians; do not bring your problems to everybody).

Along with practical intelligence is the ability to be a person of vision. Vision is the ability to form plans and remain ahead of the people. For the sake of the people, leaders must be people of vision: "Where there is no vision, the people are unrestrained . . . " (Proverbs 29:18). The effective leader must be able to communicate the vision at the right time, to the right people, and in the right way. Of course, this would include the ability to give direction that comes from the heart of God. Also, vision will see the consequences of an action before it happens. In this way the leader who has vision can protect his people. Finally, it must be understood that real vision includes action. Vision without action is only a dream.

Vision + faith + energy = a movement of God. That is the power of vision!

Leaders must be able to extend sympathy and compassion; the ability to understand, appreciate, and help others in their problems. Many times, the best leaders (at least with regard to this leadership quality) are those who have had a difficult life. Through experience, they can relate to the problems of others (Matthew 9:36; Hebrews 4:15). Leaders also need to be productive and energetic. Energy includes the action and works side of obedience. There is no such thing as a lazy leader! (Acts 16:9-12).

Let's close this discussion by opening an "**IRA**" account for effective leadership (*I*nitiative; *R*eliability; *A*ccountability). *I*nitiative is the ability to start new things. Leadership without initiative results in confusion and a lack of order/organization (Joshua 1:10-18). *R*eliability is the ability to follow through on commitments. It is motivated by a refusal to compromise, an insistence on being integral, and the ability and motivation to manage oneself. *A*ccountability, first of all, assumes that you are doing something to be accountable for. To account for something, then, is to be answerable for it and responsible for it.

It is very important for leaders to have a growing **IRA** account. So, leaders, keep contributing into your **IRA**.

MARCH 14

COMMON TRAITS FOUND IN GROWING CHURCHES

". . . multitudes of men and women, were constantly added to THEIR NUMBER . . . "

Acts 5:14

The church is meant to grow. We see this very emphatically in the book of Acts: "And all the more believers in the Lord, multitudes of men and women, were constantly added to their number

. . . " (Acts 5:14). What makes a church grow? Are there some common traits found in growing churches? Yes!

One definite common trait is that the church experiences the ministry of the Holy Spirit. It is open to the power and movement of the Spirit. That this is a common trait found in growing churches is not surprising. After all, it is the Spirit who grows the church! In Acts 9:31 we read, "So the church throughout all Judea and Galilee and Samaria enjoyed peace, being built up; and going on in the fear of the Lord and in the comfort of the Holy Spirit, it continued to increase."

Another common trait is having the attitude to build for growth. In general, when eighty percent of the space in the church building is filled with people, plans to build a larger building should begin (the idea here is to stay ahead of the growth). In other words, the church has vision. It looks toward the future. Another trait is what might be referred to as the ability to have flexibility in church government and structure so that as the church goes through changes, the way it organizes itself can change also. This includes an emphasis put on the multiplication of leadership. Responsibility and authority are given to others. New leaders are raised up and released to minister. Another trait is the existence of small cell groups of ten to fifteen people each. These groups function as "little churches" or sub-congregations within the church. In these smaller groups, there can be a stronger emphasis put on people/relationships. The ministry and outreach of the church can become much more personal. There is a real sense of cooperation between church members. The idea of working together in a body is emphasized.

Another trait that is common to growing churches is that they have a variety of ministries. The ministry of the church includes many different ministries (evangelism, visitation, teaching, etc.). Each member of the church participates in some form of ministry (or at least is encouraged and equipped to participate). The people of the church trust each other. The people trust the leaders. The leaders trust the people. Therefore, the people are willing to participate, and the leaders allow the people to participate. This leads to the development of a variety of ministries. Another trait is doing everything with excellence. This does not necessarily require spending a lot of money. Another trait seen in growing churches is practical biblical preaching and teaching that provides real answers to real problems in life. Another trait is that goals are well defined. There is no confusion concerning what the church is trying to do. This includes ministry to all ages as children and youth, as well as adults, have their needs met through specially designed ministries for them.

Another common trait is that the purpose of the church is known and understood by its members. There is the sense that covenants are established between people. The church is not an organization. You do not "sign up." You make commitments to other people. It is a family. Another trait found in growing churches is that there is an emphasis on people. People are more important than programs. One final common trait is that the church is willing to do things differently. It is creative. It is willing to be unique. It has a pioneering spirit. Each year there may be new ministries and new programs.

Ministries that have outlived their usefulness are allowed to end. New ministries are started. The church is doing things it did not do last year. These are just some of the common traits found in growing churches.

MARCH 15

GOD CREATED OUT OF . . . NOTHING!

"IN THE beginning God created the heavens and the earth.
The earth was formless and void . . . "

Genesis 1:1-2

What was in the beginning? The very first words in the Bible answer this cosmic question of *bereshit* ("beginnings" in Hebrew) or *Genesis* (the Greek translation). Beyond human comprehension, God existed even before "the beginning" since "In the beginning God" (Genesis 1:1). He is preexistent (more precisely, He is self-existent). Paradoxically, He exists before existence; He never began. However, the "heavens and the earth" did have a beginning. God created them. How did He create them? Get ready for another paradox of sorts. He created out of . . . **nothing**! The Scripture reports that "The earth was formless and void" (Genesis 1:2); it was empty, nothing, broken. Since we cannot comprehend this, we must look at it through the lens of faith: "By faith we understand that the worlds were prepared by the word of God, so that what is seen was not made out of things which are visible" (Hebrews 11:3). If the things that are visible are not made out of things that are visible, then what are they made out of?! The "heavens and the earth" came into being by the Word of God (by divine command) and were not constructed out of any preexisting matter or energy. They were created "ex nihilo" (out of nothing). Before there was a universe, there was this ultimate Being we call God whose existence is not dependent on matter (He is transcendent) nor time (He is omnipresent). It is this God, in all His wonder, who "created the heavens and the earth"!

Just as God worked "weaknesses/brokenness/emptiness/nothingness" into something "good" (Genesis 1:31: "God saw all that He had made, and behold, it was very good"), He also works "good" out of our weaknesses, brokenness, emptiness, and nothingness (Romans 8:28:

"And we know that God causes all things to work together for good to those who love God, to those who are called according to His purpose"; 2 Corinthians 12:9: "And He has said to me, 'My grace is sufficient for you, for power is perfected in weakness'"). If He can make something as big as the world out of nothing, then He surely can make something out of our nothingness. More generally, He can take the brokenness of the fallen world and recreate it (Galatians 6:15; Isaiah 65:17). Even as the original heavens and earth were created by the Word of God (the *logos* or "Word" that implies order, organization, logic), and sin moves everything more and more toward entropy (disorder, chaos, breaking apart), God's creation (His redemption or recreation) will ultimately move back to Christ, the logos: Ephesians 1:10: "with a view to an administration suitable to the fullness of the times, "the summing up of all things in Christ things in the heavens and things on the earth."

God created in six days. In the first three days, He created realms or molds that were previously unformed (pre-solar light in Genesis 1:3-6; the firmament or expanse in Genesis 1:6-8; and the seas and land in Genesis 1:9-13). In the final three days, He created rulers or fillings to fill that which was previously unfilled (luminaries in Genesis 1:14-19; fish/birds in Genesis 1:20-23; and the animals and man in Genesis 1:24-31). God is a "mold former" and then a "mold filler." He might form a home (actually an empty house), but then fill it with a husband and a wife, and then children. A baby was first conceived and then formed "in his mother's womb" before he was "filled with the Holy Spirit" (Luke 1:15). God Almighty is the mold former and mold filler. All glory and praise be unto Him!

MARCH 16

OH MY WORD! . . .

"Your word is a lamp to my feet And a light to my path."

Psalm 119:105

The greatest thing about life is that we can know God. One of the best ways to know God is to know His Word; that is to know the Bible. The Bible is blessed, and it is a blessing; it is "perfect," "sure," "right," "pure," "clean," "enduring forever," "true," "righteous altogether," "more desirable than gold" . . . and "sweeter also than honey." Not only is it blessed, it is also a blessing: "rejoicing the heart," "enlightening the eyes," "by them Your servant is warned," and "in keeping them there is great reward" (Psalm 19:7-11). Oh my Word! The Bible "is inspired by God" (2 Timothy 3:16-17). The Bible exists because it is "the will of God" (2 Peter 1:21). It is dangerous not to know the Bible (Matthew 22:29). The Bible is my "lamp/light" that is "true" and "eternal" (Psalm 119:105, 160). So, how can we know the Bible? We can know the Bible by hearing the Word, reading the Word, studying the Word, memorizing the Word, meditating on the Word, and applying the Word.

We can know the Bible by hearing the Word. We are called to hear the Word (Jeremiah 22:29). We should listen attentively (Luke 19:48). Hearing the Word affects your prayers (Proverbs 28:9). So every time you have an opportunity to hear the Word (going to church, going to a Bible study, listening to CDs in your car, etc.), seize that opportunity and hear the Word. We can also know the Bible by reading the Word. There are blessings in reading the Bible (Revelation 1:3). It should be read carefully (1 Timothy 4:13). We should try to read it daily (Deuteronomy 17:19). So every time you have an opportunity to read the Word (in your "quiet time," in a Bible study, to your children or students, etc.), seize that opportunity and read the Word.

We can know the Bible by studying it. It is good to do Bible study (Acts 17:11). Studying the Bible is like searching for treasure (Proverbs 2:1-5). Ezra provides us with a great example (Ezra 7:10). So every time you have an opportunity to study the Word (in a class, in a Bible study, reading commentaries, etc.), seize that opportunity and study the Word. We can also know the Bible by memorizing it. Moses strongly encourages it (Deuteronomy 6:6-7) and Jesus is our ultimate example (Matthew 4:4). The Word must be inside of us (Proverbs 7:1-3). It gives us stability (Psalm 37:31) and certainly can help us (Colossians 3:16). So every time you have an opportunity to memorize the Word (when preparing to teach, by keeping Scripture cards in your pocket, etc.), seize that opportunity and memorize the Word.

We can know the Bible by meditating on the Word. There are promises that come with meditation (Joshua 1:8) as well as results (Psalm 1). Meditation on the Word brings joy (Jeremiah 15:16). Meditation can be a constant mental discipline (Philippians 4:8). Every time you have an opportunity to meditate on the Word (in your "quiet time," in your study of the Word, etc.), seize that opportunity and meditate on the Word. We can also know the Bible by applying the Word to our lives. Meditation naturally leads to application (Psalm 119:56-60). We must **do** what the Word says (James 1:22-25). The Word of God is profitable and practical (2 Timothy 3:16-17). Obedience is a sure foundation. We must hear and do the Word (Luke 6:46-49). So every time you have an opportunity to apply the Word to your life (in your daily activities, in your teaching, etc.), seize that opportunity and apply the Word to your life. Perhaps, all that is left to say is . . . **Oh, my Word!**

MARCH 17

NEWSFLASH . . . JESUS CLAIMS TO BE GOD!

"'I and the Father are one.' The Jews took up stones again to stone Him."

John 10:30-31

The most obvious basis for the radical nature of Christianity is the claim made by Jesus Himself that He is God. He is very clear about this. He claims to be God! He claims that He is the Messiah (John 4:25-26) and in so doing declares His divinity. He describes His understanding of His own divinity when He declares where He came from; Jesus claimed to have come down out of heaven (John 6:33-35). Who is this Person? Where are you from? I was born in Teaneck, New Jersey, and grew up near Baltimore, Maryland. So when people ask that oft-asked question, "Where are you from?" I would say, "the Baltimore area via north Jersey." Where are you from, Jesus? The answer: "I Am from heaven." Jesus claims, "I Am God." "Are you really?" the chief priests and scribes inquired . . . "Yes, I am," Jesus responded (Luke 22:70-71).

Jesus clearly claimed to be God when He said that He "and the Father are one." This is a very radical statement and those who heard it understood its claim. For this statement the Jews tried to stone Him. Why? Because He was saying that He was a great teacher or a prophet or a special man? No! They would not have stoned Him for that. They tried to stone Him for blasphemy; "they took up stones again to stone Him" because He claimed that He was God (John 10:31-33). Again? Is this something that happened to Jesus often? Yes, because this is something He claimed often. The Jews "picked up stones to throw at Him" because, again, He was claiming to be God (John 8:51, 58-59). In that confrontation, Jesus claimed His Divinity in three different ways. First, He claimed that He existed before the birth of Abraham (who lived 2000 years before Him). Second, He used God's personal name "I Am" for Himself (in such a way that it was either a serious grammatical error or, if true, a radical theological truth). Third, He claimed to have the authority to save people from death and only God Himself has this authority. The Pharisees were well aware of this, and so they tried to stone Him for blasphemy (claiming to be God).

Christianity is radical because Jesus' claims about Himself are radical. You are not a Christian because you follow a great teacher or a respected prophet or a nice guy. It is impossible to say that you believe the words of the Bible but that you do not believe that Jesus is God. The Pharisees themselves would laugh at you. It is obvious what Jesus was claiming. It was so obvious that the Jews tried to kill Him many times, and then at Calvary, they finally did kill

Him on the cross. That is the most obvious basis for the radical nature of Christianity. There is no in-between!

MARCH 18

THREE KEY HABITS TO DEVELOP IN A NEW BELIEVER

"Iron sharpens iron, So one man sharpens another."

Proverbs 27:17

It is important that new believers develop certain key "habits" that will help them to begin their faith journey on top of a firm foundation. More mature believers (disciples) should look to help new believers along the way. The first, and perhaps foremost, key habit is to learn to be in communion with Christ. The new believer must solidify his/her relationship with Jesus. Certainly, the disciple can pray for the new believer that he/she will develop his/her relationship with the Lord: " . . . we have not ceased to pray for you and to ask that you may be filled with the knowledge of His will in all spiritual wisdom and understanding, so that you will walk in a manner worthy of the Lord, to please Him in all respects, bearing fruit in every good work and increasing in the knowledge of God" (Colossians 1:9-10). Disciples can explain their own motives to have a relationship with Jesus, and can describe the importance and the benefits of their relationship with the Lord. Be specific when you are explaining the benefits. Tell the new believer about specific answers to prayer you have received. You might share some specific revelations that you have received recently in your Bible study and prayer times. Introduce him/her to other Christians who have a relationship with the Lord. Encourage him/her to have times of Bible study and prayer with other Christians.

A second key habit is to maintain accountability to other believers. A new believer, especially, needs strong relationships with other believers. Within these sets of relationships, there need to be some that provide for an accountability of thoughts, actions, and time. Accountability creates an atmosphere where Christians can challenge one another to confront sin and keep sin from gaining a foothold in their lives (James 5:16; Ephesians 5:21). Accountability helps to strengthen and sharpen believers—"iron sharpens iron, so one man sharpens another" (Proverbs 27:17)—to become more Christ-like and more obedient in their lifestyle. New believers can look to more mature Christians as a source of accountability. They can provide wisdom and encouragement, while helping to create discipline in the new believer (1 Peter 5:5; Hebrews 13:17). A good example of accountability and discipleship in the New Testament can be seen in Paul's Christian life as he became acquainted with Barnabas (Acts 9 and 11). Paul was converted when he encountered Christ personally on the road to Damascus (Acts 9). He also had an individual period of training in the Arabian Desert. Yet, when Paul first came to Jerusalem to meet with the disciples, they did not trust him and doubted his sincerity. However, Barnabas brought Paul to the apostles and made it possible for him to stay with them (Acts 9:26-31). Barnabas later went and found Paul in Tarsus (Acts 11:25) and brought him to Antioch. He gave him an opportunity to teach for a year with him as his partner. They became a ministry team, taking the gospel to the gentile world. As time went on, Paul became the more well-known and prominent apostle. Yet Paul, the mightiest of the apostles, needed an accountability structure and relationship with Barnabas early on to help him grow, gain credibility, and eventually be sent out to the mission field. Paul also maintained his relationship with the church at Antioch, providing accountability even as he traveled in his missionary work.

A third key habit to develop in new believers is consistency. It is critical to develop faithfulness in the small things for "he who is faithful in a very little thing is faithful also in much" (Luke 16:10). So, a disciple might give as "assignments" short Bible studies that can later be studied together. The goal of the disciple is to develop good habits in the new believer, so offer a lot of encouragement.

––––––––––––

MARCH 19

REJOICE, PRAY, PEACE . . .

"Rejoice in the Lord always . . . in everything by prayer and
supplication with thanksgiving let your requests be made
known to God. And the peace of God, which surpasses all comprehension,
will guard your hearts and your minds in Christ Jesus."

Philippians 4:4, 6-7

After Paul gives specific instructions to the Philippians concerning the importance of unity, he makes reference to another thing he clearly considers to be of great importance; that is, rejoicing: "Rejoice in the Lord always; again I will say, rejoice!" (Philippians 4:4). Why is it so important for the Philippians to rejoice? It seems to be relevant to evangelism. Paul concludes his admonition to rejoice by proclaiming that "the Lord is near" (Philippians 4:5). Rejoicing in the context of having a "forbearing spirit" is connected to the idea of expediting evangelism. This forbearing spirit is to "be known by all men" (Philippians 4:5). It is to be a witness. They are to rejoice always. This includes rejoicing in the midst of persecution. Surely Paul is reflecting on the example he left them during his original visit when he and Silas were imprisoned, yet they rejoiced in/praised God, and the jailer and his household were saved (Acts 16:25-34). To have a "forbearing spirit" is to be satisfied with less than you deserve—a humble and patient steadfastness which can submit to injustice without reacting in hatred—as it trusts in the sovereignty of God. Their self-restraint against hatred and bitterness ("forbearing") toward those who persecuted them must be seen by all men. This is accomplished by rejoicing *in* all things. Thus, the importance of rejoicing is due to the need for urgent evangelism; "The Lord is near."

Is there an alternative to rejoicing? Yes! Paul says to "rejoice always." He then says to "be anxious for nothing" (Philippians 4:6). The alternative to rejoicing is worrying. How can they avoid this anxiety? Anxiety can be avoided through prayer and thanksgiving (Philippians 4:6). If we pray and give thanks, then we will not worry. If we worry, then we will not pray and give thanks. They are opposites! And so, replacement is the solution. Anxious thoughts are replaced with good thoughts: "Finally, brethren, whatever is true, whatever is honorable, whatever is right, whatever is pure, whatever is lovely, whatever is of good repute, if there is any excellence and if anything worthy of praise, dwell on these things . . . and the God of peace will be with you" (Philippians 4:8-9). More succinctly, "Set your mind on the things above, not on the things that are on earth" (Colossians 3:2). Worrying about things is replaced by praying about things. The result of this method of replacement is the opposite of anxiety. The result is "the peace of God, which surpasses all comprehension, will guard your hearts and your minds in Christ Jesus" (Philippians 4:7). The word guard was a military term that was used to describe the job of soldiers who stood guard *inside* of the city gates. They controlled what went out of the city. The peace of God does not depend on outside circumstances. It is within us. The peace of God is like a guard on the inside that controls what goes out. It does not allow to exit those words, thoughts, and actions that would produce worry.

What about you? Do you realize that your testimony is greatly affected by your disposition? An attitude of rejoicing is important in evangelism. Are you a person of joy? Can you rejoice in the Lord in the worst of times? Do you practice replacement with respect to worry? Do you waste time worrying or do you replace it with time spent in prayer? Do you replace negative thoughts with positive thoughts? Do you know the peace of God? This peace is a result of prayer because prayer releases things to God and rests in His sovereignty. Could you be at peace even in the midst of suffering?

———————

MARCH 20

WE WANT TO FELLOWSHIP LIKE
THE EARLY CHURCH!

"Day by day continuing with one mind in the temple,
and breaking bread from house to house,
they were taking their meals together with gladness and sincerity of heart."

Acts 2:46

The accounts and descriptions of the early church in the book of Acts paint an incredible and desirable picture of a high quality of fellowship. After all, "day by day continuing with one mind in the temple, and breaking bread from house to house, they were taking their meals together with gladness and sincerity of heart" (Acts 2:46). We sometimes respond by saying, "We want to fellowship like the early church!" What was their secret formula for such a high quality of fellowship?

First, all Christians became witnesses. The Acts 2 description continues, " . . . and having favor with all the people. And the Lord was adding to their number day by day those who were being saved" (Acts 2:47). It was commonly accepted and understood then that a Christian was a witness. The common practice of "witnessing"—of giving public testimony for Christ—naturally formed strong relationships between Christians. This is still true for Christians today. Fellowship in a church is strengthened when evangelism is a focus of its members.

Second, owners became stewards. There was a renewal of the mind in the area of money and possessions (Acts 2:44-45). Christians understood that God owned everything. They viewed themselves as stewards of material things. This, of course, affected their fellowship greatly. It was much easier for them to share their things because they had the perspective of a steward. This is still true today. The more we see ourselves as stewards, the more likely it is that we will share. Sharing, of course, is the essence of fellowship and, so, the quality of fellowship increases.

Third, self-interest was lost due to a holy passion for Jesus (Acts 2:42). The cross was embraced. Early Christians understood that the Christian life was a life that took up the cross daily. They gave up their own lives. It is much easier to share (fellowship) with others after you have let go of yourself. Selfless people are relationally superior people since they are more likely to not let themselves "get in the way" within their relationships. For example, think about what the tendency to not claim and defend your rights (1 Corinthians 6:7-8) does for the quality of a relationship. Consider what not thinking more highly of yourself than you ought (Romans 12:3) does for a relationship. Think about how considering someone before yourself and not focusing so much on your own needs (Philippians 2:3-4) or not having to talk about yourself so much provides more of a path for quality interaction. This is still true today. The cross frees us to have sincere and fruitful fellowship. The direction of fellowship is toward others. The direction of the cross is toward others. The cross and fellowship are brothers.

Fourth, they interacted in small groups: "day by day . . . breaking bread from house to house" (Acts 2:46). The early church understood that without small groups fellowship would simply become a theory (or just an idea). They practiced their Christianity in the context of small house churches. Their fellowship was real and operative. This is still true today. We cannot have the intimate relationship that the New Testament commands require in the midst of hundreds of people. In some way, we must be a part of a smaller group so that we can truly (not just theoretically) enter into fellowship.

Secrets? There are not really any "secrets" to fellowship, just revealed truth. The early church did not have any secrets. If "we want to fellowship like the early church," we can . . . we are not in the dark. It is clear for all to see. So, **fellowship**!

––––––––––

MARCH 21

WHO WANTS TO BE THE GREATEST?!

"You call Me Teacher and Lord; and you are right, for so I am.
If I then, the Lord and the Teacher, washed your feet,
you also ought to wash one another's feet.
For I gave you an example that you also should do as I did to you.
Truly, truly, I say to you, a slave is not greater than his master,
nor is one who is sent greater than the one who sent him."

John 13:13-16

How can you become the greatest? (How can you become the leader?). Of course, we'll have to start with Jesus. Jesus became the greatest through His death (study Philippians 2:5-11 and Luke 22:26). The example of service in humility (the foot washing) was done by Jesus in response to the disciple's questions concerning who was the greatest. The disciples appeared to have been very concerned about who was the greatest: Matthew 20:25-28; Mark 9:33-37; Mark 10:35-45; Luke 9:46-48; and Luke 22:25-27. Finally, Jesus decided to answer their question (see Luke 22:25-27 and note how it is connected to the foot washing in John 13:12).

Who was the greatest? Jesus systematically answered their question: 1) I am the greatest (John 13:13); 2) I serve you (John 13:14); 3) Imitate me (John 13:15); 4) The slave is not greater than his master (John 13:16). So, who is the greatest? Of course, only Jesus is the greatest. They are not greater than Him. I serve you. Imitate Me. The answer is clear. Jesus is the greatest. Why is Jesus the greatest (the leader)? Because He serves. How can the disciples be great? They must imitate Him. They must serve. This is "the how" of leadership or greatness.

How is greatness measured? Is it measured in centimeters or pounds or liters? No! It is measured in humility and service. Jesus created a ruler to measure greatness. Greatness is calculated in units of humility and service. Greatness is a relative concept. Unfortunately, we tend—like the disciples—to make it relative in terms of other people. We compare ourselves to others. This is what the disciples were doing. However, Jesus substituted the comparison to others with a comparison to Himself. Jesus challenges the disciples to look to Him only. When we apply this to our own lives, we are released from the bondage of competition and we are presented with a great challenge. The result is humility.

It is interesting to note that as much as the disciples argue over rank, Jesus never actually rebukes them for lobbying for such a haughty position. The reason for this is that Jesus does not simply rebuke them, but rather, He turns the tables on them. Who is the greatest? Whoever is the least! Who is the greatest? That position is relative to Jesus, not each other! Who is the greatest? It is defined in terms of responsibility, not authority! It is not that Jesus does not want them to want to be the greatest. Rather, He wants them to understand how "the greatest" is defined . . . what it really means to be the greatest. So when He had washed their feet, and taken His garments and reclined at the table again, He said to them:

> Do you know what I have done to you? You call Me Teacher and Lord; and you are right, for *so* I am. If I then, the Lord and the Teacher, washed your feet, you also ought to wash one another's feet. For I gave you an example that you also should do as I did to you. Truly, truly, I say to you, a slave is not greater than his master, nor *is* one who is sent greater than the one who sent him. If you know these things, you are blessed if you do them (John 13:12-17).

It is not wrong to want to be the greatest. It is just that you must understand how "the greatest" is identified. Jesus, the greatest, becomes the servant. Who is the greatest? Perhaps, Jesus answers the question most concisely when He states, "So the last shall be first . . . " (Matthew 20:16).

SO, YOU WANT TO
BE SUCCESSFUL . . .

"I am the vine, you are the branches; he who abides in Me
and I in him, he bears much fruit,
for apart from Me you can do nothing."

John 15:5

What is success? Of course, our culture fashions a certain picture for us with respect to the answer to this question. The American dream has become much more (in terms of worldly acquisitions) than simply owning your own home. Success is pictured in terms of becoming rich, living in luxury, and being famous. Timeout! It may be helpful (if not ironic) to first say what success is *not* according to the Scripture. The comforts and luxuries of this world as well as the fame and popularity in this world do not mark true success (Luke 6:24-26). The successful Christian life will not result in comfort, luxury, or popularity (Luke 6:20-23).

So, what does success look like? In general, the key to a successful life is to seek the glory of God and not your own. Thus, a successful life is the life that is lived to glorify God (John 7:18). More specifically, success is found only in Jesus (John 15:5) for it is the person who abides in Him who bears much fruit (is successful!). Thus, the successful life is the life that seeks after God; "He is a rewarder of those who seek Him" (Hebrews 11:6).

Ultimately, then, our success is His success; "it is no longer I who live, but Christ lives in me" (Galatians 2:20). And so, success is not associated with boasting, declaring your success, or counting yourself as "superior." "For who regards you as superior? What do you have that you did not receive? And if you did receive it, why do you boast as if you had not received it?" (1 Corinthians 4:7). Man is completely dependent on the sovereignty of God. Ultimately, success in ministry—or in life, in general—depends on God since a man cannot receive if it is not first given to him (John 3:27). Even with respect to Jesus' own ministry while on earth, the key to His success was that He saw what the Father was doing (John 5:19). Similarly, the key to any successful teaching ministry is that it is not your teaching, but rather the teaching of God (John 7:16). Furthermore, it should be noted that success in evangelism depends on being "in God" (John 17:21-23).

And so, you want to be successful . . . well, know that success is described most biblically as being in Christ; being in the truth (John 14:6). To prosper is to be "walking in the truth" and thus the Scripture exhorts: "Beloved, I pray that in all respects you may prosper and be in good health, just as your soul prospers. For I was very glad when brethren came and testified to your truth, that is, how you are walking in truth. I have no greater joy than this, to hear of my children walking in the truth" (3 John 2-4).

―――――――

CHRISTIANITY CANNOT BE LIVED OUT ON AN ISLAND!

". . . we are to grow up in all aspects into Him, who is the head, even Christ, from whom the whole body, being fitted and held together by that which every joint supplies, according to the proper working of each individual part, causes the growth of the body for the building up of itself in love."

Ephesians 4:15-16

Fellowship is a requirement for successful Christian living. The Christian life, because of the nature of its various mandates, requires a social context; it cannot be achieved on a private island. Interpersonal relationships build the venue in which Christian life can be lived out since those relationships both lay their claims upon one Christian and at the same time welcome the other to respond. Minus those relationships, those claims, and their corresponding responses, have no track to run on. That venue that is necessary for Christian life to be lived out is, by definition, non-existent on an island. Christianity, by definition, cannot be lived out alone on an island! Fellowship is a requirement, not an option.

Interaction with others (fellowship) is necessary if "we are to grow up in all aspects into Him, who is the head, even Christ, from whom the whole body, being fitted and held together by that which every joint supplies, according to the proper working of each individual part, causes the growth of the body for the building up of itself in love" (Ephesians 4:15-16). The concept of the body of Christ assumes and requires interaction (fellowship) between its various members even as "iron sharpens iron, so one man sharpens another" (Proverbs 27:17). The church (body of Christ) is the *ekklesia*, the gathering together of "the called out ones." When Paul writes to "the called out ones" in Ephesians 4:1—"I, therefore, the prisoner of the Lord, entreat you to walk in a manner worthy of the calling with which you have been called"—it is in the context of the instructions given in Ephesians 4:2-3 ("with all humility and gentleness, with patience, showing forbearance to one another in love, being diligent to preserve the unity of the Spirit in the bond of peace").

To be called out (to be in the church) necessarily involves fellowship with other "called out ones." Fellowship becomes an obvious requirement when we begin to see the nature of many of the instructions that are given to the church. As is the case in Ephesians 4:2 ("showing forbearance to one another"), many instructions to the church are "one another" oriented. There exist in the New Testament at least twenty-three different *alaython* ("one to another") commands. These "one to another" commands, of course, require interaction (fellowship) to achieve. Whether it is to "be kind to one another" (Ephesians 4:32), or to "bear the burdens of one another" (Galatians 6:2), or to "give preference to one another" (Romans 12:10), or to "encourage and build up one another" (1 Thessalonians 5:11), the same thing is true. You cannot respond to these commands by yourself. You need to interact with and be in fellowship with others.

Christianity, by definition, cannot be lived out alone on an island! Fellowship is a requirement, not an option; thus, fellowship must become a priority for the Christian. So, **fellowship**!

MARCH 24

GOD'S WORLD VISION AND HIS VISION BEARERS . . .

"And Jesus came up and spoke to them, saying, 'All authority has been given to Me
in heaven and on earth. Go therefore and make disciples of all the nations,
baptizing them in the name of the Father and the Son and the Holy Spirit,
teaching them to observe all that I commanded you; and lo, I am with you always,
even to the end of the age."

Matthew 28:18-20

What is God's primary way in which He desires to use His people? Well, it goes all the way back to the initial calling of a people—God's calling of Abraham. This calling is similar to God's greatest ("Great") calling ("Commission") in Matthew 28:18: "Go therefore and make disciples of all the nations, baptizing them in the name of the Father and the Son and the Holy Spirit, teaching them to observe all that I commanded you; and lo, I am with you always, even to the end of the age." The way in which God says it to Abraham is basically "I'll bless you so that you can be a blessing to all the nations" (Genesis 12:1-3). He repeats His missiological covenant with His people in Genesis 28:14-15 when He says to Jacob in his ladder dream " . . . and you will spread out to the west and to the east and to the north and to the south [sound familiar? "Go . . . all the nations"] and in you and in your descendants shall all the families of the earth be blessed [sound familiar? "make disciples/baptizing/teaching all nations"] . . . Behold, I am with you . . . [sound familiar? "and lo, I am with you always . . . "]." Genesis 28 (missiological covenant) is consistent with Matthew 28 (missiological covenant).

Remember, it is true that "God so loved the world" (John 3:16). His is a "world vision," and He enacts that vision through His people. And so, we must be willing to go if God calls us (Isaiah 6:8) to go. We are to "pray for laborers" (Matthew 9:35-38) and "preach the gospel to all people" (Mark 16:15) as the Holy Spirit "empowers us to bring the gospel to the ends of the earth" (Acts 1:8). And so, we are to be His witnesses. We should proclaim Christ in a natural way (Colossians 1:28-29). Do not be ashamed of the gospel (Romans 1:16). Be consistent and eager to spread the good news (2 Timothy 4:1-2). Remember, it is the wise man who wins souls (Proverbs 11:30). Use the Bible when witnessing (Acts 8:35). Boldness is necessary (Proverbs 28:1). The Holy Spirit will give you boldness (Acts 4:31). We should look for people to witness to (Luke 19:10). Finally, as witnesses we should be sure to make Christ the focus of our testimony. Sometimes it is best to just keep it simple: what you were like before your conversion to Christ; how you got converted to Christ; and how your life has changed after your conversion to Christ. Remember, it is ultimately your personal testimony that is your most powerful tool in your evangelistic/ missiological toolbox.

The gospel is powerful. People will be converted. Thus, we must be prepared to follow up with those we witness to. This is based on God's "ministry of multiplication" (2 Timothy 2:2). And so, prayer is involved in follow up (2 Timothy 1:3). We are called to "present every man perfect in Christ" (Colossians 1:28) for "there is joy in seeing someone walking with God" (3 John 4).

God continues to say, "go therefore . . . " What is the "therefore" there for? It is there for "all authority has been given to me in heaven and on earth" (Matthew 28:18-19). At the end of the day, that is why we **go**. We go because the One we are testifying about is none less than God Himself. Jesus is God. That is the foundation of this divine world vision!

———————

MARCH 25

LEADERS IN TRAINING . . . ATTITUDES AND ACTIONS

"Not that I have already obtained it *or have already become perfect, but I press on . . .*
I do not regard myself as having laid hold of it yet;

but one thing I do: *forgetting what* lies *behind and reaching forward*
to what lies *ahead . . . "*

Philippians 3:12-13

How can leaders get themselves more prepared to lead? How can they be readier? How can they further develop their abilities? Leaders in training may do so via working on both their attitudes and actions.

Attitudes are foundational components in the life of a leader. Leaders must develop the attitude that moves them toward a striving for excellence in all they do. Mediocrity does not honor God or man. Paul encourages zeal and excellence; "So also you, since you are zealous of spiritual gifts, seek to abound for the edification of the church" (1 Corinthians 14:12).

Paul provides what we might call a healthy attitude to have as he encourages the Philippians in 1 Corinthians 3:12-14: "Not that I have already obtained it or have already become perfect, but I press on so that I may lay hold of that for which also I was laid hold of by Christ Jesus. Brethren, I do not regard myself as having laid hold of it yet; but one thing I do: forgetting what lies behind and reaching forward to what lies ahead, I press on toward the goal . . . "

A healthy attitude realizes that we all have need for improvement. One might say, "If you stop learning, then you stop leading." Paul said, "Not that I have already obtained it." He realized and accepted that he was not perfect. This attitude enables the leader to continue to grow and to improve. This attitude protects the leader from the destruction of pride. Without this attitude you stop growing . . . and your attitude takes on the expression, "I have arrived!"

At the same time, you should be satisfied with only the best from yourself. Paul said, "But I press on." He kept his eye focused on perfection. This attitude enables the leader to continue to grow and to improve. This attitude protects the leader from the destruction of mediocrity. Without this attitude you stop growing . . . and your attitude will take on the expression "I cannot arrive!"

These attitudes balance each other out and form a healthy attitude. If you have one without the other, then you will have an unhealthy attitude. You will either want to quit, or you will never be able to say that you are wrong or that you made a mistake. Paul could say that he was not perfect. However, that did not stop him from striving for perfection. He had a healthy attitude.

Leaders can also grow based on their actions. Prepare thoroughly for every act of service, however humble it may be: "He who is faithful in a very little thing is faithful also in much" (Luke 16:10). Study the field that you are in. Read! Develop your natural talents. How? Use them (Matthew 25:14-30). Develop good work habits. Be systematic in Bible study and in prayer. Organize your time. Do not procrastinate (2 Timothy 2:15). Ask for counsel, direction, advice, and criticism from successful people in your field. Be a learner (Proverbs 13:10). Observe a good leader in action. If possible, be an apprentice. Finally, make your time spent with God a priority.

MARCH 26

GREATNESS IS MEASURED IN HUMILITY . . .

"Whoever then humbles himself as this child,
he is the greatest in the kingdom of heaven."

Matthew 18:4

Muhammad Ali was a great boxer in this world. He was not, however, great as it is measured in the kingdom of God. His often-repeated proclamations about his own accolades sometimes rhymed—"Float like a butterfly, sting like a bee, the hands can't hit what the eyes can't see"—but were never said with the humility of a child. Wrought with biblical irony, then, His most famous self-promoting statement, "I am the greatest," survives as a sort of antithesis to the biblical description of "greatness."

It is the one who humbles himself like a child who is the greatest in the kingdom of God (Matthew 18:4). A child is humble in that he is totally dependent on his parents, he innocently trusts them, he naturally desires their affection, and he is willing to obey them. These are biblical attributes of greatness. Furthermore, Jesus established a new principle. The greatest is the servant (Luke 22:26-27). Greatness in the kingdom of God does not equal the exercise of authority. It does not manifest itself in lording it over others (Matthew 20:25-27). Greatness in the kingdom of God equals being the servant (Matthew 23:11). It does manifest itself in serving others. The *first* shall be the *last* of all; the servant of all (Mark 9:35).

And so, to be great in the kingdom you must serve. Service includes being willing to make your life a ransom for others. It includes the willingness to give up your life for others (Mark 10:45) . . . to be a "witness" (Acts 1:8) or as in the Greek text, a *"martus"* (from which we get the English word "martyr"). And so, greatness is associated with giving up your life for the sake of Jesus and the gospel.

Those who are first will be last and the last will be first (Matthew 19:30). The concept of the last being first and the first being last is set in the context of leaving behind everything for Jesus (Mark 10:28-31). Leaving everything behind in this world will result in being last in this world; however, you will then be first in the kingdom of God. Another way to express this is that those who try to hold onto everything will advance in this life but will be last in the age to come. And so, the Scripture says:

> For whoever wishes to save his life will lose it, but whoever loses his life for My sake and the gospel's will save it (Mark 8:35).

Greatness, in the Kingdom of God, requires humility; thus, it involves sacrifice. So, if you want to be great, heed these words:

> Peter began to say to Him, 'Behold, we have left everything and followed You.' Jesus said, 'Truly I say to you, there is no one who has left house or brothers or sisters or mother or father or children or farms, for My sake and for the gospel's sake, but that he will receive a hundred times as much now in the present age, houses and brothers and sisters and mothers and children and farms, along with persecutions; and in the age to come, eternal life. But many *who are* first, will be last, and the last, first' (Mark 10:28-31).

MARCH 27

FAITH RESULTS IN . . .

"And He said to the woman, 'Your faith has saved you; go in peace.'"

Luke 7:50

Faith is powerful; "Your faith has saved you" (Luke 7:50). Faith leads to salvation (Mark 16:16). Faith in Jesus results in eternal life (John 3:36).

The Scripture speaks of salvation as already and not yet. And so, you "have been saved" (Romans 8:24) and you "are being saved" (1 Corinthians 1:18). Salvation in us is an ongoing process. In theological terms, this is called "sanctification" (which means to be "set apart"). It is faith that leads to sanctification. It is faith that leads to being set apart or "sold out" more and more for Jesus (to a large degree, to grow in sanctification is to grow in commitment or dedication to God). The importance of eternal life should make everything else relatively unimportant (another way to describe being "sold out"). Our commitment to God (our sanctification) depends on our understanding of this truth. It depends on how much we believe it (Matthew 16:26; Mark 8:36-37). And so faith results in sanctification.

Faith results in prayer. Consistent prayer is a result of faith (Luke 18:8). Moreover, answered prayer is a result of faith (Matthew 21:21-22). Faith is the key to success with respect to your prayers (Mark 11:24).

Faith results in miracles. It can move mountains (Matthew 21:21; Luke 17:6). Faith can result in healing (Mark 5:34). All things can be done through faith (Mark 9:23). Faith is powerful!

When they came to the crowd, a man came up to Jesus, falling on his knees before Him and saying, Lord, have mercy on my son, for he is a lunatic and is very ill; for he often falls into the fire and often into the water. I brought him to Your disciples, and they could not cure him." And Jesus answered and said, "You unbelieving and perverted generation, how long shall I be with you? How long shall I put up with you? Bring him here to Me." And Jesus rebuked him, and the demon came out of him, and the boy was cured at once. Then the disciples came to Jesus privately and said, "Why could we not drive it out?" And He said to them, "Because of the littleness of your faith; for truly I say to you, if you have faith the size of a mustard seed, you will say to this mountain, 'Move from here to there,' and it will move; and nothing will be impossible to you (Matthew 17:14-21).

MARCH 28

THE ERROR OF POSTMILLENNIALISM . . .

"They will say to you, 'Look there! Look here!' Do not go away, and do not run after them. For just like the lightning, when it flashes out of one part of the sky, shines to the other part of the sky, so will the Son of Man be in His day."

Luke 17:23-24

Dominion theology, also known as "kingdom now" theology, states that biblical Christianity will rule all areas of society. It is based on a postmillennial interpretation of the end times. Jesus' teaching on the kingdom of God, however, completely contradicts the postmillennial position that says that the church age will bring in the kingdom of God (thus, Jesus will return "post" or after the millennium). It is clear that the kingdom of God will grow. However, it is also clear that the kingdom of Satan will grow (Matthew 24:12). Note that both are described as leavens (Matthew 13:33; Matthew 16:6). The biblical picture is not one of the world getting better and better; rather, it is one of the world getting worse and worse (Matthew 24:12) as the kingdom of God grows at the same time. It should also be noted that man does not cause the growth of the kingdom of God (Mark 4:26-29). Its key ingredient is not found in man's actions but in God's sovereignty (Mark 4:30-32).

The kingdom of God is not of this world. It is not physical. It is spiritual (John 18:36). Since the kingdom of God is not of this world, it will not be established in this world. It is established within its own realm; the spiritual realm. Notice that Jesus says the kingdom of God will not come with physical signs (Luke 17:20). He says that the kingdom of God is within us; it is spiritual (Luke 17:21). Since the kingdom of God is not of this world, it will not be observable in a geographical, political, or economic sense. We will not come to a place in any of these spheres and say, "Here is the kingdom of God" (Luke 17:20-21). The kingdom of God is not something to be observed—"Look, there it is"—amid the realms of this world because it is an inner kingdom and not an outer kingdom (Luke 17:21). It is a spiritual kingdom and not a physical kingdom. Thus, "the kingdom of God is not eating and drinking, but righteousness and peace and joy in the Holy Spirit" (Romans 14:17). This peace and righteousness does not necessarily correlate to an outer peace or a just society. The closer you get to the kingdom of God the more persecution you experience (2 Timothy 3:12; Matthew 5:10). Remember, Jesus did not come to bring peace, but a sword (Matthew 10:34). He guarantees inner peace in His kingdom because His is a spiritual kingdom. However, He does not guarantee outer peace because His is not a physical kingdom. Thus, the physical sword comes against those in the spiritual kingdom (Hebrews 11:37). At the same time, the spiritual sword is used by those in the spiritual kingdom (Ephesians 6:17). The spiritual kingdom of God will positively affect/impact the physical kingdom of Satan. However, simply because there is the possibility of having a better society does not mean that the society is the kingdom of God. This would make the kingdom of God equal to the world. Yet, the kingdom of God and the world always collide with each other. They are always in opposition to each other (2 Timothy 3:8).

Finally, it should be realized that the kingdom of God is not something that is brought into being by man. It is not something that man can create and say, "Look, here it is." There will be those in the last days who will take advantage of the great desire to see the kingdom of God. They will try to argue that the kingdom of God can be observed in the physical realm. They will say that man can create it. However, the Scripture is clear. It says to not follow them. This is not how the kingdom of God will be established. It will be established by God in the blink of an eye (Luke 17:22-24). Remember: A postmillennial type of eschatology was the great error of the Jews. They thought that the kingdom of God would be established in the physical realm. They were looking for a political, economic, and nationalist kingdom (Luke 19:11). The tragic result of this erroneous expectation was that they "missed Jesus." With the existence of postmillennial thinking in the church, Christians are vulnerable to the same error.

———

MARCH 29

THE LEADER IS THE SERVANT ...
HERE AM I, SEND ME!

"But it is *not this way with you, but the one who is the greatest*
among you must become like the youngest,
and the leader like the servant."

Luke 22:26-27

Perhaps more than any other character trait a leader must have is that of being a servant. This, of course, is foreign to worldly descriptions of leadership. In the world it is the leader who is served, not the leader who is the servant. And so, Jesus explains this to His disciples—who are in the midst of a worldly argument about leadership—when He says, "The kings of the gentiles lord it over them; and those who have authority over them are called 'Benefactors'" (Luke 22:24-25). In the kingdom of God, however, leadership is service, and the leader is the servant. So, Jesus continues in His teaching: "But it is not this way with you, but the one who is the greatest among you must become like the youngest, and the leader like the servant" (Luke 22:26-27). Jesus once again pits the world's understanding of leadership against the kingdom of God's understanding: "Calling them to Himself, Jesus said to them, 'You know that those who are recognized as rulers of the gentiles lord it over them; and their great men exercise authority over them. But it is not this way among you, but whoever wishes to become great among you shall be your servant ...'" (Mark 10:42-44). And so, leadership potential depends greatly on having a servant's heart. Jesus, who was the greatest leader in history, described His life by saying, "even the Son of Man did not come to be served, but to serve" (Mark 10:45).

Biblical leadership (authority) is not a cause. It does not, in and of itself, demand respect. The action of leading does not necessarily cause others to follow. No, biblical leadership (authority) is a result. It is a result of service. Carnal leadership exercises authority instead of exercising service. And so it goes, " ... those who are recognized as rulers of the gentiles lord it over them; and their great men exercise authority over them ... " (Mark 10:42).

Since in God's economy, God is not so much interested in our "greatness" as He is interested in our availability, it makes complete sense that the greatest is the servant. It is not so much that the servant becomes great, as it is that the servant becomes available; available for the Great One to work greatness through him. Isaiah was one of these types of leaders. He experienced, in quite a dramatic way, the availability versus greatness distinction:

Then one of the seraphim flew to me with a burning coal in his hand, which he had taken from the altar with tongs. He touched my mouth *with it* and said, 'Behold, this has touched your lips; and your iniquity is taken away and your sin is forgiven.' Then I heard the voice of the Lord, saying, 'Whom shall I send, and who will go for Us?' Then I said, 'Here am I. Send me!' (Isaiah 6:6-8).

The bottom line: We are not the service that fills others or provides the filling. We dispense or give out only that which we have been filled with from the Lord. We are not the contents. We are the containers (vessels). We are not the source. We are the instrument. We are not the living water. We are the river bed that contains and carries the living water to the dry and thirsty lands. We are referring here to what we might call "vessel theology": "But we have this treasure in earthen vessels, so that the surpassing greatness of the power will be of God and not from ourselves" (2 Corinthians 4:7). Servants of God are vessels of God more than anything else! They, like Isaiah, say "Here am I, Send me!"

MARCH 30

DID YOU CHOOSE GOD OR DID GOD CHOOSE YOU?

"You did not choose Me but I chose you . . . "

John 15:16

Did you choose God? Jesus answers that question. The answer is "No, God chose you" (John 15:16). We are lost sheep. A sheep that is lost not only does not find its way home by itself, but it does not even know that it is lost so as to start looking for home. As part of a testimony of salvation, someone might talk about the time in their life when they "found" God. With respect to salvation, however, it is God who finds us and takes us home. Lost sheep do not find the shepherd . . . the shepherd has to "go after the one which is lost, until He finds it" (Luke 15:4-6).

This, of course, is true because God is the source of all good things. He is the source of salvation. It is God who draws the person to Himself. The person does not come in his own ability: "No one can come to Me, unless the Father who sent Me draws him . . . " (John 6:44). Salvation is impossible if it depends on man and his choice; it is only possible through God, and thus finds its source in God (Mark 10:27). And so, we are not born again by our own free will but by the will of God (John 1:13). Our free will is not a will that creates. It is a will that receives or rejects that which is already created and offered. The paradox that is formed by the free will of man existing together with the sovereignty of God is seen in the fact that God gives the right of salvation to those who receive Him yet it is according to His will (John 1:12-13).

Who chose who? Who found who? God chooses. God finds. The Scripture reports that the Father "gave some" to Jesus. Herein, we see the idea of God's "choosing" (John 17:2, 6, 9). The free will of man is so powerfully influenced by God's sovereignty as to allow man to freely accept or reject, and yet conclude what God has concluded beforehand. This is difficult for man, in his finiteness, to fully understand/accept. Jesus, seemed to be making His point about the need for God to draw a man to Himself and man's inability to come to God on his own in the context of responding to those who were "grumbling" (John 6:41-66). They were grumbling because they could not accept the words of Jesus, "no one can come to Me, unless the Father who sent me draws him . . . unless it has been granted him from the Father" (John 6:44, 65). The implication seems to be that Jesus was explaining why some could not accept His words: "Jesus answered and said to them, 'Do not grumble among yourselves . . . As a result of this many of His disciples withdrew, and were not walking with Him anymore" (John 6:43, 66). They could not accept His words because they were not being drawn by the Father. This points to the sovereignty of God with respect to salvation; "you did not choose Me but I chose you" (John 15:16).

MARCH 31

THE WAY UP IS DOWN . . .

"Whoever exalts himself shall be humbled; and whoever humbles himself shall be exalted."

Matthew 23:12

The way up is down (the way of humility) and the way down is up (the way of pride). Whoever humbles himself will be exalted (Luke 14:11; 18:14) while pride comes before a fall (1 Timothy 3:6). It is pride (the lack of humility) that is the essence of sin. Sin is very closely linked to a lack of recognition of need; it is associated with a lack of recognition of "blindness" or a lack of broken-ness/humility (John 9:41). Instead, the way up (to success) is the way down. It is opposite from the world's system. To reach success in the kingdom of God it is necessary to lower yourself down. To reach success in the organizations of the world it is necessary to fight your way up (Matthew 23:12). The one who humbles himself like a child is the greatest in the kingdom of God. A child is humble in that he is totally dependent on his parents, he innocently trusts them, he naturally desires their affection, and he is willing to obey them. To be great you must be humble. Therefore, the way up is the way down (Matthew 18:4).

Success in ministry requires humility. Another way to say this is that in order for Jesus to increase, we must decrease. For our ministries to be successful, Jesus must increase (John the Baptist understood that this required that he must decrease). Thus, humility in ministry is essential (John 3:30). Humility is required to minister to others. To help someone else with their faults, you must first be humble enough to consider your own faults and correct them. Then you will be able to help others instead of judging them (Luke 6:42).

Humility is essential. If human righteousness prevails and we do not embrace God's righteousness that He has provided for us, then we cannot be saved. Humility is needed to embrace God's righteousness and to accept the work that he has done (John 13:8). Being justified and forgiven is associated with humility and brokenness before God. It is associated with trusting only in God and refusing to trust in yourself. Humility is essential (Luke 18:10-14). Humility is needed to live in the kingdom of God. Only the humble can reject themselves and embrace Jesus. Only the humble (poor in spirit) can reject the temptation to rule themselves—to be your own king ruling your own kingdom—and accept the rule of Jesus (Matthew 5:3). Jesus ministers to those who are in need. Humility—the perception that you are in need of Jesus—is necessary to receive from Jesus and to be ministered to by Him (Luke 4:18; 5:31-32). And so, the way up is the way down. The way to heaven/God is the way of humility.

NOTES

April

IF THERE IS NO RESURRECTION
. . . PITY THE FOOL!

" . . . and if Christ has not been raised, your faith is worthless; you are still in your sins. Then those also who have fallen asleep in Christ have perished. If we have hoped in Christ in this life only, we are of all men most to be pitied."

1 Corinthians 15:17-19

The importance of the resurrection of Jesus Christ is clear. If Christ did not rise from the dead, then "you are still in your sins" and your faith is a sham; You are "of all men most to be pitied" (1 Corinthians 15:17-19)! The Christian faith is not a sham, however, and believers are not to be pitied for "Christ has been raised from the dead" (1 Corinthians 15:20). Certainly, this is the proclamation of the Bible as the resurrection is presented in the Psalms (Psalm 16:10-11; Acts 13:34-35), in the Prophets (Isaiah 53:10-12; 1 Corinthians 15:4), in the Gospels (Mark 9:9-10; John 2:19-22), and in the proclamations of the apostles (Acts 2:32; 3:15).

What caused the resurrection and what did the resurrection body look like? The resurrection came about by the power of God (Acts 2:24), by the power of Christ (John 10:18), and by the power of the Holy Spirit (Romans 8:11). The form of the resurrection was that of a body (John 20:27; Luke 24:39-43); more specifically, it was a spiritual body (Luke 24:31-36; John 20:19; 1 Corinthians 15:44). And so, there remains a sense of mystery regarding exactly what the resurrection body looks like (Luke 24:16; Mark 16:12; John 20:14).

The importance of the resurrection can especially be seen through its plethora of purposes. The purposes of the resurrection are to fulfill the Scriptures (Luke 24:45-46), to forgive sins (1 Corinthians 15:17), to justify the sinner (Romans 4:25; 8:34), to give hope (1 Corinthians 15:18-19), to make faith real (1 Corinthians 15:14-17), to prove that Jesus is the Son of God (Psalm 2:7; Romans 1:4), to prove the divinity of Jesus (John 20:26-29), to prove the Lordship of Jesus (Acts 2:24-34), to break the power of death (Acts 2:24; 1 Corinthians. 15:20-22, 54), to put Jesus on the throne of David (Acts 2:30-32), to insure the exaltation of Jesus (Acts 4:10-11; Philippians 2:9-10), to guarantee the coming judgment (Acts 17:31), and to seal the resurrection of believers (Acts 26:23; 1 Corinthians 15:20-23).

What a list of purposes! What a plan! Could you imagine sitting in a celestial board meeting and the Chairman of the Board declares that they must come up with one thing that will satisfy all the purposes listed above? That would not be an easy assignment. The resurrection is that one thing! How important is the resurrection?

APRIL 2

PROSPERITY THEOLOGY . . . WHAT JESUS ARE YOU LOOKING AT?

"Do not be afraid, little flock, for your Father has chosen gladly to give you the kingdom.
Sell your possessions and give to charity . . . "

Luke 12:32-33

The emphasis that "prosperity theology" proponents place on gaining wealth seems to claim that the good news of the gospel is material in nature. It could be said that it is the "developed" world's version of the "developing" world's "liberation theology"—salvation is liberation from the injustices of poverty—in which the good news of the gospel is, again, material in nature. These materially focused theologies, ironically, both claim to be founded on biblical "kingdom teaching." Of course, the irony comes in the fact that Scripture describes the kingdom of God and the good news of the gospel as being spiritual in nature. Jesus clearly states, "My kingdom is not of this world" (John 18:36). The kingdom of God is a spiritual reality (1 Corinthians 2:9-16; 2 Corinthians 10:3-5; Colossians 1:13) not a materially focused entity "for the kingdom of God is not eating and drinking, but righteousness and peace and joy in the Holy Spirit" (Romans 14:17). The irony is most emphatic—and startling to the prosperity theology proponent—as Jesus reports that God "has chosen gladly to give you the kingdom" and then says, "so gain many possessions and live luxurious lifestyles . . . " That is what the prosperity theologian would have expected Jesus to say, but of course, that is not what He said. He says that you will be given the kingdom so "sell your possessions and give to the poor" (Matthew 11:12). What? "Kingdom" juxtaposed with "sell your possessions"? It is a different kind of kingdom!

The false teaching that focuses on receiving everything you want from a "Santa Claus" type of God and obtaining great wealth and possessions because "you are a king's kid . . . on top, looking down . . . the head not the tail" is not consistent with Jesus' teaching on the kingdom of God. Even the announcer of the kingdom of God does not "wear soft clothing" (Matthew 11:8) but wears "a garment of camel's hair" and eats "locusts and wild honey" (Matthew 3:4). This is not to say that those who live in the kingdom of God must walk the streets naked and eat crumbs for lunch, but it certainly does not support the prosperity picture of luxury and its materialistic focus. The kingdom of God is more characterized by sacrifice and is not so concerned with material/physical comfort (Luke 18:29-30; Luke 6:20-26; 2 Timothy 2:3-4).

Prosperity theology teachers often defend their position by saying that Christians are "children of the King," and therefore, should live the life of a king. Of course, they forget that the King whom they are referring to spoke of material sacrifice, not comfort, when He spoke of those who would follow Him (Matthew 8:19-20). Perhaps, the most dramatic way to challenge prosperity theology is to ask whether the picture of a materialistic lifestyle that focuses on wealth and material luxury is the picture of Jesus' lifestyle. Can you picture Jesus living in the lap of luxury? Can you picture Jesus living in excess and waste? Can you picture Jesus focusing His life on gaining possessions and storing up more and more wealth for Himself? Does that look like Jesus? Does that sound like Jesus' message? Herein is the gravest of all the problems with "prosperity theology"; it is built on another Jesus, not the one we see in the Gospels. What Jesus are you looking at?

APRIL 3

UTILITARIAN THINKING CAN SEEM SO WISE, BUT . . .

"Where is the wise man? Where is the scribe? Where is the debater of this age?
Has not God made foolish the wisdom of the world?"

1 Corinthians 1:20

Where is wisdom? Wisdom begins at "the fear of the Lord" (Proverbs 9:10). The "wisdom of the world" is foolish (1 Corinthians 1:20) because it tries to begin somewhere else. A form of worldly wisdom is sometimes called utilitarianism. It can seem so wise, but it is foolishness. It does not begin with God. It begins with results. Truth is determined by the usefulness of results. A successful outcome justifies any method used to arrive at that outcome; the end justifies the means. Results replace God. Results become god. Results drive and define what is true, what is valued, and what is ultimately done.

Consider the absurdity of utilitarianism in the case of Esau and his willingness to give away his birthright for a bowl of soup (Genesis 25:29-34). Esau became so focused on the result that he was willing to engage in any method to achieve that result. The result became his god. The bowl of soup drove and defined truth, value, and action for him. Should I cheat on the test? Be careful. Don't let the result of a better grade become your definer of truth and action. It may seem so wise. Why not? Good grades are important. If cheating gets you a better grade, then . . . ! It seems so wise, but it is so foolish.

The wisdom of the world can be so deceptive. Consider the deception of utilitarianism in David's life with respect to his need for a solution to his problem (created by his sin with Bathsheba); his justification of his actions (the murder of Uriah) based on the desired result of ridding Bathsheba of a husband (2 Samuel 11:26-27). It seems so wise. After all, it did resolve the issue . . . didn't it? It seems so wise, but it is so foolish.

In response to the deception and absurdity of utilitarianism let us consider the "great cloud of witnesses" of Hebrews 11. Certainly, they show us that "results" do not act as our primary authority. Thus, one of them by faith "escaped the edge of the sword" while another by the same faith was "put to death by the sword" (Hebrews 11:34, 37). Many of the greatest people of faith did "not receive what was promised" (Hebrews 11:39). Their faith was not in a certain result or outcome, but in the One who provides those results; their faith was in the Word of God. This is where wisdom begins. It does not begin with results. Certain results, outcomes, or circumstances must not become your god. That is not wisdom. That is foolishness! This is Paul's point that he makes so clearly to the Philippians:

> I have learned to be content in whatever circumstances I am. I know how to get along with humble means, and I also know how to live in prosperity; in any and every circumstance I have learned the secret of being filled and going hungry, both of having abundance and suffering need. I can do all things through Him who strengthens me (Philippians 4:11-13).

What is the point? The point is that results or circumstances are not the point. Results do not drive and define what is true, what is valued, and what is ultimately done. That is foolishness (wisdom of the world). I can engage in all circumstances through Christ. Christ drives and defines what is true, what is valued, and what is ultimately done. That is wisdom!

———————

APRIL 4

THE WHEN OF CHURCH LEADERSHIP . . .

" . . . but if a man does not know how to manage his own household, how will he take care of the
church of God?"

1 Timothy 3:5

A young potential leader in the church might have, at some point, the question, "When will I have the opportunity to be a leader?" Paul seems to address this question in 1 Timothy 3:5 when in the context of listing criteria for leadership in the church He says, " . . . but if a man does not know how to manage his own household, how will he take care of the church of God?" Paul is making a definitive comparison between the family ("household") and the church: "His own household" is to "God's church" what "manage" is to "care for." The comparative structure shows an even more direct analogy than, perhaps, first seen. First, "God's church" could be likened to "God's household" as seen in Ephesians 2:19: "So then you are no longer strangers and aliens, but you are fellow citizens with the saints, and are of God's household . . . " Furthermore, the Greek word for "manage" that describes the work of family leaders is the same Greek word ("take care of") that is used to describe the work of church leaders; they are to "rule" well as in 1 Timothy 5:17.

Paul is saying here, "If you cannot govern that which is your own, how can you govern that which is God's?" Luke says it this way: "Whoever can be trusted with very little can also be trusted with much" (Luke 16:10). In other words, "If you cannot do a little thing, why do you want to try to do a big thing?" So where do young potential leaders begin? They begin with the basics. Potential church leaders must begin with their own families. Be a good leader with what God has already given you and then you will be a legitimate candidate to be given more.

We can prove ourselves as good leaders. Our potential ability can be indicated by our actual ability in a similar but less complex situation. We can practice and develop leadership skills. "He who is faithful in a very little thing is faithful also in much" (Luke 16:10) because being faithful in a little produces the ability to be faithful in much. Good ways are developed in doing the little or routine things. Bad ways are developed in doing the little or routine things. One way or another you will develop your abilities within those every day, routine, and basic areas of your life.

And so, if I do not lead well in the home (or in other areas where God has given me authority), I have no reason to believe that I will lead well in the church. If I do lead well in the home, then I can at least be assured that I am developing the proper skills to lead well in the church.

———————

STEPS TO HONOR IN THE LIFE OF JOSEPH (GENESIS 39) . . .

"Now Joseph had been taken down to Egypt . . . he left his garment in her hand and fled, and went outside."

Genesis 39:1, 12

All good things begin with God. So, the first step to honor in the life of Joseph is nothing less than godly influence. Initially this comes via what happened to him: "Now Joseph had been taken down to Egypt. Potiphar, an Egyptian who was one of Pharaoh's officials, the captain of the guard, bought him from the Ishmaelites who had taken him there" (Genesis 39:1). Godly influence then begins to build success in life: "The Lord was with Joseph and he prospered, and he lived in the house of his Egyptian master" (Genesis 39:2). Godly influence as a step to honor in the life of Joseph is then seen with respect to how other people viewed his life: "When his master saw that the Lord was with him and that the Lord gave him success in everything he did, Joseph found favor in his eyes and became his attendant. Potiphar put him in charge of his household, and he entrusted to his care everything he owned (Genesis 39:3-4).

A second step to honor in the life of Joseph is business integrity and honesty. First, with respect to blessing others: "From the time he put him in charge of his household and of all that he owned, the Lord blessed the household of the Egyptian because of Joseph. The blessing of the Lord was on everything Potiphar had, both in the house and in the field" (Genesis 39:5). Second, business integrity and honesty is seen with respect to acquired responsibility: "So he left in Joseph's care everything he had; with Joseph in charge, he did not concern himself with anything except the food he ate" (Genesis 39:6).

A third step to honor in the life of Joseph is resistance to temptation. We see this resistance, with respect to avoiding pride and lust: "Now Joseph was well-built and handsome, and after a while his master's wife took notice of Joseph and said, 'Come to bed with me!' But he refused. 'With me in charge,' he told her, 'my master does not concern himself with anything in the house; everything he owns he has entrusted to my care. No one is greater in this house than I am. My master has withheld nothing from me except you, because you are his wife. How then could I do such a wicked thing and sin against God?'" (Genesis 39:6-9). Note that loyalty is based on an acceptance of responsibility and a commitment to it. Also note how the contents of verse nine represent a practical redemption of what happened in Genesis 2:16-17. God withheld no tree from Adam and Eve with the exception of the tree of the knowledge of good and evil.

Adam and Eve sinned against God when they took fruit from the only tree that was forbidden. Similarly, Potiphar withheld nothing from Joseph except his wife. Unlike Adam and Eve, Joseph did not sin against God because he resisted the temptation to have the one thing that was forbidden.

Joseph's resistance to temptation is also seen with respect to being steadfast and consistent: "And though she spoke to Joseph day after day, he refused to go to bed with her or even be with her" (Genesis 39:10). Ultimately, resistance to temptation is manifested in fleeing from it: "One day he went into the house to attend to his duties, and none of the household servants was inside. She caught him by his cloak and said, 'Come to bed with me!' But he left his cloak in her hand and ran out of the house" (Genesis 39:11-12). At the end of the day, there really is only one response to temptation. Flee from it! Flee from it and embrace honor.

APRIL 6

THE GREAT GENERATOR, REGENERATOR, AND RE-REGENERATOR

"IN THE beginning God created the heavens and the earth.
The earth was formless and void,
and darkness was over the surface of the deep,
and the Spirit of God was moving over
the surface of the waters.

Genesis 1:1-2

When the power goes out it is nice to have a generator. The generator turns on and power is restored; the lights go on and all is brought back into order. The Spirit of God is the Great Generator (creator), Regenerator (recreator), and Re-regenerator (re-recreator).

The Spirit generates/creates (Genesis 1:1-2). Through the activity of the Spirit of God ("and the Spirit was moving"), Deity brings creative order ("God created the heavens and the earth"). The generating Spirit does not then go away. The Great Generator is involved in creation and in the maintaining of that creation. Man depends on the Spirit of life (2 Corinthians 3:6) "for in Him we live and move and exist" (Acts 17:28). The Great Generator creates initially and then retains that creation: "If He should determine to do so, if He should gather to Himself His spirit and His breath, all flesh would perish together, and man would return to dust" (Job 34:14-15). And so, because of the Great Generator, the lights go on and stay on.

Nevertheless, the lights did go out; man sinned (Romans 3:23) and died spiritually (Romans 6:23). The Great Generator, then, became the Great Regenerator as those who were generated (born) needed to be regenerated (born again). Just as the power of the Spirit was used to create the original creation, it is also the power of the Spirit that creates a new creation in Christ:

> Jesus answered and said to him, 'Truly, truly, I say to you, unless one is born again he cannot see the kingdom of God.' Nicodemus said to Him, 'How can a man be born when he is old? He cannot enter a second time into his mother's womb and be born, can he?' Jesus answered, 'Truly, truly, I say to you, unless one is born of water and the Spirit he cannot enter into the kingdom of God. That which is born of the flesh is flesh, and that which is born of the Spirit is spirit' (John 3:3-6).

Originally, there was creation or generation. The light bulb turned on. Now there is recreation or regeneration. The light bulb is changed. Of course, the lights will go out again. Those who were regenerated will die physically. The Great Regenerator, then, will become the Great Re-regenerator as those who were regenerated (born again) will be re-regenerated (raised from the dead). At the resurrection of the dead, that which was "sown a natural body . . . is raised a spiritual body" (1 Corinthians 15:44) by the power of the Spirit of God (Romans 8:11).

The Spirit creates (the lights go on). He recreates (the lights go back on). He re-recreates (the lights go back on forever). The Spirit of God is the Great Generator (creator), Regenerator (recreator), and Re-regenerator (re-recreator).

APRIL 7

WHAT COMES BEFORE A REVIVAL?

"Jesus wept."

John 11:35

Sometimes society needs revival. Sometimes the church needs revival. And sometimes, you and I need revival. Sometimes we just need to be woken up from our spiritual slumber. But what comes before a revival? What precedes it? In order to answer this question, we may be able to rely on descriptions of physical revival to understand principles of spiritual revival. So, what comes before a revival?

First, it can be said that **compassion**—in John 11:35, "Jesus wept"—precedes a revival:

> Soon afterwards He went to a city called Nain; and His disciples were going along with Him, accompanied by a large crowd. Now as He approached the gate of the city, a dead man was being carried out, the only son of his mother, and she was a widow; and a sizeable crowd from the city was with her. When the Lord saw her, He felt compassion

for her, and said to her, 'Do not weep.' And He came up and touched the coffin; and the bearers came to a halt. And He said, 'Young man, I say to you, arise!' The dead man sat up and began to speak. And *Jesus* gave him back to his mother. Fear gripped them all, and they *began* glorifying God, saying, 'A great prophet has arisen among us!' and, 'God has visited His people!' This report concerning Him went out all over Judea and in all the surrounding district" (Luke 7:11-17).

As it was with Lazarus, it also was with this "only son of his mother." Before Jesus revives them, He feels compassion on them. Compassion precedes a revival which then leads to Jesus being glorified and His reputation being magnified.

Early on in Jesus' ministry, there was a great revival in Galilee: "Large crowds followed Him from Galilee" (Matthew 4:25). In studying this passage, we see that what preceded revival was **teaching** and **preaching**: "Jesus was going throughout all Galilee, teaching in their synagogues and proclaiming the gospel of the kingdom . . . " (Matthew 4:23). There were also **signs and wonders** that preceded the revival (see Matthew 4:23-24). This all, once again, led to Jesus' reputation being magnified.

It has been the testimony of church history that prayer and spiritual warfare have always preceded revivals. In other words, God uses his people to do something before he sends a revival. In the remarkable revival of Lazarus we see this to be true. Jesus said: "Remove the stone" (John 11:39). He used them, and then revival came. Obedience can also be seen as that which precedes revival (see Luke 6:46-49). Laying down your life for Jesus' sake (dying to self) can also be seen to precede revival inasmuch as revival is to find life: "He who has found his life will lose it, and he who has lost his life for My sake will find it (Matthew 10:39).

Revival is when, after a period of inactivity, people begin to hunger and thirst for righteousness—"Blessed are those who hunger and thirst for righteousness, for they shall be satisfied" (Matthew 5:6)—hungering for personal righteousness (individual revival), righteousness in others (evangelistic revival), or hungering for righteousness in society (social revival). Each one of these categories of revival necessitates spiritual warfare. Revival is the plundering of the kingdom of Satan, and thus, it must be preceded by spiritual warfare. First, Satan must be bound, "And then he will plunder his house" (Matthew 12:29). Satan's house plundered. God's kingdom advanced. Revival experienced!

———————

APRIL 8

WHO DO YOU BELIEVE THIS JESUS TO BE?

"Thomas answered and said to Him, 'My Lord and my God!'
Jesus said to him, 'Because you have seen Me, have you believed?
Blessed are they who did not see, and yet believed.'"

John 20:28-29

What does it mean to believe in Jesus? Maybe you believe in Santa Claus. Or maybe you believe in "justice for all." But what does it mean to believe in Jesus? Most foundational to what constitutes "belief in Jesus" is necessarily consistent with what is most foundational about the nature of Jesus; that is, Jesus is God. To believe in Jesus, at its very core, is to believe that Jesus is God. You cannot believe in Jesus and simply believe that He is a nice guy who is to be respected because of His nice teachings. No! Christianity is much more radical than that because who Jesus is, most fundamentally, is much more radical than that. Jesus is God!

This is not something that is a hidden or contrived point according to the Bible, or more specifically, according to Jesus Himself. The Bible paints Jesus as being equal to God. When Jesus said that God was His Father it was understood that He was making Himself equal with God (John 5:18). Jesus understood Himself to be equal to the Father. According to Jesus, the honor of the Son must be **equal** to the honor of the Father (John 5:23). And so, when Thomas called Jesus, "God," Jesus did not correct him. Why? Because Jesus is God. Being in God (knowing God) has its purpose in testimony to the world that Jesus is God (John 17:21).

In the Scripture, Jesus speaks as God. He says, "I am the way, and the truth, and the life . . . " (John 14:6). The way is not simply the "ways" of Jesus. Jesus **is** the way. Only God can speak like this! The truth is not simply the concepts that Jesus talked about that are true. Jesus **is** the truth. Only God can speak like this! The life is not simply the life of Jesus. Jesus is the life. Who else can speak like this but God Himself? Jesus speaks as God.

He references ancient history and His ancient historical desire to be the God of Jerusalem when He addresses the city and cries out, "O Jerusalem, Jerusalem, the city that kills the prophets and stones those sent to her! How often I wanted to gather your children together, just as a hen gathers her brood . . . " (Luke 13:34). Who is this that speaks to cities in this way? Could you imagine walking down the main street of your town and seeing someone standing up on a bench in the park and yelling, "O Philadelphia, Philadelphia, the city that cracked the Liberty Bell! How often I wanted to gather colonial Philadelphians under my wings like a hen gathers its chicks . . . " What would you think of this person? This person is either something beyond just a man (God Himself) or this person is a raving lunatic! Jesus, according to the way he speaks in the Scripture, is either God Himself or a raving lunatic. But He is not something in-between. He is not, as lukewarm Christianity often tries to depict Him, simply a great teacher or prophet or nice guy with admirable ethical teaching. Jesus is God and to believe in Jesus is to believe He is God. This makes Christianity radical and the follower of Christ, then necessarily, a radical person inasmuch as he or she is a person that is following God Himself. What does it mean to believe in Jesus? It means something very radical and, thus, the believer's life is, by definition, a radical life!

———————

APRIL 9

LET JESUS BE THE ONLY STUMBLING BLOCK . . .

"Woe to the world because of its stumbling blocks!
For it is inevitable that stumbling blocks come . . ."

Matthew 18:7

The cross of Jesus is described as a "stumbling block" (Matthew 11:12; Galatians 5:11). The cross is a stumbling block to our flesh—it offends us—because it is difficult for us to accept the fact that God Himself had to die for our sins . . . that God had to save us. This, of course, is actually good news ("gospel") since we could not/would not save ourselves. This is the gospel message; that God did it all for us. It stands, however, as a stumbling block to our flesh. It is difficult (if not seemingly impossible) for man to accept this "good news/gospel" (Matthew 19:23-26).

People need to be presented with this stumbling block. The presentation of the gospel to others (through our words and actions) needs to be done in such a way as to allow the stumbling block of the cross to be the only stumbling block presented. In evangelism, when we offer the gospel to others, we need to try to avoid creating other stumbling blocks (misunderstandings, cultural insensitivities, and religious requirements). Jesus must be the only stumbling block. In this way, the person who receives the message is forced to accept or deny Jesus (and not your cultural insensitivity or religious rules). If Jesus offends them, then the blood is on their own hands (John 3:17-18). In Matthew 17:25-27, Jesus Himself avoids offending others ("but lest we give them offense"). He does not allow the trivial things of this world (the paying of taxes) to become a stumbling block. Thus, the real issue or stumbling block—His being Savior and Lord—can be the focus when His gospel message is presented.

Unfortunately, other stumbling blocks are inevitable (Matthew 18:7). In our own lives, we must be "militant" against these stumbling blocks. Anything that blocks our way to God must be destroyed. Do whatever it takes to move forward in Christ and closer to God (Matthew 18:8-9). We can allow our own righteousness to be a stumbling block. Self-righteousness denies the need for God's help. Peter fell over this stumbling block (John 13:8). We must avoid it. We must also understand that Satan will try to tempt us with the comforts and success of the world to keep us from the way of God (which is the cross). The temptation of a comfortable life is a common stumbling block that must be avoided (Mark 8:31-33).

Another potential stumbling block to be aware of is the fear of man. The world does not want to hear people crying out for Jesus. They will try to silence you. This can be a stumbling block if we focus on men instead of Jesus. We must continue calling on Him no matter what the world says (Matthew 20:31). More specifically, hypocritical leaders can be a stumbling block (Matthew 23:13). A blind leader causes others to stumble with him (Luke 6:39). People who cause "little ones" (new believers) to stumble will pay a great price (Matthew 18:5-6; Mark 9:42). We may be susceptible to these sorts of stumbling blocks—wrongly following others—because we are so susceptible to wanting to please men.

The desire and temptation to please men may be one of the greatest stumbling blocks. The person who only wants to please men will always be found stumbling (Mark 11:29-32). We should not, however, fear men. We should fear the "Rock" who is sovereign over us. Other men are not sovereign over us. As long as we are pleasing the one who is sovereign over us, then we do not have to worry about whether the ones who are not sovereign over us are pleased or not (Luke 12:4-7). Seeking glory for yourself from others can result in an inability to believe (John 5:44). So, avoid these stumbling blocks and, instead, embrace the stumbling block of the cross. Embrace Jesus; your need for Him, and therefore, your trust in Him. Embrace Him and you will be held up and kept from stumbling!

APRIL 10

WALKING AND TALKING WITH OTHERS . . .

"They were continually devoting themselves to the apostles' teaching and to fellowship."

Acts 2:42

A significant part of life—certainly a big part of the Christian life—could simply be described as "walking and talking." "Successful talking" has to do with how we use our words while "successful walking" has to do with how we engage in fellowship with others. The Scripture tells us in Psalm 133 that it is good to have fellowship with one another; it is a "blessing":

> BEHOLD, HOW good and how pleasant it is For brothers to dwell together in unity! It is like the precious oil upon the head, Coming down upon the beard, *Even* Aaron's beard, Coming down upon the edge of his robes. It is like the dew of Hermon Coming down upon the mountains of Zion; For there the LORD commanded the blessing—life forever.

Our walking with each other is based on our walking with God: " . . . so that you too may have fellowship with us; and our fellowship is with the Father, and with His Son Jesus Christ" (1 John 1:3). We can go all way the back to the earliest church in the New Testament to see an example of this walking/fellowship: "They were continually devoting themselves to the apostles' teaching and to fellowship . . . " (Acts 2:42). The Scripture is clear as to the importance of fellowship as it admonishes us that we should not be "forsaking our own assembling together . . . " (Hebrews 10:25). It is also clear regarding the desire we should have for fellowship: "I was glad when they said to me, 'Let us go to the house of the Lord'" (Psalm 122:1). So be sure you are "walking." Walk. Walk. Walk!

So, as much as we emphasize walking, we must also emphasize talking—the use of our words—which is referred to in James 3:2-10 as "the tongue":

> For we all stumble in many *ways*. If anyone does not stumble in what he says, he is a perfect man, able to bridle the whole body as well. Now if we put the bits into the horses' mouths so that they will obey us, we direct their entire body as well. Look at the ships also, though they are so great and are driven by strong winds, are still directed by a very small rudder wherever the inclination of the pilot desires. So also the tongue is a small part of the body, and *yet* it boasts of great things. See how great a forest is set aflame by such a small fire! And the tongue is a fire, the *very* world of iniquity; the tongue is set among our members as that which defiles the entire body, and sets on fire the course of *our* life, and is set on fire by hell. For every species of beasts and birds, of reptiles and creatures of the sea, is tamed and has been tamed by the human race. But no one can tame the tongue; *it is* a restless evil *and* full of deadly poison. With it we bless *our* Lord and Father, and with it we curse men, who have been made in the likeness of God; from the same mouth come *both* blessing and cursing.

A World War II story is told that metaphorically describes what James is talking about:

> On May 21, 1941 the "unsinkable" German battleship, the Bismarck, was sighted in the North Atlantic. Planes and ships from the British Navy sped to the area. The Bismarck sped toward the German controlled French coast looking like it would be safe. Suddenly it turned around, began zigzagging about and headed directly into the

mass of British ships. It was sunk. Why? One reason. A torpedo had hit its rudder . . . it went out of control. Such a little thing, the rudder. But like the little part of us called the tongue, it is that little thing that controls all else. Without that control we can easily be sunk!

Talking is emphatically significant. Almost thirty percent of the 1 Corinthians 13 description of love is linked to our words. And so, we should speak words that edify (Ephesians 4:29) and use our tongue to praise God (Psalm 71:15). We should not use our tongue to spread rumors (Proverbs 26:20). If not controlled, our mouth can make our religion worthless (James 1:26), and actually lead to our ruin: "A fool's mouth is his ruin, and his lips are the snare of his soul" (Proverbs 18:7). So be sure you are "talking" right. Talk. Talk. Talk!

––––––––––––

APRIL 11

NO WORRIES . . . GOD IS STILL ON THE THRONE!

"Are not two sparrows sold for a cent? And yet not one of them
will fall to the ground apart from your Father.
But the very hairs of your head are all numbered.
So do not fear; you are more valuable than many sparrows."

Matthew 10:29-31

Unless you live in Jamaica and are heavily impacted by that "don't worry . . . be happy" culture, you probably tend to struggle with worry and fear. The Scripture offers us a variety of antidotes to fear and anxiety. The Scripture tells us that all things will be revealed. Nothing will remain hidden. This understanding can be used as medicine to cure a fear of people and their power and influence that may lead to injustice (Matthew 10:26). More generally, focusing on God and His sovereignty over your life can be a cure for fear (Matthew 10:28). God is in complete control. He is aware of and in control of every detail. And so, what do we have to fear? (Matthew 10:29-31).

We should respond to God's sovereignty by seeking the kingdom of God. Too often, we worry about things that we cannot control. Instead of worrying, we should realize that God is sovereign. This will free us to control what we can (what we are responsible for); to seek the kingdom of God (Luke 12:26, 31). In any case, it is helpful to realize that anxiety cannot add time to your life. So why worry? (Matthew 6:27). Furthermore, we cannot be persecuted without it being God's will. If it is God's will then it is the best thing for us. Thus, we should not worry. God is in control (John 7:30; 8:20).

In a specific application of these principles, the Scripture reminds us that anxiety about the future should not be a motive to save money. Money cannot cure anxiety (Luke 12:16-21). More generally, we must avoid being anxious with the worries of this world or the end could come as a trap. We should be alert. We should always be praying so that we will be strong and prepared when Christ comes (Luke 21:34-36). Prayer, then, replaces worry: "Be anxious for nothing, but *(instead)* in everything by prayer and supplication with thanksgiving let your requests be made known to God" (Philippians 4:6). Prayer prevails as a potent medicine to take in order to combat fear and worry, as well as the potential discouragement that may accompany both. Consistent prayer will lead to justice. God responds to consistent prayer, so do not give up when injustice seems to have won the fight. Do not get discouraged (Luke 18:7-8).

No worries . . . God is still on the throne. So "let us therefore draw near with confidence to the throne of grace" (Hebrews 4:16) for when we enter His throne room, we are especially reminded that He is still there, and fear and anxiety will begin to fade away.

APRIL 12

LORD OF THE LAW . . .

"For the Son of Man is Lord of the Sabbath."

Matthew 12:8

Jesus is the Lord of the Sabbath; He is Lord of the law. Accordingly, the law and its application to our lives are to be understood through Jesus. Thus, for example—according to Jesus' explanation in Mark 2:22-28—man does not need to serve the Sabbath; rather, the Sabbath should serve man since it is made for him. Does this mean that the law (Sabbath) can be broken? Not at all! We must obey the law of God as we are to obey the laws of man (consider Luke 20:24-25). We are to pay taxes in obedience to the government as we are to obey the law of God in obedience to God (Mark 12:12). Give to Caesar what is Caesar's, and to God what is God's. We take nothing away from God by obeying the civil law as long as we understand that civil law is limited by God's law. That is, the right of the state is limited by what the individual owes to God since He is Lord of the law (Matthew 22:21). The law is not to be broken. The law is perfect in quality and quantity and not one part of it will pass away (Luke 16:17). A lack of the law leads to rebellion and hatred. When lawlessness increases the love of people grows cold (Matthew 24:12). No law, no love. Conversely, the existence of law implies the existence of love.

Here we see the connection that is most emphatic in the application of the law as understood through Jesus, the Lord of the law; that is the connection between the law and love. The law is summarized in this way: love God and love others (Matthew 22:37-39). Thus, Jesus indicated that working on the Sabbath is permitted if the work is to do good unto others; if the work is to show mercy and love that seeks to glorify God and meet the needs of others (John 5:15-17). Hence, the higher law of love/compassion is always above the secondary laws which illustrate it/God's character (Matthew 12:7). Another way to describe this dynamic is to understand that God's law is not of the letter, but of the heart—it is reality not superficiality (Matthew 5:22, 28).

And so, does Jesus as Lord of the law, bring forth a new law? Certainly, new wine goes into fresh wineskins. Thus, the coming of the new covenant (law) with the coming of Jesus to earth is accompanied by new ways (Luke 5:36; Mark 2:21-22). The new law is to love others as Jesus loved us (John 13:34). It is a new law in the sense that there is a new (better/fuller/clearer) covenant. God's incarnation in Christ gives us the perfect example of how to love. Thus, we are better equipped to love others because we have a better idea of how to love others. Therefore, we are not under the law, not because we are exempt from it, but rather, because we are enabled to do it. And so, the Lord of the law is asked a question and then answers:

Teacher, which is the great commandment in the Law? And He said to him, 'YOU SHALL LOVE THE LORD YOUR GOD WITH ALL YOUR HEART, AND WITH ALL YOUR SOUL, AND WITH ALL YOUR MIND.' This is the great and foremost commandment. The second is like it, 'YOU SHALL LOVE YOUR NEIGHBOR AS YOURSELF.' On these two commandments depend the whole Law and the Prophets (Matthew 22:36-40).

APRIL 13

TYPES OF LEADERSHIP . . .

"Where there is no vision, the people are unrestrained."

Proverbs 29:18

The term "elders" is used twenty-one times in the New Testament and every time it is used it is in the plural form. Church leadership is described as a plurality of leadership. Some of this is routed out of the fact that there are different types of leadership. A priestly type of leadership—one who has a "pastor's heart"—might be described as being "**a**ffiliative," having an emphasis on people and fellowship. The key word here would be *relationship* (John 13:35). A prophetic type of leadership might be described as focusing on "**a**chievement," having an emphasis on goals and tasks. The key word here would be *vision* (Proverbs 29:18). A kingly type of leadership might be described as focusing on "**a**uthority," having an emphasis on power and hierarchy. The key word here would be order or organization (1 Corinthians 14:40). The priestly emphasis might be described as a social club/social director, or a family/parent (Ephesians 2:19). The prophetic emphasis might be described as a building/architect, or a business/entrepreneur (1 Corinthians 3:9). The kingly emphasis might be described as a factory/foreman, or an army/general (2 Timothy 2:3-4).

Another way to describe these different types of leadership is to picture a hypothetical situation in a church and then determine how each type of leader might respond to that situation. You go to the leaders in the church and explain that you are having marriage problems. The "priest" says, "Let me give you a hug and we can talk about it over a cup of coffee." The "prophet" says, "Well you need to get your marriage right so go home and do these three things." The "king" says, "Let me get you in touch with Fred and Jane who head up our marriage ministry." Another analogy (a bit more ridiculous but nonetheless descriptive) might have to do with you going to the leaders of the church and asking, "Where is the bathroom?" The "priest" says, "Let me take you there myself." The "prophet" says, "I will draw you a map." The "king" says, "Let me introduce you to the head of our bathroom ministry."

In terms of the ministry of the church, priests are more naturally inclined toward counseling, visitation, and other more pastoral functions, whereas prophets focus on pointing toward the way to go, establishing goals and plans, and giving direction.

Kings, in turn, are more inclined toward the administration and management of the church looking to establish a chain of command and delegating authority. The strengths of the priestly type of leadership are typically discipleship and community/fellowship. Prophets are strong in achieving good works and enjoying many accomplishments. Kings develop very stable, well defined, and controlled environments for ministry to thrive. On the other hand, the vulnerability of the priestly type of leadership is that they can become too inward ("implosion"). Prophets can become too busy and insensitive to the needs of people ("explosion"). Kings must be careful not to abuse power as they might tend to not be open to new ideas and become inflexible ("nonplosion").

An emphasis on relationships (priests), an emphasis on vision (prophets), and an emphasis on order and organization (kings) are all very different. They are also all very necessary. All these aspects of the church and its leadership must exist to some degree at all times in every church. Healthy and balanced leaders need each other. They understand that "different is good" and are not intimidated by differences but have an appreciation for them. It is easy to see that priests need prophets to shake up that which they have put to sleep. Prophets need kings to put in order that which they have shaken up. And kings need priests to personalize that which they have put in order. Different types of leaders need each other. It is a healthy church whose leaders understand this, accept it, and put it into practice.

APRIL 14

TWO ADAMS . . . TWO NATURES . . . ONE WINNER!

"So also it is written, 'The first MAN, Adam, BECAME A LIVING SOUL.' The last Adam became a life-giving spirit. However, the spiritual is not first, but the natural; then the spiritual."

1 Corinthians 15:45-46

At our physical birth we have a first Adam experience. To be saved is to be born again. It is to have a second or last Adam experience: "The first man, Adam, became a living soul. The last Adam became a life-giving spirit" (1 Corinthians 15:45). Because we have two births, we have two natures: "The first man is from the earth, earthy; the second man is from heaven. As is the earthy, so also are those who are earthy; and as is the heavenly, so also are those who are heavenly. Just as we have borne the image of the earthy, we will also bear the image of the heavenly" (1 Corinthians 15:46-49). These two natures tend to battle each other (Romans 7:18-19; Galatians 5:17). Nonetheless, those who are born again can rejoice in the second Adam's superiority over the first Adam, and therefore the superiority of our "new" nature over our "old" nature. For the Christian, there is a fight (for there are, two natures). However, it is in no way an even battle, for the One is superior to the other. Christ is superior to Adam.

The power resulting from the second Adam's accomplishment is superior to the power resulting from the deeds of the first Adam. The power of grace is greater than the power of sin (Romans 5:20). The second Adam is "much more" (Romans 5:9, 10, 15, 17, 20) and is superior to the first Adam. The first Adam is created in God's image, according to God's likeness (Genesis 1:26), while the second Adam is the radiance of God's glory and the exact representation of God's nature (Hebrews 1:3). The first Adam received his life from God who breathed into his nostrils the breath of life

(Genesis 2:7), while the second Adam became a life-giving Spirit (1 Corinthians 15:45). The first Adam is from the earth, while the second Adam is from heaven (1 Corinthians 15:47).

Christ is not the New Adam. He is the second Adam; He is the original Adam in His perfection. Christ is not so much the representative of a **new humanity** as He is the representative of perfect humanity—of everything Adam should have been. Pilate did not know how profoundly correct he was when he looked at the suffering Christ and proclaimed, "Behold, the Man!" (John 19:5). Humanism is confused about humanity. The humanist looks to the first Adam as representative of what humanity should be. He believes him to be good and without need for redemption. In reality, he deifies something that is broken, fallen, and corrupt. The first Adam is his god. Therefore, he dies with the first Adam (Romans 6:23). The Christian looks to the second Adam. He desires a real humanity. The second Adam is his God. He is, therefore, raised with Jesus (1 Corinthians 15:2, 20, 23).

Adam failed. Christ succeeded. To the degree that we allow the new nature (Christ) to govern our lives is the degree to which we will succeed also. Two Adams, two natures, but **one winner**!

APRIL 15

JESUS, THE ULTIMATE MISSIONARY, BECOMES ALL THINGS TO ALL MEN!

"To the weak I became weak, that I might win the weak; I have become all things to all men, that I may by all means save some."

1 Corinthians 9:22

God is a missionary God. He is a "sent One." A "missionary" is a "sent one" as the word stems from the Greek derived "apostle" (*apo* = "from" and *stello* = "to send"); "For God so loved the world, that He gave His only begotten Son . . . For God did not send the Son into the world to judge the world, but that the world should be saved through Him" (John 3:16-17). Herein lies one way to express the paradox of the Trinity; God sending Himself to the needy to provide for their needs. God is the mission sending agency as well as the missionary Himself. We are the needy because we cannot, in ourselves, reach God. Thus, He must come to us . . . He must send Himself. Even the ability to know Him begins with Him. God provides knowledge of Himself because He must provide knowledge of Himself. There is no other way that finite and sinful man can know Him. God must provide revelation of Himself to those who need His provision. In order to do this, like a missionary, He must go to them . . . even become like them.

The ultimate revelation of God is Jesus Christ (John 1:14, 18). He, then, becomes the ultimate missionary. Missionary methodology is expressed in 1 Corinthians 9:22: "To the weak I became weak, that I might win the weak; I have become all things to all men, that I may by all means save some." Christ ultimately solves the problems that prevent man from knowing God by "becoming all things." Man's problem in knowing God is that God is infinite, and man is finite. God's solution is that He becomes finite. He becomes man. Through the incarnation, God becomes knowable and visible to men (John 14:7). God reveals Himself in Christ in a way that man can understand and relate to (Philippians 2:7). The finite could not reach the infinite, so the infinite becomes finite. What a miracle! What a price that is paid! It is impossible for the finite to fully comprehend the price that was paid by the infinite "who, although He existed in the form of God, did not regard equality with God a thing to be grasped, but emptied Himself, taking the form of a bond-servant, and being made in the likeness of men" (Philippians 2:6-7). Even if we metaphorically compare this to man becoming a cockroach to save the cockroaches, we would still be comparing the sacrifice of the finite for the finite and not nearly arrive at a comparison of the price that was paid by the infinite becoming the finite. Would you be willing to pay the incredible fees—fees that would still be incredibly less than the fees paid by the infinite becoming the finite—you would incur in becoming a cockroach to save the cockroaches? You would not even be born into a relatively cozy house—perhaps, in a crevice in the kitchen wall—but in the mud in a dangerous open field. The cockroaches you came to save would not even honor and thank you but would step on you and spit on you and stick pins in you. Would you do it? Thankfully, God did! He came to us and paid a price that is incomprehensible.

Christ ultimately solves the problems that prevent man from knowing God by "becoming all things." Man's problem in knowing God is that God is holy, and man is sinful. God's solution is that He becomes sin. Through the atonement—"He made Him who knew no sin to be sin on our behalf, that we might become the righteousness of God in Him"—God becomes knowable and visible to men (2 Corinthians 5:21). God reveals Himself in Christ in a way that man can understand and relate to (Hebrews 4:15-16). He again becomes the ultimate missionary by "becoming all things to all men." Miraculously and incomprehensibly, the infinite becomes finite and the holy becomes unholy as God says to those He comes to, "To the weak I became weak, that I might win the weak; I have become all things to all men, that I may by all means save some." Glory be to our great missionary God!

APRIL 16

PAUL'S DESCRIPTIONS OF CHRIST . . .

". . . our Lord Jesus Christ . . . only Sovereign, the King of kings and Lord of lords, who alone
possesses immortality . . . To Him be *honor and eternal dominion! Amen."*

1 Timothy 6:14-16

Paul, in his writings, offers a description of Jesus that serves to view Him from multiple angles, and thus, becomes for the Bible student a relatively comprehensive description of Jesus. These descriptions might be placed under three categories: 1) actions/functions; 2) titles; 3) characteristics/nature. Regarding how Jesus might be described according to His actions/functions, we see that He is the **peacemaker**: "Therefore, having been justified by faith, we have peace with God through our Lord Jesus Christ" (Romans 5:1). Similarly, He is the **liberator**: "It was for freedom that Christ set us free; therefore keep standing firm and do not be subject again to a yoke of slavery" (Galatians 5:1). He is the **conqueror of death** (1 Corinthians 15:24-26) and the **redeemer**: " . . . our great God and Savior, Christ Jesus, who gave Himself for us to redeem us from every lawless deed, and to purify for Himself a people for His own possession, zealous for good deeds" (Titus 2:13-14). Jesus functions as God's provided substitute, so He is described as "the sacrificial lamb" (1 Corinthians 5:7). He then becomes for us the *author and perfecter of faith* (Hebrews 12:2). Someday, of course, He will return; thus, He is described as "the coming Lord" (1 Thessalonians 4:16) who will be the *Judge* of all men (2 Timothy 4:1).

Jesus is described by Paul via his use of a variety of titles. He is "the Lord of glory": " . . . the wisdom which none of the rulers of this age has understood; for if they had understood it they would not have crucified the Lord of glory" (1 Corinthians 2:8). Jesus is also given the title, "the only foundation": "For no man can lay a foundation other than the one which is laid, which is Jesus Christ" (1 Corinthians 3:11). Furthermore, He is the **head of the church**: "He is also head of the body, the church" (Colossians 1:18). In addition, He is nothing less than the **author of salvation**: "For it was fitting for Him, for whom are all things, and through whom are all things, in bringing many sons to glory, to perfect the author of their salvation through sufferings" (Hebrews 2:10). Finally, Jesus is described with perhaps the ultimate title: " . . . which He will bring about at the proper time—He who is the blessed and "only Sovereign, the King of kings and Lord of lords" (1 Timothy 6:15-16).

Paul also describes Christ in terms of His characteristics or nature. In a very profound statement, Paul gives Jesus the title "the image of God": "see the light of the gospel of the glory of Christ, who is the image of God" (2 Corinthians 4:4). This image of God, then, is the goal or

standard of maturity: " . . . until we all attain . . . to a mature man, to the measure of the stature which belongs to the fullness of Christ" (Ephesians 4:13). Furthermore, Paul describes Jesus by calling Him the great **high priest**: "Therefore, since we have a great high priest who has passed through the heavens, Jesus the Son of God, let us hold fast our confession" (Hebrews 4:14). Finally, Paul describes Christ with a title we might put forth as "the ultimate reward of a believer": "More than that, I count all things to be loss in view of the surpassing value of knowing Christ Jesus my Lord, for whom I have suffered the loss of all things, and count them but rubbish so that I may gain Christ" (Philippians 3:8).

Through Paul's descriptions, we see, from many angles, just who Christ is, but perhaps the most profound is Paul's description of Christ as redeemer in the midst of referring to Him as " . . . our great God and savior, Christ Jesus" (Titus 2:13). At the end of the day, above all else, Jesus is God!

APRIL 17

WHERE, OH WHERE, IS THE GOD OF JUSTICE??

"You have wearied the L*ORD* *with your words. Yet you say,*
'How have we wearied Him*?' In that you say,*
'Everyone who does evil is good in the sight of the L*ORD,*
and He delights in them,' or, 'Where is the God of justice?'"

Malachi 2:17

In Malachi 2:17, God was wearied by the sinful words of a self-deceived, hypocritical people. His patience was coming to an end. He was impatient with His people who were not holy themselves, but still questioned the holiness of God. The people of Israel were not atheists. Thus, when they said "Where is the God of justice?" they were not questioning whether He existed or not. They were questioning the character of the God whom they knew existed. This was even worse than atheism just as hypocrisy is even worse than pure unbelief (Mark 12:40). Israel's questions did something worse than doubt God. They mocked God. Israel mocked the holiness of God.

The priests were weary of their own religiosity because they felt its emptiness (Malachi 1:13). God was weary of their hypocrisy. More specifically, He was weary of the deception generated by hypocrisy that did not allow them to see their own sins, but only to see the sins of others, and worse yet, to accuse God of wrong. Of course, this is ridiculously ironic! The sinner (Israel) desires that God would punish the sinners and accuses God of being unjust. The sinner wants justice, yet his own hypocrisy blinds him to the fact that he is the sinner. They were asking for their own judgment (Matthew 7:1-5; Romans 2:1-3). It is like a child who disobeyed his father who told him not to play in the street. When the child runs to the father to complain that his older brother was doing something wrong, the father looks at him and says, "Why are you so worried about your brother when you cannot obey me yourself?"

Where is the God of justice? God's justice is most profoundly found in His coming to us: "'Behold, I am going to send My messenger, and he will clear the way before Me. And the Lord, whom you seek, will suddenly come to His temple; and the messenger of the covenant, in whom you delight, behold, He is coming,' says the Lord of hosts" (Malachi 3:1). This is a picture of the coming of Jesus Christ, the Lord God. Paradoxically (as the Trinity remains a paradox), what we see here is God sending God.

Mercifully, this God of justice will come as Savior and not yet as Judge. The God of justice comes "like a refiner's fire and like fuller's soap" (Malachi 3:2). Herein, we see the mercy of God. A refiner does not destroy. He purifies; he burns away everything that is not pure (Matthew 3:11-12; 1 Peter 4:12-13; 1 Corinthians 3:13). A fuller's soap is the soap that can clean even the worst stain. It is what makes clothes white again. God the Savior is pictured as a "smelter and purifier" who "purifies" and "refines" His people so that they can be right with Him again and "so that they may present to the Lord offerings in righteousness" (Malachi 3:3). God the Savior is also pictured as One who sits as He works on His people showing the patience and concern that God has for His people.

It is because God does not change that the "sons of Jacob" are not consumed (destroyed): "For I, the Lord, do not change; therefore you, O sons of Jacob, are not consumed" (Malachi 3:6). Where is the God of justice? God's justice is defined in terms of His faithfulness and loyalty to His promises. God does not change. He is faithful to His covenant and His "work" (Philippians 1:6). Thus, God's people are refined and purified instead of being consumed. Here we see a good definition of the pure justice of God: "I do not change." This is the ultimate in justice or "fairness." Thanks be to God!

APRIL 18

THE ROAD THAT A DISCIPLE WALKS . . .

"The things which you have heard from me in the presence of many witnesses,
entrust these to faithful men who will be able to teach others also."

2 Timothy 2:2

What is a disciple? He is a follower. What is a disciple of Jesus? She is a follower of Jesus. That discipleship is a process. You might say it is a road. So what does Discipleship Road look like? In perhaps the most general sense, there is the Christian life in which there is the initial establishing of the disciple and then the more defined establishing of that disciple. And so, Jesus declares, "make disciples . . ." (Matthew 28:19). The establishing then moves down the road to equipping laborers. The Christian life part of the highway then becomes the Christian ministry part of the highway. And so, Jesus says to His disciples, "The harvest is plentiful, but the workers are few. Therefore beseech the Lord of the harvest to send out workers into His harvest" (Matthew 9:37-38).

This threefold general description of the discipleship road (initial establishing, establishing, and equipping laborers) is most clearly expressed as: **d**iscovery, **d**evelopment, **d**eployment. The **d**iscovery stretch of the road is paved with statements like "come and see" (John 1:35-41; Acts 2:42-47; 1 Thessalonians 2:7-12) in which the focus is the Person of Jesus Christ. The **d**evelopment stretch of the road is paved with statements like "follow Me, and I will make you become fishers of men" (Mark 1:16-20; Luke 5:1-11) in which the focus is a Christ-centered life. The **d**eployment stretch of the road is paved with statements like "that they would be with Him and that He could send them out to preach" (Mark 3:13-19; Luke 6:12-17) in which the focus is a fruitful life. This threefold highway is most succinctly expressed in 2 Timothy 2:2: "The things which you have heard from me (**d**iscovery) in the presence of many witnesses, entrust these to faithful men (**d**evelopment) who will be able to teach others also (**d**eployment)."

Another way to describe the discipleship road is to picture the disciple as: rooted, built up, overflowing. The disciple who is being "rooted" especially focuses on the following contents: who is Jesus Christ, who we are in Christ, and who we are in His body. The disciple also develops assurances: salvation (1 John 5:11-12), answered prayer (John 16:24), victory (1 Corinthians 10:13), forgiveness (1 John 1:9), and guidance (Proverbs 3:5-6). He also begins establishing the following disciplines (Acts 2:42): study of the Word, partaking in fellowship, praise and worship, and prayer.

The disciple who is being "built up" focuses more on the type of contents that form the foundations of biblical doctrine and theology. He becomes even more consistent in the Acts 2:42 disciplines. He begins to realize an even deeper level of personal maturity in terms of obedience, devotion, character, pursuit of the will of God, love for others, and working in harmony with others.

Finally, the disciple who is "overflowing" begins to move into more of the ministry side of discipleship. Some of the aspects of this part of the road include: the use of gifts for ministry, the establishing of goals for ministry, the receiving of vision for ministry, the development of skills for ministry, a more defined calling to ministry, an enabling for ministry, and a clear contribution to the ministry of Jesus Christ. So, the disciple who is walking down Discipleship Road moves from functioning as a Christian to contributing as a Christian. The disciple moves from "come and see" to sending "them out to preach." They move from discovery to deployment . . . from being rooted to overflowing!

APRIL 19

WHEN LOOKING FOR SALVATION, AVOID MIRRORS!

"So Jesus said to them, 'Truly, truly, I say to you, unless you eat the flesh of the Son of Man and drink His blood, you have no life in yourselves.'"

John 6:53

Nothing is more important to you than your salvation. Salvation is so important that even some of the most incredible things (like the supernatural power of God in signs and wonders) pale in comparison. Your joy is not based on seeing the power of God manifested over evil spirits, but in seeing your name "recorded in heaven" (Luke 10:20). The church is built on salvation. It is built on the confession of salvation; that Jesus is the Savior (Matthew 16:18). Nothing is more important than salvation. Salvation is the forgiveness of sins (Luke 5:20; 7:50). Nothing is more important than the forgiveness of sins. Everybody wants to be forgiven . . . is looking for forgiveness/salvation. Tragically, it is often looked for in the wrong place.

When looking for salvation, avoid mirrors! No matter how hard you try—and people have all kinds of ways in which they try hard—you cannot save yourself. Apart from Jesus, "you have no life in yourselves" (John 6:53). There is nothing in the mirror that will save you, so stop looking there! There is no way to pay for your own forgiveness with your own money (Matthew 18:34). You cannot be good enough to earn your way into heaven. Only Jesus is good enough and, is therefore, the only way (John 14:6). Jesus proclaims this truth as He uses sarcasm to rebuke unbelievers who would think there is some kind of way other than to follow Him (Matthew 19:17-21). Salvation is impossible if we only depend on man and his free will. It is only possible through God, and thus finds its source in Him (Mark 10:27). He has to provide it. It is not anywhere in the mirror, so stop looking in there! It is not even in your family's mirror or in your culture's mirror. You cannot simply inherit it (Luke 3:8). "You have no life in yourself" so stop looking in the mirror. Where shall you look? From whence shall your help come? Look to the Lord (Psalm 121:1-2).

Mirrors are useless when it comes to salvation. The Humanist Manifesto is as wrong as it gets. It states, "No God will save you. You must save yourself." This is a lie from the pit of hell that goes all the way back to the Garden of Eden when the serpent said to Eve—while tempting her to eat the forbidden fruit—"You surely will not die! For God knows that in the day you eat from it your eyes will be opened, and you will be like God . . . " (Genesis 3:4-5). Evil says, "Go ahead . . . look in the mirror. There you see your salvation. You see your divinity." Jesus says, "Look to Me. I am the way. I am the life. You can only come to the Father's salvation through Me. In the mirror you only find death!"

So choose life (John 14:6). Break the mirrors (Galatians 2:21)!

———————

APRIL 20

THE CRISIS OF DEPENDENCE UPON GOD . . . IT'S ALL AND NOTHING!

"Apart from Me you can do nothing . . . in all your ways acknowledge Him."

John 15:5; Proverbs 3:6

Did Jesus really say, "I am the vine, you are the branches; he who abides in Me, and I in him, he bears much fruit; for apart from Me you can do nothing"? (John 15:5). He did not really mean nothing, did He? It must be the translation. Aren't there other versions of the Bible? Maybe the NSE (Not So Extreme version) which says, "apart from Me you cannot do *much*," or the NCO (New Chill Out version) which must say, "apart from Me you can do *almost* nothing." Did Jesus really say "nothing"?

If this statement is true, then every moment of your life is a crisis of dependence upon Jesus. This is, of course, truer than we care to admit even as we know that "If He should determine to do so, if He should gather to Himself His spirit and His breath, all flesh would perish together, and man would return to dust" (Job 34:14-15). Every moment of every day we are in a crisis of dependence upon God. Nevertheless, many people only come to God in times of an emergency (a perceived crisis) because that is when they feel the urgency of their helplessness. The reality of life is that every moment leaves us in reliance upon God and represents our complete helplessness without Him. In this sense, logically and reasonably, every moment is a crisis of dependence. Perhaps for this very reason, Paul says "I beseech you therefore, brethren, by the mercies of God, that you present your bodies a living sacrifice, holy, acceptable to God, which is your reasonable service" (Romans 12:1; NKJV). Every moment we must come to God because every moment we need God. When we begin to see every moment as a crisis, we begin to see the crisis of dependence in our relationship with God. Perhaps it is then that worship of God is no longer merely an event, but rather becomes a lifestyle! The more that you see yourself as helpless without God, the more you will seek God. To say "God, increase my relationship with You," is to say "God, increase my awareness of how helpless I am without You. Increase my awareness of my need for You!"

Once there was a king who had a son to whom he gave a yearly allowance. He paid him the entire allowance on the first day of each year. As the years passed, the king began to realize that the only day that he saw his son was on the first day of the year. So the king changed the payment schedule. He began to pay his son day by day. He paid him what was sufficient for the day. The king began to see his son every day! Inappropriately, some Christians have a sort of "deistic" view of God. They act as if God is far away and unconcerned about their daily lives. Perhaps, God is not involved at all or He is only involved in crisis situations. Perhaps, God is involved with us in "serious" things but not "commonplace" things. Perhaps, we should not bother God too often. However, God is like the king in the story. He is the God of John 15:5. He makes it so that we are in constant need of Him, so that we might remain in constant fellowship with Him. We may want more of a "microwave God" (give it all to us now), but we have more of a "crock pot God" (slow cooking always results in food that is better looking and tasting!). God's greatest goal for us is to transform us into Jesus' image (Romans 8:29) while His greatest desire of us is to know us, to spend time with us, and to be in relationship with us (Hosea 6:6). Amazingly, His greatest strategy is to achieve His greatest goal for us by manifesting His greatest desire of us; thus, "we shall all be changed" (1 Corinthians 15:51) "when He appears" (1 John 3:2).

Each and every moment, we are experiencing the crisis of dependence upon God because every moment we are in need of God. If you can do nothing without Him (John 15:5), then "in all your ways acknowledge Him" (Proverbs 3:6). The crisis of dependence upon God is an all *and* nothing dynamic. God really said "nothing," and so God really said "all"!

APRIL 21

WHAT? NO ACTUAL FELLOWSHIP?
. . . FALSE ADVERTISING!

"By this all men will know that you are My disciples, if you have love for one another."

John 13:35

Fellowship is crucial to the life of the church and it is essential in the witness of the church. The church is the body through which Jesus continues to work on the earth. Fellowship is not simply extra weight to carry on the body. Fellowship is like the ligaments and sinews which connect the different parts of the body together. If there are no ligaments, then the body cannot hold together (Ephesians 4:15-16). If there is no fellowship, then the church will fall apart. For the body to keep functioning, the parts need to stay connected. For the church to keep functioning as it should, the members must remain in unity. They must stay connected to each other. This is done though fellowship.

The exhaustive nature of the modern electronic social media craze that, ironically, only seems to exacerbate the epidemic of loneliness, provides a platform used to desperately try to escape an age of personal insignificance and damaging isolation. More than ever, the church needs to reestablish the primacy of fellowship as people more and more, whether they realize it or not, are starving for actual and authentic community. The church has a great opportunity. The world has left many people lonely and hungry for genuine fellowship. The church is the only entity that can truly fill these empty lives.

Fellowship is the ultimate goal of evangelism. The main focus is not on converting individuals. It is not even on discipling individuals. The effort of evangelism is to bring others into the family of God. It is to bring others into the body of Christ and into its fellowship. Jesus came to build His church (Matthew 16:18). He came to form a people (community) of God. And so, this must be the primary goal and motivation of biblical church growth. Fellowship is the basis of evangelism. We must have something to offer to people.

Our love for one another—"By this all men will know that you are My disciples, if you have love for one another" (John 13:35)—is the world's evidence that we are the children of God. The church's credibility—and therefore the credibility of the gospel message itself—depends on how well Christians can demonstrate love for one another. If the world cannot see us showing love to each another, then why would they believe our message about love? The nature of God is embedded in the Trinity and the essence of the Trinity is perfect relationship and fellowship. If the church wants to present a God of fellowship, then it must demonstrate that same spirit of fellowship.

A business that does not exist does not conduct advertising to promote itself; a nonexistent business never advertises. Evangelism without a corresponding community is like an advertisement without a corresponding business. The customer is attracted to the business because of the advertisement. However, when he arrives at the advertised location of the business, he finds that it does not exist. This is false advertising! Unfortunately, the same thing happens sometimes with Christianity. The new believer hears the evangelism and is attracted to the church. However, when he arrives, he can immediately see that the family of God that was part of the "advertising" (evangelism) is cold and uncaring. What? No actual fellowship? He could understandably shout, "False advertising!" Fellowship is crucial to the life of the church and it is essential in the witness of the church. So, **fellowship**!

APRIL 22

POWER LINE-UP: PURITY, FAITHFULNESS, AND INTEGRITY

"Blessed are the pure in heart, for they shall see God."

Matthew 5:8

Certain character traits are critical to have when playing in the game of life (life in the kingdom of God). They form a "power line-up" in the character batting order. Up first is purity/holiness. God is holy and pure. In order to see Him, you must be pure (Matthew 5:8). We might say impurity cannot see purity, and purity cannot see impurity (Habakkuk 1:13). And so, God is in the business of purifying us. The baptism Jesus gives seems to include an empowering of the individual to come to Jesus (Holy Spirit) as well as a judgment, disciplining, or refining (fire). The fire may point to the process of purifying the person (Luke 3:17). Holiness or purity must be real. You can change the outward appearance and still be polluted inside, but if you clean up the pollution inside, then it will also change the outward appearance (Matthew 23:25-26). Defiling yourself is the result of what is said, thought, and done (reality). It is not the result of what is eaten (superficiality). It has to do with what comes out of the heart. Purity/holiness (or the lack of it) is very real/profound. It comes from the heart (Matthew 15:11). Man is defiled or stained (made impure) by what comes out of his own heart (Mark 7:18-20). And so, purity/holiness is critical in the game of life (life in the kingdom of God).

Batting second is faithfulness/dedication. To be in the kingdom of God takes extreme dedication (Luke 9:62). Faithfulness in little things leads to faithfulness in bigger things. The implication is that as we prove ourselves to be faithful in the "little things," God will entrust us with authority and responsibility over "bigger" things (Luke 16:10). And so, faithfulness/dedication is critical in the game of life (life in the kingdom of God).

Batting third is integrity. The very action of repentance includes integrity towards others (Luke 3:10-13). It might be said that integrity is the greatest cure for hypocrisy. Those who practice and treasure integrity will avoid hypocrisy. Hypocrisy begins when you allow your "yes" to be something less than "yes" or your "no" to be something more than "no." Integrity is that aspect of your character that makes your "yes" and "no" have value (Matthew 5:37). And so, integrity is critical in the game of life (life in the kingdom of God).

Do you see these traits in your character batting order? Do you have this power line-up? The more you can insert these "players" into your daily line-up, the more likely you will be scoring runs and winning in the game of life . . . life in the kingdom of God.

———————

APRIL 23

SIN IS UGLY . . .

"Because lawlessness is increased, most people's love will grow cold."

Matthew 24:12

Love is beautiful (Song of Solomon 4:10). God is love (1 John 4:8). Sin is ugly (Psalm 39:11). Sin is lawlessness (1 John 3:4). And so, it is no surprise that when lawlessness (sin) increases, "most people's love will grow cold" (Matthew 24:12). Sin paints an ugly picture.

Some moments in history are uglier than others. Some might point to the ruthlessness of Robespierre and his "Reign of Terror," others to the brutality of Stalin and his "Purges," others to the callousness of Hitler and his "Final Solution," and still others to the cold-bloodedness of Osama Bin Laden and his "9/11 Attacks." Perhaps, the ugliest picture in all of history, however, came between noon (the sixth hour) and three p.m. (the ninth hour) on Good Friday; God gives "beauty instead of ashes" (Isaiah 61:3) . . . He turns the ugly into the beautiful . . . the "Bad Friday" into the "Good Friday." In Mark 15:33-34 we see utter ugliness: "When the sixth hour came, darkness fell over the whole land until the ninth hour. At the ninth hour Jesus cried out with a loud voice, "Eloi, Eloi, lama sabachthani?" which is translated, "My God, My God, why have You forsaken Me?"

There can be nothing uglier than God forsaking Himself. Yet, this is the ultimate reality of the result of sin. Sin is ugly! What killed Jesus; the nails, the spear, the thorns, the beatings?

Actually, our sins killed Jesus. The cross of Jesus was made from our sins that He had to carry upon Himself. Thus, as He paid the wages (Romans 6:23) of sin (that is, death/separation), He felt the separation from the Father. This was the ugliest picture in all of history. God was separated from Himself as "He made Him who knew no sin *to be* sin on our behalf, so that we might become the righteousness of God in Him (2 Corinthians 5:21). In the paradoxical way that is the way of the gospel, utter ugliness (God becomes sin) becomes utter beauty (we become righteous)!

Sin is ugly. Sin results in ugly things; things that are not beautiful as God intended them to be. Sin can result in the ugliness of physical sickness (John 5:14). Moreover, sin results in the ugliness of spiritual sickness. Spiritual sickness is the inability to see and hear God (Matthew 5:8; 13:13). Ultimate spiritual sickness—and the ultimate picture of ugliness—is hell, a place of "eternal destruction, away from the presence of the Lord and from the glory of His power . . . " (2 Thessalonians 1:9). It is a place where there is the absence of God and, thus, the absence of love (Matthew 24:12). Love is beautiful. Sin is ugly! Choose your picture.

APRIL 24

ASPECTS OF GOD'S PLAN OF REDEMPTION IN GENESIS . . .

"Now the Lord said to Abram, 'Go forth from your country, And from your relatives And from your father's house, To the land which I will show you; And I will make you a great nation, And I will bless you, And make your name great; And so you shall be a blessing; And I will bless those who bless you, And the one who curses you I will curse. And in you all the families of the earth will be blessed.'"

Genesis 12:1-3

Perhaps, the earliest point in Scripture in which we see the two part nature of God's plan of redemption is in God's covenant He made with Abraham. This Abrahamic covenant included both Abraham being blessed *and* Abraham being a blessing to others; Abraham knowing God *and* Abraham making God known. It included both Abraham enjoying privileges *and* Abraham taking responsibility; Abraham receiving promises *and* Abraham shouldering obligations. God will make Abraham "a great nation" *and* in Abraham "all the families of the earth will be blessed" (Genesis 12:2-3). The plan of redemption included God's promises to Israel so that they can bless the nations. God loved Israel. As Scripture progresses, God consistently repeated His promise to give Abraham (Israel) land and descendants (a multitude of nations). God also loved the nations. Abraham interceded for Sodom (Genesis 18:22-33). God showed great interest and compassion for

Ishmael (Genesis 21:19-21). Jacob's staircase dream seemed to be related to the evangelism of others (Genesis 28:10-14). God blessed Egypt through Joseph (Genesis 50:20).

The plan of redemption includes God's sovereign choosing and activity. God did not choose Israel based on some predictable characteristic or typical attribute from which someone might cast favor on someone else. No, God choose Israel in His sovereignty which was consistent with His two part plan of redemption: "The Lord did not set His love on you nor choose you because you were more in number than any of the peoples, for you were the fewest of all peoples, but because the Lord loved you and kept the oath [*the missiological Abrahamic covenant*] which He swore to your forefathers" (Deuteronomy 7:7-8). In His sovereign choosing, God chose Israel to be loved by Him *and* He chose Israel to be the missionary nation through whom He would shine His love on the nations.

God's sovereign choosing is seen in the preference of the second born over the first born. Seth over Cain. Shem over Japheth. Isaac over Ishmael. Jacob over Esau. Judah and Joseph over the other brothers. Ephraim over Manasseh. In addition, God's sovereign activity is seen in the repetition of the number seven (symbolic for perfection for ancient Hebrews). Seven words in Genesis 1:1 (in the original Hebrew). Seven times two (fourteen) words in Genesis 1:2 (in the original Hebrew). Seven days of creation (Genesis 1:3-31). Seven years of abundance (Genesis 41:34). Seven years of famine (Genesis 41:54). Seventy descendants of Noah's sons (Genesis 10:32). Seventy descendants of Jacob (Genesis 46:27). Lamech lived to be seven hundred and seventy-seven years old (Genesis 5:31)—and many more examples of the number seven in Scripture.

And so, God's plan of redemption is seen throughout the Bible, and perhaps, most profoundly in the New Testament. Nonetheless, in order to read about His Story (History) one does not need to wait until the reading of Matthew or Romans. God's story of redemption can be read about in the book of beginnings . . . the book of Genesis!

———————

APRIL 25

WHO IS THE GREATEST? . . .

"Not that I have already obtained it *or have already become perfect, but I press on*
so that I may lay hold of that for which also I was laid hold of by Christ Jesus."

Philippians 3:12

Greatness is a relative concept. We tend to make it relative to others. We live in the bondage of competition. There are always those who are better than us in certain things. We can easily become discouraged. Then we are not able to say: "But I press on" (Philippians 3:12).

We also can live in the bondage of pride. There are always those who are worse than us in certain things. We can easily become arrogant. We are not able to say: "Not that I have obtained it yet" (Philippians 3:12).

In performing the foot washing in John 13, Jesus forevermore makes greatness relative to Himself. In so doing, He releases us from the bondage of competition. We cannot compete with Jesus! So, there is no reason to be discouraged. Instead, we are free! We are able to say: "But I press on" (Philippians 3:12).

We live with a great sense of challenge. We cannot be better than Jesus! We are not arrogant, we are humble! We can say: "Not that I have obtained it yet" (Philippians 3:12).

The disciples maintained a carnal sense of greatness (leadership). They defined greatness in terms of authority and made it relative to each other. Jesus turned the tables. He defined it in terms of service and responsibility and made it relative to Himself. Judson Cornwall said, "God is not interested in our greatness. He is only interested in our utility. The greatest is the servant. But even then the servant does not become great, he just makes greatness available."[2]

Who is the greatest? Jesus! (John 13:13). How is He the greatest? How does He lead? He leads via service in humility by example (John 13:14-15a). How can we become great? How can we lead? By imitating Jesus (John 13:15b). How can we imitate Jesus? The slave is not greater than his master (John 13:16). Notice how this concept is explained in John 13:20. It is explained in terms of Jesus in us. This is consistent with the biblical understanding of the imitation of Christ. We cannot reduplicate what Jesus has done. In this sense we cannot imitate Jesus. Biblical imitation has to do with allowing Christ to live in us. Thus, the only biblical way to imitate Jesus, the only biblical way to lead others, and the only biblical way to be great is to allow the One who is great to live in you: "I have been crucified with Christ; and it is no longer I who live, but Christ lives in me; and the life which I now live in the flesh I live by faith in the Son of God, who loved me and gave Himself up for me" (Galatians 2:20).

As death to self increases, potential greatness increases, because potential to allow in the only One who is great increases (Mark 10:18). The difference between potential and actual greatness is the difference between the dedicated eastern mystic and a dedicated Christian. As death to self and living for Jesus increases, actual greatness increases, because the actuality of allowing in the only One who is great increases. The dedicated eastern mystic dies to self in order to find self. The dedicated Christian dies to self in order to find and live for Jesus.

APRIL 26

GOD'S WILL, IF YOU WILL . . .

"If anyone is willing to do His will . . . "

John 7:17

If God is perfect—and, of course, He is (Matthew 5:48)—then the only logical "will" to desire is the will of God. The Holy Spirit can help us find that will (John 16:13). We find direction through God's Word (Psalm 119:105) and through others who can offer us biblical counsel (Proverbs 15:22). Perhaps, the initial key to knowing God's will is to believe God has His own will for you and will guide you into that will: "For I know the plans that I have for you, declares the Lord, plans for welfare and not for calamity to give you a future and a hope" (Jeremiah 29:11). To know "the Word's will" you need to know the Word. Know the Bible and you will know God's will: "If you continue in My word, then you are truly disciples of Mine; and you will know the truth, and the truth will make you free" (John 8:31-32). Sometimes it's helpful to request counsel from others: "For where two or three have gathered together in My name, I am there in their midst" (Matthew 18:20). Of course, it's not just what to include but also what to exclude. To know God's will you have to get rid of sin, so it does not blind you to His will (Romans 1:24-32). Finally, to know God's will and follow it you must be willing to surrender to His will (John 7:17). To say, "God let me know your will" is to say "God, I surrender to you."

Seeking the will of God assumes seeking the Lordship of Christ. Jesus must be more important than anything else: "He is also head of the body, the church; and He is the beginning, the firstborn from the dead, so that He Himself will come to have first place in everything" (Colossians 1:18). The road to God's will is the road to radical commitment to Him: "Therefore I urge you, brethren, by the mercies of God, to present your bodies a living and holy sacrifice, acceptable to God, which is your spiritual service of worship. And do not be conformed to this world, but be transformed by the renewing of your mind, so that you may prove what the will of God is, that which is good, acceptable and perfect" (Romans 12:1-2). To say, "God let me know your will" is to say "God, you are my boss . . . my Lord."

The result of all this is obedience. Desiring God's will and making Him Lord of your life does not really make any sense at all without obedience: "Why do you call Me, 'Lord, Lord,' and do not do what I say?" (Luke 6:46). Love is proved by obedience (John 14:21). Strength comes from obedience (Job 17:9). Obedience is even better than sacrifice (1 Samuel 15:22). Obedience pleases God and results in fruitfulness (John 15:10-14). Incentive for obedience (John 14:23) is not only the realization that disobedience is sin (James 4:17) but, more importantly, the realization that God desires our obedience (Psalm 119:59-60). To say, "God let me know your will" is to say "God, I will obey you."

And so, the saying, "God's will, if you will" is not only a proper English way to request God's will, but it is also a realization that your will has a lot to do with experiencing God's will.

APRIL 27

WHY GOLD, FRANKINCENSE, AND MYRRH FOR A BABY?

" . . . they fell to the ground and worshiped Him. Then, opening their treasures, they presented to Him gifts of gold, frankincense, and myrrh."

Matthew 2:11

Not every leader leads in the same way. Leaders have their own style and their own area of emphasis. Different leaders possess different gifts and have different personalities. We might say, at least in general, that there are three different types of leadership. There is kingly leadership, prophetic leadership, and priestly leadership. These three "types of leadership" are based on the three different offices of Christ; King, Prophet, and Priest.

The different types of leaders are different! That is not to say that their distinctions are absolute or that there is no crossover in the actions of their leadership. They are, in no way, mutually exclusive from each other. Nevertheless, the different types of leadership have their emphases or styles that do stand out from the other types. The king tends to *d*elegate the *a*uthority of the church, whereas the prophet tends to *d*irect the *a*ctivities of the church. The priest, it might be said, tends to *d*istribute the *a*bsolution (grace) of the church.

These three types of leadership are seen throughout the Scripture as they are based on the three offices of Christ. Jesus is King: " . . . took the branches of the palm trees and went out to meet

Him, and began to shout, 'Hosanna! BLESSED IS HE WHO COMES IN THE NAME OF THE LORD, even the King of Israel'" (John 12:13). Jesus as Prophet is seen in Acts 3:22: "Moses said, 'THE LORD GOD WILL RAISE UP FOR YOU A PROPHET LIKE ME FROM YOUR BRETHREN; TO HIM YOU SHALL GIVE HEED to everything He says to you'" (Acts 3:22). Jesus is also seen as Priest: "YOU ARE A PRIEST FOREVER ACCORDING TO THE ORDER OF MELCHIZEDEK" (Hebrews 5:6).

There are three types of leadership because there are three offices of Christ: "The crowds going ahead of Him, and those who followed, were shouting, "Hosanna to the Son of David . . . [king] . . . And the crowds were saying, This is the prophet Jesus, from Nazareth in Galilee . . . [prophet] . . . And Jesus entered the temple; And He said to them, It is written, 'MY HOUSE SHALL BE CALLED A HOUSE OF PRAYER" [priest] (Matthew 21:9-13). Another way, perhaps, that we see the three offices is in the gifts that were brought by the magi to the baby Jesus: " . . . they presented to Him gifts of gold, frankincense, and myrrh" (Matthew 2:11). Why these three gifts? Why not diapers, a pacifier, and a crib? These gifts were not meant to be practical. They were meant to be symbolic. Of course, gold was the appropriate gift for a **king**. Myrrh was used in the burial process of which Jesus the **prophet** would later prophesy concerning His own death. And, frankincense was used by the **priest** in the temple.

Christ holds all three of these offices. He is the perfect leader. The leadership of a man will usually emphasize one of these offices. There are leaders who focus on power and influence (the Kingly office). There are other leaders who focus on vision and direction (the Prophetic office). Other leaders focus on the practical lives of the people and the grace of God which is available to those people (the Priestly office). Not exclusively, but as tendencies, "kingly leaders" emphasize authority and might be said to be system or power-oriented leaders. "Prophetic leaders" emphasize tasks and might be said to be task oriented leaders. "Priestly leaders" emphasize relationships and might be said to be people-oriented leaders. These three types of leadership are different and are needed in the church. Different is good!

———

APRIL 28

BE A MISSIONARY BY BEING A GOOD EXAMPLE!

"'I have loved you,' says the LORD . . . Your eyes will see this and you
will say, 'The LORD be magnified beyond the border of Israel!' . . . 'And if I am a

master, where is my respect?' says the Lord *of hosts to you,*

'O priests who despise My name . . . '"

Malachi 1:2, 5-6

Why did God choose you? First, He chose you because of His unconditional and unmerited love for you ("'I have loved you,' says the Lord of hosts . . . " Malachi 1:2). Second, He chose you so that He could use you to include others ("And your eyes will see this and you will say, 'The Lord be magnified beyond the border of Israel!' . . . " Malachi 1:5). He chose Israel (and then the church) because He loved them, and He wanted to hold to the Abrahamic covenant in which Israel would be blessed so that she could be a blessing to others (Genesis 12:1-3). Similarly, God speaks to Israel again saying, "The Lord did not set His love on you nor choose you because you were more in number than any of the peoples, for you were the fewest of all peoples, but because the Lord loved you and kept the oath which He swore to your forefathers" (Deuteronomy 7:7-8). Our response to God choosing us should be that of gratitude and thankfulness. This gratitude should motivate us to go beyond ourselves and to the person (nation) beyond ourselves (our own borders). Paul writes to the church, "For all things are for your sakes, so that the grace which is spreading to more and more people may cause the giving of thanks to abound to the glory of God" (2 Corinthians 4:15).

So, Israel (God's missionary nation), "will say, 'The Lord be magnified beyond the border of Israel!'" if they are in a proper relationship with God (Malachi 1:5). However, the priests (Israel's representatives) being addressed in the book of Malachi are ignoring God. The problem is not that the priests are unwilling to *say* that God is their "father" and "master" (a priest would proclaim these things as part of his job when he recited the creeds in the temple). The problem was not in their words but in their behavior. Their words and their actions were two different things. They were not atheists, but backsliders. Thus, we see that the ignoring of God is not being done on the level of pure rebellion. It is being done on the level of pure hypocrisy. In any case, THE LORD OF HOSTS the Lord of the nations—is not being magnified "beyond the border of Israel." Israel, God's chosen missionary people, is not being a good example to the nations, and thus, the Lord is not being "magnified beyond the border of Israel!" (Malachi 1:5). A bad example results in bad missionary work! It results in God's purposes not being realized.

Sometimes, being a good missionary revolves around being a good example. How could Israel have been a good example to the nations? By ascribing to God His proper worth and not undervaluing Him. Another way to say this is: by showing God honor and not despising Him. In Malachi 1:6 we read, "A son honors his father, and a servant his master. 'Then if I am a father, where is My honor? And if I am a master, where is My respect?' says the Lord of hosts to you, 'O priests who despise My name.'" It is the "Lord of hosts" or "Lord of the nations" who should receive honor.

Then the name of the Lord of the nations would be magnified not just in Israel but beyond the border of Israel. To "despise" is to give little worth to something and to undervalue it. The priests were undervaluing God. They were not giving Him His proper value or worth (they were not engaging in proper *worthship* of God). If the God of the nations does not receive honor from His own children, then how will the nations learn to give Him honor? If God's missionary people do not provide a good example, then their effectiveness in magnifying God's name beyond the border of Israel will be severely diminished.

APRIL 29

A MULTIPLICITY OF BIBLICAL FORMS OF WORSHIP . . .

"Meanwhile, David and all the house of Israel were celebrating before the Lord with all kinds of instruments made of fir wood, and with lyres, harps, tambourines, castanets and cymbals."

2 Samuel 6:5

Form follows function . . . form follows substance. Forms or styles of worship must be an expression of, or response to, the nature or substance of God. That which is external must not exist apart from that which is internal. The opposite of this is religiosity or hypocrisy (empty forms; forms without substance). Form but no substance is mere appearance. And so, we might "dance before the Lord" (a form of worship), but only if it is an expression of, or response to the majesty of the Lord (substance of worship). If we are dancing before the Lord void of an expression of, or response to Him, then we might look like we are worshiping but we might just be engaging in some sort of ritual or the mechanics of worship. Having established the point that forms without substance are worthless, it must also be said that forms that do follow substance are important and valid. There exists a multiplicity of biblical forms of worship.

Standing can be a form of worship (1 Kings 8:22; Romans 5:2) as it may be out of respect that we stand and show that we are attentive to the Lord. Kneeling could be a form of worship as it might reflect reverence and submission to God. Bowing down is a biblical form of worship (Isaiah 45:23; Romans 14:11) that might be an expression of honor. Dancing can be a form of worship (Exodus 15:20) as it responds to God's deliverance, or victory, or majesty. It could even be said that laughing is a biblical form of worship (Psalm 126:2) as it becomes an expression of the joy of God.

Shouting (1 Samuel 4:5), loud noise (2 Chronicles 20:19), and solemn sound and procession (Ezekiel 46:9) could be forms of worship. The use of banners in worship might be an expression of

God's victory (Isaiah 31:9). Singing is, of course, a biblical form of worship (in the Bible there are over 120 references to the use of singing in worship). The use of a variety of instruments can be seen as a form of worship in Scripture (Psalm 150:3-6). Tambourines, stringed instruments, pipes, cymbals, horns, trumpets, harps are all seen in Scripture being used in the context of worship; a complete symphony is used as "David and all the house of Israel were celebrating before the Lord with all kinds of instruments made of fir wood, and with lyres, harps, tambourines, castanets and cymbals" (2 Samuel 6:5)! The lifting of hands (Psalm 44:20; Psalm 143:6; 1 Timothy 2:8) is a biblical form of worship as it might serve as an expression of prayer, penitence, and thirsting for God). Clapping of hands is also a biblical form of worship and can be an expression of, among other things, rejoicing (Isaiah 55:12), triumph (Psalm 47:1), and making a pledge (Proverbs 11:21).

Forms without substance are worthless, even dangerous. However, forms that do follow substance are important and valid. There exists a multiplicity of biblical forms of worship. The point is not so much which forms of worship we use, but that we do use them; that we do worship!

APRIL 30

IS BEING "CHOSEN" AN EXCLUSIVE IDEA NECESSARILY?

"'I have loved you,' says the Lord. But you say, 'How have You loved us?' 'Was not Esau Jacob's brother?' declares the Lord. 'Yet I have loved Jacob; but I have hated Esau . . .'"

Malachi 1:2-3

The Lord says to Israel, "I have loved you" and they, then, question that love saying, "How have You loved us?" (Malachi 1:2). God responds to their doubts by putting forth a contrast. The contrast is between Jacob (whom He loves) and Esau (whom He hates). How could this be? Not only was Esau the brother of Jacob, but he was his twin brother who was older. The troublesome aspect of this discussion is that we cannot deny that God uses a *relative* argument to prove His love for Israel; His "love" for Israel is demonstrated by His lack of love for Esau. There are no conditions or criteria for how God chooses. We simply read: "I have loved Jacob . . . I have hated Esau" (Malachi 1:3). Surely, God cannot actually mean that He emotionally hated Esau. After all, the Scripture is very clear that God loves all people: "For God so loved the world . . . " (John 3:16).

Does God love (choose) Jacob at the expense of Esau? The ideas of "loving" and "choosing" are associated with each other:

For you are a holy people to the Lord your God; the Lord your God has chosen you to be a people for His own possession out of all the peoples who are on the face of the earth. The Lord did not set His love on you nor choose you because you were more in number than any of the peoples, for you were the fewest of all peoples, but because the Lord loved you and kept the oath which He swore to your forefathers . . . (Deuteronomy 7:6-8).

Here we see that "set His love on you" and "choose you" are interchangeable. God did not choose (love) Israel because of anything they did or were that was greater than what others had done or were. He simply chose them for *two* reasons: 1) because He loved them; *and* 2) because He wanted to keep His covenant with Abraham.

And so, in order to more fully understand the biblical idea of "chosen" we must consider the contents of the Abrahamic covenant: "I will make you a great nation, and I will bless you, and make your name great; And so you shall be a blessing; and I will bless those who bless you, and the one who curses you I will curse. And in you all the families of the earth will be blessed" (Genesis 12:2-3). Note how there are two parts to the covenant. One part focuses on how God will bless Abraham. The other part focuses on how Abraham will be a blessing to the nations. Abraham was not chosen at the expense of the nations. God did not choose Abraham in order to exclude the nations. Quite the contrary . . . He chose Abraham in order to include the nations. When God says that He loved (chose) Jacob, it does not mean that He rejected Esau. It means that He did not choose Esau. However, Esau does not have to be excluded. He can be included according to the very reason (missiological) God chose Israel. Thus, Esau can be rejected in the very same way that he can be accepted. God "will bless those who bless you" (Esau would be accepted) or God "will curse those who curse you" (Esau would be rejected). God's choosing is not exclusive; rather, it is inclusive.

The Abrahamic covenant is a missionary covenant. God chooses Israel as a missionary nation to be a conduit (John 20:23) through whom others can be chosen. And so, the concept of being chosen is not an exclusive one; it is, rather an inclusive one. We who are "chosen" need to put as much (if not more) emphasis on the responsibility of being chosen (being a blessing) as on the privilege of being chosen (being blessed). This is God's *worldwide* missionary plan (since "God so loved the world"). And so, He said to Abraham the missionary, "Go forth from your country" (Genesis 12:1), and to His disciples the missionaries, "Go therefore and make disciples of all the nations" (Matthew 28:19). He says to you His missionary, "Go" so you who are chosen can include others . . . *not* exclude them!

NOTES

May

SECRETS TO GOOD LEADERSHIP . . .

"So when He had washed their feet, and taken His garments and reclined at the table again, *He said to them, "Do you know what I have done to you? "You call Me Teacher and Lord; and you are right, for so I am. "If I then, the Lord and the Teacher, washed your feet, you also ought to wash one another's feet. "For I gave you an example that you also should do as I did to you. "Truly, truly, I say to you, a slave is not greater than his master, nor is one who is sent greater than the one who sent him. "If you know these things, you are blessed if you do them. "I do not speak of all of you. I know the ones I have chosen; but* it is *that the Scripture may be fulfilled, 'HE WHO EATS MY BREAD HAS LIFTED UP HIS HEEL AGAINST ME.' "From now on I am telling you before* it *comes to pass, so that when it does occur, you may believe that I am* He. *"Truly, truly, I say to you, he who receives whomever I send receives Me; and he who receives Me receives Him who sent Me."*

John 13:12-20

What do good leaders do? Good leaders stay informed about developments in their own field (read books, magazines, talk to other leaders). Good leaders make it a habit to always hear both sides of a problem. They do not act on the information of only one person. Furthermore, good leaders never betray a confidence. If someone asks you to keep something confidential and you agree then you must keep it confidential. If your people cannot trust you then your ministry will be ineffective.

Learn how to be a good loser. Sometimes this includes trying to negotiate differences between people; that is, be a peacemaker (Matthew 5:9). Be careful to control your temper. Do not think too seriously about yourself, or you will become puffed up (like a balloon, some people will love to pop you). Be able to laugh at yourself.

Do not try to run away from your troubles (failures, objections, complaints, criticisms). Remember: problems do not disappear . . . problems are solved. Do not allow your own personal gain to determine your decisions.

Show equal respect to those who are under your authority as to those who are over you in authority. Accept responsibility for failure as well as for success. Search for and create opportunities for growth in those whom you lead.

So based on our look at Jesus in John 13, how do we lead? We lead through service in humility by example. We are motivated by love and security in God, and our leadership must be symbolic of the cross. According to the Christ-like example, the leader (or the greatest) is the servant. Greatness is measured by service and humility. Greatness is relative to Jesus. It is not relative to others. Jesus is the greatest. If we want to be great, we must allow Him to be great through us. If we want to lead, we must allow Him to lead through us. Finally, remember Jesus' conclusion with respect to these things: "If you know these things you are blessed if you do them" (John 13:17).

MAY 2

WHAT FOLLOWS REVIVAL?

"Will You not Yourself revive us again,
That Your people may rejoice in You?"

Psalm 85:6

What is revival? Revival is defined in the dictionary as "to live again," or "to restore to consciousness or life something that is not wholly or permanently lifeless." It is when ordinary spiritual conditions are intensified and become extraordinary. In revival, God pours out the Holy Spirit and phenomenal results follow. What are some of these results? First, and foremost, is the extraordinary growth of the church via extraordinary conversions of people to the Christian faith: "And all the more believers in the Lord, multitudes of men and women, were constantly added to their number . . ." (Acts 5:14). In the eighteenth century, American revivals led by preachers such as Jonathan Edwards and George Whitfield, it was estimated that at one point in New England some 40,000 souls were converted in less than three years. With this comes a new multitude who give thanks to Him, praise and worship Him, and rejoice in Him: "Will You not Yourself revive us again, that Your people may rejoice in You?" (Psalm 85:6). Many times, what also comes with the growth of the church is the restructuring or reforming of the church—as in one of the greatest revivals ever, the Reformation of the early sixteenth century—"Those from among you will rebuild the ancient ruins; you will raise up the age-old foundations; and you will be called the repairer of the breach, the restorer of the streets in which to dwell" (Isaiah 58:12).

Even as obedience leads to revival, it also is what follows revival. In a sense, Joseph was revived. The result is that Joseph obeyed God: "And Joseph awoke from his sleep and did as the angel of the Lord commanded him, and took Mary as his wife . . ." (Matthew 1:24). Another work of God that is often seen to follow revival is the liberating of people from addictions and bondage. People are set free. The "wrappings of death" are removed: "The man who had died came forth, bound hand and foot with wrappings, and his face was wrapped around with a cloth. Jesus said to them, 'Unbind him, and let him go'" (John 11:44). It is important to note here that Jesus uses His people in what follows revival. Just as He said to His people, "Remove the stone" (John 11:39), He also said to them, "Unbind him, and let him go." There is much work to be done after a revival (especially concerning the need for biblical teaching), and Jesus uses His church (His people) to ensure that the positive impact of the revival is secured.

This is very important. The revival needs to be fed (Mark 5:43). Revival results in an extraordinary hunger for spiritual things. If that hunger is not filled, there is the risk that those hungry people may accept tainted spiritual food. The spiritual high needs to be guided and steered toward truth, otherwise the spiritual high may consume false teaching. Do you remember the "revival" in Luke 9:32? "Now Peter and his companions had been overcome with sleep; but when they were fully awake, they saw His glory and the two men standing with Him."

Peter, John, and James were revived and saw the glory of Jesus at His transfiguration. How beautiful and marvelous! However, read the next verse. In the excitement and spiritual high of the moment "Peter . . . not realizing what he was saying" tried to worship Moses and Elijah. These heretical actions came as a result of a revival. The testimony of church history has sometimes been the same. Sometimes cults are formed immediately after great revivals. The Mormon church began in America immediately after the great revivals of the early 1800s. The heretical Kimbanguist movement began in the Congo in the early 1920s after a revival movement there. Man is overwhelmed with the glory of God. With this spiritual intoxication comes a fascination with other spiritual entities besides Jesus. This is what happened to Peter at the transfiguration. To avoid this, biblical teaching must be offered to "fill up the spiritually hungry." The revival must be fed (Luke 9:35)!

MAY 3

AND THE ANSWER IS . . . HAVE FAITH IN GOD!

"And Jesus answered saying to them, 'Have faith in God.'"

Mark 11:22

The question: "What shall we do, that we may work the works of God?"

The answer: Have faith in God (John 6:29).

That is a great answer . . . "And Jesus answered saying to them, 'Have faith in God'" (Mark 11:22).

That is a great answer because faith is powerful. Faith has no limits for him whose faith believes before seeing the results (Mark 11:24). Faith is the conviction of things not yet seen (see Hebrews 11:1). Faith can move mountains. And so, we come to our next logical question (as did Jesus' disciples in Luke 17:5): How do we get more of that powerful thing . . . more faith? Paradoxically, we increase our faith by having "mustard seed faith." When Jesus' apostles asked Him to increase their faith, He answered by saying they needed to have "faith like a mustard seed" (Luke 17:6). He then told them a story that describes the nature of this "mustard seed faith":

> Which of you, having a slave plowing or tending sheep, will say to him when he has come in from the field, 'Come immediately and sit down to eat'? But will he not say to him, 'Prepare something for me to eat, and *properly* clothe yourself and serve me while I eat and drink; and afterward you may eat and drink'? He does not thank the slave because he did the things which were commanded, does he? So you too, when you do all the things which are commanded you, say, 'We are unworthy slaves; we have done *only* that which we ought to have done' (Luke 17:7-10).

If you want to have more faith in God ("Increase our faith") you will have to have less faith in yourself ("We are unworthy slaves"). You will have to decrease, so that God will increase (John 3:30). In order to increase your faith, you will have to decrease your view of yourself. That "mustard seed faith" is a faith that enables you to see yourself as a mustard seed; to see yourself as the smallest or the least. When you see yourself in this way, you will tend not to rely on yourself and you will, instead, be more inclined to rely on God; to look to the largest or the greatest. Another way of saying this is that the person with the most faith is the person who looks to God the most.

Who is the greatest? God is the greatest. Great faith, then, is associated with seeing Jesus as the greatest . . . as God (John 8:19-24). Faith is proven when you act on your belief that Jesus is God (Luke 7:6-9). Faith is linked to being focused on Jesus (seeing Him only). Doubt is linked to looking away from Jesus and focusing on your circumstances or other things around you (Matthew 14:26-31). And so, prayer and fasting can produce or release greater faith (Matthew 17:20-21). Prayer and fasting tend to help us along the way to viewing ourselves as mustard seeds and, then, our faith is increased. God is increased as we are decreased. This is the essence of increased faith, the increase of God Himself. How do we increase our faith? The answer is, "Have faith in God!"

———

MAY 4

THE IMPORTANCE OF KNOWING GOD . . .

*"So let us know, let us press on to know the L*ORD*. His going forth is as certain as the dawn; And*
He will come to us like the rain, Like the spring rain watering the earth . . . For I delight in loyalty
rather than sacrifice, And in the knowledge of God rather than burnt offerings."

Hosea 6:3, 6

A recently married man wanted so much to please his new wife. He worked two jobs so that he could buy her the best home, the nicest clothes, and anything else that she might want. He did not have much time to spend with her, but he thought that there would be more time in the future once they were financially stable. After a few years, his wife left him. She did not leave him for more money or for more material things. She left him for a man who would spend time with her. We, also, are often so busy in the things that we are doing for God that we fail to spend time with Him. Yet our cry should be "let us know, let us press on to know the Lord" because God "delights in loyalty rather than sacrifice, and in the knowledge of God rather than burnt offerings" (Hosea 6:3, 6). The heart of God beats with the desire to spend time with us. His greatest desire is to have an intimate and constant relationship with us.

God is not so interested in us doing something for Him, as He is in Him doing something through us. For Him to do something through us, we must be in relationship with Him: "it is no longer I who live, but Christ lives in me; and the life which I now live in the flesh I live by faith in the Son of God" (Galatians 2:20). It is interesting to note that Christ's disciples never asked their Master how to preach, or what were the five steps to church growth; they did, however, ask Him how to pray! (Luke 11:1). Martin Luther, the great sixteenth century German theologian and re-former, understood the importance of his relationship with God relative to his ministry for God. The more Martin Luther had to do in a day, the longer he prayed in the morning. He would say, "I have so much to do that I must spend the first three hours of each day in prayer."

Physical food is necessary for physical health. Spiritual food is necessary for spiritual health. Would you cook a meal for yourself even if it seemed like you did not have time to or if you simply did not feel like cooking? Most people would answer by saying, "no matter if you feel like cooking or not, food is still necessary!" Would you spend time with God even if you did not feel like it? Our answer should be the same.

Job declared, "I have treasured the words of His mouth more than my necessary food" (Job 23:12). For the follower of Christ, seeking God should be like breathing. Just as breathing is the response of physical life to the presence of air, so prayer should be the response of spiritual life to the presence of God. So "let us know, let us press on to know the Lord" (Hosea 6:3).

MAY 5

MEN AND WOMEN ARE EQUAL BUT NOT THE SAME (DIVINELY ORDAINED AUTHORITY STRUCTURE . . .

"But I want you to understand that Christ is the head of every man,
and the man is the head of a woman, and God is the head of Christ."

1 Corinthians 11:3

There is a divine order within the family unit in which the wife is subject to the husband (Ephesians 5:22) as the children are subject to the parents (Ephesians 6:1-2). There exist divinely ordained authority structures. This is not to say that certain family members are superior or inferior to others. No, they are equals in their nature as human beings. Nevertheless, they are not the same. They are equal in their identity within the family and, at the same time, different in how they function in that family. Divinely ordained authority structures are indicative of functions or roles. In the order of the Trinity the Father has a precedence relative to the Son and the Spirit although all three are equally God. One is not superior or inferior to the other (they are equal), yet they are distinct (not the same); they are equal in identity or nature, and different in function or role. As it is in the human family, the divine family (the Trinity) exists in a divinely ordained authority structure: "But I want you to understand that Christ is the head of every man, and the man is the head of a woman, and God is the head of Christ" (1 Corinthians 11:3). The husband, wife, and children are equal in identity while remaining different in function, role, and relational order. The Father, Son, and Holy Spirit are equal in identity while remaining different in function, role, and relational order. And so, God the Father sends and begets God the Son (John 3:16; Acts 13:33), God the Son sends God the Spirit from God the Father (John 15:26), and God the Son glorifies God the Father (John 17:1) while God the Spirit glorifies God the Son (John 16:14). The Trinity is the ultimate "divinely ordained authority structure."

So, what is meant, then, by "divinely ordained authority structure" with respect to the human family? First, it should be understood that it is not a reference to what men and women are worth. It does refer to the position that each takes according to God's established order. It does not imply inferiority and superiority because it is an order of function, not an order of identity, dignity, or value. Marriage roles exist in reference to a hierarchy of function and order because they represent a hierarchy of responsibility and authority that was established at creation.

And so, Paul says that "the husband is the head of the wife"—the husband takes the lead/ initiative and goes ahead of the wife—he does not say that the husband is "over" or superior to the wife (Ephesians 5:23). The husband is "the head" in his functional and relational position; he goes ahead of the wife and takes the lead in his role as initiator. He is not superior in his identity or nature. Paul speaks of two different functions of two equal beings; the functions (roles) of husband and wife are different, not uneven. Simply because they are different and have different functions within God's order does not mean that they are not equals. Again, the reason for this is because men and women are at the same time equal and different. To say one is inferior to the other is the common error of proud and oppressive men. To say that one is the same as the other is the popular error of rebellious and confused women (commonly seen in the women's liberation movement in the Western world).

It seems so obvious just in a natural kind of way. Nevertheless, it is not often understood or accepted. Men and women are equal. That seems like it should be understood naturally. Men and women are not the same. Even more so, that seems like it should be understood naturally. However . . . ?

MAY 6

THE SECOND GENERATION CHURCH . . . A HISTORICAL STUDY

"Beware of the . . . false circumcision; for we are the true circumcision,
who worship in the Spirit of God and glory in Christ Jesus and put no confidence in the flesh."

Philippians 3:2-3

When we think of the New Testament church, we most likely think of the first-generation church. We might think of some of the major events that occurred soon after the resurrection of Christ in which we see multiple believers gathered together: "When the day of Pentecost had come, they were all together in one place . . . " (Acts 2:1). This is the beginning of the church at Jerusalem that grew very quickly: " . . . and that day there were added about three thousand souls. They were continually devoting themselves to the apostles' teaching and to fellowship, to the breaking of bread and to prayer" (Acts 2:41-42). This was about 30 A.D. . . . certainly part of the first-generation church.

By the time such books as 1 Peter and 1 John were written (around 65 A.D. or later), the first generation of Christian believers was giving way to the second generation. The first generation was marked by great enthusiasm, energy, and power. Everything was fresh and pure. The second generation began with certain different variables that changed the focus and emphasis of the life of the church. The final separation of Christianity from Judaism had occurred. The Christian church began as a Jewish church. The gospel was taken primarily to the Jews. In the Roman world, early Christianity was probably considered a sect of Judaism. The first-generation church adapted Jewish customs and struggled with allowing the church to become universal (Galatians 2); members being both Jew and gentile.

It did not take long, however, for the second-generation church to become increasingly universal. And so, it came against a new struggle. Instead of seeking the way in which to incorporate itself into Judaism, it sought a way to distinguish itself from Judaism: "Beware of the dogs, beware of the evil workers, beware of the false circumcision; for we are the true circumcision, who worship in the Spirit of God and glory in Christ Jesus and put no confidence in the flesh" (Philippians 3:2). With this new struggle came another more serious struggle. The new universal church opened the "universal door" to the problems associated with worldliness.

The first century church was persecuted, mostly, by the Jews. The Roman world saw the church as a Jewish sect and was not intimidated or bothered by it. In the second generation, the church became universal. It began to intimidate and bother the universal authorities. This was the beginning of a larger persecution of the church. This persecution was intensified when the Roman position of favor towards the Jews began to deteriorate. Finally, Jerusalem and the temple were destroyed in 70 A.D. Although this increased the spread of the gospel (by scattering the Christians), it may have also contributed to the increase of false doctrines especially with respect to eschatology (the end times). Many Christians were waiting for the immediate return of Christ. They associated His return with the destruction of the temple. When He did not return after this event, it promoted confusion, doubt, and error, which lead to false doctrine. With respect to authority, the leaders of the first-generation church were those who had walked and talked with Christ. They were eyewitnesses of the death, resurrection, and ascension of Jesus. As the majority of these people died, it became easier and easier to distort the truth. Heresy became an increasingly serious problem. The threat of false doctrine became more and more real. Hence, the addressing of those issues in second generation church Scripture like 1 Peter and 1 John.

MAY 7

THE NATURE OF THE CHURCH . . .

"Jesus . . . was asking His disciples, saying, 'Who do people say that the Son of Man is? . . .' He said to
them, 'But who do you say that I am?' And Simon Peter answered, 'Thou art the Christ, the Son of the
living God.' And Jesus answered and said to him, 'Blessed are you, Simon Barjona, because flesh and
blood did not reveal this to you, but My Father who is in heaven. And I also say to you that you are
Peter, and upon this rock I will build My church and the gates of Hades shall not overpower it. I will
give you the keys of the kingdom of heaven; and whatever you shall bind on earth shall be bound in
heaven, and whatever you shall loose on earth shall be loosed in heaven.'"

Matthew 16:13, 15-19

What is the "church"? The first time we see it mentioned in the Bible (and the first of only two times it is mentioned in the Gospels) we find a significant description of the nature of the church (Matthew 16:13-19). Most significantly, it is most directly associated with Jesus. It is His church ("My church") and He is the One who will build it ("I will build My church"). Furthermore, it is built on who He is ("Who do you say that I am?"); it is built on the fact that Jesus is the divine Christ ("Thou art the Christ, the Son of the living God"). More specifically, it is built upon the "rock" of divine revelation of this truth ("flesh and blood did not reveal this to you, but My Father who is in heaven") and human confession of this truth ("Thou art the Christ, the Son of the living God"). Even more specifically, it is built on divine revelation to and human confession of an individual ("But who do you say that I am?"), not a group ("Who do people say . . . But who do you say . . . "). The church is built on salvation and that salvation cannot be inherited from your parents or passed on to you via any other group, but it must be received via your own individual/personal decision. The nature of the church is that its central theme is salvation; the forgiveness of sins that comes through revelation and confession (Peter's answer to Jesus' question is famously called "The Great Confession").

And so, the proactive activity of the church—it should be noted that the church is on the offensive since it is the "gates/defensive structures of Hades" that "shall not overpower it"—revolves around the declaration of salvation; the declaration of the forgiveness that comes through revelation and confession. And so, the church holds "the keys of the kingdom of heaven." What opens the door? The keys of divine revelation and human "confession" open it. And the church (the heavenly Christ's earthly "body") is the earthly entity (Christ's people, Christ's ministry, Christ's ongoing life) that provides a context for this declaration of salvation via revelation and confession.

"Whatever you shall bind (not confess) on earth shall be bound in heaven, and whatever you shall loose (confess) on earth shall be loosed in heaven."

The only other time we see the term church in the Gospels is in Matthew 18:17-18. Here is also the only other time we see the "binding and loosing" that was first mentioned in Matthew 16:19. Interestingly, the common topic found in both Matthew 16 and Matthew 18 is confession. The context of Matthew 18 is that of church discipline; the church being used in the context of confession. If there is sin in the "body" then there should be correction (Luke 17:3). Ultimately, the goal of the church is forgiveness via confession. The church holds the keys; "whatever is loosed" is associated with the one who needs forgiveness who is "listening" or confessing, and "whatever is bound" is associated with the one who needs forgiveness who is "refusing to listen" or not confessing (Matthew 18:15-18).

The focus of the church is its authority to declare the forgiveness of sins. Christ, the source of forgiveness, declares forgiveness through His body (John 20:23). And so, Jesus breathes upon the new church in a context of evangelistic commission (it is an "apostolic" church); the church of the Lord Jesus Christ is a sent one into the world (John 20:21-22). It is sent out with the "keys." May God continue to use the church to open the door to many for salvation (Luke 10:2).

———————

MAY 8

BE SURE TO PREPARE GOD'S WAY . . .

"As it is written in Isaiah the prophet: 'BEHOLD, I SEND MY MESSENGER AHEAD OF YOU, WHO WILL
PREPARE YOUR WAY; THE VOICE OF ONE CRYING IN THE WILDERNESS,
MAKE READY THE WAY OF THE LORD, MAKE HIS PATHS STRAIGHT.' John the Baptist appeared in
the wilderness preaching a baptism of repentance for the forgiveness of sins."

Mark 1:2-4

In the ancient world, when a dignitary was approaching a city, city workers would go out and level the path on which the dignitary would enter. They would prepare the way for the dignitary to come into the city. They would make his paths straight. What is it that prepares God's way to enter our "city" . . . into our lives? It is repentance (Mark 1:2-4). Repentance is to turn to God. It is the turning to Him that prepares His way to you; all He needs in order to come to you, as the prodigal son found out, is for you to turn to Him (Matthew 7:7; Luke 15:20). Of course, this turning to Him (repentance) includes more than a superficial curiosity; it must include actions/

results/fruit (Matthew 3:8; Luke 3:8-10; Luke 15:21). And so, to prepare the way of the Lord, John the Baptist came preaching "a baptism of repentance for the forgiveness of sins" (Mark 1:4). There is no actual forgiveness without repentance, only potential forgiveness (Luke 17:3). Repentance is critical.

God "is not far from each one of us" (Acts 17:27). The question is, "Do we believe that God is really there?" This is critical for repentance. Why would we repent? We repent "for the kingdom of heaven is at hand" . . . it is near (Matthew 3:2). As a child, what would make me turn from doing something that my parents would not want me to do? The nearness of my parents! Would I steal the proverbial "cookie from the cookie jar" if my parents were not in the room? Maybe. Would I steal it if they were standing right next to the cookie jar? Definitely not! What do you do that you would not do if you realized that Jesus was standing right there? And so, it is a question of belief. Do you really believe Jesus is there? If so, you repent because Jesus is near . . . He is "at hand" (Mark 1:15).

It does not take much . . . just a turn toward Him. God's mercy is great. He does not need much of a response from you to be able to bless you. As with Sodom, the existence of a "smoldering wick" is enough. He will not put it out. His great mercy allows Him to respond to the smallest sign of repentance (Matthew 12:20). Of course, God is not pleased when we do not repent . . . when we wrongly think we do not need to turn to Him (Luke 15:7). However, when we do turn to Him there is great joy in heaven: " . . . there is joy in the presence of the angels of God over one sinner who repents" (Luke 15:10). So be sure to "prepare God's way" and start some parties in heaven!

———————

MAY 9

THE IMPORTANCE OF HUMILITY IN THE LIFE OF A LEADER

"But to this one I will look, To him who is humble and contrite of spirit, and who trembles at My word."

Isaiah 66:2

The leader must be humble. Leaders must live for others, and thus, get their eyes off themselves and onto others. As leaders walk in that attitude, they put themselves in position to prosper. And so, it is the humility of leaders that enables them to focus on others. Moreover, it is humility that enables leaders to put the focus on God. Of course, God uses leaders. Thus, it is especially true that humility is so essential in the life of a leader. Why? Because it is very easy for leaders to point to themselves and not to God when God does something great through them. Consider Daniel in his response to King Nebuchadnezzar (Daniel 2:25-30):

> Then Arioch hurriedly brought Daniel into the king's presence and spoke to him as follows: "I have found a man among the exiles from Judah who can make the interpretation known to the king!" The king said to Daniel, whose name was Belteshazzar, "Are you able to make known to me the dream which I have seen and its interpretation?" Daniel answered before the king and said, "As for the mystery about which the king has inquired, neither wise men, conjurers, magicians *nor* diviners are able to declare it to the king. "However, there is a God in heaven who reveals mysteries, . . . He who reveals mysteries has made known to you what will take place. "But as for me, this mystery has not been revealed to me for any wisdom residing in me more than in any other living man . . . "

It certainly should be noted that Daniel resisted the temptation to point to himself. Surely the temptation was significant for Daniel to, at least, take some of the credit. God did miraculous things through Daniel, yet Daniel did not point to himself, but emphatically pointed to God. The wise leader will consider the implications of Isaiah 42:8: "I am the Lord, that is My name; I will not give My glory to another, nor My praise to graven images."

A lack of humility will produce two root problems in the life and ministry of a leader: **ignorance** and **insecurity**. First, leaders cannot afford to be *ignorant*. However, leaders who are not humble are leaders who cannot be taught. They cannot receive counsel from others. They cannot learn and grow. Proud leaders are not learners; they have a hard time taking counsel from others. This is a problem for leaders: "Where there is no guidance the people fall, but in abundance of counselors there is victory" (Proverbs 11:14), and "Without consultation, plans are frustrated, but with many counselors they succeed" (Proverbs 15:22). Proud leaders will inevitably be ineffective. Second, without humility, pride rises and eventually manufactures *insecurity*. Pride forces leaders to focus on themselves. They worry about how they appear to others, always looking in the mirror. Inevitably, they become paranoid. They are not sure of themselves or their positions. They become very *insecure*. Insecurity tends to result in an attempt to control everything and everyone. They begin to oppress instead of lead.

And so, it is humility that will sustain leaders. Without humility, leaders will be overwhelmed by their success. They will begin to think too much of themselves. Their leadership will be destroyed. For this reason, Paul strongly suggests not to put new converts into leadership lest they "become conceited" (1 Timothy 3:6). Instead, God says, "But to this one I will look, to him who is humble and contrite of spirit, and who trembles at My word" (Isaiah 66:2). And so, it is not accidental that one of the Bible's greatest leaders (Moses) was also the humblest man "on the face of the earth" (Numbers 12:3).

MAY 10

WHAT'S IN A NAME . . . ?

"Then Moses said to God, 'Behold, I am going to the sons of Israel, and I will say to them, "The God of your fathers has sent me to you." Now they may say to me, "What is His name?" What shall I say to them?' God said to Moses, 'I AM WHO I AM'; and He said, 'Thus you shall say to the sons of Israel, "I AM has sent me to you."'

Exodus 3:13-14

Especially in Hebrew culture, a name was very significant. It denoted the very existence of a person and indicated the nature or character of that individual. Moses understood this and responded to it when he was commissioned by God to deliver His people. Moses felt like he needed to carry with him God's name—" . . . they may say to me, 'What is His name?' What shall I say to them?"—and so, God revealed His name to Moses, "I AM WHO I AM" (Exodus 3:13-14). The significance of God's name is extensive. It is the name of God that we are warned about (Exodus 20:7). We are instructed to pray, "Hallowed be Your name" (Matthew 6:9). We are called to love His name (Psalm 69:36), to glorify His name (2 Thessalonians 1:12), to praise His name (Psalm 18:49), to act upon His name (Acts 2:21), to give thanks to His name (Hebrews 13:15), and to believe on His name (1 John 3:23).

God uses His names as a way of revealing Himself to us. It is the meaning of the name that adds to our knowledge of Him. Moreover, with respect to being aware of those aspects of God that will enable us to know Him better, it is experiencing in our own lives the need for God with respect to what a particular name of God represents that increases our knowledge of Him; we need to have an experiential awareness of the names of God. Thus, as we say "El Shaddai" (God Almighty) we remember Abraham, who was too old to have a son (Genesis 17:1). We realize that God's power is made perfect in man's weakness. It is when we are aware of that power in our own lives that we begin to grow closer to God. As we become aware in (as opposed to only being aware of) the names of God, we will necessarily know Him more fully.

Suggested Activity #1: Use a topical index or other encyclopedic reference tool to find the various names of Jesus that are in the Bible. There are at least fifty-two different names ("The Lord of Peace"; "The Good Shepherd"). Memorize one name each week for a year. During the week take time during your prayer time to meditate on the significance of the name. At the end of your prayers, use that name of Jesus. If you are praying for the peace of God in your life, then end the prayer in the name of the Lord of Peace. When your prayer is answered you will begin to experience (and therefore know) God more specifically in that area.

Suggested Activity #2: Use the following diagram to study the "Jehovah" names of God. Apply what you have studied to your own life. Look to God to be "Jehovah-Jireh" your Provider/Father. As you become experientially aware of the names of God, your relationship with Him will grow. You will know Him more fully. Can you say that you know God as your Father? Your Doctor? Your Warrior? Your Sanctifier? Your Comforter? Your Advocate? Your Pastor? Your Shadow?

NAME OF GOD	MEANING	SCRIPTURES	DESCRIPTION
Jehovah-Jireh	Jehovah sees; provides	Genesis 22:14	God my Father
Jehovah-Rophe	Jehovah heals	Exodus 15:26 Isaiah 61:1	God my Doctor
Jehovah-Nissi	Jehovah my banner	Exodus 17:15 Psalm 20:5	God my Warrior
Jehovah-M'Kaddesh	Jehovah who sanctifies	Leviticus 20:7-8	God my Sanctifier
Jehovah-Shalom	Jehovah is peace	Judges 6:24 Isaiah 9:6	God my Comforter
Jehovah-Tsidkenu	Jehovah our righteousness	Jeremiah 23:5-6	God my Advocate
Jehovah-Rohi	Jehovah my shepherd	Psalm 23 1 Peter 2:25	God my Pastor
Jehovah-Shammah	Jehovah is there	Ezekiel 48:35	God my Shadow

MAY 11

YOU'RE DEDICATED TO WHAT YOU BELIEVE . . .

"For what does it profit a man to gain the whole world, and forfeit his soul? For what will a man give in exchange for his soul?"

Mark 8:36-37

The ultimate importance of eternal life tends to make everything else relatively unimportant (Mark 8:36-37). Your commitment and dedication to God depends on your understanding of this truth. It depends on how much you believe it! The quantity and quality of your commitment to God depends on the quantity and quality of your faith. The quantity of your commitment to the world depends on the quantity of your doubt. If you have no doubt, then you will logically give everything that you have to move toward the goal of eternal life (Matthew 16:26). You would "give your all" knowing that there is no risk of being wrong (knowing that in the end you will see that what you believed was really the truth). People of faith are committed/dedicated people because they know that there is no risk of losing. There is no risk of regretting or being disappointed with your life of faith. Doubt leads to the fear of regret. The fear of regret leads to the attempt to get satisfaction and comfort in this world just in case you die and realize that your faith was not the truth (a sort of odd "faith insurance"). Thus, a lack of belief in the importance of eternal life will result in a lack of commitment to God. To be completely dedicated to God is to believe His Word completely.

The more dedicated you are to God, the more you will know God (Luke 18:29-30); the more you will have "eternal life" (which is defined, according to John 17:3, as knowing God). To know God is to be like Him; it is "to walk in the same manner as He walked" (1 John 2:6). Thus, the more dedicated you are to God, the more you will lead a selfless life (Philippians 2:3-5); a life that esteems other people. Dedicated people treat others the way they themselves would like to be treated; they prefer/esteem others (Luke 6:31). To know God is to be like Him; it is "to walk in the same manner as He walked." The more dedicated you are to God, the more you will lead a servant's life (John 13:13-15).); a life that serves other people. Dedicated people are servants who prefer/esteem others to the point of being willing to give up (ransom) their lives for others (Mark 10:43-45). Your love for Jesus can be measured by your willingness to serve others (John 21:15; 15:13).

You're dedicated to what you believe. People who believe God are dedicated to God. People who are dedicated to God are like God. Are you like God? Are you dedicated to Him? Do you believe?

MAY 12

THE NEED TO PERCEIVE OUR NEED . . .

". . . for apart from Me you can do nothing."

John 15:5

What does the name *Jesus* mean? In Hebrew it is *Yeshua*. In Greek it is *Iesus*. In Spanish it is *Dios*. In Lingala it is *Yesu*. No matter the language, it means the same thing. It means, *"God saves."* Thus, God is God (and you are not), and God must save us (because we cannot save ourselves). The core of the meaning of the name of Jesus with respect to how we should respond to it is that we desperately need Him. Without Him, there is no other way; thus, "Jesus said to him, 'I am the way, and the truth, and the life; no one comes to the Father but through Me'" (John 14:6). This reality is *exhaustive*; thus, Jesus said "I am the vine, you are the branches; he who abides in Me and I in him, he bears much fruit, for apart from Me you can do nothing" (John 15:5).

There is the need to perceive our need. That is the crux of our situation relative to God. We have to see our need and admit it (confess it): "Jesus said to them, 'If you were blind, you would have no sin; but since you *say*, '*We see*,' your sin remains'" (John 9:41). Similarly, He said, "It is not those who are healthy who need a physician, but those who are sick; I did not come to call the righteous, but sinners" (Mark 2:17). So, the questions the gospel message demands we ask ourselves are: "Do I see my sin?," "Do I see my need for my sins to be forgiven?," and "Do I see my need for a Savior?" Those who perceive their need are blessed: "Blessed are the poor in spirit, for theirs is the kingdom of heaven" (Matthew 5:3).

The story is told of a man who desperately needed to get to the top of an extremely high mountain. The problem was he was dead. Every day friends, family, and strangers would pass by where his body was lying at the foot of the mountain and scream at him to get up and hike up to the top of the mountain. Sometimes they would cheer him on while other times they would ridicule him screaming, "Get up you fool, you lazy and incompetent scoundrel!" No matter which attitude the passers-by happened to have that day, the man did not move. No wonder . . . he was dead, and a dead man cannot climb a mountain! There was a man, however, who lived at the top of the mountain. He looked down the mountain from his mountain top mansion and saw the situation; he took his cart and began to make the long trip down the mountain. He arrived at the bottom, approached the dead man, picked him up and placed him in his cart; he then began the hike back up the mountain. When they arrived at the top, the dead man came back to life. Together, they entered the man's mansion and the revived man lived there with his rescuer forever. This is our exact situation. We are dead in our sins, separated from God, and have no way to "climb up the mountain" to get back to Him. So . . . God climbs down the mountain to get us! It is truly the only way to resolve our massive/extremely high mountain problem (Philippians 2:5-11). We need Him to come to us!

Sometimes it is more difficult to perceive our need for God in the "bigger things" of life because they make us feel so uncomfortable that we do not choose God's help since we greatly fear the unknown. The story is told of a spy who was captured and then sentenced to death by a general in the Persian army. This general had the strange custom of giving condemned criminals a choice between the firing squad and a big black door. As the moment for execution drew near, the spy was brought to the Persian general, who asked the question, "What will it be: the firing squad or the big black door?" The spy hesitated for a long time. It was a difficult decision. He chose the firing squad. Moments later shots rang out confirming his execution. The general turned to his aide and said, "They always prefer the known way to the unknown. It is characteristic of people to be afraid of the undefined. Yet, we gave him a choice." The aide said, "What lies behind the big black door?" "Freedom," replied the general. "I've known only a few brave enough to take it." In need of God's grace, we must remember we need Him in the "known" and the "unknown."

––––––––––

MAY 13

WHAT IS WORSHIP? . . .

"God is spirit, and those who worship Him must worship in spirit and truth."

John 4:24

What is worship? It is not immediately obvious. It is a spiritual activity that is directed at an intangible entity—"God is spirit, and those who worship Him must worship in spirit and truth" (John 4:24)—and is, therefore, to some degree, otherworldly. Are all the following activities considered to be acts of worship: the singing of hymns or choruses, shouts of celebration, kneeling in reverence, dancing, the raising of hands, or silence? Is worship more fundamental than its many forms?

There are a variety of biblical words used to depict the idea of worship in the Scripture. Most often used is the word *proskuneo*, which means to "kiss toward" and can be translated "to adore." Another often used word is *sebezomai*, which alludes to an act of "reverential awe" or respectful reverence. Sometimes used is the word *eusebeo*, which points to a lifestyle of godliness or piety. The word *therapeuo*, which literally means "to heal by manipulation with the hands"—in Acts 17:25

such worship, often practiced by idolaters, was denied as being a legitimate form of worship of the living God—is sometimes used to depict worship. Then there is the word *latreuo*, which refers to "an act of priestly service" rendered to a deity. Similarly, the word *leitourgeo*, suggests a fulfillment of a representative office of worship.

From this linguistic foundation we see that worship affects outward forms and postures, but by looking more closely, we understand that "bowing" and "kissing" are outward responses to inner attitudes that stem from perceived value or worth. A servant bows to a king because he recognizes the king's worthy position. A man gives a kiss out of a deep inner desire to communicate preciousness to the beloved one. An act of worship (an expression of the "worth" of something or someone) is rooted in an attitude of worship (a perception of the "worth" of something or someone). The essence of "worship" is "worth" ship!

What is worship? We might say, in summary, that worship is the adoration of God accompanied by reverence; it includes inspired thoughts, words and deeds. To *worship* God is to agree with and proclaim His *worth*!

MAY 14

GOD BECAME FLESH . . .

"And the Word became flesh, and dwelt among us, and we saw His glory . . . "

John 1:14

The Word is God and it became flesh (John 1:1, 14). This is the definition of the incarnation. Since we could not get to God, God came to us. The incarnation is not just a possibility, it is a necessity. God come in the flesh. It is a wondrous thing to consider the actuality of the incarnation. God Himself (Jesus) clothed Himself in our skin and "dwelt among us." Jesus is to the New Testament what the tabernacle was to the Old Testament. The word "dwelt" is literally "to tabernacle," which means "to make his tent among us." The reference to "His glory" reminds us of the "shekinah" glory of the presence of God in the tabernacle. Make no mistake about it. The incarnation is integral to His Story. Jesus claimed to have come down out of heaven (John 6:33-35). This not only points to His deity but to the wondrous picture of the incarnation.

The mystery of the incarnation is like the mystery of the new birth. In the incarnation it is proclaimed that Jesus **came from heaven**. In the new birth it is proclaimed that we are **born from above** (John 3:13). What is salvation? What is it to have eternal life? It is to know God (John

17:3). The main idea of the incarnation is that God Himself has become visible (knowable) to men (John 14:7).

Herein, we understand the necessity (not just the possibility) of the incarnation. How can we know what to do in this darkened world? It does not take a whole lot of living life in this world to realize that the fog is thick and that, in general, we encounter "low visibility." How can we know where to go? What to do? How to do it? The answer to all those questions is found in the incarnation. And so, our most practical encouragement in the Scripture is to "fix our eyes on Jesus" (Hebrews 12:2). This is how we can know where to go. This is how we can know what to do. This is how we can know how to do it. This is how we can "run with endurance the race that is set before us" (Hebrews 12:1).

And so, when life is foggy, see the incarnation . . . see God in the flesh . . . see Jesus . . . and the fog lifts!

MAY 15

THE SOVEREIGN GOD AND YOU . . .

"So Pilate therefore said to Him, . . . 'Do You not know that I have authority to release You, and I have authority to crucify You?' Jesus answered, 'You would have no authority over Me, unless it had been given you from above . . .'"

John 19:10-11

God's sovereignty can be defined as His unchallengeable power for good. It is described by His "three C" actions: He Creates, He Causes, and He Controls. Nothing exists apart from Him. Nothing is set into motion that did not begin with His action. And nothing is outside of His control.

God is in control regarding authority in our lives. The fact that the Pilates in our lives that exercise authority over us can only exercise that authority if it is given from above should stand as a comfort in the midst of oppression. At the same time, submission to authority begins with an awareness of the existence of the sovereign authority giver.

God is sovereign over revelation. Sometimes we might not see because a veil covers our face. God can **re**move that **veil** ("**re**" "**vela**"). He can take away the cover ("apo" = take away and "kalupsis" = cover; thus, apokalupsis or "apocalypse" is a synonym for "revelation"). In any case, revelation or the withholding of it, is controlled by God (Luke 9:45). As the sovereign God removes our veils, we are blessed like Simon Barjona, since flesh and blood does not reveal the wonders of God to us but God Himself is the sovereign Revealer (Matthew 16:17).

As an awareness of the sovereignty of God may promote our submission to authority and our expectation of revelation, an awareness of the sovereignty of God in evangelism may promote our evangelistic activity. We may not evangelize as much as we could because we think we are sovereign over evangelism. If I believe I control—via my effectiveness or lack thereof—someone's acceptance of Christ, I may shy away from witnessing to that person in fear of failing (as if the results depend on me). However, we do not have to be great preachers—only available ones—to be effective in evangelism. Why? Because God is sovereign in evangelism. The key is the soil, not so much the preacher (Mark 4:30-32). God prepares and is sovereign over the preparation of the soil. Thus, the key is God, not so much man. "Neither the one who plants nor the one who waters is anything, but God who causes the growth" (1 Corinthians 3:7).

So, take "the heavy" off yourself as you consider God's sovereignty and you may find yourself sharing the gospel with more people.

MAY 16

YOU HAVE TO KNOW WHERE THE POWER COMES FROM . . .

"But when Peter saw this, he replied to the people, 'Men of Israel, why are you amazed at this, or why do you gaze at us, as if by our own power or piety we had made him walk?'"

Acts 3:12

Jesus told His followers that they would "receive power when the Holy Spirit has come upon you" (Acts 1:8). The word "power" is translated from the Greek word *dunamis* (from which we get our words "dynamic" and "dynamite"). Where does this "power" come from? It comes from and is found in God. It is not resident in us to use at will. God chooses who gets the *dunamis* and why he gets it (Romans 9:17), to what degree the *dunamis* is given (Matthew 25:15), and when to manifest the *dunamis* (Luke 5:17).

After a great manifestation of the dynamic power of God in which a lame man began to walk, Peter explained once and for all that the *dunamis* is not our own: " . . . why do you gaze at us, as if by our own power or piety we had made him walk?" (Acts 3:12). Peter goes on to explain that it is from "the God of Abraham, Isaac, and Jacob" (Acts 3:13). Peter was simply used as a vessel for the dynamic power to flow through; "we have this treasure in earthen vessels, so that the surpassing greatness of the power will be of God and not from ourselves" (2 Corinthians 4:7).

A story is told of a man who was walking down the street when he saw a very strange sight. There was a man pumping a hand pump at an incredible rate of speed. He went on for quite a long time and did not seem to get tired. The man who saw this decided to take a closer look. When he got closer, he realized that what he thought was a man was only a wooden figure that was painted to look like a man. The wooden man was connected to the handle of the pump in a way that made it look like he was pumping. The water was pouring forth. However, it was not because the wooden man was pumping. It was an artesian well and the water was pumping the man.

It is the same way with the power of God. A man who works for God and gets results is a man who the Holy Spirit is working through. The only thing the man must do is to keep his hand on the handle. And so, it is important to know where the power comes from. If you think it comes from yourself, then you will look to yourself. However, if you understand that it comes from God, then you will look to God . . . you will stay focused on keeping your hand on that handle!

MAY 17

WHO YOU ARE SPEAKING WITH MAKES A DIFFERENCE . . .

"Then those who feared the LORD spoke to one another, and the LORD gave attention and heard it, and a book of remembrance was written before Him for those who fear the Lord and who esteem His name. 'They will be Mine,' says the LORD of hosts . . . "

Malachi 3:16-17

In the book of Malachi there are two different groups of people. One group speaks against God (Malachi 1:13) while another group "who feared the Lord spoke to one another, and the Lord gave attention and heard it" (Malachi 3:16). Here we see the importance and efficacy of fellowship amongst believers. It very well may have been this fellowship that strengthened the God-fearer's faith and kept them from falling into doubt (like the other group). Moreover, it was in the midst of this fellowship that God "gave attention and heard it, and a book of remembrance was written before Him . . . " (Malachi 3:16). Fellowship is effective, "For where two or three have gathered together in My name, I am there in their midst" (Matthew 18:20).

The group that did not fear God (Malachi 1:6) wearied God with their words (Malachi 2:17; Malachi 3:13), despised (Malachi 1:6), profaned (Malachi 1:12), and did not give honor to God's name (Malachi 2:2). They saw no value or profit in serving God (Malachi 3:14), and so they were cut off (Malachi 2:12) having only given attention to themselves (2:15-16).

This contrasts with the group that did fear God (Malachi 3:16; Malachi 1:14). God gave attention to their words and heard them (Malachi 3:16) as they esteemed His name (Malachi 3:16), and so they would be spared (Malachi 3:17). God says "They will be Mine" (Malachi 3:17) and they are remembered (Malachi 3:16) instead of being "cut off" (Malachi 2:12) as God gives attention to them (Malachi 3:16) instead of them giving attention to themselves (Malachi 2:15-16).

We might point to four ways in which God distinguishes between those whom He "spares" and those whom are "cut off." They are distinguished by their **attributes** (they serve God versus they do not serve God), **actions** (they are obedient versus they are disobedient), **attitudes** (they fear God versus they do not fear God), and **results** (meaning/fullness versus futility/emptiness).

An **attribute** is that which characterizes someone and belongs to his or her character. It is more than what someone does. It is what someone is. It is more than doing acts of service. It is being a servant. The murmuring Israelites claimed that "it is vain to serve God" (Malachi 3:14). They placed conditions on their service. They did acts of service, but they were not servants. Servants say, "We have done only that which we ought to have done" (Luke 17:10). Since it is something they are and not simply something they do, they do not expect or demand a reward. Attributes lead to **actions**. Servants are obedient because they have laid down their rights, whereas those who merely do acts of service lend themselves more to disobedience as their service is often empty. The **attitude** of fearing God is the attitude of seeking and walking with God (Proverbs 2:5). The lack of a fear of God **results** in the lack of a relationship with God. The results are that those who fear the Lord will be "spared" or "saved," even if it be "so as through fire" (1 Corinthians 3:15); they will be purified and refined (disciplined) instead of being consumed as is the case with those who do not fear God.

MAY 18

YOU ARE A GOOD WORK THAT IS BEING PERFECTED . . .

"FOR I AM confident of this very thing, that He who began a good work in you will perfect it until the day of Christ Jesus."

Philippians 1:6

Paul writes to the Philippians and tells them that he is praying for them with faith that God will complete in them the process which He began—"always offering prayer . . . for you all . . . confident of this very thing, that He who began a good work in you will perfect it until the day of Christ Jesus" (Philippians 1:4-6)—and then further describes this "process" when he explains what exactly he prays for them. So, what is the good work that is being perfected? The good work that God began and will complete is the work of love: "And this I pray, that your love may abound still more and more" (Philippians 1:9).

This process of beginning and completing the "good work" of love is, ultimately, something that is being done in the Philippians. Nevertheless, it should be noted that all the causal focus is on Jesus. The perfecting of love is done in the Philippians. Yet, it is God who is doing it; "He . . . will perfect it."

It is care, compassion, and love that Paul has for the Philippians. Yet, it is actually "the affection of Christ Jesus" (Philippians 1:8); it is actually Christ's love. The increased love is the result of the Philippians "having been filled with the fruit of righteousness." Yet, that fruit of righteousness "comes through Jesus Christ" (Philippians 1:11). So, who is who and what is what in this process? The Philippians are the containers and Christ is the contents. The Philippians are the instruments and Christ is the source.

Christians are involved in a process. We must realize this and have patience. At the same time, we must seek to move ahead. We must do it by faith. Faith in what or who? In ourselves? No! We are the instruments. Christ is the source. And so, our faith must be in God. He began the process (He began the good work). He will lead us through the process (He will perfect/complete it). He will end the process (it will continue *until* the day of Christ Jesus). Are we conscious of the process? Is there growth? Are we patient? Are we willing to have faith that will let God begin the process on Friday at the cross and end it on Sunday at the resurrection while we wait through the process on Saturday? You are a good work that is being perfected. So, hold on!

MAY 19

WHAT DID YOU DO WITH WHAT I GAVE YOU? . . .

"To one he gave five talents, to another, two, and to another, one, each according to his own ability; and he went on his journey . . . For to everyone who has, more shall be given, and he will have an abundance; but from the one who does not have, even what he does have shall be taken away."

Matthew 25:15, 29

Success is measured in obedience, obedience of a steward (one who is responsible with someone else's resources). The issue is not so much a quantitative issue; rather, it is qualitative. The criteria for the success of a steward is not measured in terms of how much resource the steward is responsible for (that is the sovereign choice of the owner), but in what the steward did with whatever resources he has been entrusted with. And so, "justice" is not defined in "sameness" (everyone getting the same resources), but in terms of faithfulness (how responsible you are with what you have been given). Some people have one talent, others two, and yet others five . . . different ones have different "abilities" (Matthew 25:15). The measurement of success is not determined by the quantity of your "abilities" but by the quality of your use of those abilities; "everyone who has, more shall be given . . . but from the one who does not have, even what he does have shall be taken away" (Matthew 25:29). What did the successful one "have" and what did the unsuccessful one "not have"? The successful one had the responsibility to use and, therefore, multiply his ability (obedience of a steward) while the unsuccessful one did not (Matthew 25:14-30).

Good stewards are obedient. We are called to be good stewards. We desire to walk in obedience. So, what produces obedience? Revelation and understanding can lead to obedience (John 7:17). Remorse leads to obedience (Matthew 21:30). Fellowship with God leads to obedience (John 8:29). Love for God leads to obedience (John 14:15, 21). And so, the good steward should pray for and put into practice these "obedience producers." Pray that God would "grant you" understanding and revelation of Himself (Ephesians 3:16-19). Pray for the conviction that comes from the Holy Spirit that leads to remorse. Spend more time with God and express your love for Him. In so doing, you will walk in greater obedience to the Owner and, thus, be a more successful steward.

This obedience yields success. What are some of the results of obedience? Inasmuch as food can be a symbol of energy and satisfaction, we can say that obedience results in energy and satisfaction in life (John 4:34). Obedience results in joy (John 15:7-11). Moreover, obedience leads to wisdom (Matthew 7:24), leads to more fellowship with God (John 8:29), and results in God hearing us when we pray (John 9:31). It leads to receiving more revelation (John 14:21). It results in being in God's family (Matthew 12:50; Mark 3:35). Most significantly, obedience results in glorifying God (John 17:4). Oppositely, a lack of obedience weakens the foundation and yields weak/unsuccessful stewards (Matthew 7:26-27). Without obedience worship is not valid; it is useless, meaningless, and futile (Matthew 15:8-9; Mark 7:7). Most significantly, a lack of obedience results in the wrath of God (John 3:36).

The successful steward accepted the responsibility to use and, therefore, multiply his ability (obedience of a steward) while the unsuccessful one did not (Matthew 25:14-30). Success is measured in obedience; the obedience of a steward (one who is responsible with someone else's resources). Are you ready for the question that the Owner will inevitably ask, "What did you do with what I gave you?"

———————

DOES JESUS BRING PEACE? . . .

"Do not think that I came to bring peace on the earth; I did
not come to bring peace, but a sword."

Matthew 10:34

Did Jesus come to bring peace? Seemingly, the business of making peace stands as God's "family business" as it is associated with those who are "blessed" to be called family members (Matthew 5:9). And so, it is not surprising that when Peter takes out his sword in the garden of Gethsemane to fight off the soldiers who have come to arrest Jesus that Jesus tells him to "put your sword back into its place" (Matthew 26:52). Why, then, does Jesus say that He has "not come to bring peace, but a sword" (Matthew 10:34)? It is because the gospel divides believers and unbelievers. It forms very clear cut "teams" (Luke 12:51-53; Mark 3:6; Luke 23:12). These teams are not necessarily formed in keeping with this life's natural relationships (like family relationships), and yet may be formed regardless of this life's natural relationships (like the unnatural alliance between the Pharisees and the Herodians, or the unlikely friendship between former enemies Herod and Pilate).

The existence of a common enemy can result in strange partners (as the saying goes, "Politics makes for strange bedfellows!) As we see with the Pharisees and Herodians or with Herod and Pilate, people who are normally enemies can find unity in their common opposition to Jesus. At the same time, people who are normally enemies can find unity in their common acceptance of Jesus (the division that existed between Jew and Gentile is broken down by the message of the gospel as seen in Ephesians 2:11-22). Does Jesus come to bring peace? Does He come to bring unity or division? He brings both because the gospel message, and the response to it, divides people into teams.

How should those on Jesus' team respond to the reality of "peace" . . . to the existence of unity and division . . . to those who are with you and those who are against you? First, Christians must understand the importance of unity. Unity is essential for the success of any group or organization (Matthew 12:25). If the kingdom (group) is divided against itself, then its strength is wasted and its structure falls (Luke 11:17). Thus, he who is not against you is for you (Luke 9:50). Unity is critical. Success in evangelism depends on unity (John 17:23). Furthermore, it should be noted that Jesus dwells in the midst of unity (Matthew 18:20). There is power in the midst of agreement (Matthew 18:19). And so, Christians must understand the importance of unity and take advantage of its potential power!

Second, Christians must respond to enemies—those who are against you because of the gospel—with the understanding that they are not your enemies ("put away your sword"), rather, you are their enemies ("I came to bring a sword"). And so, Christians are not called to come against others ("put away your sword") even though others will come against them ("I came to bring a sword"). Jesus challenges us to not hate our enemies. Beyond that, He challenges us to go out of our way to do something for them; we are to feed them, love them, forgive them, and pray for them (Romans 12:20; Luke 6:27-35; Matthew 6:12-15; Luke 23:34). We are commanded to not resist evil but turn the other cheek. We are to be willing to love our enemies, suffer, and persevere (Matthew 5:38-42). This, then, is the Christian response to the reality of "peace."

MAY 21

WHAT IS IMPORTANT? . . . WELL, WHAT IS ETERNAL?

"This is eternal life, that they may know You, the only true God,
and Jesus Christ whom You have sent."

John 17:3

What is important? Certainly, whatever is not simply temporary is more important than what is temporary. The question is, "What is eternal?" What is eternal life? The dictionary definition of eternal life is found in the Bible; eternal life is to know God (John 17:3). So, what is important? Seeking and knowing God (relationship with God) is important!

A man came to Jesus and wanted to know the "bottom line." He asked, "What shall I do to work the works of God? What is really important?" Jesus answered, "Believe (seek/know) God" (John 6:29). Being with Jesus (relationship with Him) precedes doing the work of Jesus (Mark 3:14). Sometimes we don't understand this. We are often distracted by the things we do for God. We try to make our lives complicated. Yet, Jesus is calling us to sit with Him like Mary did (seek/know Him) and realize the simplicity of our lives (Luke 10:38-42). We should respond to God's sovereignty by seeking the kingdom of God. We worry about things that we cannot control. Instead of worrying, we should realize that God is sovereign. This will free us to do what we can control (what we are responsible for); to seek the kingdom of God as our first priority (Luke 12:26-31). Actually, it goes beyond the idea of priority. The word "first" might be better translated "only." Seeking God should be our **only** concern (Matthew 6:33). And so, of Mary who was "listening to the Lord's word, seated at His feet," Jesus said, " . . . but only a few things are necessary, really only one, for Mary has chosen the good part, which shall not be taken away from her" (Luke 10:39, 42). Mary was doing what was important . . . what was not simply temporary, but what was eternal!

What is important? Even for Jesus, the key to the success of His ministry was that He "saw what the Father was doing." He understood the importance of seeking God (John 5:19). And so, worthiness is based on our response to God's call, whether or not we come to Him/seek Him (Matthew 22:8).

What is important? Whatever is eternal . . . heavenly! So, invest in heaven! Put your time and focus into heavenly things and your heart will remain in heaven. Where you put what is important to you is where your heart will be (Matthew 6:21). Certainly, whatever is not simply temporary is more important than what is temporary. So, follow Paul's suggestion in Colossians 3:2 and "set your minds on the things above (eternal/not simply temporary), not on the things that are on earth (temporary)." Seek and know God. Live eternal life. Live an important life!

MAY 22

DO YOU LONG TO SEE THE RETURN OF CHRIST?

"And He said to the disciples, 'The days shall come when you will long to see one of the days of the Son of Man . . .'"

Luke 17:22

No one but the Father knows the day or hour of the return of Christ (Mark 13:32). However, Christians can know the "signs of the times" (Luke 21:29-31). Moreover, Christians should long for His return (Luke 17:22). That desire is emphasized in the Scripture by way of it being the very issue that ends the Bible: "He who testifies to these things says, 'Yes, I am coming quickly.' Amen. Come, Lord Jesus" (Revelation 22:20).

Believers must always be alert and looking for the return of Christ. Since we do not know when He will come, we must be sure that we are always ready (Luke 12:35-40). Being ready does not mean that we will have to decide or figure out if Jesus has returned or not, for the coming of Christ will be like lightning and those who claim that they are Jesus are all impostors (Matthew 24:27). Instead, we must be ready in the sense that we avoid being anxious over the worries of this world or the end could come as a trap. We should be alert. We should always be praying so that we will be strong and prepared when Christ comes (Luke 21:34-36). Thus, being ready and alert is associated with being a good steward with respect to the things that God has given us to do (Luke 12:42). We stay encouraged knowing that Jesus prepares a place for us in heaven and will return to take us there (John 14:2-3).

Not everyone, however, longs for the return of Christ. The world will not be expecting the return of Jesus. It will come suddenly without a special warning or announcement (Luke 17:26-30). The one who is not ready and watching for Christ's return will be the one who is surprised and disappointed when He comes (Luke 12:40, 46). Before the end, unbelievers will be troubled by problems with the oceans, and by miracles in the sun, moon, and stars. As the heavens are shaken, they will have a great fear concerning the things that are coming upon the world (Luke 21:25-27).

This is not the response of those who long for His return . . . those whose cry is "Maranatha . . . Come, Lord Jesus" . . . for "then they will see the Son of Man coming in a cloud with power and great glory. But when these things begin to take place, straighten up and lift up your heads, because your redemption is drawing near" (Luke 21:27-28).

MAY 23

PURE MOTIVES FOR ENGAGING IN MARRIAGE ROLES

". . . be filled with the Spirit . . . making melody with your heart to the Lord; always giving thanks for all things . . . and be subject to one another in the fear of Christ. Wives, be subject to your own husbands, as to the Lord. For the husband is the head of the wife . . . "

Ephesians 5:18-23

The commands to be filled with the Spirit and to submit to one another in the fear of Christ— "be filled with the Spirit . . . and be subject to one another in the fear of Christ" (Ephesians 5:18-21)—serve as the introduction to Paul's declaration of the marriage roles: "wives, be subject to your own husbands . . . the husband is the head of the wife" (Ephesians 5:22-23). This statement puts the focus on who is under Christ, not on who is over another. The point is that husband and wife must relate to each other according to the desire of Christ. They must obey His ordained structures. The correct motive, then, with respect to functioning in your marriage role, is the motive of being obedient to Christ.

A husband who does not selflessly love, serve, and lead his wife disobeys Christ. A wife who does not submit to and respect her husband disobeys Christ. If we do not make surrender and obedience to Christ our ultimate motivation to engage in our marriage roles, then we will begin to focus on the responsibilities of our mate instead of focusing on our own responsibilities. We will begin to make the performance of our role dependent on the demonstration of the other's role. We will begin to focus on our "rights" in our marriages, instead of focusing on our individual responsibilities in our marriages. This all leads to a selfish, false love. In a healthy marriage, a husband and wife are motivated to function in their roles by the responsibilities of their roles, not by the privileges of their roles. More than anything, they are motivated by their desire to obey and please Christ.

And so, a wife must understand her role of submission in terms of the divine order. She must see it as the way in which she can assume her own divinely ordained position. Thus, her submission to her husband must be based on freedom and love, and not on compulsion and apprehension. He church is not forced into submission. She submits out of her own free will and desire to be obedient to Christ, the Head. Similarly, a wife's motivation to submit to her husband must be based on her love and fear of God (Ephesians 5:21); it must be based on her desire to obey God. A wife must understand and accept that her submission to her husband cannot simply depend on her husband's willingness to fulfill his role. Her motives must be pure, based on her desire to please Christ. Her eyes must be on Him, not so much on her husband. If her eyes are on her husband, then she will fail because her husband will fail. If her eyes are on Christ, then she will not fail because Christ and His love never fail (1 Corinthians 13:8). And so, her act of submission must be an unconditional one. It must be motivated by her desire to operate in the divine order. It must be motivated by her desire to be **right**eous (to stand in her **right** position before God).

Both husband and wife must fulfill their roles without expecting or requiring anything in return. Their motives must be pure. Husbands and wives must relate to each other according to the desire of Christ. They must obey His ordained structures. The correct motive, with respect to functioning in your marriage role is, ultimately, obedience to Christ. So, obey!

———————

MAY 24

THE CLAIMS AND COMFORTS
OF GOD'S JUSTICE

"So when those came who were hired *first, they expected to receive more. But each one of them*
also received a denarius . . . So the last will be first, and the first will be last."

Matthew 20:10, 16

God's justice is different from man's justice. Man often insists on a certain view of fairness
that is not necessarily consistent with God's view. In the Parable of the Prodigal Son the frustra-
tion that results from this disconnect is vividly heard in the voice of the older son who did not
stray from his father's house:

> For so many years I have been serving you and I have never neglected a command
> of yours; and yet you have never given me a young goat, so that I might celebrate
> with my friends; but when this son of yours came, who has devoured your wealth
> with prostitutes, you killed the fattened calf for him.' "And he said to him, 'Son, you
> have always been with me, and all that is mine is yours. 'But we had to celebrate and
> rejoice, for this brother of yours was dead and has begun to live, and was lost and
> has been found' (Luke 15:29-32).

In the Parable of the Laborers (Matthew 20:1-16), the disagreement with a "flip-flopped" view
of justice ("the last will be first . . . ") is evident as the laborers "began to grumble against the
landowner." The question of fairness is again at stake here. Nevertheless, God's view of justice
and fairness is not necessarily consistent with man's view that often defines justice/fairness
in terms of sameness. God makes everyone equal by offering the same reward to those who
begin with different abilities. Those different abilities are especially apparent in the Parable of
the Talents (Matthew 25:14-30): "And to one he gave five talents, to another two, and to another,
one . . . " Herein, it might be said that God's view of justice is more concerned with quality than
quantity. God does not evaluate our success according to how much we have been given, but according to what we did with that which He gave us. Justice and fairness are more viewed from
the lens of stewardship than from the lens of sameness. The more authority you are given, the
more responsibility you have. The more opportunities you are given, the more that is expected
from you (Luke 12:48).

God's view of justice/fairness is not necessarily consistent with man's view. Selflessness towards others reflects a higher law than what we might call "fairness" (Luke 6:30). Unity among
God's people may also reflect a higher law than what we might call fairness and so the Scripture

reprimands: "The very fact that you have lawsuits among you means you have been completely defeated already. Why not rather be wronged? Why not rather be cheated? Instead, you yourselves cheat and do wrong, and you do this to your brothers" (1 Corinthians 6:7-8). Here we might conclude that we cannot demand justice at any price.

Will there be justice, then? Persistent prayer will lead to justice. God responds to consistent prayer, so do not discontinue in prayer when injustice seems to have won the fight (Luke 18:7-8). Moreover, all is revealed in the end as nothing will remain hidden (Matthew 10:26). So, hypocrites may deceive others now, but their folly will ultimately be exposed (Luke 12:2). Everything will be revealed for what it really is in the end. Thus, the "final justice" of God brings comfort to the righteous who sometimes feel like Habakkuk felt (Habakkuk 1:1-4, 12-14).

MAY 25

THE PARADOX OF THE INCARNATION CLARIFIED AT THE TRANSFIGURATION

"And He was transfigured before them; and His face shone like the sun, and His garments became as white as light . . . they fell down to the ground and were terrified. And Jesus came to them and touched them and said, 'Get up and do not be afraid.' And lifting up their eyes, they saw no one, except Jesus alone."

Matthew 17:2, 6-8

At a very fundamental level, the theological lifeblood of Christianity is wrapped up in a paradox, the doctrine of the incarnation. God reveals Himself to man in an ultimate way by coming to man, taking on flesh, and becoming a man Himself in Jesus Christ. The somewhat paradoxical dynamic of the incarnation can be expressed by saying that when God became man, He did not stop being God and the fact that He did not stop being God did not preclude Him from becoming man. Jesus is fully man as He took on "the form of a bond-servant . . . made in the likeness of men" (Philippians 2:7). Yet, He is not only man as He is One existing "in the form of God" (Philippians 2:6). He is fully God. Although He "did not regard equality with God a thing to be grasped, but emptied Himself" (Philippians 2:6-7), His letting go of the right to express His divinity was not tantamount to losing His divinity; "in Him all the fullness of Deity dwells in bodily form" (Colossians 2:9). This is the paradox of the incarnation.

The paradox of the incarnation is clarified at the transfiguration of Jesus (Matthew 17:1-9). The Greek term translated as "transfiguration" or "transformation" comes from the same Greek term translated as "form" in Philippians 2:6 and 2:7 ("He existed in the form of God" and He took "the form of a "bond-servant . . . made in the likeness of men"). It signifies being, essence, or the mode of **expression** of that essence. The form of something is the perfect **expression** of a perfect essence. It is the outward expression of someone's inmost nature. If someone **expresses** the nature of something, then it implies that person has that nature. So, to say that Jesus existed in the form of God is to say that Jesus **expressed** divinity; His outward divine expression is an expression of His inward divine reality or essence. And to say that Jesus existed in the form of man is to say that Jesus **expressed** humanity; His outward human expression is an expression of His inward human reality or essence. This is somewhat paradoxical. The paradox is clarified at the trans**form**ation of Jesus as "he was transfigured before them; and His face shone like the sun, and His garments became as white as light" (Matthew 17:2). The transfiguration was actually a change ("trans") in outward expression ("figure" or "form"). It was the reversal of what happened in Philippians 2:6-7. In the Matthew 17:2 "change" we see the outward expression of deity (proof that the deity of Jesus still existed). Then we see another "change" as "Jesus came to them and touched them and said, 'Arise, and do not be afraid.' And lifting up their eyes, they saw no one, except Jesus Himself" (Matthew 17:7-8). Here, we see the outward expression of Jesus as man. He can go back and forth in His expression because He actually is the full nature of both. The expression is dependent on the nature. The nature is not dependent on the expression. Thus, Jesus can have two natures at the same time while only outwardly expressing one of them. Another way to say this is, "you can be what you are not expressing."

Paul used Jesus as the ultimate example of the "attitude" he exhorted the Philippians to have when he charged them to "have this attitude in yourselves which was also in Christ Jesus" (Philippians 2:5). What is this attitude that Christians must have in order to "conduct yourselves in a manner worthy of the gospel of Christ" (Philippians 1:27)? It is an attitude that is willing to give up the expression of who you are or what you have in order to take on the expression of something lower or less. Note that it does not mean that you give up who you are. This is the key to having a true and balanced "incarnational ministry" in which you might "become all things to all men, that I may by all means save some" (1 Corinthians 9:22) without losing who you are "for though I am free from all men, I have made myself a slave to all , that I might win the more . . . to those who are under the Law, as under the Law, though not being myself under the Law . . . to the weak I became weak" (1 Corinthians 9:19-22). It is also the way in which someone can truly "regard one another as more important than himself" (Philippians 2:3). This is the paradox of "incarnational ministry." It is the paradox of the incarnation!

———————

THE KEY TO DISCIPLESHIP . . .

"He must increase, but I must decrease."

John 3:30

A Christian disciple is a follower of Jesus Christ. A disciple is someone who willingly disciplines their life to pattern the character and message of Jesus Christ. We are able to do this as Christians because we have Christ living within us, enabling us to draw closer to Himself and become more like Him, "Christ in you, the hope of glory" (Colossians 1:27). Of course, to help other people become disciples, we must first be disciples ourselves. The things we say and teach must be demonstrated in our lives. Otherwise, our words will be hypocritical and meaningless, and we will have very little impact on others. If our life does not point toward Jesus and reflect His message and values, then how can we expect anyone else to listen to what we say? Making disciples begins with being honest with ourselves. We must live for Jesus and be an example of the things we teach to others.

The process of discipling someone is natural. It is the process of leading a person toward a life of increased commitment to Jesus Christ by showing that person how to die to himself. As Paul would say, " . . . for if you are living according to the flesh, you must die; but if by the Spirit you are putting to death the deeds of the body, you will live" (Romans 8:13). Much of discipling another person comes via the study of the Word of God and through experiencing life together. Every day offers many obvious and practical opportunities to die to yourself and to live for Christ: "I affirm, brethren, by the boasting in you which I have in Christ Jesus our Lord, I die daily" (1 Corinthians 15:31-32).

The key to discipleship is to form an attitude in the disciple that Jesus is *worthy*. It is *worth* it to follow Jesus and therefore natural to "*worth*ship" Him. It will be a natural scene in heaven to hear the proclamation, "Worthy are You, our Lord and our God, to receive glory and honor and power; for You created all things, and because of Your will they existed, and were created" (Revelation 4:11). And so, the potential disciple must be willing to pay whatever price there is in order to follow Jesus. A disciple must be willing to even die for Christ (John 11:16). To teach and model this attitude of total commitment to Jesus is the key to the successful process of discipling someone. A growing disciple is one who is retaining fewer and fewer options and holding on to more and more of Jesus Christ (John 3:30). He is one who says, "But seek first His kingdom and His righteousness, and all these things will be added to you" (Matthew 6:33).

History shows us cases of building commitment in the lives of those who are followers of someone else. Cortez, the infamous Spanish explorer, knew how to disciple conquistadors. He created increased commitment in the lives of his soldiers by reducing their available options. When Cortez arrived on the beaches of Vera Cruz in 1519 in order to conquer the land of Mexico, he burned each one of the eleven ships that he and his men sailed on. The soldiers stood on the beach watching as their only form of retreat sank into the Gulf of Mexico. The soldiers had only one direction to go. They began to march straight ahead toward the interior of Mexico. Cortez created commitment in his men by reducing their options.

In the same way the process of discipleship must build more commitment to Christ by reducing the person's options. The process of discipleship must teach others how to die to themselves and to leave Christ as the only option. The process of discipleship must burn the ships of retreat in a person's life. It must destroy all routes of retreat and encourage others to march straight ahead toward Jesus. You might say that for the disciple of Jesus, the ships are sin! Disciples must reduce their options by burning (dying to) their ships of sin: " . . . and He Himself bore our sins in His body on the cross, so that we might die to sin and live to righteousness . . . " (1 Peter 2:24). Ultimately then, the disciple is one who can say, "I have been crucified with Christ; and it is no longer I who live, but Christ lives in me . . . " (Galatians 2:20).

MAY 27

THE QUESTION OF APOSTASY: CAN YOU FALL AWAY?

"Those on the rocky soil are those who, when they hear, receive the word with joy; and these have no firm root; they believe for a while, and in time of temptation fall away."

Luke 8:13

There exist several topics that, historically, have been categorized under the "classic" theological debates. Often, these debates are rooted in the theological paradox that is formed by the free will of man existing together with the sovereignty of God. One of these debates, the possibility or impossibility of apostasy, includes one side that emphasizes the free will of man and concludes that a person can fall away and "lose their salvation." This Conditional Security position is put up against the Eternal Security position that emphasizes the sovereignty of God and concludes "once saved, always saved." So, what about the question of apostasy? Can you fall away or not?

Scripture seems to point to the possibility of apostasy. Some people are described as those who "receive the word with joy . . . believe for a while, and in time of temptation fall away" (Luke 8:13). At the same time, Scripture seems to support the idea of "eternal security." Jesus speaks of His sheep (followers) as those whom He gives eternal life to and who "shall never perish, and no one shall snatch them out of My hand" (John 10:28).

Judas, of course, is the classic example of apostasy (John 6:70). With respect to his eternal situation we need only to refer to the obvious implication of the words, "better for him to have not been born" (Mark 14:21). The question, however, that the proponent of eternal security would ask is whether Judas was ever a "firm" believer to begin with, or was he simply a "temporary" believer (Matthew 13:21)? The argument here would be, "How can someone lose their salvation if that person never had it to begin with?"

And so, we see the essence of the debate. Perhaps, the best way to answer the question of apostasy ("Can you fall away or not?") is to say that apostasy is theoretically possible (John 17:9-12; Hebrews 6:4-6; 10:26-39; 2 Peter 2:20-22) but practically impossible (John 10:28-29; Jude 24; Ephesians 4:30; Romans 8:38-39). And so, the believer must understand and appropriately respond to the fact that he must finish the race (Matthew 24:13; 1 Corinthians 9:24; Hebrews 12:1) while, at the same time, can gain comfort from knowing that he is protected by God while in that race until the end (Matthew 28:20).

MAY 28

PROPER CONDUCT REQUIRES A PROPER ATTITUDE

"Only conduct yourselves in a manner worthy of the gospel of Christ . . . Have this attitude in yourselves which was also in Christ Jesus . . ."

Philippians 1:27; 2:5

A manner of conduct that is consistent with Christ requires an attitude that is consistent with Christ. Christian conduct requires Christian attitude. So, when Paul exhorts the Philippians to "conduct yourselves in a manner worthy of the gospel of Christ" (Philippians 1:27), he also charges them to "have this attitude in yourselves which was also in Christ Jesus" (Philippians 2:5). If you are going to engage in proper conduct, you are going to have to embody a proper attitude.

What is "this attitude" that will enhance our ability to engage in proper conduct? Paul previously referred to the "attitude" when he said, "make my joy complete by being of the same mind, maintaining the same love, united in spirit, intent on one purpose" (Philippians 2:2). In the Greek, the word translated as "attitude" is the same word that is translated as "mind" and "purpose." By the time Paul charges the Philippians to "have this attitude" (verse 5), he has already told them (verse 2) to be "of the same mind (attitude)" and to be "intent on one purpose (attitude)." With this understanding, we can see that what comes before Paul's charge to "have this attitude" is the definition and description of the "attitude" and what comes after the charge is a picture of the perfect example of the "attitude" (Christ's attitude as the perfect example).

The "attitude" is one that would "do nothing from selfishness or empty conceit, but with humility of mind let each of you regard one another as more important than himself" (Philippians 2:3). The attitude is further described as that which would "not merely look out for your own personal interests, but also for the interests of others" (Philippians 2:4). It is not a divisive attitude. It does not focus on personal gain—a divisive attitude is the enemy of Christian unity—and so avoids being the friend of Christian opposition (there is, perhaps, nothing the devil hates more than to see Christians selflessly showing preference for each other!). It is an attitude that considers the other person's needs and interests as more important than one's own (Romans 12:10). It directs its concern toward others (Galatians 5:13). It is an attitude that gives others preference (1 Peter 5:5).

Can this really be done? How can we have this attitude? How? We have to do it *with* a certain tool? What is that tool? We have to do it "with humility of mind." This literally means "to bring low." Only with a bringing low of ourselves can we focus our attention on others. Only with a self-decrease can we enact an other-increase (John 3:30). This "bringing low" is quite profound in its degree. It is not simply a little bit of a reduction of self. We see how profound it is when we see how Jesus himself enacted this attitude. What did He do? He "emptied Himself" or laid down His rights (Philippians 2:7). He "humbled Himself" and became "obedient" even "to the point of death" (Philippians 2:8).

Can you lower yourself in order to serve someone else? Can you give preferential treatment to others? Do you always try to get the first place in line or the best seat in church? Do you live an individualistic lifestyle? Do you say, "I will take care of myself and you can take care of yourself?" Or do you recognize that you live in a family—the family of God—and forego your individual preferences/interests for the sake of the bigger family and the preferences/interests of others? Of course, that would be proper conduct in a family. But that proper conduct is not possible without a proper attitude. Do you "have this attitude in yourselves which was also in Christ Jesus"? That is the question!

MAY 29

THE HEART OF KOINONIA (FELLOWSHIP) IS . . . SHARING!

"And the congregation of those who believed were of one heart and soul; and not one of them claimed that anything belonging to him was his own; but all things were common property to them."

Acts 4:32

Only after the day of Pentecost when "they were all filled with the Holy Spirit" (Acts 2:4) is the word *koinonia* used to describe the fellowship of believers. It certainly is a radical type of fellowship that is pictured in the New Testament church (Acts 4:32), and the only way to have that type of fellowship is to have it by the power of the Spirit evidenced in transformed lives.

The essence of the meaning of the Greek term *koinonia* revolves around the idea of sharing. Christians have a shared faith (Titus 1:3), a shared grace (Philippians 1:7), and a shared salvation (Jude 3). Christian fellowship (*koinonia*) is, then, a radical manifestation of that which is shared, and thus, can be defined as having "all things in common." Christians have a common problem and a common solution; thus, there is "a sharing in the blood of Christ . . . a sharing in the body of Christ . . . we all partake of the one bread" (1 Corinthians 10:16-17). Christian fellowship is based on what is shared and is manifested in a radical sharing. The heart of *koinonia* is sharing!

Perhaps the most radical picture of this sharing in the New Testament church is seen in the sharing of material possessions as "the congregation of those who believed were of one heart and soul; and not one of them claimed that anything belonging to him was his own; but all things were common property to them" (Acts 4:32). The sharing of possessions was not a law. It was a desire. It was not done with respect to obligation. It was done with respect to opportunity (Acts 2:43-47; Acts 4:32-35). The sharing of possessions was an outpouring of love. It was a free, logical response to a sincere belief and understanding of being part of a family. Family members share their things. They share everything.

The sharing of possessions in the New Testament church was an acknowledgment and manifestation of the heightened unity the early Christians knew in Christ through the power of the Holy Spirit. The practice of sharing possessions—"While it remained unsold, did it not remain your own? And after it was sold, was it not under your control?"—was not forced upon the community (it was not Communism). It was not an end. It was not a goal. Rather, it was a natural response to a sincere acknowledgment of the existence of the relationship of actual brothers and sisters; those who have the same Father. They shared their things because they shared their Dad. *What* they shared was based on *Who* they shared! The heart of *koinonia* is sharing!

———————

MAY 30

KEEP A GOOD ECCLESIASTICAL REPUTATION . . .

"Your boasting is not good. Do you not know that a little leaven leavens the whole lump of dough?"

1 Corinthians 5:6

Church discipline—a very difficult and complicated subject—is, perhaps, in its simplest form, that which maintains the good reputation of the church. The church must maintain a good reputation in order to grow. Existence of sin without repentance within the church is not consistent with the message of the church. This can, of course, affect the validity of the message of the church and when the validity of the message of the church suffers, the growth of the church also suffers. Paul (1 Corinthians 5:1) firmly states that the church cannot be allowed to be shamed by the sin of its members. He exclaims, "it is actually reported" and, in so doing, references the effect that sin has on the reputation of the church. He adds, "of such a kind as does not exist even among the gentiles" and, thus, points to the extent of the repercussions that sin has on the reputation of the church. How important is the reputation of the church? (1 Corinthians 6:1-5). Sin in the church gives the enemies of God an opportunity to blaspheme (consider Romans 2:24 and 1 Timothy 6:1). The sin must be removed (consider 1 Corinthians 5:7a) in order to restore the honor of God (consider 1 Corinthians 5:7b). Only then, can the testimony of the church shine again.

The reputation of the church is very important with respect to evangelism and missions. The church represents the witness of God to the world. God has chosen to use the church to make known His glory and His name. The world's view of God depends on the world's view of the church. It must be a clean church that results in the world glorifying God when Christ returns: "Keep your behavior excellent among the gentiles, so that in the thing in which they slander you as evildoers, they may because of your good deeds, as they observe them, glorify God in the day of visitation" (1 Peter 2:12). The reputation of the church must be that it is holy, because God is holy; He (and therefore the church) is *separated* (a more literal translation of the word "sanctified" or "holy"). The church must be separated from sin. The basis for discipline in the church is the holiness of God. A lack of discipline indicates a lack of understanding regarding the holiness of God. Managing or governing the church must include discipline. Our motivation must be to maintain the reputation of the church (1 Timothy 5:19-20).

In the midst of a serious church discipline situation, Paul metaphorically explains how church discipline is motivated by the need to maintain the reputation of the church as he references "leaven": "Your boasting is not good. Do you not know that a little leaven leavens the whole lump of dough?" (1 Corinthians 5:6). Leaven was a symbol for wickedness. Paul's motivation for discipline has to do with maintaining the reputation of the church. To some degree, to understand this fully, one needs to understand the church as a "body." The church is one! The leaven leavens the whole lump of dough because of its bad influence. It also leavens the whole lump because the church is "one body." It could be said that one unrepentant sinner in the church is the same as all being unrepentant sinners: "And if one member suffers, all the members suffer with it; if one member is honored, all the members rejoice with it" (1 Corinthians 12:26). In an individualistic society (like the United States), this concept is very hard to understand and accept. Nevertheless, the need to keep a good ecclesiastical reputation is essential. Sin ignored or simply accepted reflects badly on the whole "body." Hence, the need for ecclesiastical discipline is essential: "Your boasting is not good. Do you not know that a little leaven leavens the whole lump of dough?" (1 Corinthians 5:6-7).

––––––––––––

MAY 31

FOR WHOM OR FOR WHAT DO YOU USE YOUR FAITH?

"For I know that this shall turn out for my deliverance through your prayers and the provision of the Spirit of Jesus Christ, according to my earnest expectation and hope . . . "

Philippians 1:19-20

Paul was in prison. No problem. He rejoiced! While in prison, he wrote to the Philippians, " . . . and in this I rejoice, yes, and I will rejoice" (Philippians 1:18). Why did Paul rejoice? He said he would rejoice "for I know that this shall turn out for my deliverance" (Philippians 1:19). How would Paul's deliverance be accomplished? It was accomplished "through your prayers and the provision of the Spirit of Jesus Christ, according to my earnest expectation and hope" (Philippians 1:19-20). Paul believed in the efficacy of prayer and trusted in the power of the Holy Spirit. He also believed in the power of faith—"faith is the assurance of things hoped for" (Hebrews 11:1)—which he described as his "earnest expectation and hope."

What did Paul have faith for? For whom or for what did he use his faith? His "earnest expectation and hope" (faith) was "that I shall not be put to shame in anything, but that with all boldness, Christ shall even now, as always, be exalted . . ." (Philippians 1:20). Paul's faith was being used so that he would not fail Christ. He remained bold for Him in whatever circumstance that he was in. For whom or for what would he use his faith? He would use his faith to exalt Christ. The focus of Paul's faith was grounded in Christ and was designed to benefit Christ. He did not concentrate on his own benefit. Even while in prison he did not look to God simply in terms of what God could do for him. He looked to God with a focus on what could be done for Christ. His faith went beyond believing for what God could do for him; it believed for what God could do through him for the glory of Christ.

When you are in a difficult position what do you use your faith for? Is it simply used to get out of the uncomfortable situation? Is that your focus and motivation? Or is your faith pure enough to focus on what can be done for Christ regardless of what the results may be for you personally or situationally? Is the focus of your faith on how God can benefit you? Or on how Christ can be exalted regardless of how that may or may not benefit you? When you have a problem does all of your faith depend on and point to your physical circumstances? Are you primarily concerned with the removal of the problem or does your faith go beyond the problem and enable you to pray like Jesus—"My Father, if it is possible, let this cup pass from Me; yet not as I will, but as Thou wilt" (Matthew 26:39)—and answer the Nebuchadnezzar's of your life like Shadrach, Meshach, and Abednego did when they faithfully proclaimed "our God whom we serve is able to deliver us from the furnace of blazing fire; and He will deliver us out of your hand, O king. But even if He does not, let it be known to you, O king, that we are not going to serve your gods or worship the golden image that you have set up" (Daniel 3:16-18).

Sometimes, a sort of "hyper-faith pop theology" rebukes us for praying "if it be thy will" and encourages us to insist on our own will as being of primary importance. Some "hyper-faith, victory/prosperity" types of theologies have told us for so long that faith is used for us, that it is now difficult to think about using our faith for Christ. Not so for Paul! His faith for his deliverance was nothing less than his knowing that he would be used to glorify Christ—no matter what the side-effects or ensuing circumstances would be for his own personal situation—as he clearly answered the question, "For whom or for what do you use your faith?" consistent with Habakkuk 3:17-18, "Though the fig tree should not blossom, and there be no fruit on the vines, though the yield of the olive should fail, and the fields produce no food, though the flock should be cut off from the fold, and there be no cattle in the stalls, yet I will exult in the Lord, I will rejoice in the God of my salvation."

NOTES

June

YOU NEED TO BELIEVE SO . . . AKT!

"Even so faith, if it has no works, is dead,
being by itself."

James 2:17

What is man's response to God's offer of salvation? The proper response is to "repent and believe" (Mark 1:15). What does it mean to "believe"? The Greek term *pistis* is translated "to believe" or "to have faith" or "to trust." In any case, *pistis* implies action because faith implies obedience. "Faith, if it has no works, is dead, being by itself" (James 2:17). "Faith" without obedience is proof that it is not faith at all (James 2:14-19). And so, it might be said that to "believe" is to "AKT" ("A" for Agreement; "K" for Knowledge; "T" for Trust).

First, in order to believe you must have knowledge: "faith comes from hearing, and hearing by the word of Christ" so the information or content of the message is necessary (Romans 10:17). However, knowledge by itself is not enough (James 2:19). In order to truly believe you must also be in agreement; you must give assent to the information/knowledge you have. To recognize, acknowledge, and agree with the truth of the gospel, then, certainly implies obedience to the gospel. To recognize, acknowledge, and agree with your need for Christ's saving work implies that you have a sense of reliance on the gospel. And so, genuine belief must include trust. There is a personal relationship aspect of faith in which you look away from yourself (Proverbs 3:5-6) and you look to Christ (Hebrews 12:2). You have knowledge **about Him**, you agree **with Him**, and you trust **in Him**.

How can someone be saved who needs to jump out of a window from the fifth floor of a burning building? Perhaps, there is a big, strong, willing man on the street below who could catch you if you jumped. Of course, you would have to **know** that the man was there. Furthermore, you would have to **agree** that the man is able to catch you. Moreover, you would have to **trust** that he will catch you. You would have to "believe." When all is said and done, of course, that "belief" would require that you jump. *Pistis* implies action because faith implies obedience (James 2:17).

And so, to believe is to "AKT." Ultimately, however, we must be motivated by the "white flag of surrender." Our part in the salvation process is to receive (John 1:12). In order to receive, we must believe. In order to believe, we must surrender. We must stop fighting against God. The essence of faith is the action of surrendering (Matthew 16:24-25) and the result of that action is that "we have peace with God" (Romans 5:1).

JUNE 2

COUNT THE COST TO FOLLOW JESUS . . .

"For which one of you, when he wants to build a tower, does not first sit down and calculate the cost, to see if he has enough to complete it? . . . So then, none of you can be My disciple who does not give up all his own possessions."

Luke 14:28, 33

Jesus did not "pull any punches" with what He was offering to those who would want to be His disciple. If you want to follow Him you cannot follow anything else (Matthew 6:24); thus, you must count the cost to follow Jesus (Luke 14:28, 33). You want to follow Jesus? You have to consider who you are looking to follow. You must understand that you are following One who is highly mobile and who often had no permanent home. He challenges those who would want to follow Him to consider the implications (count the cost) of this fact before they decide to follow Him (Matthew 8:20).

So, let's count the cost. What does it take to be Jesus' disciple, to follow Him? Following Jesus includes denying yourself and carrying your cross (Matthew 16:24; Mark 8:34). Whoever does not carry his cross (become a sacrifice) **cannot** be His disciple (Luke 14:27). To follow Jesus is to be willing to own nothing. It is to be willing to have nothing that is your own. All is God's. The flesh owns nothing (Luke 9:57-58). You cannot be a disciple unless you release control of your own possessions. We must consciously decide to give everything to God. He will decide what we should do with it (Luke 14:33). To be a follower of Jesus you must love Him more than anything or anyone (Matthew 10:37). Furthermore, disciples of Jesus must love other disciples of Jesus (John 13:35). Ultimately, to be a disciple you must obey the Bible . . . you must obey Him (John 8:31).

What might hinder us from being Jesus' disciple . . . from following Him? First, we should note that if you cannot first admit that you are sick (in need), then you will not be able to be a disciple of Jesus (Matthew 9:12-13). In addition, we should be aware that one of Satan's greatest weapons against us is to encourage us to focus on man's interests. This can cause us to deny suffering and hardship which can lead us away from following Christ. The offer of a comfortable life has always been one of Satan's most used weapons (Matthew 16:23).

We must be "militant" against any hindrance to being a disciple. Do whatever it takes to move forward in Christ and closer to God (Matthew 18:8-9). Count the cost and then pay whatever price is necessary!

———————

JUNE 3

BEING ALONE WITH GOD . . .

"After He had sent the crowds away, He went up on the mountain by Himself to pray; and when it was evening, He was there alone."

Matthew 14:23

God calls us to be alone with Him. Even Jesus "often withdrew to lonely places and prayed" (Luke 5:16, NIV). He calls us to a time when it is just "us and him." After we have, in a sense, sent everything else away, we climb up to God's presence to just talk with Him by ourselves: "After He had sent the crowds away, He went up on the mountain by Himself to pray; and when it was evening, He was there alone" (Matthew 14:23).

The reason that we are called to this "quiet time" with God is because we are called to have a relationship with Jesus: "God is faithful, through whom you were called into fellowship with His Son, Jesus Christ our Lord" (1 Corinthians 1:9). This goes all the way back to the example of Abraham: "Now Abraham arose early in the morning and went to the place where he had stood before the Lord . . ." (Genesis 19:27). There is also the example of Moses (Exodus 34:2-3: "So be ready by morning, and come up in the morning to Mount Sinai, and present yourself there to Me on the top of the mountain. No man is to come up with you . . . "), David (Psalm 5:3: "In the morning, O Lord, You will hear my voice; in the morning I will order my prayer to You and eagerly watch"), and Daniel (Daniel 6:10: "Now when Daniel knew that the document was signed, he entered his house [now in his roof chamber he had windows open toward Jerusalem]; and he continued kneeling on his knees three times a day, praying and giving thanks before his God, as he had been doing previously").

Thus, we make it our practice to begin our days "up on the mountain" having a "quiet time" alone with our Lord and Savior. He, Himself, modeled this for us: "In the early morning, while it was still dark, Jesus got up, left the house, and went away to a secluded place, and was praying there" (Mark 1:35). Of course, God has nothing against us praying with others; He encourages it (Acts 12:12: " . . . he went to the house of Mary . . . where many were gathered together and were praying"). Nevertheless, there seems to be something special in the eyes of God when we spend time with Him all alone: "But you, when you pray, go into your inner room, close your door and pray to your Father who is in secret, and your Father who sees what is done in secret will reward you" (Matthew 6:6).

This, of course, is not to say that the seclusion of the morning is the only time we are to pray. The goal of the one who prays is to pray constantly: " . . . pray without ceasing" (1 Thessalonians 5:17). Prayer may sometimes be done alone but it is never done by itself. It is done with obedience and faith. Obedience and answered prayer go together: " . . . and whatever we ask we receive from Him, because we keep His commandments and do the things that are pleasing in His sight" (1 John 3:22). Faith and answered prayer go together: "And all things you ask in prayer, believing, you will receive" (Matthew 21:22). The bottom line is that prayer can yield some incredible results: "Elijah was a man with a nature like ours, and he prayed earnestly that it would not rain, and it did not rain on the earth for three years and six months. Then he prayed again, and the sky poured rain and the earth produced its fruit" (James 5:17-18).

God calls you to be alone with Him to talk . . . a time when it is just "you and him." So, get in the practice of climbing up the mountain early in the morning for that quiet time with God!

JUNE 4

JESUS IS REAL AND JUDGMENT IS REAL . . .

"He who believes in Him is not judged; he who does not believe has been judged already, because he has not believed in the name of the only begotten Son of God."

John 3:18

It is a lack of belief in Jesus that results in judgment (John 3:18). Unbelief leads to condemnation (Mark 16:16). Moreover, unbelief and disobedience result in receiving the wrath of God (John 3:36). How is this unbelief manifested? Our words are not insignificant! They can be very costly. They can result in judgment: "But I tell you that every careless word that people speak, they shall give an accounting for it in the day of judgment. For by your words you will be justified, and by your words you will be condemned" (Matthew 12:36). Perhaps a specific application of this warning concerns how we interact with those whose "believing" should be protected: "Whoever causes one of these little ones who believe to stumble, it would be better for him if, with a heavy millstone hung around his neck, he had been cast into the sea" (Mark 9:42).

Judgment is more concerned with quality than quantity. Jesus will not judge us when He comes again according to how much we have in the end, but according to what we did with that which He gave us in the beginning (while He was gone). To some degree, obedience is measured in terms of stewardship. Some people are afraid to fail (which is a form of pride and unbelief). Thus, they never use what Jesus gave them. They will suffer loss and judgment (Luke 19:12-26). God allows us a certain amount of time (grace) to bear fruit. If we continue to be useless, then at some point we will be cut down; that is, judged (Luke 13:6-9).

There seem to be different degrees of condemnation or judgment (Luke 20:47). Jesus' actions, attitudes, and words towards hypocrites seem to indicate that they will be judged with a greater degree of judgment (Mark 12:40). The issue of stewardship (using what Jesus gave us) and this issue of different degrees of condemnation seem to be linked together:

> And the Lord said, 'Who then is the faithful and sensible steward, whom his master will put in charge of his servants, to give them their rations at the proper time? Blessed is that slave whom his master finds so doing when he comes. Truly I say to you that he will put him in charge of all his possessions. But if that slave says in his heart, 'My master will be a long time in coming,' and begins to beat the slaves, *both* men and women, and to eat and drink and get drunk; the master of that slave will come on a day when he does not expect *him* and at an hour he does not know, and will cut him in pieces, and assign him a place with the unbelievers. And that slave who knew his master's will and did not get ready or act in accord with his will, will receive many lashes, but the one who did not know it, and committed deeds worthy of a flogging, will receive but few. From everyone who has been given much, much will be required; and to whom they entrusted much, of him they will ask all the more' (Luke 12:42-48).

JUNE 5

THE SON IS INTERCHANGEABLE
WITH THE FATHER

*"'Return to your house and describe what great things **God** has done for you.' So he went away, proclaiming throughout the whole city what great things **Jesus** had done for him."*

Luke 8:39, emphasis author's

Jesus is God. It is not a hidden mystery of the Scripture. The deity of Jesus is put forth quite plainly and in a variety of ways. One way in which the Scripture asserts this is through the way in which the Son is interchangeable with the Father, without the loss of meaningful distinctiveness of either. Jesus and God are interchanged quite naturally and without justification. For example, "the gospel of Jesus" is said in the same breath as "the gospel of God" (Mark 1:1, 14). References to Jesus and God are easily interchanged because Jesus is God.

Believing in Jesus and beholding Him is the same as believing in God and beholding Him (John 12:44-45).It is not as though Jesus Himself was confused about this or was not aware of His own divinity. Jesus (who knew the Scriptures) would know that "no one can share God's glory" (Isaiah 42:8; 48:11). Yet Jesus said that Lazarus was sick for the glory of God, and then, in the same breath, said that it was for His own glory (John 11:4).

We often search for the right thing to do. We want to know the godly way . . . the way that is consistent with the final authority of the universe . . . the way of the Father. Where should we look? To understand the deity of Jesus is to understand how to answer this question. Jesus clearly states, "He who has seen Me has seen the Father" (John 14:9). The Father has given His name to Jesus (John 17:11). The deity of Jesus is not an interpretive aspect of Christianity. It is not a doctrine that was contrived by scholars in recent centuries, and is now, blindly accepted as part of the faith having been forced or imposed upon us by those who made it up. The Scripture is matter-of-fact about the deity of Christ, even to the point that the Son is interchangeable with the Father.

Jesus claims to be God. Others refer to Him and address Him as God. The Scriptures describe Him in divine terms. He does actions that are put forth as proof of His divinity. He, in many ways, is the fulfillment of scores of Old Testament Scriptures that point to His divinity. God the Son is interchangeable with God the Father. Jesus is God!

JUNE 6

TRUE OR FALSE CIRCUMCISION ... THE DIFFERENCE?

" . . . beware of the false circumcision; for we are the true *circumcision . . . "*

Philippians 3:2-3

In Philippians 3, Paul talked quite extensively about the "false circumcision" and the "true circumcision." He defined and described them both by comparing one to the other. So according to Paul, what does it mean to be of the false circumcision? In order to answer this, Paul contrasted it with the true circumcision. Those of the true circumcision are those who: 1) worship in the Spirit, 2) glory in Jesus, 3) put no confidence in the flesh. Thus, it could be said that those of the false circumcision are those who: 1) worship in the flesh, 2) glory in self, 3) put confidence in the flesh. False circumcision puts confidence in the flesh. What does that mean? We can answer this question by observing a repetition where Paul gave a list of reasons why he could easily "put confidence in the flesh" (Philippians 3:4). He was "a Hebrew of Hebrews; as to the Law, a Pharisee . . . as to the righteousness which is in the Law, found blameless." Notice what is emphasized. The term "Law" is repeated in Paul's list (Philippians 3:5-6). "Confidence in the flesh" is confidence in yourself through the "Law." This is stated more clearly in Philippians 3:9 when Paul says: "not having a righteousness of my own derived from the Law." To be of the "false circumcision" is to trust that your right standing with God is attained and maintained by your good works.

Do you have any "false circumcision" in you? Maybe you feel good about yourself because you see yourself as a "Methodist of Methodists" or a "Baptist of Baptists." Do you glory and put confidence in the flesh? Do you trust in yourself and in your own abilities, accomplishments, and good works (maybe you're a home group leader, or a deacon, or you play in the worship band)? All those things are not bad things and could be good things (just like Paul being found "blameless" as to the Law was not a bad thing but a good thing)? Whether the act/work is a good or bad thing is not the point. The point is whether you trust in them or not. Do you receive salvation from God freely through faith? Or do you try to earn it through your good works in order to feel good about yourself? Do you receive forgiveness for a sin through faith? Do you then respond to God with thanksgiving in a continued relationship with Him that results in Him doing good works through you? Or do you first try to feel good about yourself by paying for your sin with good works (perhaps like a husband who wants his wife to forgive him for some hurtful act and so before asking for forgiveness he has flowers sent to her, trusting that the sending of the flowers will earn him forgiveness)? Do you forgive yourself by your works or do you allow God to forgive you by his grace? Do you try to send God flowers to gain favor with Him and feel good about your status with Him or do you receive your positive status only by "the rose of Sharon, the lily of the valleys" (Song of Solomon 2:1)?

What does it mean to be of the "true circumcision"? Those of the true circumcision "put no confidence in the flesh" (Philippians 3:3). They give up confidence in the flesh in order to gain Christ (Philippians 3:7). They trade one thing for another. For Paul, this trade was not an equal trade. It was far more valuable to gain Christ than to keep the flesh. We might compare this trade to a trade that gets the leading scorer in the NBA in exchange for a junior high school basketball player. It was a great trade! Self-righteousness (which is unprofitable according to Isaiah 57:12 and like a filthy garment according to Isaiah 64:6) is traded for God's righteousness (which is salvific according to Jeremiah 33:16). The Law (which cannot save according to Acts 13:38-39) is traded for faith (which can save according to Mark 16:16). It is a trade of the false for the true!

JUNE 7

ULTIMATE EXAMPLE OF LEADERSHIP: FOOTWASHING . . .

"Then He poured water into the basin, and began to wash the disciples' feet and to wipe them with the towel with which He was girded . . . He said to them, 'Do you know what I have done to you? You call Me Teacher and Lord; and you are right, for so I am. If I then, the Lord and the Teacher, washed your feet, you also ought to wash one another's feet. For I gave you an example that you also should do as I did to you. Truly, truly, I say to you, a slave is not greater than his master, nor is one who is sent greater than the one who sent him. If you know these things, you are blessed if you do them.'"

John 13:5, 12-17

American General Dwight Eisenhower used a piece of string to demonstrate how to lead others. He would put the string on a table and say: "If you pull it then it will follow you. If you push it then it will not go anywhere." The same thing is true with people. They need to have an example to follow. (Consider John 10:4 and Luke 22:25-26). Eisenhower would say, "You do not lead people by hitting them over the head. That is assault, not leadership."

A study of John 13:1-17 yields a variety of leadership principles with respect to how to lead. In one phrase: Service (the action), in humility (the attitude), by example (the avenue or form or medium). The foot washing is not only an insightful example of leadership, but it stands as a powerful and multi-faceted symbol of leadership. If you want to serve then you have to wash! The foot washing was symbolic of the cross (leadership must be symbolic of the cross). The context of the foot washing is that Jesus was going back to God. His hour had come. He was going to the cross (John 13:3). While washing Peter's feet Jesus said, "If I do not wash you, you have no part with me" (John 13:8). We know that it is the work of the cross that washes us. Without the shedding of blood on the cross, there is no forgiveness of sins (Hebrews 9:22). While washing Peter's feet Jesus said, "What I do you do not realize now, but you shall understand hereafter" (John 13:7). It was the cross that the disciples did not yet understand.

In the same way, Christian leadership should symbolize the cross. Leadership should be the result of death to self. Our service and leadership should be the outward manifestation of the inward death that we have experienced. F.B. Meyer understood that the foot washing service symbolized the cross (the greatest act of service in humility by example; the greatest act of leadership). Meyer offers this version of John 13:4-5: "He rose from the throne, laid aside the garments of light which He had worn as His vesture, took up the poor towel of humanity, and wrapped it about His glorious Person; poured His own blood into the basin of the cross, and set Himself to wash away the foul stains of human depravity and guilt."[3]

In the context of the foot washing, Jesus responded to the ongoing question among His disciples, "Who is the greatest among us?" The answer was clear although it was questionable whether the disciples wanted to hear it. The greatest is the one who gives up his life for his friends: "Greater love has no one than this, that one lay down his life for his friends" (John 15:13). The disciples appeared to have been very caught up in the debate over who would be the greatest. The real question, however, was who would die to self! Who would wash feet?

JUNE 8

CHRISTIAN FELLOWSHIP BASED ON THE CROSS . . .

"But it is not the way among you . . . whoever wishes to be first among you shall be slave of all. For even the Son of Man did not come to be served, but to serve, and to give His life as a ransom for many."

Mark 10:43-45

Christian fellowship must be a Christ-centered fellowship. It must be a fellowship ("a sharing") of the life of Christ, which is identified, perhaps most primarily, by the cross; thus, **Christ**ian fellowship must be based on the cross. What does fellowship based on the cross look like? It must look like what the cross looks like; it must be rooted in selflessness and service.

The cross generates selflessness. Jesus' life was a life of selflessness, a "ransom for many" (Mark 10:45). His coming was an act of selflessness, one that "did not regard equality with God a thing to be grasped, but emptied Himself, taking the form of a bond-servant" (Philippians 2:6-7). His death on the cross was the climax of selflessness, "a ransom for all, the testimony borne at the proper time" (1 Timothy 2:6). Without a denial of self, a laying down of rights, and a dying to self, it is impossible to have Christian fellowship. Instead, we will only have a Christianized humanistic community. Christian fellowship is a cross-centered fellowship that is based on "agape" (divine) unconditional love. It builds itself because it gives of itself. Humanistic fellowship is a cross-less fellowship that is based on "phileo" (human) conditional love. It destroys itself because it takes for itself. A Christian community is distinguished by its members who willingly lay down their rights for the sake of the community. It is not to say that we have no rights. It is to say that we are willing to lay them down for the sake of fellowship (1 Corinthians

9:4-12; 2 Thessalonians 3:9). When rights are selfishly held onto, then service, love, and fellowship are usually let go of—fellowship decreases because the cross decreases—as opposed to fellowship that increases when rights are laid down (when the cross increases).

The cross yields service. The selflessness of the cross must, ultimately, yield service. If self-denial is practiced without service, then there is the danger of moving into mysticism. Christianity must not stop at self-denial. It must continue in service. The Christian community is an "other" oriented community. It is a community whose members try to "outdo one another in showing honor" (Romans 12:10). It is a community whose members think of each other as more important than themselves (Philippians 2:3). It is a community that focuses on the good of the other. More than anything else, the members of the Christian community should put into practice a willful desire to put each other first instead of putting themselves first. And so, "it is not so among you . . . whoever wishes to be first among you shall be slaves of all" since its members imitate its founder who "did not come to be served, but to serve" (Mark 10:43-45).

Christian fellowship is manifested in the sharing of the life of Christ. The life of Christ is centered on the cross. Thus, *Christ*ian fellowship must be based on the cross. Engage in fellowship. Engage in selflessness and service. To engage in **Christ**ian fellowship is to be like Christ!

JUNE 9

AND SO, WHAT ABOUT MONEY? . . .

"Then He said to them, 'Beware, and be on your guard against every form of greed;
for not even when one has an abundance does his life consist of his possessions.'"

Luke 12:15

The Scripture does not demonize money. It is not simply money that is "a root of all sorts of evil," but it is the "love of money" (1 Timothy 6:10). The point is not so much that we don't have or use money ("when one has an abundance" assumes that one may have/use money), but that we don't define ourselves by, trust in, or give ourselves over to money (Luke 12:15). And so, how should we think about money?

First, we should understand that God is our provider. We are promised if we seek God's kingdom, then our needs will be met (Matthew 6:33). Of course, that does not warrant a lifestyle of excess and waste. On the contrary, it seems to point more to a simple lifestyle as the idea of needs is more descriptive of the basic necessities of life (food, covering, shelter) than it is descriptive of the luxuries of life (Matthew 6:31-32). We should have what one might call "a healthy disinterest in money" knowing your life does not consist of your possessions (Luke 12:15). A disinterest does not negate the having or using of money, but it does include a perspective about money rooted in a focus or preference for something else. Money, like anything else, only has worth (finds its reason or purpose for being) in terms of how much it points/moves toward the kingdom of God; thus, "the master praised the unrighteous steward" (Luke 16:1-12). We see in Luke 3:10-14 that the action of repentance includes compassion and generosity (verse 11), integrity towards others (verse 13), and justice (verse 14). All these actions focus on having a lack of interest in material things as it is manifested in a desire for something else that is more associated with the kingdom of God. As Zacchaeus exhibited after coming down from the tree, how we view money may be associated with repentance not so much because we negate the having or using of money, but because we have a perspective about money that is rooted in a focus or preference for something else . . . the kingdom of God (Luke 19:8).

And so, what about saving money? First, we must remember that anxiety about the future should not be our motive to save money. The implication is that money cannot cure anxiety (Luke 12:16-21). Kingdom teaching does not focus on having riches here on earth. It does include having our needs met but is in opposition to storing away and accumulating excess possessions (Luke 12:31-33). Kingdom teaching is more concerned with giving than with taking and keeping (Acts 20:35). It is so associated with giving that it is linked to being willing to give everything. To follow Jesus is to be willing to own nothing. It is to be willing to have nothing that is your own. All is God's (Luke 9:57-58). You cannot be a disciple unless you release control of your possessions. We must consciously decide to give everything to God. He will decide what we should do with it (Luke 14:33). Why is this? It is because it is impossible to serve two masters. It is one or the other (Matthew 6:24). You cannot serve God and money because, ultimately, one will become conditional with respect to the other. There can only be *one* Lord (Luke 16:13). And so, what about money? It is a tool, not the boss. It is a servant, not the master. Allow *the* boss (Lord) to dictate its use!

HEALED, DIED, REWARDED . . . GOD IS IN CONTROL

"One day He was teaching; . . . and the power of the Lord was present *for Him to perform healing."*

Luke 5:17

Before speaking at a conference in Bulgaria, I was asked to visit one of the members of the church who was gravely ill. I entered the room where this man lay with the hope of comforting him with the Word of God and praying for him. As I talked with him, it became increasingly obvious that his primary suffering was not physical but emotional/psychological. He was distraught, utterly depressed. Why? I came to find out that his depression was rooted in bad theology. He perceived himself to be a failure simply because he was sick. Some friends of Job had bombarded him with the understanding that if you are sick it is only because of your own sin and if you are not healed it is only because of a lack of faith. He was told that it was all his fault that he could not get out of that bed.

In Scripture, faith is clearly a significant part of receiving healing from God. However, we must understand that God is sovereign over healing. Jesus certainly healed many people. Even His healing ministry is presented to us with the explanation that the power of the Lord must be present to heal. The implication is that sometimes that power may not be present. Healing is not automatic. God is sovereign over healing. Sickness is not always the direct result of one's own sin (Luke 13:4-5) and the lack of healing is not always the result of a lack of faith. It can be the result of nothing more than the sovereignty of God. Its purpose can be to glorify God through the manifestation of His power in healing; "Jesus answered, 'It was neither that this man sinned nor his parents, but it was in order that the works of God might be displayed in him'" (John 9:3; John 11:4).

You will not die outside of the sovereignty (control) of God (Matthew 10:29-31). No one can kill you unless God allows it (Luke 12:4-7). God is sovereign over sickness, healing, and death. Moreover, God is sovereign over rewards after our death. Even rewards in heaven have been prepared beforehand by God (Mark 10:40).

God's sovereignty over our sickness, our healing, our death, and our rewards after death does not negate our participation in those things. So, even though it is only God who can heal, we are still called to pray for healing. The sovereign God includes us in His sovereignty!

JUNE 11

SHUTTING THE BACK DOOR
OF THE CHURCH . . .

"So the church . . . continued to increase."

Acts 9:31

We should expect that the church will grow: "So the church throughout all Judea and Galilee and Samaria enjoyed peace, being built up; and going on in the fear of the Lord and in the comfort of the Holy Spirit, it continued to increase" (Acts 9:31). There are two ways to grow: get more *or* lose less! Often in a church there is a "back door" problem. Many people who come into the church do not stay very long. Somehow, they "slip out through the back door." Subtraction can stop growth just as quickly as the lack of addition. It may not be that your church is not growing because people are not coming in the front door. Rather, it may be that there is a lack of growth because too many people are going out the back door. So, the bottom line is you have to shut the back door!

Why does this subtraction of people out the back door happen? The person may have a disagreement or get offended by another member of the church. The person begins to not attend worship services. Perhaps, the person waits to see if anyone cares enough to notice that he is gone. When no one responds, the person leaves. What is the solution to this problem? How do we close the back door? First, and foremost, are friendliness and the establishing of relationships. Research has shown that friendliness is the key to getting visitors to stay. When people have established at least three significant relationships in the church they tend to stay away from the back door. It is easy to leave a program. It is difficult to leave a relationship!

Many times, a church is controlled by one core group of people. This core group does not allow others to enter their group. Therefore, it is difficult for others to become a real part of the church. Revival in a church can begin when the core group members let go of the church and give it back to Jesus. The core group might include twenty percent of the members. A main group of people who faithfully attend but are not involved in the main flow of church activities might include sixty percent of the members. A fringe group of people who come and go at various times might include twenty percent of the members. Then, of course, there are the billions of people in the world outside the church.

It might be said that the key to church growth is to move each group of people closer to the center. The main group moves into the core group. The fringe group moves into the main group. The world moves into the fringe group. One way to do this is by starting "home cell groups" or fellowship groups. Two or three core group members can host seven to ten main and fringe group members. The core group members can help to move the others into the life and flow of the church. They can serve as bridges by sharing their responsibility and authority with others.

Another solution to the back door problem is to be open about it from the pulpit. Tension always exists between church members (they are human). The leadership of the church must try to promote opportunities for reconciliation. An opportune time to do this is when the church gathers together for the Lord's Supper (1 Corinthians 11:17-34). Remember, problems do not disappear; rather, problems are solved. The leadership always needs to be creating opportunities or channels for reconciliation to take place. This can often be done through fellowship. When people have to work together, minister together, eat together, and play together, they often can solve their differences.

In conclusion, let us stress again the importance of community and fellowship. People are looking for it. The church must make sure that it is available. If it is not available, we will continue to have many people who leave the church through the "back door." So, let's grow the church and keep it healthy by making sure we shut and lock the back door of the church.

JUNE 12

FAITHFULNESS: A LITTLE LEADS TO A LOT . . .

"He who is faithful in a very little thing is faithful also in much . . ."

Luke 16:10

A brief Bible study of a portion of David's life in 1 Samuel 17 clearly affirms a principle regarding faithfulness, that a little leads to a lot, or how being faithful in small things leads to faithfulness in greater things, or how "He who is faithful in a very little thing is faithful also in much . . ." (Luke 16:10).

In 1 Samuel 15, the prophet Samuel anointed David to become King over Israel. However, David spent the next twelve to fourteen years in preparation before becoming the king. After being anointed, in 1 Samuel 17:15, we find that David went back and forth from the sheep fields to play music for King Saul: " . . . but David went back and forth from Saul to tend his father's flock at Bethlehem." He was faithful as a shepherd even though he had the opportunity to play music for the king and had been anointed to become the future king. One thing to note is that David's faithfulness was effective in that while serving as Saul's musician David learned a lot as he observed how the King administrated His kingdom. In 1 Samuel 17:20, David left the sheep with another shepherd when he went to deliver food to his brothers, who had gone off to war. He remained faithful to his responsibility for the sheep: "So David arose early in the morning and left the flock with a keeper and took the supplies and went as Jesse had commanded him."

David left the food supplies with a keeper, when he went to investigate the possibility of confronting Goliath. "Then David left his baggage in the care of the baggage keeper, and ran to the battle line and entered in order to greet his brothers" (1 Samuel 17:22). Even in an extreme situation, David was faithful with his responsibilities. David volunteered to face Goliath in battle (1 Samuel 17:37). He reflected on how God had taught him to kill lions and bears while he tended his father's sheep. He knew God had prepared him to face a greater opponent, Goliath, by helping him against lesser opponents.

> Then Saul said to David, 'You are not able to go against this Philistine to fight with him; for you are but a youth while he has been a warrior from his youth.' But David said to Saul, 'Your servant was tending his father's sheep. When a lion or a bear came and took a lamb from the flock, I went out after him and attacked him, and rescued it from his mouth; and when he rose up against me, I seized him by his beard and struck him and killed him. Your servant has killed both the lion and the bear; and this uncircumcised Philistine will be like one of them, since he has taunted the armies of the living God.' And David said, 'The Lord who delivered me from the paw of the lion and from the paw of the bear, He will deliver me from the hand of this Philistine' (1 Samuel 17:33-37).

Throughout 1 Samuel 17, David demonstrated faithfulness in the relatively little tasks he had been assigned. This resulted in him being able to defeat the nation's biggest enemy and eventually to become king over all of Israel. So, David, in a variety of ways, clearly shows us "Whoever can be trusted with very little can also be trusted with much" (Luke 16:10).

———————

REMEMBER, YOU WORK IN ACCOUNTS RECEIVABLE!

"But as many as received Him, to them He gave the right to become children of God . . . "

John 1:12

God is sovereign. We are not. We are not creators and so, ultimately, we are not saved by our own means. We are those "who were born not of blood, nor of the will of the flesh, nor of the will of man, but of God" (John 1:13). Nevertheless, we do have a free will. So, what is our part in salvation? It is the act of receiving. We must *receive* what He has already provided. Our free will is not a will that creates. It is a will that receives or rejects that which is already created and offered (John 1:12). The paradox that is formed by the free will of man existing together with the sovereignty of God is seen in the fact that God gives the right of salvation to those who receive Him, yet it is according to His will (John 1:12-13). We are receivers because we cannot provide for ourselves, and so, we must be careful not to allow our own righteousness (our perceived own provision) to be a stumbling block. Self-righteousness denies the need to receive God's help . . . God's provision. Peter fell over this stumbling block. We must accept the fact that we need God and His provision for salvation (John 13:8); we are receivers not quarterbacks!

So, what is our part in salvation? Receiving . . . and giving. We must *give* everything to Jesus (Mark 10:21). Our part includes not holding onto anything other than Him who is offered to us (Matthew 13:44). The rich ruler was found lacking because he was holding onto; he was not willing to give everything to Jesus (Luke 18:22).

So, what is our part in salvation? Receiving, giving . . . and denying. Jesus says, "If anyone wishes to come after Me, he must deny himself, and take up his cross daily and follow Me" (Luke 9:23). The key to finding life is to lose (deny) your life for the sake of Jesus (Matthew 10:39). We might call this the "inverted principle" (Mark 8:35). If you try to save, keep, or hold onto your own life, then you will lose your life. If you do not try to hold onto your life and you are willing to give it away for the sake of Jesus, then you will find it (Matthew 16:25).

So, what is our part in salvation? Receiving, giving, denying . . . and repenting/believing. Jesus proclaims, "The time is fulfilled, and the kingdom of God is at hand; repent and believe in the gospel" (Mark 1:15). Belief leads to salvation. Unbelief leads to condemnation (Mark 16:16). Forgiveness of sins comes by faith (belief) in Him (Luke 5:20). Salvation comes by faith in Him (Luke 7:50). Belief in Jesus for salvation includes belief in His deity. In the context of Jesus' claim that He is "from above" (divine) and "not of this world," He says that unless people "believe that

I am" (God's divine name) they shall die in their sins (John 8:19-24). And so, "as many as received Him, to them He gave the right to become children of God, *even* to those who believe in His name" (John 1:12).

So, what is our part in salvation . . . in becoming those "children of God"? We must become like children (Matthew 18:3; Luke 18:16-17). Children are those who remember that they "work in accounts receivable"; they are ready and able to **receive**!

JUNE 14

HYPOCRISY AND GOD'S MISSIONARY PLAN DON'T MIX

" . . . nor will I accept an offering from you.
For from the rising of the sun even to its setting,
My name will be *great among the nations."*

Malachi 1:10-11

Why will God not accept an offering from His people (Malachi 1:10)? The answer has something to do with His missionary plan (His universal plan of redemption). It is "for" or because His "name will be great among the nations and in every place . . . for My name will be great among the nations, says the LORD of hosts" (Malachi 1:11). The Lord of hosts or Lord of the nations will not accept impure offerings from His own people when His ultimate goal is to receive pure offerings from all the peoples of the earth. Moreover, the sins of Israel are providing a bad testimony to the nations. This is opposite of what God's plan was for Israel the missionary nation (Genesis 12:1-3). The lack of authentic worship negatively affects God's universal plan of redemption. There is a contrast between what God hopes for ("My name will be great" in verse 11) and what is actually happening ("You are profaning it" in verse 12).

Some things just don't mix. Hypocritical worship and God's missionary plan do not mix! Furthermore, hypocritical worship is useless. It is downright boring or "tiresome" (Malachi 1:13). The priests are bored with religiosity. They are bored with empty worship. Religion is boring. True and sincere worship of God is not boring because it bears fruit. Hypocrisy, however, bears no fruit ("and as for its fruit, its food is to be despised" . . . Malachi 1:12). Hypocritical religiosity is boring because it is empty. This is the tragic reality of empty religion. It is dead. Nothing real goes in so nothing real comes out. Boredom and empty religion always exist together. When there is no real meaning (hypocrisy results in a very real sense of futility), then there is no life or excitement. You can only go so long eating empty pie shells before you will tire of them. If there is no fruit, then it becomes boring.

Most significantly, this "fruitless boredom" born in insincerity does not mix well with God's proclamation that "'I am a great King,' says the Lord of hosts, 'and My name is feared among the nations'" (Malachi 1:14). And so, God is calling Israel to a sincere and authentic life of worship for their own good (because He loves them), and for the good of the "nations" (because He was keeping the missiological covenant He made with Abraham in Genesis 12:1-3). The nations receive their testimony of God through Israel (Deuteronomy 7:8).

People admire the dedication of an athlete or a musician, but they think it is "weird" or "legalistic" to be dedicated to God. They watch five hours of television each day, but they cannot find time to read the Bible. They spend thousands of dollars on toys, but cannot give God ten percent of their income. What is God worth to us? Have we undervalued ("despised") God? Do we give God what He deserves? Do our offerings smell of hypocrisy? Are we willing to count the cost of authentic worship? If you are not living a true Christian life, then it would be better to "shut the gates" (Malachi 1:10) and stop calling yourself a Christian. Why? Because His name is to be feared among the nations. Hypocrisy and God's missionary plan do not mix.

JUNE 15

REDEMPTION . . . A STUDY IN CONTRASTS

"For as through the one man's disobedience the many were made sinners,
even so through the obedience of the One the many will be made righteous."

Romans 5:19

The study of redemption is a study in contrasts: 1) Sinner versus Righteous ("many were made sinners" versus "many will be made righteous"), 2) Disobedience versus Obedience ("through the one man's disobedience" versus "through the obedience of the One"), 3) Death versus Life (1 Corinthians 15:22: "For as in Adam all die, so also in Christ all will be made alive."), 4) The First Adam versus The Last Adam or Adam versus Jesus (1 Corinthians 15:45: "'The first man, Adam, became a living soul.' The last Adam became a life-giving spirit."). The method of redemption is a study in contrasts. The fallen Adam is contrasted with the risen Christ. The first Adam fell; he was disobedient. The last Adam rose; He was obedient. Redemption necessitates an opposite. Falling, to be turned around (redeemed), needs a rising; disobedience, to be turned around (redeemed), needs obedience. The fallen needs the risen . . . mankind needs Jesus!

Similarly, pride, to be turned around (redeemed), needs humility. The first Adam wanted to rise (pride); he wanted to be God (Genesis 3:5: " . . . and you will be like God"). This desire to rise resulted in the Fall. The last Adam was willing to fall (humility); God became a man (Philippians 2:6-8: "although He existed in the form of God, did not regard equality with God a thing to be grasped, but emptied Himself, taking the form of a bond-servant, and being made in the likeness of men. Being found in appearance as a man, He humbled Himself . . . "). This willingness to fall resulted in the rise.

Pride (which results in the fall) is contrasted with humility (which results in the rise). Philippians 2:9-11 states: "For this reason also, God highly exalted Him, and bestowed on Him the name which is above every name, so that at the name of Jesus every knee will bow, of those who are in heaven and on earth and under the earth, and that every tongue will confess that Jesus Christ is Lord, to the glory of God the Father."

Redemption, as a study in contrasts, reflects the upside-down nature of the kingdom of God, "whoever exalts himself shall be humbled; and whoever humbles himself shall be exalted" (Matthew 23:12). And so, the contrasting nature of redemption points to the reality of the counter-intuitive for those who live in God's "flip-flopped" kingdom. If you want to be first, you have to be last (Matthew 20:16). If you want to be filled, you have to be emptied (Matthew 5:3). If you want to live, you have to die (Matthew 16:25). The study of redemption is a study in contrasts!

JUNE 16

OH MY WORD (OF GOD) . . .

"In the beginning was the Word, and the Word was with God, and the Word was God."

John 1:1

What is the Word of God? Jesus is called the Word of God. The Bible is also referred to as the Word of God. The Bible is the Word of God in its written form and Jesus is the Word of God in its incarnate form. They are both described in the same way: The written Word of God is eternal (Psalm 119:89; Mark 13:31), conceived by the Holy Spirit (2 Timothy 3:16), written in common language (2 Peter 1:20-21), and fully perfect (Psalm 19:7-8). The incarnate Word of God is eternal (John 1:1), conceived by the Holy Spirit (Luke 1:35), born a common man (Philippians 2:7), and fully perfect (Hebrews 4:15).

The Word of God is God Himself even as Jesus, the Incarnate Word of God, is God, "and the Word was God . . . all things came into being through Him, and apart from Him nothing came into being that has come into being . . . He was in the world, and the world was made through Him . . . and the Word became flesh, and dwelt among us" (John 1:1, 3, 10, 14).

The written Word of God (the "Law and the Prophets and the Psalms" or the "Scriptures" or the "Bible") is consistent with and points to the incarnate Word of God. And so further on in John 1 we read, "Philip found Nathanael and said to him, 'We have found Him of whom Moses in the Law and also the Prophets wrote—Jesus of Nazareth, the son of Joseph'" (John 1:45). Jesus, in rebuking the Pharisees, equates the Scriptures (written Word of God) with Himself (incarnate Word of God) when He says, "You search the Scriptures because you think that in them you have eternal life; it is these that testify about Me . . . For if you believed Moses, you would believe Me, for he wrote about Me (John 5:39, 40, 46). Similarly, on the road to Emmaus after the resurrection, He clearly connects the Scriptures to Himself:

> Then beginning with Moses and with all the prophets, He explained to them the things concerning Himself in all the Scriptures . . . Now He said to them, 'These are My words which I spoke to you while I was still with you, that all things which are written about Me in the Law of Moses and the Prophets and the Psalms must be fulfilled.' Then He opened their minds to understand the Scriptures . . . (Luke 24:27, 44-46).

To understand the Scriptures (Bible) is to understand Jesus. To obey Jesus is to obey the Bible. To believe in the Bible is to believe in Jesus. To follow Jesus is to follow the Bible. To know the Bible is to know Jesus. To love Jesus is to love the Bible. To make Jesus yours is to make the Bible yours . . . Oh *my* Word (of God)!

JUNE 17

THE SLIPPERY SLOPE OF BEING "LUKEWARM" . . .

"So because you are lukewarm, and neither hot nor cold,
I will spit you out of My mouth."

Revelation 3:16

God does not accept the halfway/half-hearted thing. He is not interested in a "going through the motions" type of "obedience." He requires an obedience that includes faith and relationship with Him. "Without faith it is impossible to please Him, for he who comes to God must believe that He is and that He is a rewarder of those who seek Him" (Hebrews 11:6). Obedience that is grounded in faith and relationship is an obedience that includes repentance (turning to Him or "coming to Him") and, thus, forgiveness (2 Chronicles 7:14). The problem is that when we have a halfway commitment to begin with, we can lose that which will lead us to repentance. The halfway person can be deceived and ruined:

Why do you call Me, 'Lord, Lord,' and do not do what I say? Everyone who comes to Me and hears My words and acts on them, I will show you whom he is like: he is like a man building a house, who dug deep and laid a foundation on the rock; and when a flood occurred, the torrent burst against that house and could not shake it, because it had been well built. But the one who has heard and has not acted accordingly, is like a man who built a house on the ground without any foundation; and the torrent burst against it and immediately it collapsed, and the ruin of that house was great' (Luke 6:46-49).

A young man went to the same restaurant every week. About halfway through the meal he would take whatever remained on his plate and in his glass and throw it at the waiter. He would apologize profusely, explaining it was a compulsion he had for years that embarrassed him terribly. The waiter told him to see a psychiatrist and warned him not to return until he had done so. A few months later the man came back to the restaurant and the same thing happened. The waiter shouted, "I told you not to come back until you went to a psychiatrist!" "I have been going to one," the guy replied indignantly. "Well, it has not done you any good," said the waiter. "Yes, it has . . . I'm not embarrassed about it anymore."

That is the way we can be when we are not steadfast in our mind about obedience. Little by little we become desensitized to sin when our obedience is not rooted in faith and relationship with God. Whereas once we were embarrassed (convicted), sin soon becomes not so bad. Why? God knows the deception of a halfway heart: "I know your deeds, that you are neither cold nor hot; I wish that you were cold or hot. Because you are lukewarm, and neither hot nor cold, I will spit you out of My mouth" (Revelation 3:15-16). Lukewarm/halfway/half-hearted is simply not accepted by God:

> *You* are presenting defiled food upon My altar. But you say, 'How have we defiled You?' In that you say, 'The table of the LORD is to be despised.' But when you present the blind for sacrifice, is it not evil? And when you present the lame and sick, is it not evil? . . . With such an offering on your part, will He receive any of you kindly?, says the LORD of hosts. Oh that there were one among you who would shut the gates, that you might not uselessly kindle fire on My altar! I am not pleased with you, says the LORD of hosts, nor will I accept an offering from you (Malachi 1:7-10).

Sometimes it just may be necessary to "shut the gates." It may be necessary to reevaluate your "obedience" to God. It may be time to take off the masks of religion, repent, and get back to an obedience that is rooted in faith and relationship with God. Then you can reopen the gates to a revived religion!

PRACTICAL STATEMENTS ABOUT LEADERSHIP . . .

". . . they are not of the world . . . I do not ask You
to take them out of the world . . ."

John 17:14-15

Leadership is critical to any group. Good leadership is healthy for any group. Good Christian leadership is provided, by Christ, for the multifaceted ministry of the body of Christ. How might we describe this Christ-sourced leadership? Perhaps, we might begin with three practical statements: 1) You cannot lead anyone until you are going somewhere yourself, 2) Christian leaders have the unique ability to keep perspective of the overall vision, while at the same time remaining practical on a day to day basis, and 3) If you stay one step ahead of your people then you are a leader. If you stay too many steps ahead of your people, then you become separated and become like a martyr.

First, you cannot lead anyone until you are going somewhere yourself. A leader directs. Therefore, the leader must know what direction to go in. Effective leadership is prefaced by the assumption that leaders know where they are going so that they can lead others there also. Furthermore, a leader must be a person of vision. They must be able to look ahead in order to see what is needed and, in so doing, be prepared. A mother leads her infant by being prepared ahead of time for what a baby does best, and thus, gets an extra diaper ready. In addition, leaders must be dedicated people. They must be committed to their goals and push for their completion. Lastly, leaders must have energy and motivation. They must be moving forward. They cannot be lazy. Sometimes, they must do the things that the others are not willing to do.

Second, Christian leaders have the unique ability to keep perspective of the overall vision (that is, to "be a visionary"), while at the same time remain practical on a day to day basis. One might say, leaders have the unique ability to "keep their heads in the clouds" while also "keeping their feet on the ground." Leaders are "spiritual," but they are also practical. Christian leaders "live with" God and with men. They are not so "holy" that they cannot relate to people. Yet, they are not so concerned about being accepted by people that they forget about godly things. Of course, another way to say this is that leaders are in the world, but not of the world: "the world has hated them, because they are not of the world, even as I am not of the world. I do not ask You to take them out of the world, but to keep them from the evil one. They are not of the world, even as I am not of the world" (John 17:14-16). Leaders lead holy lives before God. Having said this, it must be said also that leaders are still people. Leaders must be open (vulnerable) with their people. In many ways, it is an issue of humility. They identify with their people and their people can identify with them. Of course, the greatest example of this is Jesus Himself who, " . . . existed in the form of God, did not regard equality with God a thing to be grasped, but emptied Himself, taking the form of a bond-servant, and being made in the likeness of men. Being found in appearance as a man, He humbled Himself . . . " (Philippians 2:5-8).

Third, if you stay one step ahead of your people then you are a leader. If you stay too many steps ahead of your people, then you become separated and become like a martyr. Leaders must be out in front. However, they must remain close enough that they are not separated from the people. Both physical separation and ideological separation must be avoided. The leader must remain close to his people for their protection and for his own protection.

And so, consider the impact of these statements on your leadership roles. You cannot lead anyone until you are going somewhere yourself. Keep your head in the clouds and your feet on the ground. Do not stay too many steps ahead of your people lest you become like a martyr. Now go ahead and lead!

JUNE 19

THE BRIDE COMPLETES THE GROOM . . .

"Then the Lord God said, 'It is not good for the man to be alone;
I will make him a helper suitable for him.'"

Genesis 2:18

Marriage is referred to as a "divine institution" because it is established by God Himself (Genesis 2:18-24). It is not an invention of man. Rather, there is a divine process in its establishment. The process begins when God Himself brings the couple together, original family ties are replaced with new ones, and a new permanent relationship comes into being: " . . . and God brought her to the man . . . for this cause a man shall leave his father and his mother, and shall cleave to his wife; and they shall become one flesh" (Genesis 2:22, 24). God establishes this new relationship because it is necessary. God sees that "it is not good for the man to be alone" and, thus, makes "a helper suitable for him" (Genesis 2:18). The man needs a "helper" or a "completion." And so, God "fashioned into a woman the rib which He had taken from the man" (Genesis 2:22) and the man, then, understands her to be his completion: "And the man said, 'This is now bone of my bones, and flesh of my flesh; she shall be called Woman, because she was taken out of Man'" (Genesis 2:23). And so, marriage provides a way for the man to be completed—the word "helper" is a translation of the Hebrew word *ezer* which means "completion"—via the woman completing him. The bride completes the groom.

The Scripture uses this God-ordained marriage relationship as an analogy to describe the relationship between Christ and the church. In Paul's discourse concerning marriage in Ephesians 5:22-33, Christ is compared to the husband and the church is compared to the wife as he remarks that this mystery (the marriage relationship) "is great; but I am speaking with reference to Christ and the church" (Ephesians 5:32). The church (Christ's body) is described as "the fullness of Him who fills all in all" (Ephesians 1:23). The body is "the fullness" of Christ, the completion of Christ. The bride completes the groom. The church completes Christ in the sense that Christ continues to live and work through the church. Thus, Paul says "I rejoice in my sufferings for your sake, and in my flesh I do my share on behalf of His body (which is the church) in filling up that which is lacking in Christ's afflictions" (Colossians 1:24). The bride completes the groom.

Whether that is the church completing Christ or the woman completing the man, it is God's doing and His choice. It is not an invention of man. God's plans to use for His glory both your marriage and your ministry in His church are divinely instituted. The home and the church both are divine institutions! Herein lies the primary rationale for a high view of marriage (Hebrews 13:4) and a high view of the church (1 Corinthians 11:29). Your marriage and your ministry should in no way be viewed lightly or flippantly.

———————

JUNE 20

THE SHOW IS ON NOW . . . DOES YOUR ANTENNA WORK?

"And without faith it is impossible to please Him, *for he who comes to God must believe that He is and that He is a rewarder of those who seek Him."*

Hebrews 11:6

God is known by faith. Faith is the instrument or the vehicle through which the knowledge of God is manifested. Still, there is mystery in the knowledge of God because it is the knowledge "of things not seen" (Hebrews 11:1). Nevertheless, when revelation passes through the instrument of faith, it produces a beautiful song of the knowledge of God.

Faith is necessary in the process of knowing God in the same way that a gift needs a recipient before it is really a gift. Faith is like the antenna of a television. The show may be being transmitted over the airways, but if your antenna does not work, then your television will not receive the program. It is the same way in knowing God. Does your antenna work? Is your faith operational?

Faith is the exact opposite response to what we see in Romans 1:18-25 with respect to man's response to general revelation. Instead of suppressing the truth (verse 18), faith recognizes the truth (2 Thessalonians 2:13). Instead of showing dishonor and ingratitude to God (verse 21), faith glorifies and thanks God for His manifestation of Himself (Colossians 2:7). Instead of exchanging the truth for a lie (verse 25), faith affirms and responds to God's self-disclosure (Hebrews 11:8). Faith is not a vehicle associated with general revelation (you cannot be saved via your recognition of God in nature) because sin has clouded that revelation. And so, faith is a vehicle associated with special revelation. "Faith comes from hearing, and hearing by the word of Christ" (Romans 10:17).

The result of faith is to know God. In Hebrews 11:6—"And without faith it is impossible to please Him, for he who comes to God must believe that He is, and that He is a rewarder of those who seek Him"—faith and relationship with God (knowing God) are directly connected ("faith" = "believe that He is"; "please God" = "he who comes to God" = "those who seek Him"). Faith starts the receiving part of the process. Faith pleases God because faith results in knowing God, and knowing God is what God wants for us and from us more than anything else.

God is known by faith. If God is the "television program" then faith is the "antenna" used to tap into the airways that transmit that program. Like "Gilligan's Island," the show that metaphorically could be called "Knowing God" is always on somewhere. The question is, "Is your antenna up so as to tune into that program?" The show is on right now . . . does your antenna work?

JUNE 21

STAND FIRM!

"THEREFORE, MY beloved brethren whom I long to see, my joy and crown,
so stand firm in the Lord, my beloved."

Philippians 4:1

What's the "therefore" there for (Philippians 4:1)? Paul has just finished encouraging the Philippians to look to the future in order to understand how Christ will bring his work in them to a completion. The "therefore" then introduces the result of that encouragement. The result should be to "stand firm." The implication of what will surely happen in the future is that the Philippians should certainly "stand firm in the Lord" now. Endurance comes from hope. And so, toward the end of Paul's letter to the Philippians, he exhorts them to "stand firm" (Philippians 4:1) and then pleads for unity between two specific people in the church (Philippians 4:2). Near the beginning of the letter, he similarly exhorts them to ". . . conduct yourselves in a manner worthy of the gospel of Christ . . . that you are standing firm in one spirit, with one mind . . ." (Philippians 1:27). Stand firm and remain in unity . . . that is Paul's focus.

And so, what is included in "standing firm" is seen throughout the letter. What are some of those things and how do they apply to our lives? In the beginning of chapter three, Paul describes standing firm in terms of the relative value of Christ when he writes, "But whatever things were gain to me, those things I have counted as loss for the sake of Christ" (Philippians 3:7). Herein, we might put forth some challenging questions to ourselves in order to apply the idea of standing firm. How valuable is Christ to you? Would you consider everything of worldly value in your past as being garbage relative to gaining Christ? How about your accomplishments? How about your money? How about your reputation?

As we read on in the letter, we see other ideas (and, thus, coinciding application questions) that may be included in what makes up "standing firm." What is your purpose in life? Is it to know God (Philippians 3:8, 10)? Or is it to be "successful" according to the world's definition of success? When you wake up in the morning, what do you consider to be the purpose for being alive that day? Is it to know God? Do you accept that the only way to know God is through the death of Christ? Do you understand that this includes your own "death" (Philippians 3:10-11)? You must die to self in order to know Jesus! Is your goal in life Christ's goal for you (Philippians 3:12)? Remember that God's goal for you is to be transformed into the image of Christ (Romans 8:29). Do you consider this goal in all aspects of your life? Is it a reality to you? Do you realize that you are being changed (Philippians 3:12)? Do you want to be changed? Do you judge the success or failure of each day according to that goal? Do you see this as a process (Philippians 3:12-14)? Are you willing to pay the price of time in order to see results?

What kind of attitude controls your life? Is it a healthy attitude? Can you accept that you make mistakes (Philippians 3:12)? Can you learn from those mistakes and press on without being discouraged? Or are you willing to do only the things that you can do "perfectly"? Or do you simply do nothing because you have an attitude of hopelessness that controls your actions? What does the picture of your Christian life look like? Are you intense like a runner who is stretching toward the finish line and who has his eyes fixed on it (Philippians 3:13-14)? Or is the picture more akin to you lounging on a hammock? Do you gain practical hope in your life from the future hope of being transformed in your body? Does the hope of the future allow you to stand firm today (Philippians 3:20-21; 4:1)? Or are you weak today because your focus is on the past or on present circumstances? God exhorts you: "Stand firm!"

JUNE 22

MINISTRY IS BUILT ON FAITHFULNESS . . .

"He who is faithful in a very little thing is faithful also in much; and he who is unrighteous in a very little thing is unrighteous also in much."

Luke 16:10

You may have a sincere desire to have a bigger, more influential ministry. Your hope as an active believer is marked by the cry, "God use me more!" How does a ministry grow? God will trust you with greater responsibilities (ministries) as you prove your faithfulness in lesser responsibilities. Ministries are built on faithfulness (Luke 16:10). The most important area of your life to be faithful in is your relationship with the One you have faith in. And so, spending time with Jesus is the most essential part of preparing for ministry (Mark 3:14). During ministry, you must spend time with God (Luke 5:16). You cannot allow the things that you do for God (ministry) to distract you from spending time with God (Luke 10:41-42). This is an essential aspect of ministry especially because Jesus Himself is the source and content of ministry; ministers are vessels.

Ultimately, success in ministry depends on God since a man cannot receive (which is his responsibility) if it is not first given to him (God's responsibility). God works ministry *through* people (John 3:27). Even Jesus' own earthly ministry was sourced out of His relationship with the Father: "Truly, truly, I say to you, the Son can do nothing of Himself, unless *it is* something He sees the Father doing; for whatever the Father does, these things the Son also does in like manner" (John 5:19). Jesus was a vessel of the Father. Disciples of Jesus are representatives of Jesus; they are vessels through whom Jesus works (ministers). Thus, listening to or rejecting the gospel proclamation of a Christian is the same as listening to or rejecting the proclamation of Jesus Himself (Luke 10:16).

Because we are His vessels, Jesus' ministry continues through us. Thus, some of the same signs that accompanied His ministry will accompany our ministries (Mark 16:17-18). We cannot simply say that our individual ministries are equal to or greater than the ministry of Jesus when He was on earth. Jesus simply cast out the demon; however, He told His disciples that they could do it only after much prayer and fasting (Mark 9:29; Matthew 17:21). Having said that, it is understood that Jesus no longer walks this earth Himself in singular places (He has "gone to the Father"), but walks now, in many more places by the Holy Spirit, as He walks through those He lives in (Galatians 2:20). Jesus sums up this escalation of ministry that occurs via "vessel ministry":

> Do you not believe that I am in the Father, and the Father is in Me? The words that I say to you I do not speak on My own initiative, but the Father abiding in Me does His works. Believe Me that I am in the Father and the Father is in Me; otherwise believe because of the works themselves. Truly, truly, I say to you, he who believes in Me, the works that I do, he will do also; and greater *works* than these he will do; because I go to the Father (John 14:10-12).

Perhaps you have a sincere desire to have a "greater" ministry. Your cry is, "God use me more!" Remember, "He who is faithful in a very little thing is faithful also in much" (Luke 16:10). The most important area of your life to be faithful in is your relationship with the One you have faith in. It is "he who believes in Me" (has faith in Jesus/has relationship with Jesus) who will do "greater works" (John 14:12). So, build your ministry. Build your relationship with God!

JUNE 23

FREE WILL OF MAN VERSUS THE SOVEREIGNTY OF GOD

"But as many as received Him, to them He gave the right to become children of God,
even to those who believe in His name, who were born, not of blood nor of the
will of the flesh nor of the will of man, but of God."

John 1:12-13

It is true that man has a free will. However, this free will is not a creative will. It is a receptive will. Man has a free will in terms of what he can receive from God, not in terms of what he is able to create apart from God. And so, the Scripture explains that "as many as received Him" can be saved and "become children of God," but the receptive free will that "believes in His name" (John 1:12) is *not sourced* by "the will of the flesh nor the will of man, but of God" (John 1:13). And so, man's free will and God's sovereignty are not so much opposed to each other as they are reflections of each one's nature; man as creation (receiver) and God as Creator (source). Thus, man's free will is that which can respond (or not respond) to that which only the sovereign God can offer. However, man's free will cannot "will himself" into anything he chooses.

The Edomites could not use their free will to insure their security. Their destiny is not under their control (they are not sovereign): "Though Edom says, 'We have been beaten down, but we will return and build up the ruins;' thus says the Lord of hosts, 'they may build, but I will tear down'" (Malachi 1:4). The Psalmist states it this way: "Unless the Lord builds the house, they labor in vain who build it; unless the Lord guards the city, the watchman keeps awake in vain" (Psalm 127:1). Of course, this kind of understanding of how man can have a free will and God can still be sovereign, and how God can be sovereign, and man can still have a free will, is not exactly the kind of understanding that a motivational speaker wants to hear. It is, certainly (at least in a human sense), very encouraging (motivating) to proclaim to young people, "You can be anything you want to be!" However, what is truer (and even more motivating) is to proclaim to young people, "You can be anything God made you/wants you to be!"

Did the Edomites not have a free will? Yes, they certainly did, but their free will could not be something outside of, or inconsistent with, their nature (who they were). You cannot be something you are not. You cannot have something you don't have! In other words, a *receiver* can only have a free will to receive (or not receive). The Edomites free will could have been used to respond positively to God through responding positively to Israel, but they rejected God through rejecting Israel (Genesis 12:3). Their free will alone is not enough to save them. God is sovereign over man's attempt to save himself, to try to use his receptive free will as though it were a creator free will. In terms of salvation, it is expressed by saying: "I do not nullify the grace of God (God's sovereign provision/source for salvation), for if righteousness comes through the Law (man's attempt to save himself and be self-provider/source for salvation through good works), then Christ died needlessly" (Galatians 2:21). But, of course, Christ did not die needlessly. Salvation could only come down to man through a sovereign God's provision; Christ on the cross. Man could not save himself through the Law (since man's receptive free will is involved in the salvation process, it could not be what man provides but would have to be what man receives).

God actually uses man to offer His sovereign provision; thus, Israel was a missionary people (Genesis 12:1-3) and now the church is that missionary people, those who *go* and proclaim God's good news/sovereign provision (Matthew 21:43; Matthew 28:18-20). Man, who has a free will, can accept God's provision or reject it by rejecting those whom God sends to him: "Go; behold, I send you out . . . The one who listens to you listens to Me, and the one who rejects you rejects Me; and he who rejects Me rejects the One who sent Me" (Luke 10:3, 16). Use your free will to *receive*!

———————

CHURCH HISTORY AND THE IMPORTANCE OF SMALL GROUPS

"Day by day continuing with one mind in the temple, and breaking bread from house to house, they were taking their meals together with gladness and sincerity of heart . . . "

Acts 2:46

In the New Testament church, community was practiced in small groups as "day by day continuing with one mind in the temple, and breaking bread from house to house, they were taking their meals together with gladness and sincerity of heart" (Acts 2:46). The result was that there was a great revival as they were "having favor with all the people. And the Lord was adding to their number day by day those who were being saved" (Acts 2:47). From the beginning of the organizing of the church, fellowship in small groups has proven to be of great value, "Behold, how good and how pleasant it is for brothers to dwell together in unity . . . for there the Lord commanded the blessing" (Psalm 133:1).

It is true that whenever spiritual awakenings have occurred throughout the history of the church, they have always been accompanied by a restoration of the idea of community or fellowship. Confession of sins to one another becomes a focus. Bearing one another's burdens becomes a focus. Therefore, the use of the more intimate and manageable small group becomes a focus. The Wesleyan revival in the eighteenth century used the dynamics of small groups to feed itself. One of the revival's leaders, George Whitefield, wrote to his converts:

> My brethren, let us plainly and freely tell one another what God has done for our souls. To this end, you would do well, as others have done, to form yourselves into **little companies** of four or five each, and meet once a week to tell each other what is in your hearts; that you may then also pray for and comfort each other as need shall require. None but those who have experienced it can tell the unspeakable advantages of such a union and communion of souls. None, I think, that truly loves his own soul and his brethren as himself, will be shy of opening his heart, in order to have their advice, reproof, admonition and prayers, as occasions require. A sincere person will esteem it one of the greatest blessings.[4]

The Wesleyan revivals grew out of John Wesley's understanding of the need for small groups. Wesley saw through the superficial attempts of the church of his day to have community. He realized that without the organization of small groups, community would only be a theory and not actual. The revived church needed to have a real and strong sense of relationship and community. In 1742, Wesley began to organize what were called "class meetings."

These meetings were house churches. Each group usually had about twelve members from the same neighborhood. It was led by a pastoral leader or leaders. Within this intimate form of community, *koinonia* or fellowship (sharing) became a reality (not simply an abstract theory) to bear one another's burdens, encourage and exhort one another, and begin to form relationships that would allow the needed atmosphere to speak truth in love and confess sins to one another. This structure and practice of community allowed the group to begin to function as a church. The group became the body of Christ as genuine fellowship (sharing) became possible.

It is not realistic to think we can effectively pray for 250 people. It is not healthy to bear the burdens of 300 people. It is unlikely that a person will feel comfortable enough to confess his sins in front of 750 people. Building a sense of community can become very unrealistic if we only try to practice it amid a large group of people. For community to be practical and real, we must practice it in a small group. And so, church history has always born out the need for and use of small groups. Are you a part of a small group where you can practically engage in actual fellowship?

JUNE 25

METHODS AND STYLES OF EVANGELISM . . .

"Then the head of the household became angry and said to his slave,
'Go out at once into the streets and lanes of the city and bring in here
the poor and crippled and blind and lame.'"

Luke 14:21

To continue to invite (evangelize) those who make excuse after excuse for why they are not willing to hear, nor respond, to the invitation is not an effective method of evangelism (Luke 14:16-20; Matthew 7:6). Instead, it is better to go to the needy (Luke 14:21). Focus on those who admit that they are in need (Matthew 9:12-13). Evangelists should focus on the needy as a method of evangelism by focusing on needs. The central need of all people is forgiveness. And so, a method of evangelism is to simply challenge people with the question: "Have you been forgiven?" (Matthew 26:28). Of course, the most foundational method of evangelism is to keep the focus on Jesus. When we lift Him up people are drawn unto Him (John 12:32).

There are different styles of evangelism. Sometimes those with a "religious spirit" may not be very open to the invitation. Inviters (evangelists) should have two attitudes toward the religious community (Matthew 10:16). They should be wise as serpents (sly, cunning, crafty, shrewd), and harmless as doves (patient, submissive, faithful). Certainly, a legitimate style of evangelism can be an "offering style," a style that simply proclaims and invites (Matthew 22:9). A legitimate style can also be a "convincing style" that debates, convinces, and compels (Acts 9:29; Luke 14:23; Acts 17:17). Another style can be a "testimony style" that shares personal experience (John 4:39-42). Another legitimate style of evangelism due to the principle that Jesus calls people to respond to Him publicly (Matthew 10:32-33; Luke 9:26; 12:8-9) is what might be called an "altar call style." That can include the mass evangelism technique where people are called to gather at the front of an assembly (near the "altar," hence "altar call") to respond publicly and to receive personalized counseling and prayer. Or it can simply be the individual evangelism technique of challenging someone to make a decision.

And so, there are various methods and styles of evangelism. Of course, the most foundational method of evangelism is to keep the focus on Jesus. So, lift up Jesus (John 12:32) and "do the work of an evangelist" (2 Timothy 4:5)!

JUNE 26

STRENGTHEN YOUR MARRIAGE BY NOT BEING A HYPOCRITE!

"And why do you look at the speck that is in your brother's eye,
but do not notice the log that is in your own eye?
Or how can you say to your brother, 'Let me take the speck out of your eye,'
and behold, the log is in your own eye? You hypocrite, first take the log out of your own eye,
and then you will see clearly to take the speck out of your brother's eye."

Matthew 7:3-5

Jesus could have very well said, "And why do you look at the speck that is in your [wife's or husband's] eye, but do not notice the log that is in your own eye . . . You hypocrite, first take the log out of your own eye, and then you will see clearly to take the speck out of your [wife's or husband's] eye" (Matthew 7:3-5). Embedded in this statement is a principle for a healthy marriage. The husband and wife must focus on their own responsibilities instead of on the other's responsibilities. Parents often chastise their children instructing them to "worry about yourself . . . don't worry about your brother . . . Daddy will deal with him . . . it's between him and Daddy . . . you just worry about yourself!" As adults, however, we often manifest the same childish tendencies yet perceive them as being more sophisticated and, thus, more elusive or hidden. You can easily forget that it is really God's place to deal with your mate regarding their performance of their role in your marriage and that you "just need to worry about yourself!"

The somewhat ironic aspect regarding this principle is that, if it is applied, it usually will heal an, otherwise, unhealthy marriage; "divine irony" is often in play with respect to the way God deals with His people as He often "waits" for you to surrender/let go of something before He then provides you with what you want/need. The submission of a wife to her husband naturally motivates a husband to love and lead her. The love and leading of a husband naturally motivates a wife to submit to him. An unhealthy marriage is often the result of a husband or a wife who focuses on the responsibilities of the other instead of focusing on his or her own responsibilities. When this happens, a husband tries to force a wife to fulfill her role of submission, and a wife tries to manipulate a husband into fulfilling his role of headship. This is consistent with how the Fall of man and its judgments distorted the marriage roles. The husband looks to "rule over" or oppress the wife and the wife looks to manipulate or "desire" to control the husband (Genesis 3:16; Genesis 4:7).

There is a clear difference between godly love and carnal love. A worldly or carnal love can be described as a "50/50" kind of love, while a godly (*agape*) love can be described as a "100/100" love. Carnal ("50/50") love is the type of love that is self-interested. Each partner gives half of their total being or makes a fifty percent effort in the marriage. Each person gives with the expectation that the other person must give an equal share (you scratch my back, I'll scratch yours). Of course, the tragic result is a stalemated marriage as each "fifty" is waiting for the other's "fifty" to happen first. Each person is waiting for the other to scratch their back! This is a form of selfishness. Jesus exposed the hypocrisy that is associated with this type of love when He explained "for if you love those who love you, what reward have you? Do not even the tax-gatherers do the same?" (Matthew 5:46). Godly love, on the other hand, is unconditional ("100/100") love. This type of love is unconditionally committed to the success of their partner, without self-concern. Each partner gives their total being, or one hundred percent of their effort in the marriage. Each partner desires to help the other partner without any expectation of a return, even when the giving is at their own expense and is at great cost. Paul described this love when he explained that love "does not seek its own, is not provoked, does not take into account a wrong suffered" (1 Corinthians 13:5).

A Christian marriage must be full of "agape love" and, thus, engage in "100/100" love. Both husband and wife must fulfill their roles without expecting or requiring anything in return. Their motives must be pure and not hypocritical. So, strengthen your marriage by not being a hypocrite!

———

FROM DEATH TO LIFE . . . FROM FIRST ADAM TO THE LAST!

"So also it is written, 'The first MAN, Adam, BECAME A LIVING SOUL.' The last Adam became a life-giving spirit."

1 Corinthians 15:45

Redemption is the plan or strategy of salvation. It is the process of bringing back that which was lost. To redeem is to regain, to take back or reclaim that which was originally yours. One way in which the Scripture describes the story and process of redemption is its depiction of the "first Adam" to the "last Adam"; in its depiction of the process from death to life. Much of what God had originally given to Adam was lost in the Fall of man in the Garden of Eden. It needed to be redeemed. Jesus Christ, the "last Adam" (1 Corinthians 15:45), came to redeem what the first Adam had lost.

The Bible describes the unfolding of the story of redemption beginning with the life of the first Adam and following all the way through the life of the second Adam. It unfolds the story of redemption from death to life, or from what was lost to what was regained, the story of Scripture (it is His Story) from cover to cover even as it is the story from originally being in the midst of the tree of life (Genesis 2:9) to once again being in the midst of the tree of life (Revelation 22:14).

Paul referred to this perspective of redemption in 1 Corinthians 15:20-28, 42-49 and Romans 5:12-21 as he developed what we might call an Adam-Christ theology. For Jesus to qualify conclusively as the Messiah, He would have to return (redeem) to the human race those aspects of humanity that Adam lost when he rebelled against God. Jesus was the fulfillment of the purpose that God originally had for man. And so, the relationship between the first Adam and the second Adam is analogous to the relationship between fallen man and redeemed man. This picture of redemption is pre-figured by previous pictures like the "kinsman redeemer" (Ruth 2:20; 3:2-13; 4:1-22) and the redeemer of the land (Leviticus 25:25-28). It is seen, however, in its fullness and culmination in Christ the Redeemer, the "last Adam."

And so, redemption moves from the "first Adam" to the "last Adam," from death to life. And "so also it is written, 'The first Man, Adam, became a living soul.' The last Adam became a life-giving spirit" (1 Corinthians 15:45). Jesus Christ, the "last Adam," came to redeem what the first Adam had lost. Do you realize what you have regained in Christ?

CROSS BEARING IS IMPLICIT TO FOLLOWING THE CROSS BEARER

"And he who does not take his cross and follow after Me is not worthy of Me."

Matthew 10:38

What is your "M.O." . . . your *"modus operandi"* . . . your "method of operation"? That Latin phrase, "modus operandi," is used to describe a way or method of doing something that is distinctive and well-established. What is God's M.O.? What is the method or way He does things? It is the way of the cross; the *method* of Christianity is the cross! Thus, to carry your cross is an essential part of following the one who has already carried it for you. Cross bearing is implicit to following the Cross Bearer (Matthew 10:38). Whoever does not carry his cross (become a sacrifice) and follow Jesus cannot be His disciple (Luke 14:26-27).

The M.O. in the business of imperialism is to conquer other nations. The M.O. in the business of monopolization is to buy out all other businesses that operate in a particular market. The M.O. in the business of espionage is to deceive people to obtain information. The M.O. in the business of redemption (God's business) is to sacrifice (carry a cross). To a large degree to be involved in that business requires that one operates in that mode, the method of the cross (Mark 10:28-29). The concept of the "last being first and the first being last" (Mark 10:31) is set in the context of forsaking (sacrificing) everything to obey/follow Jesus.

Sacrifice, as a method of operation, requires an attitude that leads one to be willing to lay down his rights. Thus, Christians are called to have this "attitude" (Philippians 2:5-7). This M.O. is ironically powerful; it is counter-intuitive to what is normally understood to be an efficacious method. The Christian response to being wronged is the opposite of how the world responds. The typical response resists being wronged via insistence on defending one's rights. Christians are called to lay down their rights and "turn the other cheek" (Matthew 5:39-42). Ultimately, the earth is to be taken or "subdued" (see Genesis 1:28). However, that commandment (like the life of Jesus) is not consistent with aggression. Instead, we inherit the earth through meekness (Matthew 5:5); as we give up our rights, we then gain the right to inherit the earth!

What is your M.O.? Is it the way/method of the cross? Cross bearing is implicit to following the Cross Bearer (Matthew 10:38). Whoever does not carry his cross **cannot** be Jesus' disciple (Luke 14:26-27).

JUNE 29

THE BAPTISM AND LEADING
OF THE HOLY SPIRIT . . .

"As for me, I baptize you with water;
but One is coming who is mightier than I . . .
He will baptize you with the Holy Spirit and fire . . .
to gather the wheat into His barn;
but He will burn up the chaff with unquenchable fire."

Luke 3:16-17

Jesus baptizes with the Holy Spirit and He baptizes with fire. The baptism with the Holy Spirit seems to include an empowering of the one baptized to come to Jesus ("gather the wheat into His barn"), while the baptism with fire seems to include a judgment, disciplining, or refining ("burn up the chaff with unquenchable fire"). The receiving of the Holy Spirit results in the reality that "it is no longer I who live but Christ who lives in me" (Galatians 2:20). Jesus is in me because the Holy Spirit is in me (John 14:17, 20).

The receiving of the Holy Spirit has to do with coming to Jesus. Some may speak of a baptism, filling, or gift of the Holy Spirit as a "second experience" subsequent to salvation (coming to Jesus), and thus, in addition to the receiving of the Holy Spirit for salvation (that is, for coming to Jesus). In Luke 11:11-13, a story about a son who asks his father for a gift is presented as an analogy for receiving the gift of the Holy Spirit. In keeping with the analogy, a son (someone who already is a Christian) asks the Father (God) for a gift (the Holy Spirit) and the gift is given to "those (sons/Christians) who ask Him." Herein, we may see the gift of the Holy Spirit being referenced as a "second experience" subsequent to salvation.

In any case, the baptism (submerging/overwhelming) of the Holy Spirit is associated with power (Acts 1:8). Some may speak of being "slain in the Spirit" as a result of the power of the Holy Spirit coming upon them. Perhaps this is what happened in John 18:4-6 when "they drew back and fell to the ground" (also consider Acts 9:3-4; Acts 22:7; 2 Chronicles 5:14; Matthew 28:4; Revelation 1:17; John 18:5-8). Regardless of the possible biblical support of these sorts of experiences, it should be understood that the power associated with the Holy Spirit is used to point to Jesus. It is the Holy Spirit who bears witness of Jesus (John 15:26), glorifies Jesus (John 16:14), and defends/supports Jesus' honor (Mark 13:11; Luke 12:11-12).

The power that points to Jesus necessarily points to the cross for the sake of the spread of the gospel: "Jesus, full of the Holy Spirit, returned from the Jordan and was led around by the Spirit in the wilderness for forty days, being tempted by the devil . . . and Jesus returned to Galilee in the power of the Spirit, and news about Him spread through all the surrounding district" (Luke 4:1, 14). And so Jesus says in Acts 1:8, "you will receive power when the Holy Spirit has come upon you; and you shall be My witnesses both in Jerusalem, and in all Judea and Samaria, and even to the remotest part of the earth" ("witnesses" comes from the Greek word "*martus*" from which we get our word "martyr"; one who dies to self for the sake of the gospel just as Jesus commands in Mark 8:34-35, "take up your cross . . . for My sake and the gospel's"). And so, the Spirit does not always lead us into the things that the world calls good or desirable because He has in mind the things of God and not the things of men (Matthew 16:21-25).

JUNE 30

THERE IS THE NOW AND THERE IS THE NOT YET . . .

"Beloved, now we are children of God, and it has not appeared as yet what we will be . . ."

1 John 3:2

The Scripture declares what we are "*now*" while also referring to "*yet* what we will be" (1 John 3:2). There exists in Scripture an "already *and* not yet" dynamic. Salvation is already and not yet (Romans 8:24; 1 Corinthians 1:18). The "appearing of God" is already and not yet (Titus 2:11-13). The kingdom of God is already and not yet: "he left nothing that is not subject to him" and "now we do not yet see all things subjected to him" (Hebrews 2:8-9).

The kingdom of God is "already." The proof of the existence of the "kingdom now" is found in the working of His power. Jesus prophesied that the kingdom of God would come with power. This prophecy was fulfilled at the Transfiguration of Jesus and, then, on the Day of Pentecost (Mark 9:1; Acts 1:8; 2:4). The presence of the kingdom of God is related directly to the power of God and the working of miracles among both the Jews (Matthew 10:5-8) and the gentiles (Luke 10:8-9). The proof of the existence of the "kingdom now" is also found in the establishment of His victory. The presence of the kingdom of God is proven by the reign of God over Satan (Luke 11:20; Matthew 12:26-29). At the same time, the presence of the kingdom of God is proven by the fact that the kingdom of God grows together with the kingdom of Satan. In the end they will be separated, but for now we can distinguish them by the different fruit that is produced (Matthew 13:24-30, 48).

The kingdom of God is "not yet." It has not yet come in its fullness. And so, the reference to the judgment day in Luke 10:14 is linked to "that day" in Luke 10:12. "That day" is linked to Luke 10:11 and implies "that the kingdom of God has come near" but has not yet come in its fullness. It will come in its fullness on the judgment day. The kingdom of God does not "appear immediately" (Luke 19:11); it does not appear in its fullness. Jesus must first go away "and then return" (Luke 19:12). He will return as Judge with full reign (Luke 19:11-27). There are two comings of the kingdom of God because there are two comings of the King. Ultimately, the kingdom of God will be separated from the kingdom of Satan. This will happen in the future when the kingdom comes in its fullness (Matthew 13:24-30). And so, there is a future feast that is associated with the kingdom of God. People will come from everywhere and will dine at the table together with Abraham, Isaac, Jacob, and the Prophets (Matthew 8:11; Luke 13:28-29). Jesus says He will not drink wine again until He drinks it in the kingdom of God (Matthew 26:29; Mark 14:25) and will not eat the Passover again until it is fulfilled in the kingdom of God (Luke 22:16). Jesus refers to the future when He says that the apostles will eat at the table in His kingdom. They will sit on thrones and judge the 12 tribes of Israel (Luke 22:29-30).

The entrance into the kingdom of God is placed in the future (Mark 9:43-45). So too, the awarding of positions in the kingdom of God is spoken of in terms of a future event (Matthew 20:21-23). It should be noted that your position in the "kingdom not yet" is directly correlated to your actions in the "kingdom already." There is the "now" and there is the "not yet," but in no way are they mutually exclusive. So, the question is, "What are you doing with your time in the 'kingdom already'?" since it will affect your status in the "kingdom not yet." Be exhorted as Paul exhorted the Corinthians: " . . . we also urge you not to receive the grace of God in vain – for He says, 'At the acceptable time I listened to you, and on the day of salvation I helped you'; behold, now is 'the acceptable time,' behold, now is 'the day of salvation . . .'" (2 Corinthians 6:1-2). And finally, "encourage one another day after day, as long as it is *still* called 'Today,' so that none of you will be hardened by the deceitfulness of sin" (Hebrews 3:13).

There is the "now kingdom" and the "not yet kingdom" since there are two comings of Christ. He came in the incarnation and He will come again when He returns. Be ready!

NOTES

July

BIBLICAL POSITIVE THINKING . . .

"I said, 'I beseech You, O Lord God of heaven, the great and awesome God, who preserves the covenant and lovingkindness for those who love Him and keep His commandments . . . '"

Nehemiah 1:5

Nehemiah was a positive thinker. He was a man of faith. What was this positive thinking and faith based on? It was based on three things (Nehemiah 1:5):

It was based on his firm belief that his God was able to meet his need. Faith starts with who God is. His prayer began with a statement of who God is, which focused on God's ability: "O Lord God of heaven, the great and awesome God."

It was based on his firm belief that his God was faithful and willing to answer his prayer. Faith continues with the belief that God is for you, not against you. His prayer continued with a reminder that God is a God of justice and love "who preserves the covenant and lovingkindness."

It was based on his confidence of being in the right position himself. Faith includes an understanding of who you are. Nehemiah's prayer ended with a description of the people who God was willing to help. They were the ones who had a relationship with God and who obeyed Him; He was "for those who love Him and keep his commandments."

This definition of "positive thinking" is somewhat different than some popular, philosophical teachings about positive thinking. The biblical definition focuses on the promises of God and what God has already said. Popular/philosophical teaching often focuses on the desires of man and what man says. This type of teaching in the church has sometimes been referred to as "positive confession."

Although the "positive confession" movement is not wholly representative of biblical teaching on faith, it still points to a biblical attitude that believers should have, an attitude of confidence:

> Now suppose one of you fathers is asked by his son for a fish; he will not give him a snake instead of a fish, will he? Or if he is asked for an egg, he will not give him a scorpion, will he? If you then, being evil, know how to give good gifts to your children, how much more will your heavenly Father give the Holy Spirit to those who ask Him? (Luke 11:11-13).

An earthly father loves his son and, therefore, has a great desire to respond to his son's requests. How much more does our heavenly father love us? How much more does our heavenly father desire to give us good things? How much more is our heavenly Father able to do? How much more ability does He have to answer our requests? The answers to these questions form the basis for confidence in prayer. God is for us. God is able. What are we, then, as His children going to be? Timid? Uncertain? No! We are going to be confident! Like Nehemiah, we are going to be positive thinkers. We are going to be people of faith.

––––––––––

JULY 2

WE MUST BE A MISSIONARY PEOPLE . . .

" . . . but you will receive power when the Holy Spirit has come upon you;
and you shall be My witnesses both in Jerusalem, and in all Judea and Samaria,
and even to the remotest part of the earth."

Acts 1:8

Two of the major themes in the book of Acts, the power of the Holy Spirit and the spread of the gospel, go together like a fan and the circulation of air. The purpose of a fan is to circulate air. The purpose of the power of the Spirit is to spread the gospel. And so, the gospel is to be spread to all levels of society and to all locations. According to Acts 1:8, the gospel would be spread to Jerusalem, Judea, and Samaria, and to the ends of the earth. This meant the gospel was to be spread in the local community, in the surrounding provinces, and to the most distant places as well. The spread of the gospel in Jerusalem (Acts 1-7) was accomplished at some cost. There was much persecution as we can see from the various jail experiences (Acts 4-5) and the death of Stephen (Acts 7). In the midst of persecution, the church at this time began to develop more of a structure or order (note the appointment of deacons in Acts 6). The spread of the gospel in Judea and Samaria (Acts 8-9) had as its focus Philip's ministry in Samaria (Acts 8). One might note here how, perhaps, African Christianity had its roots in this phase of early church outreach (consider the account of the Ethiopian eunuch). Meanwhile, Paul was ministering in Damascus (Acts 9:19-31) and Peter was ministering in Lydda, Sharon, and Joppa.

The spread of the gospel (Acts 1:8) was going "even to the remotest part of the earth" (Acts 10-28). Peter went to Caesarea (Acts 10), and Antioch (Acts 11:19). Then on Paul's first missionary journey He ended up in Cyprus (Acts 13:5-13), Perga (Acts 13:13), Antioch Pisidia (Acts 13:14), Iconium (Acts 13:51), and Lystra and Derbe (Acts 14:6). On Paul's second missionary journey he went to Asia Minor and Greece, including places like Syria and Cilicia (Acts 15:41), Lystra (Acts 16:1), Phrygia and Galatia (Acts 16:6), Troas (Acts 16:9), Philippi (Acts 16:12), Thessalonica and Berea

(Acts 17:1, 10), Athens and Corinth (Acts 17:16 and 18:1), and Ephesus (Acts 18:19). On Paul's third missionary journey he traveled to Asia Minor and Greece again: to Galatia (Acts 18:23), to Ephesus (Acts 19:1), to Greece (Acts 20:2), to Troas (Acts 20:6-12), to Tyre (Acts 21:1-4), to Caesarea (Acts 21:8), and to Rome (through Paul's imprisonment). Paul testified before many influential people such as Felix and Agrippa (Acts 26:18) as God sovereignly used Paul's imprisonment to bring the gospel to Rome (Acts 26:32). Finally, tradition tells us that Paul even got as far as Spain (Romans 15:24-28).

Certainly, the New Testament church responded to the instructions of Acts 1:8. The gospel was spread from Jerusalem to the known ends of the earth. The high priest said, "you have filled Jerusalem with your teaching" (Acts 5:28; Acts 6:7). Due to persecution in Jerusalem, Christians were scattered throughout Judea and Samaria (Acts 8:1; Acts 8:14; Acts 9:31). The gospel then began to be spread to the "end of the earth" (Acts 13:47) by those who "upset the whole world" (Acts 17:6) and more specifically, Paul, who stirred up "all the Jews throughout the world" (Acts 24:5). And so, the obvious application question to ask ourselves is: Are we going to our Jerusalems, Judeas, Samarias, and even to the remotest parts of the earth? The question is as foundational as God's heart (John 3:16 . . . "He so loved the **world**") . . . **We must be a missionary people!**

JULY 3

JESUS: THE CLIMAX OF REVELATION (REMOVING THE VEIL)

"And the veil of the temple was torn in two from top to bottom."

Mark 15:38

The symbolic tradition of yester-year wedding ceremonies in which the bride wore a veil as she walked down the aisle only to have it lifted by her father as he passed her over to the groom represented the revealing of the bride to the groom; the *re* . . . moving of the *veil* or *re* . . . *vela* . . . *tion*. All of history is the story of God increasingly revealing Himself to man. This progression is seen in the ongoing development of covenants made by God with man . . . covenants that all point to and culminate in the new covenant that is associated with the coming or revealing of God in the most direct and complete way; God revealed in Jesus Christ. The new covenant is not "new" in the sense of being separate from or unrelated to the old covenant; rather, it is "new" in the sense of being a better (Hebrews 7:22; 8:6; 12:24) or more complete revelation of the same thing that God has always been revealing. There is no God of the old covenant who is separate from or unrelated to the God of the new covenant, "God is the same today, yesterday, and forever" (Hebrews 13:8). He is, has been, and will continue to be in the same business. The name of His business is *Revelation, God and Son.*

Jesus (meaning "God Saves") is the focus of all of the covenants, who/what is being revealed. He is seen in all of Scripture (Luke 24:27, 44; John 5:39). The coming of the divine Messiah/Savior (God Saves) is not only reflected in the old covenant but is predicted by it (John 1:41, 45). The "progression of revelation" is descriptive of the idea that Jesus is to the new covenant what the tabernacle was to the old covenant: "And the Word became flesh, and dwelt (or tabernacled) among us, and we saw His glory, glory as of the only begotten from the Father, full of grace and truth" (John 1:14). The dwelling (or "tabernacling") of God with man, which in the old covenant found its expression in the "holy of holies" that was set behind a veil, is now expressed in the new covenant by a clearer, fuller, more complete revelation; God Himself come in the flesh. The climax of this ongoing/progressive revelation then results in the complete removing of the veil (revelation): "And the veil of the temple was torn in two from top to bottom" (Mark 15:38).

It is revelation that brings life/transformation; "we know that, when He appears, we shall be like Him, because we shall see Him just as He is" (1 John 3:2). And so, we walk down the aisle as the Father approaches and removes the veil. Jesus is the climax of that revelation and, thus, we can be in relationship with God. That is the fruit of His business. So, let us draw near . . . .

Therefore, brethren, since we have confidence to enter the holy place by the blood of Jesus, by a new and living way which He inaugurated for us through the veil, that is, His flesh, and since we have a great priest over the house of God, let us draw near with a sincere heart in full assurance of faith, having our hearts sprinkled clean from an evil conscience and our bodies washed with pure water (Hebrews 10:19-22).

JULY 4

EPITAPH ON JESUS' TOMB: HE IS NOT HERE!

"And he said to them, 'Do not be amazed; you are looking for Jesus the Nazarene, who has been crucified. He has risen; He is not here; behold, here is the place where they laid Him.'"

Mark 16:6

When we wander through a graveyard and read what is engraved on the tombstones, we see one heading that is common to them all, "Here lies . . ." How different is the epitaph on the tomb of Jesus! It is not written in gold nor cut in stone . . . it is spoken by the mouth of an angel: "He has risen. *He is not here!*" (Mark 16:6). There are "many convincing proofs" (Acts 1:3) for the resurrection of Jesus . . . many points that can be made to build the argument. Perhaps most significant is the empty tomb.

How can you explain the empty tomb? Jesus' disciples preached the resurrection in Jerusalem (where the tomb was). Certainly, if the tomb was not empty it would have at least been refuted by those there in Jerusalem, but it was not. Other historical sources besides the Bible report the empty tomb (it is not a historical question). Found in the empty tomb were the grave clothes (John 20:5-7) still in place after 100 pounds of embalming spices were put on the body (John 19:39-40).

How can you explain that the enemies of the gospel could never successfully prove that the resurrection was false? The body was never found! Well, maybe the body was stolen? That, however, is not a reasonable explanation. How could the thieves make the body appear alive? Moreover, how could they roll the two-ton rock up a hill (Mark 16:3-4) and break the Roman seal (how could they even have had an opportunity)? How did they get by the professional/motivated Roman guards (Matthew 28:11-15) whose very lives depended on their success in guarding the tomb? In any case, why would they invent a story that contradicted their own expectations? Moreover, why would they then be willing to die for a lie? Okay, so the body was not stolen! Maybe "witnesses" of the resurrected Christ were having hallucinations. But, why would so many different people see similar hallucinations, many of them at the same time? Furthermore, the tone of the testimonies does not fit hallucinations. Okay, so it was not hallucinations! Maybe, instead, Jesus simply swooned on the cross and did not actually die (thus, He would not have been raised from the dead). This, of course, is absurd! The Romans were professional executioners. How could Jesus escape from the Roman crucifixion? How could Jesus have appeared healthy (to appear raised) so quickly after such torture? And so, the resurrection has never been shown to be false even though there have been many enemies of the Gospel that would be highly motivated to disprove it . . . they just never could!

How can you explain the historical response to the witnesses? People heard the testimony and evaluated it. They accepted the credibility of the witnesses and their testimony. They believed.

How can you explain the incredible growth of the first 300 years of Christianity? The most reasonable answer to these questions is that Jesus Christ truly rose from the dead.

There are evidences . . . there are proofs. Ultimately, however, we come back to the bottom-line question in the "resurrection trial": Is Jesus *alive* in your life? What is really on trial? Relationship with God! Is Christianity a creed **or** a relationship? Do you know about God **or** do you know God? Is Jesus dead **or** alive in your life? And so, the closing argument in the trial ends with this statement: "If you confess with your mouth Jesus as Lord, and believe in your heart that God raised Him from the dead, you shall be saved" (Romans 10:9).

JULY 5

WORSHIP—THE NEW NORMAL THAT IS . . . NORMAL!

"After this I looked and there before me was a multitude that no one could count, from every nation, tribe, people, and language, standing before the throne and in front of the Lamb . . . and they cried in a loud voice: 'Salvation belongs to our God, who sits on the throne, and to the Lamb.' . . . they fell down on their faces before the throne and worshipped God . . . "

Revelation 7:9-11

Have you ever asked yourself: "Why did God make the world? Why did He make man? Why did He create me?" Certainly, great philosophers like Socrates, Plato, and Aristotle have asked the same questions. This curiosity about our origin, existence, and destiny is very normal. These are the critical questions with which the Bible concerns itself. The answer to those questions is found in one single concept in the Scriptures; the worship of God. Worship is normal!

Creation's reason for existence is tied to a worshipful response to God, our Creator, and Redeemer. This is evident on a universal/creational level, "the heavens are telling of the glory of God; and their expanse is declaring the work of His hands" (Psalm 19:1). If there was no man ever to lift a voice of adoration to God, it would be enough that the heavens forever declare His worthiness and glory.

Worship as the definitive reason for existence is also apparent on a global level; "they sang a new song, saying, 'Worthy art Thou to take the book, and to break its seals; for Thou wast slain, and didst purchase for God with Thy blood men from every tribe and tongue and people and nation" (Revelation 5:9). The culmination of all world history is a multi-ethnic, multi-linguistic, multi-national celebration of the worthiness of the Creator. Similarly, the preeminence of worship is manifest on a national/state level: "therefore, O kings, show discernment; take warning, O judges of the earth. Worship the Lord with reverence, and rejoice with trembling. Do homage to the Son, lest He become angry, and you perish in the way, for His wrath may soon be kindled. How blessed are all who take refuge in Him!" (Psalm 2:10-12). Leaders of nations and peoples are warned about being in conflict with the very purpose—worship of God—for which they were authorized to serve.

The prominence of worship is obvious on a church level. The first distinctive of the newly Spirit-baptized church was its remarkable multi-linguistic worship of God unto witness and redemption (Acts 2:1-21). Most specifically, the supremacy of worship is unmistakable on an individual worshiper level, "an hour is coming, and now is, when the true worshipers shall worship the Father in spirit and truth; for such people the Father seeks to be His worshipers. God is spirit, and those who worship Him must worship in spirit and truth" (John 4:23-24). Jesus removed all doubt about what God is seeking on the earth. He is seeking true worshippers; His very mission was linked with finding true worshipers.

Certainly, in heaven, that is what will be going on—worship—as "there before me was a multitude that no one could count, from every nation, tribe, people, and language, standing before the throne and in front of the Lamb . . . and they cried in a loud voice: 'Salvation belongs to our God, who sits on the throne, and to the Lamb.' . . . they fell down on their faces before the throne and worshipped God" (Revelation 7:9-11). Worship will be, as it were, the "new normal." Having said that, it should be said that worship has always been . . . normal! It is only logical and natural (normal) for that which is created to worship Him who is the Creator. And so, the Psalmist proclaims, "By Thee I have been sustained from my birth; Thou art He who took me from my mother's womb; my praise is continually of Thee" (Psalm 71:6). Worship is as natural/normal as breathing. And so, we cry out "I will praise the Lord while I live; I will sing praises to my God while I have my being" (Psalm 146:2). The worship of God. What could be more normal?

JULY 6

PRAYER RESULTS IN . . .

"The effective prayer of a righteous man can accomplish much."

James 5:16

Prayer is efficacious, "the effective prayer of a righteous man can accomplish much" (James 5:16). Prayer yields results. What are some of those results?

Prayer can help you not fall into temptation. Especially since the "flesh is weak," you need to "keep watching and praying, that you may not enter into temptation" (Matthew 26:41). Prayer gives you a greater sense of success, and therefore, confidence—"And he continued to seek God . . . and as long as he sought the Lord, God prospered him" (2 Chronicles 26:5)—since prayer represents your seeking of the Lord. There is a sense of peace and security (being "anxious for nothing") that comes from spending time with God in prayer (Philippians 4:6).

Prayer keeps you broken and humble before God; thus, prayer results in a greater sense of God's favor (1 Peter 5:5; Matthew 23:12). Prayer can provide you with an increased perception of **total** reality. It enables you to see the invisible dimension of reality (2 Kings 6:17; 2 Corinthians 4:18). Prayer gives you a greater sense of intimacy and closeness to God. Prayer enables you to know God and His ways. Knowing someone's ways is a result of spending a lot of time with that person. It is the same with God.

Prayer helps you to die to self. It helps you to develop a greater sense of selflessness as you focus your prayers on behalf of others. Prayer brings you into unity with others (those whom you pray with and those whom you pray for). Prayer helps you to know the purposes and will of God. There is joy in the presence of God through prayer.

Of course, the idea of the efficacy of prayer (it "can accomplish much") revolves around the fact that God answers prayer (James 5:16). Nevertheless, the "results of prayer" are not only wrapped up in God's answers but are also packaged in what prayer accomplishes" in us. Prayer is efficacious. It changes us!

JULY 7

YOUR SALVATION IS BOTH DONE AND IN PROCESS

"The wind blows where it wishes and you hear the sound of it,
but do not know where it comes from and where it is going;
so is everyone who is born of the Spirit."

John 3:8

The "new birth" (salvation) is mysterious. It is like the blowing of the wind; it is not easy to understand or observe its origin or its destination (John 3:8). Where does it come from? Where is it going? When does it blow? With respect to "time," the Scripture speaks of your salvation from various points of reference. You "have been saved" (Romans 8:24), you "are saved" (1 Corinthians 15:2), you "are being saved" (1 Corinthians 1:18), and you "shall be saved" (Mark 13:13).

Certainly, in a sense, salvation is "already"; it is not an "after you die" issue or determination (Luke 2:29; Luke 10:20; Philippians 4:3). That is, in part, because salvation is not based on what you have done or will do but, rather, on what God has already done. The "jury is not still out" waiting for your final tally that can only be "counted" after your life is over because the court decision has already been made as the "count" that comes from Calvary (Jesus has already died for your sins) has already been made. The work of salvation is already accomplished. It has been completed. And so, on the cross long ago Jesus said, "It is finished" (John 19:30). The Greek word *tetelestoi* means "paid in full." No more work is necessary.

At the same time you must continue to "work out your salvation" (Philippians 2:12). This is not because you are saved by your works (Ephesians 2:8-9), but because Jesus continues to work His works in you (Galatians 2:20; John 6:29). You continue in your salvation in "fear and trembling" because it is "God who is at work in you, both to will and to work for His good pleasure" (Philippians 2:12-13). And so, salvation is a process that includes perseverance and "endurance" (Luke 21:19).

You have been saved and you are saved; yet, you are also being saved and shall be saved. And so, "it is the one who has endured to the end who will be saved" (Matthew 10:22). Your salvation is both "done" and "in process." And so, "Brethren . . . **press on**!" (Philippians 3:13).

———————

JULY 8

BE A PERSON OF PROVEN WORTH
. . . BE A TIMOTHY!

"But I hope in the Lord Jesus to send Timothy to you . . . for I have no one else *of kindred spirit . . . but you know of his proven worth . . ."*

Philippians 2:19-22

There exists in "church work" a very curious statistic. It is sometimes referred to as the "20/80 rule"; that is, twenty percent of the people do eighty percent of the work. Church leaders must watch out for these "twenty percent" so that they do not burn out. Pastors have to be careful to not over work those that are most naturally looked to for work to be accomplished. Of course, it is natural for leaders to look for dependable people and delegate work to them. Leaders naturally look for people of "proven worth." What puts someone in that class?

Paul needs to send someone to the Philippians for a ministerial visit. Who will he send? Who can he trust? Who is of proven worth? Paul writes to them,

> But I hope in the Lord Jesus to send Timothy to you shortly, so that I also may be encouraged when I learn of your condition. For I have no one *else* of kindred spirit who will genuinely be concerned for your welfare. For they all seek after their own interests, not those of Christ Jesus. But you know of his proven worth that he served with me in the furtherance of the gospel like a child *serving* his father. Therefore I hope to send him immediately, as soon as I see how things go with me; and I trust in the Lord that I myself also shall be coming shortly (Philippians 2:19-24).

Paul has confidence in Timothy. He is like himself. He is a "kindred spirit." What spirit is that? It is the spirit of someone who has sincere motives—someone who is not simply concerned about his own interests—and is concerned about the interests of others. It is someone who does "nothing from selfishness or empty conceit . . . not merely look[ing] out for your own personal interests, but also for the interests of others" (Philippians 2:3-4). The most likely person to be able to do this is the person who seeks after the "interests . . . of Christ Jesus" (Philippians 2:21). This is a person of "proven worth" (Philippians 2:22). The person of "proven worth" is able to work with others ("he served with me in the furtherance of the gospel") and is able to submit to others ("like a child serving his father"). Church leaders are thrilled to find dependable people to whom they can delegate ministry. They are looking for the twenty percent (wishing they were the one hundred percent!). It would be ideal if church leaders could choose from anyone in the congregation to do the "work of service" (Ephesians 4:12) because all members were of "proven worth." Are you of proven worth? Are you a Timothy? Be sure to look to the interests of Christ and not simply to your own interests. This will make you usable. This will make you of **proven worth**!

JULY 9

THAT'S JUST NOT HIS WAY . . .

"For forty years I loathed that *generation,*
And said they are a people who err in their heart,
And they do not know My ways."

Psalm 95:10

To know God we must be aware of His ways. We grow in our relationship with God as we grow in our awareness of His ways. So, we pray with Moses, "Now therefore, I pray Thee, if I have found favor in Thy sight, let me know Thy ways, that I may know Thee" (Exodus 33:13), and we cry out with David, "Make me know Thy ways, O Lord; teach me Thy paths" (Psalm 25:4). Our relationship with God is intensified when we know His ways: "Yet they seek Me day by day, and delight to know My ways . . . they delight in the nearness of God" (Isaiah 58:2). Knowing God and knowing His ways run parallel to each other and impact each other. The more we know God's ways, the more we know God; likewise, the more we know God, the more we know His ways.

Just as we come to know someone better as we begin to know that person's "ways," so too we will know God better as we become aware of His ways. God has certain ways that He does things (many followers of God might describe one of God's ways with regard to Him as Provider by saying that He is "never late, but often last minute"). We might say something like, "that does not seem like God." This type of statement is an evaluation of God's ways. How do we know someone's "ways"? We are most aware of the "ways" of the people who we spend the most time with. I am very aware of the ways of my wife. I spend a lot of time with her. I know her habits, customs, and style of doing things. She tends to be very calm and is not inclined to lose her temper. If someone told me that they saw her on the street shouting at someone in anger, then I would have a difficult time believing it. Why? Because that is not like her! That is not her way. It is the same with God. The more time we spend with Him, the more we will come to know His ways. As we come to know His ways, we will grow in relationship with Him.

How important is it to know God's ways? Well, how important is it to know the ways of your wife? Your husband? Your best friend? Someone whom you seek an intimate relationship with, yet you do not know their "ways" would probably be met with a rhetorical rebuke like, "Don't you know me?" God says it this way: "For forty years I loathed that generation, and said they are a people who err in their heart, and they do not know My ways" (Psalm 95:10). So, let us pray to God along with Moses and David so we do not "err" in our hearts: "let me know Thy ways, that I may know Thee" (Exodus 33:13) . . . "Make me know Thy ways, O Lord; teach me Thy paths" (Psalm 25:4).

JULY 10

WHAT GOD LOOKS FOR IN A LEADER . . .

"Do not look at his appearance or at the height of his stature,
because I have rejected him; for God sees not as man sees,
for man looks at the outward appearance,
but the LORD looks at the heart."

1 Samuel 16:6-7

A leader's character and conduct is like a clock in an airport. The clock in an airport is more important than our own watches because many people set their watches according to the time on that clock. The same thing happens with the character of a leader. Many people set their own standards of conduct according to the conduct of the leader. Leaders have a great responsibility. Why does God choose certain people to be leaders? The answer is not found on the outside of a person. It is found in the inside of a person.

Samuel was looking for a king. He did not consider David. He was too small. Samuel thought it would be Eliab. Eliab was tall. Then God spoke. He told Samuel that He does not choose leaders according to what is on the outside. He chooses leaders according to what is in the inside of a person: "When they entered, he looked at Eliab and thought, 'Surely the Lord's anointed is before Him.' But the Lord said to Samuel, 'Do not look at his appearance or at the height of his stature, because I have rejected him; for God sees not as man sees, for man looks at the outward appearance, but the Lord looks at the heart'" (1 Samuel 16:6-7). Men often choose leaders according to what is on the outside. They look for the best and the most; they look for the "*ests.*" Often men choose those who are the smart*est*, the strong*est*, the fast*est*, the rich*est*, the pretti*est*, the loud*est*, and a variety of other "*ests.*" Many times, however, these traits are strong on the outside, but lacking on the inside.

These leaders who are only outwardly gifted might be compared to cheaply made sports cars. They look great but they smash easily. Using more biblical language we might say that these outwardly gifted leaders are like houses that are built upon the sand: "Everyone who hears these words of Mine and does not act on them, will be like a foolish man who built his house on the sand. The rain fell, and the floods came, and the winds blew and slammed against that house; and it fell—and great was its fall" (Matthew 7:26-27). When the rain, wind and floods come, then the house falls. It was beautiful on the outside, but weak on the inside. The rain, wind, and floods of life have an uncanny way of concentrating on leaders. And so, the leader must be more than an attractive person, and even more than a "gifted leader."

So, why does God choose certain people to be leaders? What are the most significant characteristics that God is looking for in a leader? Perhaps, we can begin to answer this question by using the following definition: A biblical leader is a pure, humble servant who seeks and knows God. The leader is really an instrument through which God leads others. Leadership begins and ends with seeking and knowing God. And so, the leader who seeks God will know God: "I love those who love me; and those who diligently seek me will find me" (Proverbs 8:17). In turn, the leader who knows God will seek God: "When he puts forth all his own, he goes ahead of them, and the sheep follow him because they know his voice" (John 10:4). The leader is an instrument through which God leads others. Therefore, the key word is "empty."

First, purity removes that which is negative. It prepares for emptiness. Second, humility establishes emptiness. Third, service uses the emptiness in a positive way. It points the emptiness towards God and others. Man looks at the outward appearance, but the Lord looks at the heart!

———————

JULY 11

FACES OF LEADERSHIP . . .

"Within it there were figures resembling four living beings.
And this was their appearance: they had human form.
Each of them had four faces . . . As for the form of their faces,
each *had the face of a man; all four had the face of a lion on the right*
and the face of a bull on the left, and all four had the face of an eagle. Such were their faces."

Ezekiel 1:5-6, 10-11

There is a very odd picture of some sort of "living beings" that is painted by Ezekiel in the Old Testament and then by John in the New Testament. In both cases, these living beings each had four faces: "Each of them had four faces . . . each had the face of a man; all four had the face of a lion on the right and the face of a bull on the left, and all four had the face of an eagle" (Ezekiel 1:5, 10). The question is, of course, "What do these 'four living beings' who each have four faces represent?" Maybe we can answer this question by answering a few other questions: "Why are there four Gospels?" and "How might the four Gospels relate to the four faces?" The four Gospels each represent a different type of leadership. Jesus is King. He is Prophet. And He is Priest. He functions in all of these as a Man. Here we have the four Gospels: Matthew (King); Mark (Priest); John (Prophet); Luke (Man). In an allegorical interpretation we might also connect the four faces: Matthew (Lion); Mark (Ox); John (Eagle); Luke (Man).

Matthew's gospel was written for Jews. It focused on Jesus as the bold King and the triumphant Messiah. Matthew is distinct in his use of the title *"Son of David"* for Jesus which focuses on Jesus' *King*ly ministry. He is seen as the *Lion* of Judah. Mark's gospel is the shortest gospel. It provides a list of Jesus' actions without extra commentary. Why? It focuses on Jesus the servant like one would focus on the service of an *Ox*. His life is a service for people as the role of the *Priest* was supposed to be. And so, Mark is distinct in his use of the title *"Son of God"* for Jesus as he focuses on Jesus the servant (Philippians 2:22) who serves the people like the yolk on the ox serves out in the fields. Luke's gospel is the universal gospel. It was written for all mankind. It focuses on Jesus' compassion for human needs. We see Jesus the *Man*. Luke's favorite title for Jesus is *"Son of Man"* which focuses on the humanity of Christ. We see his deity in the form of a *Man*. Jesus becomes the perfect vessel.

Finally, John's gospel focuses on Jesus *"The Word of God"* as he emphasizes the mystery of Christ and spotlights His ministry as *Prophet*. One might say, metaphorically, that John's gospel—which is so simple yet so profound—soars like an *Eagle*. It is like the "seer" who soars in the skies and sees like a Prophet.

There are four different Gospels which demonstrate three different types of leadership and one type of vessel through which they all function. The four faces in Ezekiel 1:5, 10 and Revelation 4:7 might allegorically represent this reality. The Lion represents the Kingly ministry (Matthew). The Eagle represents the Prophetic ministry (John). The Ox (who is gentle yet strong as is a faithful, consistent servant who is slow and patient) represents the Priestly ministry (Mark). The Man represents the vessel through which all of these ministries function (Luke). They functioned perfectly and completely in the perfect and complete Man. Now they function, in part, through the vessel made in His image—man.

And so, the "faces of leadership" seen in Revelation 4:7—"The first creature was like a lion, and the second creature like a calf, and the third creature had a face like that of a man, and the fourth creature was like a flying eagle"—perhaps, are symbolic of the full ministry of Jesus Christ on earth. Of course, no one human being is Christ. This "full ministry of Jesus Christ on earth" now through the church requires a plurality of leadership as was practiced in the New Testament church. A "one-man pastor" situation in a church would not be able to encompass all four faces of leadership.

JULY 12

TO KNOW (GOD) OR NOT TO KNOW (GOD) . . . THAT IS THE QUESTION!

"Oh that I knew where I might find Him, That I might come to His seat."

Job 23:3

What is the question that has gripped humanity throughout history? History shows us that man has always been preoccupied with the question of the knowledge of God. Regardless of whether the search to answer this question has come through religion or philosophy, the fact remains that man has always considered as his greatest priority the question of how to know God. Inevitably, there is something in man that reaches out for this supreme knowledge. That "something" is nothing less than the idea of divinity itself; the concept of eternality. Man was made by God (it is inside him) with "eternity in their heart" (Ecclesiastes 3:11). He was made with the inclination to know God since eternality is to know God (John 17:3). And so, *the question* is a question of the finite reaching out to the infinite.

The importance of knowing God is clearly seen from the human perspective. Job cries out, "Oh that I knew where I might find Him, that I might come to His seat" (Job 23:3). Philip expresses the heart of man to know God when he makes his request of Jesus saying, "Lord, show us the Father, and it is enough for us" (John 14:8).

The importance of knowing God is also seen—of course—from the divine perspective. God expresses this clearly when He says, "Let not a wise man boast of his wisdom, and let not the mighty man boast of his might, let not a rich man boast of his riches; but let him who boasts boast of this, that he understands and knows Me" (Jeremiah 9:23-24). What is God's ultimate desire and intention for man? It is that man would know Him. And so, God says, "They will not hurt or destroy in all My holy mountain, for the earth will be full of the knowledge of the Lord as the waters cover the sea" (Isaiah 11:9) and "They will not teach again, each man his neighbor and each man his brother, saying, 'Know the Lord' for they will all know Me, from the least of them to the greatest of them" (Jeremiah 31:34). What does God want from His people more than anything else? God's answer is, "For I delight in loyalty rather than sacrifice, and in the knowledge of God rather than burnt offerings" (Hosea 6:6). The passion God has for being in relationship with His people (knowing them) is especially seen in the Song of Solomon:

> "You have made my heart beat faster, my sister, *my* bride; You have made my heart beat faster with a single *glance* of your eyes, With a single strand of your necklace. How beautiful is your love, my sister, *my* bride! How much better is your love than wine, And the fragrance of your oils than all kinds of spices!" (Song of Solomon 4:9-10)

What is the question? It is the question of knowing God. Tragedy is the result of a lack of knowledge (Isaiah 1:2-7; Hosea 4:1-6). Why is the question of knowing God the critical question for man? It is because of the way man was made by the Creator (Ecclesiastes 3:11). God initiated it (Jeremiah 31:33; 32:40) as it is His desire/heartbeat (Jeremiah 24:7; Hebrews 11:6) and His very purpose for man: "and He made from one man every nation of mankind to live on all the face of the earth, having determined their appointed times and the boundaries of their habitation, that they would seek God, if perhaps they might grope for Him and find Him" (Acts 17:26-27). To know God or not to know God . . . *that* is the question!

———————

THE METHOD AND RESULT OF CHURCH GOVERNMENT

"The things which you have heard from me in the presence of many witnesses, entrust these to faithful men who will be able to teach others also."

2 Timothy 2:2-3

The method of church government and the way to gain authority is through being a servant (Matthew 23:11-12; John 3:30; Luke 22:25- 26). A leader must lead through *service*. The result is that the leader gains a natural authority. The formation of church government is a very natural process (1 Timothy 3:13). Servants gain ("obtain") something. They gain a "high standing" (respect). This respect includes a "great confidence in the faith" (natural authority). This is the method of church government.

What is the result of church government? It is the multiplication of leadership (the delegation of responsibility and authority). Multiplication is the result of organization (government); see 2 Timothy 2:2. It is like a tree. It grows through reproduction/multiplication (see Mark 4:30-32). In the world, men try to hold onto their authority and privileges while in the kingdom of God it is required to release or let go of authority and privileges. You must give away that which has been given to you, for only when you let go of something will it produce fruit (John 12:24-25).

This is one of the lessons that can be learned from the parable of the talents. We are required to reproduce that which has been given to us (Matthew 25:14-30). Having the right attitude or perspective is critical here: "For who regards you as superior? What do you have that you did not receive? And if you did receive it, why do you boast as if you had not received it?" (1 Corinthians 4:7). In the world, men think that those who have more authority and privileges have earned the right to relax. In governing the church, we can see the opposite principle is actually true (Luke 12:48). This principle is true because: 1) The result of authority (government) must be the multiplication of that authority; and 2) That which we receive (authority/privileges) has been given to us freely. Therefore, we must give it and multiply it freely (Matthew 10:8; 1 Corinthians 4:7).

Multiplication is not only spiritual. It is also logical. D. L. Moody said: "I would rather get ten men to do the job than to do the job of ten men." Leaders must do their ministry as well as reproduce their ministry in others (Ephesians 4:11-12). Woodrow Wilson said: "I not only use all the brains that I have, but all that I can borrow also." How do you multiply leaders? The current leadership and the people of the church must be willing to work together. The leaders must be willing to multiply leadership. They must be willing and able to say what Moses said: "Eldad and Medad are prophesying in the camp. Then Joshua the son of Nun, the attendant of Moses from his youth, said, 'Moses, my lord, restrain them.' But Moses said to him, 'Are you jealous for my sake? Would that all the Lord's people were prophets, that the Lord would put His Spirit upon them!'" (Numbers 11:27-29). The people must not be lazy. They must be able to say what the Israelites said to Moses in Deuteronomy 1:13-14: "Choose wise and discerning and experienced men from your tribes, and I will appoint them as your heads. You answered me and said, 'The thing which you have said to do is good.'"

The current leadership and the people of the church must develop ways to include all the members of the body in the ministry of the church. The job of the leader is not to protect his/her "authority turf," but it is to multiply that turf.

JULY 14

WHO'S YOUR DADDY? . . .

"For they exchanged the truth of God for a lie, and worshiped and served the creature rather than the Creator, who is blessed forever. Amen."

Romans 1:25

It is the most unfortunate of facts that we have a sin nature. Thank you, Adam and Eve! Through them, it is a fact that we *all* sin. Thus, "If we say that we have no sin, we are deceiving ourselves . . . " (1 John 1:8). That does not mean that we cannot have victory over sin. Actually, the Scripture tells us that we can "escape" the temptation to sin: "No temptation has overtaken you but such as is common to man; and God is faithful, who will not allow you to be tempted beyond what you are able, but with the temptation will provide the way of escape also, so that you will be able to endure it" (1 Corinthians 10:13). Of course, the Word of God is crucial here: "How can a young man keep his way pure? By keeping it according to Your word . . . Your word I have treasured in my heart, that I may not sin against You" (Psalm 119:9-11).

God promises to help (Isaiah 41:13). Specifically, there is victory through Jesus (1 Corinthians 15:57). In the first Adam we are bound to sin, but in the "last Adam" (1 Corinthians 15:45) we are separated from sin (2 Corinthians 6:14-16). We are called to "persevere under trial" (James 1:12), "abide in the light" (1 John 2:10), "abstain from wickedness" (2 Timothy 2:19-22), and not "love/ be conformed to the world" (1 John 2:15; Romans 12:2). We may sin but sin should not dominate us; "sin shall not be master over you" (Romans 6:12-14). Instead, through confession (1 John 1:9), "watching and praying" (Mark 14:38), and trusting God (Romans 13:14), we must be holy (1 Peter 1:14-16) as we live a new life by putting on "the new self" (Colossians 3:9-10).

Sin is a **lie** and obedience is the **truth**. Satan is "the father of **lies**" (John 8:44) and God is the "Father of our spirits" (Hebrews 12:9). Herein lies the crux of the issue: "For they exchanged the **truth** of God for a **lie**, and worshiped and served the creature rather than the Creator . . . " (Romans 1:25). Which way are you going to go today (it is a daily battle)? Are you going to go the way of the lie or the way of the truth; the way of sin or the way of obedience? Ultimately, it is a fight between "the father of lies" (Satan) and the "Father of our spirits" (God). It is a fight to see "who's your daddy."

Satan wants to be your "daddy." You must be aware of him and his ploys: " . . . so that no advantage would be taken of us by Satan, for we are not ignorant of his schemes" (2 Corinthians 2:11). We see him in the wilderness tempting Jesus (Matthew 4:1-11) with the same three temptations he used to tempt Adam and Eve in the Garden of Eden; what John calls "all that is in the world" (1 John 2:16). It is important to learn from Jesus here. In each case of temptation, He uses the Word of God to overcome Satan. Fighting temptation is a spiritual war; thus, we must know our spiritual weapons that need to be used in the war (Ephesians 6:10-18). Perhaps most importantly, we must understand that Satan does not have to be our daddy. His power is limited (1 John 4:4) and ultimately his works will be destroyed (1 John 3:8) as he is a fallen foe (Isaiah 14:12-15).

So, who's your daddy? God is your daddy. The Holy Spirit decrees this: "God has sent forth the Spirit of His Son into our hearts, crying, 'Abba! Father!'" (Galatians 4:6). The Holy Spirit directs us away from the lie and toward the truth. He is the comforter (John 14:6), He helps us to pray (Romans 8:26), He is a "Helper" who convicts us of sin (John 16:7-8), He gives gifts (1 Corinthians 12:4-10), and He has power (Acts 1:8) and fruits (Galatians 5:22-23). It is the Spirit who fights against our flesh (Romans 8:5-6) and it is the Spirit who glorifies Christ (John 16:13-15). So why not be filled with the Spirit (Ephesians 5:18)? Why not choose God as your **Daddy**?

JULY 15

ALL RISE. HERE COMES THE JUDGE!

" . . . in the future there is laid up for me the crown of righteousness,
which the Lord, the righteous Judge, will award to me on that day;

and not only to me,

but also to all who have loved His appearing."

2 Timothy 4:8

Judges pronounce judgments. When a Judge enters the chambers, all rise as they anticipate hearing the pronouncement. Some love the appearing of the Judge . . . some not so much. Who is the Judge? It is Jesus (John 5:22, 27). When Jesus returns, He will return as Judge. The kingdom of God is already (Jesus has come) and not yet (Jesus will come again). The kingdom of God has not yet come in its fullness but will come in its fullness when the Judge and His judgment come (Luke 10:11-14). Jesus' first coming begins or prepares for coming judgment. The wood of the cross is like the kindling wood of a fire (Luke 12:49-50). However, Jesus will not come as the Judge until His second coming. Meanwhile, we judge ourselves (John 3:17-20). Certainly, the umpire makes the call ("Out!") when the runner runs out of the base path. Nevertheless, it is the runner who "judges" himself when he runs outside the lines.

Until Jesus comes as Judge, we judge ourselves. Those who do not properly represent the Lord will have the Lord's things taken from them. They will be given to others (Matthew 21:43). Another way to say this is, "we reap what we sow." As we do to others, it will be done unto us. We determine how we will be judged by how we judge others (Luke 6:36-37). In other words, we judge ourselves.

The idea that final judgment (via the final coming of the Judge) has not yet come does not, however, negate the defining and evaluating of that which is right and wrong. The reason why we should not judge others is because we have sin in our own lives (John 8:7). In order to help someone else with their faults you must first consider your own faults and correct them. Then you will be able to help others instead of judging them (Luke 6:42). A tree bears fruit according to what kind of tree it is. Men are the same way. They bear fruit according to what kind of men they are. Thus, we can and should judge others in the sense of discerning and evaluating but not in the sense of condemning (Luke 6:43-44). Even in Jesus' first coming, He made evaluations of unrighteousness and expressed righteous anger toward it. The righteous anger of Jesus came against those who were using the temple for their own selfish interests and benefits (John 2:14-16). Christians should understand that they are now the temples of God (1 Corinthians 3:16). God's righteous anger can also burn against us if we use our lives (temples) for our own selfish interests and benefits.

———————

IF GOD (JESUS) BECAME MAN, DID HE STOP BEING GOD?

". . . Christ Jesus, who, although He existed in the form of God, did not regard equality with God a thing to be grasped, but emptied Himself, taking the form of a bond-servant, and being made in the likeness of men."

Philippians 2:5-7

At a very fundamental level, the theological lifeblood of Christianity is wrapped up in the doctrine of the incarnation. God reveals Himself to man in an ultimate way by coming to man, taking on flesh, and becoming a man Himself in Jesus Christ. This is, on a theological and philosophical level, revolutionary in its implications. It implies that man could not "reach up" to God, so God had to "reach down" to man. The question, "How could God have become a man?" is changed to "How could God NOT have become a man?" Man has no possibility to climb up to heaven, so God drops down from heaven to earth. This relief maneuver is what is called the "gospel"; that is, "good news!" (Phew!—what seemed hopeless is now full of hope). So, if God became man, did He then stop being God?

The Scripture tells us that although Jesus "existed in the form of God, did not regard equality with God a thing to be grasped, but emptied Himself, taking the form of a bond-servant, and being made in the likeness of men" (Philippians 2:6-7). The Greek term translated as "form" is a philosophical term (not simply a physical term as in "the form or shape" of something). It signifies being, essence, or the mode of **expression** of that essence. It is the perfect **expression** of a perfect essence. It is the outward expression of a person's inmost nature. The expression is separate from its corresponding nature as light is separate from its corresponding fire. They are not identical. Yet they are one. If someone expresses the nature of something then it implies that person has that nature. So to say that Jesus existed in the *form* of God is to say that Jesus *expressed* divinity; His outward divine expression is an expression of His inward divine reality or essence.

The Greek term translated as "existed" is a present active participle indicating that the action of "existing" continues and does not cease. In other words, Jesus never stopped being God. He only laid aside ("emptied") the right or privilege of expressing that essence or nature (2 Corinthians 8:9). Jesus emptied Himself of His right to express

His essence (His "Godness"). He did not empty Himself of His deity. He did not stop being God. He stopped His outward expression (form) or "glory" of deity and took instead the outward expression (form) of a bond servant (John 17:5). Jesus, still "existing" (present active participle) as

God with the ability to express His deity, freely chose to let go (to empty Himself) of that ability. In that sense, He "did not regard equality with God a thing to be grasped" (Philippians 2:6), but He was still God as the continuous nature of the term "existing" suggests.

If Jesus did not stop being God, did He actually become man? Again, we must understand the definition of the term "form" as it is used in Philippians 2:7 ("taking the form of a bond-servant, and being made in the likeness of men. And being found in appearance as a man . . . "). He laid aside one outward expression of who He was (remaining who He was) and accepted another outward expression (becoming the essence or nature of that expression). Because of the definition of the word "form" (the reality of the outward expression assumes the existence of the inward nature), we must say that Jesus became a man. In addition, the term "likeness" (physical identity of a man) shows us that He was not simply a man. He was more than a man. However, He had the same physical appearance of a man. Finally, the term "appearance" (experiential identity of a man) shows us that He experienced the same things that a man experiences. So, if Jesus did not stop being God, did He actually become man? Yes. If God (Jesus) became man, did He stop being God? No. Jesus is God incarnate. What a relief! He is the God-man. That is gospel. That is good news! That is the lifeblood of Christianity.

JULY 17

YOU ARE NOT THE DEFINER . . . YOU ARE NOT GOD!

" . . . everyone did what was right in his own eyes."

Judges 21:25

The Humanist Manifesto states, "No deity will save us. We must save ourselves." For the humanist, man is God. Man is his own solution and man is his own definer of truth. Instead of Jesus being "the way, and the truth, and the life" (John 14:6), man becomes his own way and his own truth. Augustine said, "Sin is believing the lie that you are self-created, self-dependent, and self-sustained." In this sense, humanism is the ultimate sinful ideology. It is the ultimate idolatry (man worshipping man). It is the ultimate deception. It is the ultimate foolishness that masquerades as wisdom; yet, it is only the wisdom of this world!

Situational ethics defines the moral code of humanism. It says that truth is relative. There are no absolutes. It yields an egotistical morality; since man is God, man makes the rules. The rules depend on what benefits man the most. It also results in a utilitarian philosophy (the result justifies the method). Morality is judged in terms of the result. If the result is positive for the individual, then the action is considered moral. A humanist might say, "If it feels good then do it" (certainly hedonism is a natural outworking of humanism). A humanist would definitely say, "Do whatever works out best for you."

Perhaps the clearest picture of a people being taken over by the deception of humanism is the picture of God's own rebellious people, the Israelites. "Everyone did what was right in his own eyes" (Judges 21:25). Humanism makes man the definer of truth. Thus, truth is relative. What is right and what is wrong depends on what is best for man's situation; what is right in man's own eyes (situational ethics). This creates some perplexing views of truth, and some bizarre definitions of right/wrong and good/bad. Perhaps, this explains the otherwise seemingly unexplainable reason why a society can view the killing of one's own child as the morally correct thing to do. On the face of it, abortion seems to be an act that is so obviously wrong. However, in the wisdom of the world shaped by humanism, abortion is an act that can so oddly be considered good, moral, and right.

The Scripture inquires, "Where is the wise man? Where is the scribe? Where is the debater of this age? Has not God made foolish the wisdom of the world?" (1 Corinthians 1:20). Humanistic philosophy seems so wise but it is so foolish. And so, the Scripture warns, "See to it that no one takes you captive through philosophy and empty deception, according to the tradition of men, according to the elementary principles of the world, rather than according to Christ" (Colossians 2:8-9). And yet, man, in his own wisdom, approves evil; the Scripture rebukes the humanist saying, "and, although they know the ordinance of God, that those who practice such things are worthy of death, they not only do the same, but also give hearty approval to those who practice them" (Romans 1:32).

Humanism and its situational ethics yields a confused, if not, bizarre morality. But God says, "Woe" . . . "Woe to those who call evil good, and good evil; who substitute darkness for light and light for darkness; who substitute bitter for sweet, and sweet for bitter! Woe to those who are wise in their own eyes, and clever in their own sight!" (Isaiah 5:20-21). God rebukes human wisdom when He says, "He who justifies the wicked, and he who condemns the righteous, both of them alike are an abomination to the Lord" (Proverbs 17:15). At the end of the day, you are *not* the definer. Thank God!

———————

HOW TO KEEP GOING IN THE MIDST OF IMPERFECTION

"Not that I have already obtained it *or have already become perfect, but I press on*
so that I may lay hold of that for which also I was laid hold of by Christ Jesus.
Brethren, I do not regard myself as having laid hold of it *yet; but one thing* I *do: forgetting*
what lies *behind and reaching forward to what* lies *ahead, I press on toward the*
goal for the prize of the upward call of God in Christ Jesus."

Philippians 3:12-14

Paul has a healthy attitude in living out his Christian life. It is a balanced attitude. He understands he is still a sinner (not perfect), but that does not stop him from pressing "on toward the goal for the prize of the upward call of God in Christ Jesus" (Philippians 3:14). How does Paul remain motivated in the midst of his imperfection? Paul seems to refer to his motivation as a *logical* motivation. He says that he presses on "in order that I may lay hold of that for which also I was laid hold of by Christ Jesus" (Philippians 3:12). In other words, Paul is saying what motivates him is to remain consistent relative to Christ's purpose for him (Paul's goal is Christ's goal for him). He is motivated by the hope and desire that the reason God chose him would be realized; that he may obtain that which represents the whole reason he was chosen in the first place; seems very logical.

There is a very important implication buried within Paul's description of this healthy attitude; that salvation is a process. Paul already stated: "For I am confident of this very thing, that He who began a good work in you will perfect it until the day of Christ Jesus" (Philippians 1:6). He also proclaimed: "work out your salvation with fear and trembling; for it is God who is at work in you, both to will and to work for His good pleasure" (Philippians 2:12-13). In chapter three, Paul uses phrases like "press on" (Philippians 3:12), "reaching forward" (Philippians 3:13), and "toward" (Philippians 3:14) to imply the existence of a process. We "are saved" (1 Corinthians 15:2) *and* we are "being saved" (1 Corinthians 1:18).

This healthy attitude is not simply conceptual. It should be applied to your life. The concept "not that I have already obtained it" is applied by admitting that you do not have the attitude in every aspect of your life (Philippians 3:15). The concept "but I press on" is applied by being determined to at least live out the attitude in the areas that you have already attained (Philippians 3:16). In doing this, you will not remain stagnant for "God will reveal that also to you" (Philippians 3:15). You will grow and advance because God will lead you to growth and advancement.

And so, how do you keep going in the midst of imperfection? You say with Paul:

> Not that I have already obtained it or have already become perfect, but I press on so that I may lay hold of that for which also I was laid hold of by Christ Jesus. Brethren, I do not regard myself as having laid hold of it yet; but one thing I do: forgetting what lies behind and reaching forward to what lies ahead, I press on toward the goal for the prize of the upward call of God in Christ Jesus (Philippians 3:12-14).

JULY 19

WHAT ARE THE CONDITIONS FOR REVIVAL?

"... and My people who are called by My name humble themselves and pray and seek My face and turn from their wicked ways, then I will hear from heaven, will forgive their sin and will heal their land."

2 Chronicles 7:14

For certain things to grow there needs to exist the right conditions. Even something seemingly as unsophisticated as *grass*, needs certain conditions to be able to grow. In the Outer Banks of North Carolina because of, among other things, the sand and salt, it is difficult to grow grass. It is not often that one sees grass anywhere in Kitty Hawk, Kill Devil Hills, or Nags Head. It's so rare that, whereas in other places, people might say they married into money or into a certain business, in the Outer Banks they say they married into grass! Grass needs certain conditions (like the presence of dirt) to grow—not found in much quantity in the Outer Banks—which, as the legend has it, is why the Wright Brothers came to Kill Devil Hills to try to fly their airplane. The "Hills" were grassless hills of sand. These grassless hills of sand would be better for launching the craft and safer for potentially crashing the craft. So, as it is with growing grass, there are certain conditions that are necessary for revival. What are some of those conditions?

One condition for revival is that we must first perceive our need for God. It needs to be as if there is a large stone that appears too big to be removed. If we think that we can do everything then there will never be a revival. We need to see the immovable stone in front of the tomb: "They were saying to one another, 'Who will roll away the stone for us from the entrance of the tomb?' Looking up, they saw that the stone had been rolled away, although it was extremely large" (Mark 16:3-4). Of course, the extremely large stone is associated with the greatest "revival" ever.

Another condition for revival is obedience:

Why do you call Me, 'Lord, Lord,' and do not do what I say? Everyone who comes to Me and hears My words and acts on them, I will show you whom he is like: he is like a man building a house, who dug deep and laid a foundation on the rock; and when a flood occurred, the torrent burst against that house and could not shake it, because it had been well built. But the one who has heard and has not acted accordingly, is like a man who built a house on the ground without any foundation; and the torrent burst against it and immediately it collapsed, and the ruin of that house was great (Luke 6:46-49).

Revival is to "rebuild the house." What is the difference between the two builders in this passage? One is obedient and the other is not. One acted upon the word and the other did not act on the word (obedience versus disobedience). We might say then that a condition for revival is obedience.

So, a partial recipe for revival includes the ingredients of "perceived need for God" and "obedience toward God." Another way to express these conditions is to "humble yourself and pray and seek His face" and to "turn from your wicked ways." This "recipe" results in a passionate seeking of God and a hunger for righteousness; it results in revival: " . . . and My people who are called by My name humble themselves and pray and seek My face and turn from their wicked ways, then I will hear from heaven, will forgive their sin and will heal their land" (2 Chronicles 7:14). Perceived need for God and obedience = revival!

JULY 20

THERE ARE TREASURES IN THE "LOST AND FOUND!"

"He who has found his life shall lose it, and he who has lost his life for My sake shall find it."

Matthew 10:39

The key to finding life is to lose your life for the sake of Jesus (Matthew 10:39). We might call this the "inverted principle." If you try to save, keep, or hold onto your own life, then you will lose your life. If you do not try to hold onto your life and you are willing to give it away for the sake of Jesus, then you will find it (Matthew 16:25). A saved life is a life that has died to itself (Mark 8:35). Eternal life requires that you first hate your life in this world (John 12:25). It requires that you can truly say, "I am just dying to live!" The principle of dying in order to live is seen in the life of a shepherd who gives his life for the sheep in order to receive life back (John 10:17). This takes humility (Philippians 2:8). Humility is needed to live in the kingdom of God. Only the humble can reject themselves and embrace Jesus. Only the humble can reject the temptation to rule themselves and accept the rule of Jesus. Only the humble can die to themselves in order to live to God (Matthew 5:3). Losing is finding.

So how does this "losing is finding" thing work? The action in focus is the action of self-denial. Following Jesus includes denying yourself and carrying your cross (Matthew 16:24; Mark 8:34). It is this denying of yourself that leads to treasure in heaven (Matthew 19:21). Ultimately, Jesus is our model. It is He who most perfectly shows us how to deny ourselves. He did not seek His own will but the will of the Father (John 5:30). He continuously died to Himself during His life (Hebrews 5:8). And so, it is with us. There is a constant process of death that God works in us. Death is replaced with life. Areas of our lives that bear fruit are continuously being pruned to produce more fruit. God cuts away (kills) the things that are not needed in our lives (John 15:2).

The Christian life is a radical life. To follow Jesus is to be willing to own nothing . . . to be willing to have nothing that is your own (no self-interest). Instead, all is God's (Luke 9:57-58). The Christian is a "witness" (a "*martus*"); one who lives for and represents someone else . . . a "martyr" (Acts 1:8). The Christian is the temple of God (1 Corinthians 3:16). The temple of God must be used for the interests of God. The righteous anger of Jesus came against those who were using the temple for their own selfish interests and benefits (John 2:14-16). Christians are now the temples of God and God's righteous anger can also burn against us if we use our lives (temples) for our own selfish interests and benefits (1 Corinthians 3:17).

The life of the Christian is a life that denies self-interest and lives for the interests of God. It is a life that is found because it is lost. There are great treasures in the "lost and found" (Matthew 19:21). Be a treasure hunter!

JULY 21

JESUS CALLS EVERYONE TO OBEDIENCE . . .

"While Jesus was saying these things, one of the women in the crowd raised her voice and said to Him, 'Blessed is the womb that bore You and the breasts at which You nursed.' But He said, 'On the contrary, blessed are those who hear the word of God and observe it.'"

Luke 11:27-28

Every human being is equally responsible to obey God. Obedience is not partial, and no one is exempt from its call. Jesus makes this clear when He refers to His own earthly mother and family (Luke 11:27-28). To obey is simply what we are obligated and expected to do (Luke 17:10). It is not extra-credit nor is it optional. It is the regular assignment for all the students and there are no "teacher's pets."

Coming to God and hearing His voice is analogous to building a house. Obeying Him is analogous to building the foundation of the house. The lesson is clear in Luke 6:46-49. Without obedience nothing will endure (not even coming to Him and hearing His voice). Obedience is foundational . . . it is of critical importance. And so, even when obedience does not seem logical, we must obey anyway (Luke 5:5-7). Even when it is not consistent with what is otherwise good and proper (like obeying authorities and showing courtesy to others), we must obey anyway (Acts 5:29; Luke 10:4).

Obedience is essential in the kingdom of God. Entering the kingdom depends on knowing God which, in turn, depends on obedience (Matthew 7:21-23). Living the kingdom life is marked by living a life that glorifies God (1 Corinthians 10:31). To glorify God is to complete the work that He has here on earth for you to do; it is to live a life of obedience (John 17:4). Ultimately, the entire life of faith must be marked by obedience. Obedience must define faith and inform its use (Mark 14:33-36). Jesus' faith was dependent on God's will being done ("not what I will, but what Thou wilt"). It was based on obedience and not necessarily on desire or on what might be preferred (that "the hour might pass Him by").

Obedience . . . it is the regular assignment for all the students and "blessed are those who hear the word of God and observe it" (Luke 11:28). So, keep working on your assignment and be blessed!

JULY 22

YOU ARE A CHRISTIAN? YOU WILL BE PERSECUTED

"Indeed, all who desire to live godly in Christ Jesus will be persecuted."

2 Timothy 3:12

You are a Christian? According to the Scripture, you *will be* persecuted (2 Timothy 3:12). You cannot be persecuted outside of God's will (John 7:30). God is in control (John 8:20). Nevertheless, persecution is not optional for a Christian.

Who persecutes you? The world persecutes you because you are chosen out of this world, and so, you are not of the world; thus, the world hates you (John 15:19). Those who live under the rule of God practice righteousness and since the world cannot see the rule of God, they persecute the righteous (Matthew 5:10). Worldly groups who are normally enemies can find unity in their common opposition to and persecution of Jesus and His followers (Luke 23:12). Family members persecute you because spiritual bonds are stronger than natural bonds; thus, your own family members may hate you because of Jesus (Matthew 10:21, 34-36). It is even possible that family members might betray and kill you (Luke 21:16-17). Religious people persecute you because they think you are "crazy" as they thought Jesus was crazy (Mark 3:21-22). If they thought Jesus was crazy, they will think you are crazy; if they persecuted Jesus, they will persecute you (John 15:20). People who kill Christians will think that they are doing a service to God; they will kill for religious reasons (John 16:2). Of course, this is why Jesus Himself was killed.

Why are Christians persecuted? You, as a Christian, should not be surprised that you are persecuted since you know that Christ lives in you. The persecution of Christians is the continuation of the persecution of Jesus Himself (Colossians 1:24; Romans 8:17). The world hates Jesus; thus, the world hates Jesus in you (John 15:20). Christians are persecuted because of the name of Jesus (Matthew 10:22). Christians are persecuted because they are of the household of Jesus (Matthew 10:25). Worldly people cannot understand Christians. Christian actions and ways can appear "insane" to them which sometimes leads to persecution (Mark 3:21-22). And so Christian sacrifice is associated with persecution (Mark 10:28-30). It could simply be said that Christians are persecuted because the world is spiritually blind (John 16:2).

Persecution is not in and of itself a "holy" thing that should be desired or sought after. Persecution might be purposely avoided (John 7:1; John 8:59). It should also be understood that an insistence on the avoidance of persecution is one of Satan's greatest weapons against us as he incites us to focus on man's interests (Matthew 16:23). This can cause us to deny persecution, suffering, and hardship, which can lead us away from Christ. The offer of a comfortable life (the lack of persecution and hardship) has always been one of Satan's most used weapons against God's people. Of course, there is a great irony in the effectiveness of this weapon since it is during persecution that you find Jesus' help (Matthew 10:19-20; Mark 13:11; Luke 21:10-15). There is great reward for those who are persecuted for the sake of Jesus (Luke 6:20-23).

You are a Christian? You *will be* persecuted (2 Timothy 3:12) and you *will be* victorious (1 Corinthians 15:54-57). Ultimately, " . . . you will be hated by all on account of My name, but the one who endures to the end, he shall be saved . . . by your endurance you will gain your lives" (Mark 13:13; Luke 21:17-19).

———————

JULY 23

PRINCIPLES OF CHURCH GROWTH . . .

"The things which you have heard from me in the presence of many witnesses,
entrust these to faithful men who will be able to teach others also."

2 Timothy 2:2

Perhaps the most significant principle for church growth is the principle of multiplication or reproduction. As more members of the church are equipped and trained, the church will grow. As the church grows, more leaders need to be equipped and trained.

Multiplication/reproduction → Growth.

More multiplication/reproduction → more growth.

Even more multiplication/reproduction → even more growth.

This process is seen very clearly in 2 Timothy 2:2: "The things which you have heard from me in the presence of many witnesses, entrust these to faithful men who will be able to teach others also." It is also seen in Ephesians 4:11-12: "And He gave some as apostles, and some as prophets, and some as evangelists, and some as pastors and teachers, for the equipping of the saints for the work of service, to the building up of the body of Christ."

In terms of structure, there are three major ways to make room for growth in a church: the "mega-church" method, the "extension" method, and the "meta-church" method. The "mega-church" method looks to add full-time ministers to the staff of the church. With every additional 200 people who join the church, the church adds another full-time pastor. The idea here is that one pastor cannot equip and train all of the people. The "extension" method looks to form "daughter churches" once the size of the original church gets to a certain point. When the church grows to 300 people a new church is started in a different location. This method can lead to the beginning of a "movement." The "meta-church" method (sometimes called the "cell group" method) looks to do intentional discipleship via the use of small groups within the church body. The term "meta" can mean "between" as it refers to things that stand in relation to each other. Thus, a "metaphor" is a figure of speech that represents a link between one thing and something else it can be compared to. Meta-church, therefore, represents a church structure that builds a link between the smaller group and the larger group.

Inevitably, regardless of which church growth structure is used, it is the **equipping principle** that must be practiced in order for the church to grow. In Ephesians 4:1-16, we see a description of how the church (body of Christ) will grow. Leaders "equip" the body by reproducing their ministries in others. An evangelist should not only evangelize but should also train others to evangelize (Ephesians 4:11-12). It is this equipping principle that grows a church because it is this principle that multiplies or reproduces leaders. If you want to grow your family you are going to need to do some multiplying; reproducing. The reproduction must include equipping; passing things on to others. This "passing on" results in what was done originally being done again. Thus, things grow or are multiplied: "The things which you have heard from me in the presence of many witnesses, entrust these to faithful men who will be able to teach others also" (2 Timothy 2:2).

This equipping principle assumes unity in diversity: " . . . from whom the whole body, being fitted and held together by what every joint supplies, according to the proper working of each individual part, causes the growth of the body for the building up of itself in love" (Ephesians 4:16). So, the body grows by experiencing unity within diversity. There is only one body (unity); however, there are many different members in that one body (diversity). For the body to grow, all the different members must be willing—and must be allowed—to work together (unity in diversity): "For even as the body is one and yet has many members, and all the members of the body, though they are many, are one body, so also is Christ" (1 Corinthians 12:12).

JULY 24

WHO'S WHO IN THE SPIRIT WORLD . . . ANGELS AND DEMONS KNOW!

"Let us alone! What business do we have with each other, Jesus of Nazareth?
Have You come to destroy us? I know who You are—the Holy One of God!"

Luke 4:34

Angels and demons are spiritual beings created by God who are aware of and can recognize "who's who." The Scripture tells us that when a sinner repents there is joy in heaven among the angels (Luke 15:7, 10). They know who's who and who's on what "team." "Little ones" (understood to be Christians within the context of Matthew 18:10) seem to have their own angels; Christians seem to have angels assigned to them (in this sense there is validity to the idea of "guardian angels").

Demons (fallen angels) also know who's who and who's on what team. On the defensive (Matthew 16:18), Satan and his demons must ask permission from God with respect to what they can do to those on God's team (Luke 22:31-32). They know who's who in the spirit world. They are aware of the presence of Jesus and know who He is and tremble (Matthew 8:29; Luke 4:34). They recognize Jesus and must submit to Him (Mark 5:6-7; 1:24). Jesus commands evil spirits to come out and depart into the "abyss" (Luke 8:31). He also commands them not to enter in again (Mark 9:25).

When a demon is cast out it is like Satan is being dethroned; he falls (Luke 10:18). Why? Because he knows who's who! It's all about recognition. And so, a lack of faith or a lack of prayer and fasting (in a very real sense, a lack of recognition) can result in the inability to cast out a demon (Matthew 17:20-21; Luke 9:41). Demons can return after being cast out. They can also bring other demons with them (Luke 11:24-26). Demons travel and seek to rest in a vessel. If the person who had a demon cast out of him does not fill himself with Jesus (does not apply proper recognition of who's who), then the demon will return again to his original vessel (Matthew 12:43-45).

Angels and demons certainly know who's who and who's on what team. You are recognizable in the spirit world. The question is, "On what team will you be recognized?"

JULY 25

WHY SERVE OTHERS? . . . TRY LOVE AND SECURITY!

" . . . Jesus knowing that His hour had come that He would depart out of this world to the Father, having loved His own who were in the world, He loved them to the end."

John 13:1

In one of the greatest biblical teachings on "how" to serve (John 13:1-17), Jesus prefaces His example with a brief discourse that addresses the "why" of the "how." He expounds on the motivation behind the example of service in humility done at the foot washing. What motivated or enabled Jesus to lead in this way? According to the text, there are two prompters: **love** and **security**. Most immediately, **love** motivated Jesus to wash the disciples' feet: "Now before the Feast of the Passover, Jesus knowing that His hour had come that He would depart out of this world to the Father, having loved His own who were in the world, He loved them to the end" (John 13:1). Love motivated Jesus to wash the disciples' feet. The depth of His love becomes more obvious when we realize the nature of the situation. Jesus knew He was going to be killed soon. However, He forgot about His own needs in order to focus on the needs of

His disciples. In a moment when He might have been understandably selfish, He performed the most unselfish act of service. Love is a very powerful force. It can enable us to serve others in the midst of the most difficult circumstances. Love never fails (1 Corinthians 13:8).

Love, certainly is the great motivator, but perhaps, just as equally important is . . . **security**. Of course, the greatest enemy of service is insecurity. Insecure people are not able to serve others because their insecurity forces them to focus on themselves. In order to be free to serve others, you must be sure of who you are in God. You must know that you know. Jesus was free to serve because of His security in God the Father. He knew that He knew! What did He know? "Jesus, knowing that His hour had come that He should depart out of this world to the Father" (John 13:1). Like Jesus, we must know where we are going. We must be secure in our salvation. Jesus knew where He was going. There was no doubt. Thus, He was free to serve others. A lack of security in this area will result in the tendency to serve yourself. What else did Jesus know? "Knowing that the Father had given all things into His hands" (John 13:3a). We must know what we have in Christ. We must know the benefits of being a child of God. We must be secure in who we are in Christ. Jesus knew what He had been given. There was no doubt. He was free to serve others. Without this security you will want to try to gain benefits. You will serve yourself. Finally, Jesus knew: "And [knowing] that He had come forth from God, and was going back to God" (John 13:3b). We must know how we relate to God. We must be secure in our relationship with God. Jesus knew how He related to the Father. There was no doubt. He was free to serve others. People who are insecure in their relationship with God are insecure with people. They are unable to serve.

Our insecurities force us to focus on self, hindering our ability to serve others. Security provides motivation and freedom to serve. A woman and two men are standing at a bus stop. The woman has a small child in one arm and a large pocketbook in another. It is raining. The child suddenly jumps out of her arms and runs across the street. The women must put down her pocketbook and run after the child. She turns to the first man and asks him to hold her pocketbook. He refuses. She asks the second man. He gladly holds it. The first man could not serve the woman. Why? He was insecure in his manhood and so he was concerned about what others might think. The second man could serve the woman. Why? Because he was secure in his manhood. He was free to serve and focus on the need of the woman.

———————

THE TENDENCY TOWARD MAN-CENTERED WORSHIP

*"Cain brought an offering to the L*ORD *of the fruit of the ground.*
Abel, on his part also brought of the firstlings of his flock and of their fat portions.
*And the L*ORD *had regard for Abel and for his offering; but for Cain*
and for his offering He had no regard."

Genesis 4:3-5

Worship often tends to drift away from being God-centered and becomes man-centered. There are several reasons for this. First and foremost is the very nature of man, his fallen nature. Man embodies a carnal tendency. Man has been so created as to be able to transcend time and eternity through the act of worship, or prayer, or through illumination from the Bible. We would think that this tremendous ability would make us more noble, but we tend to prefer the flesh, that which can be seen, and that which makes us feel better about ourselves (1 John 2:15). We tend towards carnality. In matters of worship, this tendency is evident in man's ability to make the worship experience something which is convenient for man: "Cain brought an offering to the Lord of the fruit of the ground. And Abel, on his part also brought of the firstlings of his flock and of their fat portions. And the Lord had regard for Abel and for his offering; but for Cain and for his offering He had no regard" Man-centered worship that is rejected by God stands in contrast to God-centered worship and its offering that is enjoyed by God (Genesis 4:3-5).

One manifestation of man's carnal tendency in worship is his tendency to add to what God has directed for worship. This tendency is based on the false notion that "Jesus is not enough." The Galatian church was corrected by the apostle Paul – "how is it that you turn back again to the weak and worthless elemental things, to which you desire to be enslaved all over again? You observe days and months and seasons and years" (Galatians 4:10) – because they departed from true worship by adding features that would make worship "more interesting" or "more mystical" than God had intended. Often times, these sorts of "additions" are rooted in worldliness and the tendency to copy or imitate the ways of the world. A worship service can become more of an "entertainment event" than a response to God!

Another manifestation of man's carnal tendency in worship is his tendency to subtract from what God has directed for worship. Undue limitations are placed upon the believer's worshipful expression in the name of the Law. Certain worship elements and forms are censured from use, not from a biblical rule, but from traditions of men, denominational regulations, or cultural preferences. The scribes and Pharisees of Jesus' time—"But woe to you, scribes and Pharisees, hypocrites, because you shut off the kingdom of heaven from men; for you do not enter in yourselves nor do you allow those who are entering to go in" (Matthew 23:13)—were chastised for this tendency to limit the approach to God. Often times, these sorts of "subtractions" are rooted in religiosity; the tendency toward control of others, and the focus on legalistic rules. This was seen in the tendency of the institutional church for a long time in its history to not make the Scripture available to the laity in the vernacular (the preventing of common people from reading or hearing the Bible in their own language at worship gatherings), or the tendency of some churches to not allow the use of musical instruments.

Worship often tends to drift away from being God-centered and becomes man-centered. This is not only an oxymoronic issue, and thus absurd, but ultimately results in us being "driven . . . from Thy face" (Genesis 4:14) as was Cain as a result of his man-centered worship (Genesis 4:3-5). Flee from Cain-worship and embrace Abel-worship. Flee absurdity and embrace the reasonable. Remain God-centered!

JULY 27

TAKE GOD BEYOND YOUR BORDERS . . .

"Your eyes will see this and you will say, 'The Lord be magnified beyond the border of Israel!'"

Malachi 1:5

Like many other Old Testament prophets (Isaiah 1:9, Jeremiah 6:6, Haggai 1:2, Zechariah 1:3), Malachi repeatedly (24 times in four chapters) refers to God as "the LORD of hosts." This is a very important title with respect to the message of the book of Malachi. The term "hosts" signifies the idea of heavenly powers. It points to the universal and sovereign rule of God. Yahweh is the Lord of all powers, the Lord of the universe, or the Lord of the nations. Malachi wants to revive in the Israelites God's plan to use them **beyond their own borders**. The manifestation of the sovereignty and power of the Lord against those (Edom) who reject whom He has chosen (Israel) will result, in effect, in Israel's proclamation of the greatness of God. God says, "Your eyes will see this and you will say, 'The Lord be magnified beyond the border of Israel!'" (Malachi 1:5). Israel was chosen to be a blessing (testimony) to the "nations" (Genesis 12:1-2). It is the Lord of hosts or the Lord of the "nations" who is the subject of the proclamation. It is Him who is to be magnified beyond Israel. God is a missionary God who always wants to include—John 3:16: "For God so loved the world . . . "—*not* exclude. And so, yes He loves Israel, but He also wants His love to go "beyond the border of Israel." Thus, God is trying to move Israel in the right direction. They must fulfill their part of the Abrahamic covenant by functioning as a missionary nation (Genesis 12:1-3). They are the light that must shine in the world in order for God to be "magnified beyond the border of Israel." They should be proclaiming these truths to the "nations."

God opens up this missiological discussion with Israel by saying, "I have loved you" (Malachi 1:2). Why is this so important with respect to the success of the missiological endeavor? First, we must remember that God's redemptive plan is based on a chosen people who will be a missionary people. Next, we must apply the principle of 1 John 4:19: "We love because He first loved us." If it is true that we can love others only because God first loved us, then it is essential that we know that God loves us if we have any hope of ever loving others. It is with this understanding that we see Paul pray for a greater revelation of God's love before he directs the church/God's witnesses (Ephesians 4-6) to go forth in ministry as lights to the world: " . . . so that Christ may dwell in your hearts through faith; and that you, being rooted and grounded in love, may be able to comprehend with all the saints what is the breadth and length and height and depth, and to know the love of Christ which surpasses knowledge, that you may be filled up to all the fullness of God" (Ephesians 3:17-19). And so, this was the problem with Israel; Israel failed to see that God loved her. The result was that she was not able to love others. She was not able to bless others. She was not only unable to receive God's blessings, but she was unable to be a blessing to "all the families of the earth" (Genesis 12:3).

If you are not a receiver then you cannot be a supplier. If you do not receive God's love, then you cannot give that love to others. If you do not receive God's word, then you cannot offer that word to others. In many ways, the greatest prayer you can pray for yourself is Ephesians 3:17-19. Pray that for yourself and get ready to see "the Lord be magnified beyond" your borders!

———————

JULY 28

THE NATURE OF THE CHURCH . . .

"For just as we have many members in one body and all the members do not have the same function, so we, who are many, are one body in Christ, and individually members one of another."

Romans 12:4-5

What are some ways in which the church is understood? What are some popular images of the church (people's perceptions of the church with their positive and negative aspects)? Some people metaphorically think of the church as a "train station." This model is positive in that it promotes and focuses on the hope within the church, it diminishes the fear of death, and it establishes a positive offer for those who are currently not in the church. It is somewhat negative in that it projects an attitude of holding on instead of overcoming. It might tend to deny the power and fruit of the church, and thus, people can become lazy!

Another metaphor to describe the church is a crutch. Of course, this is true to a significant degree (Galatians 6:2). It is true that we are weak and that we do need Jesus. A negative tendency of this metaphor is to use the church in place of your own responsibilities yielding a lack of overcomers. Sometimes the church can be seen as a ticket. The church is a vehicle used to draw people to Jesus. This can mix with the misunderstanding that there is salvation through the church. Another descriptive metaphor is a fort. This positively depicts security in God, dependence on God, and the strength of the community. This wrongly, however, depicts the church as being on the defensive (Matthew 16:18), and never leaving the fort. How about seeing the church as a gas station? The church can and should be a place to get filled up with the things of God, yet that image may promote seeing the church only in terms of what someone gets from it.

The church is sometimes pictured as a refuge where the focus is on acceptance and safety. At the same time, it might negatively depict the church as a place to escape from the world instead of engaging it. Certainly, an often-used metaphor for the church is a community center. Here we embrace the aspect of the church that focuses on fellowship, community, and service for its members. A vulnerability, however, can be a tendency to become a club and become closed off to those outside. Finally, the church may be understood and depicted as a theater. The church is seen as an exciting and popular place, but there may be a tendency for it to become worldly.

Many people think of the church as nothing more than simply a building. However, the church is not simply a building. If the church is simply a building, then that means there were no churches until the fourth century. The early church did not meet in buildings. They met in houses. The favorite question of these people is, "Where is your church?" But, when they say "church" they think "building."

Other people think of the church as a denomination. They think of it as another organization or institution. The favorite question of these people is, "What is the name of your church?" When they say "church" they think "institution."

Some people think of the church as the professional ministry. The full-time, ordained ministers make up what would be called the church. The others can help sometimes, but they are not in the church. They think of the church as a profession or a business. The favorite question of these people is, "What is your title?" When they say "church" they think "profession."

So, what is the church? In Greek, it is the "ek" (out of) . . . kaleo (called), or "the called out ones." There are called out ones in "the universal church" (Ephesians 1:22), "the local church" (Romans 16:1), "the meeting of believers for worship" (1 Corinthians 11:18), and "the place of the meetings" (Romans 16:5). The "church" in New Testament times was understood as the meeting or assembly of those who were called out of the world.

JULY 29

THE LEADER IS THE SERVANT . . .

"But it is not this way with you, but the one who is the greatest among you
must become like the youngest, and the leader like the servant. For who is greater,
the one who reclines at the table or the one who serves? Is it not the one who reclines at the table?
But I am among you as the one who serves."

Luke 22:26-27

Jesus was among us "as the one who serves" and, thus, the leader is the servant (Luke 22:26-27). Greatness (leadership) in the kingdom of God does not equal the exercise of authority. It does not manifest itself in "lording it over" others. It does manifest itself in serving others (Matthew 20:25-27). Greatness (leadership) is tantamount to being the servant (see Matthew 23:11). The first (the leader) shall be the last of all; the servant of all (Mark 9:35). Jesus is our model and our standard. Since He is our Lord (He is above us/we are below Him) and since He has served all men, it only makes sense that we should serve others (John 13:13-14).

What is the nature of service as it is exemplified in the "Jesus model"? To serve is to give away your life for others (Matthew 20:28). In the "Jesus model," service includes being willing to make your life a "ransom" for others (Mark 10:45). And so, it might be said that service (leadership) requires death. Leadership, by definition, cannot be done on an island . . . it cannot be done alone. Leadership, by definition, results in multiplication or reproduction and reproduction begins with death: "Truly, truly, I say to you, unless a grain of wheat falls into the earth and dies, it remains by itself alone; but if it dies, it bears much fruit" (John 12:24).

Jesus' model of leadership is the model of a shepherd. He is the "good shepherd" and "the good shepherd lays down His life for the sheep" (John 10:11). This leadership model includes a full picture of leadership (John 10:3-4) as it portrays all three leadership offices (priest, prophet, and king). The shepherd leads as a priest ("he calls His own sheep by name"), as a prophet ("he leads them out"), and as a king ("he puts forth all His own"). In addition, the shepherd does not push from behind, but he pulls from the front; "he goes before them" as He leads by example. This is another way of saying that he lays down his life for the sheep.

Jesus is *the* leader. He is our model. He was among us "as the one who serves" and, thus, the leader is the servant (Luke 22:26-27). Are you following the model? Are you a servant?

JULY 30

THE CROSS OF JESUS . . .
IT'S DOWNRIGHT SCANDALOUS!

" . . . but we preach Christ crucified, to Jews a stumbling block and to Gentiles foolishness . . . "

1 Corinthians 1:23

The cross of Jesus is described as a "stumbling block" (Galatians 5:11). It is in the Greek text, an *"eskandalon."* It is a scandal to our flesh . . . a pride-laden flesh that cannot stomach the idea that it is unable to save itself. The cross is a stumbling block to our flesh—it offends us—because it is difficult for us to accept the fact that God Himself had to die for our sins. Until the end, Peter was falling over this stumbling block (John 18:10-11). He had continuously wrestled with it (Matthew 16:23; John 13:6-8). Eventually he would have to submit to the inherent offensiveness of the cross so as not to be crushed by it (1 Peter 2:4-8; Matthew 21:44).

The very coming of Christ is a stumbling block (John 7:7). The world hates Jesus because people hate to be told that they are evil. Of course, the incarnation—the fact that God had to come to man because man in his sin would/could not come to God—points directly to the reality that man is a sinner. It points to the fact that man is evil and in desperate need of a Savior. Sinful/prideful man stumbles over that truth. Jesus is a stumbling block to men because the sinful nature of the human being is naturally offended by the perfect life of Christ. However, blessed is anyone who keeps from stumbling over Him (Matthew 11:6).

For people who do not know Jesus, the power of God can be frightening (intimidating). It can be so intimidating (offensive) that they do not want any part of it; they are crushed by it. It becomes the stumbling block (Luke 8:35-37). That power of Jesus, most immediately and emphatically, is His very presence. His presence in this world shook the world to its core (Acts 17:6). It turned it upside-down as His coming pointed to the absurdity of the idea that man could save himself and the necessity of the idea that God had to save man (the name "Jesus" means "God saves"). It is this presence . . . this reality . . . this call . . . that each individual needs to acknowledge.

The questions, then, simply are: "What are you going to do with 'Jesus'? What are you going to do with 'God saves'? What are you going to do with 'you cannot save yourself'? Who do you say that 'I AM'?" (Luke 9:20). It is scandalous . . . a stumbling block. Don't let it crush you! Don't let "offense" become "a fence" between you and God. He has come to break down the dividing wall . . . to bring peace . . . to bring near to Him those who were far off . . . to abolish the enmity . . . to reconcile man to God . . . to give him access to the Father . . . to be no longer strangers but members of God's household "having been built upon the foundation of the apostles and prophets, Christ Jesus Himself being the corner stone . . . " (Ephesians 2:13-20).

For *this* is contained in Scripture: "Behold, I lay in Zion a choice stone, a precious corner *stone*, And he who believes in Him will not be disappointed." This precious value, then, is for you who believe. For those who disbelieve, "The stone which the builders rejected, This became the very corner *stone*," and, "A stone of stumbling and a rock of offense"; for they stumble because they are disobedient to the word, and to this *doom* they were also appointed (1 Peter 2:6-8).

JULY 31

GIVING IS A HEAVENLY THING . . .

"Looking at him, Jesus felt a love for him and said to him, "One thing you lack:
go and sell all you possess and give to the poor,
and you will have treasure in heaven; and come, follow Me."

Mark 10:21

The Scripture famously proclaims, "It is more blessed to give than to receive" (Acts 20:35). It might be said that giving is a heavenly thing. When you "give to the poor" you "will have treasure in heaven" (Mark 10:21). Giving "in secret" is linked to laying "up for yourselves treasures in heaven" (Matthew 6:4, 20). Receiving the kingdom of heaven is consistent with "give to charity" (Luke 12:32-33). Giving is so "heavenly" that when we give to others we are giving to God (Matthew 25:37-40).

Giving may be prompted by repentance (Luke 19:8). It certainly should be prompted by love; "For God so loved the world, that He gave . . . " (John 3:16). And so we give to support ministries; to support and help the spread of love . . . the spread of the gospel (Luke 8:3). Giving is the focus of ministry itself. Pastors are ones who give their lives for their sheep (John 10:11).

How is giving measured? Giving is measured, to some degree, by how much it cost you to give (Luke 21:1-4; Mark 12:41-44). Ultimately, we should give because God has given to us. We have received from God and so we are now obligated to give to others (Matthew 10:8). According to Jesus, the reason to give is simply because someone has asked you to give (Luke 6:30). Giving to others should not be determined by their character or by how much they appreciate it (Luke 6:35). Giving must be unconditional. Having said this, it might be noted that Jesus does seem to emphasize the importance of appropriate timing in giving (Luke 12:42).

Giving is one of those "God things." It is "blessed" (Acts 20:35). Giving is a heavenly thing. How is your heavenly thing going?

NOTES

August

WHAT DOES IT TAKE TO BE NOTICED BY GOD?

"... and they cried out; and their cry for help because of their bondage rose up to God. So God
heard their groaning... God saw the sons of Israel, and God took notice of them."

Exodus 2:23-25

Everyone wants to be noticed. What does it take to be noticed by God? The Scripture says regarding the persecuted Israelites that "God heard ... God saw ... God took notice" (Exodus 2:23-24). What did God take notice of? He took notice of their need. More specifically, He took notice of their realization and confession of their need for Him. What does God ultimately require of us so that He would pay attention to us ... so that He would help us? Is it really true that "God helps those who help themselves" (Proverbs 1,547,268:17 ... the most often quoted verse that is not in the Bible anywhere ... not even if there were 1,547,268 chapters in the book of Proverbs!)? It is true that "God helps those who humble themselves and confess their need for His help" (John 13:5-8). The truth of the matter is that man is in complete need of God. Man cannot save himself. Apart from Jesus, man has no life in himself (John 6:53). He is in desperate need of God. Man is helpless without Jesus ... apart from Him man can do nothing (John 15:5).

And so, the question is not whether we need God or not; rather, the question is, "Do we perceive and confess that need?" Jesus came for those who are lost; that is, in need (Luke 19:10). Jesus' ministry is to those who are in need (Luke 4:18). He came not for those who are well but for those who are sick (Luke 5:31-32). Is there anyone who is not spiritually sick? Is there really anyone who does not need Jesus (does not need "God saves")? No, there are only those who do not realize/confess their need (those who would save themselves). So, what does God require of us that He would pay attention to us ... that He would help us? The Scripture answers clearly, "He has told you, O man ... what does the Lord require of you ... to walk humbly with your God" (Micah 6:8). Sin is very closely linked to a lack of recognition of your need; it is associated with a lack of brokenness and humility (John 9:41). Our greatest need is to see that we are in need of God; to be humble.

Not seeing your need for God is disastrous. The principle of going to those in need because they will respond is set in the context of a reference to those who do not perceive their need and, thus, make absurd excuses (Luke 14:18-21). Similarly, your love for God will depend on your perception of how much you have been forgiven; your perception of the degree to which you *need* forgiveness (Luke 7:40-47). Moreover, we can allow our own righteousness to be a stumbling block. Self-righteousness denies the need for God's help. Peter fell over this stumbling block. We must accept/confess the fact that we need God and His provision for salvation. Those who cannot see that they have need, like Peter, will "have no part" with Jesus (John 13:8). Disastrous! Read John 9:39-41. Those who say that they do not have need (they say that they see) will not have their needs met (they will remain blind). Those who are willing to say they have need (they say that they cannot see) will have their needs met (they will no longer be blind). The truth is that we are all blind. The only difference is in whether we admit it or not. Read Matthew 9:12. It is not those who are healthy (who say that they do not have need) who need a physician (who receive help). It is those who are sick (who perceive and admit their need) who need a physician (who receive help).

Everyone wants to be noticed. What does it take to be noticed by God? What does God ultimately require of us so that He would pay attention to us . . . so that He would help us? Blessing comes to those who are in need because Jesus meets needs (Luke 6:20-21). Thus, to be helped by Jesus, we must perceive our need. We must confess that we are desperately needy people. In a very real sense, this is God's only requirement of us!

––––––––––

AUGUST 2

THE NEED FOR UNITY . . .

"I urge Euodia and I urge Syntyche to live in harmony in the Lord."

Philippians 4:2

What is Paul's focus in his letter to the Philippians? Toward the end, he exhorts them to "stand firm" (Philippians 4:1) and then pleads for unity between two specific people in the church (Philippians 4:2). Near the beginning of the letter, he similarly exhorts them to " . . . conduct yourselves in a manner worthy of the gospel of Christ . . . that you are standing firm in one spirit, with one mind . . ." (Philippians 1:27). standing firm and remaining in unity . . . that is Paul's focus.

So, who are these two specific people in the church who Paul is "urging" to "live in harmony" (Philippians 4:2)? One is named Euodia and the other is named Syntyche. They are Christians; their "names are in the book of life" (Philippians 4:3). Moreover, they are active in the ministry of the church, perhaps even part of its leadership, having "shared Paul's struggle in the cause of the gospel" (Philippians 4:3). How important is unity? It, obviously, is of prime importance as Paul repeats his admonition to stand firm and remain in unity. It may even be that in order to stand firm, they need to remain in unity. A divided team has a hard time winning the game! Do you understand the importance in your life and ministry of remaining in unity with fellow believers? Sometimes we are willing to sacrifice unity for relatively insignificant reasons . . . even downright silly reasons! I will not talk to or work with this or that brother or sister in Christ because they don't root for our hometown football team. What? You are willing to risk being able to stand firm and keep the unity in the family amongst the Father's children because of a football team?

Of course, a lot of times it's a little more complicated than that. Sometimes we struggle with unity due to a personality conflict. The name "Euodia" means "prosperous journey" or "successful" while the name "Syntyche" means "pleasant acquaintance" or to "meet with someone." The conflict between these two may have been a conflict that was consistent with the meaning of their names. The task oriented leader ("successful") versus the people-oriented leader ("pleasant acquaintance/meet with someone"). The task-oriented leaders (*Euodia*) become *odious* in their insensitivity while the people-oriented leaders (*Syntyche*) become *soontouchy* in their over sensitivities. In any case, different personalities or gifts sometimes result in disunity (quite ironically, since it is those very differences that we need to be successful, and thus, should appreciate differences rather than being turned off by them). Are you a "Euodia" or a "Syntyche" in your church? Do you allow personality conflicts to be a source of disunity? Are you able to walk and work with others who are different than you? Do you work alone or as part of a team? Do you realize that the church is a team? A body? Or are you willing to sacrifice unity not understanding its importance? Consider the following poem:

> To dwell above with saints we love, O that will sure be glory.
> But to dwell below with saints we know, well, that's another story!

AUGUST 3

GOD'S COMMAND AND PROVISION MUST BE TOGETHER

"*. . . so that the requirement of the Law might be fulfilled in us, who do not walk according to the flesh but according to the Spirit.*"

Romans 8:4

God's commands and provisions are unequivocally wedded together. They must be. The existence of the provision enables us to keep the command. The existence of the command demands that we receive the provision. This dynamic is seen in a variety of ways throughout the Scripture.

First, in the book of Galatians, the dynamic is seen with the use of the ideas of "freedom" and "obligation." The idea of freedom is developed by Paul in chapters 3-4 while the idea of obligation is developed in chapters 5-6. How do these ideas relate to each other? The existence of the freedom enables us to complete the obligation. The existence of the obligation leads us to receive the freedom. They are wed together.

In Matthew, we see this a bit differently, but the dynamic is still the same. Jesus says, "Do not think that I came to abolish the Law or the Prophets; I did not come to abolish but to fulfill" (Matthew 5:17). Then we read in Romans 3:31, "Do we then nullify the Law through faith? May it never be! On the contrary, we establish the Law." The Law now stands **together with** faith. By faith, Jesus is in us. Since Jesus is in us, then the Law is done through us. The existence of the faith enables us to keep the law. The existence of the law leads us to receive the faith.

The book of Ephesians, looked at in its entirety, provides a perfect example of this biblical dynamic. The first half of the book (chapters 1-3) focuses on the privileges of the believer. The second half of the book (chapters 4-6) focuses on the **responsibilities** of the believer. The existence of the privilege enables us to complete the responsibility. The existence of the responsibility leads us to depend on the privilege.

In the Old Testament, we see the same dynamic . . . promise and command. God makes a covenant with Abraham (we usually call this "The Abrahamic Covenant"). Half of this covenant is made up of promises (or privileges) like "I will bless you" while the other half is made up of commands (or responsibilities) like "and you shall be a blessing." And so it goes:

> Now the LORD said to Abram, 'Go forth from your country, And from your relatives And from your father's house, To the land which I will show you; And I will make you a great nation, And I will bless you, And make your name great; And so you shall be a blessing; And I will bless those who bless you, And the one who curses you I will curse. And in you all the families of the earth will be blessed' (Genesis 12:1-3).

Three ways of stating the promise (great nation; bless you; name great) is perfectly balanced by three ways of stating the command (you shall be a blessing; bless those who bless you and the one who curses you I will curse; in you all the families of the earth will be blessed). This existence of the promise enables us to do the command. The existence of the command necessitates that we receive what is promised.

The New Testament version of Genesis 12:1-3 is found in the provision/mission dynamic of Acts 1:8. Here, the provision of the Holy Spirit ("but you will receive power when the Holy Spirit has come upon you") is matched up with the mission of the church ("and you shall be My witnesses both in Jerusalem, and in all Judea and Samaria, and even to the remotest part of the earth"). The existence of the provision enables us to complete the mission while the existence of the mission demands that we receive the provision. And so, command and provision live together. Why? Because they must!

AUGUST 4

THE DUAL WORK OF THE HOLY SPIRIT ... TO SAVE AND TO EMPOWER

"Now when all the people were baptized, Jesus was also baptized,
and while He was praying, heaven was opened, and the Holy Spirit descended
upon Him in bodily form like a dove, and ... He began His ministry ... "

Luke 3:21-23

All four gospels depict the baptism of Jesus and the descent of the Spirit upon Him as that which precedes and leads to His ministry (Matthew 3:13-17; Mark 1:9-10; Luke 3:21-22; John 1:32-33). Jesus is baptized, the Holy Spirit descends upon Him, and then "He began His ministry" (Luke 3:23). The activity of the Holy Spirit here is the second major work of the Holy Spirit in the life of Jesus. First, He was born from above by the Spirit (Luke 1:35). Second, He was empowered by the Spirit for ministry (Luke 3:22-23). These are separate works of the Holy Spirit.

Jesus was baptized in water which is a symbol for the washing away of sin (Acts 22:16), yet Jesus had no sin (2 Corinthians 5:21). He did this "to fulfill all righteousness" (Matthew 3:15) in order to identify with sinful humanity and show the need for repentance and forgiveness (salvation). This identification precedes the coming of the Holy Spirit and the beginning of Jesus' ministry, even as the salvation of a Christian precedes that Christian's ministry. The baptism of Jesus and the descent of the Spirit upon Him were two distinct and separate events. He was baptized. He began to pray. Then the Spirit descended upon Him. Baptism is essential preparation for the empowering of the Spirit, even as salvation is essential preparation for the call and anointing for ministry of him who is saved. Similarly, the purpose of Jesus' baptism and the purpose of His anointing were different. The purpose of Jesus' baptism was to fulfill all righteousness (representing the initial work of the Holy Spirit in Jesus being born from above by the Spirit and becoming the Savior). The purpose of Jesus' anointing (the descending of the Holy Spirit upon Him) was that He would be empowered for ministry: "You know of Jesus of Nazareth, how God anointed Him with the Holy Spirit and with power, and how He went about doing good and healing all who were oppressed by the devil, for God was with Him" (Acts 10:38).

And so, there is a distinction between baptism in water and baptism in the Spirit. Baptism in water is related to repentance and righteousness. It signifies the main role of Jesus as Savior (John 1:29); being "born from above" (John 3:3) even as Jesus was "born from above" (Luke 1:35). Baptism in the Spirit is related to power in ministry. It signifies Jesus' role as "empowerer," (John 1:32-33) being empowered for ministry (Acts 1:8) even as the Holy Spirit descended upon Jesus and then He began His ministry (Luke 3:22-23). There is a dual work of the Holy Spirit . . . to save and to empower. Jesus is born from above by the Spirit, and thus, baptized (representing righteousness or salvation). He is then empowered by the Holy Spirit for ministry. So too, the believer receives the Spirit (John 20:20) and is saved. The believer is then filled with the Spirit and empowered for ministry (Acts 1:8; 2:4). And so, the Scripture refers to those who are already saved as those who *will receive* the gift of the Holy Spirit: "Peter said to them, 'Repent, and each of you be baptized in the name of Jesus Christ for the forgiveness of your sins; and you *will receive* the gift of the Holy Spirit'" (Acts 2:38).

There is a dual work of the Holy Spirit. There is a work of the Holy Spirit for salvation and a work of the Holy Spirit for ministry that is received *after believing*: "And I remembered the word of the Lord, how He used to say, 'John baptized with water, but you will be baptized with the Holy Spirit.' Therefore if God gave to them the same gift as He gave to us also *after believing* in the Lord Jesus Christ, who was I that I could stand in God's way?" (Acts 11:16-17). And so, perhaps, the question is: What stands in God's way for you to receive the dual work of the Holy Spirit? Perhaps you just need to ask for it: "If you then, being evil, know how to give good gifts to your children, how much more will your heavenly Father give the Holy Spirit to those who ask Him?" (Luke 11:13).

AUGUST 5

THE MULTI-FACETED MEANING OF THE LORD'S SUPPER

" . . . do this in remembrance of Me."

1 Corinthians 11:24

The taking of the Lord's Supper, which was actually a commandment (1 Corinthians 11:24-25), was practiced often in the early church (Acts 2:42-46). It was based on the last meal (thus, sometimes called the Last Supper) that Jesus had with His disciples (Mark 14:17-26 and Luke 22:14). The significance of the Lord's Supper includes a multi-faceted perspective including a looking behind, a looking at ourselves, a looking around us, and a looking ahead.

Let's first consider the significance of the Lord's Supper as we **look behind**. The Lord's Supper is connected to the Passover: "He reclined at the table, and the apostles with Him. And He said to them, 'I have earnestly desired to eat this Passover with you before I suffer'" (Luke 22:14-16). The Jews celebrated the Passover and told its story in memory of what God did in the Exodus (Exodus 12:8-27). More specific for the Christian is that the Lord's Supper is a memory of what Jesus did: "This cup is the new covenant in My blood; do this . . . in remembrance of Me" (1 Corinthians 11:25). Thus, it is a time to "give thanks" which is the meaning of the term "eucharist" (interchangeable with the idea of "the breaking of bread" as seen in Acts 2:42). The Lord's Supper is a memorial. The Supper is celebrated in honor and in memory of Jesus. It should reflect the complete realization of what Jesus has done for us to obtain our salvation (1 Corinthians 5:7).

Let us also consider the Lord's Supper as we **look at ourselves**. Before the day of the Passover there was a day of purification. All of the leaven (the symbol of evil) was removed from the house. So too, now, Christians must examine themselves. They must cleanse themselves by confessing their sins and by having an attitude and spirit which is consistent with the Lord's Supper and the cross (1 Corinthians 11:27- 28 and 1 Corinthians 5:7). To take the Lord's Supper is to accept and live the life of the cross. It is to share the life of Christ. Jesus invites us to eat with Him. Within the Supper is the intimate, personal relationship with Christ that defines Christianity. We "break the bread together" and we partake of "the body and the blood."

Let's next consider the Lord's Supper as we **look around us**. The Passover celebration included others. Children and the whole family participated. Moreover, it was the custom to invite any strangers who were outside of your house to come in and join the celebration. The Lord's Supper is a "koinonia" (sharing). Implied, is the communion one with another (1 Corinthians 10:16; Jude 12; Acts 2:42-46). The Supper necessitates that we are considerate of others (1 Corinthians 11:17-34). The Lord's Supper is the supper of his family. To take of the Lord's Supper is to say that your life is connected to/in common with the lives of other believers. We have a common salvation. Thus, we take of the SAME bread (sometimes referred to as "Holy Communion" or "Agape Feasts"). We are in unity. Moreover, we are saying that we give our lives as a sacrifice to serve others.

Finally, let us consider the Lord's Supper as we **look ahead**. Within the Passover celebration there was the sense of hope for the future salvation. Thus, there was always an empty seat left at the table. Within the celebration of the Lord's Supper is the hope of the Lord's return: "For as often as you eat this bread and drink the cup, you proclaim the Lord's death *until He comes*" (1 Corinthians 11:26) and "I will never again drink of the fruit of the vine until that day when I drink it *new in the kingdom of God*" (Mark 14:25). Moreover, there is the hope of the coming of the wedding supper of the Lamb (Revelation 19:9). To take of the Lord's Supper is to say that we are waiting, hoping, and looking forward to the Supper in heaven. We eat with hope and expectation for the Supper of the Lamb at the Table of the Lord.

AUGUST 6

IDOLATRY . . . WHEN WORSHIP LOSES ITS WAY!

"I hate, I reject your festivals, Nor do I delight in your solemn assemblies. Even though you offer up to Me burnt offerings and your grain offerings, I will not accept them . . . *take away from Me the noise of your songs; I will not even listen to the sound of your harps. But let justice roll down like waters, And righteousness like an ever-flowing stream . . . "*

Amos 5:21-24

It goes without saying that worship is to be a God-centered activity. The evidence of this understanding is not always present in many churches. There is a carnal tendency in mankind to relax and move toward self-centeredness. God-centered worship is a matter of diligent response to biblical revelation on church-wide, family, and individual levels. Worship transcends meeting times, or singing songs, or even orthodox formulations of the truth about God. When it does not, God rejects it. God says, "I hate, I reject your festivals, nor do I delight in your solemn assemblies. Even though you offer up to Me burnt offerings and your grain offerings, I will not accept them . . . take away from Me the noise of your songs; I will not even listen to the sound of your harps. But let justice roll down like waters, and righteousness like an ever-flowing stream . . . " (Amos 5:21-24). Since worship is a life so captivated by God's valuableness (His worth), believers respond by "bowing" with their whole life in response to the truth of Scripture.

Worship is the most God-intended response in creation. We are most human when we practice the spirit and forms of Godward worship and adoration. Because of this reality, Satan is set directly against true worship. He is committed to corrupting, disrupting, and perverting biblical worship. Due to this assault against worship in the world, it is no wonder that worshipers, and humans in general, sometimes lose their way from God-centered worship. The Scripture is clear regarding one kind of worship that is not God-centered; the worship of idols. Much of mankind's worshipful response is idolatrous.

Idolatry is to worship idols, images, or anything made by the hands, or which is not the living God revealed in the Scriptures. It involves excessive attachment, veneration, or adoration of anything. There are two kinds of idolatry. First, there is the worship of anything made by the hands or imagination of mankind (images, statues, possessions, and wealth). Second, there is the worship of things not made by man (for example, the sun, moon, earth, water, man, animals, vegetation, angels, demons, ancestors, and even "saints"). Mankind's tendency is to worship whatever is perceived to be greater than man (by its appearance, strength, or beauty), or whatever is able to help man meet his needs in this world.

The Egyptians (Exodus 12:12) venerated the sun and the Nile river as these were sources of life on which they were dependent. The Canaanites' (Genesis 38:21) worship involved religious prostitution and snake worship as these represented fertility and ecstatic mystery. The Mesopotamians (Deuteronomy 29:17) worshipped mountains, trees, and blocks of stone as they represented visible things perceived to be greater than man.

Idolatry is practiced when worship loses its way. When something other than God is the center of our worship, we practice idolatry. Whether that something else is the sun or a rock, or our possessions or our lusts, the same thing is true . . . worship has lost its way!

AUGUST 7

YOU'RE GOING TO GET A NEW BODY . . .

"But someone will say, 'How are the dead raised?' And with what kind of body do they come? . . . But God gives it a body just as He wished . . . There are also heavenly bodies and earthly bodies . . . it is sown a natural body, it is raised a spiritual body . . ."

1 Corinthians 15:35, 38, 40, 44

We do things to change our bodies. Sometimes the things we do are more extreme than other things. I guess that's why there may be a Golden Corral Buffet Restaurant and a Weight Watchers Club right next door to each other in your local strip mall. There will come a day, however, when our bodies will truly be made "new." What will that look like?

In the end, things will become new. The Scripture states that "according to His promise we are looking for new heavens and a new earth" (2 Peter 3:13). The old will pass away and the new will come (Luke 21:33; Mark 13:31). This is true of the heavens and the earth and it is true with respect to our bodies. Jesus Himself will raise up believers "on the last day" (John 6:40). As a believer, you will be given a new body . . . a heavenly body . . . a spiritual body (1 Corinthians

15:35-44). What will that look like? Perhaps the best picture we have of that is the resurrected body of Jesus Himself. The resurrected Jesus is the "first fruits" of those who will be resurrected from the dead (1 Corinthians 15:20-21); His resurrected body is not only a sure sign that there will be more resurrected bodies, but it is a prototype of those resurrected bodies to come. So, what does Jesus' resurrected body look like?

There is certainly a significant degree of continuity between Jesus' earthly body and His resurrected body. It is a physical body with physical parts and movements (Matthew 28:9; Luke 24:30). He eats and drinks (Luke 24:43; Acts 10:41). He is not simply a spirit but has flesh and bones (Luke 24:39). There do seem to be some significant differences as well regarding the way in which the body appears. Jesus, at times, seems to appear or disappear in a way that goes beyond the physical. The doors were shut yet Jesus "came and stood in their midst" (John 20:19, 26). On another occasion He simply "vanished from their sight" (Luke 24:31). Furthermore, people don't always recognize Him immediately. Mary when first seeing the resurrected Christ initially "did not know that it was Jesus . . . supposing Him to be the gardener . . . " (John 20:14-15). Later, two of Jesus' disciples who were walking on the road to Emmaus did not recognize Him as He walked along with them (Luke 24:13-16). Why does this body look/act different?

We might have a clue about the nature of the "new" body relative to the "old" body. Certainly, it is a physical body; nevertheless, the Scripture calls it a "spiritual body" (1 Corinthians 15:44). We now have a physical body and a spirit in which the physical takes precedence in terms of appearance, our spirit is subordinate to our body (or it could be said that, in terms of appearance, the physical dictates the spiritual). Perhaps, that is the difference with our new bodies (as it seems to have been with Jesus' new body); that the spirit supersedes the physical or the outward form is subordinate to the spirit. Thus, in terms of "appearance" it is the spirit that must be seen in order to see the physical. Notice how in both cases of the lack of physical recognition of Jesus He was then recognized after a more "intimate" (or perhaps, "spiritual") type of interaction. Mary does not recognize Jesus but then "Jesus said to her, "Mary!" and she then knows who He is (John 20:16) . . . the spiritual supersedes the physical. The disciples on the road to Emmaus eyes were opened to recognize Him "when He had reclined at the table with them . . . took the bread and blessed it, and . . . began giving it to them" (Luke 24:30-31) . . . the spiritual superseding or dictating the physical?

In any case, the Scripture is clear. You're going to get a new body and whatever the nature is of that new body one thing is sure: " . . . it is raised an imperishable body . . . it is raised in glory . . . it is raised in power . . . we shall be changed . . . Death is swallowed up in victory" (1 Corinthians 15:42, 43, 52, 54). So, rejoice in, and look forward to, your new body!

AUGUST 8

THE IMPORTANCE OF
UNITY IN DIVERSITY . . .

"For even as the body is one and yet has many members, and all the members of the body,
though they are many, are one body, so also is Christ . . . For by one Spirit we were all baptized
into one body, whether Jews or Greeks, whether slaves or free, and we were all made to drink of
one Spirit. For the body is not one member, but many . . . But now God has placed the members,
each one of them, in the body, just as He desired. If they were all one member, where would the
body be? But now there are many members, but one body."

1 Corinthians 12:12, 14, 18-20

As part of the same body, both the knees and the buttocks want to sit down. The knees must bend. The buttocks must sit. Each member must do its part. If the knees refuse to bend, then the buttocks will not be able to sit. If the buttocks refuse to sit, then the bending of the knees will be useless. As they work together, unity exists within diversity (knees and buttocks are very different).

The same principle of unity within diversity is true in the church, since it is a body (see 1 Corinthians 12:12). Why is unity within diversity so important? The practice of unity within diversity is the key to church growth (Ephesians 4:11-16). Different "office gifts" are given to the church (verse 11). These gifts represent the "What?" of church growth. They are the units that will be used to grow the church. These gifts are given for the same purpose (verse 12). The specific purpose is that the different members would mature together (verse 13) . . . Not to be immature (verse 14) . . . But to grow up (verse 15). This purpose represents the "Why?" of church growth. This purpose will be accomplished by experiencing unity within diversity (verse 16). This experience represents the "How?" of church growth. Without unity within diversity, the purpose cannot be fully accomplished. Church growth depends on the practice of unity within diversity. Thus, church government must promote and allow unity within diversity. This is the government of a body not the government of an individual.

Continuing with the metaphor, the brain of the body is Jesus. He tells the body (the church) to do certain things in order to grow. The church includes many different members. Some are mouths. Others are feet. Some are eyes. Others are teeth. For many different reasons, the different members of the church do not work together. The church does not grow because for a body to grow, it must work in unity. Each part depends on the other. Church government must be consistent with these principles. It must be in the form of a body. It must practice unity within diversity.

The brain says: "Eat!" But if the mouth is not willing to cooperate with the teeth, then the body will not be able to eat (and will not grow). The teeth are ready to eat, but the mouth refuses to open. It says that it will not work with the teeth because yesterday the teeth bit him on the lip (and now the mouth's wife will not kiss him). The mouth is mad at the teeth. If the teeth try to eat without the help of the mouth (it remains closed), then there will be a mess. The same thing is true in the church. Some members are ready to eat. Other members are not willing to cooperate. One is mad at the other. The result is that there is a mess and the church does not grow. The brain says: "Eat!" But if the teeth are not willing to cooperate with the mouth, then the body will not be able to eat (and will not grow). The mouth is ready to eat. It is wide open. But the teeth refuse to chew. It says that it will not work with the mouth because the mouth has bad breath (and now the teeth's wife will not kiss him). The teeth are embarrassed to work with the mouth. If the mouth tries to eat without the help of the teeth (they will not chew) then the body will choke itself. The same thing is true in the church.

———————

AUGUST 9

TWICE HIS! GOD MADE YOU AND BOUGHT YOU . . .

"Or do you not know that your body is a temple of the Holy Spirit who is in you, whom you have from God, and that you are not your own? For you have been bought with a price . . . "

1 Corinthians 6:19-20

A young boy lived by the sea. He loved boats. He would watch them come in from the ocean every day. One day he began to build his own sailboat. He worked for six days. Finally, it was finished. He could not wait to put it in the water. Just as he was putting the boat in the water the wind changed direction. It forced the boat out into the water until it was completely out of sight. The boy began to cry. Every day he returned to that point on the beach and searched for the boat. He never found it. One day he was walking downtown when he saw the sailboat in the window of a store. It was the boat that had been lost. He ran in the store and told the owner that it was his boat. The man said that he could not have it unless he paid $10 for it. The boy argued. Finally, he paid the money. It was all the money that he had. When the boy left the store with the boat he said, "Little boat, you are twice mine. You are mine because I made you, and now you are mine because I bought you." God created us (Genesis 1:27). Then he paid a great price to get us back (1 Corinthians 6:19-20). This is the story of redemption and salvation.

From the moment Adam fell into sin in the Garden of Eden, God has had one plan for mankind. It is called the plan of redemption and salvation. The unfolding of the plan can be seen in the Bible from cover to cover as it is first indicated in Genesis 3:15—with the picture of the cross being painted by God while Man stood in the midst of the "tree of life" just before having to leave "the garden"—and ultimately referenced in Revelation 22:14 (with the picture of Man entering "the garden" again in the midst of the "tree of life").

This grand divine plan is the binding that holds the Bible together. It is the structure that is the foundation for all of theology (thus, "soteriology" or the theology of salvation is often called "the grandfather of theology"). Redemption and salvation are the main themes of the Bible. It might be said that without redemption and salvation, the Bible is just history, but with it, the Bible is His Story!

Salvation is the ultimate goal of both God and man. All men want to be saved. God wants all men to be saved (1 Timothy 2:4; 2 Peter 3:9). Redemption is the plan of salvation. It is God's strategy for men to be saved. God saves us by redeeming us and our fallen situation; His plan is to restore us, and His strategy is to buy us back. Initially, He made us. Then we got lost. So, He bought us back. We are twice His!

AUGUST 10

THE KEY TO CHRISTIAN LEADERSHIP . . .

"Let them alone; they are blind guides of the blind. And if a blind man guides a blind man, both will fall into a pit."

Matthew 15:14

A car in front of me had a bumper sticker that said: "Why are you following me? I am lost, too." Motion does not always signify purpose. Therefore, we should not always follow the crowd. There are many leaders in the world (and therefore many crowds) who do not know where they are going. As Jesus explained, "Let them alone; they are blind guides of the blind. And if a blind man guides a blind man, both will fall into a pit" (Matthew 15:14). If a lost driver follows another lost driver both will become even more lost! Hence, there exists the need for strong Christian leadership.

And so, our first question is: What is Christian leadership? Let's work on a definition. First, let's formulate a definition for "leadership." Perhaps, the primary idea of leadership is to have influence upon others. To lead is to guide or direct. Next, let's propose a definition for "Christian." Of course, the main idea is a Person; that is, Christ. A Christian is a person who is Christ-centered or Christ-directed. Jesus is the centerpiece of his or her life. Now let's put these two definitions together to finalize a definition of "Christian leadership." Christian leadership is Christ-centered guidance or guidance toward Christ. It is directing someone toward Christ.

The key to Christian leadership, then, is to take a person from where they currently are in Christ and to bring them one step closer to Him. To bring someone closer to Jesus is to bring that person closer to the kingdom of God. There are other leaders who do the opposite: "But woe to you, scribes and Pharisees, hypocrites, because you shut off the kingdom of heaven from people; for you do not enter in yourselves, nor do you allow those who are entering to go in" (Matthew 23:13). In any case, let's get back to the key to Christian leadership (to take a person from where they currently are in Christ and to bring them one step closer to Him). There are two assumptions within this key: 1) "To take a person from where they currently are in Christ"—this assumes that the leader knows people. He can talk with someone and know more or less where they stand. He has wisdom and discernment; 2) "One step closer"—this assumes that the leader is not a person of extremes. He does not expect too much from people. He is patient. He goes step by step. He is willing to wait for the fruit to grow. He does not immediately try to make a new Christian one of the leaders. He does not try to push a person to have too much responsibility too soon. He is willing to let people grow. At the same time, he is secure enough in his own ministry to have the desire to see others moving into leadership positions. He does not see stagnation in the lives of the sheep as a way to have more personal control. He wants to see people grow closer to Christ.

And so, it would be a great boost to any society, if more and more cars in front of us had bumper stickers that read: "Follow me. I will direct you toward Christ!" So, don't just follow the crowd. Don't just be a blind man following a blind man unless, of course, you are an accomplished "pit swimmer" (but even then, you will not be able to climb the walls to get out of the proverbial "pit"!). Instead of following the crowd, follow the maker of the universe (I think He knows where He is going since He made it). The more *Christian leaders* we have in our communities, in our churches, in our schools, in our businesses, and in our families, the more stable and healthier of a society we will live in. And so, maybe the title should not only be "The key to Christian leadership," but should also be "Christian leadership is the key!"

———

IT TAKES TWO TO TANGO ...
AND TO BE DIVIDED!

"For He Himself is our peace, who made both groups into one,
and broke down the barrier of the dividing wall ...
you are fellow citizens with the saints, and are of God's household ... "

Ephesians 2:14, 19

The people of God are described metaphorically as "God's household" (Ephesians 2:19). It is "household" (singular) and not "households" (plural). Division can only exist amid plurality. You cannot divide "one." There must be at least two tribes for "tribalism" (division, discrimination, and prejudice) to exist. One tribe cannot discriminate against itself! In Ephesians 2:11-22, Paul applies this "division" dynamic by explaining that there is only one (tribe) in Christ. This makes the practice of prejudice or discrimination (or any form of "tribalism") impossible, since there must be at least two groups for it to exist. One group discriminates against another group. If there is only one group to begin with, then discrimination and division is not possible. It takes two to tango *and* it takes two to be divided!

In Ephesians 2:14, Paul writes about making "both groups one" by breaking "down the barrier of the dividing wall." Never in history has there been a stronger tribalism than that which existed between the tribes of Israel and the tribes of the gentiles. They hated each other. In the early church, they needed to realize that Christ came to break down the wall between them. We too, must allow Christ to break down any walls that divide us. Those walls might include denominational walls, racial walls, ethnic walls, and social class walls. These walls, and any other "tribal barriers" that stand as walls, must be broken.

Tribalism in the church is an oxymoronic idea. They cannot go together. Why? The Scripture answers, "since there is one bread, we who are many are one body; for we all partake of the one bread" (1 Corinthians 10:17). There is only one "tribe"; thus, discrimination/division is not possible since it takes two to be divided. There is only one bread because there is only one cross, and thus, only one solution. The singular nature of the people of God ("household") necessarily results in unity, not division. And so, "being diligent to preserve the unity of the Spirit in the bond of peace" (Ephesians 4:3) is directly linked to the singular nature and situation of the people of God; "one body and one Spirit, just as also you were called in one hope of your calling; one Lord, one faith, one baptism, one God and Father of all" (Ephesians 4:4-6).

You cannot divide "one." "One" cannot discriminate against itself! If there is only one to begin with, then division is not possible. This is a very practical principle. Herein lies the secret to a strong marriage. How do you look at your mate? If you are "one" then division is not possible "so husbands ought also to love their own wives as their own bodies. He who loves his own wife loves himself; for no one ever hated his own flesh, but nourishes and cherishes it" (Ephesians 5:28-29). It takes two to tango *and* it takes two to be divided! "One" cannot divorce himself from himself!

AUGUST 12

WHY ARE THERE FOUR GOSPELS? . . .

"This gospel of the kingdom shall be preached in the whole world."

Matthew 24:14

Why are there four gospels? Why Matthew *and* Mark *and* Luke *and* John? Because there are different authors who write to different audiences with different themes, emphases, and purposes. Matthew portrays Jesus as the Son of David who is the King, while Mark depicts Jesus as the Son of God who is the Servant. Luke pictures Jesus as the Son of Man who is the Savior, and John renders Jesus as the Word of God who is the divine Eternal One.

Matthew was writing to the Jews; thus, Matthew's purpose was to convince Jews that Jesus the Son of David was the King and Messiah of Jewish prophecy. Matthew, then, uses more than 100 quotes from the Old Testament, and traces Jesus' genealogy back to Abraham, the father of Israel (instead of, as in Luke, to Adam, the father of all mankind). Since he is writing to Jews, Matthew does not explain Jewish customs (as they would already be understood by his readers) but does use Jewish terms. Matthew's emphasis is on Jesus the King.

Mark was writing to Roman gentiles; his Gospel contains few references to the Old Testament. Moreover, Mark takes time to explain Jewish terms and customs. Mark's book is "event-oriented" using the term "immediately" seventeen times to show Jesus, the Son of God, as the Servant. Mark puts the spotlight on Jesus' works including nineteen miracles in only sixteen chapters. Mark's emphasis is on Jesus the Servant.

Luke writes to the gentiles providing a chronological and orderly narrative of the life of Christ with a focus on the character of Jesus the Son of Man as the Savior of the world. Luke takes Jesus' genealogy back to Adam (universal lineage) and makes the order of Jesus' temptations match that of Genesis 3:16 (resulting in a more universal presentation to all people/gentiles, not just the Jews). Luke's emphasis is on Jesus the Savior.

John was writing to Greek gentiles; he seems to focus on the heresies about Christ that began with the Greeks. John's Gospel is more spiritually philosophical than all the other Gospels, perhaps adapting the message for the Greeks. John's emphasis is on Jesus the Eternal One. In so doing, John presents Jesus as the incarnate Word of God who is the divine Eternal One:

> IN THE beginning was the Word, and the Word was with God, and the Word was God. He was in the beginning with God. All things came into being through Him, and apart from Him nothing came into being that has come into being . . . And the Word became flesh, and dwelt among us, and we saw His glory, glory as of the only begotten from the Father, full of grace and truth (John 1:1-3, 14).

So, why are there four Gospels? There are four Gospels to show four different sides or aspects of the ministry and Person of Jesus Christ. The Holy Spirit uses four different authors to write to four different audiences in order to shine the light on these four different aspects. Jesus is the Son of David (the King), the Son of God (the Servant), the Son of Man (the Savior), and the Word of God (the divine Eternal One).

AUGUST 13

THE BIBLE SCREAMS OUT, "JESUS IS GOD!"

"Jesus came up and spoke to them, saying, 'All authority has been given to Me in heaven and on earth'."

Matthew 28:18

The phrase "nominal Christianity" is, perhaps, the most oxymoronic phrase ever (even more oxymoronic than "sweet tart" or "jumbo shrimp"). Christianity is not "nominal." It is radical! Jesus is not just good. Jesus is God. To follow Jesus is not just "being good." To follow Jesus is to follow God Himself. The radical implications are obvious.

Those who wish to water down Christianity and lighten up on its obvious radical implications would like to water down the very nature of Jesus Himself. The Bible does not provide such a spray can; rather, the Bible screams out that Jesus is God. Scripture has many ways in which it points to the deity of Christ. The titles of Jesus point to His deity. When Jesus was called the "Son of God," it was understood that He was equal with God (John 5:18). Jesus was killed by the Jews because they understood that when He claimed to be the Son of God, He claimed to be God Himself (John 19:7; Matthew 14:33). Similarly, the "Son of Man" is a title that screams divinity. The healed man asked, "Who is the Son of Man?" Jesus answered that He was the Son of Man. The man immediately worshipped Jesus. Any Jew knew that only God could be worshipped (see Matthew 14:33; Revelation 22:8-9; Acts 10:25-26). Thus, the man clearly was associating his understanding of the meaning of the title, "Son of Man," with deity (John 9:35-38; Mark 2:5-11).

The pre-existence of Jesus, according to the Scripture, screams out that Jesus is God. Jesus existed before His birth on earth (John 1:1-2, 15). He existed before Abraham who lived on earth 2000 years before Him (John 8:58). He shared the glory of the Father before the world existed (John 17:5). The Bible is clear in demonstrating Jesus' deity. It also does this in its description of Jesus' role in creation. All things were created through the Word or the light; they were created through Jesus (John 1:3, 10).

The "I am" statements are also used to depict Jesus' deity. In a very dramatic way, Jesus used God's personal name for Himself (John 8:58). The Scripture does this repeatedly in a variety of ways (John 13:19; Mark 14:62; Luke 22:70; John 18:5-8; Revelation 1:18). Jesus' full authority reveals His deity. Jesus had authority to forgive sins. This was an authority that only God could have (Mark 2:5-11). Jesus had authority to save people. This was an authority that only God could have (John 8:51). Jesus had all authority in heaven and on earth.

Who is this Jesus? He is the incarnate ("all authority on earth") God ("all authority in heaven")! It is this full authority that then makes following Him a radical decision and makes "nominal Christianity" an oxymoronic phrase!

AUGUST 14

GOD: INCOMPREHENSIBLE BUT NOT IMPERSONAL

"'Am I a God who is near,' declares the LORD,
'And not a God far off.'"

Jeremiah 23:23

God is "far off" and God is "near" (Jeremiah 23:23); He is transcendent and immanent. And so, in one sense, God is incomprehensible. He is incomprehensible in the sense that there will always be those things that finite men will not be able to know or understand about an infinite God (1 Kings 8:12; Job 37:23); He is "unsearchable" and "unfathomable" (Romans 11:33). Furthermore, God is incomprehensible in the sense that He is God and cannot simply be known in the same way that we know each other (Isaiah 55:8). In addition, God is incomprehensible in the sense that the knowledge of One who is infinite must be infinite itself (Ecclesiastes 3:11); by definition, we can never come to the end of knowing an infinite God.

A doctor of Theology once described this truth in the following way: "The process of knowing God is like the process of education. I have completed my doctoral studies and the greatest thing I have learned is that the more I know, the more I know that I do not know. It is the same way with knowing God. The more I come to know God, the more I come to know how much I do not know about Him." This is certainly true in the sense that the closer we get to God, the bigger He becomes. Since there is no end to His getting bigger, He is incomprehensible! The result of the reality of God's transcendence, however, is not to run away from Him (to be afraid of Him). Rather, the one who comes to know an infinite God comes to know (to be more fully aware of) the grandeur of God; the result is to fear/respect Him, to be in awe of Him, to worship Him . . . to draw near to Him!

God is incomprehensible. At the same time, it must be said, although we cannot know everything that God knows, we can know Him. There is a great difference between our God who is incomprehensible and a God who is impersonal. Our God is incomprehensible. However, He is not impersonal. He is a personal God. He wants to have a relationship with those He created "in His own image" (Genesis 1:27). We can know God. We must know God. This is God's desire (Hosea 6:6; Hebrews 11:6). This is God's plan (John 17:3). "That I may know Him" must be my highest goal (Philippians 3:8-10). What is your response to this incomprehensible yet personal, God? What is your highest goal? What do you "seek first" (Matthew 6:33)? What do you see as personal "success"? What do you boast in?

> Thus says the Lord, "Let not a wise man boast of his wisdom, and let not the mighty man boast of his might, let not a rich man boast of his riches; but let him who boasts boast of this, that he understands and knows Me . . . " (Jeremiah 9:23-24).

AUGUST 15

MOM IS IN THE KITCHEN . . . NO HAND IN THE COOKIE JAR!

"Repent, for the kingdom of heaven is at hand."

Matthew 3:2

If mom is not in the room, then Johnny may be more inclined to stick his hand in the cookie jar and snag the proverbial prohibited cookie. Why does he not try it when mom is in the kitchen? Because she is right there . . . that's why! So too, the response to the nearness of the kingdom of God is to repent (Matthew 3:2). If God is right there ("is at hand" or "has come near"), then you are more inclined not to stick your hand in the cookie jar.

The proper response to the kingdom of God is to repent. More specifically, the response to the kingdom of God is to let go of the things of this world. That is not always easy. That's why it is hard "for those who are wealthy to enter the kingdom of God" (Mark 10:23). Certainly, living in the kingdom of God assures that your material needs will be met (Luke 12:31). However, it requires that you would be willing to let go of possessions, if necessary (Luke 12:32-33). This may even include being willing to "let go" of family members (Luke 18:29-30).

What are some other proper responses to the kingdom of God? One significant response is to be a good steward of what God has given you (Matthew 25:14-30). Use your talents and resources to advance and multiply the kingdom and the King of that kingdom will say, "Well done, good and faithful slave . . . " (Matthew 25:20-21). He will say, "That was a proper response to the kingdom!" Another proper response (Mark 4:26-29) is to "cast seed" (to testify and preach of the kingdom of God) and to "put in the sickle" (engage in evangelism and discipleship). The proper response to the kingdom of God is to look for it, wait for it, and prepare for it (Matthew 25:1-13).

And so, the proper response to the kingdom of God is to repent (Matthew 3:2). If God is right there ("is at hand" or "has come near"), then you are more inclined not to stick your hand in the proverbial prohibited cookie jar.

It is true . . . if mom is in the kitchen then there's no hand in the cookie jar! Respond to the kingdom of God. Repent, for the kingdom of heaven is at hand.

AUGUST 16

WHAT IS PRAYER? . . .

"He must increase, but I must decrease."

John 3:30

Someone once said, "Christians do not gossip. They just share prayer requests." Some people think of prayer as being nothing more than a part of their social lives. They think of it as a tool of manipulation. This is not the essence of prayer, however. Prayer is not gossip! Well, then, what is prayer? What is it that we are doing when we pray?

Prayer is humility. Prayer is the thing that says to God: "I cannot do it, but You can." Prayer becomes an expression of a humble attitude before God that recognizes the reality of Who

He is relative to who you are. It states emphatically, "He must increase, but I must decrease" (John 3:30).

Prayer is reliance. Prayer is the thing that says to God, "I need You in all my ways." In prayer, you "trust in the Lord with all your heart, and do not lean on your own understanding" while acknowledging Him in all your ways (Proverbs 3:5-6).

Prayer is trust. Prayer is the thing that says to God, "I deposit my time in Your bank." Prayer becomes an investment that is assured of a return "for everyone who asks, receives, and he who seeks, finds; and to him who knocks, it shall be opened" (Luke 11:10).

Prayer is relationship. Prayer is the thing that says to God, "I have decided to share with You my problems, my desires, my joys, and my dreams. Most importantly, I have decided to share my time in prayer with You." In prayer, you share with God your most precious commodity—you share your time—and proclaim your "fellowship is with the Father, and with His Son Jesus Christ" (1 John 1:3).

Prayer is faith. Prayer is the thing that says to God, "I realize that You are there. I believe that You hear me and I believe that You will answer me." Prayer confirms that "without faith it is impossible to please Him, for he who comes to God must believe that He is, and that He is a rewarder of those who seek Him" (Hebrews 11:6).

Prayer is love. Prayer is the thing that says to God, "I have decided to receive Your love and to show You my love through the time I spend with You." In prayer, you verify that "you have not received a spirit of slavery leading to fear again, but you have received a spirit of adoption as sons by which we cry out, 'Abba! Father!'" (Romans 8:15).

Prayer is the correct perception of yourself. Prayer is the thing that says to God, "I am the creation, and You are the Creator. You are the Vine, and I am the branch." When you understand who you are relative to God then you understand your desperate need for God, and in turn, you seek God. You go to Him (through prayer) because you perceive yourself and your abilities correctly relative to Him and His abilities. In prayer, you respond to the truth that "as the branch cannot bear fruit of itself, unless it abides in the vine, so neither can you, unless you abide in Me" (John 15:4).

So, then, what is prayer? What is it that we are doing when we pray? Jesus said, "And I, if I am lifted up from the earth, will draw all men to Myself" (John 12:32). We are drawn to God (prayer) as we lift our eyes to Him. "He must increase, but I must decrease" (John 3:30). This is prayer!

BIBLICAL MODELS OF THE CHURCH . . .

" . . . for you once were NOT A PEOPLE, but now you are THE PEOPLE OF GOD."

1 Peter 2:10

There exist a variety of biblical models to describe the church. One is the people of God or the family of God. This is depicted starting in the Old Testament, from Exodus 6:6, until the end of the New Testament, in Revelation 21:3. Israel is seen as the people of God (see Hosea 11:7; Psalm 100:3). The church is seen as the people of God (see 1 Peter 2:10; 1 Corinthians 3:9). We can say that in the spiritual sense the church is the new Israel (see Romans 9:6-8; Galatians 3:6-8; Galatians 6:16). Thus, the church has the responsibility of Israel. It has the responsibilities of the people of God. It must glorify God with its words and deeds (see Deuteronomy 4:5, 6; 1 Peter 2:9-11; Matthew 5:14-16). It must glorify God with its life (see 2 Corinthians 6:16-18; Titus 2:11-14). We must remember that the church is the people of God. It is not the person of God (although it is true that each individual Christian is the temple of the Holy Spirit). The church is made up of Christians or "saints" as the New Testament often calls them. "Saint" occurs sixty-one times in the New Testament. It is always "saints" (in the plural).

The church is not simply an individual believer. It is the community of believers. It is the family of God. Therefore, the description of the life of the church is filled with things to do "one for another." The people of God are the family of God (see 1 John 1:3; Galatians 3:29). The people of the church are sons and daughters of God. Therefore, they are brothers and sisters (Ephesians 2:19).

Another model to describe the church is the body of Christ. The idea of "body" in the Greek is the unity of something that has different members. Paul used this description of the church to emphasize: 1) The unity between the church and Jesus Christ; 2) The unity between the members within the church. The phrase "body of Christ" is also used: 1) To describe the sacrifice of Jesus on the cross (see Romans 7:4; Hebrews 10:10); 2) To describe the communion of the Lord's Supper (see 1 Corinthians 10:16; 11:23-29). We can see the idea of the body of Christ very clearly in John 15:1-6: 1) The body without the head is crippled (verse 4); 2) The branches without the vine are withered (verse 6); 3) The church without Christ is nothing (verse 5). Jesus is the Head of the body (see Ephesians 1:22, 23; Colossians 1:18): 1) The body depends upon the head; 2) The body obeys the instructions that come from the head (consider that a crippled part of the body is crippled because it no longer responds to the signals sent by the brain).

Perhaps, the most important implication of the concept of the body of Christ is the church's need for unity (see 1 Corinthians 12:12, 20). Remember, the motivation for unity is love. The idea of the body of Christ implies that there is unity within diversity in the church. There are different parts, and each have different functions. Yet, they work together (see Romans 12:4-8 and 1 Corinthians 12:14). Each member must be trained to do his part. Each member must minister (Ephesians 4:11-13). The commitment of each member is very important. Each member depends on the other members (see Ephesians 4:16 and 1 Corinthians 12:22, 26). The gifts of the Spirit are very important within the body of Christ. Each member must use his gift or gifts to edify the body (see Romans 12:6 and 1 Corinthians 12:7). The church is the light of the world because it is the body of Christ; Him who is the light (John 8:12).

Christ continues His ministry through His body. The leadership of the church must encourage diversity while also promoting unity within that diversity. After all, the church is a people, a family, a body . . . !

AUGUST 18

TO LEAD . . . NATURAL TALENTS OR CHARACTER TRAITS?

"Therefore . . . select . . . men of good reputation, full of the Spirit and of wisdom, whom we may put in charge . . . "

Acts 6:3

Many people think that you must have many natural talents to be a leader. Certainly, there is a gift of leadership: "Since we have gifts that differ according to the grace given to us . . . he who leads, with diligence" (Romans 12:6-8). However, most of the biblical requirements for leaders are *requirements of the heart.* They are *character traits.* Christian leadership requires more of a list of "*attitudes*" than it requires a list of abilities. It comes down to more of a list of *character traits* than it comes down to a list of natural talents. What does God "need" from potential leaders? Does He need your abilities or your *attitudes?* Does He need your skills or the *decisions of your heart?*

Before getting too extreme here, let's be clear. God does not despise your gift of leadership, your abilities, your natural talents, or your skills; He gave them to you and will certainly use them. However, it's a true statement to say that Christian leadership is more of an attitude than an ability. Why is this true? Because Christian leadership is actually the leadership of Jesus *through* the chosen leader. Jesus does not need your natural talents (although He will certainly use them if they are submitted to His Lordship). He *does* need your heart for that is where He will enter. Leaders need the beatitudes (attitudes of being). Then, Jesus can lead through them. This is Christian leadership.

In light of the above discourse, an interesting study to do is to look at some of the biblical passages that most directly address requirements for leadership. Let's look at Exodus 18:21-22: "Furthermore, you shall select out of all the people *able men who fear God, men of truth, those who hate dishonest gain*; and you shall place these over them as leaders." What are the requirements? Natural talents? No. They are issues of the heart; issues of character (those who fear God, who hold to the truth, and who hate dishonest gain).

Next, let's look at Acts 6:3: "Therefore . . . select . . . men of good reputation, full of the Spirit and of wisdom, whom we may put in charge . . . " Again, we do not so much see natural talents as we see the character traits; men of *"good reputation"* who are *"full of the Spirit* and *wisdom."* Another passage, 1 Timothy 3:2-7, paints an interesting picture of requirements for leaders: "An overseer, then, must be *above reproach,* the *husband of one wife, temperate, prudent, respectable, hospitable,* able to teach, *not addicted to wine or pugnacious,* but *gentle, peaceable, free from the love of money . . . And* he must have a *good reputation . . . "* In quite an extensive list we see only one ability (teach), while the rest we see are character traits.

Titus offers a similar list in 1:5-9 using words like: "above reproach, not accused of dissipation or rebellion, not self-willed, not quick-tempered, not addicted to wine, not pugnacious, not fond of sordid gain, but hospitable, loving what is good, sensible, just, devout, self-controlled." Of course, at the heavenly job interview, Jesus would not reject natural talents, but he would not hire without a healthy amount of godly character traits and attitudes.

Finally, we find a list in 1 Peter 5:2-3: " . . . exercising oversight not under compulsion, but voluntarily, according to the will of God; and not for sordid gain, but with eagerness; nor yet as lording it over those allotted to your charge, but proving to be examples to the flock." So what is the answer to our question: To lead . . . natural talents or character traits? Clearly the answer is . . . character traits!

AUGUST 19

MAKE NO MISTAKE . . . YOU ARE IMPORTANT!

"If you then, being evil, know how to give good gifts to your children, how much more will your heavenly Father give the Holy Spirit to those who ask Him?"

Luke 11:13

Do you feel important? Of course, a child is very important to an earthly father. How much more important, then, are you to your heavenly Father (Luke 11:11-13)? Your importance to God is clearly seen in the fact that He will search for you when you are lost (Matthew 18:12-14). You are important! You are important in His *story*; Your importance in the hi*story* of redemption is greater than that of John the Baptist (Matthew 11:11)! Your importance is shown in the fact that Jesus will share His glory with you since He is in you (John 17:22-23). You don't get any more important than that!

Important people are people who have authority. Of course, there is no authority except that which is established by God (John 19:11). Jesus has *all* authority in heaven and on earth (Matthew 28:18). Our authority is "ambassadorial authority" (2 Corinthians 5:20). It comes from Jesus. We are ambassadors who represent a King! Thus, our authority is based on the authority of that King (Luke 7:8). And so, we have authority in the spirit world to cast out demons (Luke 4:36) and declare forgiveness of sins (John 20:23).

Of course, authority cannot be separated from responsibility: " . . . And from everyone who has been given much shall much be required; and to whom they entrusted much, of him they will ask all the more" (Luke 12:48). In the world, authority is taken and exercised based on position. In the kingdom of God authority is earned and received based on function, based on service (Mark 10:42-44). And so, we are servants because He was a Servant (John 13:13-15). Jesus' sharing of His glory with us, then, includes the sharing of His authority and His responsibility. We must serve others by serving God, and thus, glorify Him. Like John the Baptist (John 3:30), we must decrease (serve) in order for Jesus to increase (be glorified). We should not seek our own glory; rather, we should seek the glory of God (John 7:18). This necessitates a life of service . . . a life of responsibility. To glorify God is to complete the work here on earth that He has for you to do (John 17:4). It is to do the will of God in the name of Jesus (John 14:13).

You are very important! Jesus' glory (literally, His "heaviness" or "reputation" or "importance") is shared with you because He is in you (John 17:22-23). Thus, you share in His authority and in His responsibility. You are, then, a powerful servant . . . "Christ in you, the hope of glory" (Colossians 1:27). You can't get any more glorious (important) than that!

AUGUST 20

WATCH OUT! BE SURE TO PASS THE TRUE/FALSE TEST

"FINALLY, MY brethren, rejoice in the Lord. To write the same things again is no trouble to me, and it is a safeguard for you. Beware of the dogs, beware of the evil workers, beware of the false

circumcision; for we are the true *circumcision . . . put no confidence in the flesh . . . not having a*
righteousness of my own derived from the *Law, but that which is through faith in Christ . . . "*

Philippians 3:1-3, 9

Paul challenges the Philippians to "rejoice in the Lord" and states that this challenge "is a safeguard for you" (Philippians 3:1). Who will they be safeguarded against? They are "safeguarded" when they "rejoice in the Lord" (Philippians 3:1) as opposed to rejoicing in man (see Galatians 6:12). Paul is leading into his warning against the Judaizers who wanted to rejoice in the Law and in man's accomplishments (man's ability to follow the Law). Paul warns them to "beware of" (Philippians 3:2) which means to continually be alert with a view toward avoiding. Avoiding what/who? Watch out for "the dogs . . . the evil workers . . . the false circumcision" (Philippians 3:2). More specifically, they must beware of those who "put confidence in the flesh" (Philippians 3:3). Paul would not use the term "dogs" to refer to gentiles. He possibly uses it to refer to the Jews in an attempt to make a stronger rebuke by using the Jews' own term. The Jews considered dogs that roamed the streets and ate the garbage as the most despised animals. Perhaps the picture here is of Judaizers who prowl around the Christian congregations trying to win converts to legalistic Judaism (salvation via the Law).

Also, the idea of "circumcision" could be used in the same way and for the same reason. The Judaizers (those who pushed the doing of the Law as the solution/salvation) were putting confidence in the flesh. Paul is warning the Philippians about the mixed gospel of the Judaizers which is actually a different gospel. Thus, Paul is very strong in his attitude towards this problem (see Galatians 1:8-9). He says in Philippians 3:2-3, "true circumcision" (as opposed to the "false circumcision") "worship in the spirit of God . . . and put no confidence in the flesh." The term "worship" means to serve, to minister and is specifically used to describe the service to God by the Jewish people. Thus, Paul is being very direct in his point. He uses the term "dog" which the Jews used to refer to the gentiles, the term "circumcision" which was a Jewish rite, and the term "worship" which most specifically refers to the service to God by the Jews. All of this to emphasize the great "change" that has taken place in God's redemptive plan (the inclusion of the gentiles via the gospel) and to warn against those who do not accept that change because they so passionately want to hold on to their particular ways (Judaism; hence the term "Judaizers").

We all must watch out for this and make sure we pass the true/false test. We have to avoid the false circumcision and reject the tendency to put confidence in the flesh; in our own abilities and accomplishments. We must embrace the "true circumcision" that insists on putting confidence only in Jesus; in His abilities and accomplishments. This is the essence of the gospel for you and for me; that I understand/accept/trust in the truth that I do not have "a righteousness of my own derived from the Law, but that which is through faith in Christ . . . " (Philippians 3:9).

Why am I in good standing with God? It is not because of what I have done, but because of what Jesus has done. And so, "let him who boasts, boast in the Lord" (1 Corinthians 1:31). We can finalize our discussion by simply declaring with Paul, "Finally, my brethren, rejoice in the Lord (Philippians 3:1)."

AUGUST 21

A LITTLE MORE MARY AND A LITTLE LESS MARTHA . . .

"But the Lord answered and said to her, 'Martha, Martha, you are worried and bothered about so many things; but only one thing is necessary, for Mary has chosen the good part, which shall not be taken away from her.'"

Luke 10:41-42

The Christian disciplines include the obvious inward disciplines like prayer, Bible study, and fasting but also include the lesser known outward disciplines like simplicity. What is the discipline of simplicity? We are often distracted by the things we do for God (as was Martha). We try to make our lives complicated. Yet, Jesus is calling us to sit with Him (as Mary chose to do) and realize the simplicity of our lives (Luke 10:38-42). Perhaps the best way to point ourselves toward the discipline of simplicity is to build a lifestyle that has "a little more Mary and a little less Martha!" We try to make our lives more complex than they need to be ("but only one thing is necessary"). We worry about things that we cannot control. Instead of worrying, we should realize that God is sovereign. This realization will free us to do what we can control (what we are responsible for); to seek the kingdom of God (Luke 12:26-31). It is really quite simple (not complicated) even though it is not easy to do (since we tend to focus on our own "sovereignty").

The discipline of simplicity is necessarily associated with the rejection of materialism. Kingdom teaching points us away from accumulating and storing up riches (excess/waste) in this life (Luke 12:16-21) and points us toward being content to have our needs met (Luke 12:31-33). Kingdom teaching is more concerned with giving than with taking and keeping (Acts 20:35). Certainly, in this sense, we could say that kingdom teaching promotes a simple lifestyle; a lifestyle in which we live according to our needs. The idea of "needs" is a very basic one (Matthew

6:31-32). Our needs include the basic necessities of life such as food and covering (shelter, clothes). And so, we should be content to lead a simple lifestyle.

A simple lifestyle, however, is not tantamount to being simplistic (in the sense that "simplistic" pictures a haphazard, unorganized life). The leading of the Spirit and organization exist together (Luke 9:14). And so, a simple lifestyle is not an undisciplined lifestyle. Jesus had certain customs, habits, or disciplines (Mark 1:35;Matthew 14:23; Mark 6:46; Luke 6:12; Luke 9:28; Luke 22:39). His was not an unorganized lifestyle even though it was a simple lifestyle! What is your lifestyle? Do you need a little more Mary and a little less Martha? It's your choice. Choose "the good part" (Luke 10:42)!

AUGUST 22

SOLVING THE MYSTERY OF THE KINGDOM OF GOD

"Jesus was going throughout all Galilee, teaching in their synagogues and proclaiming the gospel of the kingdom . . . And He was saying to them, 'To you has been given the mystery of the kingdom of God.'"

Matthew 4:23; Mark 4:11

The "kingdom of God" was the principal topic of Jesus' teaching ministry. What is the kingdom of God? The Greek term *basileia*, translated "kingdom," is most directly translated as "reign" or "rule." The kingdom of God is the rule of God. A kingdom is not simply a physical place . . . it is the authority or rule over people regardless of a physical place; thus, "a certain nobleman went to a distant country to receive a kingdom for himself, and then return" (Luke 19:12). God's rule is exhaustive as "the Lord has established His throne in the heavens, and His sovereignty rules over all" (Psalm 103:19). His kingdom is marked by His authority or rule in the hearts of those who yield themselves to Him; thus, the "kingdom of heaven is at hand" or "in your midst" (Matthew 4:17).

There is a certain degree of "mystery" involved in all of this (Mark 4:11). What is a "mystery"? A biblical mystery is something that has been kept secret through times eternal but is now disclosed (Romans 16:25-26). The kingdom that will one day change the entire external order has entered this Age in advance to bring the blessings of the kingdom of God to people, yet, without transforming the old order. The kingdom of God is working here among us, but God does not compel people to bow before it. They can reject it. If they are to receive it, it must be with a willing heart and a submissive will.

A mystery is to be "solved." And so, Jesus continues commenting on the idea of the "mystery of the kingdom of God" (Mark 4:11) by saying, "A lamp is not brought to be put under a peck-measure, is it, or under a bed? Is it not brought to be put on the lampstand? For nothing is hidden, except to be revealed; nor has anything been secret, but that it should come to light. If any man has ears to hear, let him hear" (Mark 4:21-23). So, how do you solve the mystery? How do you hear? Jesus answers this in a parable. Those who understand the mystery are associated with "good soil." The "good soil" is linked to those who "accept" what they hear and "bear fruit" (Mark 4:20). To accept the Word and bear fruit is to repent; it is to turn away from self and turn to Jesus (John 15:5).

Mystery solved! And so, before Jesus reports "the kingdom of God is at hand," He puts forth the command to "repent" (Matthew 4:17). Turn to Jesus. Solve the mystery. Live in the rule of God!

———————

AUGUST 23

SEE YOUR SMALLNESS TO SEE GOD'S GREATNESS

"He must increase, but I must decrease."

John 3:30

Our attitudes affect our walk with God every step of the way. "He teaches the humble His way" (Psalm 25:9). Without humility, a man cannot know God. To know God, we must be humble enough to die to ourselves and live to God. We must put on Christ. Only the poor in spirit can do this because only the poor (empty) in spirit are available for this (Matthew 5:3). A vessel must be emptied before it can be filled up with something else (2 Timothy 2:20-21). The way to know God is to be full of His Spirit, and so God is searching for empty (humble) vessels to fill up (the poor in spirit make way for the rich in Spirit).

After receiving his doctorate degree, a humbled graduate proclaimed, "the more I learn the more I find out what I do not know." There is a similar response on the road/path to knowing God. To some degree, the process of knowing God becomes the process of knowing His infinity. A very real aspect of knowing God is realizing who we are in relation to Him. We must recognize our smallness, our inadequacy, our finiteness, our imperfections, our uselessness, and our hopelessness (apart from Him) so that we can begin to see His greatness, His adequacy, His infinity,

His perfection, His effectiveness, and His hope. To see His perfect power, we must see our weakness (2 Corinthians 12:9). To see at all, we must recognize our inability to see (John 9:39-41). "He must increase, but I must decrease" (John 3:30).

So, an attitude of humility will bring us to God. We will then know God. The more we know God, the bigger God becomes. In turn, the bigger God becomes, the more we are humbled before Him. Then, of course, the more humility we have, the more we will come to God. And so, humility starts and continues us on the road/path to knowing God. No wonder Moses had such a close relationship with God. He was humbler "than any man who was on the face of the earth" (Numbers 12:3).

The Bible offers four main analogies to describe how we know God: a son knowing his father (we are children of God); a wife knowing her husband (we are the bride of Christ); a subject knowing his king (we are servants of God); and a sheep knowing its shepherd (we are the sheep of His pasture). Each one of these analogies points to the knower humbly looking to the one who is known. To know God, we must understand who we are, relative to Him. And so, let our proclamation be that of the Psalmist: "Know that the Lord Himself is God; it is He who has made us, and not we ourselves; we are His people and the sheep of His pasture" (Psalm 100:3).

AUGUST 24

GOD THE REVEALER, REVEALS . . . HIMSELF!

"AND WHEN Abram was ninety-nine years old, the Lord appeared to Abram and said to him, 'I am God Almighty; walk before Me, and be blameless.'"

Genesis 17:1

God is in the business of revelation. That's what He does . . . He reveals! What is the content of that revelation? The content is God Himself. God reveals Himself (Genesis 35:7; Exodus 3:6, 14). And so, "the Lord appeared to Abram and said to him, 'I am God Almighty'" (Genesis 17:1). This does not mean that there is no more mystery. With special revelation mystery still remains (Exodus 33:20); even in His immanence He still remains transcendent. Even with the climax of special revelation that comes in the incarnation of God (Jesus), mystery still remains (Matthew 17:2-6).

God reveals Himself. Most specifically, God reveals Himself in Jesus Christ. When the question is asked, "Who art Thou, Lord?," the answer is "I am Jesus" (Acts 9:5). God is no one else? There are no other options. God's revealing of Himself is very specific. He is Jesus! "There is no other name under heaven that has been given among men" (Acts 4:12). Perhaps the most magnificent (and mind-boggling/mysterious) dynamic of life for me, then, is that God "reveals His Son in me" (Galatians 1:16). The Scripture speaks of "this mystery . . . Christ in you, the hope of glory" (Colossians 1:27).

And so, everything in my life points to one thing; that my life is not about me but is about Him. This is not realized so much because I am good or because I am humble, but because it is true and because it is God's ultimate purpose. *The* reality show is the "show" in which "He made known to us the mystery of His will, according to His kind intention which He purposed in Him with a view to an administration suitable to the fullness of the times, the summing up of all things in Christ" (Ephesians 1:9-10).

Ultimately, revelation is life and God, as revealer of Himself, produces life as He reveals Himself; most specifically, as He reveals Himself in Christ. This is God's way. This is God's truth. This is God's life. Jesus is "the way, and the truth, and the life" (John 14:6). He is "the Alpha and the Omega" (Revelation 1:8), "Him who fills all in all" (Ephesians 1:23), and He in whom is "the summing up of all things" (Ephesians 1:10). And so, we cry out "To Him be the glory, both now and to the day of eternity. Amen" (2 Peter 3:18).

AUGUST 25

AVOIDING THE CORRUPTION OF FAITH . . .

"Peter said to Him, "Lord, if it is You, command me to come to You on the water." And He said,
"Come!" And Peter got out of the boat, and walked on the water and came toward Jesus."

Matthew 14:28-29

Faith can move mountains (Matthew 21:21; Luke 17:6). Faith can walk on water (Matthew 14:29). It is certainly an understatement to say that faith is powerful. It might be more correct to say that faith is absolutely powerful. Perhaps it is that particular aspect of the nature of faith that results in the tendency to sometimes corrupt the way in which it is taught and practiced. As the saying goes, "Power corrupts and absolute power corrupts absolutely." Abraham Lincoln was known to say, "Nearly all men can stand adversity, but if you want to test a man's character, give him power." Faith is powerful. Don't let the "power aspect" of faith corrupt your understanding of what it is and how it is used. How do we promote a "balanced" understanding of faith . . . how do we avoid corrupting what the Scripture teaches about faith?

First and foremost, it must be understood that faith is not presumption. It is based on the Word of God. Peter, in that sense, did not walk on the water; rather, he walked on the Word of God: "And

He (Jesus/God) said, 'Come!'" (Matthew 14:29). Peter walked on that Word! You cannot "faith yourself" into walking on the water or digging up dead bodies, but you can obey the Word of God to "Remove the stone" (John 11:39-40). It must be understood that obedience to God is the cornerstone of faith. Faith is not associated with getting whatever you want whenever you want it ("name it and claim it"). It is associated with getting whatever God wants (desires). A "name it and claim it" faith teacher might highlight the fact that the Scripture promises us that "He will give you the desires of your heart" (Psalm 37:4). And that is true, but it must be understood and applied within its context which is to "Delight yourself in the Lord." God gives you the desires of your heart because they are His desires. When you delight yourself in the Lord (the Word), His desires become your desires. While praying to the Father, Jesus used the phrase: "If it is your will" (Luke 22:42). Some have taught erroneously that prayer should never include the phrase, "If it is your will," because such prayers lack certainty; they say that it shows a lack of faith. Did Jesus lack faith? Of course not! Faith is built on obedience and is based on the desire for God's will . . . not simply your own!

Some corrupt faith teaching demands that strong faith is equal to receiving in prayer whatever you want. Under this type of thinking, Jesus would have never gone to the cross! He actually prays for God to remove "this cup" (Mark 14:33-36, 39). Note that He prays this in the context of "all things are possible with God" (a context of faith). If all things are possible with God, then why did Jesus not "use His faith" to make it happen . . . to believe that "this cup" would be taken from Him? First, it is because "all things are possible with God" is often set in the context of God enabling us to go through difficulties instead of simply being delivered/exempted from them (Philippians 4:12-13). Second, it is because obedience must define faith and inform its use. Jesus' faith was dependent on God's will being done ("not what I will, but what Thou wilt"). It was based on obedience and not necessarily on desire or on what might be preferred (that "the hour might pass Him by").

Ultimately, faith is not in things or particular results. They are not the objects of our faith; rather, God is the object of our faith. And so, when we talk about faith, we must talk about it most definitively in terms of "trust." Trust could be said to go beyond faith in the sense that faith believes for something while trust may have to believe when there is nothing to believe for. Trust puts its confidence in God instead of man or things or results. Trust cries out to God instead of relying on self (Luke 18:10-14). Faith is powerful but don't let the "power aspect" of faith corrupt your understanding of what it is and how it is used. How do we avoid corrupting what the Scripture teaches about faith? Faith is not presumption. Obedience to God is the cornerstone of faith. God, Himself, is the object of our faith (not things or particular results). Faith is, more than anything else, trust in God!

AUGUST 26

ASSURANCES AND THE BELIEVER . . .

"NOW FAITH is the assurance of things hoped for,
the conviction of things not seen."

Hebrews 11:1

In many ways, faith and Christianity go hand in hand. According to Christian belief "it is impossible to please God without faith" (Hebrews 11:6). The entire chapter (Hebrews 11) provides a multitude of portraits of faith. It is introduced by the definition of faith; that it "is the assurance of things hoped for, the conviction of things not seen" (Hebrews 11:2). Faith = Assurance! Assurance of what? Just to name a few things: faith can be used to have an assurance of victory over Satan (Ephesians 6:16); faith can be used to have an assurance of overcoming the world (1 John 5:4); and faith can be used to have an assurance that there is a God worthy of being glorified (Romans 4:20-21).

A variety of assurances come with being a believer, not the least of which is the assurance of salvation. How do you know that you are a Christian? You know because you know your own *testimony*. You know and can describe your own conversion *experience*. The Bible proclaims that we can know that we are Christians (1 John 5:13) most significantly because assurance is based on the work of Christ (John 1:12-13). Assurance of salvation for the Christian is based on the promise of the Bible (1 John 5:11-12) and the witness of the Spirit (Romans 8:16).

Closely related to the assurance of salvation is the assurance of forgiveness. Christians can know they are forgiven and, therefore, should be the first to forgive others (Matthew 5:23-24; Matthew 18:15). Of course, this assurance of forgiveness begins with the need for and action of confession (1 John 1:9) that then yields the blessing of forgiveness (Psalm 32:1).

Another important assurance for Christians is that Jesus is going to return; the assurance of the Second Coming of Christ. This assurance, especially, has definite pragmatic applications for the Christian. Referencing the Second Coming, Peter emphatically exhorts:

Since all these things are to be destroyed in this way, what sort of people ought you to be in holy conduct and godliness, looking for and hastening the coming of the day of God, because of which the heavens will be destroyed by burning, and the elements will melt with intense heat! But according to His promise we are looking for new heavens and a new earth, in which righteousness dwells. Therefore, beloved, since you look for these things, be diligent to be found by Him in peace, spotless and blameless . . . (2 Peter 3:11-14).

The assurance of His return began at His going (ascension) when two angels said, "Men of Galilee, why do you stand looking into the sky? This Jesus, who has been taken up from you into heaven, will come in just the same way as you have watched Him go into heaven" (Acts 1:11). The return of Christ is a promise (1 Thessalonians 4:16-17). He will come to receive us (John 14:2-3). It is a challenge for our lives now (1 John 3:2). We must live godly lives (Titus 2:11-14).

The assurance that He will come is the assurance that he will come in glory (Revelation 19:11-16). The shout of every believer's heart is the word "Maranatha" (1 Corinthians 16:22); "Come Lord Jesus." And so, the Scriptures come to a close with this assurance as their final thought: "He who testifies to these things says, 'Yes, I am coming quickly.' Amen. Come, Lord Jesus. The grace of the Lord Jesus be with all. Amen" (Revelation 22:20-21).

AUGUST 27

CHURCH GOVERNMENT: UNITY IN DIVERSITY . . .

"He must increase, but I must decrease."

John 3:30

What happens to the church if its members reject a "body" form of government (unity in diversity)? What happens if the church looks at the gifts in an unbalanced way? What happens if the planter is looked at as being greater than the one who waters (1 Corinthians 3:4-7)? The result is that the church will not grow, because it will only be able to drink milk like babies (1 Corinthians 3:1-3). The form of church government is important. It must be in the form of a body because the church is a body (a unity in diversity).

Imagine that a long time ago fire and water were great enemies. The fire said that he was a great friend of people. He kept them warm. He cooked their food. He also said that water was an enemy of people. Sometimes it would rush down the mountain and destroy their houses and kill them. However, the water said that he was a great friend of people. He quenched their thirst. He washed their clothes. He also said that fire was an enemy of people. Sometimes it would lose control and burn down their houses and kill them.

Then one year there was no rain. It changed the weather. It became very cold. The babies were crying. The people were beginning to die. The water on the mountain was desperate. There was nothing that he could do. Suddenly, the fire ran toward the people and began to warm them. They were saved. The water said: "The fire is good to the people."

However, after some days, the babies began to cry again. People began to die because there was no water. The fire was desperate. There was nothing that he could do. Suddenly, the water ran down the mountain. The people drank it and they were saved. The fire said: "The water is good to the people." The fire and the water looked at each other. They confessed that they were wrong to think badly about each other. They embraced. As they embraced two things happened. First, the fire lost some of its force and the water lost some of its weight. Second, a cloud of steam rose up over them.

The cloud of steam that was created might be seen to represent the Holy Spirit. Also, the first thing that happened was a result of the teaching found in John 3:30. The fire and the water had to decrease for the steam to increase. It is the same with the members of the church. They are as different from each other as fire and water. They tend to focus on their differences in a negative way instead of focusing on what they have in common. They do not realize their desperate need for each other. Finally, they begin to appreciate each other. They unite. God is glorified and lifted up like the cloud of steam. However, both members had to die to themselves. They had to lose a little bit of themselves (John 3:30).

AUGUST 28

DADDY PROVIDES IT ALL (HE HAS TO ... THERE'S NO OTHER WAY)!

"And Abraham called the name of that place The Lord Will Provide, as it is said to this day,
'In the mount of the Lord it will be provided'."

Genesis 22:14

Children need their parents to take care of them. Why? Because they are unable to take care of themselves. Infants need an "all-inclusive" degree of care. Why? Because they are unable to take care of themselves in an "all-encompassing" way. Parents see this reality. It is obvious to them. Since they see it then they understand they must be seen – they must show up – since they must provide. The provider might say: "Since apart from me you can do nothing (John 15:5), then from me you must get everything." It is an inescapable formula. Total need requires total provision. God's revealed name in Genesis 22:14, Jehovah Jireh ("The Lord Sees" or "The Lord Will Be Seen" or "The Lord Will Provide"), embodies this inevitable formula. God sees man's complete need, so God provides in a complete way by showing up completely. God (Abba Father, Daddy) provides it all because he has to . . . there's no other way.

Can God be known by man? No and yes. No, in the sense that God is transcendent (beyond). The finite cannot reach the infinite. Yes, in the sense that God is immanent (near). The infinite comes to the finite. Man can know God (and receive God's provision) because God has chosen to reveal Himself (to make Himself known); God has seen the reality of the situation (complete need) and has shown up (revealed Himself/involved Himself) provided for that need. God has to do it.

A shepherd watches and provides for his sheep. If a sheep gets lost, he does not search for the shepherd. The sheep does not even know he is lost. His need is complete. He not only needs to be found, but he needs to know that he needs to be found. We, like lost sheep, do not find God. In ourselves, we don't even know we are lost. It is the shepherd who must go and find the lost sheep. The shepherd must show up (Luke 15:4). We do not choose God. God chooses us: "You did not choose Me, but I chose you" (John 15:16). We do not come to God. God draws us: "No one can come to Me, unless the Father who sent Me draws him" (John 6:44). We are not saved by our own will. It is God's will: " . . . who were born not of blood, nor of the will of the flesh, nor of the will of man, but of God" (John 1:13).

These truths are hard for man to accept. It means that Jesus (the all-encompassing provision) is the stumbling block for all mankind; yet, only through Him can man know God. Like a child, we need "Daddy" to provide not just ninety percent, but one hundred percent. We earn nothing. We provide nothing. We deserve nothing. This is the stumbling block; that it is not our works/provision but God's works/provision (Romans 9:32). We must come to God as children who have complete need: "Truly, I say to you, whoever does not receive the kingdom of God like a child shall not enter it at all" (Mark 10:15). God provides completely. God is the source of all good things (James 1:17). He is the Alpha and the Omega, the beginning and the end (Revelation 1:8). It is God who "fills all in all" (Ephesians 1:23). Even the ability to know Him begins with Him (Ephesians 2:8). God provides knowledge of Himself because He must provide knowledge of Himself. There is no other way that finite and sinful man can know Him. God must provide revelation of Himself. He must show up. God (Abba Father, Daddy) provides it all because he has to . . . there is no other way!

CHURCH GOVERNMENT:
UNITY IN DIVERSITY . . .

"And He gave some as apostles, and some as prophets, and some as evangelists, and some as pastors

and teachers, for the equipping of the saints for the work of service, to the building up of the body

of Christ; until we all attain to the unity of the faith, and of the knowledge of the Son of God, to a

mature man, to the measure of the stature which belongs to the fullness of Christ. As a result, we

are no longer to be children, tossed here and there by waves and carried about by every wind of

doctrine, by the trickery of men, by craftiness in deceitful scheming; but speaking the truth in love,

we are to grow up in all aspects into Him who is the head, even Christ, from whom the whole body,

being fitted and held together by what every joint supplies, according to the proper working of each

individual part, causes the growth of the body for the building up of itself in love."

Ephesians 4:11-16

Different denominations or groups within Christianity have different ways of organizing their leadership. Some focus on the title, Pastor, while others focus on the title, Elder, and yet others focus on the title, Bishop. These three Greek terms in the New Testament are used interchangeably (1 Peter 5:1) to convey the church as a body. Regardless of which interchangeable Greek term your denomination might focus on (poiman=Pastor; presbuteros=Elder; episkopos=Bishop), the church is a body. It is a unity in diversity, and not a tyrant form of government in which there is a very small group of those who have power. It is a unity in diversity, and not a dictator form of government in which one man has all the power. It is a unity in diversity, and not a central form of government in which leaders are simply replaced by others in the same family or who have "connections."

In the body form of government, all authority and responsibility starts with Jesus. It is distributed to a group of leaders whose job (function) it is to do the same thing. They distribute their authority and responsibility to others. The focus is relationships and reproduction. The idea is not to hold on to power or to maintain the system, but to let go of power and to multiply the system. It's not the Tyrant form of government with its evil system/authority that seeks to purge via oppression (power) and results in taking away leadership (subtract). It's not the Dictator form of government with its one-man/claimed authority that seeks to control via intimidation (title) and results in neutralizing leadership (zero growth). It's not the Central form of government with its elite few/received authority that seeks to maintain via received authority based on one's situation (position) and results in adding leadership.

No! The church is a body. It is not only a brain. It is not one central command center (like the Central form of government). It is not only a mouth. It is not one overwhelming, charismatic figure (like the Dictator form of government). It is not only a fist. It is not one group of fingers who unite in order to create power (like the Tyrant form of government). It is a *body*. It is a group of different members who all have the same purpose. Thus, the government of this body must be consistent with itself. It must be designed to use the different functions of its members while maintaining its united purpose. The key is that the government is based on unity in diversity. How does unity within diversity operate? The church is compared to a body. A body is one. It is unified. However, it has many different parts. Yet, these parts all have the same purpose. At the same time, they have different functions and identities. The church is a body . . . it is a *unity in diversity*!

AUGUST 30

YOU WERE MADE FOR ETERNAL LIFE . . . YOU WERE MADE TO KNOW GOD!

"This is eternal life, that they may know You, the only true God, and Jesus Christ whom You have sent."

John 17:3

What is eternal life? Sometimes, almost subconsciously, it might be metaphorically understood with a picture—a picture of someone who has passed on from this life and is now clothed in a white robe, wings sprouting from his back, sitting on a cloud and playing a harp. Is this eternal life? The Scripture provides a more precise, almost dictionary-like, definition of eternal life: "This is eternal life, that they may know You, the only true God . . . " (John 17:3). Eternal life is to know God.

The topic of knowing God is the most important topic in theology (the study of God) and anthropology (the study of man). Salvation cannot be had without it (and so Jesus says in Matthew 7:23, "Depart from Me . . . I never knew you"), and salvation (eternal life) is defined by it ("This is eternal life . . . to know God"). History shows us that man has always been preoccupied with the question of the knowledge of God. Regardless if the search to answer this question has manifested itself in the form of what one might call religion or what one might call philosophy, it is not an overstatement to say that the human quest to know God has formed cultures, nations, and eras of human history:

So Paul stood in the midst of the Areopagus and said, 'Men of Athens, I observe that you are very religious in all respects. For while I was passing through and examining the objects of your worship, I also found an altar with this inscription, 'TO AN UNKNOWN GOD.' Therefore what you worship in ignorance, this I proclaim to you. 'The God who made the world and all things in it, since He is Lord of heaven and earth, does not dwell in temples made with hands; nor is He served by human hands, as though He needed anything, since He Himself gives to all *people* life and breath and all things; and He made from one *man*, every nation of mankind to live on all the face of the earth, having determined *their* appointed times, and the boundaries of their habitation, that they should seek God, if perhaps they might grope for Him and find Him, though He is not far from each one of us; for in Him we live and move and exist, as even some of your own poets have said, 'For we also are His children' (Acts 17:22-29).

There is something in man that reaches out for this supreme knowledge . . . this eternal life. Why? Because there *is* something in man . . . ! The reason why man seeks after God is, most fundamentally, found in the way in which man was created; it is found in man. It is not only that "the Lord God formed man of dust from the ground, and breathed into his nostrils the breath of life; and man became a living being" (Genesis 2:7), but more specifically, it is that "God created man in His own image, in the image of God He created him" (Genesis 1:27). This quest to know God is in man inasmuch as God's image is in man; it is how man was created. And so, there is the human quest to know God since God has made man and "set eternity in their heart" (Ecclesiastes 3:11). The "eternity in their heart" is to know God. What is eternal life? "This is eternal life, that they may know You, the only true God" (John 17:3). Eternal life is not sitting on a cloud and strumming a harp. Eternal life is to know God!

AUGUST 31

WE ARE MADE BY AN "US" WHO IS "THREE IN ONE" . . .

"Then God said, 'Let Us make man in Our image, according to Our likeness . . .'"

Genesis 1:26

The paradoxical nature of God as a unity in diversity that is theologically understood as the Trinity is seen as soon as you turn to the first page in the Bible. As early as Genesis 1:26, we see God referring to Himself as an "Us." God refers to Himself in the plural as He said, "Let Us make man in Our image, according to Our likeness . . . " (Genesis 1:26). Later, in dealing with the issue at Babel, God spoke to Himself in the plural: "Come, let Us go down and confuse their language, so that they will not understand one another's speech" (Genesis 11:7).

The Hebrew word for "God" is "Elohim" (as in Genesis 1:31). That Hebrew word (*Elohim*) is in the plural form, yet it is followed by a singular verb. This is consistent with the concept of the Trinity. God is a plurality yet is one and acts in harmony within His plurality. He is a unity in diversity. In the Hebrew language this could be expressed in terms of the difference between "*echad*" (compound unity) and "*yachid*" (non-diverse unity). Both words are translated as "one." However, there is a big difference between the two Hebrew words. The word "*yachid*" means "one" in the sense of a non-diverse unity, while the word "*echad*" is the word used in Deuteronomy 6:4 where the Bible definitively states that God is *One*. He is an *echad*. He is one in the sense of a compound unity . . . a unity in diversity . . . an *echad*.

An example of this idea of a compound unity (an *echad*) is seen when the spies come back from the land of Canaan and "then they came to the valley of Eshcol and from there cut down a branch with a single [*echad*] cluster of grapes" (Numbers 13:23). If it was just one grape (a non-diverse unity), then the word *yachid* would have been used. It was a cluster of grapes (a compound unity), and thus the word *echad* was used. Another example of a compound unity is found connected to God's creation of a day: "God called the light day, and the darkness He called night. And there was evening and there was morning, one day" (Genesis 1:5). A "day" is a compound unity. It is evening and morning, yet it is an "*echad*" . . . it is "one" day.

More applicable concepts in the Bible where we see the idea of "one" as a compound unity are found in the nature of the idea of the body of Christ as well as in the nature of the marriage relationship. It is the body of Christ in which "many are one": "For just as we have many members in one body and all the members do not have the same function, so we, who are many, are one body in Christ, and individually members one of another" (Romans 12:4). The word "echad" is also used to describe the nature of marriage and the relationship between husband and wife. Man was created in the image of God; in the image of a compound unity. Man is created as male and female: "God created man in His own image, in the image of God He created him; male and female He created them" (Genesis 1:27). And so, it is not surprising that when male and female come together in marriage, they become a compound unity . . . they become an "echad": "For this reason a man shall leave his father and his mother, and be joined to his wife; and they shall become *one* flesh" (Genesis 2:24). Two become one.

The marriage relationship, understood as a unity in diversity, is the basis for understanding what a marriage is supposed to be and is the foundation for growing a healthy marriage. So, don't have a "yachid" marriage . . . have an "echad" marriage.

NOTES

September

MYSTERY SOLVED: GOD'S BUSINESS OF REVELATION

*"Beloved, now we are children of God, and it has not appeared as yet what we will be.
We know that when He appears, we will be like Him, because we will see Him just as He is."*

1 John 3:2

If God was said to run a business what might it be called? What would be the name of the company that would be followed, of course, by God and Son, Inc.? Perhaps, the name of the company would be Revelation. God is in the "business" of revealing Himself. The word *revelation* comes from two Latin parts, *re* (remove) and *vela* (sail or veil); thus, *revelation* is the removal of a veil. The corresponding Greek derived word, *apocalypse*, comes from two parts, *apo* (take away) and *kalupsis* (cover). *Apocalypse* is a synonym of *revelation* (and so, the last book of the Bible is sometimes referred to as the *Revelation of John* or the *Apocalypse of John*). This is what God does. It is God's business. He is in the business of removing veils and taking away covers. This implies that there is something hidden. There is a mystery that needs to be solved. God is the Great Solver of Mysteries!

Mystery is produced by the difference between God and man and is exacerbated by the Fall of man: God is holy/man is sinful, God is infinite/man is finite, God is unlimited/man is limited, God is eternal/man is temporal, and God is perfect/man is partial. One could say that mystery is bound up in the need for redemption; man was originally made in God's image according to His likeness (Genesis 1:26) but now needs to be "transformed by the renewing of your mind" (Romans 12:2) to become "conformed to the image of His Son" (Romans 8:29) which is "the will of God" (Romans 12:2) that is "according to His purpose" (Romans 8:28). What is God's will? What is God's purpose? What is God's "business"? He is the Great Solver of Mysteries—"Beloved now we are children of God, and it has not appeared as yet what we shall be"—that is accomplished through His revealing of Himself ("We know that, when He appears, we shall be like Him, because we shall see Him just as He is") to the end that the original intention of God for us (His "deeming" of us) is brought back (that is, His "redeeming" of us); he who was made in God's image/likeness, but then fell away, shall again "be like Him" (1 John 3:2).

How is all of this accomplished? God's business! It is accomplished by God revealing Himself. It is "when He appears" that we shall be like Him and it is because "we shall see Him just as He is." The mystery is solved. God is perfect and man is partial (thus, there is mystery), but "when the perfect comes, the partial will be done away" (1 Corinthians 13:10) for "we see in a mirror dimly, but then face to face" (1 Corinthians 13:12). When He appears, we shall see Him just as He is, face to face, and we shall be changed completely because we have seen Him completely. This is the power of revelation . . . the power of God's business: "But we all, with unveiled face beholding as in a mirror the glory of the Lord, are being transformed into the same image from glory to glory, just as from the Lord, the Spirit" (2 Corinthians 3:18). In referencing this great culminating event manufactured by God's business (the return of Christ or the Second Coming of Christ), Paul speaks of it as "when the perfect comes" (1 Corinthians 13:10) and John speaks of it as "when He appears" (1 John 3:2). In any case, this great revelation will solve a great mystery:

> Behold, I tell you a mystery; we will not all sleep, but we will all be changed, in a moment, in the twinkling of an eye, at the last trumpet; for the trumpet will sound, and the dead will be raised imperishable, and we will be changed. For this perishable must put on the imperishable, and this mortal must put on immortality. But when this perishable will have put on the imperishable, and this mortal will have put on immortality, then will come about the saying that is written, "DEATH IS SWALLOWED UP in victory. O DEATH, WHERE IS YOUR VICTORY? O DEATH, WHERE IS YOUR STING?" The sting of death is sin, and the power of sin is the law; but thanks be to God, who gives us the victory through our Lord Jesus Christ (1 Corinthians 15:51-57).

Mystery solved! Redemption accomplished. God's "revelation business" will ultimately be the conduit through which He does His will and accomplishes His purposes. Glory be to God!

SEPTEMBER 2

DESCRIPTIONS OF JESUS IN JOHN'S WRITING . . .

"I am the Alpha and the Omega, the beginning and the end."

Revelation 21:6

The apostle John wrote one of the four Gospels and the book of Revelation. In those writings, John lays out a very clear picture of who Christ is and the nature of His character. In his Gospel, John proclaims Christ's divinity by referencing His "I AM" statements (God's most personal name given to Moses in Exodus 3:14, "I AM THAT I AM"). Jesus says that He is the Messiah

(John 4:26). He also proclaims, "I am the bread of life" (John 6:35) and "I am from above" (John 8:23). He claims to be the eternal one when He says, "Truly, truly, I say to you, before Abraham was born, I am" (John 8:58). Jesus also describes Himself by saying, "I am the light of the world" (John 9:5), "I am the door" (John 10:7), "I am the Son of God" (John 10:36), and "I am the resurrection and the life" (John 11:25). He tells His disciples they are correct to call Him Lord and Master/Teacher "for so I am" (John 13:13). He then states, "I am the way, the truth, and the life" (John 14:6), and "I am the true vine" (John 15:1). And so, John makes it clear . . . Jesus is the great I AM!

We can also consider John's descriptions of Jesus in accordance with each chapter in his Gospel. To start with, John portrays Jesus as the "Son of God" (John 1:1-14), the "Son of Man" (John 2:1-10), the "divine teacher" (John 3:2-21), the "soul winner" (John 4:7-29), the "great physician" (John 5:1-9), and the "bread of life" (John 6:32-58). As his Gospel continues, John pictures Jesus as the "living water" (John 7:37), the "defender of the weak" (John 8:3-11), the "light of the world" (John 9:1-39), the "good shepherd" (John 10:1-16), and the "prince of life" (John 11:1-44). Then, Jesus is seen as "King" (John 12:12-15), "Servant" (John 13:1-10), and "Consoler" (John 14:1-3). Closing out, John refers to Jesus as the "true vine" (John 15:1-16), the "giver of the Holy Spirit" (John 16:1-15), the "great intercessor" (John 17:1-26), the "model sufferer" (John 18:1-11), the "uplifted Savior" (John 19:16-19), the "conqueror of death" (John 20:1-31), and the "restorer of those who repent" (John 21:1-17).

John's descriptions of Jesus from the book of *Revelation* are equally as profound as his descriptions in his Gospel. Jesus is said to be "the faithful witness, the firstborn of the dead, and the ruler of the kings of the earth" (Revelation 1:5). In a clear declaration of His divinity, Jesus states "I am the Alpha and the Omega . . . who is and who was and who is to come, the Almighty" (Revelation 1:8). Jesus is described as "the lion that is from the tribe of Judah" (Revelation 5:5). At the same time, He is described as the "Lamb": "These will wage war against the Lamb, and the Lamb will overcome them, because He is Lord of lords and King of kings" (Revelation 17:14). In addition, He is said to be the "Word of God": "He is clothed with a robe dipped in blood, and His name is called The Word of God" (Revelation 19:13). Finally, Jesus is put forth in Revelation 19:16 as being supreme: "And on His robe and on His thigh He has a name written, 'KING OF KINGS, AND LORD OF LORDS.'"

John is certainly not lacking in descriptions of Jesus. Nevertheless, it is in no way exhaustive, and so, we must find a place to end our description. Perhaps it would just be best, then, to let Jesus Himself close things out: "It is done. I am the Alpha and the Omega, the beginning and the end" (Revelation 21:6). Our response to these descriptions must be WORSHIP. Lord Jesus, we praise and worship you!

TYPES OF PRAYER . . .

"And He came to the disciples and found them sleeping, and said to Peter,
'So, you men could not keep watch with Me for one hour? Keep watching and praying . . .'"

Matthew 26:40-41

Consider some of the things that you do for one hour or more each day. What about prayer? Jesus challenges us, "could you not keep watch with Me for one hour . . . keep watching and praying" (Matthew 26:40-41). To be able to answer this challenge, it may be helpful to understand that there are different types of prayer. Praying in a variety of ways can help us to be able to spend one hour in prayer each day. Dick Eastman in his book, *The Hour That Changes the World,* identifies twelve different types of prayer and encourages his readers to pray for five minutes using each type of prayer to pray for one hour. This "hour of power clock," then, is used to say "Yes" to Jesus' question, "Could you not keep watch with Me for one hour?"

One type of prayer is praise, the action of divine adoration. You can choose a specific theme (the greatness of God or His mercy) and proclaim all that God is with respect to that theme. Another type of prayer is waiting, the action of surrender. You might simply allow yourself to rest in complete silence. Think only about God while focusing on your commitment to give yourself to Him. You might say that "praise prayer" is setting God in His proper place while "waiting prayer" is setting yourself in your proper place.

Another type of prayer is confession, the action of admitting that you are a sinner in need of God's grace. Confess your sins. Confess your need for the guidance and anointing of the Holy Spirit. An additional type of prayer is praying according to the Scriptures, the action of standing on the Word. You could examine one passage of the Bible. Pray according to the promises, commandments, and implications of the passage. You could also use the prayers of the Bible by praying the prayer as your own prayer. You could pray for wisdom and revelation (Ephesians 1:17-23) or for strength and power (Ephesians 3:14-21). Another type of prayer is watching; the action of mental awareness. Be spiritually alert. Consider the methods of attack that Satan might use against you and claim the power of God to be able to overcome the enemy. Consider world events. Pray for the nations and leaders of those nations.

Another type of prayer is intercession, the action of praying for others. Ask God to give you a greater burden for others and then petition God on behalf of them. An additional type of prayer is supplication, the action of praying for yourself. Ask for the guidance of the Holy Spirit to pray according to the will of God. Consider your schedule for the day and its corresponding needs.

Talk with God about these needs and explain your requests. Examine your motives. Make sure that they are pure. Another type of prayer is thanksgiving, the action of expressing your appreciation. Consider all the things that God has done for you over the last few days. Offer specific thanks for spiritual blessings, material blessings, and physical blessings. Give thanks in anticipation of future blessings. Every day try to give thanks for something new.

Another type of prayer might be referred to as singing, the action of worship with a melody. Choose a special theme and sing a song about that theme. An additional type of prayer is meditation, the action of spiritual evaluation. Ask God theological questions and use the Bible to search for and dwell on the answer. Another type of prayer is listening, the action of receiving from God (both mentally and spiritually). Ask God-specific questions. Ask for direction and understanding. Ask God to show you how to solve problems. Be sensitive to the "still small voice" of the Spirit. Listen. Write down the things that you believe God is saying to you. A final type of prayer is proclamation, the action of divine magnification. Proclaim God's greatness. Focus on His omnipotence, His sovereignty, and His constant presence.

Jesus' challenge continues to ring in our ears, "Can you give Me one hour of your time?" As we engage in different types of prayer, we may find that "giving Jesus one hour of our time" every day becomes more possible.

SEPTEMBER 4

CHURCH GROWTH AS SEEN IN THE BIBLE . . .

"Day by day continuing with one mind . . . And the Lord was adding to their number
day by day those who were being saved."

Acts 2:46-47

Church planting goes together with church growth like the birth of a child goes together with the growing up of that child. First a church is planted. Then the church must grow. But what exactly is church growth? What does it look like? In Western cultures, the topic of church growth has become a science. It is studied, analyzed, and to a large degree, formulized. This has some advantages. We can become aware of certain trends and begin to develop certain principles of church growth. We can also observe and use proven methods of church growth. However, church growth as a science also has some disadvantages. We can begin to see the growth of a church as a recipe (as a strict set of procedures that supposedly guarantees success). Church growth as a science sometimes results in looking at the church as a business.

Current teaching on church growth often gives principles of "marketing" as the keys that will unlock the growth of a church: 1) Inventory – the idea of a "full service" church having all types of ministries, programs, and facilities; 2) Quality – the idea that the product must be excellent; 3) Advertising – the use of mass media and social media to promote the church; 4) Service – being sensitive to the needs of members and meeting those needs; 5) Availability – having meetings at convenient times; 6) Parking – being sure it is convenient for people to park their cars; 7) Integrity – letting your yes be yes and your no be no (do what you say you are going to do).

Of course, these principles, in and of themselves, are not wrong and can be very helpful as they are, for the most part, simply logical observations and conclusions with respect to church growth. However, we must not forget that the church is not a business. **A**dvertising, **S**ervice, **A**vailability, **P**arking (certainly great business ideas) form the acronym **ASAP**. Maybe that's part of the problem with church growth being attained "scientifically." It looks to be done ASAP, quick and easy and not necessarily in need of God and His sovereignty and power.

The word "church" comes from the Greek word *"ekklesia"* which includes two parts, *"ek"* (meaning "out") and *"kaleo"* (meaning *"to call"*). Thus, fundamentally, "church" refers to "the called out ones." It was used as a word to call together an army. It also has the meaning of "assembly," "meeting," or "congregation." Therefore, we should understand the church to be "the assembling together of the called out ones." The word "growth" means to expand, to extend, to add to, or to multiply. Growth can be quantitative; to grow in size or in number. It can be qualitative, to grow in character and inner strength. It can also be multiplicative, to grow in reproduction. Putting it all together we could say that church growth is the growth, extension, or expansion of the total number of individuals in the assembly of the called out ones, as well as the growth or expansion of the inner lives and character of those individuals.

Perhaps, the purest type of church growth is when the qualitative growth leads to the quantitative growth, when the growth in the lives of those already in the assembly naturally leads to the growth of the number of people brought into the assembly. This is what happened in the New Testament church (consider how Acts 2:46-47a leads to Acts 2:47b): "Day by day continuing with one mind in the temple, and breaking bread from house to house, they were taking their meals together with gladness and sincerity of heart, praising God and having favor with all the people. And the Lord was adding to their number day by day those who were being saved." This may not be "scientific" but it sure is divine!

———

SEPTEMBER 5

REWARD OF RELATIONSHIP WITH GOD? . . . A GREATER RELATIONSHIP!

"In all your ways acknowledge Him, And He will make your paths straight . . .
He is a rewarder of those who seek Him."

Proverbs 3:6; Hebrews 11:6

The promise of consistency in your relationship with God is reward. God "is a rewarder of those who seek Him" (Hebrews 11:6) and for those who "acknowledge Him . . . He will make your paths straight" (Proverbs 3:6). What is the reward that is promised to those who consistently seek God? Brother Lawrence, the celebrated seventeenth century French monk who learned to live a life continually in God's presence, said, "There is not in the world a kind of life more sweet and delightful than that of a continual conversation with God." For Brother Lawrence the reward of seeking God was the opportunity and motivation to seek God more. The reward of having a relationship with God is to have a greater relationship with God.

The Psalmist, who said to God, "I am continually with Thee" then reflected on the result or reward of that relationship by saying, "God is the strength of my heart and my portion forever" (Psalm 73:23, 26). For that seeker of God, God Himself was his "portion" or reward/benefit. The reward of his nearness to God was a greater nearness: "But as for me, the nearness of God is my good" (Psalm 73:28).

The tribe of Levi was unique among the tribes of Israel in that "Levi does not have a portion or inheritance with his brothers" (Deuteronomy 10:9). The Levites were also unique in that they served God in a very intimate way in that they "carried the ark of the covenant of the Lord, to stand before the Lord" (Deuteronomy 10:8). Although Levi had no "portion or inheritance" (reward) like that of his brothers, the fact that his ministry revolved around his relationship or nearness to God (He stood before the Lord) resulted in his reward that revolved around greater relationship with God; "the Lord is his inheritance" (Deuteronomy 10:9). The reward of his relationship with God was God Himself.

Peter, who was inquiring about this issue of the nature of the reward associated with seeking or following God, said to Jesus "Behold, we have left our own homes, and followed You" (Luke 18:28). Jesus responded by pointing to the reward of "eternal life" for those who follow Him (Luke 18:30). Of course, "eternal life" is to know God (John 17:3). The reward of seeking, knowing, or having a relationship with God is more seeking, knowing, or relationship with God!

And so, what is the reward that is promised to those who consistently seek God? The Scripture repeatedly points to the reward of having a relationship with God as having a greater relationship with God (1 Chronicles 28:9; Matthew 7:7; James 4:8). God said to Abram "Your reward shall be very great" (Genesis 15:1). What greater reward could Abram have than his "direct communication" with God as he was most remarkably referred to as "Abraham Thy friend forever" (2 Chronicles 20:7)? The reward of being a friend of God (having a relationship with God) is being a friend of God forever (having a greater relationship with God). "He is a rewarder of those who seek Him" (Hebrews 11:6)!

SEPTEMBER 6

KNOCK, KNOCK . . . WHO'S THERE? . . . GOD!

"For everyone who asks, receives; and he who seeks, finds; and to him who knocks, it will be opened."

Luke 11:10

It is certainly biblical to say that we can know God by our own actions. Many Bible passages encourage us to seek God in order to know Him. God is still the starting point in man's quest to know Him. Jesus says, "No one can come to Me, unless the Father who sent Me draws him" (John 6:44). God says, "I will give them a heart to know Me, for I am the Lord; and they will be My people, and I will be their God, for they will return to Me with their whole heart" (Jeremiah 24:7). Even the desire and ability to seek God comes from God. It could be said that we seek God because He first sought us and gave us a desire to seek Him (1 John 4:19).

The fact that God is the initiator does not eradicate the biblical mandate that we should know God by our own actions. "Searching" is a repeated theme in Scripture with respect to our actions relative to how we relate to God. We are to act—"For if you cry for discernment, lift your voice for understanding; if you seek her as silver, and search for her as for hidden treasures; then you will discern the fear of the Lord, and discover the knowledge of God" (Proverbs 2:3-5)—and we are to act with fervency ("cry" and "lift your voice" and "seek as silver"). God rewards our actions as "He is a rewarder of those who seek Him" (Hebrews 11:6). His reward is that we "discover the knowledge of God"; that we know Him. The Psalmist declares, "But as for me, the nearness of God is my good" (Psalm 73:28). And so it goes, "for everyone who asks, receives; and he who seeks, finds; and to him who knocks, it shall be opened" (Luke 11:10).

Not only can we know God by our own actions, but we are assured of knowing God by our own actions. The mandate to seek God comes with a promise of success. God says, "And those who diligently seek Me will find Me" (Proverbs 8:17). David encourages his son Solomon with this truth as he tells him, "If you seek Him, He will let you find Him" (1 Chronicles 28:9). Success is assured: "Draw near to God and He will draw near to you" (James 4:8); "knock, and it shall be opened to you (Matthew 7:7). It's no joke. Knock, knock . . . Who's there? God!

SEPTEMBER 7

HISTORY IS ACTUALLY HIS STORY . . . HE IS SOVEREIGN!

"But when the fullness of the time came, God sent forth His Son . . . "

Galatians 4:4

The time between the final book of the Old Testament (Malachi – 430 B.C.) and the birth of Christ (4 B.C.) is sometimes referred to as the Intertestamental Period. What happened during this time period and why is it significant? In 586, Nebuchadnezzar, the Babylonian (modern day Iraq) king, burned down the Temple and took the Jewish people into exile. Eventually, the Jews returned from the exile in three stages. With Cyrus as the king of Persia and Zerubbabel as the governor of the Jews, approximately 50,000 exiles returned to Jerusalem in 538 B.C. and rebuilt the Temple. With Artaxerxes as king of Persia, Ezra the priest returned with 1750 exiles in 458 B.C. and taught the Law to the Jews. Under Artaxerxes, Nehemiah returned to Jerusalem as governor of the Jews in 445 B.C. He established, administrated, and completed the project of rebuilding the city walls.

During the Persian (modern day Iran) period (450-330 B.C.), the Persians controlled Jerusalem. Nevertheless, they allowed the Jews to worship their God and the high priests were allowed to rule the local government. During the Hellenistic (Greek) period (330-166 B.C.), Alexander the Great conquered much of the known world. He was active in spreading the Greek culture to all parts of the world. He gave a significant amount of freedom to the Jews. They could worship God and keep His laws. Greek rule led to the translation of the Old Testament into the Greek language (the Septuagint). During this period Egyptian and Syrian rule began to oppress the Jews more and more. Finally, at the end of the period, Antiochus Epiphanes defiled the temple and prohibited Judaism. During the Hasmonean period (166-63 B.C.), after years of cruel oppression, the Jews revolted against the Syrian rulers. Under the leadership of the Maccabees and John Hyrcanus, the Jews enjoyed the freedom of an independent state for 100 years. Then, in 63 B.C. the Roman general, Pompey, invaded and conquered Jerusalem and all of Palestine came under the rule of the Roman emperor. At the time of Christ's birth in 4 B.C., Herod the Great was ruler of all of Palestine. In 19 B.C. he began to rework the building of the second Temple.

This is not just secular history. Like all history, it is His Story. God in His sovereignty used a variety of dynamics found in this history as key factors that prepared for the birth of Christ. The worldwide conquest by Alexander the Great resulted in the establishment of Greek as a common language throughout the world. The unifying of culture and language prepared the way for the rapid spread of the gospel. The Roman Empire established a worldwide, stable government. Peace filled the land. The Romans built a system of laws and a system of roads that made travel and communication much more efficient and safer. These things also led to the rapid spread of the gospel. The series of persecuting rulers eventually caused the dispersion of the Jews. They were dispersed into all parts of the world spreading the messages of the unity of God, the hope of a Messiah, and the truth of the Scriptures. This also led to the rapid spread of the gospel.

History is His Story because He is sovereign: " . . . until the appearing of our Lord Jesus Christ, which He will bring about at the proper time—He who is the blessed and only Sovereign, the King of kings and Lord of lords" (1 Timothy 6:14-15). The word *proper* in this verse is from the Greek word, *kairos* (instead of *chronos* meaning chronological time), which means "time" in the sense of perfect timing. And so, during His perfect timing and sovereignty over history we conclude: "But when the fullness of the time came, God sent forth His Son" (Galatians 4:4). Amen!

SEPTEMBER 8

A LACK OF FAITH IS A LACK OF FOCUS . . . ON JESUS!

"Peter said to Him, 'Lord, if it is You, command me to come to You on the water.' And He said, 'Come!' And Peter got out of the boat, and walked on the water and came toward Jesus. But seeing the wind, he became frightened, and beginning to sink, he cried out, 'Lord, save me!' Immediately Jesus stretched out His hand and took hold of him, and said to him, 'You of little faith, why did you doubt?'"

Matthew 14:28-31

Whatever you do, don't look away . . . from Jesus! Everything was fine for Peter on the water as he "came toward Jesus." He was focused on one thing; He was focused on Jesus. Then we see the problem and the problem is in the "But": "But seeing the wind" (Matthew 14:30). Oh no, Peter, don't do it . . . don't look away from Jesus . . . stay focused! Faith is linked to being focused on

Jesus, seeing Him only. Doubt is linked to looking away from Jesus and focusing on the circumstances or the things going on around you (Matthew 14:28-31). One of the other things (other than Jesus) we can look to that will tend to reduce our faith is our own glory. Seeking glory for yourself from others can result in an inability to believe: "How can you believe, when you receive glory from one another . . . ?" (John 5:44). You're walking on the water focused on Jesus but then you see the wind . . . you see the fear of man and the desire to please man . . . and you begin to sink! Don't do it . . . don't look away from Jesus . . . stay focused!

Of course, it is very important to stay focused. Our lives and ministries are too often hindered because of a lack of faith. A lack of faith hinders miracles (Matthew 13:58). A lack of faith can hinder us in spiritual warfare (Matthew 17:20-21; Luke 9:41). A lack of faith hinders our prayers (Matthew 21:21-22). Ultimately, the result of a lack of faith is sin: " . . . and whatever is not from faith is sin" (Romans 14:23; John 16:8-9). A lack of faith results in being committed to the desires and ways of the world (Matthew 16:26; Mark 8:36-37). A lack of faith leads to judgment (John 3:18) and condemnation (Mark 16:16). It results in the wrath of God (John 3:36).

And so, whatever you do, don't look away from Jesus! In the waters of life, the winds will blow but you will walk on the water as long as you keep walking toward Him. A lack of faith is a lack of focus . . . on Jesus. Stay focused!

SEPTEMBER 9

HAVING THE HEALTHY ATTITUDE . . .

"Not that I have already obtained it, or have already become perfect, but I press on . . . have this attitude . . . "

Philippians 3:12, 15

In Philippians 3, Paul referred to a sort of "holy trade." Paul was willing to trade "confidence in the flesh" (Philippians 3:3) for knowing God (Philippians 3:10). The way in which this trade was enacted is consistent with the cross; death to self is the method! The existence of a method implies the hope for a result. What is the result? Paul introduces the answer in Philippians 3:11 with the words "in order that." The Greek is actually "if perhaps." This implies a desired or hoped for result in sight. The desired result is "the resurrection from the dead." The Greek term "**ex**anastasis" is used instead of the Greek term "anastasis" as was used in verse 10 to refer to the actual event (the resurrection). This "**ex** . . . anastasis" is the resurrection out of something or from something, from the dead. The result is to have eternal life. It is to become, as Paul says, "perfect" (Philippians 3:12).

Paul may be doing two things here. First, he is taking the opportunity to emphasize the theological connection between death and life. He is saying that in order to live one must die. The resurrection is preceded by the cross; Friday comes before Sunday. The cross is the method. The resurrection is the result. Second, he refers to the resurrection as something that can be attained now. Eternal life is a current possibility since it is a current possibility to know God; "And this is eternal life, that they may know thee, the only true God, and Jesus Christ whom thou hast sent" (John 17:3). Thus, he refers to the ultimate fulfillment of the resurrection as well as to the current possibility. This is consistent with the "already/not yet" theology of the kingdom of God. To live in God's kingdom is already (although not completed) and not yet (when it will be completed . . . heavenly . . . perfect).

Has Paul obtained it yet? No! He actually said, "Not that I have already obtained it, or have already become perfect . . . " (Philippians 3:12). So, then, did he give up? Did he quit? No! He then said, "but I press on." Paul had a healthy attitude. He accepted and admitted that he needed to improve. He also moved ahead toward the improvement. Paul said: 1) I have not yet obtained it; *and* 2) I will move forward. His having not obtained it did not discourage him from moving forward. His moving forward did not keep him from admitting his lack. This was a healthy attitude. The perspective of this attitude is to look ahead and to forget what is behind (Philippians 3:13). The imagery of this attitude—as seen in the Greek terms translated as "forgetting/reaching" and "toward the goal" in verses 13 to 14—is that of a runner who bears down and is intent on the goal but is not overwhelmed by his distance from it. At the same time, he does not fall into a false confidence; he realizes and admits that he is not yet there. So, he keeps running!

Let's end our discussion of the healthy attitude with a few other sports metaphors in the Scripture. "Do you not know that those who run in a race all run, but only one receives the prize? Run in such a way that you may win" (1 Corinthians 9:24). "Fight the good fight of faith; take hold of the eternal life to which you were called . . . " (1 Timothy 6:12). "I have fought the good fight, I have finished the course, I have kept the faith; in the future there is laid up for me the crown of righteousness, which the Lord, the righteous Judge, will award to me on that day; and not only to me, but also to all who have loved His appearing" (2 Timothy 4:7-8). " . . . let us run with endurance the race that is set before us, fixing our eyes on Jesus, the author and perfecter of faith . . . " (Hebrews 12:1-2). "But the one who endures to the end, he will be saved" (Matthew 24:13). So, retain a healthy attitude. Even though you admit your lack of perfection, keep running and fighting until "the perfect comes" (1 Corinthians 13:10).

SEPTEMBER 10

WHAT MAKES A CHURCH GROW?

"So the churches were being strengthened in the faith . . .
increasing in number daily."

Acts 16:5

Certainly, any pastor or leader of a church would desire to know what makes a church grow. Of course, the New Testament has a lot to say about this. More specifically, the book of Acts reveals some of the more often seen dynamics that are associated with church growth. So . . . what *does* make a church grow? In the book of Acts there are nine separate scenarios in which either the phrase "added to their number" or "the word of the Lord was growing mightily" is used to indicate church growth. As we study these passages, we see factors that led to church growth. The first passage is Acts 2:1-41: "and that day there were added about three thousand souls (Acts 2:41). The next passage is Acts 2:42-47: "praising God and having favor with all the people. And the Lord was adding to their number day by day those who were being saved" (Acts 2:47). Another passage is Acts 5:1-16: "And all the more believers in the Lord, multitudes of men and women, were constantly added to their number . . . " (Acts 5:14). The next passage is Acts 6:1-15: "and the number of the disciples continued to increase greatly in Jerusalem" (Acts 6:7). Another passage is Acts 9:28-35: "So the church throughout all Judea and Galilee and Samaria enjoyed peace, being built up; and going on in the fear of the Lord and in the comfort of the Holy Spirit, it continued to increase" (Acts 9:31). A sixth passage is Acts 12:1-24: "But the word of the Lord continued to grow and to be multiplied" (Acts 12:24). Another passage is Acts 14:1-7: " . . . that a large number of people believed, both of Jews and of Greeks" (Acts 14:1). The next passage is Acts 16:1-5: "So the churches were being strengthened in the faith and were increasing in number daily" (Acts 16:5). The ninth and final passage is Acts 19:1-20: "So the word of the Lord was growing mightily and prevailing" (Acts 19:20).

So, we see clearly that the book of Acts has much to say about church growth. Especially regarding these nine passages we can ask the question, "What dynamics/actions/scenarios are included in the passage that would then be used to help us answer the question, "What does make a church grow?" Perhaps, the most important factor we find in the book of Acts associated with church growth is the presence of signs and wonders. This is seen in eight out of the nine passages. Almost equally important is the action of preaching and teaching which is seen in seven out of nine passages. An especially undesirable scenario is the occurrence of persecution that seems to be involved in church growth (four out of nine passages). Judgment (church discipline) is found in three out of nine passages as is the use of the gifts of the Holy Spirit/baptism of the Holy Spirit. Generosity and the sharing of material resources turns up in two of the nine passages as does the dynamic of leadership and organization. Finally, both praise and prayer show up in one out of nine passages.

Most of these dynamics/actions/scenarios (signs/wonders, preaching/teaching, persecution, judgment, gifts/baptism of the Holy Spirit, generosity/sharing, leadership/organization, praise, and prayer) have to do either with the ministry of the church as it is empowered by God or the effects of that divine empowerment. Not that there is anything necessarily wrong with having a coffee shop outside of the sanctuary of the church, a church softball team, or facilities large enough to include a game room for the youth group, but those sorts of "science of church growth" emphases used to supposedly grow the church just do not show up in the book of Acts. Nevertheless, a lot of church growth shows up in the book of Acts (even though none of the churches seem to have a coffee shop, softball team, or game room). Let's be clear. There is nothing wrong with having a game room, but it is not a game room that is going to grow your church; rather, it is preaching and teaching the Word that will lead to church growth.

SEPTEMBER 11

GOD IN THE FLESH . . . IN THE "CARNE" . . . INCARNATION!

" . . . who, although He existed in the form of God, did not regard equality with God a thing to be grasped, but emptied Himself, taking the form of a bond-servant, and being made in the likeness of men."

Philippians 2:6-7

There is no other more alarming and assuring event in history than when God became a Man. God took on flesh in Jesus Christ, the God-Man (Jesus is fully God and fully Man). In many ways, the climax of history is the incarnation. As we see in Philippians 2:6-7, Jesus, existed (actually should be translated "existing" as the Greek verb is a present active participle) "in the form of God" (He was God, is God, and continues to be God; that is, in becoming a Man, He does not stop being God) "but emptied Himself" (He laid aside His privileges, not giving up His deity but giving up His expression or environment of deity, or glory as He took upon Himself limitations of place, knowledge, and power).

We can see the incarnation (pre-incarnation) well before the birth of Christ in the way in which the Scripture pictures "the angel of the Lord." These seem to be appearances of Jesus before the actual incarnation (Genesis 16:7-13; Genesis 32:24-30 with Hosea 12:2-5; Exodus 3:2-6; Judges 6:11-14; Joshua 5:13-15; Exodus 23:20-22). We also see the incarnation before the birth of Christ through prophecy (Isaiah 7:14). "Immanuel" or "God is with us" is a succinct definition of the incarnation. Of course, a fuller description of the incarnation is then seen in the New Testament. God became flesh (John 1:14). He was born of a woman (Galatians 4:4). He came in the flesh (1 John 4:2). He appeared in the flesh (1 Timothy 3:16). He was made in our likeness (Romans 8:3; Hebrews 2:14). He had a body (Hebrews 10:5-10; 1 John 1:1-3). He died in the flesh (1 Peter 3:18; 4:1).

Why does God become a Man? Why does God take on flesh in Jesus Christ? Jesus does this to reveal the Father (John 14:8-11), to do the will of God (Hebrews 10:5-9), to fulfill prophecy (Luke 4:17-21), to die for people's sins (1 Peter 3:18), to fulfill all righteousness (Matthew 3:15), to reconcile the world to Himself (2 Corinthians 5:18-21), to become our high priest (Hebrews 7:24-28), and to become our example (1 Peter 2:21-23). The incarnation, then, becomes the proof or evidence of the deity of Christ (Romans 9:3-5), confirms the resurrection (Acts 2:24-32), and serves as a "test" to identify believers (1 John 4:1-6).

And so, the incarnation is an essential aspect of the gospel story. Only God Himself can forgive us. Only God Himself can die for us. God "had to" become a Man. He had to come to us because we could not get to Him. So, Jesus, who is fully God (He is the Son of God) and fully Man (He is the Son of Man) is "God with us" (Isaiah 7:14) and "He who will save His people from their sins" (Matthew 1:21). "Jesus" means "God saves" and God must save because we cannot save ourselves. He is God Incarnate (Colossians 1:15; Hebrews 1:3). He is God who has come to man, as a Man (Philippians 2:5-8).

God Himself was willing to identify with us. He was willing to become one of us and live with us. The implication for His followers who represent Him and who spread His message throughout the world is clear. A missionary must follow the "incarnational model." He must be willing to identify with the people whom he goes to and take on their customs/culture. He must be willing to live with the people (1 Corinthians 9:19-23). In this sense, the incarnation informs the Great Commission. And so, as God "went from heaven" He calls us to "Go, therefore . . . " (Matthew 28:19). Where are you going?

———

SEPTEMBER 12

REDEMPTION RIGHT FROM THE BEGINNING . . .

"And I will put enmity Between you and the woman, And between your seed and her seed; He shall bruise you on the head, And you shall bruise him on the heel."

Genesis 3:15

Some of the major theological themes of the Bible are presented right away. We see a picture of the Trinity in the very initial verses of the Scripture: "Then God said, 'Let Us make man in Our image, according to Our likeness'" (Genesis 1:26). Then we see the plan of redemption in two different ways early on in Genesis, the book of beginnings.

First, we see redemption in the cross in Genesis 3:15: "And I will put enmity between you and the woman, and between your seed and her seed; He shall bruise you on the head, and you shall bruise him on the heel" (Genesis 3:15). This proclamation of "enmity" is set in the context of God speaking to the serpent; that is, the devil or Satan (Revelation 12:9). God says to Satan that He will put something called "enmity" between him and "the woman" and between his "seed" and her seed. Her "seed" (singular) is going to injure ("bruise") Satan on the head, and Satan is going to bruise him ("her seed") on the heel. The Hebrew word for "enmity" could be translated "blood feud." This is what would happen on the cross to achieve redemption. Jesus Christ would reverse what Satan had corrupted through the shedding of His own blood. The word "seed" in the singular refers to the incarnation via Mary ("her seed" is Mary's seed). It refers to the birth of Jesus Christ: "Now the promises were spoken to Abraham and to his seed. He does not say, 'And to seeds,' as referring to many, but rather to one. And to your seed, that is, Christ" (Galatians 3:16). So, "He shall bruise you on the head" is referencing Jesus' destruction of Satan, while "you shall bruise him on the heel" is referencing the redemption that Jesus achieves for believers by His shed blood. Jesus is not destroyed as Satan will be; Satan is bruised "on the head." Jesus is put to death (bruised "on the heel) only to rise from the dead.

Certainly, the death and resurrection of Jesus Christ is the specific provision for redemption for mankind. We see that right away in the Scripture. Moreover, God has a strategy for spreading that provision of redemption that we also see right away:

> Now the LORD said to Abram, 'Go forth from your country, And from your relatives And from your father's house, To the land which I will show you; And I will make you a great nation, And I will bless you, And make your name great; And so you shall be a blessing; And I will bless those who bless you, And the one who curses you I will curse. And in you all the families of the earth will be blessed' (Genesis 12:1-3).

God's strategy for spreading His redemption is based on a dual objective: "I will bless you" and "you shall be a blessing." Here we see the strategy of redemption is to choose a people and work through that people to reach other peoples (to bless a people and use them to bless other peoples). In this strategy "all the families of the earth will be blessed." God's strategy is dependent upon the obedience of His chosen people who He will work through. "So Abram went forth as the Lord had spoken to him" (Genesis 12:4). Abram obeyed God. He went forth. Why? Because the Lord had told him to "Go." He obeyed. Out of obedience God's plan of redemption goes forth; ultimately to "all the families of the earth." And so, Jesus will later speak of the same strategy: "Go therefore and make disciples of all the nations" (Matthew 28:19). Now, the chosen ones who must "Go" are Jesus' disciples . . . the church!

SEPTEMBER 13

WILL YOU BE A 60 WATT OR 100 WATT LIGHTBULB?

"If any man's work is burned up, he shall suffer loss; but he himself shall be saved, yet so as through fire."

1 Corinthians 3:15

Eternal life is a gift (Romans 6:23) that is not earned by good works (Ephesians 2:8-9). Nevertheless, there exist numerous Scriptures that point to the idea that there will be degrees of reward in heaven. Thus, someone can go to heaven (be "saved") having some of his work "burned up," and therefore, "suffering loss . . . saved, yet so as through fire" (1 Corinthians 3:15). What is the "loss"? It is the loss of opportunity, the loss of the opportunity to gain increased rewards. And so, there is a "quality of each man's work" and if, via that quality, that work "remains, he shall receive a reward" (1 Corinthians 3:12-14). In order to understand this, it might be described metaphorically by saying that all who are saved will be lightbulbs in heaven, but some will be 60 watt, some will be 75 watt, and some will be 100 watt lightbulbs.

Since there is a "degrees of reward in heaven" dynamic, your actions in this life impact eternal life. Reward in the life to come is directly correlated to action in this life. It could be said that our positions in eternity depend on what we do on earth (Matthew 20:21-22). We might say the more death (to yourself) you experience here, the more life you will experience there. Thus, Jesus indicates we should be wise in making requests with respect to position in heaven. We must count the cost of the thing we ask for. Still, Jesus encourages us to think of ways that we can receive rewards in heaven. One way is to do things in such a way that will not bring attention to yourself, to do things that will not receive rewards here on earth (Luke 14:12-14). Another way to say this is that eternal life requires that we first hate (not prefer) our lives in this world (John 12:25). Furthermore, if you are ashamed of Jesus and the gospel here, then He will be ashamed of you there (Mark 8:38).

God has prepared positions for each one in His coming kingdom (Matthew 20:21-23). Even rewards in heaven have been prepared by God beforehand, He is sovereign over these "positions" in heaven (Mark 10:40). Jesus prepares places for believers in heaven and will return to take them there (John 14:2-3). He who is currently first here on earth will be last in heaven. He who is currently last here on earth will be first in heaven (Matthew 19:30). Jesus seems to imply that to have a heavenly position close to His, you must have an earthly life—and death to self—similar to His (Matthew 20:22). And so, the bottom line is that rewards in heaven based on this life are only based on this life relative to how we interact with "life" itself; how we interact with Jesus (John 14:6). "He who plants and he who waters are one; but each will receive his own reward according to his own labor . . . let each man be careful how he builds upon it for no man can lay a foundation other than the one which is laid, which is Jesus Christ" (1 Corinthians 3:8-11).

SEPTEMBER 14

WHO DA MAN? . . . BEHOLD, THE MAN!

"Pilate said to them, 'Behold, the man!'"

John 19:5

Was universal sin and death a part of God's original plan for man? Is "fallen man" the intended picture that God originally painted on the canvas of creation? No! There was a monumental change. There was an "exchange" (Romans 1:23) in which something original/natural was given up for something not natural, something not intended. And what a foolish (Romans 1:22) exchange it was!

The discourse found in Romans 1:18-25 describing this tragic change is certainly influenced by the very contents of the creation and ensuing fall of man story found in Genesis 1-3. Man was originally made to serve the Creator. After he served the creature, man became something less than he originally was intended to be (Romans 1:25). And so, there is a vast difference between that which is "incorruptible" and that which is "corruptible"; an epic "exchange" (Romans 1:23)! The fall of man is tantamount to taking the product (mankind as intended originally) back to the store and exchanging it for something entirely less than it was intended to be. This can be described as the incorruptible for the corruptible, the truth for the lie, the real for the counterfeit, the pure for the impure, the domain of light for the "domain of darkness" (Colossians 1:12-13), the realm of life for the realm of death, and the immortal for the mortal! It can be argued that Adam originally had potential to be immortal. The "tree of life" was in the garden and was one of the trees available to Adam (Genesis 2:9, 16). If Adam did not at least have the potential for immortality, then to forfeit it would not have been a real punishment. Yet God used the possibility of death as a real punishment (Genesis 2:17).

It might be said that the first Adam could have been something other than what he became. And so, the essence of redemption (regaining that which was lost) is that the last Adam (1 Corinthians 15:45) was victorious at the crucial point where the first Adam failed. He would be what the first Adam should have, could have, would have been, He is what God originally intended in terms of His purpose for humanity. Jesus Christ, the perfect mediator, became mankind's "first fruits" (1 Corinthians 15:20). First fruits, in agricultural terms, are the first viable shoots of newly planted seeds. They are a joyful promise that more growth and fruit will follow. And so, consider this outrageous statement: It is not Adam's humanity that is natural, but Christ's. In God's eternal perspective, the humanity of Christ ("first fruits") is prior to the humanity of Adam in the sense that God's purpose for man was prior to Adam's rebellion. Adam, who apparently was the first, was the last. Christ, who apparently was the last, was the first. And so, "the last shall be first, and the first last" (Matthew 20:16).

The name "Adam" is from the Hebrew term that can be translated "mankind" or "the man." Tragically, he became "the unnatural man." Pontius Pilate, in a sort of "Caiaphasian prophecy" (John 11:49-51), unwittingly referred to Jesus correctly when he proclaimed, "Behold, the man" (John 19:5). Victoriously, Jesus became "the natural man." As the first Adam failed Christ the last Adam fulfilled all God's desire (Isaiah 53:11-12; Hebrews 12:2). He is the perfect picture of humanity. He is the intended picture that God originally painted on the canvas of creation. Behold, *the* Man!

SEPTEMBER 15

SPIRIT ACTIVITY IS ACTIVITY
THAT POINTS TO CHRIST

" . . . the Spirit of truth who proceeds from the Father, He will testify about Me . . . He will glorify Me."

John 15:26, 16:14

What is spiritual? How does one know when the Holy Spirit is at work? What kinds of activities is the Spirit of God involved in? The activity of the Holy Spirit points to Christ. Jesus describes this dynamic when He explains that "the Spirit of truth who proceeds from the Father, He will testify about Me . . . He will glorify Me" (John 15:26, 16:14). This is the activity and work of the Holy Spirit: pointing to Jesus! Throughout all His Story (history), that is the work of the Holy Spirit. The prophets of the Old Testament, by the power of the Spirit, point to Jesus (John 5:39; Luke 24:27). Then, Jesus' followers in the New Testament, by the power of the Spirit, point to Jesus (Acts 1:8).

Those who stand between the Testaments—the forerunners of the Messiah like John the Baptist, Mary, Elizabeth, Zacharias, and Simeon—by the power of the Spirit, point directly to Jesus. John the Baptist was filled with the Holy Spirit while he was still in the womb (Luke 1:15). He was a unique person with a unique Spirit anointing who was sent to do a unique ministry that pointed to Jesus and prepared the way before Him (Luke 1:16-17). The enabling work of the Holy Spirit in human beings (specifically in Mary) reached to its greatest height when a virgin was enabled to give birth to God's Son by the activity of the Holy Spirit (Luke 1:34-35). Elizabeth, the mother of John the Baptist, was filled with the Spirit and she pointed to Jesus. Elizabeth was filled with the Spirit as the Spirit-filled baby in her womb (John the Baptist) leaped when the Spirit-anointed baby in Mary's womb was present (Luke 1:41-42). Zacharias, the father of John the Baptist, was filled with the Spirit and the Spirit activity in him pointed to Jesus (Luke 1:67-68). Then there was Simeon, "a man in Jerusalem . . . looking for the consolation of Israel; and the Holy Spirit was upon him" (Luke 2:25). The activity of the Spirit in Simeon, like the activity of the Spirit in John the Baptist, Mary, Elizabeth, and Zacharias, pointed to Christ and His salvation (Luke 2:27-32).

Who is involved in this spiritual activity? Spirit activity that points to Jesus is done among the people of God (Luke 1:5, 27; 2:25). There is a strong religious character of those who are activated by the Holy Spirit. Righteousness, humility, and commitment are some of the character traits of those who are used by the Spirit (Luke 1:6, 15, 30, 38; 2:25). The activity of the Holy Spirit was done in a context of faith, expectancy, and obedience (Luke 1:38, 45). The atmosphere of the activity of the Holy Spirit was that of joy and blessing (Luke 1:41-47, 64, 68; 2:27, 28, 34).

Throughout all His Story (history), the work of the Holy Spirit is to point to Jesus. The prophets of old, the forerunners of the Messiah, the followers of Jesus all are used by the Spirit of God to point to Jesus. Are you pointing to Jesus? Are you involved in what is spiritual? Spirit activity is activity that points to Christ!

SEPTEMBER 16

PRAYER IS FAITH . . .

" . . . now, will not God bring about justice for His elect who cry to Him day and night, and will
He delay long over them? I tell you that He will bring about justice for them quickly. However,
when the Son of Man comes, will He find faith on the earth?"

Luke 18:7-8

God's people pray . . . they "cry to Him day and night" (Luke 18:7). God responds to the prayers of His people, yet questions whether He will find them praying when Jesus returns, whether He will "find faith on the earth" (Luke 18:8). Herein, we see that prayer is linked to faith to such a degree that we might say that "prayer is faith." In another context (Mark 9:18-19, 28-29) in which a similar connection between prayer and faith is made, a lack of faith that results in an inability to cast out a demon is able to be corrected with prayer (making prayer tantamount to faith). So, show me the person who prays the most ("in all your ways acknowledge Him") and I will show you the person who has the most faith ("trust in the Lord with all your heart"). The minute you pray is the minute you say: "I do not lean on my own understanding/ability/authority, but on the ability/authority of Someone I have faith in" (Proverbs 3:5-6). Prayer is faith!

If prayer is faith, then, prayer is of critical importance even as "whatever is not from faith is sin" (Romans 14:23). Thus, we cannot substitute activity for prayer. It should be noted that extended teaching on prayer is set in the context of the contrast between busy Martha and her sister, prayerful Mary (Luke 10:38-11:13). And so, during activity (even ministry) we must take time to be alone with God in prayer (Luke 5:16).

Prayer is important. Prayer is beneficial to the everyday life of the one who prays. Prayer is useful to make important decisions (Luke 6:12-13). Consistent prayer is connected to the avoidance of discouragement (Luke 18:1). Prayer is beneficial to the ministry of the one who prays. Prayer is connected to success in casting out demons (Mark 9:29). Moreover, prayer can be used to help complete the Great Commission (Matthew 9:37-38; Luke 10:2). Prayer is beneficial to the eternal situation of the one who prays. The spirit is willing, but the flesh is weak.

To protect ourselves against the flesh and avoid falling into temptation, it is necessary to keep watching and praying. Prayer protects us from temptation (Matthew 26:41; Mark 14:38). We should pray that we do not enter into temptation (Luke 22:40; Matthew 6:13). Moreover, prayer can be used to help us to be prepared for the return of Christ (Luke 21:34-36).

How important is prayer in the Christian life? How important is faith in the Christian life? Prayer is faith. Are you a person of prayer? Are you a person of faith?

SEPTEMBER 17

THE GOD OF PEACE SHALL BE WITH YOU . . .

"The things you have learned and received and heard and seen in me, practice these things,
and the God of peace will be with you."

Philippians 4:9

Much of the Christian life revolves around *replacement*. Paul contrasts being "anxious" (Philippians 4:6) with having "the peace of God" (Philippians 4:7). He then points to practical ways to achieve this transition and replacement, the transition from anxiety to peace and the *replacement* of anxiety with peace. Those practical ways are ways of replacement, replacing anxiety with "prayer and supplication with thanksgiving" (Philippians 4:6) and replacing anxious thoughts with "whatever is true, whatever is honorable, whatever is right, whatever is pure, whatever is lovely, whatever is of good repute . . . dwell on these things" (Philippians 4:8). As important as these replacements are, they are largely dependent on the greatest replacement of all. The greatest replacement is the one that Paul writes about in Galatians 2:20: "I have been crucified with Christ; and it is no longer I who live, but Christ lives in me . . ." To replace your life with the life of Christ is the majestic replacement!

Paul is an example of one who has done this. So, he exhorts the Philippians to imitate his example, to imitate Christ . . . "Be imitators of me, just as I also am of Christ" (1 Corinthians 11:1). What is the result of following Paul's advice? The result is that "the God of peace will be with you" (Philippians 4:9). The result of replacing anxiety with prayer was that "the peace of God" would be with them (Philippians 4:7). The result of replacing your life with the life of Christ is that "the God of" that "peace will be with you" (Philippians 4:9). It is one thing to have the peace of God. It is another thing to have the God of that peace. The difference is in putting action behind your prayers. Paul does not stop with the exhortation to pray. He makes that the foundation, but it is a foundation that assumes action ("practice these things"- Philippians 4:9). Prayer without action is like faith without works. It is dead. It is dead because it is not possible to have the peace of God with you without having the God of that peace with you! Do you try to have the peace of God in your life without having the God of that peace in your life? Do you put action behind your prayers? Does your faith produce works?

Paul writes about a lot of things in his letter to the Philippians. He encourages them. He instructs them. He challenges them. All of it revolves around one paramount and supreme concept; the idea and reality of Christ in him. Thus, he ends his letter with an incredible declaration: "I can do all things through Him who strengthens me" (Philippians 4:13). This wraps up all that has been said or all that could ever be said. If God is in you then . . . what else needs to be said?

Christ in you, the hope of glory (Colossians 1:27).

SEPTEMBER 18

THE WORK AND WAY OF THE CROSS . . . IT'S ALL GOD!

" . . . work out your salvation with fear and trembling; for it is God who is at work in you, both to will and to work for His *good pleasure."*

Philippians 2:12-13

There is the work of the cross, what Jesus had to do in giving up His life to save us (John 3:16). There is also the way of the cross, what Jesus continues to do in us to save us (Hebrews 2:11). The finality of the work of the cross (what God has already done for us) and the ongoing process of the way of the cross (what God continues to do in us) is seen in that you are to "work out your salvation with fear and trembling; for it is God who is at work in you, both to will and to work for His good pleasure" (Philippians 2:12-13). The bottom line is this: God does it all!

There are four things that God must do for your salvation to be accomplished. First, God must draw you (John 6:44). This is sometimes called "effectual calling." Second, God must regenerate you (John 3:1-5). You must be "born again" or "born from above." Jesus, in His humanity, is never regenerated because He is generated via the incarnation, He is not "born from above again" because He already was born from above. And so, "The angel answered and said to her, 'The Holy Spirit will come upon you, and the power of the Most High will overshadow you; and for that reason the holy Child shall be called the Son of God'" (Luke 1:35). Third, God must wash away your sins; He must atone for your sins (John 13:5-10). This is represented in water baptism (Acts 22:16). And so, even Jesus was baptized "to fulfill all righteousness" (Matthew 3:13-15). Fourth, God must give you the power to live out your salvation (Acts 1:8; 2:38). This is the issue of sanctification. God does this by baptizing the believer in the Holy Spirit. And so, even Jesus was baptized in the Holy Spirit (Matthew 3:16).

The work of the cross includes effectual calling, regeneration, and atonement; it includes what God already did for you. The way of the cross includes sanctification; it includes what God continues to do in you. In each case, the focus is on Christ. God saves you through the work of Christ and He continues to save you (sanctify you) through Christ in an ongoing process in which you increasingly learn to put on the "yoke of Jesus" (Matthew 11:29) and allow Christ to live in you (Galatians 2:20).

God does it all! And so, we fix "our eyes on Jesus, the author (the work of the cross that God has already done) and perfecter (the way of the cross that God continues to do) of faith" (Hebrews 12:2). God saves you. God continues to save you, you are to "work out your salvation with fear and trembling; for it is God who is at work in you, both to will and to work for His good pleasure" (Philippians 2:12-13). The bottom line is that **God does it all**!

SEPTEMBER 19

WHAT DOES IT MEAN TO IMITATE GOD?

"BE IMITATORS of me, just as I also am of Christ . . . You also became imitators of us and of the Lord . . . THEREFORE BE imitators of God."

1 Corinthians 11:1; 1 Thessalonians 1:6; Ephesians 5:1

Have you ever heard someone do a great imitation of a famous person? Rich Little is one of the all-time great impersonators. He could do a great Johnny Carson. If you closed your eyes while Rich Little did his imitation of Johnny Carson, you would think you were at the *Tonight Show* listening to Carson's routines. Rich Little, seemingly, could imitate anybody. The list of voices that he could do was endless. However, he never did an imitation of God (unless you count George Burns!). How do you imitate God?

The apostle Paul exhorted Christians to imitate Jesus (1 Thessalonians 1:6) and encouraged believers to imitate him (1 Corinthians 4:16) and follow his example as he imitated and followed Christ (1 Corinthians 11:1). Paul often encouraged believers to imitate those believers whose life and faith imitated that of the Lord (1 Thessalonians 1:6; 2:14; Hebrews 6:12; 13:7). He said, "Therefore be imitators of God" (Ephesians 5:1). What does it mean to imitate God? Paul's reference to "imitating an example" (2 Thessalonians 3:9) does not mean that there is a code or list of rules that must be memorized and followed. The knowledge of Christian behavior is not acquired in that type of a process. Imitation is the result of a new attitude towards God. It expresses itself, not in the following of a rule, but in the commitment to an entire lifestyle because my imitation of God can be nothing less than the continuation of the life of Christ in me as it is "no longer I who live, but Christ lives in me" (Galatians 2:20).

And so, the idea of imitation is focused on Christ as the One who enables the follower to imitate Him. Man is not the one who attains or achieves a level of imitated perfection in the likeness of God. Man, in his own ability, power, or works cannot be like God. Only as man allows Jesus to work through him can he become an imitator of that example. It is not "working" or "striving" that results in being more like Him; rather, it is the process of being formed into His image that results in being more like Him. This is done through walking with Him in relationship and obedience. It is not a "striving," but instead, it is a "surrendering" that results in the imitation of God. The imitation of God is more of a result of relationship and obedience than it is a result of certain actions that might produce a likeness. God cannot be imitated like Rich Little imitates Johnny Carson. He can, however, be allowed to mold you in His image—in 2 Thessalonians 3:9, you imitate a *tupos* or "type" or "example," a mark or brand formed by a blow or impression, a "print"—as He molds you via living in you.

Thus, to imitate God is to surrender to Him, because the only way to imitate God is to have God living in you. Consistent with this is the fact that references to the imitation of God in the Scripture are always set in the context of our "surrendering"; dying to self (Ephesians 5:1-2), suffering (1 Thessalonians 2:14), and laying down of rights (2 Thessalonians 3:8-9). This makes sense if you realize that in order to imitate God you must allow God to control your life. How do you imitate God? Perhaps, the most biblical way to answer this question is to say, "You really don't imitate God; rather, God imitates Himself as you allow Him to live in you." Rich Little could do a great Johnny Carson. God can do a great God, and He does it through you!

SEPTEMBER 20

BLESSINGS AND CURSES . . .

"If you do not listen, and if you do not take it to heart to give honor to My name,' says the LORD of hosts, 'then I will send the curse upon you and I will curse your blessings . . . Behold, I am going to rebuke your offspring, and I will spread refuse on your faces, the refuse of your feasts; and you will be taken away with it.'"

Malachi 2:2-3

The priests of Israel were engaged in disobedient practices when it came to performing their duties in the temple with regard to the sacrificial system (Malachi 1:8, 13-14). They must turn away from this disobedience, and from their hypocritical attitudes and their empty ritualism. They must "take it to heart" (Malachi 2:2). This is crucial, not only for the priests and Israel, but for the nations. It is the "Lord of hosts" (which could be translated "Lord of the nations") and His reputation ("My name") that is to "be magnified beyond the border of Israel!" (Malachi 1:5; Malachi 2:2).

Remember, this is Israel, God's missionary nation: "Go forth from your country, and from your relatives and from your father's house, to the land which I will show you; And I will make you a great nation, and I will bless you, and make your name great; and so you shall be a blessing; and I will bless those who bless you, and the one who curses you I will curse. And in you all the families of the earth will be blessed." (Genesis 12:1-3). Notice the flow of thought here as God establishes this oath or covenant with Abraham. God would bless Israel and then Israel would bless the nations. The first part of the covenant depends on the completion of the second part. If Israel does not **bless the nations,** then God will **not bless them**. Or in the words of Malachi 2:2: "if you do not take it to heart to give honor to My name" (**bless the nations** by providing a correct witness), "then I will curse your blessings" (I will **not bless you**). Historically, this principle is displayed beyond Israel. As nations were blessed by God, they retained their blessings as long as they were willing to give away blessings to the nations. If they did not bless the nations, the blessings were taken away. This is seen in the fall of Rome. It is also seen in the fall of the Goths and the Vikings. Biblically, it is seen in the Babylonian exile and the destruction of Jerusalem in 70 A.D.

And so God says in Malachi 2:3: "I will curse your blessings . . . I am going to rebuke your offspring (*the opposite of making them a great nation*), and I will spread refuse on your faces (*the opposite of making their name great*) . . . and you will be taken away with it (*the opposite of blessing them*)." God then explains His purposes: "Then you will know that I have sent this commandment to you, that My covenant may continue" (Malachi 2:4). This dual purpose is consistent with why God chose Israel in the first place: "The Lord did not set His love on you nor choose you because you were more in number than any of the peoples, for you were the fewest of all peoples, but because the Lord loved you and kept the oath which He swore to your forefathers" (Deuteronomy 7:7-8).

That missionary covenant is now made with the church of Jesus Christ, His disciples (Matthew 21:43; Matthew 28:18-20). As a disciple of Christ, the principle of blessings and curses remains the same. So, don't just keep all of God's blessings to yourself. No! Be sure to share them so they don't get cursed.

———————

SEPTEMBER 21

RESURRECTION ON TRIAL . . . DOES IT EVEN MAKE SENSE?

" . . . and if Christ has not been raised, your faith is worthless . . . If we have hoped in Christ in this life only, we are of all men most to be pitied."

1 Corinthians 15:17, 19

The resurrection is often put on trial. Some people may say that even the idea of "resurrection" does not make sense. If there is no resurrection then all of Christianity makes no sense (1 Corinthians 15:17-19). Does it make sense to believe in the resurrection? Well, it might not be as far-fetched as some might claim. Even the government seems to believe in resurrection:

A letter came from the Department of Health and Human Services to a resident of Greenville County, South Carolina: "Your food stamps will be stopped, effective March 1992, because we received notice you passed away. May God bless you. You may reapply if your circumstances change."

There are "many convincing proofs" (Acts 1:3) for the resurrection of Jesus . . . many points that can be made to build the defense's argument in the "resurrection trial."

How can you explain the detail in which Jesus foretold the resurrection? He gave a journalist's summary (the who, what, where, why, when, and how) of the entire story before it happened:

Who = done by Jesus' own power (John 2:19; 10:18).

What = resurrection after suffering/put to death (Matthew 20:18-19).

Where = in Jerusalem (Matthew 20:18).

Why = fulfill all prophecies concerning the Messiah's death and resurrection (Luke 18:31-32).

When = on the third day (Luke 18:32-33).

How = disciples will fall away but He will then appear to them in Galilee (Matthew 26:31-32; 28:16)

How can you explain the number of appearances? That precludes any single conspiracy. It could not be explained by the possibility of an illusion as there were too many people who would have had to have had the same illusion; moreover, the appearances were close up, intimate, and often lengthy.

How can you explain the quantity of the historical witnesses?

Empty tomb – Mary Magdalene/others on Sunday morning (Mark 16:1-11).

Two travelers – road to Emmaus on Sunday afternoon (Luke 24:13-32).

Peter – in Jerusalem on Sunday (Luke 24:34).

Ten disciples – in the upper room on Sunday night (Luke 24:36-43).

Eleven disciples – in the upper room one week later (Mark 16:14).

Seven disciples – by the Sea of Galilee one week later (John 21:1-23).

Eleven disciples – a mountain in Galilee some time later (Matthew 28:16-20).

More than 500 after some time (1 Corinthians 15:6).

James some time later (1 Corinthians 15:7).

Men of Galilee at the Mount of Olives forty days later (Acts 1:1-11).

Stephen and Paul some time later (Acts 7:55-56; 9:1-6).

There are evidences. There are proofs. Ultimately, however, we come back to the bottom-line question in the "resurrection trial": Is Jesus *alive* in your life? What is really on trial? Relationship with God! Is Christianity a creed *or* a relationship? Do you know about God *or* do you know God? Is Jesus dead *or* alive in your life? And so, the closing argument in the trial ends with this statement: "If you confess with your mouth Jesus as Lord, and believe in your heart that God raised Him from the dead, you shall be saved" (Romans 10:9).

SEPTEMBER 22

THE FANATICISM OF IT ALL . . . WE NEED MORE FANATICS!

"Trust in the Lord *with all your heart,*
And do not lean on your own understanding.
In all your ways acknowledge Him,
And He will make your paths straight."

Proverbs 3:5-6

Don't be a fanatic! Don't be irrational and over-zealous regarding the things of God in an undesirable way. The word "fanatic" is often directed at Christians who seem to be "too serious" about their faith . . . too involved with and focused on the things of God. The leaders of the early Methodist revival movement in the late eighteenth century were looked down upon in this way and were, in turn, derogatorily called "enthusiasts" (ironically, a word that comes from the Greek *en theos,* or "in God"!). Be real. Don't be an enthusiast or a fanatic. Don't go overboard. God,

Himself, does not want you to act like *all* things revolve around Him. Be more balanced . . . not so *extreme*! Don't be crazy.

The problem, of course, with this perspective is that God, Himself, says, "Trust in the Lord with all your heart . . . in all your ways acknowledge Him" (Proverbs 3:5-6). "All" is a quite serious and exhaustive word. "All" means . . . *all*! And so, our relationship with God must be consistent and it must cover every area of our lives. Our need to look to God in **all** ways is exhaustive since we can do **nothing** without Him (John 15:5). If this sounds extreme, well, it is—if this sounds "crazy," well it's not—and, so, the only real "crazy" thing is to try to do something without God (if "apart from Me you can do nothing" then it is only crazy to not "acknowledge Him in all your ways"). What we really need in our Christian lives is a little more of this "fanaticism." We need more "fools for Christ" (1 Corinthians 4:10). Paul, who used this phrase of Himself as opposed to those described as "prudent in Christ," is also the one who used words like "always" (Colossians 1:3), "all" (Ephesians 6:18), and "without ceasing" (1 Thessalonians 5:17) when he talked about prayer.

There is no Christian who has too much of Jesus in his or her life! Someone might have too much religiosity or too much legalism (too much hypocrisy, empty ritual, or superficial relationship), but no one can have too much genuine relationship with Jesus. Jesus is not like milk! Doctors say that milk is very healthy as long as you do not drink too much of it. They say too much of even a good thing is not healthy. Jesus is not like milk! You can't get too much! The fact that *all* things are "God things" does not mean we must carry a pulpit onto the basketball court and drag it around while we are dribbling down the court, but it does mean that we carry around on the court a perspective, a spirit, a witness, a light, a worship . . . a difference!

The theological idea and process of "sanctification" can be described in many ways. One of the clearest ways to describe it is in terms of consistency in our relationship with God. Sanctification is the process of spending less time out of fellowship with God, and more time in fellowship with God. To spend time with God is to acknowledge Him (Proverbs 3:6). To acknowledge Him is an attitude and awareness (Colossians 3:1). As Brother Lawrence would say in his classic work penned hundreds of years ago, it is to practice His presence. Oh, the fanaticism of it *all* . . . well, we need more "presence-practicers" . . . more enthusiastic fanatics!

———————

SEPTEMBER 23

PARADOXICAL MANNER OF CHRISTIAN CONDUCT

"Only conduct yourselves in a manner worthy of the gospel of Christ . . . in no way alarmed by your opponents . . . For to you it has been granted for Christ's sake, not only to believe in Him, but also to suffer for His sake . . . "

Philippians 1:27-29

In his letter to the Philippians, Paul encourages believers to "conduct yourselves in a manner worthy of the gospel of Christ" (Philippians 1:27). That "manner" is to both stand "firm in one spirit, with one mind, striving together" and to not be "alarmed by your opponents" (Philippians 1:27-28). In a sort of paradoxical way, the manner of conduct of a Christian is both to be in unity with others and to be in disunity with others!

Why is this paradoxical "manner" the proper conduct of a Christian? Paul explains it by saying "for to you it has been granted for Christ's sake, not only to believe in Him, but also to suffer for His sake" (Philippians 1:29). Unity with others corresponds to faith in Christ (1 Corinthians 10:16-17) while opposition from others corresponds to suffering for Him (2 Timothy 3:12). The nature of the gospel causes seemingly opposing themes to exist within the "manner" of Christian conduct. The gospel represents salvation for believers and a stumbling block for unbelievers (1 Corinthians 1:21-23). Thus, unity and disunity exist together. And so, Jesus instructs His disciples, "This I command you, that you love one another. If the world hates you, you know that it has hated Me before it hated you . . . if they persecuted Me, they will also persecute you" (John 15:17-20).

Can you accept the fact that to live the Christian life you must unify with your brethren and you must stand opposed to the world (not because you *hate* others but because others stand opposed to you and hate you)? Or do you only see God as "love" and therefore desire to unite with all people? Can you accept the fact that not all people are brethren (children of God)? Can you accept the fact that there will be opposition? How do you look at Christian suffering? Is it something to be avoided at all costs? Do you despise it as if it can only be a work of the devil? Or can you accept suffering for Christ as a gracious gift, saying with Paul, "For to me it has been granted . . . to suffer for His sake"?

To some degree, to understand and accept this paradoxical manner of conduct is to be willing to find ourselves "standing firm in one spirit, with one mind striving together for the faith of the gospel" (Philippians 1:27). The Greek term translated as "striving together" is used to describe the cooperation of a team of athletes who were competing against another team of athletes in an athletic contest. There is an opposing team. The struggle against this opponent is placed in the context of a description of Christian duty. Christians are mandated to be in unity and to be in disunity.

Part of the specific instructions given to Christians who are mandated to engage in this "opposition" is that they in no way should be "alarmed" by their opponents (Philippians 1:28). The Greek term translated as "alarmed" means to be startled or terrified and may be used by Paul here to describe the terror of a startled horse. Paul may have also had Cassius in his mind when he used this term. History tells us that at the battle of Philippi, Cassius committed suicide when he became terrified of the possibility of defeat. Here, Paul warns against the danger of allowing the enemy to scare you. Perhaps not so paradoxically, an important manner of conduct that should be practiced by Christians in order to avoid this danger is to remain in unity/fellowship (Hebrews 10:25). And so, in a sort of paradoxical way, the manner of conduct of a Christian is both to be in unity with others *and* to be in disunity with others!

SEPTEMBER 24

WHAT IS BAPTISM? . . .

"For you are all sons of God through faith in Christ Jesus. For all of you who were baptized into Christ have clothed yourselves with Christ."

Galatians 3:26-28

Baptism is a symbol and seal of a person's union "with Christ" (Galatians 3:26-28). That person is "of Christ." He is "in Christ" (Acts 8:16; Romans 6:3; Galatians 3:27). It is the union with Christ's death, burial, and resurrection (Romans 6:3). It is the union with His body, and the union with the family of God (1 Corinthians 12:13). It is a symbol and seal of the forgiveness of sins (Acts 2:38). Being baptized in Christ marks being cleansed and washed in Christ (Acts 22:16; Hebrews 10:22). It points to the believer's rebirth and regeneration (Titus 3:5; Romans 6:3, 4, 11). As a believer, a person needs to be baptized only once. However, if the baptism was done before conversion, then it should be done again. There is no magic in the water. Baptism only has meaning if that which it symbolizes exists. Baptism is much more than a religious ritual. Thus, a baptism done before conversion is no baptism at all. To be baptized "again," in that case, is to be baptized for the first time as a believer.

It is important, then, to be clear as to what baptism is not. Baptism is a symbol and seal of something real, something that has already occurred. It is not the cause of that thing. Baptism does not cause salvation, forgiveness, regeneration, rebirth, and union with Christ. Instead, baptism signifies these things are real in the life of the person. If these things are not real, then the baptism has no meaning. Again, there is no magic in the water. A symbol has meaning only when that which it symbolizes exists. Thus, the baptism of infants (who cannot repent and believe) seems unreasonable.

Furthermore, it is possible to be saved without being baptized. Consider the case of the thief on the cross (Luke 23:43). Here we might remember that we cannot directly equate baptism with Hebrew circumcision. A Hebrew was circumcised after his physical birth because he was physically born into the people of God. However, no one is born a Christian. A Christian is baptized after his spiritual birth because he is spiritually born into the people of God. If a person is spiritually born into the people of God, it does not necessarily mean that the person has been baptized.

Even though we might emphasize that baptism is a symbol, it is not to say that it is not an important act (Mark 16:16; Acts 2:38; Matthew 28:19). It is a commandment. Baptism identifies a person with Christ. It is an official and public declaration of the decision and commitment to make Jesus your Lord and Savior. In baptism, the person publicly makes known his decision to follow Christ. This part of the meaning of baptism is much more important and real in places where Christians are being persecuted.

Finally, although baptism is a symbol and a seal, we are not saying that nothing happens during the event. If the symbol really has something to symbolize, then the action of the symbol can have an effect on that something. A handshake in many cultures is a symbol of friendship (or at least the willingness to be friends). If the friendship is not real, then the handshake has no meaning. If the friendship is real, then the handshake does have meaning. Moreover, the action of the handshake can affect the friendship. The symbol can make that which it symbolizes stronger if that which it symbolizes exists in the first place. It is the same in baptism. The action of the baptism can increase the commitment to Christ if the commitment to Christ is already present.

SEPTEMBER 25

ARE YOU SIGNED UP FOR THE REWARDS PROGRAM?

"But when you give a reception, invite the poor, the crippled, the lame, the blind, and you will be blessed, since they do not have the means to repay you; for you will be repaid at the resurrection of the righteous."

Luke 14:13-14

Are you signed up for the rewards program? Jesus encourages us to think of ways that we can receive rewards in heaven. He points to doing things that will not bring attention to yourself;

do things that will not receive rewards here on earth (Luke 14:12-14). The "formula" is clear: For whom do you perform? From them shall you receive your reward (Matthew 6:1-8). The New Testament includes a "doctrine of rewards." Of course, we must realize that the greatest reward is eternal life (Matthew 19:29; Luke 18:29-30). However, there seem to be "other" aspects of rewards. The Scripture speaks of receiving back 100 times what you have given up (Mark 10:30).

How is it determined who will receive what rewards? We must remember that each reward in heaven has been prepared beforehand by God (Mark 10:40). At the same time, we should understand that rewards in the life to come are directly correlated to action in this life. Our positions in eternity depend on what we do here on earth. We might say that the more death (to yourself) that you experience here, the more life you will experience there (Matthew 20:21-22). Denying yourself leads to treasure in heaven (Matthew 19:21). Rewards are for those who sacrifice for Jesus (Matthew 19:29; Mark 10:30).

What else is associated with rewards? Great rewards in heaven can be the result of being shamed for the name of Jesus in this life (Luke 6:22-23). Evangelism results in eternal rewards (John 4:36). Giving on earth results in rewards in heaven (Mark 10:21; Matthew 6:4, 20). Giving to the poor results in rewards (Luke 18:22). Whoever does good in the name of Jesus will receive a reward (Mark 9:39-41; Matthew 10:41-42). Ultimately, rewards in heaven are most directly associated with sacrifice in this life. And so, the concept of the "last being first" and the "first being last" is set in the context of forsaking everything for Jesus (sacrifice). Leaving everything behind in this world for the sake of Jesus will result in being last in this world. However, you will then be first in the kingdom of God. Those who try to hold onto everything now might advance in this life but will be last in the age to come. Reward in heaven is very closely associated with denying yourself here on earth (Mark 10:28-31).

And so, there are rewards to be had . . . Are you signed up for the rewards program?

SEPTEMBER 26

WHAT IS YOUR WORLDVIEW . . . YOUR "WHO SAYS"?

"No servant can serve two masters; for either he will hate the one, and love the other, or else he
will hold to one, and despise the other. You cannot serve God and mammon."

Luke 16:13

Everybody has a "who says"; everybody has a worldview. Your worldview is your "who says"; your worldview is what you view to be authoritative. Someone may speak of having a "biblical worldview." This means they view all of life with the Bible as their ultimate authority, their "who says." What a person does is derived from what that person values, and what a person values is derived from what a person believes to be true, and what a person believes to be true is derived from what a person perceives to be authoritative (their "who says"). The most visible thing about a person may be their actions. However, the most profound influence upon a person is what they view as authoritative; so authority (or worldview) is really a deeper issue. It precedes and determines actions.

How many different authorities can a person adhere to? Jesus answered this question when He said, "No servant can serve two masters, for either he will hate the one, and love the other, or else he will hold to one, and despise the other. You cannot serve God and mammon" (Luke 16:13). What authority structure establishes your worldview? What determines truth for you? What is your life subordinated to or ultimately based upon? What do you see as authoritative? What is your "who says"? Many different authorities attempt to gain your allegiance. The challenge for the Christian is to be in allegiance to God alone, as He has revealed Himself and His will in His Word. It is a "Lordship" issue, and for the Christian, Jesus (the Word of God) is Lord!

And so, for the Christian, the Word of God must be the basis for what is true. Who says? The Word of God says . . . that's who says! It is authoritative. It is what the philosopher calls "ultimate (or prime) reality." Thus, it defines truth, and that truth dictates what is valued, and that which is valued is ultimately acted upon. And so, a "biblical worldview" leads to a "biblical lifestyle" (or a "Jesus worldview" leads to a "Jesus lifestyle"). The Word of God is manifested in its Incarnate form (Jesus) and in its written form (the Bible). Jesus is consistent with the Bible. Thus, Jesus says, "You search the Scriptures, because you think that in them you have eternal life; and it is these that bear witness of Me" (John 5:39) and "He explained to them the things concerning Himself in all the Scriptures . . . these are My words which I spoke to you while I was still with you, that all things which are written about Me in the Law of Moses and the Prophets and the Psalms must be fulfilled" (Luke 24:27, 44). The Incarnate Word is eternal (John 1:1), conceived by the Holy Spirit (Luke 1:35), born a common man (Philippians 2:7), and fully perfect (Hebrews 4:15). So, too, the written Word is eternal (Psalm 119:89), conceived by the Holy Spirit (2 Timothy 3:16), written in common language (2 Peter 1:20-21), and fully perfect (Psalm 19:7-8).

What is your worldview? What is your "who says"? For the Christian (a biblical worldview person) it can be nothing less than the Word of God. It is a Lordship issue. Who says? Jesus says! The Bible tells me so.

SEPTEMBER 27

WHAT IN THE WORLD IS REVIVAL?

"Our friend Lazarus has fallen asleep; but I go, so that I may awaken him out of sleep."

John 11:11

What is "revival"? It can be defined from a physical perspective. There are multiple accounts in the Gospels when someone was brought back to life (physically revived). It can also be defined from a spiritual perspective, when people who had been "spiritually dead, lethargic, or asleep" begin to hunger for God's presence again. We may be able to understand principles of spiritual revival by applying to them principles of physical revival. Let's see!

So, what is revival? Revival is defined in the dictionary as "to live again," or "to restore to consciousness or life something that is not wholly or permanently lifeless." The focus can be on those outside of the church. In this sense, revival is to plunder the kingdom of Satan. The book of Jonah gives us a good example of this type of revival as it is the pagan city of Nineveh that experienced a great revival (Jonah 3:5). The focus can also be on those inside the church. In this sense, revival is to "rebuild the house." The book of Ezra gives us a good example of this type of revival as it is Ezra who leads the people of Israel in a revival. In any case, revival happens when God becomes the CENTER of our attention, when an extraordinary hunger for and manifestation of God's presence (His glory/His weight/His reputation) draws people to Him and leads them to repentance and faith. Revival is when, after a period of inactivity, people begin to hunger and thirst for righteousness—"Blessed are those who hunger and thirst for righteousness, for they shall be satisfied" (Matthew 5:6)—as they yearn for personal righteousness (individual revival), righteousness in others (evangelistic revival), and righteousness in society (social revival).

Revival means "to wake up." Someone was asleep but now he is awake: " . . . and after that He said to them, 'Our friend Lazarus has fallen asleep; but I go, so that I may awaken him out of sleep'" (John 11:11). Revival is to see the glory of Jesus: "Now Peter and his companions had been overcome with sleep; but when they were fully awake, they saw His glory . . ." (Luke 9:32). This is the very purpose of revival—to give glory to God—as Jesus proclaimed concerning Lazarus who He would later raise from the dead: "This sickness is not to end in death, but for the glory of God, so that the Son of God may be glorified by it" (John 11:4).

This way of defining revival is consistent with the event in which Jesus "revived" the twelve-year-old daughter of Jairus, the synagogue official (Mark 5:35-43). In verse 39, we have what is in effect a definition of revival. Jesus said, "The child has not died, but is asleep." The implication here is that she needs to be awakened. She needs to be revived. The question that Jesus asks before this "definition" is very important for the church today. Jesus asked, "Why make a commotion and weep?" The implication is that there is a solution. In many places in the world today, the church is asleep. We weep about it. There is a commotion. But Jesus has the solution. Revival is the solution! More specifically, perhaps you are somewhat asleep today in your walk of faith. No need for a commotion. Just ask God for revival in your life. He is the Reviver and He will revive you!

SEPTEMBER 28

PLURALITY OF LEADERSHIP IN THE NEW TESTAMENT CHURCH . . .

"THEREFORE, I exhort the elders among you, as your fellow elder and witness of the sufferings of Christ . . . and a partaker also of the glory that is to be revealed, shepherd the flock of God among you, exercising oversight . . . "

1 Peter 5:1-2

The New Testament clearly teaches a plurality of leadership in the church. This has not always been understood, in part because of a misunderstanding of biblical terminology. Three Greek terms are used interchangeably in the New Testament to describe the leadership of a local church: 1) bishop (*episkopos* in Greek), 2) pastor (*poiman* in Greek), 3) elder (*presbuteros* in Greek). Many church governments are based on the misunderstanding that these three terms signify three different positions or levels. One position is represented by the bishop (or overseer) who has authority over several different churches. Unfortunately, his position often becomes a very hierarchical and political position. He uses his influence and power to keep others from threatening his position. He begins to resemble a tyrant. Another position is represented by *the* pastor who has authority over the local church. Unfortunately, he is often a "one-man pastor" who has all the authority and responsibility. He begins to resemble a dictator. Another position is represented by an elder who is under the pastor. Unfortunately, they are often elected democratically, nominated, or gain their position because of who they know, who they are (financially/influentially), how successful they are in the world, or because of what family they are in.

Now let's consider a brief study of Acts 20:17, 18, 28. In verses 17 and 18 we see that Paul was talking to the "*presbuteros*" (elders) of the church. In verse 28, he told them that they were "*episkopos*" (bishops or overseers). Then, he instructed these elders who were bishops to "*poiman*" (pastor) the church. A study of 1 Peter 5:1-2 finds, Peter, in verse 1, exhorting the "*presbuteros*" (elders) of the church. Then in verse 2, he told them to "*poiman*" (pastor) the flock, and then he instructed these elders who pastor to be *"episkopos"* (bishops). In a study of Zephaniah 2:6-7, notice how the whole idea of *"poiman"* (pastor) in verses 6 and 7a is interchanged with the idea of being an *"episkopos"* (bishop) in verse 7b ("to care for"). Now study 1 Timothy 3:1 and Titus 1:5-9. The list of requirements in 1 Timothy 3 is for *"episkopos"* (bishops). We see the same list of requirements in Titus 1. However, in verse 5, Paul says that the requirements are for *"presbuteros"* (elders). Then in verse 7 he continues with the same list but says it is for *"episkopos"* (bishops).

Was Paul confused? No! Paul was not confused with his own teaching. He was simply using three different terms to describe the same office or position in a more complete way. I am a father. My children may use three different terms to describe who I am. Head of the family (this describes my job position). Father (this describes my function or action). Daddy (this is a title or an affectionate name). Paul appointed leaders in each church. He used three different terms to describe those leaders: 1) Bishop (this describes the job position of the leader), 2) Pastor (this describes the function or action of the leader), 3) Elder (this is a title or a name of respect of the leader).

Plurality of leadership is emphatic in the New Testament. The term "elder" (and remember according to Paul this was to be interchanged with pastor and bishop) is used more than twenty times in the New Testament to refer to a church leader. The term "elder" is always plural. It is never singular. There was no hint of a one-man pastor in the New Testament. There was a plurality of leadership. Each New Testament church had a plurality of elders/leadership. Elders were appointed in every church (see Acts 14:23). Paul went to Ephesus and called to him the elders of the church (see Acts 20:17). Paul greeted the overseers of the church at Philippi (see Philippians 1:1). Paul referred to the elders who direct the affairs of the church (see 1 Timothy 5:17 and Titus 1:5). And so, leadership in the church consists of a plurality of pastors who bishop (oversee) the church as those who are elders.

SEPTEMBER 29

ON THESE TWO COMMANDMENTS DEPEND THE WHOLE . . .

"YOU SHALL LOVE THE LORD YOUR GOD . . . This is the great and foremost commandment.
The second is like it, YOU SHALL LOVE YOUR NEIGHBOR AS YOURSELF."

Matthew 22:37-40

How are Christian leaders different than non-Christian leaders? Christian leaders seek and know God. Leadership potential begins here. It begins with the greatest commandment: "Teacher, which is the great commandment in the Law? And He said to him, 'YOU SHALL LOVE

THE LORD YOUR GOD WITH ALL YOUR HEART, AND WITH ALL YOUR SOUL, AND WITH ALL YOUR MIND'" (Matthew 22:36-37).

David spent a considerable amount of time alone with God as a shepherd boy. This prepared him to be a leader. God is the leader's source of power. Fellowship with God is the access to that power. God has found a leader when He finds someone who is willing to make fellowship with Him a priority in his life, a person who focuses his life on an intimate, personal and dynamic relationship with God. This is what we might call the "who" of leadership, the common characteristics of "who" become leaders. This "who" of leadership assumes the existence of faith since "... without faith it is impossible to please Him, for he who comes to God must believe that He is and that He is a rewarder of those who seek Him" (Hebrews 11:6-7). Through such a person, God will manifest His power (this is the "how" of leadership). He will give His guidance (this is the "what," "when," and "where" of leadership). He will display His wisdom (this is the "why" of leadership).

A biblical leader is a pure, humble, servant, who seeks and knows God. Of course, embedded within the very fibers of this limited definition of leadership must be the manifestation of love. For purity without love is self-righteousness. Humility without love is false humility or hypocrisy. Service without love profits nothing. Seeking and knowing God without love is nothing. The Scripture presents it like this: "If I have the gift of prophecy, and know all mysteries and all knowledge; and if I have all faith, so as to remove mountains, but do not have love, I am nothing. And if I give all my possessions to feed the poor, and if I surrender my body to be burned, but do not have love, it profits me nothing" (1 Corinthians 13:2-3). Love must be included in all the qualities that might define a servant.

A leader's love for the Lord will produce a zeal for God. This love and this zeal will be passed on to those whom he is leading. To begin with, Christian leaders must be close to God. They must love the Lord with all their hearts. To end with, they must be close to those whom they are leading. They must love their neighbor as themselves.

So, where does Christian leadership begin and end? Perhaps, we can apply the two greatest commandments to this question:

YOU SHALL LOVE THE LORD YOUR GOD WITH ALL YOUR HEART, AND WITH ALL YOUR SOUL, AND WITH ALL YOUR MIND. This is the great and foremost commandment. The second is like it, YOU SHALL LOVE YOUR NEIGHBOR AS YOURSELF. On these two commandments depend the whole Law and the Prophets (Matthew 22:37-40).

Perhaps, it would not be too far of a stretch to say, "On these two commandments depend the whole of Christian leadership." Christian leadership begins with loving God and ends with loving people.

SEPTEMBER 30

WHAT A BENEFICIAL RETURN POLICY!

"'Return to Me, and I will return to you,' says the LORD of hosts."

Malachi 3:7

God is faithful. He is not fickle. He does not change (Malachi 3:6). He has consistently proven His faithfulness. Contrarily, Israel has consistently proven her lack of faithfulness (Malachi 3:7). This contrast serves as the basis for the amazing divine "return policy." The fact that we are often faithless necessitates the call from heaven to "return to Me" while the fact that God is always faithful establishes the promise from heaven that "I will return to you" (Malachi 3:7). "If we are faithless, He remains faithful, for He cannot deny Himself" (2 Timothy 2:13).

And so, how do we make a "return"? To return means to change direction; this is the meaning of "repentance." The idea is that the Israelites were going away from God. God challenges them to "return" or to change their direction. He wants them to turn and come back to Him. If they turn back to Him then He will turn back to them. What kind of return might Israel make? And how will God then return to them?

One type of return might have to do with the need to stop robbing God: "'Will a man rob God? Yet you are robbing Me!' But you say, 'How have we robbed You?' 'In tithes and offerings . . . Bring the whole tithe into the storehouse, so that there may be food in My house'" (Malachi 3:8-9). Israel is challenged to turn away from their robbery of God and return to God by returning to giving financially to God's work. If Israel returns to God's Lordship over their finances, then God will return to them with material blessings: " . . . 'test Me now in this,' says the Lord of hosts, 'if I will not open for you the windows of heaven and pour out for you a blessing until it overflows'" (Malachi 3:10).

God is pleased to return to those who return to Him. Not only does He want to show "the returners" His love for them, but He also wants to keep His covenant that He made with Abraham and fulfill its missiological purposes (Deuteronomy 7:8). And so, there is a very interesting result of this divine return policy: "All the nations will call you blessed, for you shall be a delightful land," says the Lord of hosts (Malachi 3:12). The general flow of the Abrahamic covenant is that God will bless Israel and Israel will then be a blessing to the nations (Genesis 12:1-3). In the Old Testament this missiological dynamic especially happened through the building up of the reputation of Israel. As Israel was obedient, God was able to bless her. This resulted in a testimony to the nations of the reality of God (2 Chronicles 9:1-8). In this way the nations were blessed.

God is always faithful. We are often faithless. Thankfully, "If we are faithless, He remains faithful" (2 Timothy 2:13). The return policy is such that the "return line" is never closed. God is always there with arms wide open beckoning us to get into the return line and get rid of all those things that move us away from Him. The fact that we are often faithless necessitates the call from heaven to "return to Me" while the fact that God is always faithful establishes the promise from heaven that "I will return to you" (Malachi 3:7). What a beneficial return policy!

NOTES

October

KNOWING GOD VERSUS KNOWING ABOUT GOD (CHRISTIANITY VERSUS RELIGIOSITY)

"So let us know, let us press on to know the LORD."

Hosea 6:3

To know God is very different than to know about God. The difference is between being saved and being lost. It is the difference between Christianity and religiosity (outward religious practice, without an inward relationship with God). Christians are not simply involved in religion. Christians are involved in relationship. In salvation (that is, in Jesus), the knowledge of God is revealed to us (Matthew 11:27). It is in Christ that we can know God (not just know about Him), since "we know that the Son of God has come, and has given us understanding, in order that we might know Him who is true, and we are in Him who is true, in His Son Jesus Christ. This is the true God and eternal life" (1 John 5:20). Salvation (eternal life) is to know God through His Son Jesus. The only way to know God is to know Jesus (John 14:6; John 8:19; 2 Corinthians 4:6). "There is salvation in no one else; for there is no other name under heaven that has been given among men, by which we must be saved" (Acts 4:12).

This "high definition" of God (unique, "onlyness" nature of a definition of God) flies in the face of our secular humanistic style of "Christianity" that champions pluralism's rejection of definition as it discards the absolute nature of truth and embraces the political correctness of neutrality (relative nature of truth). The modern trend is toward a deification of humanistic tolerance and worldwide "brotherhood." However, the modern church must return to an understanding of the truth.

The church must not weaken amid the worldly temptation to accept the false love of humanism. This false love says that a definition of God as the One who had to come to man/provide for man is not necessary. It says that a definition of man as a sinner who is in absolute need of provision/salvation is not necessary. This false love says that Jesus—which means "God Saves"—is not necessary. The religious application to this humanistic mindset is embodied in the statement, "I'm okay, you're okay." It is understood that God's love is demonstrated in "tolerance" and God's holiness is exhibited in "situational ethics." Christianity must stand strong against religiosity and worldly wisdom. It must hold strongly to the implications of the truth that Jesus is the only way;

hence, Christianity is more than knowing about God . . . it is knowing God through a relationship with Jesus Christ.

Christianity is marked by an actual relationship with God. It is not just an intellectual or cultural knowing about God. It begins at the cross of Christ and continues by His Spirit. It is a spiritual thing (Ephesians 1:17). The Holy Spirit moves us along the road (path) to knowing God. He is the motivator and the One who enables us to have a growing relationship with God. Spiritual Christianity (knowing God) is very different than worldly religiosity (knowing about God):

> AND WHEN I came to you, brethren, I did not come with superiority of speech or of wisdom, proclaiming to you the testimony of God. For I determined to know nothing among you except Jesus Christ, and Him crucified . . . and my message and my preaching were not in persuasive words of wisdom, but in demonstration of the Spirit and of power, so that your faith would not rest on the wisdom of men, but on the power of God. Yet we do speak wisdom . . . a wisdom, however, not of this age nor of the rulers of this age . . . For to us God revealed *them* through the Spirit . . . Now we have received, not the spirit of the world, but the Spirit who is from God . . . But a natural man does not accept the things of the Spirit of God, for they are foolishness to him; and he cannot understand them, because they are spiritually appraised. But he who is spiritual appraises all things . . . we have the mind of Christ (1 Corinthians 2:1-16).

OCTOBER 2

JESUS IS THE GOOD SHEPHERD . . . SEEK AFTER HIM!

"What man among you, if he has a hundred sheep and has lost one of them, does not leave the ninety-nine in the open pasture, and go after the one which is lost, until he finds it?"

Luke 15:4

Jesus is the Good Shepherd (John 10:11). Shepherds understand that lost sheep do not have the capacity to find their way home. They do not seek to be found as they do not even know they are lost. So, the shepherd must seek after them. Eventually, sheep do tend to seek after their shepherd, but the initial "seeking" begins with the shepherd. So it is with the Good Shepherd and His followers. It is we who are lost. God is not lost. We do not "find" God. God finds us. Thus, the process of seeking God begins with God (Luke 15:4-6; John 15:16). The baptism which Jesus gives seems to include an empowering of the individual to come to/seek after Jesus as it is the Holy Spirit who draws the individual to Jesus (Luke 3:17).

The process of seeking God begins with God. It continues with where you are now; God accepts us where we are. And so, a continuation or increase in your desire to seek/know God begins when you act on the current desire that you have. If you do not act on your current desire (no matter how small it is), then you will lose even the little bit you had (Mark 4:24-25). Moreover, the amount that you seek God will be directly associated with your obedience to Him (John 8:29). Without obedience (the foundation of the "seeking God house") your seeking God will fall (Luke 6:46-49).

We are able to seek God through "Jesus our veil" (Mark 15:38; Luke 23:45). We can enter the presence of God because Jesus' death on the cross has abolished the dividing wall between us (Ephesians 2:14). Jesus became the veil of the temple that was torn in two by the cross allowing us to draw near to God (Hebrews 10:19-22). And so, we who are the lost sheep can seek God. We can also seek God along with other sheep (fellowship is important in the sheepfold) "for where two or three have gathered together in My name, there I am in their midst" (Matthew 18:20).

Seeking God yields desirable results. Seeking God leads to revelation being "about Him." It results in understanding mysteries (Mark 4:10-11). Jesus calls us by name and touches our hearts (He reveals Himself to us) via His relationship with us (John 20:16). In addition, joy is associated with seeking God and having a relationship with Him (John 15:7-11). Fulfillment and satisfaction are results of seeking God (Matthew 5:6). Seeking God results in our needs being met (Matthew 6:33). Answered prayer is associated with seeking God (John 15:7). Seeking God results in testimony to the world that Jesus is the Messiah; thus, the result of knowing God is that you will make Him known (John 17:20-21).

And so, seeking (God seeks us) results in seeking (we seek God) results in seeking (others seek God). So, respond to God's seeking after you with your own seeking after Him and watch, then, how others seek after Him as well!

OCTOBER 3

JOSEPH'S CHRIST-LIKE SPIRIT . . .

"As for you, you meant evil against me, but God meant it for good in order to bring about this present result, to preserve many people alive."

Genesis 50:20

It is beneficial to study the life of Joseph and observe how it compares with that of Jesus Christ. Of course, Joseph is not like Christ with regard to sin. He is not perfect. Nevertheless, many of his actions compare favorably to the ways of Christ. In an incredible act of mercy Joseph forgave the sins of his brothers which they so brutally enacted against him. Joseph had done nothing against them, but "his brothers were jealous of him . . . " (Genesis 37:11). The result of this jealousy was that they said to each other "let us kill him and throw him into one of the pits" (Genesis 37:20). Eventually, they decided to get money for him instead of killing him: "Then some Midianite traders passed by, so they pulled him up and lifted Joseph out of the pit, and sold him to the Ishmaelites for twenty shekels of silver. Thus they brought Joseph into Egypt" (Genesis 37:28). Incredibly, Joseph prospered in this foreign land and it was not long before the tables turned dramatically against His brothers as they were forced by a great famine to go to Egypt to buy grain. Little did they know when they got there that they were standing before Joseph: "Now Joseph was the ruler over the land; he was the one who sold to all the people of the land. And Joseph's brothers came and bowed down to him with their faces to the ground. When Joseph saw his brothers he recognized them, but he disguised himself to them . . . " (Genesis 42:6-7).

This same Joseph who was thrown into a pit by his brothers to be eventually sold can now throw those same brothers into a "pit" of hopelessness by *not* selling to them! It would, in a sense, be understandable for Joseph, at least, not to help them. However, Joseph forgave his brothers:

> THEN JOSEPH could not control himself before all those who stood by him . . . Joseph made himself known to his brothers. He wept so loudly that the Egyptians heard *it* . . . Then Joseph said to his brothers, 'Please come closer to me.' And they came closer. And he said, 'I am your brother Joseph, whom you sold into Egypt. Now do not be grieved or angry with yourselves, because you sold me here' . . . He kissed all his brothers and wept on them, and afterward his brothers talked with him (Genesis 45:1-15).

Like Jesus, Joseph had a love and compassion for sinners; "He wept so loudly" (Genesis 45:2). Like Jesus, Joseph did not try to take advantage of the sinners. He forgave and forgot without showing bitterness; "Now do not be grieved or angry with yourselves, because you sold me here . . . " (Genesis 45:5).

Two more ways in which Joseph exhibited a Christ-like spirit are in his devotion and respect to his parents—"Joseph prepared his chariot and went up to Goshen to meet his father Israel; as soon as he appeared before him, he fell on his neck and wept on his neck a long time" (Genesis 46:29)—and in the way in which he returned good for evil. He showed mercy, grace, compassion and love to sinners: "'So therefore, do not be afraid; I will provide for you and your little ones.' So he comforted them and spoke kindly to them" (Genesis 50:21). He recognized God's sovereignty and understood that God changes evil into that which is good: "As for you, you meant evil against me, but God meant it for good in order to bring about this present result, to preserve many people alive" (Genesis 50:20). And so, Joseph reflects Christ even as Christ, in the ultimate way, turns evil into good as He turns sin around on the cross and replaces the Fall of man with the redemption of man. The "last Adam" (1 Corinthians 15:45) (Jesus and His righteousness) replaced the first Adam (mankind and his sin): "For as in Adam all die, so also in Christ all will be made alive" (1 Corinthians 15:22). All glory and praise be to God!

OCTOBER 4

THE PURPOSE AND METHOD OF CHURCH GOVERNMENT

"And He gave some as apostles, and some as prophets, and some as evangelists, and some as pastors and teachers, for the equipping of the saints for the work of service, to the building up of the body of Christ; until we all attain to the unity of the faith, and of the knowledge of the Son of God, to a mature man, to the measure of the stature which belongs to the fullness of Christ."

Ephesians 4:11-13

The purpose or form of church government is understood in terms of being a "body" because the church is a body, no one man is Christ. Christ has different offices or ministries (Prophet, Priest, King). No one leader will have all these offices. However, a team of leaders can include all of them. The church needs all these different types of leaders because there are many different types of ministries in the church. The church will go through different "seasons" when it will need to emphasize one certain type of leadership. The seasons change and the emphasized type of leadership must change.

What are the goals of church government? The purpose of church government is to equip the saints (see Ephesians 4:12). The word "equip" in the original Greek was a medical term which meant "to set a bone." It is the idea of putting a bone in the right place in the body relative to other parts. The same Greek word is used in Mark 1:19 ("mending nets"). Here again we see the idea of matching or connecting parts. To equip the body is to train, organize, and help the body grow (the building up of the body). "Building up" is an expression of development. The body is being developed and unified (see Ephesians 4:13).

What is the method of church government? The one word answer is . . . **service**. The true governor of the church had one method of government. He described this method when He said: "For even the Son of Man did not come to be served, but to serve (Mark 10:45). Biblical government (authority) is not a cause of service. Rather, service is a cause (or method) of biblical government. Worldly government exercises authority and calls it service (Mark 10:42). Biblical church government exercises service that results in authority (Mark 10:43-44). Church government is based on action or function. It is not based on oppressive power, title, or position.

Church government is rooted in what might be called "natural authority." The Bible teaches that the way to gain authority is through being a servant (Matthew 23:11-12; John 3:30; Luke 22:25-26). A leader must lead through service. The result is that the leader gains a natural authority. The formation of church government is a very natural process: "Those who have served well gain an excellent standing and great assurance in their faith in Christ Jesus" (1 Timothy 3:13, NIV). Servants "gain" something. They gain an "excellent standing" (respect). and this respect includes a "great assurance in their faith" (natural authority). And so, the method of church government is service. **Service** leads to **respect** and that respect leads to **natural authority**.

OCTOBER 5

IT'S GOD HIMSELF WHO INVENTED MARRIAGE . . .

"For this cause a man shall leave his father and his mother, and be joined to his wife; and they shall become one flesh."

Genesis 2:24

Marriage is often referred to as a "divine institution." Why? It is a *divine* institution because it is God Himself who invented marriage. Marriage is defined; it's defined by God! God ordains what we have come to call "marriage" in Genesis 2:24: "For this cause a man shall leave his father and his mother, and shall cleave to his wife; and they shall become one flesh." The most fundamental human relationship, marriage is the initial building block of human society as it is the initial block that God, Himself, ordered into society. It is integral to and part of the creation story itself.

God created the world in six days. On the sixth day, He created man and "then the Lord God said, 'It is not good for the man to be alone; I will make him a helper suitable for him'" (Genesis 2:18). The word translated "helper" is a word that means "completion or complement." The woman is the completion of the man. She complements him and completes him. The man's response to the fashioning of this "helper" from his own rib (Genesis 2:21-22) is very logical: "And the man said, 'This is now bone of my bones, and flesh of my flesh; she shall be called Woman, because she was taken out of Man'" (Genesis 2:23). The commonsensical nature of the man's response revolves around the conclusion that the man and the woman are naturally related to each other because the woman was taken from the man. The relationship is natural and intimate. It is in this context that we see the ordaining of the institution of marriage in Genesis 2:24. Marriage is defined as it is "for this cause." For what cause? Because of what? It is because of God's choice as the sovereign Creator. Marriage is established because ("for this cause") of how God created the man and the woman. Because God created the woman from the man, there is marriage. It is logical, natural, and intimate.

And so, "a man shall leave his father and his mother." The man takes the initiative. He must leave his original family to begin a new family. His new priority must be to this new family. And the man "shall cleave to his wife." The new beginning includes both the man and the woman. The man must leave and cleave; he must leave behind the old and cling to the new. The word "cleave" signifies the idea of permanence. This is not a temporary arrangement. It is a permanent and strong relationship. "They shall become one flesh." The result is that the man and the woman become so united as to reflect the original design of creation (Genesis 1:27: "And God created man in His own image, in the image of God He created him; male and female He created them."). They were originally and literally one (the woman was taken out of the man). Here, the use of the word "become" is important as it points to what we might call the process of marriage. The relationship is built; it is worked on, improved, and perfected over time. The idea of "one flesh" signifies that the marriage relationship depicts a single identity. It also points to the sexual aspect of the marriage relationship. Most generally, it points to a unified and intimate relationship. The word "they" is very important. Although they become one flesh (singular identity) through their relationship, they do so as a "they"; there are two of them, unified yet distinct, together yet as individuals, equal yet not the same! There can be different roles that each one plays in the marriage without those roles delineating superiority or inferiority.

The marriage relationship was instituted by God. It was defined by Him. It is the beginning or foundation of all human relationships, and thus, human society rises and falls on the stability of that foundation. To redefine it is not man's prerogative because man did not invent it. It is God Himself who invented marriage!

PRINCIPLES AND DYNAMICS
OF MINISTRY . . .

"Jesus said to Simon Peter, 'Simon, son of John, do you love Me more than these?' He said to Him,
'Yes, Lord; You know that I love You.' He said to him, 'Tend My lambs.'"

John 21:15

Disciples of Jesus do ministry. Disciples of Jesus love Jesus and loving Jesus includes loving those who are His, doing ministry . . . "Tend My lambs" (John 21:15). Our love for Jesus can be measured by our willingness to give our lives for those who are the people of Jesus (John 15:13). And so, shepherds must give their lives to their sheep (John 10:11). The pivotal biblical principle of dying in order to live is seen in the life of the "good shepherd" who gives his life for the sheep in order to receive his life back (John 10:17). And so, a pastor need not think of his calling as a mere "job" or "career" for which he receives a salary; it is so much more! He must be the shepherd of his own sheep. He cannot simply be a "hireling" (John 10:12-13). Of course, "the laborer is worthy of his wages." This, however, does not mean that a pastor should demand a high "salary." The "laborer is worthy of his wages" statement is made in the context of "carry no money belt, no bag, no shoes" when you go to minister (Luke 10:4-7). The idea is that a minister is worthy of having his needs met (note the words "eating and drinking").

Perhaps the most important principle for ministers to remember is that it is not so much "their ministry" but the ministry of Him who lives and works in them (Galatians 2:2; Philippians 2:13). The key to a successful teaching ministry is an understanding that it is not your teaching, but the teaching of God (John 7:16). This principle (that it is not "your ministry") should result in your ability to avoid controlling and holding onto "your ministry." When you "hold on" you don't "let go" and, in turn, you don't multiply; yet, ministry should result in reproduction (Luke 6:40; 2 Timothy 2:2; Ephesians 4:11-12). The "not your ministry" principle may also help you to not press so hard in ministry that you get "burned out." If you are less inclined to control and hold onto "your ministry" you will be more inclined to get away from it and rest. A critical part of effective ministry is to "Come away by yourselves to a lonely place and rest a while" (Mark 6:31). An exhausted minister does not help anyone!

Another important principle of ministry is that ministry, by its very nature, is that which is done to meet needs. Christians are called to love their neighbor (Luke 10:27). Sometimes we try to justify our lack of ministry to others by limiting our definition of "neighbor" as we rhetorically ask the question asked by the lawyer, "And who is my neighbor?" (Luke 10:25, 29). However, Jesus provides us with a clear definition which has very broad parameters. Our "neighbor" is anyone who is in need (Luke 10:29-37). As Christians, we must respond to the needs of others; we minister to those who are in need.

The reality of the "power" of God makes for an interesting, albeit controversial, dynamic that is sometimes a part of ministry. There can be—although it is not necessary and we should say that it is not common—a physical feeling when God uses believers as ministers of His power (Luke 8:46). Some people testify of being "slain in the Spirit" as a result of the power of the Holy Spirit. Perhaps there is biblical precedent for this as seen in a variety of situations (John 18:6; 2 Chronicles 5:14; Matthew 28:4; Acts 9:4; Acts 22:7; Revelation 1:17).

OCTOBER 7

EVEN PHYSICAL HEALTH IS NOT THE PRIMARY THING

"But I thought it necessary to send to you Epaphroditus . . . receive him in the Lord with all joy, and hold men like him in high regard; because he came close to death for the work of Christ, risking his life . . ."

Philippians 2:25, 29-30

Some faulty theologies put such an emphasis on certain aspects of "blessing" that they end up creating an idol out of something that is good. For example, "prosperity theology" or "liberation theology" puts such an emphasis on material blessing—equating it with salvation—that it places material blessing over spiritual blessing. The "health and wealth" gospel adds physical health to the list of that which is of primary importance. The problem with these theologies is not with respect to the desire for God's blessing in terms of wealth or health, but with the insistence on placing those things as equal to or above God. It is an issue of idolatry!

As much as we would look at physical health as a desirable thing, it is still not the primary thing. And so, Paul writes to the Philippians, "I thought it necessary to send to you Epaphroditus . . . because you had heard that he was sick . . . he was sick to the point of death . . . therefore receive him in the Lord with all joy, and hold men like him in high regard because he came close to death for the work of Christ, risking his life" (Philippians 2:25-30). Some theologies would chastise, demean, or dishonor Epaphroditus because he was sick. Sickness is not of God, they would say. Where is your faith? God is a God of blessing, pouring out upon His people wealth and health. They would say, if you do not have those things, then you are not right with God!

What in the world is Paul doing then? He is telling the Philippians to *honor* ("hold men like him in high regard") Epaphroditus *because* he was deathly sick (Philippians 2:29-30). Epaphroditus gave himself for the cause of the gospel. He risked his life in the ministry of the gospel. Paul does not have the attitude that the sickness should be viewed in a negative way. Instead, he says that Epaphroditus should be honored because of his sickness. Should we all try to get sick then? As Paul would say, "May it never be!" This is not the point. It is not that sickness itself is a positive thing. It is only that health, like everything else, is subordinate to the Lordship of Christ in importance and value. If the expense of following and serving Christ is the loss of health, then we must be willing to pay the price.

Of course, many theologies would disagree with this interpretation. However, they would also have to disagree with Paul. Paul does not enter into a long discourse here on how divine health is for us to claim. He does not say that Epaphroditus had a lack of faith and that's why he got sick. He does not argue that the sickness should not have happened. He does not look at it negatively. He actually looks at it positively. Why? Because for Paul, physical hardship was a possible consequence of following Christ (Philippians 4:12; 1 Corinthians 4:11-13; 2 Corinthians 6:3-5; 2 Corinthians 11:23-27). Paul's positive reaction to Epaphroditus' sickness is not because of the sickness. It is not honorable, in and of itself, to be sick. Paul's perspective is built on what the sickness represented. It represented total commitment and dedication to Christ. Paul could speak like this because he did not have a theology that put physical health on the same level with salvation. Salvation, and therefore the Lordship of Christ, stood far above any circumstances.

Could you honor someone for being sick? Or does your theological view make it impossible to follow Paul's instructions? Are you more concerned about your health than you are about giving everything for the cause of Christ? Are you willing to give everything for the cause of Christ? What about your health? What about your life? For Paul, even physical health is not the primary thing. It, like everything else, is subordinate to the Lordship of Christ. Can you say that?

OCTOBER 8

TEMPTATION OF THE CHRIST ... AS REAL AS IT GETS!

"In the days of His flesh, He offered up both prayers and supplications,
with loud cries and tears, to the One able to save Him from death

and He was heard because of His piety. Although He was a Son, He learned obedience through what He suffered."

Hebrews 5:7-8

Jesus was "born from above" (Luke 1:35) and was, thus, sent "in the likeness of sinful flesh" (Romans 8:3) and not the exactitude of sinful flesh. And so, He, like Adam, was born without a sin nature. The first and last Adams (1 Corinthians 15:45) were the only men who had the potential to lead a perfect life. Where Adam failed, Jesus succeeded. This is one way to describe what happened for redemption to become a reality.

However, Jesus, like Adam, was tempted and the temptations were very real. Jesus did not simply walk easily over them; rather, He battled through them. "He learned obedience through what He suffered" (Hebrews 5:8). What did he suffer through? He suffered through the temptations "of His flesh" (Hebrews 5:7). Redemption has a price. The price was not paid at the cross only but was paid throughout Jesus' life as He prepared for the cross. He learned obedience (He overcame temptation) through the things that He suffered; "In the days of His flesh (in the days of His temptation), He offered up prayers and supplications, with loud cries and tears" (Hebrews 5:7).

Redemption is more of an addition than it is a subtraction. God redeems man by adding that which was originally meant to be (the natural) into the equation of human history without necessarily subtracting that which was not meant to be (the unnatural); thus, the natural is reclaimed in the context of the unnatural and so the natural must come against the unnatural (which is one way to explain suffering in the world). Certainly, to reclaim the natural while not completely destroying the unnatural resulted in suffering for Jesus. This is true in us also, as God works out His redemption in us. And so, the Scripture tells us that "all who desire to live a godly life in Christ Jesus will be persecuted" (2 Timothy 3:12). Surely, we must remember that in our redemption we have been made an alien race (this world is not our home). We are new creatures (who still battle against the old creature in us), living in a world filled with old creatures. It is the natural against the unnatural . . . the original against the counterfeit. As it was with Jesus, this dynamic results in suffering (John 15:20). Thus, in a certain sense (in the sense that Galatians 2:20 is true), redemptive suffering continues because the fight of the natural against the unnatural continues (Colossians 1:24; Galatians 6:17).

The first Adam was born without a sin nature yet with real temptation. It was so real, that he fell to it. Jesus was born without a sin nature yet with real temptation. It was so real, that in His battle against it "His sweat became like great drops of blood falling down to the ground" (Luke 22:44); yet, He did not fall to it (Hebrews 4:15). This is redemption! You need to be redeemed because the first Adam lost. You are redeemed because the last Adam won. All glory and honor be to that last Adam!

———

OCTOBER 9

BEWARE OF HAVING YOUR EARS TICKLED . . .

"For the time will come when they will not endure sound doctrine;
but wanting *to have their ears tickled, they will accumulate for themselves teachers*
in accordance to their own desires . . . "

2 Timothy 4:3

Beware of having your ears tickled! Sometimes fleshly or worldly desires motivate people to look to others who will legitimatize, confirm, and substantiate their desires; that is, they look for those who will "tickle their ears." The modern, Western church sometimes looks like those who do "not endure sound doctrine, but wanting to have their ears tickled, they will accumulate for themselves teachers in accordance to their own desires" (2 Timothy 4:3). Some teachers then develop theologies that attempt to deny the very method of the gospel itself; the cross. They try to legitimatize an easy, comfortable Christian life that is void of problems, persecution, and suffering. And so there is the "name it and claim it" teaching and the "positive confession" theology that tickle many ears.

Jesus' teaching on the kingdom of God, however, runs counter to these false theologies of "victory only" and "problemless" Christianity. These theologies propose that Christians should always be "living in victory" and should never have any problems. The existence of "negatives" is merely the result of a lack of faith that should be positively confessed away . . . name the positive and claim the positive. Every moment is to be lived in the resurrection. There is no life of the cross. However, Jesus indicates that a proof of the kingdom of God in your life is that you are being persecuted and insulted (Matthew 5:10) and the Scripture states that "all who desire to live godly in Christ Jesus will be persecuted" (2 Timothy 3:12). Does this mean that Christians lead a life of defeat? Of course not! It simply means that on the way to the resurrection there is the cross. Friday always comes before Sunday; the way to victory is through the cross.

Jesus' teaching on the kingdom of God runs counter to false teaching that implies the Christian life is an "easy" life that includes no hardship and has no opposition. The kingdom of God is opposite of the kingdom of this world and in opposition to it. Therefore, the kingdom of God "suffers violence" (Matthew 11:12) and advances forcefully because it is not of this world; it has an opponent. Forceful ("violent") people must take it by force (Luke 16:16) because people have opponents; Satan, the world, and their own flesh. The kingdom of God does not enter this world naturally; thus, there is conflict (Matthew 11:12; 1 Corinthians 9:27). Notice the forceful picture we have of Jesus "in the days of His flesh" (Hebrews 5:7-8; 12:4). Jesus does not casually come against His flesh. This is a picture of intensity or forcefulness. It is not a picture of "the easy life."

There is great victory and triumph in the Christian life. There are many blessings to be had and God certainly comforts His people. However, it is not a life that gets whatever it desires simply by naming and claiming it or positively confessing it, and it is not a life void of hardship and suffering. It may be nice to tickle your ears with such theologies but at the end of the day what you really need to do with your ears is . . . hear! "He who has ears to hear, let him hear!" (Matthew 11:15).

OCTOBER 10

IS YOUR "SECT" MORE PRIMARY THAN JESUS . . .

Then they sent some of the Pharisees and Herodians to Him in order to trap Him in a statement . . .
Some Sadducees (who say that there is no resurrection) came to Jesus, and began questioning Him . . ."

Mark 12:13, 18

As a reaction to the influence of the Greeks upon the Jews, several different "sects" (for the sake of analogy, you might call them "denominations") developed within Judaism. These included the Pharisees, Sadducees, Essenes, Herodians, Zealots, and Scribes. All of them, in one way or another, represented the empty religion of the Jews at the time of Christ. All of them, in the future, represent, to some degree, the empty religion of many Christian churches. The sect of the Pharisees, meaning "separated ones," probably started about 150 years before Christ as a reaction to the corrupting influences of Greek culture. Originally, the purpose of this sect was to promote holiness and separation from the world. Unfortunately, however, it was not long before it had as its focus, a superficial legalism regarding the law. Today, the Pharisees may be compared to "religious Christians."

Another sect, the Sadducees, represented the organization of the Jewish upper class and high priests. They cooperated with the secular rulers and enjoyed the benefits of wealth and influence. They were responsible for the administration of the temple and its rituals. They resisted the Pharisees' application of the law, and did not believe in the resurrection, angels, or spirits. The Sadducee sect ended with the destruction of the temple in 70 A.D. Today, this sect may be compared to "worldly Christians."

If the Sadducees separated themselves from others on the social level and the Pharisees separated themselves from others on the religious level, then the Essenes separated themselves from others on the geographic level (they physically withdrew from society). They lived in monastic communities in the mountains and caves (the Dead Sea scrolls were found in the Qumran caves where a group of Essenes lived). The Essenes lived a hard life that was very disciplined and simple. They did not take part in worship at the temple because they viewed themselves as the only true and pure Israel. They were experts in intricate warfare techniques, always practicing war games as they eagerly waited for the Messiah to come and deliver Israel via conquering their enemies. Today, this sect may be compared to "mystical, out of touch Christians."

Other sects within Judaism included the Herodians, the Zealots, and the Scribes. The Herodians were an elite group of politically oriented Jews who supported the government of the Herods. Today, this sect, perhaps, may be compared to "politically warped liberal Christians." On the other hand, the Zealots were politically opposed to the Roman rulers. As the Pharisees were opposite from the Sadducees, the Zealots were opposite from the Herodians. Today, this sect, may be compared to "politically militant Christians." Their extreme patriotism had a part to play in the eventual destruction of Jerusalem in 70 A.D. The final sect, the Scribes, consisted of religious "lawyers" who copied the Scriptures.

In order to truly follow Jesus fully, you must make sure your primary allegiance is not given to a religious group. Your primary allegiance must be given to the "sect of Jesus." So, "seek first his kingdom and his righteousness" (Matthew 6:33). This, ultimately, is the Christian's "sect"!

OCTOBER 11

A WALK WITH GOD REQUIRES REMEMBERING AND FORGETTING!

"... but one thing I do: forgetting what lies behind and reaching forward to what lies ahead,
I press on toward the goal for the prize of the upward call of God in Christ Jesus."

Philippians 3:13-14

In order to walk with God, you must **remember** and **forget**. You must "forget what lies behind" as the old man is buried/forgotten in the waters of baptism. You must "reach forward to what lies ahead" as you remember Christ who you have been raised up with (Philippians 3:13-14). And so, Paul declares in Galatians 2:20, "I have been crucified with Christ, and it is no longer I who live . . . " (I **forget** myself) **and** " . . . Christ lives in me; and the life which I now live in the flesh I live by faith in the Son of God" (I **remember** God). Seemingly opposite dynamics of thought are both significant aspects of a relationship with God and growing in that relationship.

Being aware of God requires remembering God and his past actions. Knowing is historical. As we remember God and His acts, we draw closer to Him and our relationship with Him is strengthened (1 Chronicles 16:10-12). If we do not remember God and His actions, then we more easily fall into sin (Judges 8:33-34). This is what happened to the Israelites. They did not remember how God had delivered them miraculously from Egypt. They began to murmur against God because they did not remember His way of provision. So, only four months after the parting of the Red Sea, they committed the infamous act of idolatry with the gold calf (Exodus 32:31). We, so often, are just like the Israelites. We tend to not engage in active remembering.

The solution is to continually remind yourself of God and His past actions. Cultivate an awareness (a knowing of God) in terms of remembering (journaling and a discipline of thanksgiving can be very helpful in cultivating this awareness). Of course, the single most important act of God to remember is the resurrection of Christ; thus, "if you . . . believe in your heart that God raised Him from the dead, you will be saved" (Romans 10:9). To be aware of the resurrection is to be aware that **He is alive**. To know God, you must be able to say that Jesus is alive in your own life. You cannot have a relationship with a lifeless god. You cannot know something that is not alive. The first disciples were radically changed when they became aware of the resurrection.

They went from being a defeated, depressed, and confused group of doubting "disciples" to a victorious, joyful, and mission-oriented group of believing disciples. How? They became aware of the resurrection. This same thing happens to us when we increase our awareness and remembering of the resurrection. We grow in our relationship with God.

Being aware of God requires forgetting. To know God better we must forget ourselves. We must forget what we have "lost" in giving our lives to God. We must practice the awareness of Paul in this regard, who was more than willing to forget himself and his past in order to gain Christ (Philippians 3:7-10). Sometimes we live dysfunctional lives simply because we are not willing to forget . . . to let go of the past. God shouts out to us, "Do not call to mind the former things, or ponder things of the past. Behold, I will do something new" (Isaiah 43:18-19). Forgetting is important in your walk with God. "No one, after putting his hand to the plow and looking back, is fit for the kingdom of God" (Luke 9:62). In order to move forward, we need to let go. We need to forget. Certainly, Lot's wife needed to forget, "but his wife, from behind him, looked back; and she became a pillar of salt" (Genesis 19:26).

The dynamics of remembering and forgetting are rooted in the very response required of us by the gospel. If you want to gain your life (remembering) you have to lose it (forgetting) . . . "he who has lost his life for My sake shall find it" (Matthew 10:39). I remember God as "Christ lives in me" and "I live by faith in the Son of God," and I forget myself as "I have been crucified with Christ, and it is no longer I who live . . . " (Galatians 2:20). A walk with God requires remembering and forgetting!

THE ENEMY OF YOUR RELATIONSHIP WITH GOD IS **SIN**!

" . . . and whatever is not from faith is sin."

Romans 14:23

Juxtaposed with knowing God (faith) is sin: "whatever is not from faith is sin" (Romans 14:23). It is certainly biblical to say that we can know God by our own actions. Many Bible passages encourage us to seek God in order to know Him (1 Chronicles 28:9; Luke 11:10). Some of our actions can hinder our relationship with God. It is just as important to the health of our relationship with God to not do these actions as it is to do the actions that lead us to God. These negative actions that negate faith (knowing God), according to Romans 14:23, are encapsulated in one word . . . **SIN**! The word itself can be used as an acrostic for outlining three major categories of negative actions with respect to knowing God:

Sin **I**dolatry **N**eglect

The tragic reality of Sin is that it separates us from God (Romans 6:23). It does this by darkening or hardening our heart toward God (Romans 1:21; Hebrews 3:13). God does not so much cut us off from Himself, as we cut ourselves off; God does not so much judge us, as we judge ourselves (John 3:18). We do this via our own actions which begin to desensitize us to God. The Scripture warns us about being "excluded from the life of God . . . because of the hardness of their heart . . . having become callous" (Ephesians 4:18-19).

Idols hide God from us. They become a false substitute (an "anti-revelation" of God) and lead us away from God. God is a jealous God. What is He jealous for? He is jealous for His people to know Him and only Him (Ezekiel 39:23-29). He is jealous for His plan of revelation. Remember, idols come in many different forms. In a pagan culture they may take the form of trees or stones. In a religious culture they may take the form of jewelry, paintings, or statues. In a hedonistic culture they may take the form of drugs/alcohol, sex, or money. In the life of a Christian they may take the form of a habitual sin, or even a vision from God, or the ministry itself (this is, perhaps, why so often we must die to the vision or to the ministry before God brings it to pass).

Anything that is put ahead of God, or instead of God, can be an idol and can separate us from God by hiding God from us; idols become false substitutes.

The lack of action (that is, Neglect) is perhaps the most negative action of all. Many psychologists say that the opposite of love is not hate, but apathy (not caring about or not being interested in). Neglecting God is the quickest way to destroy a relationship with Him. We must habitually remind ourselves of the presence of God. The ancient mystic, Brother Lawrence, called this kind of habit "practicing the presence of God." We must realize it is rude and insulting to ignore someone who is "with you always" (Matthew 28:20). Stereotypically, wives despise it when their husbands are so absorbed in a football game that is on television that they do not even acknowledge their presence in the room or know that they are talking to them. Negligence destroys marriages. At times, husbands should be ashamed of themselves. How much more does God despise it when we simply ignore Him? How much more should we be ashamed of ourselves? We are so often like Martha (Luke 10:38-42). We are so busy in what we are doing for God that we forget that He is right next to us trying to get our attention. Perhaps we should learn from Martin Luther who rejected the idea that he had too much to do for God, to spend much time with Him, and instead, said "I have too much to do for God, not to spend much time with Him." Negligence not only makes no sense, but more notably, it grieves the Spirit (Isaiah 54:6).

OCTOBER 13

GOD HAS ALWAYS BEEN IN THE BUSINESS OF REVELATION . . .

"For since the creation of the world His invisible attributes,
His eternal power and divine nature,
have been clearly seen,
being understood through what has been made,
so that they are without excuse."

Romans 1:20

God is known by revelation. He makes Himself known to man. The word "revelation" means "a removing of the veil." In Greek, the word is *apokalupsis* (which means uncovering). The uncovering or revelation is done by God Himself. It is God's manifestation of Himself (Matthew 16:17; John 1:13; John 6:44). God has always been in the business of revelation. There is a "general" revelation that reveals God to all people. The general revelation of God is expressed through the heavens (sun, moon, stars, etc.) and the earth (sea, mountains, forests, harvests, etc.). God (the designer) is seen in what He has created (designed). The painting points back to the painter (Psalm 19:1-2; Romans 1:20; Acts 14:17). General revelation of God is also expressed through mankind. Man was made in the image of God (Genesis 1:26) and is therefore a reflection of God. That reflection is seen in the fact that man can reason, he has a sense of morality (Romans 2:15) and free will, and he is given dominion over creation. General revelation of God is also expressed through history. History is truly "His Story," the story which belongs to God. God is revealed in it. The justice of God is revealed in the rise and fall of nations (Proverbs 14:34). The content of general revelation includes God's eternal power and deity (Romans 1:20), His benevolence and concern for man (Psalm 145:15-16; Matthew 5:45), and His righteousness (Proverbs 14:34).

Man, because of his sin, rejects general revelation (Romans 1:18-32). He suppresses the truth, although God has made it obvious (verses 18-19). He dishonors God and does not show gratitude to God (verse 21). Man is futile in his thinking and his heart is darkened (verse 21). He cannot know God. General revelation is not enough. Man needs something else. The tragedy of this whole process is caused by man's desire to be wicked (his sin nature). He exchanges the truth about God for a lie (verse 25). Man is no longer able to know God (verse 28). It must be remembered that man is without excuse (verse 20). He is guilty by his own choice.

Man cannot know God, not because God has not revealed Himself, but because man's sin clouds his ability to see God via general revelation. "Natural theology" is erroneous in its conclusion (that God can be known through general revelation). Although there is general revelation, man's sinfulness keeps him from knowing God through it. If man were sinless, then He could know God through natural theology. It is interesting to think about the symbolic language that is used in various Psalms (65:12-13; 66:1-4; 96:12-13; 97:1, 6). Perhaps when Adam walked the earth before the Fall (and in the new heavens and the new earth) the natural creation of God actually spoke forth the greatness of God in a way that enabled Adam to know God (consider Psalm 19:1-2). It is also interesting to realize that knowledge of God through special revelation (the incarnational Word and the written Word) allows us to be much more aware of general revelation. Ultimately, we need special revelation to know God, not just general revelation; nevertheless, God has always been in the business of revelation and, thus, "they are without excuse."

OCTOBER 14

I'M JUST DYING TO HAVE MORE POWER!

"... but you will receive power when the Holy Spirit has come upon you; and you shall be My witnesses both in Jerusalem, and in all Judea and Samaria, and even to the remotest part of the earth."

Acts 1:8

Where is the power of God? How do I get it? There is one word that summarizes the answer: "death." The power of God is directly connected to your death; you can get it by dying to yourself. God's power begins to be released when we begin to release our lives to God. And so we see in the Scripture that God's power is linked to my "weakness" or humility; God's power begins to be released when I begin to die to my pride and my self-sufficiency (1 Corinthians 2:3-5). "Power is perfected in weakness" (2 Corinthians 12:9). This is why it is the "poor in spirit" who get the kingdom of God (Matthew 5:3).

The question is not so much, "Where is the power of God?" as it is instead "Am I willing to die to myself?" In Acts 1:8, the Greek word *dunamis* (translated "power") is linked to the Greek word *martus* (translated "witnesses"; one who testifies to what has been seen or experienced). From this Greek word we get our modern word "martyr," which signifies one who has been so convinced by what has been seen or experienced that he would risk death to assert the reality of that testimony. Death to self and *dunamis* are inseparable: "but you will receive power when the Holy Spirit has come upon you; and you shall be My witnesses" (Acts 1:8); people who die to themselves for the sake of another. Power and death are necessarily linked together. For Paul, they are very much linked together in terms of the way he views his ministry and his purpose in this life: "that I may know Him and the power of His resurrection and the fellowship of His sufferings, being conformed to His death" (Philippians 3:10). Certainly, "unless a grain of wheat falls into the earth and dies, it remains alone; but if it dies, it bears much fruit" (John 12:24). Yes, "every branch that bears fruit, He prunes it so that it may bear more fruit" (John 15:2). Ultimately, "Worthy is the Lamb that was slain to receive power" (Revelation 5:12).

Where is the power of God? It is at your "funeral!" It is at the cross where I put self to death that I find the power of God in my life. What a paradox! It is as paradoxical as the gospel itself: "For whoever wishes to save his life will lose it; but whoever loses his life for My sake will find it" (Matthew 16:25-26). Jesus calls us to be ones who are "just dying to live." And so we joyfully proclaim, "I'm just dying to have more power!"

LOOKING FOR THE BLESSED HOPE . . .

"For the grace of God has appeared,
bringing salvation to all men,
instructing us to deny ungodliness and worldly desires
and to live sensibly, righteously and godly in the present age,
looking for the blessed hope and the appearing of the glory of our
great God and Savior, Christ Jesus . . . "

Titus 2:11-13

Who are you looking for when you are looking for "the blessed hope"? You are looking for God who "has appeared" already and who will appear again (Titus 2:11-13). Jesus came into the world initially as Savior (incarnation), and He will come again (return of Christ) as Judge (John 3:17; Matthew 25:31-33). That future "day" is described variously as "the day of the Lord" (1 Thessalonians 5:2), "the day of the Lord Jesus" (1 Corinthians 5:5), "the day of God" (2 Peter 3:12), "that day" (2 Thessalonians 1:10), and "the last day" (John 12:48). In each case, the context of "the day" is judgment and the timeframe is "the end." Exactly when that "day" will come is not able to be known (Matthew 24:27, 36, 42), but its purposes are very clear.

Jesus will return to fulfill His Word (John 14:3), to raise the dead (1 Thessalonians 4:13-18), to destroy death (1 Corinthians 15:25-26), and to gather the elect (Matthew 24:31). He will come to judge the world (Matthew 25:32-46); hence, He comes as Judge (John 3:17). He will come to glorify believers (Colossians 3:4) and to reward them (Matthew 16:27); He comes as "the blessed hope" (Titus 2:13).

So, who are you looking for? When He comes, He will come "in the clouds" (Matthew 24:30) "with the angels" (Matthew 25:31). He will come "like a thief" (1 Thessalonians 5:2-3) "in flaming fire" (2 Thessalonians 1:7-8). Most significantly, He will come "in His glory" (Matthew 25:31). While you are looking for that blessed hope, you are called to stay busy and productive (Luke 19:13-18). Otherwise, you are to wait for it (1 Corinthians 1:7), look for it (Titus 2:13), be ready for it (Matthew 24:42-51), love it (2 Timothy 4:8), and pray for it to come (Revelation 22:20; Luke 18:7-8).

And so, when you are looking for "the blessed hope," you are looking for God Himself (Titus 2:13). He is coming! Are you ready?

———

OCTOBER 16

KNOWING GOD BY KNOWING HIS ATTRIBUTES . . .

"I will betroth you to Me forever; Yes, I will betroth you to Me in righteousness and in justice,
In lovingkindness and in compassion, And I will betroth you to Me in faithfulness.
Then you will know the Lord."

Hosea 2:19-20

The aspects of God's Person that define who He is may be referred to as His attributes. Throughout the Bible, we notice that these attributes are linked to knowing God (Jeremiah 9:24). We can know God by knowing His attributes. God says, "I will betroth you to Me forever; yes, I will betroth you to Me in righteousness and in justice, in lovingkindness and in compassion, and I will betroth you to Me in faithfulness. Then you will know the Lord" (Hosea 2:19-20). You will know the Lord as you know His attributes (He is righteous, just, exhibits lovingkindness, compassionate, and faithful). When we know God by knowing His attributes, His attributes, then, begin to be lived out in us. This results in a greater knowing of God (Jeremiah 22:16; 1 John 4:7). How does this process begin? Can man know God through his attempt to live out His attributes? The answer is clearly "No, God must first make Himself known!" (Isaiah 19:21). God must act in order for us to know Him. The process begins with God. It is because He first shines His attributes on us that we are able to know His attributes experientially in our own lives.

Perhaps, God's most resounding attribute is His love. In 1 John 4:19, we see that we are able to love only because He first loved us. How can our love increase? According to the principle found in 1 John 4:19, our love could only increase if God's love for us increased. Can God's love for us increase? No (He loves us perfectly)! Then what must increase? Here we see the importance of revelation in knowing God. God's love for us cannot increase, but our perception (or revelation) of that love can increase. If the revelation of God's love for us increases, then our love for God and others can increase since "we love because He loves us." Paul understood this principle (that our love increases as our perception or revelation of God's love for us increases); he prayed that the Ephesians would be able to comprehend and know the love of Christ (Ephesians 3:18-19). Only in this way would they be able to love others. We must apply this prayer to our lives while on the road (or path) to knowing God through knowing His attributes.

More thoroughly, we can use 1 John 4:7-19 and the divine attribute of love to show how the process of knowing God through His attributes works. The process begins with the existence of an attribute of God—"God is love" (1 John 4:8). We can know God through knowing His attribute—"And we have come to know the love that God has for us" (1 John 4:16). When we know

God's attribute, we can then experience that attribute in us—"We love" (1 John 4:19). When we experience that attribute in us we can, then, know God more fully—"Everyone who loves knows God" (1 John 4:7). And so, our relationship with God grows through knowing His attributes.

To more specifically show the flow of the process, let us now use one specific verse (1 John 4:16—"We have come to know and have believed the love which God has for us. God is love, and the one who abides in love abides in God, and God abides in him"):

The attribute: "God is love."

We know God by *knowing* the attribute: "we have come to know and have believed the love."

We experience the attribute working in us: "the One who abides in love."

We know God more fully: "God abides in him."

We can know God by knowing His attributes. He is the reviver. Do you know Him as Reviver? (Hosea 6:1-3). He is the provider. Do you know Him as Provider? (Exodus 16:12; Deuteronomy 29:5). He is the deliverer. Do you know Him as Deliverer? (1 Kings 20:13; Ezekiel 13:21). We cry out with Hosea (6:3), "Let us know, let us press on to know the Lord."

OCTOBER 17

BIBLICAL ANALOGIES OF THE MARRIAGE RELATIONSHIP

"But I want you to understand that Christ is the head of every man,
and the man is the head of a woman, and God is the head of Christ."

1 Corinthians 11:3

Analogies are helpful in understanding relatively complex ideas. Famously, Forrest Gump explained that "life is like a box of chocolates" when he used an analogy to depict the variety (or even randomness) that is sometimes experienced in life. The Bible uses analogies (although it does not mention chocolate!) to depict the nature of marriage. The marriage relationship, in some way, is like the relationship between the members of the Trinity. It is also like the relationship between God and Israel, and the relationship between Christ and the church.

The marriage roles of husbands and wives (headship and submission, respectively) are compared to the roles of the various members of the Trinity. It should be understood "that Christ is the head of every man, and the man is the head of a woman, and God is the head of Christ" (1

Corinthians 11:3). The husband and wife find their equality in terms of their identity in Christ, and their headship and submission roles in terms of their relationship to each other. This same dynamic is true in the Trinity. The Father, Son, and Holy Spirit are equal. They are all God, equal but not the same—the Son depends on/is in submission to the Father (John 5:19), and the Spirit depends on/is in submission to the Son (John 16:13-14)—as it is seen that God (the Father) is the head of God the Son. Similarly, the cross reveals the equality of men and women (Galatians 3:28). That does not nullify the divine structure of the relationships within the marriage. The cross reveals the equality of the Son and the Father that exists within the Trinity (Philippians 2:6). That does not nullify the divine structure of the relationships within the Trinity (1 Corinthians 15:27-28). This is the paradox of the Trinity. The three members of the Trinity are equal, yet different (not the same). This is the paradox or "mystery" (Ephesians 5:31-32) of marriage also. The husband and wife are equal, yet they are not the same. They are equal in identity relative to each other, and different in the way they function relative to each other. This is the very idea of marriage *roles*; they are *functional roles,* not superior or inferior statuses!

Marriage, in the Old Testament, revealed the nature of the relationship between God and Israel. In general, we can study the book of the Song of Solomon to see how this analogy is used. Specifically, we can study various prophets who often refer to this analogy (consider Isaiah 54:1-8; Isaiah 62:4-5; Jeremiah 2:2; Jeremiah 3:6-14; Jeremiah 31:32; Ezekiel 16; Ezekiel 23; Hosea 1-3). Marriage, in the New Testament, revealed the nature of the relationship between Christ and the church. Christ the Head is analogous to the marriage role of the husband while the submissive church is analogous to the marriage role of the wife. This "mystery is great" (Ephesians 5:32) and may be better understood through the use of the analogy. In any case, some concluding statements with respect to marriage roles may be in order here:

Christ must be the focus of every marriage. Obeying and pleasing Him must be what motivates each partner to function in their respective marriage role.

The headship/submission relationship of husband and wife must not be understood in terms of what the husband **is** and what the wife **is not**. It must be seen as the divine order that allows each partner to complete the other. Each partner is equally important. Although they are equal, they are not the same.

Gender equality or "freedom" is not established by trying to be what one is not. Men are men and women are women. A man can only be a free man. A woman can only be a free woman. Fulfillment and freedom are found within the divine order of relationships, not outside of it. Fulfillment/freedom for men and women is available because they are equal, not because they are the same.

When husbands and wives accept and practice the divine order established by God, then they do not view headship as oppressive and submission as slavery. They do view headship and submission as the open door into a marriage of freedom and joy.

OCTOBER 18

YOU NEED TO REPENT SO . . . GET A "GRIP!"

"Therefore repent and return, so that your sins may be wiped away,
in order that times of refreshing may come from the presence of the Lord."

Acts 3:19

What is man's response to God's offer of salvation? The proper response is to "repent and believe" (Mark 1:15). What does it mean to "repent"? It means to "return" (Acts 3:19); to turn from the old to the new or from the bad to the good. More specifically, it is to "return to the Lord" (Hosea 6:1). To repent is not simply to feel sorry (it is not simply "regret") nor is it simply to feel bad (it is not simply "remorse"), but it is to turn to God and His abilities.

Why should I repent? It might be said that to be motivated to repent is to get a "GRiP" ("G" for **G**ratitude; "R" for **R**elational; "P" for **P**ractical). First, we should be motivated to repent simply out of Gratitude. The impact of what God did for us relative to what we deserve, along with the impact of what we should do for God relative to what He deserves, leads us to repentance. And so, we are presented with the question, "Or do you think lightly of the riches of His kindness and forbearance and patience, not knowing that the kindness of God leads you to repentance?" (Romans 2:4). An evidence of that gratitude that leads to repentance is a lack of being judgmental of others (note how gratitude is set in the context of not judging others in Romans 2:1-4). The one who repents out of gratitude is the same one who, when considering others' need for that same repentance, says, "But for the grace of God, there go I!"

Second, we should be motivated to repent due to the Relational aspect of the gospel. God has come to us. He is near. We are motivated to repent. Why? Because the kingdom of God "is at hand" or in your midst (Matthew 3:2). Since He is right there, we are motivated to turn to Him both because we are so readily convicted of our need for Him and so definitively convinced of His ability. Due to His closeness, we turn to Him and His abilities.

Third, and perhaps most significantly, we should be motivated to repent due to the Practical dynamic of the gospel, the reality of the situation. The truth of the matter is, we have a desperate need to have our sins forgiven (Acts 2:38; 3:19). Moreover, we have no way, in ourselves, to achieve and realize that forgiveness (Psalm 51). At the end of the day, we have no choice. It is only logical to repent. It is simply a practical thing to do! What other hope do we have?

And so, to be motivated to repent, we truly need to get a "GRiP." Ultimately, however, we must be motivated by the "white flag of surrender." Our part in the salvation process is to receive (John 1:12). In order to receive, we must repent. In order to repent, we must surrender. We must stop fighting against God. The essence of repentance is the action of surrendering (Matthew 16:24-25) and the result of that action is "that times of refreshing may come from the presence of the Lord" (Acts 3:19). So, get a grip and surrender!

———————

OCTOBER 19

THE CHURCH: A UNITY IN DIVERSITY . . .

"Since we have gifts that differ according to the grace given to us,
each of us is to exercise them accordingly."

Romans 12:6

The church is a "body." So, in order to grow, different members of the body must cooperate with each other . . . they must work together. Many times a church will not grow because the different types of leaders cannot work together. The prophets do not like the way that the pastors do things (they think pastors are too easy on the people). The pastors do not like the style of the prophets (they think prophets are too hard on the people). The evangelists do not like the teachers (they think teachers do not have a burden for lost souls). The teachers do not like the evangelists (they think evangelists do not have a burden to feed the sheep). The irony of these problems is that it is obvious that each one needs the other. After someone has been challenged by the prophet, he will soon need to be comforted by the pastor or he might become overwhelmed. After someone has been comforted by the pastor, he will soon need to be challenged by the prophet or he might fall asleep. After someone has been evangelized by the evangelist, he will soon need to be taught by the teacher or he might fall away from the Lord. After someone has been taught by the teacher, he will need to be led out in evangelism by the evangelist, or he might become a lazy Christian. Perhaps even more obvious is that the teacher needs the evangelist to evangelize so that he can have people to teach!

A church will grow when the different types of leaders learn how to work with each other as they see their need for the other person's ministry. The government of the church will be in the form of a body. Each part will be allowed to do his or her "part."

Each leadership part will train others in the church to do their "parts." The church will grow because the leadership parts will reproduce themselves. This can only happen if the government of the church is in the form of a body.

The church must go through the following processes to establish the right environment for the government of the church to exist in the form of a body. First, what the church must know or believe: 1) God's great desire for unity in the body (John 17:11, 21-22) and 2) God's great desire for diversity in the body (1 Corinthians 12:18). Second, what the church must do: 1) Each member must use his gift for the building up of the body (Romans 12:6) and 2) Each member must be allowed and encouraged to use his gift for the building up of the body (Romans 12:6). Third, what the church must think (be renewed in their minds): 1) Do not think too much of yourself (Romans 12:3) and 2) Think more highly of others (Philippians 2:3). Fourth, what the church must understand (received revelation): 1) Each member must recognize and accept his critical need for the ministries of the other members who are different from him (1 Corinthians 12:19-22) and 2) Each member must understand the need for unity within diversity in the body of Christ (Romans 12:4-5).

This is a process. The way someone believes will affect what he does. The things a person does will affect how the person thinks. The way the person thinks will affect what the person is able to understand. The people of the church must believe that God wants unity. If they believe that, then they will want to be part of the team. They will want to contribute by using their gift. If they do that, then they will not think too highly of themselves. They will see the difference between their fleshly efforts and the efforts of Christ in them (which is their gift). The people of the church must believe that God wants diversity. If they believe that, then they will allow and encourage others to use their gifts. If they do that, then they will think more highly of others because they will see Christ in them through their gifts.

All of this will have a great result. There will be new life because there will be fresh revelation: 1) Through this process, the members of the church will begin to understand that they need each other, 2) Their own gifts will not operate correctly without the operation of the gifts of others, 3) The correct climate will be established for the government of the church to exist in the form of a body. The result will be that the "body" can be what it truly is . . . a **unity in diversity**!

———————

OCTOBER 20

HEY, I'VE GOT GOOD NEWS . . . THAT'S GOSPEL!

" . . . for our gospel did not come to you in word only, but also in power and in the Holy Spirit and with full conviction; just as you know what kind of men we proved to be among you for your sake."

1 Thessalonians 1:5

What is the "gospel"? Of course, there are "the Gospels" (the first books of the New Testament: Matthew, Mark, Luke, and John). If a family had four sons, they could be named Matthew, Mark, Luke, and John so when they had to be called in from playing outside to eat dinner, the mom could save time and just yell, "Gospels . . . time to eat." What is the "gospel"? It is, literally, "good news" or "glad tidings." Biblically, it finds its roots in the Hebrew term *bisar* that was used to describe the proclamation of the "good news" concerning a victory in a battle (2 Samuel 4:10), the "good news" concerning God's deliverance from personal distress (Psalm 40:10), and the "good news" concerning the anticipated deliverance that would be achieved by the long-awaited Messiah (Isaiah 52:7).

In the New Testament, the "gospel" comes from the Greek term *euangelion* that was used to describe the proclamation of the "good news" concerning the birth of Jesus (the incarnation), the death of Jesus (the cross), and the exaltation of Jesus (His resurrection, ascension, session, and return). The basic "gospel" message states: God was born into the world and lived as a Man; He died on the cross in order to redeem man; He rose from the dead, ascended into Heaven, is now seated at the right hand of the Father, and will come again to judge the living and the dead. Hey, I've got good news . . . that's gospel!

We find a three-fold perspective of the gospel in I Thessalonians 1:5, the "Objective Gospel" ("Our gospel came to you not simply with words"), the "Subjective Gospel" ("but also with power, with the Holy Spirit, and with deep conviction."), and the "Gospel Lived Out" ("For you know how we lived among you for your sake"). The "Objective Gospel" is the oral/written speaking or proclaiming of the gospel. Jesus Christ represents the message and content of this announced good news. The gospel proclamation is a divine Word that reveals God's purpose and calls those who hear it to a responsive action. The "Subjective Gospel" is the dynamic portion of the gospel that goes beyond spoken words or theological doctrines. Within the proclaiming of the message, God breaks through to man with revelation that changes the hearts of those who receive it (Romans 1:15-17). In preaching the gospel, the power of God which raised Christ from the dead (Romans 1:4, 1 Corinthians 15:4) is activated in order to save people from death. This power may be demonstrated inwardly by the transformation of human hearts, or outwardly by supernatural signs and wonders. This mysterious power causes the Christian faith to move beyond doctrinal beliefs to an experiential event. This event is centered upon an encounter with Jesus Christ, followed by an ongoing relationship with Jesus in the life of the believer. The "Gospel Lived Out" happens when a person receives the objective/proclaimed gospel and has been transformed by the power of the subjective gospel. An encounter with Jesus Christ produces a conversion experience, which results in a lifestyle that permanently reflects the gospel.

Paul was so impacted by the revelation of Jesus (Acts 9:22, 26; 1 Corinthians 9:5) that his actions and his behavior became a statement of the gospel itself. Paul later compared all messengers' lifestyles to the actual dynamic subjective power of the gospel. The gospel became present not only in their words, but in their lives as well. Paul's life became so interwoven with the gospel he had received (as a result of meeting Jesus) that he exhibited a lifestyle that was parallel to the lifestyle of Jesus Christ Himself (1 Thessalonians 1:6). The gospel messenger's lifestyle becomes an equal portion of the total gospel expression. And so, the total "gospel" may be understood from a three-fold perspective: the Objective, Subjective, and Lived Out Gospel.

OCTOBER 21

THE DIVINITY OF CHRIST . . .

"IN THE beginning was the Word, and the Word was with God, and the Word was God . . . And the Word became flesh, and dwelt among us."

John 1:1, 14

Who is Jesus? The Bible is *very clear* about the identity of Jesus. It is not as though it is a mystical secret or an issue that is "interpretive." Jesus is God! His divinity is seen in the opening verse of the Gospel of John: "In the beginning was the Word, and the Word was with God, and the Word was God" (John 1:1). Later, Jesus is called God by Thomas: "Thomas answered and said to Him, 'My Lord and my God!'" (John 20:28). In an amazing passage that points to the Trinity, Jesus is even called God by God the Father: "YOUR THRONE, O GOD, IS FOREVER AND EVER . . . THEREFORE GOD, YOUR GOD, HAS ANOINTED YOU . . . " (Hebrews 1:8-9).

Other divinity passages are rooted in Jesus' "history," and in His actions. John tells us that He was with the Father before creation: "Now, Father, glorify Me together with Yourself, with the glory which I had with You before the world was" (John 17:5). He is the Creator of all things: "He is the image of the invisible God, the firstborn of all creation. For by Him all things were created, both in the heavens and on earth, visible and invisible, whether thrones or dominions or rulers or authorities—all things have been created through Him and for Him. He is before all things, and in Him all things hold together" (Colossians 1:15-17). He is before Abraham who lived 2000 years before Him: "Truly, truly, I say to you, before Abraham was born, I am" (John 8:58). In addition to His "history" there are His actions. He forgave sins: "And Jesus seeing their faith said to the paralytic, 'Son, your sins are forgiven'" (Mark 2:5). Beyond this, He claimed to have "all authority" on earth and in heaven (Matthew 28:18). Jesus received worship: "And those who were in the boat worshiped Him, saying, 'You are certainly God's Son!'" (Matthew 14:33). Only God can be worshipped (Acts 10:25-26). And only God can be said to be sustainer and controller of all things: " . . . has spoken to us in His Son, whom He appointed heir of all things, through whom also He made the world. And He is the radiance of His glory and the exact representation of His nature, and upholds all things by the word of His power" (Hebrews 1:2-3).

Who is Jesus? He is God. In His own words, "I and the Father are one" (John 10:30), and "He who has seen Me has seen the Father" (John 14:9). Many times He used God's most personal name ("I AM") to refer to Himself (John 8:58). The words "Jesus" and "God" are often interchanged in the Bible: "The beginning of the gospel of Jesus Christ . . . Jesus came into Galilee, preaching the gospel of God" (Mark 1:1, 14).

He walked on water. Nature obeyed Him. He healed the sick. He gave sight to the blind. He made the lame to walk and the deaf to hear. He cast out demons. He turned water into wine, and He multiplied food. He raised the dead. Who could this Jesus be? It's not that hard to see . . . Jesus is God!

OCTOBER 22

THE BOTTOM LINE FOR KNOWING GOD . . . OBEDIENCE!

"By this we know that we have come to know Him, if we keep His commandments."

1 John 2:3

We can refer to those actions that lead to knowing God as actions of obedience. Obedience is the foundation of the knowledge of God. It is the bottom line. Outside of obedience there is no knowledge of God . . . relationship with God . . . following of God. And so, "when they had brought their boats to land, they left everything and followed Him" (Luke 5:11). No leaving, no following. No obedience, no knowing. What is the bottom line for knowing God? Obedience!

Obeying God is directly connected to knowing God in a variety of ways. How do we even know that we know God? John tells us, "And by this we know that we have come to know Him, if we keep His commandments" (1 John 2:3). Jesus said it this way, "For whoever does the will of God, he is My brother and sister and mother" (Mark 3:35). What are the conditions for knowing God? The "if" connected to the "then" with respect to knowing God is related to obedience: "My son, if you will receive my sayings, and treasure my commandments within you . . . then you will discern the fear of the Lord, and discover the knowledge of God" (Proverbs 2:1-5). Even the condition for receiving the Holy Spirit is obedience: "And we are witnesses of these things; and so is the Holy Spirit, whom God has given to those who obey Him" (Acts 5:32). How do we fight for the knowledge of God? Paul explains, "We are destroying speculations and every lofty thing raised up against the knowledge of God, and we are taking every thought captive to the obedience of Christ" (2 Corinthians 10:5).

Obedience and intimacy/relationship are naturally linked. Even Pharaoh understood that there was a direct connection between obedience and knowing God. After Moses challenged Pharaoh to "Let My people go . . . Pharaoh said, 'Who is the Lord that I should obey His voice to let Israel go? I do not know the Lord, and besides, I will not let Israel go'" (Exodus 5:1-2). Pharaoh understood that you obey out of relationship. If there is no relationship, then there is no obedience. If there is a relationship, then obedience is natural. And so, friendship and love (two strong descriptions for the idea of intimacy/relationship) stand in direct correlation to obedience. And so, "You are my friends, if you do what I command you" (John 15:14) and "If you love Me, you will keep My commandments" (John 14:15).

Do I want to know God? Do I want to strengthen my relationship with God? Do I want to walk with God? So, tell me what to do. What is the bottom line? Obey!

OCTOBER 23

THE BIBLE IS ALIVE . . . IT IS POWERFUL!

"For the word of God is living and active and sharper than any two-edged sword, and piercing as far as the division of soul and spirit, of both joints and marrow, and able to judge the thoughts and intentions of the heart."

Hebrews 4:12

The purpose of the written Word of God, the Bible, is to reveal the living Word of God, the Lord Jesus Christ. To love the Bible is to love Christ. To love Christ is to love the Bible. The Bible is not just another book. It is God's Word. It is alive. Yes, "the word of God is living" (Hebrews 4:12). God's purpose is to transform us into the image of Jesus Christ (Romans 8:28-29) who is the

Word of God (John 1:1). In order to do this, He uses the Word of God (the Bible), and in so doing, the Word of God (written Word/Bible) yields the Word of God (incarnate Word/Jesus in us)!

There is power in the Word of God; it is "active and sharper than any two-edged sword, and piercing as far as the division of soul and spirit, of both joints and marrow" (Hebrews 4:12). It can change us; it is "able to judge the thoughts and intentions of the heart" (Hebrews 4:12). It can help us to know God. The degree to which you believe this and desire to know God and be transformed into His image is the degree to which you will be motivated to read and study the Bible.

The Bible helps us to initially know God. Paul said, "I am not ashamed of the gospel, for it is the power of God for salvation to everyone who believes" (Romans 1:16), and Peter told us, "you have been born again not of seed which is perishable but imperishable, that is, through the living and abiding word of God" (1 Peter 1:23). The Bible helps us to grow in our knowledge of God; we are instructed to "like newborn babes, long for the pure milk of the word, that by it you may grow in respect to salvation" (1 Peter 2:2).

How does the reading and studying of the Bible do this? How does the Bible help us grow in our relationship with God? One way is that if we put the Word of God in us, then we will be less likely to sin against God (Psalm 119:11). Of course, it is our sin that separates us from God (Romans 6:23; Isaiah 59:2), and since the Bible can help us not to sin (and therefore not be separated from God), then it is the Bible that can help us to know God. Another way the Bible helps us grow in our relationship with God is that it washes us; it cleanses, purifies or sanctifies us (Ephesians 5:26). Of course, the pure see God (Matthew 5:8), and since the Bible can make us pure, then it is the Bible that can help us to see or know God.

The Bible is alive. It is powerful. It can help us to know God. The degree to which you believe this and desire to know God is the degree to which you will be motivated to read and study the Bible!

OCTOBER 24

THE "FOUR F'S" OF REVIVAL . . .

"Do not be afraid any longer, only believe . . . something should be given her to eat."

Mark 5:36, 43

God is sovereign when it comes to revival (John 11:4). He is in control of all our "revival needing situations" and will use those situations for His purposes. At the same time, we see how man is used in the process of revival with what we might call "The Four F's of Revival" (consider Mark 5:35-43). First, we must **F**ight. Second, we must have **F**aith. Third, we must **F**eel. Fourth, we must **F**eed.

We must fight. In the reviving of Jairus' daughter we see in Mark 5:35 the need for spiritual warfare in revival. From the beginning it was a fight. The devil tries to stop a revival before it begins. Sure enough, here we see the spirit of Satan at work. Note the interruption ("While he was still speaking . . . "); not surprising since we know that Satan is rude. The only other place in the Scripture we see Jesus being interrupted is when Judas, who Satan had just previously entered (Luke 22:3), betrayed Jesus as the scene unfolded in the Garden of Gethsemane . . . "while He was still speaking, Judas, one of the twelve, came up . . . " (Mark 14:43). Satan is rude and he is also a liar. Note the lie in Mark 5:35 ("Your daughter has died; why trouble the Teacher anymore?"). The implication that nothing can be done is a lie. Satan must be fought against if revival is going to take place.

We must have faith. Jesus said, "Do not be afraid any longer, only believe" (Mark 5:36). This is in contrast to the unbelief seen in Mark 6:5-6 that resulted in no revival: "And He could do no miracle there . . . and He wondered at their unbelief." We can see the need for faith also in Mark 5:37 when Jesus created an atmosphere of faith. He only allowed those who had faith to enter the room with him. As we can also see in the revival of Lazarus (John 11:40), faith is very important in revival.

We must feel. Here we are talking about the need for compassion. Jesus created an atmosphere for faith by taking with him those who believed in Him. He created an atmosphere of compassion by taking with Him those who loved the child, the father and the mother. We also see how compassion worked in the revival as we read, "They entered the room where the child was. And taking the child by the hand . . . " (Mark 5:40-41). Jesus cared enough to go. He touched her hand. This genuine compassion was in contrast to the "people loudly weeping and wailing" (Mark 5:38) who did it as a job (hiring "professional mourners" was a somewhat common practice in that culture at that time). What a concept! Hired weepers and wailers—maybe from "Jonah's Weepers and Wailers Unlimited"—where they could possibly get a package deal (buy ten weepers and get two wailers free!). What a contrast between "God sourced burden/compassion" and "man sourced burden/compassion." A notable historical example of God sourced/burden compassion leading to revival has to do with the Scottish revivals of the sixteenth century. John Knox was instrumental in leading those revivals and is famous for his genuine words, "Give me Scotland, or I die!"

We must feed. After such an emotional and exciting event, why did Jesus simply say "that something should be given her to eat" (Mark 5:43)? Just as someone who comes out of a coma will die if they are not fed, so too, a revival that is not followed with teaching/discipleship will die. Perhaps, even worse, a revival that is not fed can result in the formation of cults. When people are starving, they do not care what kind of food they eat. If we do not feed the revival, someone else will feed it. In one of the last commands Jesus gave to His disciples, He said, "Feed my sheep" (John 21:17, NIV).

OCTOBER 25

THERE IS A NEW MAN (THE MAN) TO PUT ON . . .

"But you did not learn Christ in this way, if indeed you have heard Him and have been taught in Him, just as truth is in Jesus, that, in reference to your former manner of life, you lay aside the old man, which is being corrupted in accordance with the lusts of deceit, and that you be renewed in the spirit of your mind, and put on the new man, which in the likeness of *God has been created in righteousness and holiness of the truth."*

Ephesians 4:20-24

The Scripture instructs us to look to "lay aside the old man . . . and put on the new man" (Ephesians 4:22-24). Why? Because the original and intended condition of life for Adam (mankind) has been fulfilled in the life of Jesus. Ironically, Pilate was absolutely accurate when he proclaimed, "Behold, the man!" (John 19:5). Jesus is everything God originally intended man to be . . . He is, *the* Man!

This understanding helps us to realize the great price that Jesus paid on the cross. In His role as the "last Adam" (1 Corinthians 15:45), Christ had potential immortality (even as the first Adam had before the Fall). It is sin that leads to death (Romans 6:23), and Christ had no sin (Hebrews 4:15); He did not have to die. He died voluntarily. This points to the profound love God has for His creation, "For God sooooooooooooo loved the world . . . " (John 3:16). This also points to the astonishing soteriological dynamic that positions Christ as our substitute. He chose to ransom Himself on our behalf . . . as our substitute.

This understanding (that Jesus is everything God originally intended man to be) also helps us to recognize the creativity and sovereignty found in God's plan of redemption. Jesus, who was born as the last Adam, was not born with a sin nature (even as the first Adam was not created with a sin nature). He was not born as just another fallen man. He fulfills the nature of man as it was originally intended instead of simply destroying it. And so, the Scripture says that He was sent in the *likeness* of sinful flesh (Romans 8:3); He was sent in the *omoi* (Greek for "likeness"), not in the *omo* (Greek for "exactitude"). The only difference in the Greek words is that there is one extra "iota" in *omoi* . . . but oh what a difference one iota makes! The significance of this is that the creativity and sovereignty of God in redeeming man does not simply destroy what man became; it fulfills what man should have been. Redemption reclaims that which man lost. It does not simply reverse that which man has done. This necessitates a greater sense of God's sovereignty, and results in a greater sense of God's victory as God is bigger than the Fall (to simply eradicate would be, in a sense, to be on par with or smaller than the Fall). Redemption works despite the Fall, not simply in the absence (eradication) of it. And so Jesus does not simply abolish the Law, but He fulfills it (Matthew 5:17). Redeemed man is not simply exempt from doing the Law but is enabled to do the Law; redeemed man is not "under the Law" but over it! (Romans 6:14-18; Galatians 5:16-18).

Redemption is more of an addition than it is a subtraction. It adds (or reclaims) what should have been in the first place without necessarily subtracting—until the Lord returns and recreates the heavens and the earth—what came into being in the second place. It is redeemed man who still lives in a fallen world. Redemption does not yet negate the fallen world, and so, the tares continue to grow among the wheat (Matthew 13:24-30). We can experience redemption in our lives while still having to confront the consequences of our past evil actions and the ongoing inclination toward them. And so, Paul had to speak about the realities of the two natures "living together" (Galatians 5:17; Romans 7:14-20). "The good that I wish, I do not do; but I practice the very evil that I do not wish" (Romans 7:19) as "the flesh sets its desire against the Spirit, and the Spirit against the flesh" (Galatians 5:17). So what is a redeemed man to do? Look to "lay aside the old man . . . and put on the new man" (Ephesians 4:22-24); look to "Behold, *the* Man!" (John 19:5).

OCTOBER 26

WHAT KIND OF WALK DO YOU HAVE?

"Brethren, join in following my example, and observe those who walk according to the pattern you have in us. For many walk, of whom I often told you, and now tell you even weeping, that they are enemies of the cross of Christ . . . "

Philippians 3:17-18

In chapter three of Philippians, Paul refers to two different groups of people: the *true circumcision* and the *false circumcision*. Are they all Christians? Paul answers this question very directly. In verse 18 he says that they (the false circumcision) are "enemies of the cross of Christ." They are not Christians. Paul distinguishes between the two groups of people by referring to two different "walks." First is the walk according to the example of Paul and the pattern of others (verse 17). Second is the walk of those who are enemies of the cross of Christ (verse 18). Their end is destruction. They walk according to their appetites and earthly things (verse 19). They have a fleshly or worldly walk.

Why do Christians need to avoid this fleshly or worldly walk? This is the question that Paul begins to answer when he uses the connecting term *"for"* in verse 20: "For our citizenship is in heaven . . . " Christians are not worldly. They are heavenly. As Paul often says in other Bible passages—in Ephesians 5:8 "for you were formerly darkness, but now you are Light in the Lord; walk as children of Light"—he says here again: "Walk according to who you are!" For Paul, it is black and white. Who you are dictates how you walk because of where you are from? Those of the false circumcision have a false walk because they are from the world/flesh. Those of the true circumcision have a true walk because they are from heaven.

How will this "heavenliness" finally be realized completely? Paul answers this question in verses 20 and 21: "For our citizenship is in heaven, from which also we eagerly wait for a Savior, the Lord Jesus Christ; who will transform the body of our humble state into conformity with the body of His glory, by the exertion of the power that He has even to subject all things to Himself." Our bodies will be changed from fleshly bodies to spiritual bodies; the spirit will be primary. The spirit is now housed by the body (fleshly body), but after it is transformed the body will be housed by the spirit (spiritual body). Our "heavenliness" is not yet complete because we still have fleshly bodies. Simply because we will eventually be made perfect does not mean that we are currently perfect and do not sin. Sometimes, in our walk, we stumble: " . . . the spirit is willing but the flesh is weak" (Matthew 26:41); "For we know that the Law is spiritual, but I am of flesh, sold into bondage to sin. For what I am doing, I do not understand; for I am not practicing what I would like to do, but I am doing the very thing I hate . . . For I know that nothing good dwells in me, that is, in my flesh; for the willing is present in me, but the doing of the good is not. For the good that I want, I do not do, but I practice the very evil that I do not want" (Romans 7:14-19); "For the flesh sets its desire against the Spirit, and the Spirit against the flesh; for these are in opposition to one another, so that you may not do the things that you please" (Galatians 5:17).

There is often a stumble in our walk; nevertheless, someday our bodies will be changed and will be in harmony with the change in our spirits. This will be done through the sovereignty of God (Philippians 3:20-21). God is sovereign in the beginning of the work in us (Philippians 1:6). He is sovereign during the process (Philippians 1:6; 2:13). He is also sovereign in the completion of the work in us (Philippians 1:6; 3:20-21). God is the Alpha and Omega, the beginning and the end. Thus, all praise be to God!

AN HOUR BY HOUR ACCOUNT OF JESUS' CRUCIFIXION

"Then they brought Him to the place Golgotha . . . And they crucified Him . . .
It was the third hour when they crucified Him."

Mark 15:22-25

The climax of the incarnation is the crucifixion of Jesus Christ. A general chronological survey of the crucifixion paints for us a vivid account of some of the particular events that preceded the crucifixion, some of the events during the crucifixion, and some of the events immediately following the crucifixion. Preceding the crucifixion of Jesus was the Last Supper (Luke 22:14) on Thursday night. After that, Jesus and His disciples went to the garden of Gethsemane (Matthew 26:36) where Jesus was arrested (John 18:12) and taken to the house of Caiaphas the high priest (Mark 14:53-65).

It may be correct to say that the initial event during the crucifixion was Jesus being sent before Pilate at approximately 6:30 a.m. on Friday morning (Mark 15:1). Next, Jesus was sent to Herod at 7:00 a.m. (Luke 23:6-10), and then returned to Pilate at 7:30 a.m. (Luke 23:11). At approximately 8:00 a.m. Jesus was sentenced to death on the cross (Luke 23:23-24). At 8:30 a.m. Jesus began the short walk up to Calvary (Luke 23:26). Jesus was put on the cross at 9:00 a.m. (Mark 15:25), and soon after, He asked the Father to "forgive them" (Luke 23:34). At approximately 10:00 a.m. the soldiers cast lots for Jesus' clothes (Mark 15:24). Then, between 10:00 and 11:00 a.m. Jesus was insulted and mocked by the general public (Matthew 27:39-40 . . . perhaps representing humanity, in general), the chief priests (Mark 15:31 . . . perhaps representing religion), the soldiers (Luke 23:36-37 . . . perhaps representing political power), and one of the criminals who hung next to Him (Luke 23:39 . . . perhaps representing unrepentant sinners). At 11:00 a.m. Jesus responded positively to the request of the other criminal who was hanging next to Him (Luke 23:40-43). At 11:30 a.m. Jesus gave instructions to John to care for His mother (John 19:26, 27). At 12:00 p.m. it became dark and remained that way until 3:00 p.m. (Mark 15:33). At 1:30 p.m. Jesus cried out to God the Father: "My God, My God, why have You forsaken Me?" (Matthew 27:46). Then at 2:00 p.m. Jesus said, "I am thirsty" and "it is finished" (John 19:28-30). At approximately 3:00 p.m. Jesus said His last words and died (Luke 23:46).

Immediately following the crucifixion, there was an earthquake and the veil of the temple "was torn in two from top to bottom" (Matthew 27:51 . . . perhaps representing victory over separation from God). Next, the tombs were opened and many who had died were raised (Matthew 27:52 . . . perhaps representing Jesus' victory over death). Then, the centurion proclaimed the divinity of Jesus (Matthew 27:54 . . . perhaps representing Jesus' victory over unbelief). Next, the Scripture tells us the multitudes were grieved (Luke 23:48). The legs of the thieves were broken to accelerate their death (John 19:31-32). Jesus was already dead so they did not have to break His legs (fulfilling the Scripture "Not a bone of Him shall be broken" . . . John 19:36). Then His side was pierced (fulfilling the Scripture "They shall look on Him whom they pierced" . . . John 19:37). Finally, Jesus was buried (John 19:38-42), and the tomb was sealed, and a guard was posted (Matthew 27:66), and then, of course . . . **the resurrection!**

Of course, the ultimate "event" associated with Christ's crucifixion comes in the form of the offer of forgiveness for all mankind. It is the blood shed on the cross that saves us. And so, Jesus "said to them, 'This is My blood of the covenant, which is poured out for many'" (Mark 14:24). When someone is broken, they need to be **fix**ed. It is only by the cruci**fix**ion that we can be **fix**ed! Glory be to God!

OCTOBER 28

THE KINGDOM OF GOD IS GOSPEL . . . IT IS GOOD NEWS!

"And He sent them out to proclaim the kingdom of God, and to perform healing . . . And departing, they began *going about among the villages, preaching the gospel and healing everywhere."*

Luke 9:2, 6

To "proclaim the kingdom of God" is interchangeable with "preaching the gospel" (Luke 9:2, 6). The kingdom of God is gospel; it is "good news" (Acts 8:12). The kingdom of God is also interchangeable with "Paradise" (Luke 23:42-43). The kingdom of God is good news that is consistent with Paradise; It is eternal (2 Peter 1:11).

What is the nature of the kingdom of God? It should be understood that the kingdom of God is not so much a place as it is a rule or a reign (Luke 19:12-14); wherever the rule of God exists, there is the kingdom of God (Matthew 3:2). The kingdom of God is mysterious, and God is sovereign over it (Psalm 103:19); to see and hear (understand) the mysteries it must be granted to you (Matthew 13:11). God causes the growth in the kingdom of God. The followers of God are obedient vessels (not sources/causers) as they proclaim the Word. They are like farmers who must trust in God for the results. The farmer cannot control the growth of his crops nor understand how that growth occurs . . . it is mysterious. Nevertheless, he still plants the seed. So it is with the kingdom of God (Mark 4:3-8, 26-29).

Perhaps most descriptive of the nature of the kingdom of God is that it is "not of this world," not of this realm or order . . . it is not so much a physical kingdom as it is a spiritual kingdom (John 18:36). The one who announced the arrival of the kingdom of God did not wear "soft clothing" consistent with those who are in "kings' palaces" but wore camel hair and ate locusts (Matthew 11:8; Matthew 3:4). The kingdom of God is opposite of the kingdom of this world and in opposition to it. Therefore, the kingdom of God "suffers violence" (Matthew 11:12) and advances forcefully (because it is not of this world; it has an opponent). Forceful ("violent") men must take it by force (because men have opponents, Satan, the world, and their own flesh). The kingdom of God does not enter this world naturally; there is conflict (Matthew 11:12; 1 Corinthians 9:27). And so it is hard for rich people to enter the kingdom of God because to enter you must leave behind the world and the more of the world you possess (or perceive you possess), the more difficult it is to leave it behind (Matthew 19:24; Mark 10:23). God's desire "to give you the kingdom" is mentioned with the command to "sell your possessions and give to charity" (Luke 12:32-33).

The most foundational aspect of the nature of the kingdom of God is that it advances (Matthew 11:12) and grows (Mark 4:26-29). It may appear to be insignificant at first, however, it grows to be most significant (Matthew 13:31-32). It may even be hidden like leaven in dough; it expands the dough "until it is all leavened" (Matthew 13:33). And so, the prayer "Thy kingdom come" can be rightly translated from the Greek text "Thy kingdom is coming and will continue to come" (Matthew 6:10). Ultimately, when Jesus returns, the kingdom will come in its fullness "with power" (Mark 9:1) as it will appear suddenly "in the blink of an eye" (Luke 17:22-24). That is "gospel." That is good news! Maranatha. Come, Lord Jesus (Revelation 22:20).

OCTOBER 29

THE DISCIPLINE OF KNOWING GOD . . .

"At night my soul longs for You, indeed, my spirit within me seeks You diligently."

Isaiah 26:9

Successful athletes tend to be disciplined people. They must discipline themselves to practice regularly and remain committed to staying in shape. This is no different with the "knowing God practitioner." Successful followers of God must be disciplined in their seeking of Him by being committed to, and consistent in, that seeking. When we speak of consistency we must also speak of commitment. Consistency is not possible without commitment. Consistency is the manifestation of discipline. Commitment is the foundation and motivation of discipline.

We can decide to be committed to practical efforts of seeking God. Our motivation must be our love and desire for God. By faith, we must act. We do not necessarily need to understand how we are being transformed into the image of Jesus or how we are growing in our knowledge of God. We simply must act in faith that God is transforming us and that we are growing closer and closer to Jesus. Our sense of commitment in this process keeps us moving forward; it keeps us disciplined in the practice of knowing God. We cry out to Him, "At night my soul longs for Thee, indeed, my spirit within me seeks Thee diligently" (Isaiah 26:9).

We must be consistent in our practical efforts of seeking God. Each one of the four basic activities of knowing God alluded to in Acts 2:42 ("And they were *continually devoting themselves to* the apostles' teaching and to fellowship, to the breaking of bread and to prayer") includes within its biblical instructions a sense of consistency and regularity. In each case (Bible study, fellowship, praise and worship, and prayer), the Scriptural instructions include phrases like "always," "day and night," and "day by day." We are to be consistent in Bible study (2 Timothy 2:15). Consistent in fellowship (Acts 2:46). Consistent in praise and worship (Psalm 35:28). Consistent in prayer (1 Thessalonians 5:17). The process of knowing God must be a continual process. You must seek God consistently (Proverbs 8:17). You must try to be consistent in a general sense; you must be consistent in keeping your mind set on the things of God throughout the entire day (Colossians 3:1-2) and "in all your ways acknowledge Him" (Proverbs 3:6). You must also try to be consistent in a specific sense; you must be consistent in your devotional times with God and develop good habits of seeking God at planned times of the day.

It is amazing to calculate what the fruit is of the combination of consistency and commitment. With respect to Bible study, if you discipline yourself (remain committed and stay consistent), you can read the entire Bible in one year by reading three chapters each day (15-20 minutes per day). If you could discipline yourself to read the New Testament for 30 minutes each day, then you could read through the entire New Testament seven times each year or seventy times in a decade. You would be an expert (a "Ph.D.") in the New Testament. Moreover, the fruit of that discipline with respect to knowing God is not able to be calculated.

Successful athletes tend to be disciplined. How much more should we, successful followers of God, be disciplined in knowing God (1 Corinthians 9:25). May it be that we would cry out to Him, "At night my soul longs for Thee, indeed, my spirit within me seeks Thee diligently" (Isaiah 26:9).

WHAT IS THE CHURCH? . . .

"And He put all things in subjection under His feet, and gave Him as head over all things to the church, which is His body, the fullness of Him who fills all in all."

Ephesians 1:22-23

What is the church? The word "church" in Greek is ekklesia. It has two parts: "ek" which means "out of" and "klesia" which means "to be called." The church is the gathering together of the people who have been called out of the world (called out ones). "Ekklesia" is used in the New Testament in four different ways: 1) The universal church (see Ephesians 1:22; 1 Corinthians 10:32), 2) The local church (see Romans 16:1; Colossians 4:16), 3) The meeting of believers for worship (see 1 Corinthians 11:18; 14:19). 4) The place of the meetings, typically a house (see Romans 16:5; 1 Corinthians 16:19). Most definitively the church is the people of God and the fullness of Him who fills all in all.

Many people think of the church as nothing more than a building. Other people think that the church is a denomination. Some people think of the church as the professional ministry. Others think of the church in terms of popular images or common perceptions that people associate with the church. Each one of these images promotes both accuracies and inaccuracies with respect to the nature of the church. When the church is viewed as a "train station" it promotes and focuses on the hope within the church with its reduced fear of death and its positive offer for others. Oppositely, it promotes an attitude of holding on instead of overcoming. It can deny the power and fruit of the church and may promote laziness. Another view of the church might be that it is like a "crutch." Of course, this is true as we are weak and need help: "Bear one another's burdens, and thereby fulfill the law of Christ" (Galatians 6:2). The negative side of this image is the tendency to use the church in situations that require your own actions and abilities, resulting in a lack of overcomers. Another popular image of the church is "a ticket." The church is a vehicle used to draw people to Jesus. Taken too far this results in the misunderstanding that there is salvation through the church. Some people view the church as a "fort." This image highlights security in God, dependence on God, and the strength that is in the community. Negatively, the "fort" image results in the tendency to think of the church as being on the defensive team, and the tendency for people to not leave the fort. An appropriate metaphor of the church is a "gas station." The church can and should be a place to get filled up as long as that image of the church does not yield a lack of responsibility (members only "get" and do not "give'). Another image is "a refuge." This picture promotes acceptance and safety but may also promote a mentality of escaping. The church is sometimes described as a "community center." This is positive inasmuch as it promotes fellowship, community, and services for its members. It can be negative, however, as it promotes a tendency for the church to become a club and for it to forget to reach out to others. Lastly, the church might be viewed as a "theater." The church is seen as an exciting and popular place, but there can be the tendency for it to start acting like the world.

Of course, the usefulness of these popular images to depict the nature of the church is surpassed by the biblical images, or models, of the church. The image of the church as the "people of God" (1 Peter 2:10) points to the church as a community of believers that functions evangelistically and missiological. The image of the church as the "body of Christ" (Ephesians 4:12) paints the picture of God's people in union with Him and in union with each other. The image of the church as the "household of God" (1 Timothy 3:15) reflects on the reality of the presence of God and the fact that God dwells with His people. The image of the church as the "bride of Christ" (Revelation 19:7) represents the relationship and intimacy that God's people have with Him, as well as their purity. The image of the church as the "army of God" (2 Timothy 2:3-4) pictures the reality of the spiritual war that God's soldiers engage in as they fight the enemy of their souls.

So, what is the church? Most definitively, it is "the fullness of Him who fills all in all" (Ephesians 1:23). May God bless His church!

OCTOBER 31

THE "CAN GOD BE KNOWN?" FORECAST = CLOUDY WITH A CHANCE OF SONSHINE!

"Then Solomon said, 'The Lord has said that He would dwell in the thick cloud'."

1 Kings 8:12

Can God be known by man? We must understand and accept that God cannot be known in the exact same way that other things or persons can be known; He dwells with us yet in a "thick cloud" (1 Kings 8:12). God's actions always include a certain aspect of mystery. There is "the mystery of His will" (Ephesians 1:9). There is "the mystery of Christ" (Ephesians 3:4). There is "the mystery of the gospel" (Ephesians 6:19). God is "beyond" us, and thus, mysterious; He says to us, "My thoughts are not your thoughts, nor are your ways My ways . . . for as the heavens are higher than the earth, so are My ways higher than your ways and My thoughts than your thoughts" (Isaiah 55:8-9).

Regarding our ability to know God, there are two problems that add to the transcendent "mystery aspect" of God's nature. God is infinite and man is finite. The finite, by definition, cannot reach the infinite. The finite tries to understand the infinite, but like the mathematician, is ultimately reduced to using a line over a number and although the line over the third three after the decimal point seems to explain what one divided by three is (.333), the fact of the matter is that man (and the mathematician) are left wanting as the 3 goes on forever and ever. Alas, the mathematical line is not as powerful of an epistemological symbol as we might hope! Man, by himself, is not capable of knowing God. And so, one of Job's comforters rhetorically asks, "Can you discover the depths of God? Can you discover the limits of the Almighty?" (Job 11:7). Another one proclaimed, "The Almighty—we cannot find Him" (Job 37:23). Man (the finite), by himself, is not capable of knowing God (the infinite), or put another way, "the world through its wisdom did not come to know God" (1 Corinthians 1:21).

The second major problem man has in knowing God that adds to the "mystery aspect" of God's nature is that God is holy, and man is sinful. With regard to knowing God, then, we, like Isaiah, must cry out "Woe is me, for I am ruined" (Isaiah 6:1-5). Our sinfulness results in God "hiding His face" from us (Isaiah 8:17). Man's sin (impurity) keeps him from knowing God (Him who has no impurity). Certainly, purity can see purity (Matthew 5:8) and impurity can see impurity (Proverbs 17:4; 1 Corinthians 15:33), but purity cannot see impurity (Habakkuk 1:13) and impurity cannot see purity (Proverbs 17:20; Ephesians 4:17-19).

So what is the forecast? Can God be known by man? It's cloudy! It is cloudy because God is beyond us. He is transcendent. Nevertheless, He is also immanent; He is near because He has chosen to be near. The finite cannot reach the infinite, so the infinite came to the finite; in a paradoxical way (the paradox of the gospel itself) the infinite *became* finite (God became man). Perhaps in an even more mind-boggling sense (as if something could be more mind boggling/paradoxical than the incarnation) the unholy cannot reach the holy so the holy *became* unholy, "He made Him who knew no sin to be sin on our behalf" (2 Corinthians 5:21).

Can God be known by man? No and Yes. No, because of who God is versus who man is . . . and yes because of what God has done despite that disconnect: "For God so loved the world, that He gave His only begotten Son" (John 3:16). Perhaps, this is the greatest paradox of all; that God cannot be known by man and, yet, can be known by man. This is the gospel message. This is the good news—what man could not do, God did—and so the clouds break, and the Son shines through!

NOTES

November

INTIMACY . . . WITH GOD!

"That they may all be one; even as You, Father, are in Me,
and I in You, that they also may be in Us;
so that the world may believe that You sent Me."

John 17:21

The biblical concept of knowing God ("to know" with respect to God in the Hebrew Old Testament is *yada* and in the Greek New Testament is *ginosko*) is not a superficial one—it is, rather, profound—for it includes a sense of intimacy. The New Testament explains that eternal life is to "know" (*ginosko*) God (John 17:3). This means to know through personal experience or to know experientially ("to know intimately" not simply "to know about"). It suggests the intimate aspect of knowledge and relationship. The Old Testament exhorts us to acknowledge (*yada*) God (Proverbs 3:6). This means to know intimately. The same word (*yada*) is used in Genesis 4:1 to refer to the most intimate relationship that is possible between two people: "Now the man had relations (*yada*) with his wife Eve" (NASB) or "Now Adam knew (*yada*) his wife" (NKJV).

Our relationship with God is not to be a superficial one. It is described as analogous to the most intimate relationship that is possible between human beings (physical sexual intimacy). We might say that the Bible encourages us to have "spiritual intercourse" with God. We are to be united with Him intimately. We are to be one with Him as Jesus prayed "even as Thou, Father, art in Me, and I in Thee, that they also may be in Us" (John 17:21). And so, intimacy in our relationship with God ("Christ in you") is "the hope of glory" (Colossians 1:27).

The intimacy of the human marriage relationship ("the two shall become one flesh") is a shadow of the type of relationship that should exist between "Christ and the church" (Ephesians 5:31-32). We are, in essence, to have a love affair with Jesus. There is nothing superficial, institutional, or mechanical about our relationship with God. Our relationship with Jesus must be intimate. In Revelation 2:4, Jesus reprimands the church of Ephesus because "you have left your first love." This implies that at one time, they were intimate with God and that they should return to that intimacy.

Our relationship with Jesus needs the romance of a first love (Psalm 77:6). This romance leads to intimacy (Psalm 63:6). This intimacy leads to conception (Jeremiah 24:7). This conception leads to birth and life; "The people who know their God shall be strong, and carry out great exploits" (Daniel 11:32, NKJV). Here we might consider the vigor and vitality of a young man who is in love. A shy, weak, young man may live his life as a coward until he falls in love with a girl. If the girl is threatened, the coward can suddenly turn into a lion. We are spiritually weak when we do not have an intimate relationship with Jesus. The devil beats us down until we fall in love with Jesus. Suddenly, we become like lions. We become "the people who . . . carry out great exploits" (Daniel 11:32).

God calls you to relationship with Him. He calls you to spend time with Him. He calls you to intimacy with Him. He calls you to be "in Christ." In that calling is your hope . . . "Christ in you, the hope of glory" (Colossians 1:27).

NOVEMBER 2

WHO IS YOUR BEST FRIEND? (WHO KNOWS YOUR SECRETS?)

"But you, when you pray, go into your inner room, and when you have shut your door,
pray to your Father who is in secret, and your Father who sees what is done in secret will reward you."

Matthew 6:6

Who is your best friend? One way to define the idea of a best friend is to think in terms of secrecy. A best friend is the person who knows your secrets. That person knows the personal details of your life. Best friends know more about you than anyone else, because they spend more time with you than anyone else, and because you tell them your secrets. Secrecy breeds intimacy; it breeds devotion and allegiance as it builds the intensity of relational bonds.

God wants to be your best friend! (John 15:15). And so, He calls you to secrecy in prayer: "But you, when you pray, go into your inner room, and when you have shut your door, pray to your Father who is in secret, and your Father who sees in secret will repay you" (Matthew 6:6). He calls you to secrecy in fasting, "But you, when you fast . . . you may not be seen fasting by men, but by your Father who is in secret, and your Father who sees in secret will repay you" (Matthew 6:17-18). He calls you to secrecy in giving, "But when you give alms . . . your alms may be in secret; and your Father who sees in secret will repay you" (Matthew 6:3-4).

God wants to be your best friend! He wants to build an intimate relationship with you through secrecy. There is a bond between you and God that forms and becomes strong when you share your secrets with Him (when only you and He know). One very practical application of this dynamic is to develop a "lonely place" (or "secret place" or "private place") where you go to seek God. Jesus often went to a "lonely place" to pray (Mark 1:35), a place to pray to the Father privately (or secretly). This type of setting can help to establish the intimate relationship that is desired by God.

In calling us to secrecy in relationship with Him, God is not calling us to a denial of public affirmation or public confession of Him. Jesus says "Everyone therefore who shall confess Me before men, I will also confess him before My Father who is in heaven. But whoever shall deny Me before men, I will also deny him before My Father who is in heaven" (Matthew 10:32-33). Secrecy in relationship with God does not negate our evangelistic call as "ambassadors for Christ" (2 Corinthians 5:20; Ephesians 6:20). Secrecy is related to having intimacy with God but has nothing to do with being embarrassed of God! Secrecy breeds devotion and allegiance as it builds the intensity of relational bonds. Who is your best friend? Who knows your secrets? Best friends know more about you than anyone else, because they spend more time with you than anyone else, and because you tell them your secrets. So, go ahead. Tell God your secrets!

NOVEMBER 3

THE 7 P'S OF PRAYER . . .

"Pray, then, in this way: 'Our Father who is in heaven, Hallowed be Your name. Your kingdom come. Your will be done, On earth as it is in heaven. Give us this day our daily bread. And forgive us our debts, as we also have forgiven our debtors. And do not lead us into temptation, but deliver us from evil. [For Yours is the kingdom and the power and the glory forever. Amen.']"

Matthew 6:9-13

Lord, teach us to pray! (Luke 11:1). Jesus responds to this request and says, "Pray, then, in this way" (Matthew 6:9). What is "the way" that Jesus suggests? We might summarize "that way" by looking at seven aspects of prayer, or "the 7 P's of prayer": Praise, Petition, Provision, Pardon (received), Pardon (given), Protection, and Proclamation.

Prayer starts with praise. We "enter His gates with thanksgiving and His courts with praise" (Psalm 100:4). And so, Jesus says to pray in this way: "Our Father who art in heaven, hallowed be Thy name" (Matthew 6:9).

Prayer continues with petition. We certainly are called in prayer to "let your requests be made known to God" (Philippians 4:6) as we remain "on the alert with all perseverance and petition for all the saints" (Ephesians 6:18). We petition for ourselves and for others. Intercession stands as a significant part of petition; a substantial majority of all prayers recorded in the Bible are prayers of intercession for others. And so, Jesus says to pray in this way: "Your kingdom come. Your will be done, on earth as it is in heaven" (Matthew 6:10).

Prayer includes provision. It is God who "shall supply all your needs according to His riches in glory in Christ Jesus" (Philippians 4:19). And so, Jesus says to pray in this way: "Give us this day our daily bread" (Matthew 6:11).

Prayer includes pardon that we receive from God. In prayer we confirm what Nehemiah declared to God, "You are a God of forgiveness" (Nehemiah 9:17). And so, Jesus says to pray in this way: "And forgive us our debts" (Matthew 6:12).

Prayer also includes pardon that we give to others. We understand that "if you forgive men for their transgressions, your heavenly Father will also forgive you. But if you do not forgive men, then your Father will not forgive your transgressions" (Matthew 6:14-15). And so, Jesus says to pray in this way: "as we also have forgiven our debtors" (Matthew 6:12).

Prayer includes protection. In prayer we sing the song of David, "The Lord is my rock and my fortress and my deliverer . . . my shield . . . my stronghold and my refuge . . . Thou dost save me from violence" (2 Samuel 22:2-3). And so, Jesus says to pray in this way: "And do not lead us into temptation, but deliver us from evil" (Matthew 6:13).

Prayer includes proclamation. "Let them give glory to the Lord, and declare His praise" (Isaiah 42:12). And so, Jesus says to pray in this way: "For Thine is the kingdom, and the power, and the glory, forever. Amen" (Matthew 6:13).

And so, we request "Lord, teach us to pray!" (Luke 11:1), and Jesus responds, "Pray, then, in this way" (Matthew 6:9). Pray with "the 7 P's of prayer": Praise, Petition, Provision, Pardon (received), Pardon (given), Protection, and Proclamation.

———————

NOVEMBER 4

PROPER CONDUCT OF A KINGDOM OF GOD CITIZEN . . .

"Only conduct yourselves in a manner worthy of the gospel of Christ . . . "

Philippians 1:27

Paul's letters to the churches he founded are full of instruction, both doctrinal and behavioral. In his letter to the Philippians, Paul encourages them to "conduct yourselves in a manner worthy of the gospel of Christ" (Philippians 1:27), telling them to "do nothing . . . " (Philippians

2:3), and to "do all things . . . " (Philippians 2:14). The well-known Christological passage in Philippians 2:3-13 certainly contains profound doctrine but is purposed by Paul as the ultimate example, illustration, and manifestation of conduct/behavior that he wants the Philippians to practice. To conduct yourself as a Christian is, after all, to conduct yourself like *Christ*!

Paul instructs the Philippians to conduct themselves "in a *manner* worthy of Christ" (Philippians 1:27). The suggestion that springs from the term "manner" is all that would be indicative of the conduct of a citizen, all that would be required of a member's conduct that would rightly represent a group of people. The idea here is to conduct yourself as a responsible citizen of heaven. Paul plays upon the fact that Philippi was an official Roman "colony." He uses the metaphor to magnify the importance of their heavenly responsibilities as citizens of the kingdom of God. The Greek word (that is translated as "manner") is in the present middle imperative. The present imperative indicates a continual and habitual manner of conduct. The middle voice makes it more than an exhortation to be obeyed. It puts more responsibility on the person. Each individual is responsible to realize his own position and to hold himself accountable for the appropriate actions. They are to conduct themselves in a manner that is "worthy of"—corresponding to and consistent with—Christ.

What is included in this manner of conduct? Paul lists three points: "standing firm in one spirit," "with one mind striving together for the faith of the gospel," and "in no way alarmed by your opponents" (Philippians 1:27-28). These three points have two main themes: unity ("one spirit"; "one mind . . . together"; "your [common] opponents") and disunity or struggle against an adversary ("stand firm"; "striving"; "opponents"). The conduct of a citizen in the kingdom of God is to be in unity with others *and* to be in disunity with others! For Paul, the Christian life is foreign to this world. It assumes opposition and warfare. The correct response (or manner of conduct) is to "stand firm against" and to "stand firm with." The manner of conduct that is worthy of the gospel reflects both a life of unity and a life of opposition. This is true because the gospel has brought peace between God and man (John 14:27). There is peace that is brought between men (Ephesians 2:14-18), and at the same time, a sword that is brought between men (Matthew 10:34-36).

Do you consider yourself a citizen of the kingdom of God? Can you accept the fact that the Christian life must unify with its brethren *and* must stand opposed to the world? Or do you only see God as "love" and therefore desire to unite with all people? Can you accept the fact that not all people are brethren (children of God)? Can you accept the fact that there will be opposition? To conduct yourself as a Christian is, after all, to conduct yourself like *Christ*! And so, Jesus exhorts Christians to "love one another, even as I have loved you, that you also love one another"

(John 13:34), and at the same time reminds Christians, "Remember the word that I said to you . . . if they persecuted Me, they will also persecute you" (John 15:20). Christians are warned against breaking fellowship/unity with each other (Hebrews 10:25), and at the same time, Christians are warned that they will be persecuted (2 Timothy 3:12). And so, the proper conduct of a citizen in the kingdom of God includes both unity and disunity!

———

NOVEMBER 5

LIFE IN THE FAST(ING) LANE . . .

"Whenever you fast, do not put on a gloomy face as the hypocrites do,
for they neglect their appearance so that they will be noticed by men
when they are fasting. Truly I say to you, they have their reward in full.
But you, when you fast, anoint your head and wash your face so that your
fasting will not be noticed by men, but by your Father who is in secret;
and your Father who sees what is done in secret will reward you."

Matthew 6:16-18

Fasting is a biblical practice. It is mentioned often in the Scripture. Jesus assumes in His instructions regarding fasting, that His followers will fast. He said, "Whenever you fast . . ." clearly implying that He expects that they will fast. Paul (2 Corinthians 11:27), the apostles (2 Corinthians 6:4-5), the early Christians (Acts 13:2), and Jesus Himself (Matthew 4:1-2) all fasted as did many before them like Moses (Exodus 34:27-28), David (2 Samuel 12:16), Elijah (1 Kings 19:8), and Nehemiah (Nehemiah 1:4).

Biblical occasions for fasting are numerous and diverse. Fasting is done, among other things, in response to public disasters (1 Samuel 31:11-13), potential danger (Esther 4:16), sad news (Nehemiah 1:4), and the need for national repentance (1 Samuel 7:5-6). The Scripture indicates a variety of activities that may accompany fasting like prayer (Luke 2:37), confession (Nehemiah 9:1-2), mourning (Joel 2:12), humiliation (Nehemiah 9:1), distress (Psalm 69:10), and humility (Psalm 35:13).

The Bible offers a variety of safeguards or warnings with respect to the practice of fasting. Do not put your fasting on display (Matthew 6:16-18). Focus your fasting on God (Zechariah 7:5). Consider and implement the true essence of fasting (Isaiah 58:1-14). The Scripture also alludes to a variety of results that are connected to fasting including, among other things, divine guidance (Judges 20:26) and victory over temptation (Matthew 4:1-11).

Fasting should be thought of as a channel through which God can work in your life. It is a means of grace. To fast is to prepare the way for God. It is to make yourself more available to hear from God and to be used by God. Many fasting practitioners report of receiving critical guidance at transitional times of their lives through fasting. Fasting highlights the sense of your desperate need for God. You feel this need physically, which helps you to feel it spiritually. It also highlights your sense of appreciation for God. Typically, you appreciate more what you sometimes take for granted (both physical food and spiritual food).

Do not allow fasting to become an empty ritual or a legalistic burden. Be led by the Holy Spirit. God can show you when it is time to fast. At times, He may show you to fast systematically (one day each week or every other weekend). Whatever the case, do not fast unless you are led to fast and your heart is in it (Isaiah 58:1-14). Fasting, done rightly, can serve as a powerful spiritual discipline in your life. And so, consider getting in the fast(ing) lane!

NOVEMBER 6

HEADSHIP . . . THE AUTHORITY/ RESPONSIBILITY TO INITIATE

"For the husband is the head of the wife,
as Christ also is the head of the church . . . "

Ephesians 5:23

According to the Bible, marriage roles do exist and should be put into practice. The role of the husband is that he is to be "the head of the wife" (Ephesians 5:23). What does it mean to be "the head"? The Greek word, *kefalay*, is descriptive of someone who has authority to initiate (the opportunity of the role of headship) and, therefore, should take the initiative to direct (the responsibility of the role of headship). It is not so much the idea of "head" in the sense of identity—it is not an issue of superiority—as it is the idea of "head" in the sense of function; it is not so much that the husband "hovers over" the wife as it is that the husband "goes out in front of or ahead of" the wife. And so, the role of the husband in the marriage is summed up in his opportunity to be responsible, in his authority to initiate or direct.

Authority is not a result of domination. It is a result of service (Matthew 23:11). It is natural (developed), not forced (fabricated). When a husband views authority as his "right" then he, inevitably, will begin to demand it. He will tend to practice domination instead of service. This will result in an unhealthy marriage. When a husband views authority as his responsibility, then he will work for it and earn it. He will serve instead of dominate. This will result in a healthy marriage. The authority (headship) of the husband is natural as it was instituted by God at creation and not simply an unnatural result of the Fall of man. The man received the role of headship (authority to initiate) in the Garden of Eden. Adam was given the authority to name the animals (Genesis 2:19). He also named his wife (Genesis 3:20). In the institution of marriage, God then called the man to take the initiative to "leave and cleave" (Genesis 2:24). In the redeemed marriage of Abraham and Sarah, Abraham practiced this authority. In a passage about the submission of a wife and the authority of a husband, we see that Sarah called Abraham "lord" (1 Peter 3:1-6).

The husband's authority is the authority to initiate or direct. It must be stressed that leadership is the result of service (Luke 22:26). A husband is not the leader of his family until he is the servant of his family. Again, it should also be stressed that this leadership role is natural as it was instituted by God at creation. In Genesis 2:23 and 3:20, we see that the man takes the initiative to name the woman. Those who reject the biblical concept of the headship of the husband might argue that Adam should have consulted with Eve and allowed her to make the decision with him. In Genesis 3:17, however, it becomes obvious that the husband must lead and give direction to his wife. The man's error, according to God, is that instead of him leading his wife, he allowed his wife to lead him. The Fall of man was much more complex than the fact that he ate a piece of forbidden fruit. The Fall of man was rooted in rebellion. The man was to lead. He did not. Instead, the woman led. They rebelled against God's creation and His creative order (marriage roles)—Adam was judged "because you have listened to the voice of your wife" (Genesis 3:17)—as they inverted those roles (the essence of sin/evil is not a newly created thing but a warped, twisted, or inverted thing).

In a marriage, the husband as the "head" has authority to initiate (the opportunity of the role of headship) and, therefore, should take the initiative to direct (the responsibility of the role of headship). Husbands should not be "hovering over" their wives as if they are superiors and their wives are inferiors—husbands and wives are equal (even though they are not the same)—rather, husbands should be "going out in front of or ahead of" their wives. Husbands have an opportunity to be responsible. They have a responsibility to lead. Hey, husbands, wake up! Don't "Fall" in your "Gardens" . . . **Lead**!

———————

GOD'S SOVEREIGNTY AND MAN'S FREE WILL IN REVIVAL

"... that whoever believes in Him shall not perish, but have eternal life."

John 3:16

Spiritual revival principles may be able to be recognized through a study of physical revival events. In Mark 5:35-43 we find that both God's sovereignty and man's free will are involved in the reviving of Jairus' daughter from the dead. We see this same dynamic in an even more famous physical revival event: the revival of Lazarus from the dead in John 11:21-44. God certainly wants revival in His church. He does not want His church to be described as the "frozen chosen." He wants it to be revived and be referred to more as the "esteemed redeemed." Without God's intervention, there would be no revival. Thankfully, God wants church growth. However, he has chosen to use people to achieve it. Here we see both God's sovereignty and man's free at work in revival.

In the case of Lazarus, we see how God's sovereignty in the situation is expressed when Jesus declares, "This sickness is not to end in death, but for the glory of God, so that the Son of God may be glorified by it" (John 11:4). God is sovereign. He is in control of the situation and will use it for His purposes. At the same time, we see how man is used in the process of revival with what we might call "The Four **F**'s of Revival" (consider Mark 5:35-43). First, we must **F**ight. Many cases of church revival historically have included a focus on spiritual warfare. This might be described as the fight against hopelessness or the fight to hope. In the Lazarus event, this warfare is implied when Martha says to Jesus, "Lord, if You had been here, my brother would not have died" (John 11:21, 32). Let the **F**ight begin! Second, we must have **F**aith: "Jesus said to her, 'Did I not say to you that if you believe, you will see the glory of God?'" (John 11:40). Third, we must **F**eel. The compassion exhibited by Mary, the Jews who were with her, and Jesus Himself, was quite obvious: "When Jesus therefore saw her weeping, and the Jews who came with her also weeping, He was deeply moved in spirit and was troubled . . . Jesus wept" (John 11:33-35). Finally, we must be ready to **F**eed a revival. We must engage in ministry that will guide and help the revival along: "The man who had died came forth, bound hand and foot with wrappings, and his face was wrapped around with a cloth. Jesus said to them, 'Unbind him, and let him go'" (John 11:44).

A study of Mark 5:35-43 would reveal these same "Four F's of Revival." Man's use of his free will (his actions) is part of how revival comes about. Amid this free will, God remains sovereign. Curiously, at the end of the Mark 5 account the Scripture reads, "Immediately the girl got up and began to walk, for she was twelve years old" (Mark 5:42). Why was she revived? Because she was twelve years old? Perhaps this seemingly odd reasoning can be explained when we understand that the number twelve, in Scripture, points to God's sovereignty as it is the "number of completion" (twelve hours in a day, twelve hours in a night, twelve months in a year, twelve tribes of Israel, twelve disciples, etc.). She was revived in God's sovereign timing, His "*kairos*" (God's timing or the "fullness of time" as in Mark 1:15, Romans 5:6, and Ephesians 1:10) versus His "*chronos*" (chronological time). Immediately preceding the Jairus' daughter event is the healing of the woman "who had had a hemorrhage for twelve years" (Mark 5:25). The use of the number twelve again could be symbolically pointing to the sovereignty of God in revival. Man's free will in revival (seen in the "4 **F**'s") could also be seen in one of the most sovereign statements in the Bible—God's "vision statement"—"For God (**F**ight) so loved the world (**F**eel), that He gave His only begotten Son (**F**eed), that whoever believes in Him (**F**aith) shall not perish but have eternal life (revival)" (John 3:16). The 4 **F**'s (representing man's free will in revival) lead to the actual revival itself (representing the sovereignty of God in revival). Herein, we see the ultimate revival in that we do "not perish" but, instead, we have **eternal life**. Thanks be to God!

NOVEMBER 8

WHO GETS INTO THE KINGDOM? . . . THE BEGGARS!

"Blessed are the poor in spirit, for theirs is the kingdom of heaven."

Matthew 5:3

The initial, foundational beatitude (blessing) states that it is the "poor in spirit" who receive the kingdom of God (Matthew 5:3); it is the humble—those who are empty of themselves—who get to have the rule of God in their lives, and thus, are "happy" or "blessed." The Greek term *ptochos* ("poor in spirit") is more precisely translated as "beggar" or "pauper" denoting absolute dependency. Those who get into the kingdom of God are those who understand that apart from Christ "you can do nothing" (John 15:5).

And so, what are some of the traits or characteristics of those who do enter the kingdom of God? Those who are obedient will enter the kingdom of God (Matthew 7:21). Moreover, forceful people enter the kingdom of God (Matthew 11:12; Luke 16:16). Force must be used against the things that oppose the kingdom of God (Satan, the world, our flesh). Notice the forceful picture we have of Jesus "in the days of His flesh" (Hebrews 5:7). Jesus does not casually come against His flesh. This is a picture of intensity or forcefulness. At the same time, we must be like children to enter the kingdom of God (Matthew 18:3). We must have the purity, simplicity, and trust of a child (Matthew 19:14; Luke 18:17). Furthermore, those who are prepared and ready will enter the kingdom (Matthew 25:1-13). More specifically, those who enter the kingdom of God use the blessings that God has given to them for the purpose of producing fruit (Matthew 25:14-30).

Most fundamentally, the characteristics of those who enter the kingdom of God are rooted in faith: relationship with God and trust in Him. Those who are with Jesus ("those who were sitting around Him" as opposed to those "outside") are given understanding of the mystery of the kingdom of God (Mark 3:31-34; 4:10-11). Being with Jesus (relationship with God) opens the door to the kingdom. Paul had a very intimate relationship with Christ, and thus, he received understanding and insight into the mysteries (Ephesians 3:4). Furthermore, "kingdom people" are those who trust God. Since they are workers for God, they, like farmers, are men of action who live lives of reliance. They do their work even though they cannot cause the results; they are people who must trust God (Mark 4:26-29).

Although the kingdom is a gift (Romans 6:23), there are significant entrance standards. Righteousness must exceed "religiosity" to enter the kingdom of God (Matthew 5:20) since religiosity focuses on the rule of men while righteousness focuses on the rule of God. The kingdom of God requires significant dedication, commitment, and loyalty as "no one, after putting his hand to the plow and looking back, is fit for the kingdom of God" (Luke 9:62). And so, "blessed are the poor in spirit (beggars), for theirs is the kingdom of heaven" (Matthew 5:3). Beggars, of course, tend to be loyal to their donors since they have nowhere else to turn . . . they are empty of their own abilities. Ultimately, who gets into the kingdom of God? The beggars!

NOVEMBER 9

THE PROCESS OF CHURCH DISCIPLINE . . .

"If your brother sins, go and show him his fault in private; if he listens to you,
you have won your brother. But if he does not listen to you . . ."

Matthew 18:15

One of the more difficult practices in the New Testament to apply today is the practice of church discipline. It is clear that Paul wanted to establish the local church as the vehicle that would enforce church discipline. Leaders worked together with the congregation to enforce it. In a serious case of discipline, the phrase in 1 Corinthians 5:13 ("But those who are outside, God judges. Remove the wicked man from among yourselves") comes from Deuteronomy 17:7 in which the context was the involvement of the whole group in the action (note the movement from "witnesses" to "all the people"). In order to emphasize his point that the congregation was to be involved in the discipline process, Paul wrote the verb in its plural form making "remove" to read "we remove." Similarly, the context of 1 Thessalonians 5:14 ("We urge you, brethren, admonish the unruly . . . be patient with everyone") seems to point to the responsibility of the entire church to discipline. The church as a whole body has the responsibility to discipline. Other examples include the word "all" in 1 Timothy 5:20, the probability that the letter to Titus was read in public including the instructions to discipline in 2:15 that were for the entire church, and the implications of discipline by the church body found in 2 Corinthians 2:6 and 1 Corinthians 5:4.

The actual practice of church discipline revolves around a "warning process." The most complete biblical passage illustrating this process is Matthew 18:15-17:

> If your brother sins, go and show him his fault in private; if he listens to you, you have won your brother. But if he does not listen *to you*, take one or two more with you, so that BY THE MOUTH OF TWO OR THREE WITNESSES EVERY FACT MAY BE CONFIRMED. If he refuses to listen to them, tell it to the church; and if he refuses to listen even to the church, let him be to you as a gentile and a tax collector.

The roots of the process are found in the practice of the Jews with their Rabbi (teacher, minister). If a Rabbi did something wrong, then there were specific words and actions that were used to warn and admonish him. This was done over a period of thirty days. If the problem continued, there was another period of thirty days with the same words and actions. After that came excommunication. Similarly, we see this process in Titus 3:10, "Regarding a man who is divisive, after admonishing him once or twice, have nothing more to do with him." There are four steps in the warning process (Matthew 18): Go by yourself and confront the person in private (verse 15 and Galatians 6:1), confront the person together with one or two others (verse 16 and 1 Timothy 5:19), confront the person in front of the entire church (verse 17a and 1 Timothy 5:20), and finally, excommunication (verse 17b and 1 Corinthians 5:5 and 1 Timothy 1:20).

There is a process within church discipline. Discipline does not begin with the strongest possible confrontation. It happens step by step. Consider the case of the "unruly" (lazy) ones in 1 and 2 Thessalonians. First, Paul gave a very gentle warning to them (1 Thessalonians 4:11 and 5:14). Then, he gave a much stronger warning to them in 2 Thessalonians 3:6-15. Along with the process of discipline there is the example of discipline. Paul tells the Thessalonians to "follow our example, because we did not act in an undisciplined manner among you" (2 Thessalonians 3:7). He also highlights bad examples (1 Timothy 5:19-20) as part of the process of discipline. Both the good and the bad examples serve as tools for self-discipline. They are used to motivate others to do the right thing. It takes discipline to be a disciple. They share the same root word . . . a word meaning "to guide or to train"!

NOVEMBER 10

GOD MAKES PROMISES AND "MAKES" MEN . . .

"Your descendants will also be like the dust of the earth, and you will spread out to the west and to the east and to the north and to the south; and in you and in your descendants shall all the families of the earth be blessed. Behold, I am with you . . . for I will not leave you until I have done what I have promised you."

Genesis 28:14-15

God's promises are YES and AMEN (2 Corinthians 1:20). God's promises are made and then they are repeated and continued among successive generations. God's promise to Abram includes "all the families of the earth":

NOW THE LORD said to Abram, 'Go forth from your country, And from your relatives and from your father's house, To the land which I will show you; And I will make you a great nation, And I will bless you, And make your name great; And so you shall be a blessing; And I will bless those who bless you, And the one who curses you I will curse. And in you all the families of the earth will be blessed' (Genesis 12:1-3).

This missiological covenant is repeated to Abram in Genesis 17:2-5:

'I will establish My covenant between Me and you, And I will multiply you exceedingly.' Abram fell on his face, and God talked with him, saying, 'As for Me, behold, My covenant is with you, And you will be the father of a multitude of nations. No longer shall your name be called Abram, But your name shall be Abraham; For I have made you the father of a multitude of nations.'

Then the promise continues to successive generations:

And behold, the LORD stood above it and said, 'I am the LORD, the God of your father Abraham and the God of Isaac; the land on which you lie, I will give it to you and to your descendants. Your descendants will also be like the dust of the earth, and you will spread out to the west and to the east and to the north and to the south; and in you and in your descendants shall all the families of the earth be blessed (Genesis 28:13-14).

And so, God's promises are for the here and now while they also look ahead. It is interesting to note that what we tend to call "The Great Commission" (which is given almost 2000 years after Abraham, Isaac, and Jacob) is comparable to the promises made to Abraham, Isaac, and Jacob. The Great Commission did not begin after Jesus rose from the dead but began when God first chose Abram to "Go . . . and in you all the families of the earth will be blessed" (Genesis 12:1-3). The promise to Abraham looked ahead. Note the similar language in Genesis 28 and Matthew 28: " . . . you will spread out to the west and to the east and to the north and to the south; and in you and in your descendants shall all the families of the earth be blessed. Behold, I am with you . . . I will not leave you" (Genesis 28:14-15); " . . . make disciples of all the nations . . . and lo, I am with you always" (Matthew 28:19-20). God's promises are "for now" *and* they "look ahead." They are Yes *and* Amen!

Even as God makes promises, He also "makes" men who will then live out those promises. Sometimes He "makes" a man by "breaking" that man. Jacob is broken by God so he can be used by God. First, Jacob struggled with Esau. Then he struggled with Laban. Then he struggled with Esau again. Then he struggled with God Himself: "Then Jacob was left alone, and a man wrestled with him until daybreak . . . He said, 'Your name shall no longer be Jacob, but Israel; for you have striven with God and with men and have prevailed'" (Genesis 32:24, 28). Jacob is made by God. He was humbled and then acknowledged that the blessing must come from God: "'I will not let you go unless you bless me' . . . and He blessed him there" (Genesis 32:26, 29). Broken and made, Jacob is more available for God's promises. God makes promises and makes men!

NOVEMBER 11

THE PEOPLE OF GOD . . .

" . . . in whom you also are being built together into a dwelling of God in the Spirit."

Ephesians 2:22

The church is a dwelling in which God lives by His Spirit: "Or what agreement has the temple of God with idols? For we are the temple of the living God; just as God said, 'I WILL DWELL IN THEM AND WALK AMONG THEM; AND I WILL BE THEIR GOD, AND THEY SHALL BE MY PEOPLE'" (2 Corinthians 6:16). God dwells in the midst of His people . . . His "household": " . . . in whom you also are being built together into a dwelling of God in the Spirit" (Ephesians 2:22). This description focuses on the presence of the Holy Spirit in the church (see John 14:17, 23 and 1 Corinthians 3:16). The architect of this "household" is Jesus (Matthew 16:18). He is the builder and the building materials. Jesus is the foundation of the building (1 Corinthians 3:11). Jesus is the cornerstone (1 Peter 2:4-8; Colossians 2:6; Ephesians 2:20-22). Jesus is the center of the life of the church.

Another model of the church or the people of God is "the bride of Christ" (Isaiah 54:1-8). Jesus describes Himself relative to "the bride" as "the bridegroom": "And Jesus said to them, 'While the bridegroom is with them, the attendants of the bridegroom cannot fast, can they? So long as they have the bridegroom with them, they cannot fast. But the days will come when the bridegroom is taken away from them, and then they will fast in that day'" (Mark 2:19-20). The bride has a strong and intimate relationship with God (Song of Solomon 4:9), and embodies commitment, faithfulness, and devotion (Romans 7:1-4; 2 Corinthians 11:2-4; Matthew 21:31). The primary dynamic in the relationship between Christ and His bride (the church) is love (Revelation 2:1-7).

The church can also be visualized and experienced as "the army of God." The church is an army because there is a war (see 1 Timothy 1:18; 6:12; 2 Timothy 2:3-4; 2 Corinthians 10:3; Ephesians 6:12). Therefore, the church must understand who or what it should be fighting; that is, who its enemy is. The enemy is not other people (Ephesians 6:12). The enemy includes Satan and his demons (1 Peter 5:8; Revelation 12:9-17; Matthew 12:24) and the world, which is defined as all that is not under the Lordship of Jesus (Satan is the Lord of the world as seen in 2 Corinthians 4:4). Our own flesh, or the sin nature, is also our enemy (see Romans 8:3-8; Galatians 5:17-21). More importantly, the army must know its General (Commander in Chief). Christ is the Commander in Chief. He is the General. The Commander in Chief of the army demands discipline and obedience (Luke 7:1-10). In 1 John 5:4, we see that faith produces victory in the war against the world: "For whatever is born of God overcomes the world; and this is the victory that has overcome the world—our faith."

In Luke 7:9, faith is defined in terms of being obedient to the Commander in Chief or General. Without obedience to Jesus, the church is not able to win the war. The army must be in submission to the Commander in Chief in order to have victory over the enemy: "Submit therefore to God. Resist the devil and he will flee from you. Draw near to God and He will draw near to you" (James 4:7). The Army needs to know and use its armor (Ephesians 6:10-20). The Army needs to know and use its weapons (2 Corinthians 10:3-5): prayer and praise (see Ephesians 6:18; Acts 16:22-30), the cross (see Colossians 2:14, 15), the gifts of the Spirit (see 1 Timothy 1:18), communion, fellowship/koinonia (see Ecclesiastes 4:9-12; Luke 10:1), and a life of discipline (see 1 Corinthians 9:25-27). Every believer should be able to proclaim along with that old song: "I'm in the Lord's army, yes sir!"

STEPS TO HONOR IN THE LIFE
OF JOSEPH (GENESIS 39-41) . . .

"The Pharaoh said to his servants, 'Can we find a man like this, in whom is a divine spirit?'"

Genesis 41:38

The story of Joseph and his acquisition of honor includes, perhaps most importantly, what that honor is used for; it leads to influence through service. All good things begin with God. So, the first step to honor in the life of Joseph is nothing less than divine favor. Initially, this comes with respect to Joseph gaining favor in the eyes of others: "But while Joseph was there in the prison, the Lord was with him; he showed him kindness and granted him favor in the eyes of the prison warden" (Genesis 39:20-21). Divine favor is seen in the acquiring of responsibility and authority through being experienced. Note how Joseph was able to be used because of the experience that he already had (for example, in Potiphar's house): "So the warden put Joseph in charge of all those held in the prison, and he was made responsible for all that was done there. The warden paid no attention to anything under Joseph's care, because the Lord was with Joseph and gave him success in whatever he did" (Genesis 39:22-23). Experience and know-how is worth more than money and position. God can quickly give you money and position, but He normally does not give quick know-how!

A second step to honor in the life of Joseph is the existence of sovereign circumstances. First, with respect to what the world calls "coincidence": "Pharaoh was angry with his two officials, the chief cupbearer and the chief baker, and put them in custody in the house of the captain of the guard, in the same prison where Joseph was confined" (Genesis 40:2-3). By "coincidence" (God's sovereignty), the chief cupbearer and the chief baker were put in the same prison as Joseph which then began a string of events that ultimately resulted in Joseph being second in charge in all of Egypt!

Another way in which the existence of sovereign circumstances leads to honor in the life of Joseph is with respect to situations that make the world feel helpless: "In the morning his mind was troubled, so he sent for all the magicians and wise men of Egypt. Pharaoh told them his dreams, but no one could interpret them for him" (Genesis 41:8). Note how Pharaoh has no other alternative in such a situation but to recognize God's sovereignty:

> Then Pharaoh sent and called for Joseph, and they hurriedly brought him out of the dungeon; and when he had shaved himself and changed his clothes, he came to Pharaoh. Pharaoh said to Joseph, 'I have had a dream, but no one can interpret it; and I have heard it

said about you, that when you hear a dream you can interpret it.' Joseph answered Pharaoh, saying, "It is not in me; God will give Pharaoh a favorable answer" (Genesis 41:14-16).

It should be remembered that Joseph, even during sovereign circumstances, still had to go through hardship. Sometimes being in the limelight is preceded by being hidden (sometimes for "preparatory" purposes). It was thirteen years from the time Joseph was thrown into the pit by his brothers (Genesis 37:2) to the time when Joseph got out of prison and took a place of great honor in Egypt (Genesis 41:46). For Moses it was forty years after fleeing Egypt before he led the Exodus. David spent years serving and fleeing from Saul before he became king. Paul spent years in Arabia before he began his missionary journeys. Sovereign circumstances that, ultimately, lead to honor can be complicated!

Another step to honor in the life of Joseph is his honoring of God: "'I cannot do it,' Joseph replied to Pharaoh, 'but God will give Pharaoh the answer he desires'" (Genesis 41:16). Joseph points away from himself and points instead to God. Then God causes others to point to Joseph (honor).

One final step to honor is the receiving of divine revelation first with respect to truth, understanding, and direction (Genesis 41:25-36), then with respect to having wisdom that the world wants and needs (Genesis 41:38-39). Certainly, God's people should lead (Genesis 41:40-45) even as light leads amid darkness!

NOVEMBER 13

ABRAHAM, ISAAC, AND MOUNT MORIAH: FAITH AND FORETELLING

"Take now your son, your only son, whom you love, Isaac,
and go to the land of Moriah,
and offer him there as a burnt offering on one of the mountains of which I will tell you."

Genesis 22:2

In one of the greatest acts of faith in the Bible, Abraham responds in obedience to God's call to sacrifice his son Isaac. Even more astonishing than Abraham's faith is the uncanny resemblance between the act of sacrificing Isaac and the act of sacrificing Jesus on the cross some 2000 years later. Isaac can be seen as a *type* (a foreshadowing or example that predicts) of Jesus, and Abraham can be seen as a type of God the Father. Isaac is referred to as Abraham's *only* son: "He said, 'Take now your son, your only son . . .'" (Genesis 22:2), and "I know that you fear God, since you have not withheld your son, your only son, from Me" (Genesis 22:12). Of course, we know the New Testament verse that proclaims Jesus as God's *only* Son: "For God so loved the world, that He gave His only begotten Son . . ." (John 3:16). This is a very curious proclamation by God to call Isaac the ONLY son of Abraham since Abraham has another son (Ishmael). This is another part of the foreshadowing as it matches up Isaac (through whom will come the promise: "By faith Abraham, when he was tested, offered up Isaac, and he who had received the promises was offering up his ONLY begotten son . . ." Hebrews 11:17) with Jesus (who will be the ultimate fulfillment of the promise). In that sense they are both *only* sons. Furthermore, God says of Abraham in Genesis 22:12, "I know that you fear God, since you have not withheld your son, your only son, from Me." Similarly, in John 3:16 we see that "God so loved the world, that He gave [*He did not withhold*] His only begotten Son . . ." And so, we see numerous ways—in just the first few verses of this incredible story of faith—in which Abraham stands as a type of God the Father and Isaac a type of God the Son.

One of the most incredible aspects of this foreshadowing is seen in the geographical location in which it is taking place: "Take now your son, your only son, whom you love, Isaac, and go to the land of Moriah, and offer him there as a burnt offering on one of the mountains of which I will tell you" (Genesis 22:2). Scholars believe that the land of Moriah was in the same place as Golgotha where Jesus would be crucified nearly 2000 years later. Second Chronicles 3:1 tells us that "Solomon began to build the house of the Lord in Jerusalem on Mount Moriah." And so, Abraham and Isaac climb the same hill that the Father and Jesus would climb some 2000 years later. In addition, Genesis 22:3 seemingly pictures Palm Sunday (Jesus enters Jerusalem on a donkey) and Good Friday (Jesus becomes the ultimate sacrifice/ offering): "Abraham rose early in the morning and saddled his donkey, and . . . he split wood for the burnt offering."

In Genesis 22:3 we see that Abraham took "Isaac his son, and he split wood for the burnt offering." The burnt offering was a "sin offering" (Leviticus 4:24) that is offered "to make atonement" (Leviticus 1:4); to make payment for sin. This is what Jesus would become some 2000 years later: " . . . that He might become a merciful and faithful high priest in things pertaining to God, to make propitiation for the sins of the people" (Hebrews 2:17). Jesus, according to the Father's plan, climbs up Mount Moriah to become the payment for sin even as Isaac 2000 years earlier climbed that very same mountain with his father Abraham to serve as a burnt offering.

God, in His Word, uses many methods to point to his ways and purposes. Perhaps this story in Genesis 22 is the most powerful of those methods. One professor of theology once said to his Old Testament students, "When you study the Old Testament, look for Jesus and it will come alive!" Certainly, in a study of Genesis 22, it does not take much to see Jesus. Jesus is not just in Matthew and John. He is in Genesis and Psalms and Hebrews . . . well, of course He is . . . He *is* the Word of God. Glory be to His holy name!

NOVEMBER 14

MORE ABRAHAM, ISAAC, AND MOUNT MORIAH: FAITH AND FORETELLING

"Isaac spoke to Abraham . . . 'where is the lamb for the burnt offering?'
Abraham said, 'God will provide for Himself the lamb for the burnt offering, my son.'"

Genesis 22:7-8

In one of the greatest acts of faith in the Bible, Abraham responded in obedience to God's call to sacrifice his son Isaac. Abraham's faith is the uncanny resemblance between the act of sacrificing Isaac and the act of sacrificing Jesus on the cross some 2000 years later. Isaac can be seen as a *type* (a foreshadowing or example that predicts) of Jesus, and Abraham can be seen as a type of God the Father. Prior to the horrific climb up the mount, Jesus went to the Garden of Gethsemane " . . . and said to His disciples, 'Sit here while I go over there and pray'" (Matthew 26:36). Similarly, before climbing that same mountain, "Abraham said to his young men, 'Stay here'" (Genesis 22:5). Even the resurrection of Christ is prefigured in the Genesis 22 event. Just before climbing up Mount Moriah, Abraham said to his companions " . . . I and the lad will go over there; and we will worship and return to you" (Genesis 22:5). Abraham knew he was going up the Mount to slay his son, yet he said that both of them would return. Perhaps Abraham believed God would raise Isaac from the dead. This is the explanation in Hebrews 11:17-19: "By faith Abraham . . . offered up Isaac . . . He considered that God is able to raise people even from the dead, from which he also received him back as a type. By faith . . . " It may even be that the resurrection is alluded to when we read, "On the third day Abraham raised his eyes and saw the place from a distance" (Genesis 22:4).

Another similar scene is what is often referred to as the "Via Dolorosa, the Way of Suffering"; the path taken by Jesus as He carried His own cross up to Golgotha: "They took Jesus, therefore, and He went out, bearing His own cross, to the place called the Place of a Skull, which is called in Hebrew, Golgotha" (John 19:17-18). Isaac also carried his own "cross" (wood) up to Golgotha: "Abraham took the wood of the burnt offering and laid it on Isaac his son, and . . . the two of them walked on together" (Genesis 22:6). Before going to the cross, in the Garden of Gethsemane Jesus asked the Father if He could get out of the upcoming torture, but in the end He submitted to the Father's will: "'My Father, if it is possible, let this cup pass from Me; yet not as I will, but as You will'" (Matthew 26:39). Isaac, who was at least twelve years old and, thus, capable of, at least, trying to escape from Abraham, spoke to his father in a similar way and in the end submitted to his father's will: "Behold, the fire and the wood, but where is the lamb for the burnt offering . . . the two of them walked on together" (Genesis 22:7-8). Jesus is "the Lamb of God, who takes away the sin of the world" (John 1:29), and Isaac is told that "God will provide for Himself the lamb for the burnt offering" (Genesis 22:8). After building the altar and binding Isaac to the wood, "Abraham stretched out his hand and took the knife to slay his son" (Genesis 22:10). One might say, "Well this is where the comparison stops . . . surely God the Father does not kill God the Son . . . it was the Romans or the Jews who did the evil act." Confounding as it is, however, "the Lord was pleased to crush Him, putting Him to grief" (Isaiah 53:10).

Jesus is pictured in the New Testament as our substitute or replacement. So, too, in Genesis 22:13 we see an incredible substitute: ". . . a ram caught in the thicket . . . and Abraham . . . offered him up for a burnt offering in the place of his son" (Genesis 22:13). Genesis 22:14 records a greatly anticipated realization of a prophecy ("it will be provided") that comes out of the comparison between Abraham/Isaac and Father God/Jesus: "Abraham called the name of that place The Lord Will Provide, as it is said to this day, 'In the mount of the Lord it will be provided.'" In the future, another substitute will be provided on Mount Moriah/Golgotha. The recording of this incredible event comes to an end with nothing less than a reference to God's grand plan of redemption as He proclaims that because of Abraham's obedience He will bless both Abraham (Israel) and "all the nations of the earth" (Genesis 22:17-18). Similarly, because Jesus obeyed the Father and went to the cross, God's plan of redemption ("For God so loved the world" . . . John 3:16) would go forth (which is "the joy set before Him" . . . Hebrews 12:2). Father God, through His only Son Jesus, makes peace between God and man. Incredibly, 2000 years earlier, father Abraham and his only son Isaac are used as "types" to foreshadow the coming of this world changing peace treaty!

NOVEMBER 15

DEATH LEADS TO LIFE . . .

"The next day he saw Jesus coming to him, and said,
'Behold, the Lamb of God who takes away the sin of the world!'

John 1:29

The Hebrew toasting phrase L'Chaim ("to life") is especially poignant as it is set against Jewish history; specifically, as it is set against its most important and remembered story, the Passover, and its most important and holy day, the Day of Atonement. It is in these events that death led to life as the Passover Lamb was sacrificed so that death would "pass over" and the Hebrews could be delivered to life. The goat was sacrificed so that the sins of the people could be atoned for and they could be reconciled to God. Death leads to life; there is no life without death as there is no forgiveness without the shedding of blood (Hebrews 9:22). The death of Jesus, as the ultimate (complete and final) Lamb of God, then, becomes the death that takes away the sins of the entire world (John 1:29; 3:16). He becomes the complete and final solution to the problem of sin. He becomes the complete and final "death leading to life"; "It is finished!" (John 19:30). To know, trust in, and obey this truth results in life/freedom (John 8:31-36).

Death leads to life in us; death to ourselves leads to the life of Christ in us (Matthew 5:3; Galatians 2:20). And so, Jesus tells us (Luke 9:23), unless we deny ourselves and take up our cross daily (death to self) we cannot follow Him (life of Christ in us). It is the Spirit of God who accomplishes this death leading to life in us; "if by the Spirit you are putting to death the deeds of the body, you will live" (Romans 8:13). Death leads to life. And so, Jesus claims that "whoever wishes to save his life will lose it; but whoever loses his life for My sake will find it" (Matthew 16:26). Furthermore, "since Christ has suffered in the flesh, arm yourselves also with the same purpose, because he who has suffered in the flesh has ceased from sin" (1 Peter 4:1). Death leads to life.

Just as it is true that a grain of wheat must first be buried in the earth and die before it can bear fruit, death (to ourselves) begins the process of vibrant production in the kingdom of God (John 12:24). This "death leading to life" is an ongoing and constant process as the Vinedresser is constantly at work (in theological terms, this is called "sanctification"). There is a constant process of death that God works in us. Death is replaced with life. Areas of our lives that bear fruit are continuously being pruned to produce more fruit. God cuts away things that are not needed in our lives (John 15:1-2). Death leads to life . . . L'Chaim!

DOES THE GIFT OF THE SPIRIT COME AFTER SALVATION?

"Peter said to them, 'Repent, and each of you be baptized
in the name of Jesus Christ for the forgiveness of your sins;
and you will receive the gift of the Holy Spirit.'"

Acts 2:38

One of the more debated topics in the church today has to do with what is called the "baptism of the Holy Spirit" or "the filling with the Holy Spirit" or "the gift of the Holy Spirit." More specifically, the debate revolves around the question: Is the gift of the Holy Spirit that which comes after salvation and deemed a "second experience" or does it simply represent the indwelling Spirit within every believer? The Scripture seems to present a three-fold foundation regarding Christian conversion and the ensuing empowering or baptism of the Holy Spirit: "Repent, and each of you be baptized in the name of Jesus Christ for the forgiveness of your sins; and you will receive the gift of the Holy Spirit" (Acts 2:38). First, we see the exhortation to "repent." Second, we see the mandate to be baptized in water (both first two steps have to do with salvation/forgiveness of sins). Third, we see the promise that "you will receive the gift of the Holy Spirit." This does seem to indicate (future tense of "receive") that the receiving of the "gift" is a "second experience"; the gift of the Spirit comes after salvation, being separate from it.

The day of Pentecost account (Acts 2:1-4) also seems to present a "second experience" situation regarding the filling of the Holy Spirit in those "who were all together": "Then the day of Pentecost had come, they were all together in one place. And suddenly there came from heaven a noise like a violent rushing wind, and it filled the whole house where they were sitting . . . And they were all filled with the Holy Spirit and began to speak with other tongues, as the Spirit was giving them utterance." Who were these people "who were all together in one place"? They were not unbelievers who had not yet received salvation, otherwise, Acts 2:1-4 would be a picture of conversion or salvation. They were clearly believers who had already been converted/saved and who now were experiencing something different. This second experience, in no way, argues for the absence of the Holy Spirit in the conversion experience. The Holy Spirit is absolutely essential to that experience. And so the ones who were gathered together on the day of Pentecost, seemingly, were already saved. Perhaps their salvation experience—prior to Pentecost—is seen when they received the Holy Spirit: "And when He had said this, He breathed on them and said to them, 'Receive the Holy Spirit'" (John 20:22). This initial experience with the Holy Spirit would have been for salvation, while the second experience with the Holy Spirit at Pentecost would have been for being baptized or filled with the gift of the Holy Spirit.

Acts 4:31 and Acts 13:52 accounts show that it is not a singular "second experience," but a continual filling (see also Ephesians 5:18 and John 7:37). For further study, the following accounts all support the idea of a "second experience" (Acts 2:1-21; Acts 8:14-20; Acts 9:10-19; Acts 10:44-48; Acts 19:1-6). In the Acts 10:44-48 account the repentance and Spirit reception seem to happen simultaneously, but we later read that the "gift" was given *after* they believed (see Acts 11:17).

Perhaps, it would be appropriate to end this discussion with a story from the Scripture: "Now suppose one of you fathers is asked by his son for a fish; he will not give him a snake instead of a fish, will he? . . . If you then, being evil, know how to give good gifts to your children, how much more will your heavenly Father give the Holy Spirit to those who ask Him" (Luke 11:11-13). What is the point with respect to our discussion? It is a father who is giving "gifts" to one who is already his son. So, too, it is the "heavenly Father" who gives the gift of the Holy Spirit to those who are already his children. It seems, the "baptism of the Holy Spirit" is not the same as salvation, but is rather, a subsequent second experience.

NOVEMBER 17

CONFESS YOUR SINS TO ONE ANOTHER . . .

"Therefore, confess your sins to one another,
and pray for one another, so that you may be healed."

James 5:16

Christianity is a "one another" religion. The Christian life, because of the nature of its various mandates, requires a social context; it cannot be realized alone on a private island. And so, fellowship is a requirement, not an option. What keeps you from fellowship?

The fear of confession can steer us away from fellowship. Confession of sins one to another—"Therefore, confess your sins one to another, and pray for one another, so that you may be healed" (James 5:16)—is an essential part of fellowship. Dietrich Bonhoeffer, in his book *Life Together*, points out that "He who is alone with his sin is completely alone. In confession the breakthrough to community takes place."[5] This is certainly true in our relationship with God

(1 John 1:9). It is also true in our relationships with each other. Strong cords of fellowship are created in the midst of the confession of sins.

Why do we often have a fear of confession? A Christian may remain "alone with his sin" because of the anticipated or expressed self-righteous reaction of those in the church when sin is exposed. There can be a hypocritical and unhealthy attitude about sin in the church. Perhaps, when someone confesses their sins, others begin to not associate with that person. How ironic! In the New Testament church, the opposite was true. It was only when someone *refused to confess his sin* that others would not associate with him (Matthew 18:17). In the New Testament church, it was understood that the members of the church were sinners (1 John 1:8). It was understood that they needed to confess their sins (1 John 1:9). Moreover, it was understood that they needed to confess their sins to one another (James 5:16). The unhealthy attitude about sin in the church is often a result of a false sense of purity and righteousness. We are filthy. It is Jesus who is pure and righteous. All have sinned (Romans 3:23), and thus, all need to confess sins. This should be no great shock to us—our reaction to confession should not be one of self-righteous surprise, shock, and indignation—since we are all in the same sin boat! David Watson, in his book *Called and Committed*, concluded, "Genuine fellowship comes when Christians stop relating to one another as righteous saints, and accept one another as unrighteous sinners."[6]

Sometimes confession of sin one to another is hindered due to faulty theology. Some might say that confession of sin is a denial of faith. Ironically, a "positive *confession* theology" may not allow for *confession* of sins as it would be a "negative *confession*" and a denial of faith. What foolishness! To confess sin is not to deny faith because our faith is not in ourselves; rather, our faith is in Him who "is faithful and righteous to forgive us our sins and to cleanse us from all unrighteousness . . . if we confess our sins" (1 John 1:9)!

The community of confession must be a community that is willing to take risks. It must be a community that is open and transparent. It is a risk to be transparent. However, the alternative is to close the windows of our lives. We may all live on the same street, but no one ever comes out of their house and no one ever lets others in. We must not allow the fear of being misunderstood and wrongly judged to keep us from the fellowship of confession; "Therefore, confess your sins to one another, and pray for one another, so that you may be healed" (James 5:16).

———————

NOVEMBER 18

KINGDOM OF GOD TEACHING
RUNS COUNTER TO . . .

"BUT FALSE prophets also arose among the people, just as there will also be false teachers among you, who will secretly introduce destructive heresies . . . "

2 Peter 2:1

Biblical teaching about the kingdom of God runs counter to hyper-ecumenicalism. Unity simply for the sake of unity is false unity. Unity at the expense of truth is often the false unity that is championed in the hyper-ecumenical movement. Teaching on the kingdom of God, however, clearly defines two different "families" that have nothing in common (in unity) with each other. And so, the Scripture speaks of some as "sons of hell" (Matthew 23:15) and addresses them as being "of your father, the devil" (John 8:44). Then the Scripture tells believers (those who are sons of another Father) not to be in unity with them:

Do not be bound together with unbelievers; for what partnership have righteousness and lawlessness, or what fellowship has light with darkness? Or what harmony has Christ with Belial, or what has a believer in common with an unbeliever? Or what agreement has the temple of God with idols? For we are the temple of the living God; just as God said, 'I will dwell in them and walk among them; And I will be their God, and they shall be My people.' Therefore, 'come out from their midst and be separate,' says the Lord. 'And do not touch what is unclean; And I will welcome you. And I will be a father to you, And you shall be sons and daughters to Me,' Says the Lord Almighty (2 Corinthians 6:14-18).

We are not to fall into the trap of humanism. Humanists want to declare the brotherhood of man. This sounds nice. It almost sounds "Christian." However, it is not biblical. And so, Jesus speaks many times about the lack of unity that His kingdom brings (Matthew 10:34-36).

Biblical teaching about the kingdom of God runs counter to hyper-Arminianism (a fundamental misunderstanding about the scope of the free will of man). We do not go to the kingdom of God; rather, the kingdom of God comes to us (Matthew 6:10). We do not choose God; rather, God chooses us (John 15:16). We are not born of the free will of man; rather, we are born of God (John 1:13). Certainly, man has a free will as he has been created in the image of God (Genesis 1:27); however, he is not God and his free will is not divine. Man's free will must remain consistent with who man is/his nature, as a creation/receiver (not Creator/Source) his free will is that which accepts or rejects (receives or does not receive) what God creates or sources. And so, the hyper-Arminian misunderstanding of the scope of the free will of man must be rejected lest Christianity become indistinguishable from humanism.

Biblical teaching about the kingdom of God runs counter to those of hyper-ecumenicalism, hyper-Arminianism, and humanism! So beware of "false teachers among you" for their heresies are destructive.

NOVEMBER 19

DON'T *"DIS"* GOD!

" . . . 'if I am a father, where is My honor? And if I am a master, where is My respect?' says the
LORD of hosts to you, O priests who despise My name . . . You are presenting defiled food
upon My altar. But you say, 'How have we defiled You?' . . . 'But when you present the blind
for sacrifice, is it not evil? And when you present the lame and sick, is it not evil?
Why not offer it to your governor? Would he be pleased with you? Or would he receive you
kindly?' says the LORD of hosts."

Malachi 1:6-8

In the context of the importance of God's people being used as an example to the nations, God's people are anything but a good example. It is the "Lord of hosts" or Lord of the nations in Malachi 1:4-9 who is jealous for His reputation. He is jealous for "My name" (Malachi 1:6) so that His greatness would be made known "beyond the border of Israel" (Malachi 1:5). There is a problem with the offeror in Malachi 1:6 (" . . . where is my respect . . . O priests who despise My name"), a problem with the offering in Malachi 1:8 ("But when you present the blind for sacrifice, is it not evil?"), and an ominous result in Malachi 1:9 ("But now will you not entreat God's favor, that He may be gracious to us? With such an offering on your part, will He receive any of you kindly?" says the Lord of hosts.").

What is the problem with the offeror and the offering? The problem is that they are actually **"dis**ing" God. This type of offering was forbidden (Deuteronomy 15:21); thus, the priests were being **dis**obedient. They were also **dis**respecting God. The priests were bringing offerings to the altar of God that they would not dare bring to the civil ruler (Malachi 1:8). They showed respect to the governor and they knew that God was greater than the governor. Yet their actions toward God did not show that respect. And so, ultimately, the problem is in their faith. They can see the governor. They cannot see God. They begin to question the validity/usefulness of approaching Him (a lack of faith makes it easier to be a "men pleaser" instead of a "God pleaser").

The sacrificial system becomes a mere ritual, empty and hypocritical. An offering that is not presented in faith—it is by faith that "Abel offered to God a better sacrifice than Cain" (Hebrews 11:4)—is based on hypocrisy instead of the fear of God, and is not acceptable to God. In their offerings, the priests undervalued God. They despised Him. And so, they undervalued their own redemption and practiced hypocrisy because of their lack of faith.

God asks His faithless people rhetorical questions:

> 'But when you present the blind for sacrifice, is it not evil? And when you present the lame and sick, is it not evil? Why not offer it to your governor? Would he be pleased with you? Or would he receive you kindly?' says the LORD of hosts. 'But now will you not entreat God's favor, that He may be gracious to us? With such an offering on your part, will He receive any of you kindly?,' says the LORD of hosts (Malachi 1:8-9).

In order to see the governor, a person must bring a correct offering or gift to show his respect. It would secure entrance. In the Old Testament, the correct sacrificial offering secured entrance with respect to God. In the New Testament we could say that the correct offering is praise and worship. We enter His presence with praise (Psalm 100:4). We bring the sacrifice of praise (Hebrews 13:15). God, like the governor, will not hear our prayers and requests if we do not show Him proper and sincere worship. So be sure not to **dis** God . . . be obedient to Him and show Him respect!

NOVEMBER 20

WORSHIP PRINCIPLE #1 . . . FORM FOLLOWS SUBSTANCE!

"For you are like whitewashed tombs which on the outside appear beautiful, but inside they are full of dead men's bones and all uncleanness."

Matthew 23:27

Form must follow substance. Another way to say this, with respect to worship, is that forms or styles of worship must be an expression of, or response to, the nature or substance of God. That which is external must not exist apart from that which is internal. The opposite of this is religiosity or hypocrisy (empty forms; forms without substance). Jesus called out the hypocrites describing them as "whitewashed tombs which on the outside appear beautiful, but inside they are full of dead men's bones and all uncleanness" (Matthew 23:27). Form but no substance is mere appearance (hypocrisy).

Jesus is not against "forms" in worship; they are necessary. He is only against forms for the sake of forms, appearance for the sake of appearance, and external expression for the sake of external expression. And so Jesus admonishes the whitewashed tombs and says, "Woe to you, scribes and Pharisees, hypocrites! For you tithe mint and dill and cummin, and have neglected the weightier provisions of the law: justice and mercy and faithfulness; but these are the things you should have done without neglecting the others" (Matthew 23:23). The tithing of mint, dill, and cumin were forms of worship; they were biblical (true) forms (Deuteronomy 14:28). However, they were useless without the substance (the "weightier provisions of the law" or the more profound/internal meaning, purpose, and function of the law). It should be noted, in any case, that Jesus is not doing away with forms of worship (He says "these are the things you should have done without neglecting the others"). He is only pointing out the absurdity of forms for the sake of forms, or the absurdity of external expression for the sake of external expression . . . the absurdity of the mint and dill without the justice and mercy.

Jesus looks for those who will worship "in spirit and truth" (John 4:23) or in substance *and* forms (biblical or true forms that follow biblical or spiritual substance). Forms may change between cultures, but the substance remains; which is Christ and the gospel (John 4:22). Jesus corrected the Samaritan woman who sought to argue about the "correct" forms and locations for worship (John 4:20-24). He challenged her thinking by de-emphasizing cultural preferences (forms of worship) and emphasizing eternal realities (substance of worship). She would still worship with correct forms (worship "in truth"), but those forms (that truth) would correspond to and be rooted in actual substance (worship "in spirit").

Forms in worship are not only allowed, they are necessary. They are in no way insignificant. Forms (both individual and corporate expressions of, and responses to, the nature of God) are regulated by biblical truth, not human invention or misguided zeal. Nadab and Abihu "offered strange fire before the Lord, which He had not commanded them" and it turned out to be a fatal error (Leviticus 10:1-2). Forms are important in worship. More important, however, is that form follows substance. We certainly do not want to offer "strange fire"! More important is that if we do offer any fire at all, it is an expression of, or response to, the nature of God. And so, we might "dance before the Lord" (a form of worship), but only if it is an expression of, or response to the majesty of the Lord (substance of worship). If we are dancing before the Lord void of an expression of, or response to Him, then we might look like we are worshiping but we might just be offering really strange fire. Worship principle #1 . . . form follows function!

NOVEMBER 21

SO, WHAT'S THE MATTER?
FORGIVENESS MATTERS!

". . . for this is My blood of the covenant, which is poured out for many for forgiveness of sins."

Matthew 26:28

What matters? Forgiveness matters! The central issue associated with the new covenant is forgiveness. Above all else, the new covenant is a covenant of forgiveness (Matthew 26:28). The new covenant presents Jesus as the Lamb of God who takes away the sins of the world, as opposed to the lamb of sacrifice in the old covenant that took away the sins of Israel. Jesus is the final and complete solution to sin. He is the source of forgiveness (John 1:29). He has authority to forgive sins (Matthew 9:6). Jesus' "body," the church, then has authority to declare the forgiveness of sins. Christ, the source of forgiveness, declares forgiveness through His body (John 20:23).

How do we receive this forgiveness? Forgiveness is received through faith (Luke 5:20) and repentance. There is no actual forgiveness without repentance. There is only potential forgiveness (Luke 17:3). Being justified and forgiven is associated with humility and brokenness before God. It is associated with your trusting only in God and refusing to trust in yourself. Humility is essential in receiving forgiveness (Luke 18:10-14). Without it, you will struggle to receive forgiveness from God and, then, you will not be able to forgive others (Matthew 18:26-28) for those who do not receive forgiveness are not, then, equipped to forgive others. Herein lies a problem in the process of receiving forgiveness because you must forgive others in order to be forgiven by God (Matthew 6:14-15). And so, a willingness to forgive others is critical. Success in prayer is related to forgiving others (Mark 11:25). Forgiveness for others should not have a limit. God does not put a limit on how often He forgives us (Matthew 18:21-27).

Through forgiveness, all people have the opportunity to have their sins taken away (John 1:29). Forgiveness of sins comes by faith in Him (Luke 5:20). Salvation comes by faith in Him (Luke 7:50). We can say salvation equals the forgiveness of sins. To be saved is to be forgiven. The result of forgiveness is salvation. When we receive forgiveness ,we can then be strong, bold, and courageous. Without forgiveness we are weak, timid, and scared (Matthew 9:2). Moreover, your love for God will depend on your perception of how much you have been forgiven (your perception of the degree to which you need forgiveness). A result of forgiveness is a love for God (Luke 7:40-47). These are things that matter . . . love for God, boldness, salvation. What matters? Forgiveness matters!

NOVEMBER 22

DEVELOPING A LIFE OF PRAISE . . .

"Because thy lovingkindness is better than life, my lips will praise thee."

Psalm 63:3, KJV

We approach God and "come before His presence" with an attitude of praise (Psalm 95:1-6). God is "enthroned upon the praises" of His people (Psalm 22:3). Praise is a response to the greatness of God—it boasts of God (Psalm 106:47)—and, serves as an expression of gratefulness (Psalm 63:3). Expressions of praise are the natural response to the reality of who God is and what God does, and nature praises God (Isaiah 55:12; Psalm 148). If we do not praise God, then "the stones will cry out" (Luke 19:39-40). We do praise God as God says, "The people whom I formed for Myself, will declare My praise" (Isaiah 43:21). So, "Let everything that has breath praise the Lord. Praise the Lord!" (Psalm 150:6). Let us develop a life of praise.

We develop a life of praise as we engage in a variety of actions. First, we develop a life of praise through our actions of thanksgiving or verbal appreciation. God's Word commands us "in everything give thanks; for this is God's will for you in Christ Jesus" (1 Thessalonians 5:18), and God proclaims "he who offers a sacrifice of thanksgiving honors Me" (Psalm 50:23). Don't be a "murmurer" or a complainer. Hone a lifestyle of thanksgiving and develop a habit of being thankful. Be a "praiser"!

Second, we develop a life of praise through vocalizing adoration and recognition of God. We declare with the Psalmist, "because Thy lovingkindness is better than life, my lips will praise Thee" (Psalm 63:3). As we testify to God's great acts, we engage in a life of praise:

> I WILL extol You, my God, O King, And I will bless Your name forever and ever. Every day I will bless You, and I will praise Your name forever and ever. Great is the LORD, and highly to be praised, and His greatness is unsearchable. One generation shall praise Your works to another, and shall declare Your mighty acts. On the glorious splendor of Your majesty and on Your wonderful works, I will meditate. Men shall speak of the power of Your awesome acts, and I will tell of Your greatness. They shall eagerly utter the memory of Your abundant goodness and will shout joyfully of Your righteousness (Psalm 145:1-7).

Third, we develop a life of praise through singing to God. The Psalmist encourages us to "Sing to Him, sing praises to Him; speak of all His wonders" (Psalm 105:2), and to "Shout joyfully to the Lord . . . come before Him with joyful singing . . . enter His courts with praise" (Psalm 100:1-4). This life of praise is a joyous and celebratory life—no need to "get drunk with wine . . . but be filled with the Spirit" (Ephesians 5:18)—as we engage in "speaking to one another in psalms and hymns and spiritual songs, singing and making melody with your heart to the Lord" (Ephesians 5:19).

Finally, we develop a life of praise through practicing the presence of God. Praise brings us to where God is—He who "inhabitest the praises of Israel" (Psalm 22:3, KJV)—and where God is calls us to an attitude of praise as the Psalmist proclaims, "One thing I have asked from the Lord, that I shall seek: that I may dwell in the house of the Lord all the days of my life, to behold the beauty of the Lord, and to meditate in His temple" (Psalm 27:4). We "come into His presence with thanksgiving . . . with songs of praise" (Psalm 95:2, ESV). And so, "when they praised the Lord . . . then the house . . . was filled with a cloud, so that the priests could not stand to minister because of the cloud, for the glory of the Lord filled the house of God" (2 Chronicles 5:13-14). So, let us praise Him. Let us develop a life of praise!

NOVEMBER 23

ADMISSION TO THE MAGIC KINGDOM . . .

"Then the King will say to those on His right, 'Come, you who are blessed of My Father, inherit the kingdom prepared for you from the foundation of the world.'"

Matthew 25:34

The kingdom of God is inherited by those it has been prepared for "from the foundation of the world" (Matthew 25:34). It is available regardless of "where you are or when you started" as even "the last shall be first, and the first last" (Matthew 20:1-16). This is because it is not so much that "we go to" the kingdom of God as it is that the kingdom of God comes to us . . . "Thy kingdom come" (Matthew 6:10).

So where is the admission counter for this magic kingdom . . . the kingdom of God? How do you get a ticket to enter? First, in order to "see the kingdom of God" you must be born again of the Spirit (John 3:3, 6). It is not enough to hear the word of the kingdom of God in order to enter it; that word must be understood (Matthew 13:19). It must be sown on "good soil" in which the word is heard, understood, accepted, and bears fruit (Matthew 13:23; Mark 4:20). It is a soil of confession (I need . . .) and repentance (I turn to . . .); that which understands and accepts, and thus, abides in and bears fruit (John 15:1-5). Of course, in order to enter you need the keys. The "keys of the kingdom" that are associated with "binding and loosing" (Matthew 16:19) are confession and repentance. The context of Matthew 16:19 is Peter's confession of Christ (I need), and the context of binding and loosing in Matthew 18:18 is confession (I need) and repentance (I turn to). It is the keys of confession and repentance that unlock the kingdom of God door! And so, "tax gatherers and harlots" enter the kingdom of God before the Pharisees because they were convicted of sin and the Pharisees were not (Matthew 21:28-32). They used the keys (confession and repentance) to enter while the Pharisees tried to break down the door (with their "good works").

Not everyone enters the kingdom of God. Not everyone who speaks about God will enter (Matthew 7:21). It is difficult for rich people to enter (Matthew 19:24). In general, those who are not convicted of sin and who do not repent will not enter the kingdom of God (Matthew 21:28-32). Those who are not prepared and ready for its arrival will not enter the kingdom of God (Matthew 25:1-13). Those who do not use the blessings that God has given to them to bless others and reproduce those blessings will not enter the kingdom of God (Matthew 25:14-30). Moreover, hypocritical leaders keep their followers from entering the kingdom of God along with themselves (Matthew 23:13).

And so, it's really not magic! It is the kingdom of God . . . and admission to that kingdom is sourced by God and received by man. Do you have your ticket?

NOVEMBER 24

THE HEADSHIP OF THE HUSBAND . . . LOVE YOUR WIFE!

"Husbands, love your wives, just as Christ also loved the church and gave Himself up for her."

Ephesians 5:25

The husband is the "head of the wife" (Ephesians 5:23). His divinely ordained role is one that focuses on leadership and initiative. This leadership is not to be forced upon the wife. Instead, it is to be established by love. The Scripture declares "wives, be subject to your husbands . . . husbands, love your wives, and do not be embittered against them" (Colossians 3:18-19). The husband who is embittered against his wife may try to force his leadership on her. He might become impatient with her lack of response to him and try to force her into submission. A leadership that tries to force itself upon someone is not true biblical leadership (Matthew 20:25-28). An "embittered" leader is characterized by a leader who is irritated with the one he is leading and, in turn, focuses on the faults of that person. The husband who loves his wife, on the other hand, is patient and does not criticize her (1 Corinthians 13:4-7). The key action of headship is love and the key attitude of headship is patience and understanding.

The key action of headship is love. "Love your wives" (Ephesians 5:25) is for husbands what "be subject to your own husbands" (Ephesians 5:22) is for wives. Christ and His love for the church is the husband's model. It is *unconditional* love. It is a love without limits. This love must be motivated by a profound understanding of the great worth of the wife—as opposed to a common problem exhibited by husbands who "take their wives for granted" which is nothing less than devaluing the wife—since wives need to feel valued (as opposed to husbands, who need more to feel needed or desired)! This is consistent with Christ's understanding of the great worth of the church. It leads to a willingness to give oneself up for the other (Ephesians 5:25). This love must be a sacrificial love. It must go to the cross. This love must be a compassionate love. It must be willing to suffer with the wife to understand her and be sensitive to her. It must motivate the husband to "walk in her shoes" (an idiomatic expression that effectively expresses the idea of "compassion" which means "to suffer with"). It must enable husbands "to love their own wives as their own bodies" (Ephesians 5:28). This love a husband must have for his wife—if he truly is going to be "the head" of his wife—is nothing less than a divine "agape" love. It is most clearly pictured in the phrase, he "gave himself up for her" (Ephesians 5:25). Christ acquired the church by giving of Himself. Adam acquired Eve by giving of himself (his rib). A husband receives a wife by giving himself up for her. A man does not so much "take a wife" for himself as he gives himself for a wife.

The key attitude of headship is patience and understanding. A husband must live with his wife "in an understanding way" (1 Peter 3:7). He must understand that she is "a fellow heir" and therefore equal to him in terms of identity in Christ. He must also understand that she is "a weaker vessel" and therefore submitted to him in relational order. The husband must respond to the wife in an understanding way; he must take the initiative and lead her knowing that it is not natural for her to be leading him. The result of this kind of "understanding" on the part of the husband is "so that your prayers may not be hindered" (1 Peter 3:7). Your (plural) prayers are descriptive of the husband and wife praying together. A husband who does not understand the role of his wife (to submit to or follow him) and who does not accept his divinely ordained position of headship (to lead her) will not take the initiative to lead his wife in prayer. To a large degree, husbands and wives do not pray together because the husband lacks (or simply rejects) an understanding of marriage roles (this is especially sobering when one is aware of the statistic that fifty percent of all marriages end in divorce, but only one percent of marriages end in divorce that include husbands and wives who pray together!).

And so, the key action of headship is love and the key attitude of headship is patience and understanding. Husband . . . you are the head. So love your wife in patience and understanding!

NOVEMBER 25

WHAT IS GOD'S POWER FOR?

"To this end also we pray for you always, that our God will count you worthy of your calling, and fulfill every desire for goodness and the work of faith with power, so that the name of our Lord Jesus will be glorified in you . . ."

2 Thessalonians 1:11-12

What is God's power for? Why is God's power manifested in this fallen world? The power of God always serves as a sign that points to Jesus. This is true because God's power is associated with the Holy Spirit and the Holy Spirit always points to Jesus (John 16:14). And so, Paul prays for the Thessalonians that "God will count you worthy of your calling, and fulfill every desire for goodness and the work of faith with **POWER**." Why? What is God's power for? It is "so that the name of our Lord Jesus will be glorified" (2 Thessalonians 1:11-12).

This power for the purpose of glorifying Jesus is seen in the Scripture as it is used in a variety of contexts. Most generally, it is linked to blessings for all of mankind. God's power is linked to general revelation of God to man (Romans 1:20). So too, it is God's power that maintains, supports, and moves the world (Hebrews 1:3). God's power is used for practical blessings for the believer to have steadfastness, patience and joy (Colossians 1:11), to be protected (1 Peter 1:5), and to have hope (Romans 15:13).

In the believer, the power of God is often depicted as being manifested for the work of spreading the gospel. There is power for preaching (Acts 4:33), to turn people from their sins (Luke 1:17), and to turn people to God (Romans 1:15-16). It is the power of God that is directly linked to the spread of the gospel "throughout the whole earth" (Romans 9:17), "from Jerusalem and round about as far as Illyricum" (Romans 15:19), "in Jerusalem, and in all Judea and Samaria, and even to the remotest part of the earth" (Acts 1:8). The power of God is manifested to verify the identity of Jesus (Acts 2:22) and to confirm His gospel (Mark 16:20).

The power of God is used to build the church and its ministry. It is used to mature the members of the church (Colossians 1:28-29). It is used to do the ministry of the church in very practical ways. It is used to enact church discipline (1 Corinthians 5:4) and to prompt giving (2 Corinthians 8:3). It is used to do the ministry of the church in very mystical ways. It is used to do miracles (Luke 19:37; Acts 6:8; 1 Corinthians 12:10) and to cast out demons (Luke 4:36; Luke 10:19; Luke 9:1; Acts 19:11-12). Ultimately, God's power is associated with the end of the church age. Jesus will return with power (Matthew 24:29-30) for judgment (2 Thessalonians 1:7-8) to "raise us up through His power" (1 Corinthians 6:14) and "to reign" (Revelation 11:17).

So, what is God's power for? It is ultimately for the glory of Jesus as it is used for all of the above purposes and much more "seeing that His divine power has granted to us everything pertaining to life and godliness, through the true knowledge of Him who called us by His own glory" (2 Peter 1:3). What is God's power for? It is "so that the name of our Lord Jesus will be glorified" (2 Thessalonians 1:11-12). Amen.

NOVEMBER 26

PRAYER SUGGESTIONS . . .

"Keep watching and praying . . ."

Matthew 26:41

Jesus encourages us to "keep watching and praying" (Matthew 26:41). Prayer is a key part of the Christian life. The main suggestion regarding prayer is simply . . . keep praying (prayer is best learned by doing it). Nevertheless, it may be helpful to consider some suggestions regarding prayer.

One such suggestion is to remain unpretentious enough to pray as a child. Pray with the trust and dependence of a child. Another suggestion is to avoid selfish prayers (James 4:3). At the same time, make big requests of a big God (He can handle everything) while also making little requests of a personal God (He is interested in the details of your life).

Pray in the name of Jesus. To pray in the name of Jesus, you must pray according to the will of God. First pray to know the will of God. Then, make your request in the name of Jesus (1 John 5:14-15). Pray with faith and confidence. Trust God! (John 14:13-14; John 16:23; Matthew 18:19-20).

Confess all sins as soon as possible (Psalm 66:18). It is very important to remain in Christ and to obey Him (John 15:7; 1 John 3:22). It is helpful to plan for a specific time each day to pray (Mark 1:35; Daniel 6:10; Luke 5:16). You need to develop an attitude of prayer. You must live a general "lifestyle of prayer" that seeks to be in communion with God constantly (Proverbs 3:6; 1 Thessalonians 5:17; Ephesians 6:18). At the same time, prayer should be specific. The more specific the prayer, the more specific the answer.

Remember that there is a cost to prayer. Many times, the greater the cost, the greater the reward (Luke 21:1-4). There is, perhaps, a greater cost connected to early morning prayer, all night prayer, and prayer and fasting. It may be, also, that the results are greater.

Be intimate with God. Talk to Him in a personal way. Be natural before God. Be honest and transparent (He knows everything anyway!). Do not pray repetitive, rote, religious prayers. Try to avoid empty rituals. Be sure to take time to listen to God. Establish a minimum daily time to pray. Do not feel condemned when you lack the desire to pray. Pray anyway. The desire will follow.

Of course, the main suggestion regarding prayer is simply . . . keep praying (Matthew 26:41).

NOVEMBER 27

TRIBALISM . . . THE DEATH OF FELLOWSHIP!

" . . . that you all agree, and there be no divisions among you . . . there are quarrels among you .
. . each one of you is saying, 'I am of Paul,' and 'I of Apollos,' and 'I of Cephas,' and 'I of Christ.'
Has Christ been divided?"

1 Corinthians 1:10-13

Tribalism is the death of Christian fellowship. God calls His people (His family, His "tribe") whose "citizenship is in heaven" (Philippians 3:20) to be in unity with each other (1 Corinthians 1:10) and to not neglect fellowship with each other (Hebrews 10:25). The spirit of tribalism is the disease that fights against that calling. Paul addresses the Corinthian church regarding this cancer as he instructs them "that you all agree, and there be no divisions among you" and points out "that there are quarrels among you . . . each one of you is saying, 'I am of Paul,' and 'I of Apollos,' and 'I of Cephas'" while concluding with the rhetorical admonition, "Has Christ been divided?" Tribalism—that which divides based on systems of self-identification ("I am of the tribe of Apollos" or "I am of the Hutu tribe" or "I am of the Crips or Bloods gang")—and Christian fellowship do not mix well together. They are fundamentally juxtaposed to each other since, as Paul warned, tribalism divides Christ, and Christ must not be divided!

In East Africa there are many different tribes. There are the Batusi and the Bahutu. The Batusi are taller than the Bahutu. They are physically superior and have looked down on the Bahutu for generations. They have, to some extent, controlled the Bahutu. The Bahutu have a historic hatred for the Batusi. Loyalty to their own tribe increases the hatred toward the other tribe. They are separated by their perceptions of each other and by the loyalty/hatred dynamics. This is called tribalism. In India, it is called the caste system. In the United States, it is called racism. In high schools, it is called "cliques." In inner cities, it is called gangs. And in the church, it is called denominationalism! Whatever the name might be, the prejudice or discrimination that is inherent in tribalism comes from the same mixture of sin. It comes from selfishness and pride that are rooted in insecurity. Wherever you find this sin there is the same result, division and disunity. To say the least, the spirit of tribalism can destroy the opportunity in the church for real fellowship.

The concepts of Christian fellowship and tribalism cannot exist together. Tribalism is a very strong force in sub-Saharan Africa. It provides the various and diverse groups of people with a form of cultural identity and pride. However, it negatively affects the church and slows the progress of the gospel. When tribalism is practiced within the churches, it destroys the unity that Jesus desires (John 17:20-21). In the broader context of sub-Saharan African culture, tribalism creates significant societal problems. Many African leaders feel that there is no solution to the problem of tribalism. Christianity can provide that solution. The divisions of tribalism can be replaced by the unity of the cross (1 Corinthians 10:16-17) and the fellowship that is found in the church. The unity of the cross can effectively be applied to the other forms of prejudice and discrimination that are practiced around the world. Christianity and the true fellowship of the church represent a global solution to these problems.

Tribalism is the death of Christian fellowship. The good news is that Christian fellowship can be the end of tribalism! And so, "After these things I looked, and behold, a great multitude which no one could count, from every nation and all tribes and peoples and tongues, standing before the throne and before the Lamb, clothed in white robes, and palm branches were in their hands; and they cry out with a loud voice, saying, 'Salvation to our God who sits on the throne, and to the Lamb'" (Revelation 7:9-10).

NOVEMBER 28

LOVE AND HUMILITY ON THE WAY TO DISCIPLINE . . .

"Those whom I love, I reprove and discipline."

Revelation 3:19

Discipline is necessary for people who are prone to sin. Discipline is necessary for all of us whether it is self-discipline (with a "goal setting device" to set, measure, and achieve desired standards), parental discipline (with the "rod" to define sin and train a child in the way he/she should go), or church discipline (with the "staff" to guide away from the wrong way and nudge toward the right way). Ultimately, we know it is God who disciplines—even if He uses His vessel to enact it—as He definitively states, "Those whom I love, I reprove and discipline" (Revelation

3:19). Of course, it is understood that discipline is not a "joyful" thing. Most of us do not like it but we come to appreciate it:

> Furthermore, we had earthly fathers to discipline us, and we respected them; shall we not much rather be subject to the Father of spirits, and live? For they disciplined us for a short time as seemed best to them, but He *disciplines us* for *our* good, so that we may share His holiness. All discipline for the moment seems not to be joyful, but sorrowful; yet to those who have been trained by it, afterwards it yields the peaceful fruit of righteousness (Hebrews 12:9-11).

Perhaps you might notice a repeated theme in the previous passages, that the motive of godly discipline is love (Revelation 3:19), and the purpose of godly discipline is "for our good" (Hebrews 12:10). Church discipline must be done to benefit the individual. Motivation for discipline must be based on a desire to help the individual who is being disciplined since the discipline of the church is the discipline of the Lord of the church. This discipline must be done with the right motives. Those motives, most importantly, are love and humility.

Love is the first motive for any kind of godly discipline whether that discipline comes directly from God, "MY SON, DO NOT REGARD LIGHTLY THE DISCIPLINE OF THE LORD, NOR FAINT WHEN YOU ARE REPROVED BY HIM; FOR THOSE WHOM THE LORD LOVES HE DISCIPLINES, AND HE SCOURGES EVERY SON WHOM HE RECEIVES" (Hebrews 12:5-6) or indirectly through a vessel of God (like Paul), "For out of much affliction and anguish of heart I wrote to you with many tears; not so that you would be made sorrowful, but that you might know the love which I have especially for you" (2 Corinthians 2:4). Here we must be careful of false love. Tolerance is often a result of laziness and a lack of real concern and love. It is often a liberal, humanistic type of "love" that congratulates itself for not "judging" people but does not have enough concern for people to actually help them ("I'm okay and you're okay"; "you leave me alone and I'll leave you alone"). This was probably what Paul was referring to in 1 Corinthians 5:2-6. The Corinthians were probably proud ("arrogant" and "boasting") of their tolerance, but they did nothing to help the offender ("have not mourned"). However, tolerance of sin is not love (Habakkuk 1:13). We must accept and love the sinner, but we cannot accept and love the sin. The father who does not discipline his son, hates his son (Proverbs 13:24).

Humility is the second motive for godly discipline. The act of taking "the log out of your own eye" before taking "the speck out of your brother's eye" is rooted in humility (Matthew 7:3-5). Correction done with humility is correction done "with gentleness" (2 Timothy 2:25-26; Galatians 6:1). This humility and gentleness is practiced by Paul as he corrects others (2 Thessalonians 3:6-15). Restoration of the individual is the motivation and the method of church discipline. Even "shame" (verse 14 includes the idea of "seeing yourself"/"self-reflection") may be necessary in moving toward restoration as it may point one to repentance. When there is repentance there is forgiveness. Discipline is done in order to reform the individual. It is never done to punish or to take revenge on an individual. It is done in love and humility.

NOVEMBER 29

RIGHT METHODS . . . RIGHT RESULTS!

"For this reason also, God highly exalted Him, and bestowed on Him the name which is above every name . . . "

Philippians 2:9

Christian conduct requires Christian attitude. So, when Paul exhorts the Philippians to "conduct yourselves in a manner worthy of the gospel of Christ" (Philippians 1:27), he also charges them to "have this attitude in yourselves which was also in Christ Jesus" (Philippians 2:5). If you are going to engage in proper conduct, you are going to have to embody a proper attitude. The perfect example of the attitude we are to have as Christians is nothing less than Christ's attitude by which He "emptied Himself . . . humbled Himself by becoming obedient to the point of death, even death on a cross" (Philippians 2:7-8). Attitudes or methods yield results. Right methods yield right results.

What is the result of having "this attitude"? Christ had "this attitude" so "therefore also God highly exalted Him, and bestowed on Him the name which is above every name" (Philippians 2:9). What is the result? Exaltation! The "whoever humbles himself shall be exalted" principle (Matthew 23:12) is seen in Philippians 2:5-9 in its ultimate form. The ultimate humbling (God becoming man) results in the ultimate exaltation, "that at the name of Jesus every knee should bow, of those who are in heaven, and on earth, and under the earth, and that every tongue should confess that Jesus Christ is Lord, to the glory of God the Father" (Philippians 2:10-11).

We could refer to what might be called a "balanced gospel." The result of having "this attitude" is exaltation. The method is humility. The purpose is to glorify God. These must be kept separate. They are together in the sense that different aspects of the same event are together. Nevertheless, they must not be mixed up. If humility becomes the purpose, then we are in danger of false humility. If glorifying God becomes the method, then we are in danger of self-righteousness and salvation by works. If exaltation becomes the method, then we are in danger of superficial Christianity. If humility becomes the result, then we are in danger of a legalistic sort of Buddhist mortification Christianity. Balance in Christian doctrine and practice, to a large degree, depends on our ability to discern and apply to our lives the differences between methods, results, and purposes. The cross is the method of the gospel, it is not the result (Friday comes before Sunday). The resurrection is the result of the gospel, it is not the method. The resurrection cannot be the method lest we engage in humanistic Christianity and the cross cannot be the result lest we engage in lifeless Christianity.

The final application of this ("so then . . . ") is "just as you have always obeyed . . . work out your salvation with fear and trembling; for it is God who is at work in you, both to will and to work for His good pleasure" (Philippians 2:12-13). The method is to obey, working out your salvation with fear and trembling; to die to self so as to allow Christ to live in you (Galatians 2:20). The result is God's works (desires and actions) being worked in you; to experience resurrection or life (John 14:6; John 10:10). The purpose is "for His good pleasure"; to glorify God (1 Peter 4:11).

And so, we see that methods yield results and right methods yield right results. Are you engaging in the right method? Do you experience the right results? Jesus said it most succinctly this way: "The hour has come for the Son of Man to be glorified. Truly, truly, I say to you, unless a grain of wheat falls into the earth and dies, it remains alone; but if it dies, it bears much fruit. He who loves his life loses it, and he who hates his life in this world will keep it to life eternal" (John 12:23-25). Right methods, right results!

NOVEMBER 30

WHY DO YOU PREACH CHRIST? WHAT ARE YOUR MOTIVES?

"Some, to be sure, are preaching Christ even from envy and strife, but
some also from good will; the latter do it out of love . . . the former proclaim
Christ out of selfish ambition . . . What then? Only that in every way, whether
in pretense or in truth, Christ is proclaimed; and in this I rejoice.
Yes, and I will rejoice."

Philippians 1:15-18

Paul writes to the Philippians from prison. Yet, one of the main themes of his letter is joy and rejoicing. He rejoices over the fact that his imprisonment is resulting in "the greater progress of the gospel" (Philippians 1:12). Say what? How does Paul's imprisonment result in a greater progress of the gospel? First, there is progress ("so that . . . ") because others become aware of Paul's cause (Philippians 1:13). There is a pioneer work done amongst the Roman soldiers/guards who otherwise would have been very difficult to reach. They are now aware of Jesus Christ and the gospel. Second, there is progress ("and that . . . ") because the actuality of Paul's imprisonment provides the Roman Christians with a challenging example to speak the Word of God with boldness even in difficult circumstances (Philippians 1:14). The message is spreading as they are speaking the Word of God, as they "are preaching Christ" (Philippians 1:15).

Why are the Roman Christians preaching Christ? What are their motives? Some are preaching Christ "from envy and strife" and others "from good will" (Philippians 1:15). The latter are motivated by love and respect for Paul knowing that he is "appointed for the defense of the gospel" (Philippians 1:16). The former preach Christ with ulterior motives and self-interest (Philippians 1:17). Most probably "Judaizers," who see themselves in theological competition with Paul, they are trying to bother him (to "get under his skin"). Paul's imprisonment motivates them in the sense that it is a perceived opportunity. With Paul in prison, they can more easily preach the gospel with an emphasis on the requirements of the law (which was their "theological baby"). They are more interested in preserving their understanding of Judaism than they are interested in the gospel. They are using ("selfish ambition") the gospel to benefit themselves. They have a hidden agenda; they preach Christ "in pretense" (Philippians 1:18).

How does Paul feel about these self-proclaimed competitors of his who seek to bother him and feign ministry wrapped in a cloak of selfish ambition? Paul asks that question himself, "What then?" (Philippians 1:18). Well, what then? Discredit them? Threaten them? Mock them? Kill them? No! Instead, what does Paul do? He rejoices! He rejoices for one simple reason; Christ is being preached. Paul lived for this (Philippians 1:21). It was his true motive and goal. And so, he was able rejoice even if those who accomplish this goal are against *him*. His motives in ministry are pure. He is not in it for his own benefits; He is in it for Christ's benefits. His motives are rooted in his desire for Christ. We might say that, for Paul, the message is more than the medium!

What are your ministerial motives? Why do you preach Christ? Is it for you? Is it so that your church or denomination will grow or so that your ministry will be viewed positively by others? Or is it purely for Jesus? Do you *use* Christ for your own purposes? Or do you let Jesus use you for His own purposes? What motivates you to minister? Competition? Or the love of Christ and the desire to see His kingdom grow? How do you feel about the success in ministry of those who are not necessarily united with you? Do you secretly wish that their ministry would be destroyed? Or can you look beyond that and rejoice in the advance of the gospel? Can you rejoice even when the gospel advances in a way that is against you? What is your motive? Is it that Christ would go forth? Or is it that Christ would go forth only if it benefits you and your ministry? Why do you preach Christ? What are your motives?

NOTES

December

GOOD WORKS ARE GOD WORKS
WHICH IS TO KNOW GOD

"They said therefore to Him, 'What shall we do, that we may work the works of God?' Jesus answered and said to them, 'This is the work of God, that you believe in Him whom he has sent.'"

John 6:28-29

Because God has chosen to work through his vessels (vessel theology), good works are connected to knowing God (Jeremiah 22:16; Titus 1:16). Relationship with God that does not result in good works is no relationship at all (James 2:20). The most foundational good work that we can do is to spend time with God. To "believe/have faith" is to "come to God" and to "seek Him" (Hebrews 11:6). To believe is to be in relationship with God, and to believe is to do the work of God. So, you want to do good works? Then, walk with God . . . spend time with God . . . know God! And so, "They said therefore to Him, 'What shall we do, that we may work the works of God?' Jesus answered and said to them, 'This is the work of God, that you believe in Him whom He has sent'" (John 6:28-29). Our time spent with God (relationship with God) should be intimate and personal. It cannot be superficial and institutional. We might consider three features of our relationship with God or our time spent with God: it is private, it is public, and it is pervasive.

Our time spent with God should be *private*. Jesus had a private/intimate relationship with the Father (Luke 5:16; Mark 1:35; Matthew 14:23; Luke 4:42). God's desire for us to be alone with Him can even be understood in terms of secrecy (see Matthew 6:1-6). Best friends are often defined as those selected few who share your most treasured secrets. It is humbling to think that is what God wants from us, that He wants to be our best friend.

Our time spent with God should also be *public*. We must avoid making the same mistake that Peter made (Matthew 26:69-75). An intimate relationship with God must have a public aspect. And so, Jesus says "Everyone therefore who shall confess Me before men, I will also confess him before My Father who is in heaven. But whoever shall deny Me before men, I will also deny him before My Father who is in heaven" (Matthew 10:32-33). In our public proclamation of Him, we become more committed and devoted to Him, and we grow in relationship with Him. The better that you know Him, the better you will make Him known. The better you make Him known, the better you will know Him.

Our time spent with God should be *pervasive*. First, it must be pervasive in quantity. We are told to pray at **all** times (1 Thessalonians 5:17; Ephesians 6:18) and to acknowledge God in **all** of our ways (Proverbs 3:6). Consistency in recognition of God should be a top priority for the person on the road or path to knowing God (Deuteronomy 6:4-9). Second, our time spent with God should be pervasive in quality and variety. We might identify four distinct elements or activities in knowing God as Bible study, fellowship, praise and thanksgiving (the meaning of "breaking of bread" or "eucharist" is "to give thanks"), and prayer: "And they were continually devoting themselves to the apostles' teaching and to fellowship, to the breaking of bread and to prayer" (Acts 2:42). We are challenged to seek God in a variety of ways.

Good works are God works which is to know God. What shall I do that I may work the works of God? Seek Him. Spend time with Him. Know Him!

DECEMBER 2

ABRAHAM . . . A GREAT PEACEMAKER!

"So Abram said to Lot, 'Please let there be no strife between you and me, nor between my herdsmen and your herdsmen, for we are brothers. Is not the whole land before you? Please separate from me; if to the left, then I will go to the right; or if to the right, then I will go to the left.'"

Genesis 13:8-9

There are many ways to express faith in God. Abraham, also known as Abram, was a mighty man of faith. In a very practical use of faith, Abraham avoids disunity with his nephew, Lot. Both Abraham and Lot were quite wealthy in livestock, flocks, and herds. However, that soon posed a problem since there was starting to be a lack of space in the land: "And the land could not sustain them while dwelling together, for their possessions were so great that they were not able to remain together" (Genesis 13:6). It was the classic case of "this just ain't big enough for the two of us." Moreover, the people associated with Abraham and Lot were beginning to have conflict with each other: "And there was strife between the herdsmen of Abram's livestock and the herdsmen of Lot's livestock" (Genesis 13:7). It was like two gangs ready to brawl over the same turf.

What was going to happen? Was there a solution? Yes, as long as at least one of the "gang leaders" was willing to humble himself and exhibit selflessness. Leaders can avoid conflict even though their followers do not want to avert it. We see a clear indication that Abraham was going to humble himself when he referred to Lot as his "brother" (Genesis 13:8). Actually, Abraham was Lot's uncle—which in that culture would be equivalent to being his father—and it would have been expected that Lot would defer to Abraham. Instead, we see Abraham humble himself by being willing to lower his status and give that status to Lot (instead of demanding the honor and respect due him, he put Lot on the same level). Abraham conceded and let Lot have first choice: "Is not the whole land before you? Please separate from me; if to the left, then I will go to the right; or if to the right, then I will go to the left" (Genesis 13:9). The great irony was that with his choice of land, Lot received Sodom and Gomorrah (which Lot would have to be rescued from later by Abraham), and Abraham obtained Canaan, the Promised Land.

Abraham humbled himself and selflessly gave up his culturally-given first choice. The result was that Abraham received first choice. He was given the Promised Land! The one who humbled himself ended up getting the choice land: "Whoever exalts himself shall be humbled; and whoever humbles himself shall be exalted" (Matthew 23:12). Abraham's motive for humbling himself was to avoid conflict and retain unity. He practiced "peacemaking." And the Scripture tells us that "Blessed are the peacemakers, for they shall be called sons of God" (Matthew 5:9).

It is not easy for us to walk as peacemakers. It is not our tendency to humble ourselves, and it is certainly not our tendency to lay down our perceived "rights" and apply selflessness to situations. Abraham actually received the Promised Land via his selflessness, but this was not an easy act. It took quite a bit of faith, faith that can see the unseen. Next time you have an opportunity to die to self in order to preserve peace and maintain unity, ask God for the humility needed to be a **peacemaker**.

DECEMBER 3

THE METHOD OF GOD'S SALVATION PLAN IS THE CROSS!

"Men of Israel, listen to these words: Jesus the Nazarene, a man attested to you by God with miracles and wonders and signs which God performed through Him in your midst, just as you yourselves know—this Man, *delivered over by the predetermined plan and foreknowledge of God, you nailed to a cross by the hands of godless men and put* Him *to death. But God raised Him up again, putting an end to the agony of death . . . "*

Acts 2:22-24

The heart of the gospel message is found at the cross of Christ. The cross is God's chosen ("predetermined") method of His salvation "plan" (Acts 2:23). The method of the gospel is the cross . . . that method is death!

Jesus died in perfection; He had no sin. He died as a sacrifice (1 John 1:9; Hebrews 9:26) because He is the sacrifice (Hebrews 7:27). He is the high priest *and* the sacrifice, and so, He enters the Holy Place on our behalf with His own blood (Hebrews 9:12). His is a sacrifice without defect (1 Peter 1:19). And so, the sacrifice is final and complete (Romans 6:10; John 19:30).

Jesus had no sin. He died as a perfect substitute; a payment "in full" (Acts 20:28; Colossians 2:13-15; 1 Peter 2:22-24; 1 John 2:1-2). There was a price that had to be paid (1 Corinthians 6:20). He paid it; He received our punishment (Isaiah 53). He died in our place (2 Corinthians 5:21). Jesus is our ransom (Mark 10:45). He is our "instead of"; instead of us having to pay the price—which we were not able to do—He paid the price!

The cross of Christ is the method of the gospel. There is no other method. The cross is the *perfect and powerful* (efficacious) method. Jesus died on the cross as a perfect sacrifice (Hebrews 2:10). He died as a *powerful substitute*/payment (Romans 3:24-25). God's ways (methods) are not our ways (1 Samuel 16:7). Our ways are flawed and weak. His ways are perfect and powerful. And so, we rejoice in His method; we rejoice in the cross "for the word of the cross is foolishness to those who are perishing, but to us who are being saved it is the power of God" (1 Corinthians 1:18). We boast in His method; we boast in the cross "so that, just as it is written, 'Let him who boasts, boast in the Lord' . . . For I determined to know nothing among you except Jesus Christ, and Him crucified" (1 Corinthians 1:31-2:2).

The heart of the gospel message is found at the cross of Christ. Paradoxically, the *good news* centers on *death*! In this way, our debt has been paid. It has been "paid in full" (John 19:30).

DECEMBER 4

WHAT BIBLICAL SUBMISSION OF A WIFE IS NOT . . .

"To the woman He said . . . your desire shall be for your husband . . . sin is crouching at the door; and its desire is for you . . . "

Genesis 3:16; 4:7

The special role of the wife is to "be subject to your own husband" (Ephesians 5:22). She is to learn in submission (1 Timothy 2:11), teach about submission (Titus 2:5), and evangelize through her submission (1 Peter 3:1). It is clear that there exists a biblical marriage role of "submission," but what is it? What does it include? How is it accomplished? Perhaps, the most initial way to answer these questions is to explain what biblical submission of a wife is *not*. To walk in submission is not to walk in inferiority, subjugation, or oppression. This common distortion of "submission" is a result of the Fall of man in the Garden of Eden. Part of the judgment of the woman is that her "desire shall be for your husband" (Genesis 3:16). What is meant by the word "desire"? It is an unique word (*teshuka*) that is only used twice in the book of Genesis. The second time it appears is in the context of the dangers of sin: "And if you do not do well, sin is crouching at the door; and its desire is for you" (Genesis 4:7). First, it should be understood (as is clearly seen in Genesis 4:7) that the sentiment of "desire" is not a "positive" sense of "desire." The interpretation that equates desire in Genesis 3:16 with a woman's physical desire for her husband is the result of either wishful thinking (on the part of male interpreters) or just poor Bible study. Exegetically, the term desire is a negative concept. In Genesis 4:7, it is used in the context of sin's desire to control. In Genesis 3:16, we can conclude that the desire of the woman is not a positive one (which is no surprise as we remember that this is part of the punishment or curse of the Fall). The wife negated her natural role of submission in the garden when she took the leadership position with respect to how to handle the fruit of the forbidden tree. The wife is now punished by desiring to control her husband (the opposite of submission).

Second, as the Lord tells Cain in Genesis 4:7 to "master" or "rule" sin, so too does He judge/curse the husband in Genesis 3:16—who did not lead his wife, but instead, followed her—by giving him over to being inclined to "rule over" his wife. Natural headship of the husband—with its leadership/initiative rooted in service and love—became the unnatural subjection of the wife.

The consequence and corruption of the Fall is clear. It is not what God originally intended. The Fall has corrupted the willing submission of the wife by pushing it toward a desire to control the husband. It has also corrupted the loving headship of the husband by impelling it toward a tyrannical ruling or oppression of the wife. If we continue our comparison of Genesis 3:16 and 4:7, then we could say that if a husband does "well" (if he loves his wife as Christ loves the church), then the wife will not be "crouching at the door" or trying to control him. This is a very important truth in our discussion of marriage roles and relationships. They are very natural. Sin makes them unnatural. If the husband loves the wife as he should, then it will be more likely that there will be a natural response by the wife to be in submission to him. If the wife submits to the husband, then it will be more likely that there will be a natural response by the husband to love and lead his wife.

Punishment or judgement is to live life unnaturally. It is to go against the current of the river or to cut against the grain of the wood. It is to resist what is natural. In this sense God does not punish us at all. We punish or judge ourselves by not obeying, and experiencing the consequences (John 3:18-19; Matthew 7:1-2; 1 Corinthians 11:31). This is a profound truth of life.

Sin results in punishment not so much because God inflicts punishment upon us—although He does discipline us as seen in Hebrews 12:4-11—but because to go against God (to sin) is to go against creation and what is natural. The result is the infliction of pain upon yourself by doing something the wrong (unnatural) way. And so, if you are hammering a nail and you put your finger over the head of the nail, then you will feel pain. This punishment is not so much from God who in that moment decided to make you pay for your error. Rather, it is the result of doing something the wrong way. For a husband to be "the head of the wife" and for a wife to "be subject to your own husband" (Ephesians 5:22-23) is not to engage in superiority/inferiority, subjugation/subjection, or oppression/being oppressed. Whatever it is, this is clearly what it is *not*! What it *is* goes back to the Garden of Eden before the Fall.

DECEMBER 5

WHAT DOES GOD WANT MORE THAN ANYTHING ELSE FROM YOU?

"She had a sister called Mary, who was seated at the Lord's feet, listening to His word. But Martha was distracted with all her preparations . . . But the Lord answered and said to her, 'Martha, Martha, you are worried and bothered about so many things; but only *one thing is necessary, for Mary has chosen the good part, which shall not be taken away from her."*

Luke 10:39-42

What does God want more than anything else from you? Obedience? Honesty? Faith? Good works? There is something more important than all those things. More important than obedience? Yes, because obedience depends on something else. It depends on the strength of your relationship with God, because obedience does not depend on you but on Christ in you and is the result of relationship with God. So, more than anything else, God wants to be in relationship with you; He wants to spend time with you. He wants to know you. He wants your love (Matthew 22:37). Love is expressed by obedience (John 14:15); however, love is fostered through relationship with God (1 John 4:19).

Another way to express this idea is to say that what we need is a little more of the attitude of Mary and a little less of the attitude of Martha:

> "She had a sister called Mary, who was seated at the Lord's feet, listening to His word. But Martha was distracted with all her preparations . . . But the Lord answered and said to her, 'Martha, Martha, you are worried and bothered about so many things; but *only*

one thing is necessary, for Mary has chosen the good part, which shall not be taken away from her'" (Luke 10:39-42).

The simplicity of our lives is found in knowing God (Matthew 6:33). How could Jesus say that the only necessary thing was to spend time with Him? Because Jesus understood the reality of John 15:5 ("apart from Me you can do nothing") and the implications of Galatians 2:20 ("it is no longer I who live, but Christ lives in me"). Relationship with Jesus is the "only" thing necessary in the sense that everything else is based on it . . . everything else flows out of it. Everything else is based on Christ *in* us, and Christ in us is based on relationship with Him. And so, Mary (relationship) does not negate Martha (service); rather, she (relationship) establishes and initiates her (service).

What does God want more than anything else from you? What domino is the most important one? The first one! The first domino in the Christian life is relationship with God. Just as your ability to love flows out of God first (think dominos!) loving you (1 John 4:19), so too, ministry flows out of relationship with God. Matthew 22:37-39 tells us that the second greatest commandment (love others) flows out of the first (love God). Jesus "appointed twelve, that they might be with Him, and that He might send them out to preach, and to have authority to cast out the demons" (Mark 3:14-15). He appointed them to do ministry (preach/cast out demons), but their first activity was to simply "be with Him." It's an issue of what comes first, what leads to everything else. Ministry flows out of relationship with God. So, what does God want from you more than anything else? What domino will push over all the others? He wants the domino called "relationship with you"—a little more Mary and a little less Martha!

———

DECEMBER 6

PICTURES OF THE CHURCH . . .

"I write so that you will know how one ought to conduct himself in the household of God, which is the church of the living God, the pillar and support of the truth."

1 Timothy 3:15

The Bible includes several different models or pictures of the church. One of the most emphatic ones is the "building of God" or the "temple of God." Christ is the fulfillment of the tabernacle and the temple: "But when Christ appeared as a high priest of the good things to come, He entered through the greater and more perfect tabernacle, not made with hands, that is to say, not of this creation; and not through the blood of goats and calves, but through His own blood, He entered the holy place once for all, having obtained eternal redemption" (Hebrews 9:11-12)

. . . "Jesus answered them, 'Destroy this temple, and in three days I will raise it up.' The Jews then said, 'It took forty-six years to build this temple, and will You raise it up in three days?' But He was speaking of the temple of His body" (John 2:19-21).

Thus, the church is the house of God as it says, " . . . Christ was faithful as a Son over His house—Whose house we are" (Hebrews 3:6). Paul clearly refers to the church as the "household of God": "I write so that you will know how one ought to conduct himself in the household of God, which is the church of the living God, the pillar and support of the truth" (1 Timothy 3:15). Again, in 1 Corinthians 3:9, 16: "For we are God's fellow workers; you are God's field, God's building . . . Do you not know that you are a temple of God and that the Spirit of God dwells in you?"

The church is the holy temple: " . . . in whom the whole building, being fitted together, is growing into a holy temple in the Lord . . . " (Ephesians 2:21). The church as the Temple, then, implies that the church is a dwelling in which God lives by His Spirit: "Or what agreement has the temple of God with idols? For we are the temple of the living God; just as God said, 'I WILL DWELL IN THEM AND WALK AMONG THEM; AND I WILL BE THEIR GOD, AND THEY SHALL BE MY PEOPLE' (2 Corinthians 6:16). God dwells in the midst of His people . . . His "household": " . . . in whom you also are being built together into a dwelling of God in the Spirit" (Ephesians 2:22). This description focuses on the presence of the Holy Spirit in the church (see John 14:17, 23 and 1 Corinthians 3:16). Note: the Holy Spirit is not concerned about what the meeting place looks like. Unfortunately, some people use this description of the church to rationalize their carnal desires to build expensive buildings just for the sake of building expensive buildings.

If the church is a building, then there must be an architect. The architect is Jesus who says, "I also say to you that you are Peter, and upon this rock I will build My church; and the gates of Hades will not overpower it" (Matthew 16:18). Jesus is the builder and the building materials. Jesus is the foundation of the building (1 Corinthians 3:11). Jesus is the cornerstone (1 Peter 2:4-8; Colossians 2:6; Ephesians 2:20-22). Jesus is the center of the life of the church. The idea of the church as a building and a temple points to the reality that the church consists of many "little churches." The individual Christian is one of the stones that is used in the construction of the building of God (1 Peter 2:5). Again, we can see the importance of unity. Each member must participate. Finally, let us emphasize that the description of the church as the building of God focuses on the presence of God in its midst (see Zechariah 8:23; 1 Corinthians 14:24, 25). To be a piece of God's building (the church), we must each consider the following questions:

1) How is the quality of my construction? How is my life? (1 Peter 2:5).

2) What is my responsibility as part of the building of God? What is my ministry? (see 1 Corinthians 3:12-17).

3) Who should I work with? Who should I be unified with? (see 2 Corinthians 6:14-18).

Ultimately *you* are where God dwells; You are His building . . . His church!

———————

DECEMBER 7

TAKING A HIGH VIEW OF MARRIAGE . . .

"Marriage is *to be* held *in honor among all . . . "*

Hebrews 13:4

The most basic unit of society is the family. The most basic relationship within the family is the marriage relationship. The relationship between a husband and a wife is the most foundational human relationship. Marriage was the initial human relationship as it was ordained by God in the Garden of Eden. And so, it has been said that marriage is not finding someone whom you can live with but finding that person whom you cannot live without. This statement highlights the sovereignty of God in putting two people together. It also highlights the importance of marriage as it is marriage that represents nothing less than the completion of man. According to the Scripture, the woman was created as a "helper" or completion of the man (Genesis 2:18). Marriage paints the fullest picture of the very nature of humanity. Herein lies the "high view of marriage."

A high view of marriage that champions its importance is best expressed in the understanding that marriage is used as a way to mirror God's own image. A triune God (a plurality) who operates in unity and oneness (a singularity) creates mankind (a plurality, male and female) who must operate in unity and oneness (a singularity, "one flesh"). God (a singular plurality) creates man (a singular plurality) in His own image. "In the day when God created man, He made him in the likeness of God. He created them male and female, and He blessed them and named them Man in the day when they were created" (Genesis 5:1) for "God said, 'Let Us make man in Our image . . . and God created man in His own image, in the image of God He created him; male and female He created them'" (Genesis 1:26-27).

The importance of marriage cannot be overstated. It is fundamental in creation. And so, the divine purposes in the instituting of marriage are numerous. Marriage is instituted to multiply a godly heritage—"God said to them, 'Be fruitful and multiply and fill the earth, and subdue it; and rule over the fish of the sea and over the birds of the sky, and over every living thing that moves on the earth'" (Genesis 1:28)—and in so doing, then, marriage is ordained to be part of the way that man will manage God's creation. Additionally, marriage is instituted in order for man and woman to mutually complete one another (Genesis 2:18-24). Furthermore, marriage is figurative of God's union with Israel (Isaiah 54:5), and models Christ's relationship to the church (Ephesians 5:23-32).

On a very practical level, marriage is used to discourage immoral behavior (1 Corinthians 7:1-9). Marriage is meant to provide complete satisfaction (Proverbs 5:15-19).

The importance of marriage, from God's perspective, is best seen in His abhorrence of its destruction (Matthew 19:6). He loves marriage, and therefore, hates divorce (Malachi 2:16). On the other hand, the establishment of marriage, even the very wedding ceremony itself, is an endorsed (John 2:1-11) and joyous (Jeremiah 7:34) event. And so, we take a high view of marriage and shout from the housetops, "Marriage *is* to be *held* in honor among all" (Hebrews 13:4).

DECEMBER 8

THE APOSTLES OF JESUS . . .

"And when day came, He called His disciples to Him and chose twelve of them,
whom He also named apostles."

Luke 6:13

Who were Jesus' original twelve apostles? First, there was Simon Peter (also known as Cephas) who was a fisherman, and who became one of the three apostles in the "inner circle" (Matthew 17:1). He was affectionate and tender (Matthew 26:75) yet could be impulsive (Matthew 14:28). He would sacrifice (Mark 1:18) yet could be selfish (Matthew 19:27). He was brave (Acts 4:19) yet could be a coward (Mark 14:67-71). Peter had an evangelistic ministry to the Jews throughout Asia and Palestine and may have gone as far as Babylon to proclaim the gospel (1 Peter 5:13). Tradition says he was crucified (head downward) in Rome. Next, there was John (the beloved disciple) who was a fisherman, and who also became one of the apostles in the "inner circle." He was full of energy (Mark 3:17), but he could be intolerant of others (Mark 9:38). He was ambitious (Mark 10:35-37) but could be vindictive (Luke 9:54). Tradition says he ministered mostly in Asia Minor. At the end of his life, he was exiled by Nero to the island of Patmos and was the only apostle who was not martyred for his faith. James the elder (along with his brother John known as the "sons of thunder") was a fisherman who was the third member of the "inner circle." James was a great leader of the Jerusalem church, and was the first of the twelve to be martyred. He was beheaded by Herod sometime around 44 A.D. (Acts 12:1-2).

Andrew (the brother of Peter), also a fisherman, was originally a disciple of John the Baptist (John 1:35-40). Tradition says he preached in Greece and Asia Minor (modern Russia and Turkey), after which he was crucified on a "St. Andrew's cross" (an "X" shaped cross). Matthew (Levi) was a tax collector who responded to the call of Jesus (Matthew 9:9). Tradition says he preached in Parthia and Ethiopia where he was martyred. Thomas (also known as Didymus and "doubting

Thomas") was an apostle who was devoted to Christ (John 11:16), but slow to understand His words (John 14:5). He was absent when Christ appeared after the resurrection (John 20:25), and doubted it (John 20:26); however, he was given certain proof (John 20:27) and then believed (John 20:28; 21:2). Tradition says he ministered in Parthia and India where he was martyred by being pierced with a lance. Philip was an apostle who was tested by Christ (John 6:5) and was slow to understand (John 14:8). Tradition says he died a martyr's death after preaching in Phrygia. Bartholomew (also known as Nathanael) was an apostle who was a missionary in Armenia and then in India. Tradition says he was beaten to death and beheaded. James the younger, tradition says, preached in Palestine and Egypt where he was eventually martyred. Jude (also known as Thaddaeus), tradition says, preached in Assyria and Persia where he was martyred by being shot with arrows. Simon (the Zealot), tradition says, preached in Africa and Britain where he was crucified. Judas (Iscariot) betrayed Jesus (Matthew 27:3-4) for thirty pieces of silver and then hung himself (Matthew 26:14-16). Of course, Paul was an additional apostle who may have been Judas' replacement. He was an apostle to the gentiles (Romans 11:13) who, according to tradition, was beheaded in Rome.

There certainly are some things we learn by studying the apostle's lives. First, we realize they were human like us and strong but also weak. In addition, we see that God uses all kinds of people from all kinds of backgrounds. We also see the emphasis that God puts on spreading His gospel to the uttermost parts of the earth (missionary activity). Finally, we see that the Greek word for "witness" (Acts 1:8) is, *martus* that can be translated as "martyr." They were martyred for their faith. Ultimately "those who were sent" (apostles) lived and died for Christ.

DECEMBER 9

NOTHING MORE IMPORTANT THAN ETERNAL LIFE . . .

"For what will it profit a man if he gains the whole world and forfeits his soul?
Or what will a man give in exchange for his soul?"

Matthew 16:26

What is eternal life? Eternal life is to know God (John 17:3). It is "belief" (that is, faith/relationship) in Jesus that leads to eternal life (John 3:36). Inheriting eternal life is associated with giving everything to Jesus (Mark 10:21). More specifically, obtaining eternal life requires that we first hate our lives in this world (John 12:25); we prefer (or count as more important) the life to come after this life. Nothing is more important than eternal life (Matthew 16:26)!

The importance of eternal life is implied when Jesus explains that we should not be afraid of men or the devil. We should fear God who has power over eternal life (Luke 12:4-5). The importance of eternity should make everything else relatively unimportant. Our commitment to God depends on our understanding of this truth—it depends on how much we believe it. The quantity and quality of your commitment to God depends on the quantity and quality of your faith. The quantity of your commitment to the world depends on the quantity of your doubt. If we have no doubt, then we will logically give everything that we must toward the goal of eternal life. We would "give our all" knowing there is no risk of being wrong (knowing in the end we will see that what we believed was really the truth). People of faith are committed people because they know there is no risk of losing. There is no risk of being disappointed or of regretting your life of faith. Doubt leads to the fear of regret. The fear of regret leads to our making the attempt to get satisfaction and comfort in this world a priority just in case we die and realize our faith was not the truth. A lack of faith in the importance of eternal life will result in a lack of commitment to God (Mark 8:36-37).

To not hold onto this life seems foolish to those caught up in "this world." The world to come must either not exist or is, somehow, relatively unimportant. How important is eternal life to you? Do you understand its relative importance? Jesus uses hyperbole to express this relative importance when he challenges us to even be willing to cut out an eye if it is necessary (Mark 9:43-48). There is nothing more important than eternal life.

Do you live in that truth? Can you say, as the martyred missionary Jim Elliot was famous for saying, "He is no fool who gives what he cannot keep to gain that which he cannot lose."

Nothing is more important than eternal life (Matthew 16:26)! Nothing, then, is more practical than viewing your life through the lens of your eternal life. An otherwise non-sensible thing, this life begins to make complete sense when lived in the shining stare of eternal life. May eternal life shine on our footsteps and illuminate the path before us. Amen!

DECEMBER 10

SIX PRIMARY NEEDS OF NEW BELIEVERS . . .

". . . like newborn babies, long for the pure milk of the word, so that by it you may grow in respect to salvation . . ."

1 Peter 2:2

Maybe you have contact with a new believer in Christ. If so, it is important to know their primary needs so, perhaps, you can make provision for them or at least point them in the right direction. First, a new believer needs assurance. They need assurance that they are a new creation in Christ: "Therefore if anyone is in Christ, he is a new creature; the old things passed away; behold, new things have come" (2 Corinthians 5:17). This assurance, of course, must include a change in attitude toward Jesus Christ: "And the testimony is this, that God has given us eternal life, and this life is in His Son. He who has the Son has the life; he who does not have the Son of God does not have the life" (1 John 5:11-12). It also must include a change in attitude toward sin: "If we confess our sins, He is faithful and righteous to forgive us our sins and to cleanse us from all unrighteousness" (1 John 1:9).

Second, new believers especially need love and acceptance. A new believer needs to know the love of God as well as love from others. They need to know that "there is now no condemnation for those who are in Christ Jesus" (Romans 8:1).

> Having so fond an affection for you, we were well-pleased to impart to you not only the gospel of God but also our own lives, because you had become very dear to us. For you recall, brethren, our labor and hardship, *how* working night and day so as not to be a burden to any of you, we proclaimed to you the gospel of God . . . as you know how we *were* exhorting and encouraging and imploring each one of you as a father would his own children, so that you would walk in a manner worthy of the God who calls you into His own kingdom and glory (1 Thessalonians 2:8-12).

Third, new believers need to be protected. This protection can be offered through prayer and instruction. (2 Corinthians 13:7; 1 Timothy 1:3-4). New believers must especially be protected against: false cults (be sure to emphasize the divinity of Christ and forgiveness through the cross), bad friends and influences (it is especially important immediately after salvation to encourage the new believer to separate himself from bad influences), and Satan (warn the new believer about the reality of the attacks of the devil, and instruct him with respect to Satan's most used weapons, which are accusation and discouragement).

Fourth is the need for fellowship. The new believer must be introduced into a healthy church fellowship. He must immediately begin to be connected to other believers who will receive him warmly.

Fifth, new believers need food. Every new believer needs to eat from the Word of God: " . . . like newborn babies, long for the pure milk of the word, so that by it you may grow in respect to salvation" (1 Peter 2:2). The new believer needs to be taught the Word by a more mature believer to help them get started. You can teach them how to teach themselves; teach them how to study the Bible.

Sixth, a new believer needs some training: how to have a quiet time with the Lord, how to pray, how to memorize Scripture, how to study the Bible, how to praise and worship the Lord, how to witness, and how to have fellowship with other Christians. Note: when training a new believer, in the beginning put the focus on "How" instead of "Why" (1 Thessalonians 4:1; Philippians 4:9).

———————

DECEMBER 11

HATE THE SIN, BUT LOVE THE SINNER . . .

". . . if anyone is caught in any trespass, you who are spiritual, restore such a one in a spirit of gentleness; each one looking to yourself, so that you too will not be tempted."

Galatians 6:1

In the New Testament, church discipline is presented as inevitable. There are numerous cases of false teaching within the church which must be dealt with as serious matters. At the very least, false teaching can cause division in the church. Paul used church discipline in these types of situations. He counsels Titus to "reject a factious man after a first and second warning, knowing that such a man is perverted and is sinning, being self-condemned" (Titus 3:10-11). Elsewhere, he warns the church at Rome saying, "Now I urge you, brethren, keep your eye on those who cause dissensions and hindrances contrary to the teaching which you learned, and turn away from them" (Romans 16:17). The motive of church discipline in these situations was to protect the church:

> "I am amazed that you are so quickly deserting Him who called you by the grace of Christ, for a different gospel; which is *really* not another; only there are some who are disturbing you and want to distort the gospel of Christ. But even if we, or an angel from heaven, should preach to you a gospel contrary to what we have preached to you, he is to be accursed! As we have said before, so I say again now, if any man is preaching to you a gospel contrary to what you received, he is to be accursed!" (Galatians 1:6-9).

Yet, even in these situations Paul was concerned for the individual:

> ". . . holding fast the faithful word which is in accordance with the teaching, so that he will be able both to exhort in sound doctrine and to refute those who contradict. For there are many rebellious men, empty talkers and deceivers, especially those of the circumcision, who must be silenced because they are upsetting whole families, teaching things they should not *teach* for the sake of sordid gain . . . reprove them severely so that they may be sound in the faith . . ." (Titus 1:9-13).

Church discipline is a complicated issue. We can learn how to do it from the Scriptures. In so doing, we can also learn how to engage in interpersonal situations when we need to correct someone. We can learn something about parental discipline. So, how do we do it? To begin with, we must have the humility to examine ourselves before examining someone else: "Brethren, even if anyone is caught in any trespass, you who are spiritual, restore such a one in a spirit of gentleness; each one looking to yourself, so that you too will not be tempted" (Galatians 6:1). If there is first no self-examination, then you will not be prepared to be the vessel of God who can enforce discipline.

> DO NOT judge so that you will not be judged. For in the way you judge, you will be judged; and by your standard of measure, it will be measured to you. Why do you look at the speck that is in your brother's eye, but do not notice the log that is in your own eye? Or how can you say to your brother, 'Let me take the speck out of your eye,' and behold, the log is in your own eye? You hypocrite, first take the log out of your own eye, and then you will see clearly to take the speck out of your brother's eye (Matthew 7:1-5).

Prayer must be the foundation underneath the process of discipline. In his instructions given in the serious case of church discipline in 1 Corinthians 5, Paul seems to imply (verses 3-4) that prayer is necessary in church discipline. The church has the right to enforce church discipline because it is the body of Christ. It has a direct connection with the head. Through prayer it can reveal the will of Christ in order to discipline correctly (Matthew 18:18-20). Critical also to the discipline process are love and gentleness. Even during an extreme situation, Paul encouraged church discipline to be done with love and gentleness (2 Thessalonians 3:15). To follow this method, we should put into practice these words often attributed to Augustine: "Kill the error but love the person who made the error" (Galatians 6:1).

DECEMBER 12

JESUS THE MIRACLE WORKER . . .

"Where did this man get these things . . . such miracles as these performed by His hands?"

Mark 6:2

As we survey the Gospels, we see *many* miracles that Jesus performed. These only represent some of His miracles. As John puts it, "Therefore many other signs Jesus also performed . . . which are not written in this book" (John 20:30). Miracles of healing are the most often type of miracle performed by Jesus. Jesus healed the son of the official at Capernaum (John 4:46-54). He also healed the man with leprosy: "'Jesus . . . touched him, saying, 'I am willing; be cleansed.' And immediately his leprosy was cleansed" (Matthew 8:2-3). Jesus healed the servant of the Roman centurion (Matthew 8:5-13), the mother-in-law of Peter (Matthew 8:14-15), the paralyzed man (Matthew 9:2-7), and the woman who was bleeding: "And a woman who had been suffering, . . .

was saying to herself, 'If I only touch His garment, I will get well.' But Jesus . . . said, 'Daughter, take courage; your faith has made you well.' At once the woman was made well" (Matthew 9:20-22). Some other examples include: Jesus healing of the two blind men (Matthew 9:27-31), the sick man at the pool of Bethesda (John 5:1-9), the man with the shriveled hand (Matthew 12:10-13), the daughter of the Canaanite woman (Matthew 15:21-28), the deaf mute (Mark 7:31-37), the blind man at Bethsaida (Mark 8:22-26), the man born blind (John 9:1-7), the crippled woman (Luke 13:11-13), the man with dropsy (Luke 14:1-4), the ten men with leprosy (Luke 17:11-19), the two blind men (Matthew 20:29-34), and the servant of the high priest (Luke 22:50-51).

Jesus also performs multiple miracles of deliverance. For example, the deliverance of the possessed man in the synagogue: " . . . And Jesus rebuked him, saying, 'Be quiet, and come out of him!' . . . the unclean spirit cried out with a loud voice and came out of him" (Mark 1:25-26). Other examples include: the two men from Gadara (Matthew 8:28-34), the mute and possessed man (Matthew 9:32-33), the man who was blind, mute, and possessed (Matthew 12:22), and the boy with a demon (Matthew 17:14-18).

Some of the more astounding miracles done by Jesus are the ones related to the forces of nature. Could you imagine seeing someone walking on water? The Scripture tells us that " . . . He came to them, walking on the sea" (Matthew 14:25). Staying with the "water theme," Jesus turns water into wine (John 2:1-11), twice enables a huge catch of fish (Luke 5:4-11; John 21:1-11), calms the storm (Matthew 8:23-27), and finds a particular coin in the mouth of a random fish (Matthew 17:24-27). Lastly, Jesus performs miracles associated with "food." Five thousand people were fed with five loaves and two fish (Matthew 14:15-21), while "four thousand men, besides women and children" were fed with seven loaves and a few small fish (Matthew 15:32-38). Also, in a very prophetic miracle, Jesus curses the fig tree "and at once the fig tree withered" (Matthew 21:18-22).

Of course, when all is said and done, the most amazing miracles performed by Jesus come under the astonishing category of miracles related to raising the dead. These include: the son of the widow at Nain (Luke 7:11-15), the daughter of Jairus (Luke 8:41-56), and last, but certainly not least, the "take your breath away" account of Jesus raising Lazarus from the dead after four days in the tomb (John 11:1-44).

And so, what is the response to such a list as this? The response has to be, "WOW!" The response has to be nothing less than worship! Perhaps, on a more theological level, our response must echo that of Thomas: "Thomas answered and said to Him, 'My Lord and my God!'" (John 20:28-29). *Wow!*

———

DECEMBER 13

VERY OPPOSITE KINGDOMS . . .

"Jesus answered, 'My kingdom is not of this world . . . as it is, My kingdom is not of this realm."

John 18:36

The kingdom of God is not associated with "this world" (John 18:36). It does not come from here; rather, it is the sovereign action of God. Man cannot create the kingdom of God, he can only receive it. If he does not receive it, then he has no place within it (Mark 10:15). God is sovereign over it. God "gives" the kingdom (Luke 12:32), Jesus "grants" the kingdom (Luke 22:29), God says to whom the kingdom will come (Matthew 5:3; Mark 10:14), God gives the invitation to enter it (Luke 14:15-20), and God encourages some to enter and does not allow others to enter (Luke 14:21-24).

What is the kingdom of God like? Perhaps, the most applicable way to describe the kingdom of God is to say that it is totally opposite from "this world" (John 18:36; Luke 23:42; Acts 1:6). It is not simply a different *form* of this world, rather, it is totally different *from* this world; it is *opposite* of this world. There are different forms of this world: there is the farce of secular superficiality ("worldliness") and there is the phoniness of spiritual superficiality ("religiosity"). These may be different from each other, but at the end of the day, they are simply different forms of the kingdom of this world. The kingdom of God is fundamentally different; it is different from this world, not simply a different form of this world. The kingdom of God (relative to the world) is the fanaticism of God ruled reality (Matthew 6:10) . . . totally different from this world . . . opposite kingdoms!

And so the kingdom of God is not characterized by violent action. It is not a nationalistic or political entity. The disciples thought of it in this way and were confused (Luke 19:11). The focus of the kingdom of God is on generosity instead of greed (Matthew 5:40-42; Luke 12:32-33). It takes precedence over money and possessions (Matthew 6:19-34), rights and privileges (Matthew 5:39-41; Mark 10:42-44), family and friends (Luke 14:26; Matthew 10:34-39), and personal attitudes and hidden desires (Matthew 5:21-48). Thus, one who lives in the kingdom of God does not find his purpose for living simply in living for pleasure, status, relationships, or self. Living in the kingdom of God, then, has a totally different focus than living in the kingdom of this world (Romans 14:17) and requires a totally different commitment (Matthew 6:33; Luke 9:62).

The kingdom of God is opposite from "this world." It is the "flip-flopped" kingdom . . . the greatest will be the least, the leader will be the servant, the first will be last, the filled will be the emptied, the exalted will be the humbled, and those who live will be those who die (Matthew

23:11-12; Mark 9:35; Matthew 5:3; John 12:24; Matthew 10:39). Jesus said it best: "My kingdom is not of this world" (John 18:36).

DECEMBER 14

THE HOLY TRADE . . .

"But whatever things were gain to me, those things I have counted as loss for the sake of Christ .
. . that I may know Him . . ."

Philippians 3:7, 10

In Philippians 3, Paul refers to a sort of "holy trade." Paul is willing to trade "confidence in the flesh" (Philippians 3:3) for knowing God (Philippians 3:10). Self-righteousness—which is un-profitable (Isaiah 57:12) and like a filthy garment (Isaiah 64:6)—is traded for God's righteousness which is salvific (Jeremiah 33:16). The Law which cannot save (Acts 13:38-39) is traded for faith which can save (Mark 16:16). Hey, Paul! You probably had a lot of reasons to put confidence in the flesh. Yet you were willing to trade them "all" (Philippians 3:8). "All things to be loss" for Paul probably included much wealth. To be a citizen of Tarsus at that time (which Paul was) he would almost certainly be from a family of wealth and reputation. Surely, when we consider the impli-cations of Paul's education and status in Judaism (Philippians 3:5-6), it is not difficult to imagine the money, reputation and position that he sacrificed to become a poor and despised missionary.

Why is Paul willing to throw it all away and make this trade? Paul answers this question (Philippians 3:10) with the words "that I may know" (experiential knowledge). He hinted of this purpose earlier in Philippians 3:8 ("in view of knowing Christ") and Philippians 3:9 ("may be found in Him"). Of course, in Philippians 3:10 he is more emphatic and specific as to His purpose for the trade. It is: 1) to know "Him"; 2) to know "the power of His resurrection"; and 3) to know "the fellowship (sharing) of His sufferings." How is this a "holy trade"? It is holy because God is holy, and the trade will gain Paul relationship with God. Instead of the righteousness of self, he will gain the righteousness of God. Instead of right standing with self, he will gain right standing with God. Instead of relationship with self, he will gain relationship with God. Now that's holy!

How will Paul be able to make this trade? Paul answers this question by explaining that by "being conformed to His (that is, Jesus') death" (Philippians 3:10), he will know Him, and the power of His resurrection, and the fellowship of His sufferings. Death to self is the method. As Jesus said, "unless a grain of wheat falls into the earth and dies, it remains by itself alone; but if it dies, it bears much fruit. He who loves his life loses it; and he who hates his life in this world shall keep it to life eternal" (John 12:24-25). What a powerful description of the holy trade and what a blunt description of the method to execute that trade, death. That was Jesus' method and, thus, it must be Paul's method also. Jesus died to Himself (Philippians 2:7) and died on the cross (Philippians 2:8). When He did this: He regained a perfect relationship with the Father when He was seated at His right hand (similarly, Paul would "know Him"), He was resurrected (similarly, Paul would "know the power of His resurrection"), and He suffered (similarly, Paul would "know the fellowship of His sufferings").

Yes! The cross was for Jesus and is now for Paul (and for you and me), the one and only method for the holy trade. As Jim Elliot, the storied missionary to the Auca Indians of Ecuador, so famously said: *He is no fool who gives what he cannot keep to gain that which he cannot lose.*

DECEMBER 15

THE WHERE OF CHURCH LEADERSHIP . . .

"EVERY PERSON is to be in subjection to the governing authorities. For there is no authority except from God, and those which exist are established by God."

Romans 13:1

One of the issues of Christian leadership is the "Where?" factor: where does my leadership authority begin and where does it end? A big part of the answer to this question involves an understanding of the "Who?" factor: who is the source of authority? In Romans 13:1 we read: "Every person is to be in subjection to the governing authorities. For there is no authority except from God, and those which exist are established by God." It is God who has authority over all authorities. And it is God who has established different jurisdictions, or spheres, of authority that must not be violated. Let's now revisit the original question: "Where does my leadership authority begin and where does it end? It begins and ends where God has placed His boundaries that make up His jurisdictions or spheres.

When we look at three of the broader "spheres" of authority—family, church, and State—with regard to the authority to bear children, we find some important applications regarding how this is viewed from a biblical perspective. This authority is clearly given to the family as seen in Genesis 1:27-28: "God created man in His own image, in the image of God He created him; male and female He created them. God blessed them; and God said to them, 'Be fruitful and multiply.'" This authority, to bear children, has not been given to the church (thus, mandates by the church regarding the use of birth control are out of bounds). That same authority is not placed in the jurisdiction of the State. Thus, the law in China that regulates how many children a family can have ("one child policy") is anti-biblical as was the Romanian policy of the 1970s that wielded its authority over families regarding quotas of children that must be met in order to populate the country.

What about the authority to tax? Of course, as is true of the family, the church has no power tax; nevertheless, the church must be careful here. Although a church would never call it a tax, the reality of some systems of mandated tithing is that the tithe is a tax. Of course, it is the State that has been given the basic authority to tax: "For because of this you also pay taxes, for rulers are servants of God, devoting themselves to this very thing. Render to all what is due them: tax to whom tax is due; custom to whom custom . . . " (Romans 13:6-7).

Each of the three jurisdictions—albeit in very different ways—maintains authority to discipline or punish. The family carries the "rod" while the church holds the "staff" and the State wields the "sword." It is the family that carries the rod of discipline: "He who withholds his rod hates his son, but he who loves him disciplines him diligently" (Proverbs 13:24). Meanwhile, the church holds the staff for discipline (this is typically called *church discipline*): "But actually, I wrote to you not to associate with any so-called brother if he is an immoral person . . . not even to eat with such a one" (1 Corinthians 5:11). So, if the family has the "rod" and the church has the "staff," what does the State have? The State holds the sword. Paul is very clear here: "Every person is to be in subjection to the governing authorities . . . for it does not bear the sword for nothing . . . " (Romans 13:1-4).

Concerning a more controversial issue, it is clear in Scripture that the family does not have the authority to kill, nor does the church (perhaps non-adherence to this point resulted in the medieval Crusades). It does seem, however, that the State has the authority to kill (capital punishment): "Every person is to be in subjection to the governing authorities . . . For rulers are not a cause of fear for good behavior, but for evil . . . if you do what is evil, be afraid; for it does not bear the sword for nothing" (Romans 13:1-4).

DECEMBER 16

BASICS OF BAPTISM . . .

" . . . make disciples of all the nations, baptizing them in the name
of the Father and the Son and the Holy Spirit . . . "

Matthew 28:19

Why do Christians practice the Sacrament of Baptism? Most fundamentally, baptism is practiced because it was a commandment of Jesus (Matthew 3:15; 28:19). Beyond this, however, baptism is used as a symbol of spiritual truth. Perhaps most emphatically, it is a symbol of being buried with Christ:

What shall we say then? Are we to continue in sin so that grace may increase? May it never be! How shall we who died to sin still live in it? Or do you not know that all of us who have been baptized into Christ Jesus have been baptized into His death? Therefore we have been buried with Him through baptism into death, so that as Christ was raised from the dead through the glory of the Father, so we too might walk in newness of life. For if we have become united with *Him* in the likeness of His death, certainly we shall also be *in the likeness* of His resurrection, knowing this, that our old self was crucified with *Him*, in order that our body of sin might be done away with, so that we would no longer be slaves to sin; for he who has died is freed from sin (Romans 6:1-7).

What is the meaning of the term "baptism"? It literally means to submerge, to immerse, to dip, to sink, or to overwhelm. In Greek literature, the term is used to describe a ship filled with water. The idea of immersion or submersion is prominent. Where is the baptism? Generally, baptisms are done where there is water (Acts 8:36). However, it is not necessary to be at a certain type of body of water, like a river, sea, lake, swimming pool, or a tank (Acts 10:44-48; Acts 16:25-33). It does seem that wherever the water is it includes a public dimension; baptisms are public events.

How are people baptized? One potentially legitimate method would be "sprinkling." This could be valid in the sense that the blood of the sacrifice was sprinkled in the Old Testament with the understanding that it was inclusive in terms of redemption. Another legitimate method might be "pouring." The early church—as stated in the "Didache," which is a collection of teachings from the early church—considered pouring to be a second option. Perhaps, the most biblical method, with respect to the actual meaning of the word, would be "immersion." This would be the method most aligned with the literal meaning of the Greek term *"baptismos"* and its accompanying symbolism. It seems to be the method pictured in the New Testament (John 3:23; Mark 1:10; Acts 8:39). It was the method of the Jews who practiced baptism prior to the baptizing ministry of John the Baptist as it was also the method of John the Baptist himself. It is the best way to demonstrate the believer's burial with Christ (Romans 6:3-4).

Who should baptize? Many people think that the person who baptizes others must be a "professional" minister. However, the New Testament does not clearly teach that as a point of doctrine (Acts 8:38; Acts 9:17-18). Whatever the case, the focus should not be on the person who is baptizing. The focus should be on the person who is being baptized and the meaning of the baptism.

Finally, when is the baptism? Baptism comes after a person repents (Acts 2:38) and believes (Acts 8:12). In the New Testament a person was baptized immediately after conversion (Acts 8:12; 8:36-38; 9:17-18; 10:47-48; 16:33).

THE WORK OF GOD'S SPIRIT TO ENABLE GOD'S PEOPLE IS AT WORK IN YOU!

"Now the LORD spoke to Moses, saying, 'See, I have called by name Bezalel . . . I have filled him with the Spirit of God . . . to make artistic designs . . . that he may work in all kinds of craftsmanship.'"

Exodus 31:1-6

Under the old covenant, the Spirit of God is often seen working as the Spirit who enables God's people for God's purposes. He enabled someone to do a specific task that he would not, otherwise, have been able to do. He added something to what was natural. He worked in the supernatural. In general, the activity of the Holy Spirit was temporary and occasional. The Spirit came upon Samson from time to time. The Spirit came upon Saul, but later departed from him. The Spirit came upon a prophet at the moment of his prophesying. In any case, the activity of the Spirit always was associated with the people of God; the community of faith. In the new covenant, we see an even more emphatic role of the Spirit in the community of faith, in the life of each believer. The work of God's Spirit to enable God's people in the Old Testament on a more temporary and occasional basis points to and reflects the same sort of work of the Spirit but on a more permanent and emphatic basis as seen in the life of a New Testament Christian.

In the Old Testament, the building and eventual rebuilding of the tabernacle/temple was enabled by the work of the Spirit of God (Bezalel in Exodus 31:1-6; David in 1 Chronicles 28:12; Zerubbabel in Zechariah 4:6-7). The Christian is the temple of the Holy Spirit (1 Corinthians 3:16). This same enabling/empowering to build the temple is emphatic in the building of the New Testament temple, in the building of the Christian (John 3:3-8).

In the Old Testament, Moses (and then 70 others), is empowered by the Spirit to lead God's people (Numbers 11:17). Saul (1 Samuel 11:6) and David (1 Samuel 16:13) lead Israel when the Spirit of God comes upon them and anoints them. The Christian is led by the Holy Spirit (Romans 8:14). In the Old Testament, the Judges (Gideon in Judges 6:34; Samson in Judges 13:25) were leaders who were Spirit empowered to deliver God's people from their enemies. The Christian engages in spiritual warfare by this same Spirit empowerment (Ephesians 6:18).

History (that is, His Story) is full of the activity of the Spirit of God as He enables His people for His purposes. As the Spirit enabled and empowered individuals at specific times in particular situations in the Old Testament, He now fills each New Testament believer as the Spirit is poured out to empower Christians for His purposes. The work of God's Spirit to enable God's people has not changed; it has only become more emphatic as the Christian is now the very temple in which that enabling/empowering Spirit dwells. The Scripture proclaims, "I will pour out My Spirit on all people" (Joel 2:28) and "He will baptize you with the Holy Spirit" (Mark 1:8) and "they were all filled with the Holy Spirit" (Acts 2:4). The work of God's Spirit to enable God's people is at work in you!

DECEMBER 18

IT WOULD BE BETTER TO JUST "SHUT THE GATES"

"'Oh that there were one among you who would shut the gates, that you might not uselessly kindle fire on My altar! I am not pleased with you,' says the LORD of hosts, 'nor will I accept an offering from you.'"

Malachi 1:10

The priests of Israel were bringing offerings to the altar of God that they would not dare bring to the civil ruler (Malachi 1:8). They showed respect to the governor and they knew that God was greater than the governor. Yet their actions toward God did not show that respect. Ultimately, the problem was in their faith. They could see the governor. They could not see God. They began to question the validity or usefulness of approaching Him. The sacrificial system became a mere ritual, empty and hypocritical. In their offerings, the priests undervalued God. They despised Him. And so, they undervalued their own redemption and practiced hypocrisy because of their lack of faith. God will not accept faithless, hypocritical worship: "'I am not pleased with you,' says the Lord of hosts, 'nor will I accept an offering from you'" (Malachi 1:10). Moreover, God proclaims His desire that the priests shut down the whole sacrificial system ("shut the gates"). Why does God want them to stop the sacrifices? Would it not be better to have a partially correct system than no system at all? God keeps repeating and emphasizing that He would not accept them and their offerings almost as if He is concerned that they still do not understand. It appears that He is saying: "Do not be deceived!"

It is better to have no system of worship at all than to have a ritualistic, empty form of worship. Worship without obedience and sincerity is "useless" or in vain: "And He said to them, 'Rightly did Isaiah prophesy of you hypocrites, as it is written, This people honors me with their lips, but their heart is far away from me, but in vain do they worship me . . . '" (Mark 7:6-7). Or as Malachi says, it is "uselessly" kindling fire on God's altar (Malachi 1:10). Beyond this, however, is the problem of deception that hypocrisy and religiosity brings. False rituals often give false confidence.

Empty religion deceives people because it makes them think that they are "right with God" when they are not. God only wants the form/system if it contains the substance/contents/what Jesus calls "the weightier provisions of the law" (Matthew 23:23). Men think that the form without the substance is better than no form at all. God would rather that the gates be shut. Man would say that lukewarm is better than cold. God would rather that we be cold: "I know your deeds, that you are neither cold nor hot; I wish that you were cold or hot. So because you are lukewarm, and neither hot nor cold, I will spit you out of My mouth'" (Revelation 3:15-16). God would rather have no sacrifices at all than receive sacrifices with contempt:

> What are your multiplied sacrifices to Me?, says the Lord. I have had enough of burnt offerings of rams and the fat of fed cattle; and I take no pleasure in the blood of bulls, lambs or goats . . . Bring your worthless offerings no longer, incense is an abomination to Me . . . They have become a burden to Me; I am weary of bearing them. So when you spread out your hands in prayer, I will hide My eyes from you; Yes, even though you multiply prayers, I will not listen (Isaiah 1:11-15).

Here we should make an important application. God hates hypocrisy more than anything. He hates empty religion and ritualistic ceremonies that mean nothing. They are futile and they deceive those who practice them. He spews out of His mouth that which is lukewarm (Revelation 3:16). With God it is "yes" or "no" (Matthew 5:37). It is all or nothing (Matthew 16:24). Areas of hypocrisy in our lives must be destroyed. The "gates" must be shut! The longer that we allow hypocrisy to continue, the more likely it is that we will be fooled by its deception. Avoid it like the plague!

DECEMBER 19

AN APPLE PIE WITH NO APPLES IS . . . NOT AN APPLE PIE!

"'Your words have been arrogant against Me,' says the Lord . . . 'You have said,
It is vain to serve God' . . . Then those who feared the Lord spoke to one another,
and the Lord gave attention and heard it."

Malachi 3:13-14, 16

The attitude with which a person asks something of God is very important: "You ask and do not receive, because you ask with wrong motives, so that you may spend it on your pleasures" (James 4:3). Moreover, these "wrong attitude" people often dabble in vanity even though they may claim that it is the service unto God that is vain: "'Your words have been arrogant against

Me,' says the Lord . . . 'You have said, It is vain to serve God'" (Malachi 3:14). The people of God during the time of Malachi had fallen into empty religiosity. They practice "the form without the contents." They practice ritual without obedience. Ironically, their words ("it is vain") are true not of God, but of themselves. The type of service and worship that they are offering to God IS done in vain: "Rightly did Isaiah prophesy of you hypocrites, as it is written: 'This people honors me with their lips, but their heart is far away from me. But in vain do they worship me . . .'" (Mark 7:6-7).

In no way is it vain to sincerely worship God. It is vain to engage in a form of worship without the contents of worship. Ritual without obedience yields no results. The mold or method without its filling or substance is a "house built on sand" (Matthew 7:26). This is not to say that we should do away with forms, rituals, methods, or molds. It is to say that if they exist apart from contents, obedience, filling, or substance, then they are useless. An apple pie without the apples is . . . *not* an apple pie. Jesus put it this way to the scribes and the Pharisees: "'Woe to you, scribes and Pharisees, hypocrites! For you tithe mint and dill and cummin, and have neglected the weightier provisions of the law: justice and mercy and faithfulness; but these are the things you should have done without neglecting the others" (Matthew 23:23). Jesus uses the word "weightier" to denote contents, obedience, filling, or substance. It should be noted that His is not a discourse against forms, rituals, methods, or molds. He says the contents "should have been done without neglecting" the forms. One could imagine from Jesus' statement quite a scene at the gates of the Temple. As the Pharisee approaches the temple and the trumpet sounds to announce his arrival carrying his mint, dill, and cumin—an offering that, most probably, was given for the poor—he shushes aside the poor beggars at the gate who are bothering him and disrupting his grand entrance designed to spotlight his act of helping the poor and needy. He has a correct mold (surface) but he makes a mockery of the weightier (deeper) things that should be in that mold. And so, the mold has no purpose, and thus, no actual use.

God does not respond to those who call the worship of Him vain, and yet engage in vanity (uselessness) themselves: "'But now will you not entreat God's favor, that He may be gracious to us? With such an offering on your part, will He receive any of you kindly?' says the Lord of hosts" (Malachi 1:9). God does respond to those who worship Him in sincerity (Malachi 3:16: "Then those who feared the Lord spoke to one another, and the Lord gave attention and heard it"), not because they "deserve" it or because they have earned it, but because of His grace (Malachi 3:17: "I will spare them"). Almighty God, have mercy on us and by your grace please **spare us**! Thank you, our Savior.

———

DECEMBER 20

THE EXODUS, THE TABERNACLE, AND JESUS . . .

"But when Christ appeared as a high priest of the good things to come,
He entered through the greater and more perfect tabernacle,
not made with hands . . . "

Hebrews 9:11

The New Testament is the continuation and completion of the Old Testament even as Jesus is the continuation and completion of "God saw all that He had made, and behold, it was very good" (Genesis 1:31). And so we see Jesus in the Exodus and in the Tabernacle. This is not surprising since Jesus is found throughout the Old Testament: "Now He said to them, 'These are My words . . . that all things which are written about Me in the Law of Moses and the Prophets and the Psalms must be fulfilled'" (Luke 24:44). In an astonishing way, the Exodus is analogous to the final events of the life of Christ. The Passover prior to the Exodus of the Jews from Egypt fore-shadows Jesus death on the cross at Calvary (1 Corinthians 5:7). Even the spreading of the blood of the sacrificial lamb on the doorposts and on the lintel would create a cross of dripping blood (Exodus 12:7). The parting of the Red Sea in the Exodus (Exodus 14) anticipates the resurrection of Jesus Christ while the Law given at Sinai (Exodus 19-20) portends the Spirit given on the day of Pentecost. Incredibly, both series of events occur over a period of fifty days. With respect to the Exodus, the Passover happens on the fourteenth day of the first month (Exodus 12:6) and the giving of the Law happens on the first of the third month. That's a total of fifty days. And, yes, you guessed it: The day Jesus was crucified until the day of Pentecost is exactly . . . fifty days!

Similarly, the Tabernacle (Exodus 25-30) of the Old Testament is analogous to the redemptive work of Jesus (Hebrews 9-10). The Tabernacle represents the Old Testament's physical manifestation of the New Testament's spiritual reality concerning what Christ has done for us. Each of the seven stations of the Tabernacle has its fulfillment in Jesus. The first station of the tabernacle was the brazen altar that was used for animal sacrifices and signified repentance and payment for sins. This first station of the tabernacle had its fulfillment in the blood of Jesus Christ. The second station of the tabernacle, the Laver, was used for cleansing and washing. The people could not go beyond this point in the tabernacle. It represented the need of and provision for cleansing. It is the cross that is the fulfillment of this second station of the Tabernacle. Without Jesus' cleansing of us through His death on the cross, we would have no part with God: "Jesus answered and said to him, 'What I do you do not realize now, but you will understand hereafter.'

Peter said to Him, 'Never shall You wash my feet!' Jesus answered him, 'If I do not wash you, you have no part with Me" (John 13:7-8).

The third station of the Tabernacle was the Table of Showbread that was the representation of God's presence and provision and signified trust in God. Of course, Jesus is our provision, our trust is in Him, and He is the bread of life (John 6:48). The fourth station, the Altar of Incense, was used for intercession for the people signifying prayer and forgiveness. Jesus is a sweet smell of incense and intercession (Revelation 8:4). The fifth station, the Golden Lampstand, represented God the light signifying ministry and missions and is fulfilled in Jesus, the light of the world (John 8:12). The sixth station, the veil, represented the separation between God and man. It was torn when Jesus died on the cross now signifying relationship with God being made possible by the slaying of Jesus' flesh on the cross (Hebrews 10:19-20). The seventh station, the Ark of the Covenant, represented the presence of God. The Priest could only enter it once each year. Now, in Christ, we can enjoy the presence of God continually since Christ is in us (Colossians 1:27).

――――――――

DECEMBER 21

WHAT DOES IT MEAN TO BE RESCUED? RESCUED TO WHAT?

"... this will turn out for my deliverance ... that I will not be put to shame in anything, but that with all boldness, Christ will even now, as always, be exalted in my body, whether by life or by death. For to me, to live is Christ, and to die is gain."

Philippians 1:19-21

Paul is in prison. Things are not looking good. He needs to be rescued. How will it turn out? He believes that it "shall turn out for my deliverance" (Philippians 1:19). He believes he will be rescued. What does rescuing or "deliverance" look like? Is it simply being rescued *from* something or is it more, profoundly, being rescued *to* something? What does it mean to be rescued? Rescued to what?

Paul expects to be rescued *to* not being "put to shame in anything, but that with all boldness, Christ shall even now, as always, be exalted in my body" (Philippians 1:20). For Paul, "deliverance" is not simply that he, physically (his body), would be removed from prison, but that Christ would be exalted in his body (regardless of where his body is located!). How can Christ be exalted in Paul's body? There are two ways. Christ can be exalted in Paul's body "whether by" way number one, "life," or by way number two, "death." Way number one—resulting in Paul actually being released from prison and continuing in "fruitful labor" that will benefit and bless others (Philippians 1:22-26)—presents the picture of Paul boldly speaking out on Christ's behalf while being imprisoned for the cause of Christ. Way number two—resulting in Paul being put to death in prison—proposes a picture of Paul boldly speaking out on Christ's behalf while being imprisoned for the cause of Christ.

How can both life and death mean true deliverance and actual rescuing? Paul answers his own implied question when he says, "for to me, to live is Christ, and to die is gain" (Philippians 1:21). It is deliverance for Paul to live because he is delivered from himself through life in Christ; for Paul, he has "been crucified with Christ; and it is no longer I who live, but Christ lives in me" (Galatians 2:20). It is deliverance for Paul to die because it is "gain" or "very much better" because the result of his "departing" would be to "be with Christ" (Philippians 1:23). Can you look at death in a positive way? Can you look at life in a positive way? Are you balanced in these perspectives? Paul's desire to die was balanced by his desire to live because his love for Christ was balanced by his love for Christ's ministry to His people. Why do you want to die? Is it so that you can escape the problems of life? Or do you have a healthy desire that is purely based on your desire to be with Jesus? Why do you want to live? Is it because of your personal hopes and desires for yourself? Or do you desire to live so that you can be a blessing to others and glorify Christ?

Deliverance, rescuing, or salvation is not simply Christ getting you out of something, but it is Christ getting Himself into you! Salvation is Christ living in you not simply Christ doing something for you. This is true because, ultimately, salvation is Christ Himself—Jesus is "the life" (John 14:6), is "our righteousness" (Jeremiah 33:16), and for Simeon is "Thy salvation" only after he had actually seen Jesus (Luke 2:30)—and not simply Christ's actions or works. What does it mean to be rescued? Rescued to what? To be truly delivered, rescued, or saved is to be delivered to Christ!

DECEMBER 22

THE MEANING OF LIFE . . .

"The conclusion, when all has been heard, is: fear God and keep His commandments, because this applies to every person."

Ecclesiastes 12:13

The apparent nature of the book of Ecclesiastes is that it has a negative view of life. However, its negativity has a purpose. It is used to magnify the futility of life when it is based upon earthly ambitions and desires. The negativity is extreme. It is understandable when we realize that life without God is also extremely negative and extremely meaningless. And so, the pessimism is used to expose the futility of life without God. The word "vanity" (futility) is repeated over and over again (some thirty times) throughout the book: "'Vanity of vanities,' says the Preacher, 'Vanity of vanities! All is vanity'" (Ecclesiastes 1:2).

All of life outside the context of God is meaningless because life alone cannot explain itself or give meaning to itself. Only life in the context of God has meaning because life without God is meaningless. Life can only have meaning relative to the Creator of life and His purposes for it. Of course, this is only logical. The repeated logic is that only the eternal things are not vanity. All else is fading away and empty. And so, the conclusion and message of the book—"The conclusion, when all has been heard, is: fear God and keep His commandments, because this applies to every person" (Ecclesiastes 12:13)—sums up the meaning of life as found in this two part formula: fear God (relationship with Him) **and** obey God (serve Him/be a witness for Him); know God and make God known.

This two-part formula can be found throughout the Scriptures. In the first section of the Old Testament (the Law or Torah or Pentateuch), we see a similar two-part structure: "Now the Lord said to Abram, '. . . I will make you a great nation, and I will bless you, and make your name great; and so you shall be a blessing; and I will bless those who bless you, and the one who curses you I will curse. And in you all the families of the earth will be blessed'" (Genesis 12:1-3). God will bless Abram (he will know God), *and* God will use Abram to bless all the families of the earth (he will make God known). In other words, Abram will fear God and he will keep his commandments as a method of applying the missiological covenant. Similarly, in the section of the Old Testament called the Prophets, we see the two-part structure: "'So that you may know and believe Me . . . So you are My witnesses,' declares the Lord" (Isaiah 43:10-12). Israel is to know God (fear Him) **and** be His witnesses/make God known (keep His commandments).

In the New Testament we see the two-part formula in the teachings of Jesus: "'Teacher, which is the great commandment in the Law?' And He said to him, 'You shall love the Lord your God with all your heart, and with all your soul, and with all your mind.' This is the great and foremost commandment. The second is like it, 'you shall love your neighbor as yourself'" (Matthew 22:36-39). In other words, know God and make God known or fear God and keep His commandments. Also, in the teachings of Paul, we see a version of this two-part structure when he says, "For to me, to live is Christ . . . but if I am to live on in the flesh, this will mean fruitful labor for me" (Philippians 1:21-22): Again, know God and make God known or fear God and keep His commandments. The bottom line in all this—or as the Preacher says, "The conclusion, when all has been heard"—is that meaning in life can only be found in fearing God **and** keeping His commandments. All else besides knowing God and making God known is . . . *vanity!*

DECEMBER 23

LET'S TAKE A LOOK AT THE BIBLICAL SUBMISSION OF A WIFE!

"Wives, be subject *to your own husbands, as to the Lord."*

Ephesians 5:22

What is the biblical submission marriage role of a wife? How is it to be understood? What does it include? Let's take a look!

First, submission implies dependence. For a wife to "submit to her husband" is for her to "look to him." In Ephesians 5:21-24, Paul uses the concept of the "body of Christ" (which he had already defined/described in Ephesians 1:22-23 and 4:15-16) to explain the idea of marriage roles. It is interesting to note that in Ephesians 4:16 Paul uses the Greek word *epichoragia* (translated as "supplies") to show that the "body" receives its nourishment, life and direction from "the head." This same word was a technical word used during that time to indicate the obligation of a husband to provide basic necessities for his wife. In Ephesians 5:22-24, the husband is the head who would, as it were, supply the body (the wife), who, in her submission to him, is dependent upon that supply. A significant aspect of the submission of the wife to her husband is her acceptance of, and response to, her dependency upon him. The wife seen as being dependent on her husband is consistent with nature itself since her very formation/creation depended on the creation of the man. She was taken from him (Genesis 2:21-22).

Second, submission implies assistance. For a wife to "submit to her husband" is for her to "look to do for/with him." Again, we can refer to the analogy of the body of Christ. The body (the church) assists the head (Christ) via its love for Him and its producing on His behalf through its evangelism, testimony, and reputation. We see these same kinds of actions in the submissive wife who is referred to in Titus 2:4-5 as a woman who loves her husband, is sensible and pure, and who is productive in the home. We also see these same kinds of actions in the esteemed "Proverbs 31 woman." She is productive and affords a good reputation for her husband (Proverbs 31:11-23). The wife who assists her husband is being consistent with nature itself since her very formation/creation was motivated by the fact that the man was not complete and needed a "helper/completion." She was made to be the man's helper (Genesis 2:18).

Third, submission implies respect/honor. For a wife to "submit to her husband" is for her to "look at him." And so, Paul concludes his discourse on marriage roles with respect to the role of the wife by saying, "let the wife see to it that she respect her husband" (Ephesians 5:33). The wife who respects/honors her husband is being consistent with nature itself since she was made for him, made from him, named by him, and given to him. The man was not ashamed in the presence of his wife (Genesis 2:25).

So, what is the biblical submission marriage role of a wife? After we have taken a look, we might conclude that for a wife to "submit to her husband" is for her to "look to him" (depend on him), look to do for/with him (assist him), and to "look at him" (respect him). So, wives . . . go ahead and **take a look**!

DECEMBER 24

REDEMPTION . . . REGAINING THAT WHICH WAS LOST

" . . . for all have sinned and fall short of the glory of God."

Romans 3:23

Have you ever felt the pain of losing something that you really cherished but then felt the utter joy of finding it? Sin leads to loss (pain). Redemption regains that which was lost (joy). Redemption regains the glory of man. Man's highest identity is that he was created in the image of God (Genesis 1:27). This included a certain glory that man originally had (Romans 5:2) but lost/exchanged (Romans 1:23). Sin leads to loss: "for all have sinned and fall short of the glory of God" (Romans 3:23). The expression "fall short of" comes from the Greek word *usterontai* that can either be translated "fail to reach" or "forfeit"; the glory that man once had was forfeited in the Fall. It has been regained in Christ: "But we all, with unveiled face, beholding as in a mirror the glory of the Lord, are being transformed into the same image from glory to glory, just as from the Lord, the Spirit" (2 Corinthians 3:18).

And so, there is in redemption the "instead of" factor. The many who were made sinners are made righteous (Romans 5:19). They who were sentenced to death (Romans 5:12, 21) possess eternal life (1 Corinthians 15:26). Those who partake of the fallen nature (Genesis 5:3) are new creatures (2 Corinthians 5:17). They who are bound to constant turmoil with no rest (Hebrews 4:1-3) are free in the eternal rest found in Him (Galatians 5:1). Those who are condemned to judgement are offered justification and life (Romans 6:18). Redemption regains the glory of man.

Sin leads to loss. Redemption regains that which was lost. Redemption regains man's relationship with God. Man's highest calling is to know God. Man was meant to find purpose in life through his relationship with God. However, when Adam sinned, he formed a wall between man and God. The first Adam established the wall. The second Adam, at the cross, abolished it forever (Matthew 27:51). God's desire in redemption is to remove the veil (Isaiah 25:6-8) that separated man from Him (Hebrews 10:19-22). Jesus reveals God to man (He removes the veil). He breaks down the wall that Adam built. He now stands as the One through Whom man can fellowship with God. In a redemptive sense, Christ became the perfect mediator (1 Timothy 2:5) in order to accomplish God's highest purpose for man, to know God. Redemption regains man's relationship with God.

Have you ever felt the pain of losing something that you really cherished but then felt the utter joy of finding it? There is no greater joy than the joy of redemption/salvation. Redemption is the ultimate regaining of that which was the ultimate loss. It is the ultimate joy! And so, our hearts cry out: "Restore to me the joy of Your salvation" (Psalm 51:12).

DECEMBER 25

SPECIAL REVELATION IS . . . SPECIAL!

"He made known His ways to Moses,
His acts to the sons of Israel . . . Therefore, be sure that it is those
who are of faith who are sons of Abraham."

Psalm 103:7; Galatians 3:7

Man, because of his sin, rejects general revelation (Romans 1:18-32). Although there is general revelation (God's revelation of Himself through His creation), man's sinfulness keeps him from knowing God through it. Thus, for man to know God, he needs something more than general revelation. He needs special revelation. And so, God provides a special revelation of Himself that is progressive, saving, and verbal/personal.

Special revelation is particular. God reveals Himself to a particular people. The "people of God" include the physical and spiritual descendants of Abraham (Galatians 3:7). The particular people (physical descendants) in the old covenant are the people of Israel (Deuteronomy 7:6). The particular people (spiritual descendants) in the new covenant are the people of the church (1 Peter 2:9). "He made known His ways to Moses, His acts to the sons of Israel" (Psalm 103:7), but at the same time "the lovingkindness of the Lord is from everlasting to everlasting on those who fear Him, and His righteousness to children's children" (Psalm 103:17), and, thus, "it is those who are of faith who are sons of Abraham" (Galatians 3:7). Why is special revelation given to a particular group of people? Because God has chosen to use a "vessel methodology," which means that God works through the vessels of His choosing to make Himself known to all peoples. Special revelation is given to some, not to exclude others, but to include others. God makes Himself known through a particular people.

Special revelation is progressive. From Genesis to the book of Revelation, special revelation increases. The increase of special revelation is not from non-truth to truth, rather it is from lesser revelation to greater (more, clearer, fuller, better) revelation (Hebrews 7:22). It is not that the Law is destroyed or replaced; rather, it is fulfilled (Matthew 5:17). God does not change; rather, our ability to understand Him changes. The Law does not change; rather, our ability to do the Law changes. To not be "under the Law" is not to be exempt from it (Romans 3:31); rather, it is to be enabled to do it (Romans 6:12-18).

Special revelation is saving. General revelation reveals God as Creator and Judge. He is not revealed as Redeemer. Thus, general revelation has no saving power (note, then, someone is not a Christian simply because they believe that God created the world and is the judge of all people!). Special revelation reveals God as Redeemer. In the Old Testament through such things as the atonement sacrifices (Leviticus 5:10; 16:8-22), the Exodus (Exodus 20:2), and the kinsman redeemer (Ruth 4:1-20). And in the New Testament through Jesus Christ who is the fullest and clearest manifestation of special revelation and who all previous special revelation pointed to (John 5:39; Luke 24:27).

Special revelation is verbal and personal. The general becomes specific and defined. The indirect becomes direct. The nonverbal (Psalm 19:3) becomes verbal. Special revelation is verbal in the Word of God—both the written Word and the incarnate Word—and through the Word bearers (Old Testament prophets, and New Testament Savior, apostles, and church). Special revelation is personal. In the Old Testament, God gives His personal name to Moses (Exodus 3:1-14), speaks with Moses like a friend (Exodus 33:11), and personally appears to Samuel (1 Samuel 3:21). In the New Testament, the climax of personal revelation comes in Jesus Christ as God becomes flesh (John 1:14) and man sees God (John 14:9). Ultimately, special revelation must be personal because the revelation is to a personal being (man) and from a personal being (God). Special revelation is **special**!

———————

DECEMBER 26

THAT YOUR LOVE MAY ABOUND
STILL MORE AND MORE!

"And this I pray, that your love may abound still more and more in real knowledge and all discernment, so that you may approve the things that are excellent, in order to be sincere and blameless until the day of Christ; having been filled with the fruit of righteousness which comes through Jesus Christ, to the glory and praise of God."

Philippians 1:9-11

Paul prays for the Philippians. What does he pray for them? He prays "that your love may abound still more and more in real knowledge and all discernment" (Philippians 1:9). This increased love is built within a context of practical experience. It is "in real knowledge" (experiential understanding) and in "all discernment" (moral judgment, insight, and sensitivity that implies a need for practical experience that is activated within a process). This is true since real love requires growth and maturation (1 Thessalonians 4:9-10).

What benefit is there to an increase in one's ability to love? Abounding more and more in your ability to love has four benefits (it is "so that . . . "): more love yields a greater ability to "approve the things that are excellent"; more love yields being "sincerer"; more love yields being more "blameless"; and more love yields being readier for the return of Christ (Philippians 1:10). It is beneficial "that your love may abound still more and more." You will be more able to discern between good and evil and between right and wrong (testing/approving the purity or excellence of things). You will be purer and more unmixed (sincere). You will be more stable and less likely to stumble (blameless). Your *"love heating up"* will prepare you more for the day of Christ (for His return). "The one who endures to the end, he shall be saved" is contrasted with those in the end times whose *"love will grow cold"* (Matthew 24:12-13).

Perhaps the more important question is, "How does one's love abound still more and more?" The answer is quite clear: "having been filled with the fruit of righteousness which comes through Jesus Christ" (Philippians 1:11). How do you grow in your ability to love? You are "filled with" something, and that is how your love increases. What are you filled with? You are filled with the fruit (effects or results) of something. That something is nothing less than the "righteousness which comes through Jesus Christ";, the fruit or results of being in right relationship with God. Your increased ability to love happens because you have an active and actual relationship with God through Jesus Christ. This makes theological sense. Relationship with (love for) others is directly correlated to relationship with (loved by) God; "we love, because He first loved us" (1 John 4:19). And so, there is an order to the two "greatest commandments": first, love God and, second, love others. The one produces the other. Your relationship with God harvests your relationship with others!

Do you realize the significance of having a relationship with God? It is the starting point of the Christian life. Have you experienced an increase of love for others? If not, perhaps you need to strengthen your relationship with God. When we are in right relationship with God, we produce spiritual fruit; we have peace and joy and patience and kindness . . . and love (Galatians 5:22-23). We are enabled to love others. Many times, we are in conflict with others. Why? Perhaps it is—more than we care to admit—because we are in conflict with ourselves via being in conflict with God. We are not at peace with ourselves because we are not right (in relationship) with God. Before being able to have peace with others, we must have peace with ourselves. This only comes through peace with God. We find that the times that we are least able to love others are the times that we are rebelling against God and have sinned against Him. We are not able to love others because we are not in a right relationship with God. Paul prays that our love will abound more and more. And so, he prays that our knowledge of God's love and our relationship with Him will abound more and more (Ephesians 3:14-19). All of this points to one grand anticipated result: that it all be "to the glory and praise of God" (Philippians 1:11).

DECEMBER 27

THIS IS FOR YOUR OWN GOOD!

"All discipline for the moment seems not to be joyful, but sorrowful; yet to those who have been trained by it, afterwards it yields the peaceful fruit of righteousness."

Hebrews 12:11

Discipline can be defined as moral education. We learn obedience and gain "the peaceful fruit of righteousness" through supervision, control, and correction (Hebrews 12:11). In the New Testament, discipline has a positive nature. The source of discipline is love: "Those whom I love, I reprove and discipline" (Revelation 3:19). There are two types of discipline in the New Testament: self-discipline (discipline in order to prevent) and ecclesiastical/church discipline (discipline in order to purify). The difference between these two types of discipline has to do with the known commission of an offense.

The motives for church discipline are to restore the sinner, to maintain the purity and reputation of the church, and to give honor to Christ. All three of these basic motives have something in common. They all imply the desire for a positive result. Church discipline is not parental discipline

(discipline with the "rod"), nor is it governmental discipline (discipline with the "sword"). It is pastoral discipline (discipline with the "staff"). Sinners are to be encouraged and brought back into the community of faith instead of being excluded from the community of faith: "Take care, brethren, that there not be in any one of you an evil, unbelieving heart that falls away from the living God. But encourage one another day after day, as long as it is still called 'Today,' so that none of you will be hardened by the deceitfulness of sin" (Hebrews 3:12-13). The motive of church discipline cannot be one of retribution (wrath and punishment related to committing an offense). Retribution must be reserved for God only and in His timing (Romans 12:19; 1 Thessalonians 5:15).

To understand the importance of church discipline we must understand the power of sin. Sin is a leaven (Galatians 5:9) and without discipline sin will only grow and become unruly (this is why Proverbs 13:24 says it is a father who hates his son who withholds discipline . . . "I am doing this for your own good!"). Sin is an outside force that knows how and where to attack; evil powers that go against the authority of God (2 Corinthians 2:11; Ephesians 6:12; 2 Thessalonians 2:9). There is a constant battle between the old and new natures; between the Adamic nature and a Christ-centered nature: "For the flesh sets its desire against the Spirit, and the Spirit against the flesh; for these are in opposition to one another, so that you may not do the things that you please" (Galatians 5:17).

And so, church discipline is important. Churches that are like the liberal minded 1 Corinthians 5:1-13 church who practice a form of humanistic love, who are proud and arrogant (verse 2), and who congratulate themselves for their tolerance of sin (verse 6), do not understand the danger of sin, and therefore, do not see the importance of discipline. Oppositely, God disciplines His children and can use His church as a vessel for disciplining. Proper church discipline—as it is with proper parental discipline—can sincerely say, "This is for your own good!"

DECEMBER 28

EVIDENCE OF THE AUTHENTICITY/ AUTHORITY OF SCRIPTURE

"All Scripture is inspired by God and profitable for teaching, for reproof, for correction, for training in righteousness."

2 Timothy 3:16

Is the sacred nature of the Bible able to be proven? Are there evidences for the authenticity and authority of Scripture? Of course, for the Christian, the most compelling reason to accept the authority of the Scripture is that Jesus Himself held that view. If Jesus viewed Scripture as sacred, authentic, and authoritative, then so, too, should the Christian. According to the Scripture, this is the case. Jesus viewed Scripture as inspired by the Holy Spirit (Matthew 22:43), as the Word of God (John 10:35), as historically accurate (Matthew 12:40), as the standard for understanding (Matthew 22:29), as the final word (Matthew 4:4, 7, 10), as reliable (Matthew 26:54-56), and perhaps most significantly as consistent with Himself (John 5:39; Luke 24:27, 44).

This type of "internal evidence" is important in the debate over authenticity. If the Scripture does not view itself as sacred and authoritative then there is no reason to introduce "external evidences" into the debate. Scripture does view itself as authoritative. It views itself as "inspired by God" or "God-breathed" (2 Timothy 3:16; 2 Samuel 23:2). It views itself as being "God-sent" or "God-initiated" (2 Peter 1:20-21; Jeremiah 1:9). It even gives testimony of its own authors (2 Peter 3:15-16).

An important and unique category of evidence that spans the gap between internal and external evidences is the fulfillment of prophecy. Scripture foretells the history of nations, in general, and the history of Israel, specifically. In unexplainable ways and to a statistically impossible degree (for the connection to just be "chance"), the Scripture foretells the coming of the Messiah in Jesus Christ.

External evidence can be offered in the court of debate via a variety of "exhibits" not the least of which is the history of the Bible itself. Take its unity coupled with its diversity. The same messages are consistently expressed within the different parts of the Bible (redemption, covenant, the kingdom of God, the reality of the Messiah), yet these different parts of the Bible are written over a 1,500-year period by more than 40 different authors from completely different backgrounds. In addition, the preservation of the Bible points to its authenticity. No other book has been preserved with such careful attention as is evidenced by the discovery of the Dead Sea Scrolls. Furthermore, its distribution and influence point to its sacred nature. Its number of readers and multitude of languages it has been read in is incomparable, and it has consistently and uniquely influenced people from all cultures in a way that has radically changed their lives.

Archaeological discoveries have consistently defended its historical accuracy. The ancestors of the people of Israel have been shown to have come from Mesopotamia (Genesis 11:28). A man named Erastus was confirmed to be a high-ranking city official in Corinth consistent with the writing of Romans 16:23. Archaeological discoveries in ancient Jericho have shown that there were walls of a city that fell outward consistent with the writings of Joshua 6:20. Discoveries have shown that there were cities of the same biblical names and the same locations as Paul described with respect to his missionary trips. Even scientific discoveries are consistent with the Bible. It has been discovered that the earth "hangs on nothing" (Job 26:7) and that life is in the blood (Genesis 9:4). What is this that we call the Bible? Overall, the evidence screams out . . . It is the authentic Word of God!

DECEMBER 29

WHERE IS THE POWER? . . . IT IS IN YOU!

"And with great power the apostles were giving testimony to the resurrection of the Lord Jesus, and abundant grace was upon them all."

Acts 4:33

Jesus told His followers that they would "receive *power* when the Holy Spirit has come upon you" (Acts 1:8). The word "power" is translated from the Greek word *dunamis* (from which we get our words "dynamic" and "dynamite"). Where do we find this "power"? We find it in the church; in the ministry of the church and in its individual members.

The power of God is found in His "body"; in the ministry and activities of His people (the church). *Dunamis* is found in the unity, fellowship, and sharing that is within the church (Acts 4:32-33). It is found in the preaching of its message. *Dunamis* is found in the preaching of the cross (1 Corinthians 1:18). It is found in the preaching of the gospel (Romans 1:16; Acts 8:13; Romans 15:19; Mark 16:20). It is found in the spiritual warfare enacted by the church (Revelation 12:10). Carlos Annacondia, an Argentinean evangelist, claims that his success in having such a powerful ministry is based on successful spiritual warfare. He breaks the strongholds of demonic forces before he begins his meetings. After that the dynamite explodes. Where do we find the power? We find it in the ministry of the church; moreover, it is found in the multiplication of that ministry (consider the progression from Luke 6:12-13 to 6:19 to 9:1).

The power is found in the character of the individual members of the church. *Dunamis* is found in humility and weakness (1 Corinthians 2:3-5; 2 Corinthians 12:9). It is found in suffering (2 Timothy 1:8). It is found in relationship with Jesus (Luke 8:46; Luke 6:19). *Dunamis* is found in faith (Galatians 3:5; Hebrews 11:11; Mark 5:30, 34; Matthew 13:54-58). After Jesus' victory over the devil's temptations in the wilderness, He "returned to Galilee in the power of the Spirit, and news about Him spread through all the surrounding district" (Revelation 3:8). *Dunamis* is found in obedience (Revelation 3:8; Luke 4:14; Acts 5:32).

Where is the power? It is in the church! It is found in the place where the Holy Spirit dwells . . . in the temple of God. Perhaps, then, the more applicable question is: "Do you not know that you are a temple of God and that the Spirit of God dwells in you?" (1 Corinthians 3:16). Where is the power? It is in you!

DECEMBER 30

TO WHOM DO YOU PLEDGE ALLEGIANCE?

"For our citizenship is in heaven, from which also we eagerly wait for a Savior, the Lord Jesus Christ . . ."

Philippians 3:20

God calls His people (His family, His "tribe") whose "citizenship is in heaven" (Philippians 3:20) to pledge *allegiance* to Him before anything else. And so, He commands, "Turn to Me, and be saved, all the ends of the earth; for I am God, and there is no other. I have sworn by Myself, the word has gone forth from My mouth in righteousness and will not turn back, that to Me every knee will bow, every tongue will swear *allegiance*" (Isaiah 45:22-23). The "spirit of tribalism" fights against that calling and command. Tribalism—that which divides people based on systems of self-identification ("I am of the tribe of Apollos" or "I am of the Hutu tribe" or "I am of the Crips or Bloods gang")—and Christian fellowship do not mix well together (1 Corinthians 1:10-12). They are fundamentally opposed to each other since, as Paul warned the "tribal Corinthians," tribalism divides Christ, and Christ must not be divided (1 Corinthians 1:13). Another way to say this is to ask the question, "Who do you pledge allegiance to?" The answer for the Christian, regardless of his or her tribal affections and tendencies, must be a resounding "I pledge allegiance to God!"

When one becomes a part of the family of God, there must be a renewing of the mind (Romans 12:2) with respect to loyalty. Christians must realize that they are new creations and that all things have become new (2 Corinthians 5:17). Christians are called to a new loyalty. This does not mean that they cannot exhibit loyalty to their family, country, or culture. It does mean, however, that their new loyalty to Christ must supersede their old loyalty to their "tribe." Since "tribal loyalty" exists on three levels—loyalty to family, loyalty to government, and loyalty to community—there must be renewing of the mind on each one of these levels.

With respect to the family, loyalty to Christ must be so much greater than loyalty to the family that Luke 14:26 becomes a reality, "If anyone comes to Me, and does not hate [i.e., place below Me] his own father and mother and wife and children and brothers and sisters, yes, and even his own life, he cannot be My disciple." This is not to say that Christians should not exhibit loyalty, respect, and love for their families (Mark 7:10; 1 Timothy 5:8). Instead, there must be a higher loyalty to Christ and His family. You might say, it is a "totem-pole" issue, not a "one or the other issue." It is an issue of proper order and placement; it is an issue of hierarchy of allegiance.

With respect to country and government, the Christian must be able to say the words of Acts 5:29, "We must obey God rather than men." This is not to say that Christians do not obey authorities or show respect to rulers (Romans 13:1-7). However, there is a higher loyalty that must be given to Christ and the government of the kingdom of God. Allegiance to Christ is higher on the "totem-pole."

With respect to culture and community, the Christian must agree with the priority that is found in Galatians 6:10, "So then, while we have opportunity, let us do good to all men, and especially to those who are of the household of the faith." This is not to say that Christians must ignore their culture, ethnicity, or heritage. However, there is a higher loyalty to Christ and the Christian community. There is a hierarchy of allegiance!

Who do you pledge allegiance to? The answer for the Christian, regardless of his or her tribal affections and tendencies, must be a resounding "I pledge allegiance to God!" There is a higher loyalty—"So then you are no longer strangers and aliens, but you are fellow citizens with the saints, and are of God's household" (Ephesians 2:19)—because there is a higher citizenship. "Our citizenship is in heaven, from which also we eagerly wait for a Savior, the Lord Jesus Christ" (Philippians 3:20).

DECEMBER 31

JESUS RETURNS AS JUDGE ... AND IT'S THE END!

"But when the Son of Man comes in His glory, and all the angels with Him, then He will sit on His glorious throne. All the nations will be gathered before Him; and He will separate them from one another, as the shepherd separates the sheep from the goats; and He will put the sheep on His right, and the goats on the left."

Matthew 25:31-33

The Son (Jesus) came into the world initially as Savior (incarnation) but will come again (return of Christ) as Judge (John 3:17; Matthew 25:31-33). That "day" is described variously as "the day of the Lord" (1 Thessalonians 5:2), "the day of the Lord Jesus" (1 Corinthians 5:5), "the day of God"

(2 Peter 3:12), "that day" (2 Thessalonians 1:10), and "the last day" (John 12:48). In each case, the context of "the day" is judgment and the timeframe is "the end." Exactly when that "day" will come is not able to be known (Matthew 24:27, 36, 42). Moreover, many people will not be anticipating or understanding "that day" in any way at all "just like the days of Noah" (Matthew 24:37-39, 44). That day when "the end shall come" will not happen until "this gospel of the kingdom shall be preached in the whole world for a witness to all the nations" (Matthew 24:14). It will not come until after the rise of the antichrist (2 Thessalonians 2:2-3). It will happen "just as the lightning comes from the east, and flashes even to the west" (Matthew 24:27) "in the twinkling of an eye, at the last trumpet" (1 Corinthians 15:51-52) when "we shall be changed" because "He appears" (1 John 3:2). It will happen at the end of the age when Jesus will come as Judge.

He will come (return) to Judge along with His followers (Malachi 4:1-3; 1 Corinthians 6:2; 2 Timothy 2:12; Revelation 2:26-27; Revelation 19:7-14; 1 Thessalonians 4:14). And so, when He comes to "meet" believers "in the clouds" it will be for those believers to "escort" Him to the earth to wage war together with Him against the nations (1 Thessalonians 4:17). It should be noted that the Greek term *apantesis* ("meet") used in 1 Thessalonians 4:17 is a unique word that is only used in two other places in the New Testament (Matthew 25:6; Acts 28:15) in which the idea in each case is for people to "meet" someone who is coming to them in order to escort that someone back to where they were. The coming of Christ in 1 Thessalonians 4:17 is not designed to take away believers from the earth (as is often pictured in the "secret rapture of the church"). When the Son of Man returns it will be "like the days of Noah" in which some are "taken" and others will be "left," but the idea of being "taken" is not consistent with those who are saved but with those who are lost (Matthew 24:37-41). So when Christ returns, those who are left (believers "who remain" as in 1 Thessalonians 4:17) are not "taken" away; rather, they come with Jesus (after "meeting" Him in the clouds) to earth to wage war and enact judgment.

And so, there are no "two returns of Christ" but only one, and that return will mark the end; it will be "at the last trumpet" when judgment will come (1 Corinthians 15:51-52; Matthew 25:31-33). Jesus returns at the end (not at an interim time after which activity on earth continues on as it was before). The return of the Lord is "the last day" (John 12:48). It is not consistent with "ongoing activity" on earth since it is associated with the "suddenness" and "exhaustiveness" of lightening coming from the east that flashes even to the west (Matthew 24:17). He "gathers together" (Matthew 24:31) His saints as they are "caught up" or "gathered together" (1 Thessalonians 4:17) just like a "vulture" gathers where the "corpse" is; Christ ("the vulture") comes to where the church ("corpse") dwells (He returns to earth). He returns "after the tribulation" (Matthew 24:29) "appearing in the sky" (Matthew 24:30) as He comes "on the clouds of the sky with power and great glory" (Matthew 24:30; 1 Thessalonians 4:17) and "He will send forth His angels with a great trumpet (1 Corinthians 15:51-52) and they will gather together His elect from the four winds, from one end of the sky to the other" (Matthew 24:31).

Jesus returns as Judge . . . and it is **the end**!

NOTES

Endnotes

1. Regent University course notes, 1986.

2. Cornwall, Judson. *Profiles of a Leader.* Logos International, 1980.

3. Meyer, F.B. *Love to the Utmost.* Fleming H. Revell Co., 1988.

4. Taken from a portion of a sermon given by George Whitefield.

5. Bonhoeffer, Dietrich. *Life Together.* HarperOne, 1978.

6. Watson, David. *Called and Committed.* Shaw Books, 2000.

ABOUT THE AUTHOR

Dr. John Mannion has spent most of his life teaching the Bible. He has taught at all levels academically including middle school, high school, undergraduate, graduate, and doctoral levels. He has served on numerous college faculties including Oral Roberts University, Geneva College, Tidewater Bible College, and Bethel College. As an international Bible teacher, John has ministered on five continents in over twenty countries. He is the author of MOTMOT (a 2,000-page series of teaching curriculum designed to equip Bible teachers, consisting of 49 courses, covering six major areas of study, totaling 700 hours of teaching material, available in 10 languages, and used domestically and internationally). His ministry has included the founding of multiple Bible institutes as well as a missions organization, the planting of churches, and a variety of pastoral roles in the local church. He holds the Doctor of Ministry (D.Min.) degree from Reformed Theological Seminary.

John's greatest blessing is his wife, Audrey, and their six children and their families. His most loved hobby is anything to do with the "beautiful game," the game of soccer. John played Division I soccer at the University of Delaware in the early 1980s. He still plays, although at a much slower pace, in his over fifty-five league in Media, Pennsylvania where he also coaches at a variety of levels most notably being awarded multiple times with the Coach of the Year award for his work with his Varsity High School team. John loves to have fun and, as one of his grandchildren says, joke around. This, perhaps, still goes back to his days as an improvisational comedian in the network television comedy troupe, the L.A. Connection!

For more information about
Dr. John Mannion

and

Nuggets of Truth

please visit:

www.bibleschoolforthenations.com

To download the indices and reference material please visit
www.ambassador-international.com/books/nuggets-of-truth

For more information about
AMBASSADOR INTERNATIONAL
please visit:

www.ambassador-international.com
@AmbassadorIntl
www.facebook.com/AmbassadorIntl

If you enjoyed this book, please consider leaving us a review on
Amazon, Goodreads, or our website.